The Liturgy of Saint Gregory the Theologian

Critical Text with Translation and Commentary

The Liturgy of Saint Gregory the Theologian

Critical Text with Translation and Commentary

Nicholas Newman

Saint Dominic's Media
Belleville, Illinois

© 2019 Nicolas Newman
All Rights Reserved

This work was accepted as a PhD thesis by the Faculty of Arts and Social Sciences, University of Zurich in the spring term 2014 on the recommendation of the Doctoral Committee: Professor Ulrich Eigler [main supervisor], and Professor Manuel Baumbach.

Published by:
Saint Dominic's Media, Inc.
P.O. Box 8225
Belleville, IL 62222

www.saintdominicsmedia.com

Printed in the United States of America

19 29 21 22 23 24 25   8 7 6 5 4 3 2

BISAC Category:
Religion / Christian Rituals & Practice / Worship & Liturgy

ISBN-13: 978-1-7321784-6-5 (Paperback)
ISBN-13: 978-1-7321784-7-2 (Hardback)
ISBN-13: 978-1-7321784-8-9 (E-book)

Dedication

This book is dedicated to my parents Robert Constantine and Anna Newman for their constant support and love.

Table of Contents

Prologue 11

Introduction 12

  1. Historical Origin of the Liturgy of Saint Gregory the Theologian 12
    I.I Purpose of the Liturgy 12
    I.II. The Fourth Century 19
    I.III. Forcing a Choice: Anti-Arian and Anti- Pneumatomachianism in the Liturgy 22
    I.IV. The Place of Origin 26
    I.V. The Way to Egypt 28
    I.VI. The Liturgy in Egypt 30
    I.VII. The Question of Authorship 32

  2. Introduction to the Text 46
    II.I. Editions of the Greek text used in this critical edition 46
    II.II. Other traditions that exist alongside the Greek 48
    II.III. Manuscripts used in this critical edition 49
    II.IV. Manuscripts not obtained for this edition 49
    II.V. The textual tradition 50
    II.VI. General Introduction to the following critical edition and investigation 52

The Critical Text 55

  Part I: Pre-anaphoral Prayers 55

  Part II: The Anaphora 62

  Part III: Post-Anaphora Prayers 79

The Translation 90

  Part I: Pre-anaphoral Prayers 90

  Part II: The Anaphora 94

  Part III: Post Anaphoral Prayers 101

The Commentary 108

  Commentary Part I: The Pre-Anaphora Rites 109
    I. Pre-Anaphoral Rites 109
    I.1. Structure of the Pre-Anaphora 109
    I.II. The Εὐχὴ ἥν ποιεῖ ὁ Ἱερεὺς καθ' ἑαυτὸν ἐν ἑαυτῷ 110
    I.III. The Prayer after the Preparation of the Holy Altar 124
    I.IV. The Prayer of the Holy Gospel 131
    I.V. The Prayer of the Veil 141
    I.VI. The Other Prayer of the Veil among the Egyptians. 151
    I.VII. The Prayer of the Greeting 157
    I.VIII. The alternate Prayer of the Greeting 170

Table of Contents

Commentary Part II: The Anaphora — 176
- II.I. Introduction — 176
- II.II. The Sursum Corda. — 180
- II.III. The Ἀρχὴ τῆς προσκομίδης — 186
- II.IV. The Pre-*Sanctus* Prayer and the *Sanctus* hymn — 199
- II.V. The post-*Sanctus* prayers — 204
- II.VI. The Consecration — 222
- II.VII. The *Epiklesis* — 226
- II.VIII. The Intercessions — 234
- II.IX. The Final Benediction — 239

Commentary Part III: Post-Anaphoral Rites — 240
- III.I. Structure — 240
- III.II. The "Introduction to the Breaking" — 242
- III.III. The "Prayer of the Breaking" — 248
- III.IV. The "Other Prayer of the Breaking" — 261
- III.V. The Second "Other Prayer of the Breaking" — 269
- III.VI. The Prayer following the Lord's Prayer — 279
- III.VII. The "Prayer of the Bowing of the Head" — 284
- III.VIII. Another, similar, Prayer — 294
- III.IX. The "Prayer of Freedom" — 299
- III.X. The Preparation for the Eucharist: The Σῶμα καὶ αἷμα. — 312
- III.XI. The "Prayer of Thanksgiving" — 329
- III.XII. The Prayer of the "Bowing of the Head" — 337
- Part IV: Conclusions — 348

Appendix I: Select Bibliography — 359
- I. Monographies: — 359
- II. Articles: — 367

Register of Tables and Illustrations

1. Introduction
Table I.VII.1: The Epithets of Christ in the Pre-Anaphora   43
Table I.VII.2: The Epithets of Christ in the Post-Anaphora   44
Table III.V.1: Possible Stemma of the Manuscripts of
the Liturgy of St. Gregory the Theologian   51

3. The Commentary
I. The Pre-Anaphoral Prayers
Table I.II.1: The differences between the 'Prayer of Access' in the Liturgy of St. Gregory and the 'Opferungsgebet' in the Liturgy of St. James   111
Table I.II.2: Comparative Chart of this prayer in the Liturgy of St. Gregory the Theologian and the Liturgy ofSt. Basil the Great   113
Table I.II.3: Comparative Chart of the 'Prayer of Access' in the Liturgy of St. Gregory the Theologian and the Liturgia Praesanctificatorum of Epiphanius of Cyprus   115
Table I.II.4: The Structure of the Introductory Prayer   118
Table I.III.1: The Structure of the Prayer after the Preparation of the Holy Altar   125
Table I.III.2: The Intratextual links between Prayer I and Prayer II   127
Table I.IV.1: The Structure of the Original Prayer of the Holy Gospel   134
Table I.IV.2: The *Ekphonesis* of the Prayer of the Holy Gospel   135
Table I.IV.3: The Structure of Secondary Prayer of the Holy Gospel   136
Table I.V.1: The differences in this Prayer between the Liturgy of St. Gregory and the Liturgy of St. Basil   143
Table I.V.2: The Structure of the 'Prayer of the Veil'   145
Table I.VI.1: The Structure of the 'Other Prayer of the Veil among the Egyptians'
Table I.VI.2: Differences in the request for purification   155
Table I.VII.1: The Structure of the 'Prayer of the Greeting'   161
Table I.VIII.1: The Structure of the 'Alternate Prayer of the Greeting'   171

II. The Anaphora

Table II.I.1: The general Structure of the Anaphora	177
Table II.II.1: The Structure of the *Sursum Corda* dialogue	184
Table II.III.1: The 'Beginning of the Proskomede' in the Liturgies of St. Gregory and St. Basil	189
Table II.III.2: The Structure of the first prayer in the Ἀρχὴ τῆς προσκομίδης	192
Table II.III.3: The Structure of the second prayer in the Ἀρχὴ τῆς προσκομίδης	193
Table II.IV.1: The Structure of the pre-*Sanctus* and the *Sanctus* Hymn	203
Table II.V.1: The post-*Sanctus* prayers in the Liturgies of Sts. Basil and Gregory the Theologian	209
Table II.VI.1: The Structure of the Consecration	224
Table II.VII.1: Comparative Chart of the epiklesis in the Liturgy of St. Gregory and the Liturgy of St. Basil	230
Table II.VIII.1: The Intercessions in the Liturgy of St. Gregory	235

III. The Post-Anaphoral Prayers

Table III.II.1: The Structure of the 'Introduction to the Breaking'	244
Table III.III.1: The Structure of the 'Prayer of the Breaking'	251
Table III.IV.1: The Structure of the alternate 'Prayer of the Breaking'	264
Table III.V.1: The Structure of the other alternate 'Prayer of the Breaking'	271
Table III.VI.1: The Similarities between the Liturgies of Sts. Gregory and Mark	281
Table III.VI.2: The Structure of the Prayer following the Lord's Prayer	282
Table III.VII.1: The Structure of the 'Prayer of the Bowing of the Head'	290
Table III.VIII.1: Comparison of the texts of this prayer in the Liturgies of St. Basil and of St. Gregory	295
Table III.VIII.2: The Structure of the other 'Prayer of the Bowing of the Head'	296

Table III.IX.1: The Structure of the 'Prayer of Freedom'	302
Table III.X.1: The Greek Text vs. the Coptic Translation	312
Table III.X.2: Comparing the Parallel Dialogues in the Liturgies of St. Gregory and St. Basil	315
Table III.X.3: The Structure of the ‚Σῶμα καὶ αἷμα' Section	320
Table III.XI.1: The Structure of the ‚Prayer of Thanksgiving'	334
Table III.XII.1: The 'Prayer of the Bowing of the Head' and the 'Prayer of the Kiss of Peace'	342
Table III.XII.2: The Structure of the 'Prayer of the Bowing of the Head'	344
Table III.XII.3: The Nicene Creed and the Historical Actions of Christ	346

Prologue

  I was first exposed to the Liturgy of St. Gregory as an undergraduate attempting to find a topic for an Honors Thesis at the University of New Hampshire. While looking through a bookshelf for ideas a slim, paperback volume caught my eye. This was the Thessaloniki edition of the liturgy. I decided it would be interesting to make a translation of this work for the Thesis, little did I know, until beginning my Dissertation, how interesting this liturgy truly was, and how little is known about it.

  I owe many thanks to many people. First of all, of course, to my family, my lovely wife, Casey, my parents, the Reverend Doctor Constantine Newman and Anna Newman lic. phil. who provided many hours of discussion and suggestions, my grandparents, Orlando and Rosina Zoppi, aunt, Rosina Zoppi and siblings Elena, Dimitri and Alexander Newman, without whose support I would not have been able to write this Paper. My deepest gratitude also to my thesis directors: Professor Manuel Baumbach and Professor Ulrich Eigler for their support and guidance. There are also many other people to thank, other faculty at the University of Zürich: Professor Hermann Tränkle, Professor Christoph Riedweg, Professor Carmen Cadella, Dr. Werner Widmer and Dr. Ruth Harder for their help and support; my undergraduate professors: Professor Stephen Trzaskoma, Professor Scott Smith, Professor Stephen Brunet and Professor Richard Clairmont for continuing to take an interest in my work and continuing their guidance. Many thanks also to Professor Bruce Beck for his ideas on propaganda and to my colleagues, especially Lena Krauss and Fabian Zogg for many hours of discussion.

Introduction

1. Historical Origin of the Liturgy of Saint Gregory the Theologian

I.I Purpose of the Liturgy

Liturgy, as a literary *genre*, is often overlooked by philologists and literary theorists.[1] This is hardly surprising, as liturgies in general, and the Liturgy of St. Gregory the Theologian in particular, present the reader, and the scholar with a living text. Other texts of late antiquity may have mistakes creep into the manuscripts, or some alterations may be made by well meanings scribes, but the scholar is able to work his way back through this and create the original version in a critical edition. As a living text, used in churches over a potential period of centuries, liturgies are subject to the theological and aesthetic whims of each succeeding generation and various clerics were not shy in replacing prayers with other prayers they preferred, or with ones of their own authorship. The influence theology has on the form of liturgical texts has mostly interested theologians, or church historians, but this trend has been slowly changing, and now philologists too are looking at liturgists. The

---

[1] An interesting discussion of liturgical texts as literature can be found in Day (2014).

Introduction

process of change a liturgy goes through makes a critical edition impractical, and liturgical editions are termed comparative to note these difficulties.

The Liturgy of St. Gregory is an excellent example of a liturgy as a living text. Stylistically the liturgy contains elements from the various regions in which it was used, from Byzantine elements, from Cappadocia/Constantinople where it was written, to Egyptian elements which reflect the land in which it was used for the longest time and is still in use today. Theologically the liturgy is dominated by Nicene theology and the problems of the Arian controversy, however later theological controversies, especially the Monophysite controversy of the fifth century are also present. This liturgy, then, shows both movement in time and space as it was adapted and readapted to fit new geographic and theological situations.

The most notable aspect of the Liturgy of St. Gregory, and that which makes the Liturgy of St. Gregory nearly unique among liturgical texts, is the address of every prayer to Christ, and the Structure of each prayer in a dialogue style between the priest and Christ. What, though, prompted the author to write the text in this style? Three explanations have been postulated for this. The first is that the emphasis on Christ should be interpreted in light of the Monophysite controversies of the fifth century, this theory, however, has been abandoned since there is only one prayer in the Liturgy that can be considered Monophysite in nature.[2] Numerous other prayers, however, emphasize Christ's dual nature as man and God. Another problem with this interpretation is the date. The use of the term ὁμοούσιος in the Liturgy, for example points to the end of the fourth century as the date of authorship for this text.[3]

This leads us into the next theory, that it was not Monophysitism that the author wishes to combat, but Arianism. This theory is argued, to a certain extent, in Hammerschmidt's Commentary, in which he discusses the anti-Arian nature of several prayers.[4] We will discuss this theory at greater length later in this Introduction.[5]

Gerhards postulates a third theory, in which he interprets the "Christusanrede" and the "ich-du Stil" not as part of the polemical motivation of the author, but as part of the tradition of addressing Christ in prayer.[6] In Gerhards Commentary, he demonstrates the im-

---

[2] Bouyer, for example, considers this a late Syrian liturgy. Bouyer (1989). pg. 357
[3] See below pg. 30
[4] Hammerschmidt (1957). pp. 94-95
[5] See below pg. 11-16
[6] Especially important in this field is the work *Christusanrede* by Jungmann. Cf. Gerhards (1984). pp. 238-242 in which he sums up his findings and lays out his Biblical and early Liturgical findings, coming to the concusion that it is surprising that not more liturgies were more influenced by this tradition, perhaps because of „Konservativismus der Liturgie...die vor allem die Strukturen der jüdischen Liturgie übernommen hat."

portance of this tradition in early Christian worship by discussing its use in both a Liturgical setting, among others in the *Didache*, in the East Syrian Anaphora of Addai and Mari and the Greek Baptismal prayers.[7] He also discusses prayers "*ad Christum*"in apocryphal Scriptural works, such as the apocryphal Acts of the Apostles, the Acts of John and the Acts of Thomas.[8] He comes to the conclusion that, while: "eine ‚Geschichte des an Christus gerichteten Eucharistiegebets' ist nach dem heutigen Erkenntnisstand nicht zu schreiben."[9] He does claim, however, that: "die vorgelegten Beispiele (bieten) und weitere patristische Belege durchaus die Möglichkeit einer provisorischen Systematisierung der heutigen Erkentnisse über die Christusanrede im Eucharistiegebet..."[10] He goes on to discuss this in the tenth Chapter of his Commentary.[11] He deftly lays out the theological reasons for having a prayer addressed to Christ in a Liturgy, what he terms "Christusfrömmigkeit"and which may have to do with the "Furcht"of Christ, the absence of which he explains by the influence of the writings of Gregory the Theologian.[12] The importance of the theological background of the "Christusanrede" is not to be overlooked, however, the extreme example of the Liturgy of St. Gregory warrants a second look. Already in the pre-Anaphora of the Nestorian Liturgy (to which the Anaphora of Sts. Addai and Mari belongs)[13] we see prayers that are addressed to Christ: "Christ make true thy words and receive the fruit of thy lips and pardon the trespasses and sins of all them that hearken to thee."[14] In the Anaphora proper, several prayers are also directed to Christ. In a prayer preceeding the Breaking, for example, the text reads:

> O Christ the peace of those above and the great tranquility of those below, grant, o my Lord, that thy tranquility and peace may abide on the four corners of the world and especially within thine holy catholic church, and grant peace to the priesthood with the realm and make was to cease in all the world and

---

("Conservatism in the liturgy…which especially adopted the strucutures of the Jewish liturgy.") Gerhards (1984). Pg. 242).
[7] Gerhards (1984). pp. 180-181; 187-193 and 202-210
[8] Gerhards (1984). pp. 181-183
[9] Gerhards (1984). pp. 210 „it is not possible to establish a history of Eucharistic prayers addressed to Christ according to today's level of understanding"
[10] Ibid. „The provided examples as well as other Patristic examples certainly provide the possibility to establish a provisional systematization of prayers addressed to Christ in the Eucharist."
[11] Gerhards (1984). pp. 210-242
[12] Gerhards (1984). pp. 242
[13] Hammond and Brightman (1896). pp. 247-305
[14] Hammond and Brightman (1896). pg. 273

scatter the divided peoples that delight in war, that we may lead a quiet and peaceable life in all sobriety and godliness.[15]

Other prayers in the Anaphora are not addressed to Christ. The prayer above, for example even changes addressees, from Christ to God the Father, as follows:
> I thank thee, o Father, Lord of heaven and earth, o Father and Son and Holy Ghost, that though I be a sinner and weak, yet by reason of the multitude of thy mercifulness thou hast in thy grace accounted me worthy to offer before thee these fearful and holy and lifegiving and divine myteries of the body and blood of thy Christ that I may minister to thy people and sheep of thy pasture the pardon of their offences and the remission of thier sins and the salvation of their souls and the reconciliation of the whole world and the tranquility and peace of all the churches.[16]

The phrase: "o Father and Son and Holy Ghost" in the above text shows that not one member of the Trinity is addressed, but the Trinity as a whole. Numerous prayers throughout the Anaphora bear witness to this. So, for example, the *Cushapa* at the very beginning of the Anaphora: "O Lord God of hosts repeat, aid my weakness by thy mercy and by the help of thy grace account me worthy to offer before thee this living and holy sacrifice for the help of the whole body and for the praise of thy glorious Trinity, o Father and Son and Holy Ghost, for ever"[17] This Anaphora, while including some prayers to Christ, focuses on the Trintiy whereas the Liturgy of St. Gregory only contains prayers addressed to Christ.

West Syrian rite as well, we see prayers in various Anaphorae that are addressed to Christ, for example in the Syrian Anaphora of St. James.[18] These are, however, also not exclusive, in this Anaphora we see that most of the prayers are addressed to God the Father.[19] The same paradigm holds true for both the Eucharistic prayer of the Didache as well as the prayers of Baptism in the Byzantine tradition. While the thanksgiving for the Eucha-

---

[15] Hammond and Brightman (1986). pg. 288. Generally, with some exceptions, Greek, and Latin texts will be given in the original language with a translation provided in the footnote (unless the quotation is taken from the Liturgy of St. Gregory or is a section nearly identical to a passage from the Liturgy of St. Gregory, in which case the translation is provided in the second section of this study) while texts in other liturgical languages will be given in translation.
[16] Ibid.
[17] Hammond and Brightman (1896). pg. 282. Other prayers to the Trinity, among others, include the ‚Prayer of Incense' on the same page and the Gehantha on pg. 283.
[18] Hammond and Brightman (1986). pp. 87-88
[19] The *gehontho*, in Hammond and Brightman (1896). pg. 86, for example is addressed to the Father.

rist in the Didache can be argued to be addressed to Christ, the preparation for it is clearly addressed to God the Father:

> πρῶτον περὶ τοῦ ποτηρίον· Εὐχαριστοῦμεν σοι, πάτερ ἡμῶν, ὑπὲρ τῆς ἁγίας ἀμπέλον Δαυεὶδ τοῦ παιδός σου· σοὶ ἡ δόξα εἰς τοὺς αἰῶνας. 3. περὶ δὲ τοῦ κλάσμος· Εὐχαριστοῦμέν σοι, πάτερ ἡμῶν, ὑπὲρ τῆς ζωῆς καὶ γνώσεως, ἧς ἐγνώρισας ἡμῖν διὰ Ἰησοῦ τοῦ παιδός σου. σοὶ ἡ δόξα εἰς τοὺς αἰῶνας
> 4. ὥσπερ ἦν τοῦτο τὸ κλάσμα διεσκορπισμένον ἐπάνω τῶν ὀρέων καὶ συναχθὲν ἐγένετο ἕν, οὕτω συναχθήτω σου ἡ ἐκκλησία ἀπὸ τῶν περάτων τῆς γῆς εἰς τὴν σὴν βασιλείαν. ὅτι σοῦ ἐστιν ἡ δόξα καὶ ἡ δύναμις διὰ Ἰησοῦ εἰς τοὺς αἰῶνας.[20]

In the Baptismal prayers, in which the water is hallowed, the prayer is directed to Christ, this can be seen, for example, in the ending of the final prayer:

> ἵνα, γενόμενος σύμφυτος τῷ ὁμοιώματι τοῦ θανάτου σου διὰ τοῦ Βαπτίσματος, κοινωνὸς καὶ τῆς ἀναστάσεώς σου γένηται· καὶ φυλάξας τὴν δωρεὰν τοῦ Ἁγίου σου Πνεύματος καὶ αὐξήσας τὴν παρακαταθήκην τῆς χάριτος, δέξηται τὸ βραβεῖον τῆς ἄνω κλήσεως, καὶ συηκαταριθμηθῇ τοῖς πρωτοτόκοις, τοῖς ἀπογεγραμμένοις ἐν οὐρανῷ, ἐν σοὶ τῷ Θεῷ καὶ Κυρίῳ ἡμῶν Ἰησοῦ Χριστῷ.[21]

While the blessing of the water forms an important part of the Baptismal service as a whole, which was originally used in a Liturgical setting, during the Ressurection service on Easter morning (now celebrated on Holy Saturday morning), it is not the entirety of the

---

[20] Didache 9: 2-4 9:1
"But as touching the eucharistic thanksgiving give ye thanks thus.
9:2 First, as regards the cup:
9:3 We give Thee thanks, O our Father, for the holy vine of Thy son David, which Thou madest known unto us through Thy Son Jesus;
9:4 Thine is the glory for ever and ever.
9:5 Then as regards the broken bread:
9:6 We give Thee thanks, O our Father, for the life and knowledge which Thou didst make known unto us through Thy Son Jesus;
9:7 Thine is the glory for ever and ever.
9:8 As this broken bread was scattered upon the mountains and being gathered together became one, so may Thy Church be gathered together from the ends of the earth into Thy kingdom;
9:9 for Thine is the glory and the power through Jesus Christ for ever and ever." (Lightfoot, 2004)
[21] Μικρον Ευχολογιον (2004). pg. 71 "That, being planted in the likeness of Your death through Baptism, he (she) may become a sharer of Your Resurrection; and, preserving the Gift of Your Holy Spirit, and increasing the deposit of Grace, he (she) may attain unto prize of his (her) high calling, and accounted among the number of the first-born, whose names are written in Heaven, in You our God and Lord Jesus Christ." (Holy Cross Sacraments and Services).

Introduction

Baptism, other elements within the Baptismal service are, for example, the blessing of oil, the prayer for which is not directed to Christ, but to the Father:

> Δέσποτα Κύριε, ὁ Θεὸς τῶν Πατέρων ἡμῶν, ὁ τοῖς ἐν τῇ κιβωτῷ τοῦ Νῶε περιστερὰν ἀποστείλας, κάρφος ἐλαίας ἔχουσαν ἐπί τοῦ στόματος, καταλαγῆς σύμβολον, σωτηρίας τε τῆς ἀπὸ τοῦ κατακλυσμοῦ, καὶ τὸ τῆς χάριτος μυστήριον δι' ἐκείνων προτυπώσας· ὁ καὶ τῆς ἐλαίας τὸν καρπὸν εἰς πλήρωσιν τῶν ἁγίων σου Μυστηρίων χορηγήσας, ὁ δι' αὐτοῦ καὶ τοὺς ἐν χάριτι τελειῶν· Αὐτὸς εὐλόγησον καὶ τοῦτο τὸ ἔλαιον, τῇ δυνάμει καὶ ἐνεργείᾳ καὶ ἐπιφοιτήσει τοῦ Ἁγίου σου Πνεύματος, ὥστε γενέσθαι αὐτὸ χρίσμα ἀφθαρσίας, ὅπλον δικαιοσύνης, ἀνακαινισμὸς ψυχῆς καὶ σώματος, πάσης διαβολικῆς ἐνεργείας ἀποτρόπαιον, εἰς ἀπαλλαὴν κακῶν, πᾶσι τοῖς χριομένοις αὐτὸ ἐν πίστει, ἢ καὶ μεταλαμβάνουσιν ἐξ αὐτοῦ. Εἰς δόξαν σήν, καὶ τοῦ μονογενοῦς σου Υἱοῦ, καὶ τοῦ παναγίου καὶ ἀγαθοῦ καὶ ζωοποιοῦ σου Πνεύματος, νῦν καὶ ἀεὶ καὶ εἰς τοὺς αἰῶνας τῶν αἰώνων.[22]

Again we see that these prayers are not directed solely to Christ, but that the "Christusanrede" is only a part of the theological and stylistic whole, while in the Liturgy of St. Gregory the focus is solely on Christ and almost never, in prayers original to the Liturgy, shifts to other members of the Trinity. In 4th century homilies on Baptism too, there is an emphasis on the Trinity as a whole and not only on the person of Christ, this can be seen in John Chrysostom's second Baptismal homily,[23] in which he

The same holds true for the Apocryphal Scriptural texts that Gerhards discusses. One of these, the Acts of Thomas, is a Gnostic text which describes the journey of the Apostle Thomas to India and his work there as an apostle. In this text there are a number of prayers made by St. Thomas, most of them directed to Christ. In the first prayer made by St. Thomas, for example, he prays for a young princess who was about to be married, the plea is addressed to Christ:

---

[22] Μικρον Ευχολογιον (2004). pg. 73 „Sovereign Lord and Master, God of our Fathers, Who did send to them in the Ark of Noah a dove bearing a twig of olive in its beak as a sign of reconciliation and salvation from the Flood, and through these things prefigured the Mystery of Grace; and thereby have filled them that were under the Law with the Holy Spirit, and perfected them that are under Grace: do You Yourself bless this Oil by the power (+) and operation (+) and descent of the Holy Spirit (+) that it may become an anointing of incorruption, a shield of righteousness, a renewal of soul and body, and averting of every operation of the devil, to the removal of all evils from them that are anointed with it in faith, or that are partakers of it. To Your Glory, and to that of Your Only-Begotten Son, and of Your All; Holy, Good, and Life; creating Spirit, both now and ever, and to the ages of ages." (Holy Cross Sacraments and Services).
[23] Chrysostom. *Baptismal Homily II.* 21.

10 And the apostle stood, and began to pray and to speak thus: My Lord and MY God, that travellest with thy servants, that guidest and correctest them that believe in thee, the refuge and rest of the oppressed, the hope of the poor and ransomer of captives, the physician of the souls that lie sick and saviour of all creation, that givest life unto the world and strengthenest souls; thou knowest things to come, and by our means accomplishest them: thou Lord art he that revealeth hidden mysteries and maketh manifest words that are secret: thou Lord art the planter of the good tree, and of thine hands are all good works engendered: thou Lord art he that art in all things and passest through all, and art set in all thy works and manifested in the working of them all. Jesus Christ, Son of compassion and perfect saviour, Christ, Son of the living God, the undaunted power that hast overthrown the enemy, and the voice that was heard of the rulers, and made all their powers to quake, the ambassador that wast sent from the height and camest down even unto hell, who didst open the doors and bring up thence them that for many ages were shut up in the treasury of darkness, and showedst them the way that leadeth up unto the height: l beseech thee, Lord Jesu, and offer unto thee supplication for these young persons, that thou wouldest do for them the things that shall help them and be expedient and profitable for them. And he laid his hands on them and said: The Lord shall be with you, and left them in that place and departed.[24]

Here too, though, the apparent emphasis on Christ is not without exception, later in the narrative the king of India decides to be baptized, the baptismal prayer recited by St. Thomas ends: "Come, holy spirit, and cleanse their reins and their heart, and give them the added seal, in the name of the Father and Son and Holy Ghost."[25] The unity of style in the Liturgy of St. Gregory vs. the variation found in other Liturgical and Scriptural texts tells us that despite the existence of a tradition of "Christusanrede" laid out by Gerhards we must postulate that the author had a specific purpose in mind behind this. What is this purpose however? It is in the discussion of the date of the text that we find a possible answer. Above we discussed that the use of the term ὁμοούσιος leads us to the fourth century as a date of authorship, and to the context of the Arian and Pneumatomachian controversies.[26]

---

[24] *Acts of Thomas* (1924). 10. The translator takes the text, to a great extent, from the Syrian version.
[25] *Acts of Thomas* (1924). 27
[26] See below pg. 30

I.II. The Fourth Century

The history of the fourth century, at least the history of the Christianized Roman Empire, was defined by two emperors, Constantine the Great and Theodosius, and two theological controversies, Arianism and Pneumatomachianism.

The emperor Constantine reunited the eastern and western parts of the Roman Empire, divided by the emperor Diocletian, at the battle of the Malvian bridge.[27] It was in this battle that he, according to legend, saw a vision of the cross in the sky inscribed with, according to the source, the Latin words: *in hoc signo vinces* or the Greek: ἐν τούτῳ νίκα. This vision, or the recognition that the Christian population had grown to such a powerful segment of the empire that keeping them supressed would be impossible and dangerous, prompted the emperor to legalize Christianity with the Edict of Milan in 313.[28] Constantine decided to build a new captial for the empire over the old city of Byzantium on the Bosporus, which he called Constantinople.[29] Moving the capital of the empire also meant that the emperor was drawn more into the theological disputes that plagued the eastern part of the Empire. He was especially involved in the Arian controversy that raged throughout the fourth century.

The Christological controversy which became known as Arianism, broke out in A.D. 318. The name Arianism is taken from the priest, whose theology was the basis for the movement. Arius was the presbyter of the church and district of Baucalis in Alexandria. He was not originally from Alexandria, but, by birth, a Libyan.[30] His origins account for the staunch support he received in Libya. The controversy broke out when Arius "publically criticized the Christological doctrine of his bishop, Alexander of Alexandria."[31] The teachings of Arius himself are difficult to pinpoint, as we have only three surviving letters and a few other quotations that were written by Arius himself.[32] There is a quotation from a work by Arius, which tells us his underlying theological position: "He goes on to say that he [Arius] is being persecuted because he teaches that ‚the Son has an origin, but God is unoriginated' and also that ‚the Son derives from non-existence.'"[33] The earliest disciples of Arius expanded his theological ideas, which are summarized in the *Arius Iudaizans* and described by Hansons as:

---

[27] Eusebius, *Vita Constantini* 1.28
[32] Bettenson (1963). pg. 22
[29] Gerberding and Moran Cruz (2004). pg. 56
[30] This is recorded both by one of his biographers, Epiphanios, as well as in a letter written by the Emperor Constantine.
[31] Hanson (2005). Pg. 3
[32] Ibid.
[33] Ibid.

God was not always Father, he was once in a situation in which he was simply God and not Father...The Logos or Son is a creature. God made him out of non existence...There are two Logoi and two Wisdoms...The Son is variable by nature, but remains stable by the gift of God...The Logos is alien from the divine Being and distinct; he is not true God because he has come into existence...the Son's knowledge of God is imperfect...The Son's knowledge of himself is limited...the Son has been created for our sakes, as an instrument for creating us...[34]

This understanding of the Trinity, and the anthropocentric understanding of Christ formed the basis of Arian theology throughout the controversy.

Arius enjoyed wide support among eastern Christians, especially the bishops of his home province, Libya.[35] Many of the bishops in the west, however, such as Hillary of Poitiers, were opponents of Arianism as were some powerful theological figures in the east, such as Athanasius of Alexandria, Eustathius of Antioch and Marcellus of Ancyra.[36] The controversy raged on, nearly splitting the church and causing havoc in the empire; until Emperor Constantine convened a Council at Nicaea in 325,[37] which was charged with ending the controversy. There was amuch debate during the council[38] especially surrounding the wording of the statement of faith, the Nicene Creed. The Arians and the moderates argued that the relationship between Christ and God the Father should be termed: ὁμοιούσιος, of similar essence, while the "Nicene" party argued for ὁμοούσιος, that Christ is of the same essence as the Father.[39] The Nicenes were ultimately victorious at the Council and the term they favored was adopted into the Creed.

Even though the Nicenes defeated the Arians at Nicaea, the controversy was far from over. In the next generation, the Cappadocian Fathers in the east and Ambrose of Milan in the west were the major proponents of Nicene Christianity against the neo Arains, such as the Pneumatomachians.[40] The emperor Theodosius convened another council in 381 in Constantinople to settle the issue, the Arians were finally defeated. After this Arian-

---

[34] Ibid.
[35] Ibid.
[36] Ibid.
[37] Ibid.
[38] Growing so heated that, according to legend, St. Nicholas, the bishop of Myra, struck Arius across the face for his blasphemous attack on the divinity of Christ.
[39] Hanson (2005). pg. 193. For a history of the term ὁμοούσιος see Beatrice (2002). pp. 243-272.
[40] Hanson (2005). pg. 684

Introduction

ism in the empire was almost entirely wiped out and was restricted to the Germanic Goths, who were converted to Arianism by the missionary Ulfilas.[41]

Theodosius, like Constantine the Great, was instrumental in advancing Christianity in the Roman Empire. Where Constantine legalized, Theodosius made Christianity the official religion of the empire and closed down pagan temples and institutions such as the Academy in Athens.[42] Theodosius, like Constantine, was faced with a Christian population rent by theological dissension, a resurgent Arianism and the Pneumatomachians. This led him to call a second Council, this time in Constantinople, to deal with the problem.[43]

Pneumatomachianism, one of the offshoot branches of Arianism, which was developed by Macedonius who was Patriarch of Constantinople from 342 to 346, and from 351 until 360. These Macedonians, being semi-Arians, refused to acknowledge the validity of the term ὁμοούσιος in reference to Christ, but the main thrust of their theology was directed against the Holy Spirit, because of which they are called the Pneumatomachians. The Pneumatomachians were a group of extreme ascetics, which won them many adherents around the city of Constantinople, as well as in the surrounding provinces, such as Bithynia, Thrace, Pontos and other parts of Asia Minor.[44] This popularity prompted Theodosius to call an Ecumenical Council at Constantinople in 381, which condemned this theology by adding a section to the Nicene Creed that discusses the nature of the Holy Spirit: καὶ εἰς τὸ Πνεῦμα τὸ Ἅγιον, τὸ Κύριον καὶ Ζωοποιόν, τὸ ἐκ τοῦ Πατρὸς ἐκπορευόμενον, τὸ σὺν Πατρὶ καὶ Υἱῷ συμπροσκυνούμενον καὶ συνδοξαζόμενον, τὸ λαλῆσαν διὰ τῶν προφητῶν.[45] It is interesting to note that the term ὁμοούσιος, which was used to underscore the position of Christ in the Trinity, was not used of the Holy Spirit.

---

[41] It was the Arian Goths, who, while invading Spain, caused the Spanish bishops to meet in the Third Council of Toledo in 589. During this council the *filioque* was added to the Nicene-Constantinopolitan Creed.

[42] Hughes (1949). vol I chapter 6

[43] Williams and Friell. (1994). pg. 54

[44] Fuller, J. M. (1911). in Wace,and Piercy. *Dictionary of Christian Biography and Literature to the End of the Sixth Century*

[45] Cf. Hammond and Brightman (1896). pg. 383 "And in the Holy Spirit, the Lord and the Life giver, who proceeds from the Father, who with the Father and the Son is worshipped and glorified, who spoke through the prophets."

I.III. Forcing a Choice: Anti-Arian and Anti- Pneumatomachianism in the Liturgy

In part one of this chapter, we discussed how the author functionalizes the tradition of "Christusanrede"discussed by Gerhards by using it to excess, this unusual style would certainly have caught members of the congregation off guard, making sure that those attending would pay attention to this message, that Christ is the center of this liturgical rite. This is compounded by the dialogue style used by the author to make the connection between the congregation, through the person of the priest, and Christ closer.

Convincing the congregation of Christ's divinity is probably secondary, however, as the majority of those attending this liturgy would be Nicene Christians. More important is the ability to unify the "Nicene"Christians as a community and to marginalize those who do not conform to this theology. An Arian, after all, would not be able to attend or participate in a Liturgy during which Christ is constantly referred to as God and prayed to as such. It is in this context, that the question of audience and the communication-model of the liturgy is important. While the lay people who are present at the liturgy would certainly have noticed the way in which the liturgy had been functionalized, it is the clergy who would feel the full effect of it, as the celebrants recite the prayers which contain, at times, radical theology.[46] The clergyman is forced by this functionalization to make a choice, to embrace the Nicene theology presented in the text, or not to participate in the Eucharistic celebration at all, there is no middle ground. This way, the author communicates with the clergy through the prayers they recite and hopes to influence them and hopefully through them help to combat Arianism.

The function of this Liturgy corresponds to one of the rituals of the Jewish Liturgy, in the *Amidah*, a set of nineteen prayers recited daily. The twelfth *Amidot* of this set is the *Birkat Haminim* is a prayer against the heretics: "For the apostates let there be no hope. And let the arrogant government be speedily uprooted in our days. Let the noẓerim and the minim be destroyed in a moment. And let them be blotted out of the Book of Life and not be inscribed together with the righteous. Blessed art thou, O Lord, who humblest the arrogant."[47] The Minim, who are being prayed against here can be identified with the Christians, as is seen in two Egyptian manuscripts of the Amidah.[48] Both of these texts make it impossible for those who are considered heretics to take part in the worship of the majori-

---

[46] So for example in the *epiclesis*.
[47] Schechter. (1898), pg. 657
[48] Teppler. (2007). pp. 56 and 207

ty, in the Liturgy of St. Gregory: Arians, because they cannot acknowledge Christ as God and in the *Amidah*: Christians, because they cannot pray for their own destruction.[49]

What method does the author use to marginalize the Arians and the Pneumatomachians? In order to answer this question briefly, we will take two prayers as examples and analyze them. The first prayer we will look at is the: Εὐχὴ μετὰ τὴν ἑτοιμασίαν τοῦ Ἁγίου Θυσιαστηρίου in the Pre-Anaphora.[50] The second prayer will be the: Εὐχὴ τῆς κεφαλοκλισίας in the Post-Anaphora.[51]

a. One of the aspects of functionalization, which is difficult to pinpoint, but quite brilliant, is the way the author uses standard liturgical phraseology to emphasize Christ's position as God. In the Εὐχὴ μετὰ τὴν ἑτοιμασίαν τοῦ Ἁγίου Θυσιαστηρίου we can identify four different ways in which the author redefines the norm of liturgical phraseology: 1. Use of numerous epitheta and descriptions of Christ that underscore His divine nature as well as set up His authority. 2. Discussion of other members of the Trinity or the things usually associated with them in reference to Christ. 3. The use of terms of extreme humility when describing the ministering clergy or the people participating in the Liturgy. 4. The attribution of worship and praise solely to Christ, to the exception of other members of the Trinity.

Already in line one of this prayer the author makes clear to whom this prayer is addressed: Ἰησοῦ Χριστὲ, he accompanies this direct address with the first of the epithets: Δέσποτα Κύριε Ἰησοῦ Χριστὲ ὁ Θεὸς these opening epithets denote the power that Christ has. The positioning of these epithets is parallel to numerous other prayers in this and in other Liturgies,[52] this use here, shows us that the emphasis of the author is on Christ as Θεὸς, as God. The epithets Master and Lord come as a bundle before Christ's name, these epithets underscore Christ's power, but do not necessarily point out His divinity, since bishops, for example, are given the title Δέσποτα in the Greek speaking churches,[53] the title Κύριε, though more clear, since it is a title quite often used for God, still is not a definitive affirmation of divinity. This affirmation comes following Christ's name, where there is no room for misinterpretation, it is Christ who is God. More epithets follow in lines four and five, here Christ is termed: ζωοποιὲ, καὶ τῶν ἀγαθῶν χορηγὲ. These epithets do not have the same authoritative connotations as the ones in line one, on the other hand, they do

---

[49] ~~For a short study of some other examples of Liturgical propaganda, see Chapter two, pp. 43 ff.~~
[50] For the text see below pg. 59
[51] For the text see below pg. 143, 145.
[52] Cf. the opening of the Εὐχὴ τοῦ ἁγίου Εὐαγγελίου, which is not original to this Liturgy, but which opens in the same way.
[53] An example of this is seen in the opening exclamation of the deacon in the Divine Liturgy of St. John Chrysostom, in which the deacon proclaims: εὐλογήσον Δέσποτα.

underscore the divine nature of Christ. ζωοποιὲ refers to Christ's function as Creator, a function that is central in the epithets later in the prayer. This is an especially telling epithet because it is usually not found in connection with Christ, but with the Holy Spirit, for example, in the *ekphonesis* of the Εὐχὴ ἄλλη τοῦ ἀσπασμοῦ we see: ἅμα τῷ ἀχράντῳ σου Πατρὶ, καὶ τῷ **ζωοποιῷ** σου Πνεύματι. By transferring to Christ a function usually attributed to another member of the Trinity. This epithet, along with the other it is paired with: τῶν ἀγαθῶν χορηγὲ also serve an important function, to soften the stern and authoritative nature of the first set of epithets, this way both the authoritative nature of the "Christusanrede," and the intimate nature of the dialogue style are emphasized. The final set of epithets are found in line eight: Ἀγαθὲ Εὐέργετα Βασιλεῦ τῶν αἰώνων, καὶ τῆς κτίσεως ἁπάσης Δημιουργὲ in this set, we see a mix of the authoritarian: Βασιλεῦ τῶν αἰώνων and the intimate: Ἀγαθὲ, Εὐέργετα and τῆς κτίσεως ἁπάσης Δημιουργὲ.

  We have already discussed an instance of crossover between the use of epithets of Christ and the second type of funcitonalization, the discussion of other members of the Trinity and what is associated with them in reference to Christ. This is usually done using the qualifier σου In lines one to two the is the first time such a qualifier is used: τῆς σωτηριώδους παρουσίας σου in this case, though, the association does properly belong to Christ, it is Christ's second coming that is discussed; again, in lines four to five: τῆς καινῆς σου διαθήκης, here σου is used to link something with Christ that properly belongs to God the Father, in this case the New Convenent. Further on in line two, however, we see the Holy Spirit referred to in reference to Christ: παναγίου σου Πνεύματος, usually the Holy Spirit is referred to in reference to God the Father,[54] the same is true for a number of other instances in which the author uses the σου qualifier: in lines two and three: τοὺς ταπεινοὺς καὶ ἁμαρτώλους καὶ ἀναξίους δούλους σου and in line three to four: σου Θυσιαστηρίῳ. While it is logical that such a transference occurs in a Liturgy that is addressed to Christ, since He is the focus of the text, the transference is also used to marginalize the other members of the Trinity, in this way Christ always remains in an almost dominant position over the other members of the Trinity so that His position in the Trinity cannot be overlooked.[55]

  Twice in this prayer the priest refers to the congregation ἡμᾶς, in both of these instances the congregation is described in a manner of utter humility and self denigration. In lines two to three the congregation is described as: τοὺς ταπεινοὺς καὶ ἁμαρτώλους καὶ ἀναξίους δούλους σου and in line nine: ἀκατακρίτους. Eastern Liturgy is certainly no

---

[54] Cf. Holy Cross (1985). pg. 22
[55] Note too that God the Father is not mentioned in this prayer until the *ekphonesis*, see below pg. 77.

stranger to utter humility,[56] and the author is able to use this tradition to his advantage. One of the by products of the Arian heresy was the development of an anthropocentric view of the universe, in which Christ was created in order to facilitate the creation and later the salvation of humanity. By using the traditional language of self-abasement and humility the author is able to upend this anthropocentric view of the universe and place Christ in its center.

The author also discusses worship only in reference to Christ. In lines five and six, for example, he writes: ἐν καθαρῷ συνειδότι λατρεῦσαι σοι the choice of the term λατρεῦσαι is especially important, because *latria*, as opposed to *proskynisis*, was the type of worship reserved for God. By only directing this latria to Christ the author is able to once again underscore Christ's divinity. The author also puts Christ in the center of Liturgical worship, in line seven he writes: ταύτην σοι τὴν θείαν προσενέγκειν λειτουργίαν the author seems to sum up the function of his text here, like the Liturgy of St. Gregory as a whole, in this phrase the Liturgy, in which the entire Trinity is usually worshipped,[57] is offered solely to Christ.

b. The same themes are found throughout the text, in the Εὐχὴ τῆς κεφαλοκλισίας, for example, in the Post-Anaphora, a prayer at the very end of the text, we see the many of the same types of themes. In this prayer, the author seems to focus on the first theme. Of the seven lines, excluding the *ekphonesis*, of this rather short prayer, the first three lines are taken up with either direct epithets or more broad descriptions: ὁ κλίνας οὐρανοὺς καὶ κατελθών...ὁ τῆς σῆς χάριτος πᾶσαν ἐξαπλώσας...ὁ ποιῶν πάντα ὑπὲρ ἐκ περισσοῦ...Φιλάνθρωπε ἀγαθέ. Some of these descriptions also show a certain amount of overlap with the other themes, the first description, for example, shows Christ as the authoritative God, who has power to ‚bend the heavens,' it also places the authority over and responsibility for the incarnation and the salvation of humanity squarely in the hands of Christ. Transferring what is usually attributed to God the Father to Christ. The rest of the descriptions form part of the buildup of intimacy between the congregation and Christ, especially in the description of Him as the "lover of man." The transference of attributes from other members of the Trinity to Christ is less prominent in this prayer, despite several occasions in which the qualifier σου is used: τῆς σῆς χάριτος...σου τὴν χεῖρα... τοὺς δούλους σου... τῇ σῇ χάριτι...ἀχράντῳ σου Πατρί. these tend to discuss attributes that are

---

[56] See, as an example the *Canon of St. Andrew of Crete*.
[57] See, for example, the prayers in the *Anaphora of Sts. Addai and Mari*, in which the Trinity as a whole is the addresee.

usually associated with Christ, for example 'grace.'[58] We do see here again God the Father referred to in reference to Christ, though only in the *ekphonesis*, note that in the prayer proper there is no mention of God the Father. In the *ekphonesis* too we see the attribution of worship firstly to Christ: καὶ σοι πρέπει πᾶσα δόξα, μεγαλοσύνη, κράτος τε καὶ ἐξουσία.

I.IV. The Place of Origin

In the discussion surrounding the Liturgy of St. Gregory, the *communis opinio*[59] for the place of origin is Syria. The major commentators on this work, Jungmann, Hammerschmidt and Gerhards all agree that this Liturgy belongs to the West Syrian rite.[60] A problem presents itself in the Syrian liturgy of St. Gregory,[61] which has almost nothing in common with the Greek text.[62] It is highly unusual for a single liturgical rite, in this case the West Syrian, to contain two different texts both ascribed to the same author.[63] The Liturgy of St. James, for example, which has both a Greek version and a Syrian version, though the Syrian version is a translation of the Greek.[64] That the Liturgy of St. Gregory is part of the larger Syrian rite, however, is shown by the Anaphora, as demonstrated by Gerhards and Hammerschmidt,[65] as well as by prayers that are held in common.[66] The Greek Liturgy of St. Gregory must belong to a different subset of the Syrian rite than the Syrian Liturgy of St. Gregory. The question becomes, to which subset of the Syrian rite does the Greek Liturgy of St. Gregory belong? The opening prayer of the Greek Liturgy of St.

---

[58] Cf. the blessing of the priest in the Liturgy of St. Basil: ἡ χάρις τοῦ κυρίου ἡμῶν Ἰησοῦ Χριστοῦ...εἴη μετὰ πάντων ὑμῶν ("The grace of our lord Jesus Christ...be with all of you." Cf. Hammond and Brightman (1896). pg. 321).

[59] Older works, such as Baumstark (1908) and Beck (1959) do consider this liturgy as Cappadocian in origin: "Eine dritte griechische Anaphora der Kirche von Ägypten geht unter dem Namen des hl. Gregor von Nazianz. Auch sie soll nach A. Baumstark ein Import aus Kappadokien sein, und zwar die alte Anaphora der Kirche von Nazianz." (A third Greek Anaphora of the Egyptian Church is named after St. Gregory of Nazianzus. It is also, according to A. Baumstark, an import from Cappadocia, the ancient Anaphora of the Church of Nazianzus. Beck (1959). Pp. 240-241)." Despite the move towards the Syrian origin, I hope to show in the following section and in the Commentary that this theory bears out.

[60] Cf. Newman (2013) pp. 2-3. See also Hammerschmidt (1957). pp. 176-178 and Gerhards (1984). pp. 176-210

[61] *Anaphorae Syriacae* (1940). pp. 105-145

[62] Cf. Newman (2013) pp. 3-9

[63] Ibid.

[64] Hammond and Brightman (1896). pp. 33-68 and 74-110. An exception to this is the Liturgy of St. John Chrysostom, of which there are three versions, the Byzantine-Greek, the Syrian and the East Syrian. Renadot (1847). Volume II. pg. 253. He notes too, that a Chaldaean Liturgy also bears the name of St. John Chrysostom, this too has nothing in common with the Greek version (pp. 255-259)

[65] Hammerschmidt (1957). pp. 176-178 and Gerhards (1984). pp. 168-169

[66] Such as the opening prayer of the Liturgy, see below. pg. 73

Introduction

Gregory is almost identical with a prayer from the Greek Liturgy of St. James,[67] however, another Liturgy has a prayer which also shows common origin with the opening prayer of the Liturgy of St. Gregory, the Ἐυχὴ τῶν Πιστῶν in the Byzantine Liturgy of St. Basil:

Ὁ Θεός ὁ ἐπισκεψάμενος ἐν ἐλέει καὶ οἰκτιρμοῖς τὴν ταπείνωσιν ἡμῶν, ὁ στήσας ἡμᾶς τοὺς ταπεινοὺς καὶ ἁμαρτωλοὺς καὶ ἀναξίους δούλους σου κατενώπιον τῆς ἁγίας δόξης σου λειτουργεῖν τῷ ἁγίῳ σου Θυσιαστηρίῳ· σὺ ἐνίσχυσον ἡμᾶς τῇ δυνάμει τοῦ ἁγίου σου πνεύματος, εἰς τὴν διακονίαν ταύτην καὶ δὸς ἡμῖν λόγον ἐν ἀνοίξει τοῦ στόματος ἡμῶν εἰς τὸ ἐπικαλεῖσθαι τὴν χάριν τοῦ ἁγίου σου πνεύματος ἐπὶ τῶν μελλόντων προτίθεσθαι δώρων.[68]

Several other prayers in both the pre- and post-Anaphora are also held in common between these two Liturgies.[69] These commonalities along with the Byzantine forms found within the Anaphora itself[70] lead us to the conclusion that the Liturgies of St. Gregory and of St. Basil must have exerted great influence on one another.[71] This would be possible through one of two scenarios: 1. The Byzantine Liturgy of St. Basil, as the main Liturgical rite of the Church of Constantinople (until it was supplanted by the Liturgy of St. John Chrysostom in the year 1000)[72] exerted great influence on all the other Liturgical rites of the Eastern Church. It is possible that the Liturgy of St. Gregory borrowed prayers under influence of this Liturgy. This first hypothesis is untenable, however, since it is not the Liturgy of St. Gregory that borrows the prayers, but the Liturgy of St. Basil.[73] 2. The other possibility is that both of these Liturgies were in use in the same place, Constantinople and Cappadocia,[74] and were able to influence each other because of their common use in the

---

[67] Cf. Newman (2013). pg. 7

[68] Hammond and Brightman (1896). pg. 317 and Trempelis (1982). pg. 167. "O God, who looks upon our wretchedness in mercy and compassion, who places us, your wretched, sinful and unworthy slaves in the presence of Your divine glory to minister at Your divine table. Empower us with the power of Your Holy Spirit for this service and give us proper speech in the opening of our mouths for the calling upon of Your Holy Spirit upon the gifts about to be placed before (You)."

[69] Cf. below, the prayer of the Veil pp. 79-81, the prayer of the bowing of the head pp. 157, 159 and the prayer of the Gospel pp. 75, 77.

[70] Cf. Hammerschmidt (1957). pg. 176-177

[71] Cf. Newman (2013). pg. 9 ff.

[72] *Oxford Dictionary of Byzantium* (1991).

[73] Cf. Newman (2013). pg. 9-13.

[74] *Oxford Dictionary of Byzantium* (1991). A discussion of the origin of the Anaphora of St. Basil is beyond the scope of this paper, as it is a highly debated point. Recently, in 2004, Achim Budde has discussed the Egyptian Anaphora and the possibility that this may be the oldest form of this text: Budde, Achim. *Die ägyptische Basilios Anaphora: Text – Kommentar – Geschichte* (Münster: Aschendorff, 2004). The Armenian and Syrian influence on the Basilios Anaphora is discussed in Winkler, Gabriele. *Die Basilius-Anaphora: Edition der beiden armenischen Redaktionen und der relevanten Fragmente, Übersetzung und

same geographical area.[75] This seems to be the only way to explain how these two Liturgies, that otherwise would not have been able to mix in this way and have such an influence on each other. We must conclude, then, despite the lack of evidence, that the Liturgy of St. Gregory belongs to the Cappadocian subfamily of the West Syrian rite.

I.V. The Way to Egypt

How does a Liturgy make its way from Cappadocia to Egypt? A similar question was posed by Hugh Evelyn White, in his discussion of the textual fragments, including fragments of the Greek Anaphora of St. Gregory the Theologian, found in the St. Makarios monastery of the Wadi n' Natrun.[76] His discussion, however, departs from the assumption that the origin of this text is not in Cappadiocia, as we have discussed above, but in Syria.[77] He comes to the conclusion that the vector for bringing this Liturgy to Egypt were the Syrian monks that inhabited a monastery in the same Wadi.[78] Unfortunately there is no extant evidence to back this claim. For the lack of a better theory this idea has become the *communis opinio* and one finds it in most of the secondary literature.[79] When this adoption occured is another question, some claim that it occured relatively late, while authors such as Hammerschmidt claim an earlier date, as early as the sixth century.[80]

There are a number of problems with this theory, however, even without taking the Cappadocian origin of this Liturgy into consideration. The first is, as it was above, the Syrian Liturgy of St. Gregory. If a Liturgy were to have been brought into Egypt by Syrian monks, would it not have been that one? A second problem is presented by the research done on the Paris manuscript by H. Engberding. He comes to the conclusion that this manuscript, as opposed to the Anaphora extracts found in the Kacmarcik Codex and the fragments found in the Wadi n' Natrun, was in use by the "melkitisch-orthodoxe gemeind-

---

Kommentar. (Rom: Pontifico Instituto Orientale, 2005). These works build on the work done by Hieronymus Engberding in Engberding, Hieronymus. *Das eucharistische Hochgebet der Basiliosliturgie: Textgeschichtliche Untersuchung und kritische Ausgabe.* (Münster: Aschendorff, 1931) as well as on Schulz, Hans-Joachim. *The Byzantine Liturgy: Symbolic Structure and Faith Expression.* translated by Matthew J. O'Connell (New York: Pueblo Publishing Company, 1986). The place of origin of the Anaphora of St. Basil is not, ultimately, a deciding factor in this argument, since the majority of the prayers held in common between the two liturgies are outside of the Anaphora, and only occur in the Byzantien textual tradition.

[75] Cf. Newman (2013). Pg. 15.
[76] White (1926). pg. 200
[77] Ibid.
[78] Ibid.
[79] Cf. Cuming (1990). Introduction
[80] Hammerschmidt (1957). pp. 2-8

schaft"[81] we have, then, two textual traditions to work with then, one of which in use by the Greek population of Egypt, and one by the Coptic population. For the Syrian theory to still be viable we must assume a number of complicated steps: 1. The Greek text is brought from Syria to Egypt, to the monasteries of the Wadi n' Natrun; 2. The Greek text is adopted by the Coptic monks in the Wadi n' Natrun and spreads from there throughout the Coptic world; 3. The Greeks in Egypt adopt the Greek text from the Copts and begin to use it themselves; 4. The Greek text is translated into Coptic and the translation becomes the Liturgical norm in the Coptic Church. Why, though, would the Greek population adopt a Liturgy that was in use by the Copts and Syrians? The Melkites, the ‚king's men' belonged to the Church that accepted the Council of Chalcedon (451), while the Coptic Church did not, causing a rift between the two Churches that has not healed to this day. This rift makes a borrowing of this nature, an entire Liturgical text, unlikely. What other vector can be proposed, however, to replace this theory?

One possibility is found in the Cappadocian origin of this Liturgy. This Liturgy may have travelled to Egypt with Greeks from Constantinople and Cappadocia, who would have been familiar with this Liturgy. This introduction would have occured any time between the creation of this Liturgy (379-385) and the sixth century (the date postulated by Hammerschmidt for the translation of this Liturgy into Coptic). An early date for the introduction of this Liturgy into Egypt is preferable because of the existence of not only Bohairic Coptic translations,[82] but a Sahidic Coptic translation as well.[83] Sahidic Coptic fell out of favor for Ecclesiastical writings already in the eleventh century, so a relatively early date would be logical. An early date of introduction also circumvents the problem posed by the rift in the Egyptian Church, the Copts adopted the text before the Christological problems of Monophysitism caused the two Churches to split apart. The translation was then

---

[81] Engberding (1936). 152. Newer theories, including that of Gerhards, postulate that the Paris Manuscript belongs to the monophysite tradition rather than the melkite (pg. 15). The latest theory has been postulated by Brakmann in: Brakmann, Hieronymos. *Zur stellung des Parisinus Graecus 325 in der alexandrinisch-ägyptischen Liturgie...* 97-110, in which he discusses... Although the evidence does point to the manuscript orginating in the Macarius monastery, a Coptic monastery, the complete text found in the Paris Manuscript, as opposed to the Kacmarcik Codex and the Wadi n' Natrun fragments, which are only the text of the Anaphora inserted or to be inserted in the „Coptic Ordinary," seems to indicate a Melkite origin. If the text contained in the manuscript was that used by the Melkites (the Liturgy of St. Basil contained in the manuscript is the Egyptian Liturgy of St. Basil, which was in use by the Melkites as well, until it was replaced by the Byzantine Liturgy of St. Basil), but the manuscript a copy that had been obtained by the Copts and preserved and copied in the Macarius monastery, this would explain both the complete form of the text and its origin in a Coptic monastery also uniting the theory of Engberding with that of Gerhards.
[82] The basis of the edition put together by Hammerschmidt.
[83] Cf. Hammerschmidt (1957). pp. 104-106. Here Hammerschmidt lays out the few differences between the Bohairic and Sahidic translations of this text.

made by the Coptic Church in order to distance itself from the Chalcedonian Melkites. This theory has the following Structure: 1. Authorship of the Greek text of the Liturgy in Cappadocia; 2. Introduction of this Greek text among the Greek population of Egypt between in the fourth or fifth century; 3. Adoption of the Greek text by the Coptic population in between the fourth and sixth century; 4. Translation of the Greek text into Sahidic Coptic (probably in the sixth century) and later into Bohairic Coptic.

Unfortunately, there is as little extant evidence for this theory as there was for the theory postulated by H. E. White. The theory does, however, seem to have fewer issues than those presented by the Syrian origin theory.

I.VI. The Liturgy in Egypt

The last stage of development in this Liturgy is the reappearance of the Greek text in Egypt in the fourteenth century. Of the five extant manuscripts three, Paris Manuscript Greque 325, the Kacmarcik Codex, and the Wadi n' Natrun fragments, are dated to the fourteenth century.[84] The two remaining manuscripts are of a later date.[85] There are no extant manuscripts from before the fourteenth century, whether in Egypt, Syria or in Cappadocia.

The work of H. Engeding has shown that the Paris Codex was used by the Melkite Greeks. Who, however, used the other two manuscripts? Since the text was translated into Coptic, it seems logical that the Copts would use the Coptic text rather than the Greek, and that the other Greek manuscripts should be counted to the Melkites as well. This is not the case, however, the two other manuscripts seem to be in use among the Copts. Both of the texts consist only of the Anaphora, which is consistent with the Coptic practice of inserting various *Anaphorae* into the Ordinary of the Coptic Liturgy.[86] The Wadi n' Natrun fragments are known to originate among the Copts, because they were found in a Coptic monastery. The text of the Kacmarcik Codex, however, is more difficult to place. One aspect of the text does help to place it, the entire Greek text is written phonetically. This suggests that this text was meant for use by clergy familiar with the Greek alphabet, but unsure of the pronunciation, Coptic clergy. There are a couple of explanations as to why the Coptic Church uses this Greek text. Gerhards suggests that the manuscripts were kept in the monasteries out of tradition, and in order to be used.[87] The phonetic Kacmarcik Codex seems to

---

[84] Gerhards (1984). pp. 17-18
[85] Ibid.
[86] Cf. Hammond and Brightman (1984). pp. 144-188
[87] Gerhards (1984). pg. 6

confirm this theory. Since this was to be used liturgically, the scribe transcribing the text writes the words out so that even non Greek speaking clergymen would be able to utilize it in services. It is possible that the manuscript tradition is so strong that this phonetically written text is copied from an earlier manuscript dating to a time when Greek was still in common use among the Copts. The question is raised, however, why is there one textual tradition in which the Greek text is written phonetically and one in which it is written correctly, as is seen in the Wadi n'Natrun fragments, especially since White is uncertain when, "if ever"the Greek text was used in the Monastery of St. Macarius?[88] This seems to weaken the theory of use and point to record keeping as a basis for keeping the Greek texts.

The answer to why the Coptic Church seems to have manuscripts of the Greek text for liturgical use as well as part of their manuscript tradition must be sought in the historical occurances of fourteenth century Egypt.

The fourteenth century in Egypt was marked by several major occurences: Alexandria was conquered and abandoned by Peter of Cyprus in his short lived Alexandrian Crusade (1365).[89] The consolidation of power by the Mamluks in Egypt secured by their defeat of the Mongols and their subsequent signing of a peace treaty.[90] The fourteenth century was also marked by a decline in the Coptic community:

> During this period the Coptic Church was on the verge of experiencing its worst declining trend across all aspects of its heritage. Manuscripts production in that period were mostly of a liturgical nature There were three monumental works related to the liturgical heritage that came from that period. The first was the 14th century medieval encyclopedia of Ibn Kabar. It was titled, *Misbah al-Zulmah fi Idah al-Khidma*, or *The Lamp of Darkness for the Explanation of the Service*. The second is a work by Youhanna ibn Sabaa, titled, a*l-jawhara al-Nafisa fi 'eloum al-Kanisa*, or *the Precious Jewel in Ecclesiastical Sciences*. The third, and most important, is a work by the Coptic Patriarch Gabriel V (1409-27), intended to regulate and reform the liturgical practices of the time. This work was titled simply, *al-Tartib al-Taqsi*, or *the Ritual Order*.[91]

One possibility, that the attack on Alexandria forced some of the Greek population out of the city as refugees, who then settled with the Coptic community and prompted the

---

[88] White (1926). pg. 200
[89] For more information see: van Steenbergen (2003).
[90] Ibid.
[91] A compilation of Coptic sources was compiled by N. Takla (1996).

reestablishment of the use of Greek. This, unfortunately, cannot be the case. The sources agree that, while the Mamluk garrison of Alexandria was defeated, and a large number of the civilian population were killed, there was no lasting siege and after the city was sacked the Crusaders, not wishing to face more battles against the Mamluk armies (such as the garrison at Cairo) retreated back to Cyprus. This expedition, then, did not have any lasting effect on the population Alexandria, much less the population of Egypt as a whole. Another problem is that the Wadi n' Natrum fragments date from before this Crusade took place, the fragments bear the name of the reigning Patriarch (Patriarch Benjamin II 1327-1339).[92] The Kacmarcik Codex too is dated earlier than this crusade.[93]

That the Greek Liturgy of St. Gregory was rediscovered in the context of a liturgical renewal or reform, as undertaken by Pope Gabriel, also does not fit into the chronological context, since this reform took place early in the fifteenth century, nearly 100 years after the Wadi n'Natrun and Kacmarcik Codices were written.

It may have been the decline in influence of the Coptic community in the fourteenth century and the subsequent decline in Coptic culture that precipitated the Coptic community to attempt, as Gerhards suggests, to preserve their manuscritpt tradition by having the old Greek manuscripts rewritten along with the more common Coptic manuscripts (see the list of Coptic manuscripts of St. Gregory the Theologian listed out in Hammerschmidt (1957). Pp. 1-8). This would explain the Wadi n'Natrun codex, but where does the Kacmarcik Codex, with its phonetc spelling of the Greek alphabet (which points to what Hugh Evelyn White postulates, that there were certain occasions on which the Coptic Church used Greek in its liturgy) fit into this scheme? Perhaps it was because of this renewed interest in preserving the Greek texts, as well as the influnce of the Melkite community, that the Coptic Church was encouraged to ressurect Greek as a language used in services.

I.VII. The Question of Authorship

The Liturgy of St. Gregory, whether it be the Greek-Egyptian text, the Syrian or even the Armenian are all attributed to one of the greatest saints in the history of the Eastern Church, one of only two who were honored with the title: "the theologian."Before discussing whether or not St. Gregory could have actually written one of these texts it is important to understand why, assuming for the moment that he did not write the text, the author

---

[92] White (1926). pg. 200
[93] Cf. Gerhards (1984). pg. 17

chose to attribute his work to him. In order to understand this we must first give a brief overview of his *vita*.

1. The life of St. Gregory the Theologian.

Unlike the *vitae* of many of the less well known saints of the Eastern Church, St. Gregory's life is rather well known. St. Gregory was born in the year 330 to an aristocratic family of Cappadocia in Asia Minor.[94] His parents, who were also canonized,[95] were Gregory the Elder, biship of Nazianzen, and Nonna.[96] He received his elementary education in Nazianzen, and when he completed his studies there he went on to Caesarea in Cappadocia to continue.[97] From Cappadocia St. Gregory went on to Palestinian Caesarea and there studied under the Rhetor Thespasius.[98] He continued on from Palestine to Egypt, where he spent some time in Alexandria and from there to the Academy at Athens, where he completed his studies, remaining there for ten years.[99] Though it is not certain whether in Caesarea in Cappadocia or in Athens, it was during these years of study that St. Gregory met St. Basil the Great, who would become his lifelong friend.[100] The two of them, along with St. Gregory of Nyssa,[101] are today considered among the greatest of the Church Fathers to have come out of Cappadocia. They along with St. John Chrysostom, are termed the "Three Great Hierarchs."

After completing his education, St. Gregory returned to his family in Nazianzen, in either 358 or 359.[102] Meanwhile St. Basil the Great had founded a monastery and was compiling his rules for the monastic life. St. Gregory visited his friend regularly between the years of 359 and 362,[103] however, following his ordination in 361, the visits grew less frequent due to the increased duties in administering the diocesce of Nazianzen that went along with his new office. Soon after this, between 370 and 371, St. Basil the Great began to campaign for the diocesan see of Cesarea in Cappadocia, an extremely important see in Asia Minor. Both St. Gregory and his father, Gregory the elder, were instrumental in this campaign and St. Basil was successfully elected to the see.[104] This important diocesce had

---

[94] Synaxarion (2001). pg. 284
[95] Ibid.
[96] Hanson (2005). 701
[97] Ibid.
[98] Ibid.
[99] Ibid.
[100] Ibid.
[101] Who was the brother of St. Basil the Great.
[102] Hanson (2005). pg. 701
[103] Synaxarion (2001). pg. 286
[104] Hanson (2005). 702

lost much of its power when it was divided in half by the Emperor Valens. In order to strengthen his position, St. Basil needed to install supporters in the surrounding area, so he decided to appoint St. Gregory to the see of Sasima, a small city on the borders of Cappadocia.[105] St. Gregory did consent to the position, but refused to enter the city. Instead of staying in Sasima, St. Gregory fled to the mountains and remained there in seclusion until he heard of his fathers death in 374.[106] When he returned to Nazianzen he was put under great pressure to take his father's place as bishop of that city. Refusing, he once again fled, this time taking refuge at the monastery of St. Thekla in Selevria, remaining there until 378.[107]

The following year, 379, was a momentous one both for St. Gregory personally, as well as for the Roman Empire in general. This was the year in which St. Basil the Great died, and the year in which a new Emperor took the throne, Theodosius.

2. St. Gregory and the Arians.

Theodosius was a staunch supporter of the Nicene party, the group that espoused the position that Christ is ὁμοούσιος with God the Father, who had defeated the Arians at the First Council of Nicaea in 325. In order to meet the request for help made by the few non Arian believers in the capital of Constantinople, the emperor decided to install St. Gregory in the city, as the best candidate to counteract the Arians, who had control of the majority of the churches at this point. St. Gregory accepted the commission and went to Constantinople, setting up a house church for the Nicene Christians, the Anastasia church.[108] St. Gregory preached in this church until Theodosius forcibly expelled the Arians from the churches in Constantinople and installed Gregory as the Patriarch.[109]

Along with Arianism proper was another group that had grown powerful in Constantinople, the Pneumatomachians, also known as the Macedonians, after the developer of their theology, Macedonius, the Arian Patriarch of Constantinople 342-346 and 351-360. In 381 the Emperor Theodosius convened a council of bishops in Constantinople to decide the issue of Arianism and Pneumatomachianism once and for all.[110] Presiding over the coucil was the aging Patriarch of Antioch, who unfortunately died during the deliberations.[111] As the bishop of the city in which the council was held, St. Gregory took up the

---

[105] Synaxarion (2001). pg. 289 and Hanson (2005). 702
[106] Hanson (2005). pg. 702
[107] Synaxarion (2001). pg. 290
[108] Hanson (2005). pg. 703
[109] Hanson (2005). pg. 704
[110] This was the Second Ecumenical Council.
[111] Synaxarion (2001). pg. 292

presidency. This changed when the Egyptian bishops arrived at Constantinople.[112] They questioned St. Gregory's right to hold the presidency of the council and his right to the see of Constantinople, as he was still the bishop of Sasima. Gregory agreed to resign his position and returned to Nazianzen, where he took up the duties of bishop for the, still vacant, see of his father.[113] In 383 St. Gregory retired as bishop of Nazianzen and returned to his estates in Arianzus, where he spent the rest of his life writing many of his theological poems. St. Gregory died in the year 389.[114]

3. The works of St. Gregory.

St. Gregory, called the Theologian, certainly earned the title. His works are numerous and an integral part of the theology of the Eastern Church. The majority of his theological writings were his orations, of which there are forty five and his poetry, of which there are five hundred and seven.[115] The forty five orations are divided up as: 1. The five theological orations; 2. The two invectives against Julian; 3. The moral orations; 4. The festal orations; 5. The Panegyrics on the Saints; 6. Funeral orations and 7. Occasional orations.[116] Of these orations the five theological orations have garnered the most attention:

> These won him the title of The Theologian. They were delivered in Constantinople, in defense of the Church's faith in the Trinity, against Eunomians and Macedonians. In the First and Second he treats of the existence, nature, being, and attributes of God, so far as man's finite intellect can comprehend them. In the Third and Fourth the subject ist he Godhead of the Son, which he establishes by exposition of Scripture and by refutation of the specious arguments brought forward by the heretics. In the Fifth he similarly maintains the Deity and Personality of the Holy Ghost.[117]

The Fourth and Fifth Theological Oration are especially interesting in light of the purpose of the Liturgy of St. Gregory, which targets the same ‚heretics' as these orations do. The orations of St. Gregory also use the term ὁμοούσιος in a unique way that is also found in the Liturgy of St. Gregory: Τί οὖν; θεὸς τὸ πνεῦμα; πάνυ γε. Τί οὖν, ὁμοούσιον;

---

[112] Hanson (2005). pg. 704
[113] Hanson (2005). pg. 705
[114] Ibid.
[115] Browne and Swallow (1894). pp. 200-201
[116] Taken from Browne and Swallow (1894). pp. 200-201
[117] Browne and Swallow (1894). pg. 200

εἴπερ Θεός.¹¹⁸ The term is usually used, as is seen in the Nicene Creed, as a way to define the relationship between Christ and God the Father.¹¹⁹ St. Gregory widens the use¹²⁰ of this term to include the Holy Spirit, and in the liturgy attributed to him a similar use of the term is found: τό τε θεῖον καὶ ἅγιον καὶ **ὁμοούσιον** καὶ ὁμοδύναμον καὶ ὁμόδοξον καὶ συναΐδιον Πνεῦμα καταπέμψας.¹²¹

This connection is very important in the discussion whether or not it is possible that St. Gregory did write this liturgy. The mere fact that the term homoousios is used in a liturgical text is not itself proof of his authorship, as the term is often used in relationship to the Holy Spirit in the ekphoneseis of prayers in Coptic and Syrian liturgies.¹²² In this liturgy, however, the term is not used as a stock liturgical phrase, and the author even avoids using the phrase in prayers borrowed from Coptic or Syrian liturgies in which it is used, such as in the first prayer of the liturgy.¹²³ The use, then, is a deliberate attack on the position of the Arians and the Pneumatomachians, rather than mere liturgical convention and helps to narrow down when this work was written to the late fourth century. While this does not itself prove the authorship of Gregory, it makes his authorship a possibility.¹²⁴

The poems are also subdivided, thirty eight of them are "dogmatic"¹²⁵ forty are "moral"¹²⁶ two hundred and six are "hisorical and aubtobiographical"¹²⁷ through which we find out much of our information on St. Gregory, one hundred and twenty nine are "epitaphs"¹²⁸ and ninety four are "epigrams."¹²⁹ Browne and Swallow also discuss the quality of St. Gregory's work: "While leaving much to be desired, these verses shew much real poetic feeling, and at times rise to genuine beauty."¹³⁰

We also have a number of letters, two hundred and forty three, these are: "characterised by a clear, concise, and pleasant style and spirit."¹³¹

---

[118] Gregory Nazianzen. Theological Oration 5. 11.2 „Is then the Spirit God? Certainly. Is he of one essence? If indeed he is God."
[119] Cf. Newman (2014). pg. 2-3.
[120] For a more comprehensive discussion of this term in the Liturgy see Newman (in progress). Pp. 5-14
[121] Cf. Newman (2014). pg. 18; Cf. also below pg. 143.
[122] Cf. Newman (2014). pg. 5-12
[123] Cf. below pg. 73
[124] Cf. Newman (2014). 1-5
[125] Browne and Swallow (1894). pg. 201
[126] Ibid.
[127] Ibid.
[128] Ibid.
[129] Ibid.
[130] Ibid.
[131] Ibid.

Another text attributed to St. Gregory is the first Christian tragedy, the *Christus Patiens*.[132] This lengthy text consists mostly of quotations from Euripides, especially the *Medea*.[133] Many scholars no longer believe that text was written by St. Gregory, and some have attributed it to another Gregory, who was bishop of Antioch in the sixth century.[134]

4. St. Gregory and the Liturgy of St. Gregory.

One sees a clear movement towards an acceptance of St. Gregory as the author of this liturgy in the secondary literature. Hammerschmidt, despite several instances in which he remarks on the similarity in style and theology between this text and others of St. Gregory, claims that St. Gregory does not come into question as the author: "Es soll hier mit der Anführung des Gregor von Nazianz nicht etwa auf seine Autorschaft der Greglit angespielt..."[135] In this way Hammerschmidt distances himself from having to even suggest St. Gregory as the author in a point in the text where the theological terminology[136] corresponds exactly to that of St. Gregory. Part of the reason for this careful formulation is the assumption made by many scholars that the authors to whom liturgical texts are attributed cannot be the actual authors. One sees this, for example, in Hammerschmidt's work on the Ethiopic *Anaphorae*, in which he states that those wishing to suggest St. Basil, St. John Chrysostom or St. Gregory the Theologian bear the burden of proof in the discussion. This view has often proven to be the correct, as a number of liturgical texts are, in fact, incorrectly attributed to St. James, or to St. Mark. Other Liturgies, have been proven to, at least partially, have been composed by the authors to whom they are attributed, this is the case, for example, with the Liturgy of St. Basil.[137] Gerhards takes this change in attitude into account when he cannot stylistically and contextually exclude the possibility that St. Gregory was in fact the author.[138]

A comprehensive study of the style of the Liturgy of St. Gregory as compared to the other works of St. Gregory has yet to be done and, while some general stylistic features held in common are discussed in this investigation, it is beyond the scope of this work to fill this deficit completely. In the other commentaries to the Liturgy of St. Gregory the commentators too only discussed general similarities, Hammerschmidt, for example points

---

[132] Ibid.
[133] For more information see a dissertation in progress at the University of Zürich by Lena Krauss.
[134] Browne and Swallow (1894). Pg. 201
[135] Hammerschidt (1957). Pg. 169
[136] In this case the use of the term οὐσία.
[137] Cf. the Oxford Classical Dictionary (1991)
[138] Gerhards (1984). Pg. 104-105

out the similar use of the term οὐσιά and uses it to establish a possible time frame for the authorship of the liturgy.[139]

Gerhards, however, spends more time on this topic, especially in the discussion of an earlier work by Caro Sanchez,[140] who discusses the Post-Sanctus prayer of the Liturgy of St. Gregory, and the place of Christ in the works of St. Gregory, as compiled by Rudasso in 1968.[141] Gerhards sums up the Sanchez's theory in the following section:

> Die These Sanchez Caros lautet nun, dass die Gregoriosanaphora die so skizzierte Christusfrömmigkeit Gregors von Nazianz wiederspiegelt. Zum Beweis führt Sanchez Caro einige Themen an, die die Gregoriosanaphora mit den Schriften des Kappadokiers gemeinsam hat: die Zuordnung der Schöpfertätigkeit an den Logos, die Erschaffung des Menschen als ‚König der Schöpfung': er allein ist ‚mit der Hand und mit dem Bild Gottes geehrt',[142] der Lebensbaum als Baum der Erkenntnis: die Solidarität der Menschheit mit dem ‚ersten' und dem ‚zweiten' Adam (Christus).[143]

Caro's thesis is accepted by Gerhards: "Der...Beitrag Sanchez Caros hat überzeugend dargelegt, dass die Gregoriosanaphora ... nicht zu Unrecht mit Gregor von Nazianz in Verbindung gebracht wird."[144] The connection between St. Gregory and the liturgy is considered tentative at best by Gerhards, who postulates a range of time for the authorship of this prayer from the mid of the fourth century to the middle of the fifth century. This means that possible authors are: "...Gregor selbst, einem Zeitgenossen oder einem späteren Redaktor, der sich von den Schriften des Kappadokiers ... inspirieren liess..."[145] Gerhards is more generous in his interpretation of Caro than Caro himself is since, like

---

[139] Hammerschmidt (1957) 168-169
[140] Gerhards (1984). Ppg. 105-109
[141] Gerhards (1984). Pg. 106
[142] Gregory Nazianzus Or. 39, 13
[143] Gerhards (1984). Pp. 106-107. „Sanchez Caro's theory is that the Anaphora of St. Gregory shows the theological 'Christ piety' of Gregory Nazianzen. As evidence Sanchez Caro offers several themes, which the Anaphora of St. Gregory shares with the writings of the Cappadocian Fathers: the attribution of the fuction of Creator to the Logos; the creation of humans as the 'King of Creation:' he alone is 'honored with the hand and image of God;' The tree of life as the tree of the knowledge of good and evil; the solidarity of humanity with the 'first' and 'second' Adam (Christ)." Cf. Caro (1984). pg. 323.
[144] Gerhards (1984). Pg. 109. „The contribution of Sanchez Caro has shown convincingly that the Anaphora of St. Gregory was not connected with the Gregory Nazianzen without cause."
[145] Gerhards (1984). Pg. 109. „Gregory himself, someone from the same time or a later editor, who let himself be inspired by the works of the Cappadocian Fathers."

Hammerschmidt, he denies the possibility that St. Gregory comes into question as the author.[146]

Along with the sylistic similarities between the Post-*Sanctus* prayer and the works of St. Gregory described by Sanchez Caro above, there are a number of other points in which the writings of St. Gregory coincide, especially the *Theological Orations*, and the text of this liturgy. One of the most striking similarities is seen in the short prayers that conclude four of the *Five Theological Orations*. In the first, third and fourth Oration, the short prayer is directed to Christ: 1. ἐν αὐτῷ Χριστῷ Ἰησοῦ τῷ κυρίῳ ἡμῶν, ᾧ ἡ δόξα εἰς τοὺς αἰῶνας· ἀμήν.[147] 3. ἐν αὐτῷ Χριστῷ τῷ κυρίῳ ἡμῶν, ᾧ ἡ δόξα εἰς τοὺς αἰῶνας· Ἀμήν.[148] 4. Ἰησοῦς Χριστός, χθὲς καὶ σήμερον σωματικῶς, ὁ αὐτὸς πνευματικῶς, καὶ εἰς τοὺς αἰῶνας. Ἀμήν.[149] Since these Orations are meant to either combat the Eunomians, a subset of the Arians, or to define and defend the divinity of Christ these short prayers can be interpreted as serving the same purpose as the address of Christ in the liturgy, as polemic. That these prayers share this same specific function, rather than being coincidentally attributed to Christ, is shown by the end of the other two Orations. The *Second Theological Oration* has no concluding prayer, but the *Fifth Theological Oration*, which deals with the person of the Holy Spirit, ends with the following prayer: πατέρα καὶ υἱόν, καὶ πνεῦμα ἅγιον, τὴν μίαν θεότητά τε καὶ δύναμιν· ὅτι αὐτῷ πᾶσα δόξα, τιμή, κράτος, εἰς τοὺς αἰῶνας τῶν αἰώνων· Ἀμήν.[150] The style seen in the Orations is, then, similar to that in the liturgy, and may act as the precedent for the liturgy, providing a different precedent than the "Christusanrede"in liturgical tradition postulated by Gerhards, discussed above.[151] This assumes that the *Five Theological Orations* have an earlier date than this liturgy, which is affirmed by the date of these Orations, presented between 379 and 380[152] while internal evidence in the liturgy places the date of authorship between 380 and 385.[153] Though both the Arians and the Pneumatomachians are combated in the Orations, only Christ is addressed personally in

---

[146] Caro (1984). pg. 68

[147] St. Gregory the Theologian Theological Oration 1. 10, 21-22 "...in the Same, our Lord Jesus Christ, to Whom be glory for ever. Amen..."Browne and Swallow (1894). Pg. 288

[148] St. Gregory the Theologian Theological Oration 3. 21, 24-25 "...in Him, Christ our Lord, to Whom bet he glory for ever. Amen..."Browne and Swallow (1894). Pg. 309

[149] St. Gregory the Theologian Theological Oration 4. 21. 36-38 "...Jesus Christ is the Same yesterday and to-day in the Incarnation, and in the Spirit for ever and ever. Amen..." Browne and Swallow (1894). Pg. 318

[150] St. Gregory the Theologian Theological Oration 5. 33, 18-20 „...Father, Son, and Holy Ghost, the One Godhead and Power. To Him belongs all glory and honour and might for ever and ever. Amen." Browne and Swallow (1894). Pg. 328

[151] c.f above pg. 2-3.

[152] Browne and Swallow (1894). Pg. 196-199

[153] Cf. Newman (2014). Pg. 19-21

prayer, where we may expect a prayer to the Holy Spirit, in the *Fifth Theological Oration*, we find a prayer to the Trinity as a whole.

Another stylistic feature which the two texts share is a reliance on contradiction to underscore the interplay between the human and divine natures of Christ. So, in the *Third Theological Oration*, we read:

> ἐγεννήθη μέν, ἀλλὰ καὶ ἐγεγέννητο· ἐκ γυναικὸς μέν, ἀλλὰ καὶ παρθένου. τοῦτο ἀνθρώπινον, ἐκεῖνο θεῖον. ἀπάτωρ ἐντεῦθεν, ἀλλὰ καὶ ἀμήτωρ ἐκεῖθεν. ὅλον τοῦτο θεότητος. ἐκυοφορήθη μέν, ἀλλ' ἐγνώσθη προφήτῃ καὶ αὐτῷ κυοφορουμένῳ, κξαὶ προσκιρτῶντι τοῦ λόγου, δι' ὃν ἐγένετο.[154]

A similar juxtaposition of the divine and human natures of Christ are found in the Liturgy of St. Gregory. One way in which this contradiction is shown is in the use of divine epithets, for example in the Εὐχὴ μετὰ τὴν ἑτοιμασίαν τοῦ Ἁγίου Θυσιαστηρίου, in this prayer, Christ is referred to with titles that set him up as a divine ruler: Δέσποτα, Βασιλεῦ τῶν αἰώνων and τῆς κτίσεως ἁπάσης Δημιουργὲ as well as with titles that emphasize Christ's connection with His people and soften the strict authoritarian picture presented by the above epithets. In the same prayer Christ is also called: ζωοποιὲ, καὶ τῶν ἀγαθῶν χορηγὲ...Ἀγαθὲ, Εὐέργετα. By juxtaposing these epithets the author of the liturgy is, like St. Gregory, able to emphasise both Christ's divinity and His humanity by underscoring both His kingly and His kindly aspects.

One of the theological aspects of the Liturgy of St. Gregory, that may have been scandalous, is the tendency of the liturgy to emphasize Christ over the other members of the Trinity, especially over God the Father. This emphasis is shown in 1. the lack of discussion of the other members of the Trinity, especially the Father is almost never discussed outside the *ekphonesis*, it is not until the Εὐχὴ τοῦ ἀσπασμοῦ in the pre-Anaphora that the Father is discussed at all: ὁ τῷ Πατρὶ συναΐδιος καὶ ὁμοούσιος καὶ σύνθρονος and μεσίτης ἡμῶν γέγονας καὶ τοῦ Πατρὸς, in both of these instances it is still Christ that is under discussion, the Father is present in the text only as a reference point for the nature of Christ, and as one part of an equation, the central portion of which is Christ. In the *ekphoneseis* too, where the Father is found much more often than in the text proper, the Father is presented in a subordinate position to Christ, so, for example in the Εὐχὴ εὐχαριστίας μετὰ

---

[154] St. Gregory the Theologian Theological Oration 3. 19, 10-15 „He was born – but He had been begotten: He was born of a woman – but she was a Virgin. The first is human the second Divine. In His Human nature He had not Father, but also in His Divine Nature no Mother. Both these belong to Godhead. He dwelt in the womb – but He was recognized by the Prophet, himself still in the womb, leaping before the Word, for whose sake He came into being." Browne and Swallow (1894). Pg. 301-309

τὴν μετάληψιν τῶν ἁγίων μυστηρίων in the post-Anaphora: σὺν τῷ ἀνάρχῳ σου Πατρὶ, καὶ τῷ ἁγίῳ σου Πνεύματι a similar paradigm is found in almost every *ekphonesis* of the liturgy. The use of the qualitative σου places the rest of the Trinity in a subordinate position to Christ, they are mentioned only in reference to Christ. This subordination flies in the face of the conventional liturgical style, which usually places God the Father as the source of the Trinity and therefore in the dominant position, as in the Byzantine Liturgy of St. Basil the Great: ὅς ὢν ἀπαύγασμα τῆς δόξης καὶ χαρακτὴρ τῆς ὑποστάσεώς σου φέρων τε τὰ πάντα τῷ ῥήαμτι τῆς δυνάμεως αὐτοῦ οὐχ ἁρπαγμὸν ἡγήσατο τὸ εἶναι ἴσα σοὶ τῷ Θεῷ καὶ Πατρί.[155] Here we see the exact opposite of what is found in the Liturgy of St. Gregory, although the discussion is of Christ, He is being discussed in terms of God the Father, He is the reflection of the Father's glory and the type of the Father's person. The author also makes it clear that Christ humbles Himself, οὐχ ἁρπαγμὸν ἡγήσατο τὸ εἶναι ἴσα σοὶ and in doing so voluntarily takes a submissive role in the history of salvation and in the Trinity. This submissive role in salvation is the opposite of what is seen in the Liturgy of St. Gregory: Σὺ μοί, ὦ Δέσποτα, τὴν τιμωρίαν μετέβαλες· ὡς ποιμὴν ἀγαθὸς εἰς πλανώμενον ἔδραμες. Ὡς Πατὴρ ἀληθινὸς ἐμοὶ τῷ πεπτωκότι συνήλγησας. This section of the post-Sanctus prayer attributes salvation to Christ alone, interestingly in this section Christ is even referred to as Πατὴρ, while this does not directly equate Christ with God the Father, "as a true Father"not "as the true Father"it does suggest that the author is trying to transfer the role in salvation usually attributed to the Father to Christ. This reversal, or at least seeming reversal, of the normal roles of the Trinity is mirrored in the *Fourth Theological Oration* of St. Gregory. Though he does not go quite as far as the author of the liturgy, he does argue against the Arians, who attempt to prove that Christ is not divine by showing his subordination to God the Father: "Take, in the next place, the subjection by which you subject the Son to the Father. What, you say is He not now subject, or must He, if He is God, be subjected to God?...But as the Son subjects all to the Father, so does the Father to the Son; to One by His Work, the Other by His good pleasure..."[156] St. Gregory and the author of the liturgy are arguing the same point, that Christ is not subordinate to the Father, the extreme to which the point is taken in the liturgy can be explained as a literary device through which the author can argue the same point as St. Gregory without directly speaking to the point.

---

[155] Hammond and Brightman (1896). pg. 325. „who, being the effulgence of Your glory and the impression of Your *hypostasis* and, bearing all things by of the word of His power, He did not consider equality with You, God and Father, something to be grasped."
[156] Browne and Swallow (1894). pg. 311.

The Liturgy of Saint Gregory the Theologian

Numerous individual phrases and imagery in common between the *Five Theological Orations* and the liturgy underscore the dependance of the author of the liturgy on St. Gregory. Many of the common themes between the liturgy and the texts written by St. Gregory are discussed by Hammerschmidt and Gerhards,[157] therefore, this will not be a complete overview, but a short discussion of some of the striking similarities. In the *Fourth Theological Oration* Christ is described as a mediator between God the Father and mankind: "For He still pleads even now as Man for my salvation: for He continues to wear the Body which He assumed, until He makes me God by the power of His Incarnation..."[158] This mediation is also described in the post-Sanctus prayer discussed above,[159] St. Gregory's discussion also has another aspect to it, Theosis. This theology, better known from the writings of St. Gregory of Nyssa,[160] postulates that the Christian life proceeds in stages, that Christ's Incarnation made it possible for humans to advance in the spiritual life, becoming like God by Grace.[161] This upward journey is a major topic in the liturgy as well, uniting the salvific upward journey and the journey undergone in the liturgy that culminates in the Eucharist.

In the *Fourth Theological Oration* St. Gregory also spends a lengthy section, most of chapters 17-21, discussing the various epitheta and descriptions of Christ:

ὁ μὲν ὤν, καὶ ὁ θεός, μᾶλλόν πως τῆς οὐσίας ὀνόματα...καὶ δαπανητικὸν τῶν μοχθηρῶν ἕξεων, -- καὶ γὰρ πῦρ καταναλίσκον ἐντεῦθεν λέγεται...οἷον ὁ μὲν παντοκράτωρ, καὶ ὁ βασιλεύς, ἢ τῆς δόξης, ἢ τῶν αἰώνιων, ἢ τῶν δυνάμεων τοῦ ἀγαπητοῦ, ἢ τῶν βασιλευόντων. καὶ ὁ κύριος, ἢ σαβαώθ, ὅπερ ἐστὶ στρατιῶν, ἢ τῶν δυνάμεων, ἢ τῶν δυριευόντων...ὁ δὲ θεός, ἢ τοῦ σώζειν, ἢ ἐκδικήσεων, ἢ εἰρήνης, ἢ δικαιοσύνης, ἢ Ἀβραὰμ καὶ Ἰσαὰκ καὶ Ἰακώβ, καὶ παντὸς Ἰσραὴλ τοῦ πνευματικοῦ καὶ ὁρῶντος θεόν...Δοκεῖ γὰρ μοι λέγεσθαι υἱὸς μέν, ὅτι ταὐτόν ἐστι τῷ πατρὶ κατ' οὐσίαν...μονογενὴς δέ...λόγος δέ...σοφία δέ...δύναμις δέ...ἀλήθεια δέ...καὶ ὡς καθαρὰ τοῦ πατρὸς σφραγίς... εἰκὼν δέ, ὡς ὁμοούσιον...ζωὴ δέ, ὅτι φῶς...δικαιοσύνη δέ...ἁγιασμὸς δέ... ἀπολύτρωσις δέ...ἀνάστασις δέ...ἄνθρωπος μέν...Χριστὸς δέ...ὁδὸς δέ...ποιμὴν δέ...πρόβατον δέ...ἀμνὸς δέ...ἀρχιερεὺς δέ...Μελχισεδὲκ δέ...βασιλεὺς Σαλήμ...βασιλεὺς δικαιοσύνης.[162]

---

[157] Cf., for example, Gerhards (1984). pp. 104-165
[158] Browne and Swallow (1894). pg. 315
[159] Cf. Hammerschmidt (1957). Pg. 177
[160] For example in his teachings on *Epektasis* in his *Life of Moses*.
[161] Cf. St. Athanasius of Alexandria *On the Incarnation of the Word* 54.3
[162] Gregory Nazianzen *Theological Oration* 4. 18-21. "...He who Is, and God,[162] are special names of His Essence...He consumes evil conditions of things (from which He is called A consuming Fire)...the Almighty,

Introduction

In the Liturgy of St. Gregory, a similar focus on epitheta of Christ can be seen, many of these are the same as those found in the text above, along with the standard: Κύριε... Δέσποτα...Θεός...Φιλάνθρωπε[163] numerous prayers show rows of epitheta and descriptions, many are used to underscore the anti-Arian nature of the text, and many are used to discuss the duality of Christ's nature. In the following, the epithets used of Christ in the pre and post-Anaphora will be laid out, those within the Anaphora need not be discussed here, since they are discussed at length in Gerhards and by Sanchez.[164]

Table I: The epithets of Christ in the Pre-Anaphora.

The Pre-Anaphora	
1. Εὐχὴ ἥν ποιεῖ ὁ Ἱερεὺς καθ' ἑαυτὸν ἐν ἑαυτῷ	1. (line 1) Δέσποτα, Κύριε 2. (line 11) Κύριε 3. (line 15) ὁ Θεὸς 4. (line 20) Δέσποτα παντόκρατορ, Παντοδύναμε Κύριε 5. (line 23) φιλάνθρωπος
2. Εὐχὴ μετὰ τὴν ἑτοιμασίαν τοῦ Ἁγίου Θυσιαστηρίου	1. (line 1) Δέσποτα Κύριε...ὁ Θεὸς ἡμῶν 2. (line 4-5) ζωοποιὲ...τῶν ἀγαθῶν χορηγὲ 3. (line 8-9) Ἀγαθὲ Εὐέργετα Βασιλεῦ τῶν αἰώνων, καὶ τῆς κτίσεως ἁπάσης Δημιουργὲ
3. Εὐχὴ τοῦ ἁγίου Εὐαγγελίου	1. (line 2) Δέσποτα Κύριε...ὁ Θεὸς ἡμῶν 2. (line 7) Δέσποτα 3. (line 8-9) Κύριε ὁ Θεὸς ἡμῶν 4. (lines 10-11) ζωὴ... σωτηρία ...ἐλπὶς ...ἴασις... ἀνάστασις
4. Εὐχὴ τοῦ καταπετάσματος	1. (line 6) Δεσπότης τῶν ἁπάντων 2. (line 7) Σεραφὶμ Κύριος...βασιλεὺς τοῦ

---

the King of Glory, or of the Ages, or of the Powers, or of the Beloved, or of Kings. Or again the Lord of Sabaoth, that is of Hosts, or of Powers, or of Lords...the God either of Salvation or of Vengeance, or of Peace, or of Righteousness; or of Abraham, Isaac, and Jacob, and of all the spiritual Israel that seeth God...He is called Son...He is called Only-Begotten...He is called the Word...He is also called Wisdom...Power...Sustainer...Furnisher...Truth...the pure Seal of the Father...of one substance with Him ...Life... Light... Righteousness... Arbiter... Sanctification... Redemption... Sacrifice... Ressurection...Man...Son of Man...Christ...the Way...the Door...the Shepherd...the Sheep...the Victim...the Lamb...the Highpriest...Melchisedec...the King of Salem...King of Righteousness..." Browne and Swallow (1894). Pg. 315-318
[163] Passim.
[164] Cf. Gerhards (1984). pp. 102-105

	Ἰσραὴλ
	3. (line 8-9) μόνος ἅγιος, καὶ ἐν ἁγίοις ἀναπαυόμενος...τὸν μόνον ἀγαθόν
	4. (line 9) εὐήκοον Θεὸν
	5. (lines 15-16) ὁ ἁγιάζων καὶ ἁγιαζόμενος, προσφέρων τε καὶ προσφερόμενος, ὁ δεχόμενος καὶ δεκτός, ὁ διδοὺς καὶ διαδιδόμενος
5. Εὐχὴ ἄλλη καταπετάσματος παρ' Αἰγυπτίοις[165]	1. (line 1) Κύριε ὁ Θεὸς ἡμῶν, ὁ Παντοκράτωρ
	2. (line 6) Κύριε
6. Εὐχὴ τοῦ ἀσπασμοῦ	1. (line 1-2) Ὁ ὢν καὶ προὼν καὶ διαμένων εἰς τοὺς αἰῶνας...συναΐδιος καὶ ὁμοούσιος, καὶ σύνθρονος καὶ συνδημιουργός
	2. (line 9) Μεσίτης ἡμῶν
	3. (line 14) Δέσποτα
	4. (line 18) ὁ χορηγὸς[166] καὶ δοτὴρ πάντων τῶν ἀφαθῶν
7. Εὐχὴ ἄλλη τοῦ ἀσπασμοῦ	1. (line 1) ἡ φοβερὰ καὶ ἀπερινόητος δύναμις τοῦ Θεοῦ καὶ Πατρὸς
	2.(line 3) πῦρ καταναλίσκον
	3. (line 6) Δέσποτα

We see the same emphasis on these epitheta in the post-Anaphora as well:

Table II: The epithets of Christ in the post-Anaphora

The post-Anaphora	
1. Προοίμιον τῆς κλάσεως	1. (line 1) τὸ σωτήριον ὄνομα
	2. (line 8) Δέσποτα
	3. (line 9-10) φιλάνθρωπε, παντόκρατορ Κύριε ὁ Θεὸς ἡμῶν
2. Εὐχὴ τῆς κλάσεως[167]	1. (line 1) Ὁ ὤν, ὁ ἦν, ὁ ἐλθὼν καὶ πάλιν

---

[165] The lack of epitheta in this prayer can be explained in the same way as the ‚Prayer of the Gospel,' in that it is not a prayer original to this liturgy.

[166] *Choregos* is a term also used of Christ in the Apostolic Constitutions, Cf. Bouyer (1989). pg. 90

	ἐρχόμενος
	2. (line 2) ὁ μέγας ἀρχιερεύς
	3. (line 2-3) ὁ ἀρχηγός τῆς σωτηρίας ἡμῶν...τὸ φῶς ἀληθινὸν
	4. (line 21) φιλάνθρωπε ἀγαθέ
3. Εὐχὴ ἄλλη τῆς κλάσεως[168]	1. (line 1) ὁ Λόγος τοῦ Πατρός, ὁ προαιώνιος Θεός, ὁ μέγας ἀρχιερεὺς
	2. (line 4) Φιλάνθρωπε ἀγαθέ Κύριε
4. Εὐχὴ ἄλλη τῆς κλάσεως	1. (line 1-2) ὁ παντοκράτωρ ὁ λυτρώτης τῆς ἑαυτοῦ ἐκκλησίας
	2. (line 2) ὦ Λόγε...καὶ ἄνθρωπε
	3. (line 7) ὁ Θεός
	4. (line 9) Κύριε ὁ Θεός...Κύριε
	5. (line 13) Δέσποτα Κύριε
5. The Prayer following the Lord's Prayer	6. (line 1) Κύριε, Κύριε
	7. (line 5) βασιλεὺς ἡμετέρων πάντων
5. Εὐχὴ τῆς κεφαλοκλισίας	1. (line 2) Ὁ κλίνας οὐρανοὺς
	2. (line 3) Φιλάνθρωπε ἀγαθέ
6. Εὐχὴ ἄλλη ὁμοίως	1. (line 1) Κύριε...ὁ Θεὸς ἡμῶν
	2. (line 5) ὁ κλῶν καὶ κλώμενος καὶ ἄκλαστος
7. Εὐχὴ τῆς ἐλευθερίας	1. (line 1) ὁ ἀμνὸς τοῦ Θεοῦ
	2. (line 17) Δέσποτα Κύριε
	3. (line 20) Δέσποτα φιλόψυχε
	4. (line 22) ὁ Θεὸς ἡμῶν
	5. (line 24) ὁ Θεὸς ἡμῶν
8. Σῶμα καὶ αἷμα	1. (line 4) ὁ Κύριος
	2. (line 6). Κύριος
	3. (line 10) υἱοῦ τοῦ Θεοῦ
	4. (lines 13) υἱοῦ τοῦ Θεοῦ
	5. (line 16) Ἐμμανοὺλ

---

[167] This prayer too is probably not original to the liturgy, the number of epitheta in this prayer can be attributed to the author of this prayer attempting to match the style of the overall liturgy, especially in the opening.
[168] This prayer too is most likely not part of the original text of the liturgy.

	6. (line 19) <u>ὁ Θεὸς</u> ἡμῶν
	7. (line 29) Ἀκατάληπτε <u>Θεέ</u>, Λόγε, ἀχώρητε, ἀίδιε
9. Εὐχὴ εὐχαριστίας μετὰ τὴν μετάληψιν τῶν ἁγίων μυστηρίων	1. (line 7) <u>Λόγε</u> Θεοῦ ἀληθινὲ
	2. (line 10) Φιλάνθρωπε
	3. (line 12) Φιλάνθρωπε
10. Εὐχὴ τῆς κεφαλοκλισίας	1. (line 2) <u>ὁ ὤν</u>, ὁ ἦν, ὁ ἐλθὼν

The epithets found in the liturgy as well as in the *Fourth Theological Oration* are underlined in the tables above. Though there are a number of epithets that are in common, it is not merely the congruence of epithets that show the similarity of these two texts, it is the reliance of the authors on epitheta to underscore their theological arguing points.

The Tradition of the Church

Although not a deciding factor in this discussion, the tradition of the Church is still an interesting point of discussion. That the Liturgy is ascribed to St. Gregory the Theologian is seen in the text itself,[169] in the closing prayer: Ἐν εἰρήνῃ τοῦ Θεοῦ ἐτελειώθη ἡ θεία λειτουργία ἡ ὡρισμένη τῷ ἐν ἁγίοις πατρὶ ἡμῶν θεολόγῳ Γρηγορίῳ.[170] Along with this direct attribution is an allusions to St. Gregory in the rememberances of the saints: Καὶ τοῦ ἁγίου καὶ μακαρίου πατρὸς ἡμῶν Μάρκου τοῦ ἀποστόλου καὶ εὐαγγελιστοῦ. Καὶ τοῦ ἐν ἁγίοις πατρὸς θεολόγου Γρηγορίου.[171]

2. Introduction to the Text

II.I. Editions of the Greek text used in this critical edition

Scholarly attention to the Liturgy of St. Gregory, especially to the Greek text of the liturgy, has been notably lacking, however, there have been several important contributions beginning very early in the field of liturgical research.

1. The earliest edition of the Greek Liturgy of St. Gregory was compiled by Eusebe Renaudot in his work: *Liturgia Orientalia Collectio*.[172] This edition, based solely

---

[169] As well as in the title of the text.
[170] see below pg. 145
[171] see below pg. 113
[172] Renaudot (1847).

on the Paris Greque 325 manuscript is the only complete edition available of this liturgy. In this edition, Renaudot does not give a critical apparatus, but transcribes the manuscript available to him. The text is also accompanied by a Latin translation and commentary. This edition was reprinted by Migne in his *Patrologia Graeca*,[173] with slight alterations.

2. With the discovery of another manuscript of the Greek text of this liturgy by Frank Kacmarcik, the so-called Kacmarcik Codex, further work was done in establishing the text by Macomber, who published a critical text of this new manuscript in Orientalia Christiana Periodica.[174] This edition includes both the text of the Greek-Egyptian Anaphora of St. Basil as well as the Anaphora of the Liturgy of St. Gregory, it also includes the text of the Coptic Ordinary, into which these two Anaphorae were inserted.

3. One of the interesting aspects of the various manuscripts of the Liturgy of St. Gregory is the translations of the text into Arabic that accompany it in the margins. Classical Arabic being beyond most Ancient Greek scholars we are very thankful that Samir Khalil undertook to compile a critical edition of the Arabic text, which he published in Orientalia Christiana Periodica.[175]

3. Hugh Evelyn White, who explored and catalogued the Coptic Monasteries of the Wadi n' Natrun discovered a third manuscript of the Anaphora of the Liturgy of St. Gregory. He published a critical edition and translation into English of this Anaphora.[176]

4. The only critical edition that takes all (or all available) manuscripts of this text into account is the critical edition compiled by Alfred Gerhards.[177] This edition is part of a larger study on the Anaphora and therefore only includes the Anaphora section of the text. Along with the text of the Anaphora, Gerhards provides a lengthy and detailed commentary on the theological content of the text as well as a translation of the Anaphora into German.

5. The edition of the Liturgy of St. Gregory published in Thessaloniki (for the first time in 1981 and again in 2010) is also of interest.[178] Though this is not a critical edition, rather is designed for Church use, the text gives insight into how this service may have looked when in use by the Byzantine Churches. Similar in nature are

---

[173] Migne (1862).
[174] Macomber (1977).
[175] Khalil (1979).
[176] White (1926).
[177] Gerhards (1984).
[178] Thess (ed). (1981 and 2010)

the editions of this text compiled by the Vatican for use in the Coptic-Catholic Churches.[179]

II.II. Other traditions that exist alongside the Greek

Although the focus of this investigation is on the Greek text of this liturgy, it is important to note that there are a number of other textual traditions in which a liturgy is attributed to St. Gregory. Whether these other texts are translations of the Greek, or exist altogether independently of the Greek text, they are important in establishing the place and time of origin of the Greek text we are discussing.

1. The Coptic Liturgy of St. Gregory is a translation into Coptic of the Greek text. When precisely the translation occurred is a difficult question, but the existence of both a Sahidic Coptic and Bohairic Coptic version attests to the early date of translation. Both Coptic texts have had critical editions compiled, the Bohairic Coptic by Ernst Hammerschmidt,[180] who also includes a lengthy Commentary and a translation into German. The Sahidic Coptic version was edited by Lietzmann.[181] Hammerschmidt also includes, in his work, a comparison of the two Coptic versions. Dependant on the Coptic text is the later Ethiopic Liturgy of St. Gregory, which is discussed at length in Hammerschmidt's work: *The Ethiopic Anaphoras*.[182]

2. A second textual tradition of a Liturgy of St. Gregory exists in the Syrian rite, this text was compiled and translated into Latin in the series *Anaphorae Syriacae* by Hausherr.[183] The Syrian Liturgy of St. Gregory has very little in common with the Greek text and is one of the reasons that we can conclude that the Greek Liturgy of St. Gregory cannot belong to the Syrian rite proper, but must belong to one of the subfamilies of the rite.

3. Along with the Coptic, Ethiopic and Syrian versions there is an Armenian version, edited by Ferhat.[184] This text, like the Syrian version, is a different Liturgy than the one found in Greek, but, as is postulated by Gerhards, the Greek text may have had some influence on the Armenian.[185] If so, this would be another hint that

---

[179] Hammerschmidt (1957). Pg. 4
[180] Hammerschmidt (1957)
[181] Lietzmann (1920)
[182] Hammerschmidt (1961)
[183] *Anaphorae Syriacae* (1941)
[184] Ferhat (1911)
[185] Gerhards (1984). Pg. 199

the Greek text was in use in the Byzantine world, as the Byantine liturgies had a great influence on the Armenian.

II.III. Manuscripts used in this critical edition[186]

1. The fourteenth century manuscript *Euchologion* of the complete Liturgy of St. Gregory the Theologian, Paris Manuscript Greque 325, is the only available manuscript that gives not only the Anaphora of the liturgy, but the pre- and post-Anaphoral prayers as well. As such it is the main source in my critical edition for these sections.

2. The other manuscript used in this edition is the fourteenth century Kacmarcik Codex, in the library of St. Johns College in Minnesota. This manuscript has the text of the Anaphora of this liturgy as part of a larger Greek version of the Ordinary of the Coptic service. Especially interesting is that this manuscript was written in phonetic Greek, so that even a priest who cannot read Greek would be able to celebrate the service. This phonetic script and the fact that it is not an entire *Euchologion*, but an inserted Anaphora shows that this manuscript was most likely in use in the Coptic world as an optional Anaphora, while the Paris Manuscript was in use as a separate Liturgy by the Melkites.

II.IV. Manuscripts not obtained for this edition[187]

Unfortunately it was not possible to procure all of the manuscripts that are extant for this liturgy.

1. The Wadi n' Natrun fragments, from the fourteenth century (the text includes the the name of the reigning Patriarch Benjamin II, 1327-1339), No. 20 in the Cairo National Library was no longer available in the Cairo National Library when inquiries were made. Fortunately Hugh Evelyn White had compiled an edition of the fragments, which was used in this edition.[188]

---

[186] The limited number of manuscripts is itself of interest and may reflect the disappearance of the Greek text as a celebrated liturgy outside of Egypt, after which manuscripts may have been repurposed.

[187] The images of codices 172 and 175 taken by Dr. Budde for his study of the Lituryg of St. Basil did, unfortunately, not include the Liturgy of St. Gregory. I hope to be able to view these manuscripts in the future and revise the edition accordingly.

[188] The Paris Codex and the Fragments of the Wadi n' Natrun are postulated first by Samir Khalil to be written in the same Scriptorium as the, this is confirmed by Gerhards (Gerhards (1984). pg. 18.). The question arose about how the Wadi n' Natrun fragments and the text of the Kacmarcik Codex were related, a question

2. A codex, Manuscript number 172, from the year 1599 is kept in the Patriarchal Library formerly in Cairo and now in the Monastery of St. Mena in Alexandria.[189]

3. A codex, Manuscript 175, from the 19th century, is also kept in the Patriarchal Library in the Monastery of St. Mena in Alexandria.[190]

II.V. The textual tradition

In the following table, a possible Stemma of the various extant manuscripts of the Greek liturgy are presented, the relationships with other textual traditions are also explored. In the table, and in the rest of this investigation, the following abbreviations are used for the manuscripts and editions.

Paris Manuscript Greque 325: MS Paris.
The Kacmarcik Codex: MS Kac.
The Wadi n' Natrun Fragments: White.
Codex 173: Codex 173
Codex 175: Codex 175
Eusebe Renaudot: Ren.
Hammerschmidt: Hamm.
Gerhards: Ger.
the Thessaloniki edition: Thess.

---

which was left open. Unfortunately there is not enough information available to answer this open question. Suffice it to say that despite the similarities between the Paris Codex and the Wadi n' Natrun fragments, the lack of any hint of the pre- and post-Anaphora prayers in the Wadi n' Natrun fragments point to use in the Coptic community, while the complete Euchologion found in the Paris Codex points to use by the Melkite Greeks. One possibility is that both of these texts were written in a Greek Scriptorium, which would account for the proper Greek spelling found in both, as opposed to the phonetical spelling found in the Kacmarcik Codex, one commissioned by the Coptic Church, which eventually made it to the St. Macarius Monastery and one commissioned by the Greek population, for use in their churches..

[189] Gerhards (1984). pg. 17
[190] Ibid.

Introduction

Table III.I: The Possible Stemma of the Liturgy of St. Gregory the Theologian.[191]

(4th century)[192]

α-the original text (Cappadocian)

(5th century)[193]

β- the text as it was brought to Egypt

(6th century)

A – the Sahidic Coptic version   **β1**- the Melkite version   **β2**- the Greek-

B- the Bohairic Coptic version[194]

(14th century)

β1a- the Paris Manuscript **β2a**-the Wadi n'Natrun fragments **β2b**-the Kacmarcik Codex

---

[191] Until it will be possible to acquire the two later manuscripts: Manuscript 172 and Manuscript 175 it will be impossible to place them in the stemma. This stemma is only provisional, as it is difficult to come to conclusions with so few manuscripts.
[192] The Armenian liturgy of St. Gregory, which shows some influence from the Greek version may be dated to this time period.
[193] The Syrian liturgy of St. Gregory, which seems unrelated to the Greek and Coptic versions of the text may be dated to this time period.
[194] An Ethiopian version of the text exists as well, translated into Amharic form Bohairic Coptic.

II.VI. General Introduction to the following critical edition and investigation

The work that has been done on this liturgy, especially in the commentaries of Gerhards and Hammerschmidt, focuses mainly on the Anaphora of this text, only Cezar Login has worked on the pre-Anaphora. This investigation hopes to fill the gap left by the prior commentaries by focusing on the pre- and post- Anaphora, while spending only a little time dealing with the Anaphora itself, since it has been so thoroughly handled. The text that accompanies this commentary contains the first critical edition for the pre- and post-Anaphora, as well as a new critical edition of the Anaphora itself.

Overview of the Text[195]

Since the Anaphora of this liturgy has already garnered some attention, the text has been divided into three parts: the Pre-Anaphora; the Anaphora and the Post-Anaphora. The Pre-Anaphora consists of those prayers and rites, such as the readings from Scripture and the Entrances with the Gospel and the Gifts, that lead up to the *Sursum Corda* and the beginning of the Anaphora. In this liturgy these prayers include an initial prayer of access, a prayer of the Gospel, two prayers of the Veil and two prayers of the kiss of peace. The Anaphora section contains some of the most important prayers and hymns of the liturgy, such as the Sanctus Hymn and the Consecration of the Gifts. In the Liturgy of St. Gregory the Anaphora is set up in the fashion of a Byzantine Liturgy, beginning with the *Sursum Corda* and continuing to the pre-Sanctus, the Sanctus Hymn and a lengthy post-Sanctus prayer. Following this is the Consecration and the Epiklesis, followed by a lengthy section of commemorations and finally a closing benediction. The final section of the liturgy focuses on the final preparations for the Eucharist, in this case with three alternate prayers for the breaking of the bread, the preparation for and the recitation of the Lord's Prayer, and several prayers preceeding the distribution of the Eucharist to the people. Finally there are two prayers of thanksgiving following the Eucharist which conclude the liturgy.

List of Abbrreviations

The Manuscripts of the Liturgy of St. Gregory abbreviate a number of common liturgical terms as well as the normal *Nomina Sacra*. The Paris Manuscript contains a complete list of all abbreviations following the text of the liturgy. While the abbreviation con-

---

[195] The Paris Manuscript abbreviates a large number of words, I have represented these abbreviations by putting the parts of the words which are not in the Paris Manuscript in parenthesis. The Paris Manuscript also includes a list of abbreviated words following the text of the liturgy. I have also attempted to show what words and phrases are difficult to read or illegible in the various manuscripts by putting the illegible sections in square brackets in the apparatus.

Introduction

ventions are not standard over the manuscripts, what follows is a list of the most common abbreviations, the abbreviated section is held within the parenthesis.

ἅγ(ιος)
αἰ(νέσεως)
αἰνοῦμ(εν)
ἀμ(ήν)
ἀνατολ(ὰς)
ἀνάστ(ητε)
ἄν(θρωπ)ος
ἀποκρίνετ(αι)
ἀρχ(ὴ)
βλέψ(ατε)
δ(ιάκονος)
δίκ(αι)ον
εἰρήν(ης)
ἔλε(ός)
ἐπου(ρα)νίαις
εὐλο(γοῦμεν)
εὐχ(ὴ)
ἔχομ(εν)
Θ(εὸ)ς
Θ(εοτό)κου
θάνατ(όν)
θυσ(ίαν)
Ἱ(ερεὺς)
Ἰ(ησο)ῦ
καθήμ(ενοι)
κ(α)ὶ
κατ(ὰ)
κλίνατ(ε)
Κ(ύρι)ε
Λ(αὸς)
λέ(γει)
μετ(ὰ)
π(ατέ)ρων
Π(ατ)ρί
Π(ατ)ρ(ὸ)ς
πν(εύματο)ς
στ(αυ)ροῦ

στῶμ(εν)
συγχώ(ρησον)
σ(ωτηρ)ιώδους
σ(ωτῆ)ρ(ο)ς
τ(ὸν)
τό(τε)
Υ(ἱο)ῦ
φιλάν(θρωπ)ος
Χ(ριστ)έ

Ἡ Θεία Λειτουργία τοῦ ἐν Ἁγίοις Πατρὸς Ἡμῶν Γρηγορίου

The Critical Text

+ Ἡ Θεία Λειτουργία τοῦ ἐν Ἁγίοις Πατρὸς Ἡμῶν Γρηγορίου.

Part I: Pre-anaphoral Prayers

1. Εὐχὴ ἣν ποιεῖ ὁ Ἱερεὺς καθ᾽ ἑαυτὸν ἐν ἑαυτῷ[196]
   Ὁ ἐπισκεψάμενος ἡμᾶς ἐν ἐλέει καὶ οἰκτιρμοῖς, Δέσποτα Κύριε Ἰησοῦ Χριστέ, καὶ χαρισάμενος ἡμῖν παρρησίαν,[197] τοῖς ταπεινοῖς καὶ ἁμαρτωλοῖς καὶ ἀναξίοις

---

[196] Εὐχ(ὴ)...ἐν ἑαυτῷ om. Ren/Migne‖ Εὐχὴ ἱκετήριος, ἣν ἀναγιγνώσκει ὁ Ἱερεύς Thess.
[197] παρρησίαν MS. Par., Thess

δούλοις σου παραστῆναι τω ἁγίῳ σου θυσιαστηρίῳ, καὶ προσφέρειν σοι τὴν φοβερὰν καὶ ἀναίμακτον

5 Θυσίαν, ὑπὲρ τῶν ἡμετέρων ἁμαρτημάτων, καὶ τῶν τοῦ λαοῦ σου ἀγνοημάτων, ἄνεσιν[198] καὶ ἀνάπαυσιν τῶν προκοιμηθέντων πατέρων ἡμῶν καὶ ἀδελφῶν, καὶ στηριγμὸν παντὸς τοῦ λαοῦ σου. Ἐπίβλεψον ἐπ' ἐμὲ[199] τὸν ἀχρεῖον δοῦλόν σου καὶ ἐξάλειψόν μου τὰ παραπτώματα, διὰ τὴν σὴν εὐσπλαγχνίαν. Καὶ καθάρισόν μου τὰ χείλη καὶ τὴν καρδίαν ἀπὸ παντὸς μολυσμοῦ σαρκός τε καὶ πνεύματος. Καὶ ἀπόστησον ἀπ'

10 ἐμοῦ πάντα λογισμὸν αἰσχρόν τε καὶ ἀσύνετον. Καὶ ἱκάνωσόν[200] με τη δυνάμει τοῦ ἁγίου σου Πνεύματος εἰς τὴν Λειτουργίαν ταύτην καὶ πρόσδεξαί με διὰ τὴν σὴν ἀγαθότητα, προσεγγίζοντα[201] τω ἁγίω σου Θυσιαστηρίω. Καὶ εὐδόκησον Κύριε δεκτὰ γενέσθαι τὰ μέλλοντα προσαγόμενά σοι Δῶρα, διὰ τῶν ἡμετέρων χειρῶν, συγκαταβαίνων ταῖς ἐμαῖς ἀσθενείαις. Καὶ μὴ ἀπορρίψῃς[202] με ἀπὸ τοῦ προσώπου σου,[203] μὴ βδελύξῃς[204] με, τὴν

15 ἐμὴν ἀναξιότητα, ἀλλ' ἐλέησόν με ὁ Θεὸς κατὰ τὸ μέγα ἔλεος σου, καὶ κατὰ τὸ πλῆθος τῶν οἰκτιρμῶν σου ἐξάλειψον τὸ ἀνόμημά μου.[205] Ἵνα ἀκατακρίτως προσελθὼν κατενώπιον τῆς δόξης σου, καταξιωθῶ[206] τῆς σκέπης σου καὶ τῆς ἐλλάμψεως τοῦ παναγίου σου Πνεύματος, καὶ μὴ ὡς δοῦλος ἁμαρτίας ἀποδόκιμος[207] γένωμαι, ἀλλ' ὡς δοῦλος, ὃς εὕρω χάριν καὶ ἔλεος καὶ ἄφεσιν ἁμαρτιῶν, ἐν τω νῦν καὶ ἐν τω μέλλοντι

20 αἰῶνι. Ναὶ Δέσποτα Παντόκρατορ, Παντοδύναμε Κύριε, ἐπάκουσον τῆς δεήσεώς μου.

Σὺ γὰρ εἶ ὁ τὰ πάντα ἐνεργῶν ἐν πᾶσι, καὶ τὴν παρὰ σου πάντες ἐπιζητοῦμεν ἐπὶ πᾶσι βοήθειάν τε καὶ ἀντίληψιν. Ὅτι φιλάνθρωπος εἶ, καὶ δεδοξασμένος ὑπάρχεις Ἰησοῦ ὁ Θεὸς ἡμῶν, σὺν τῷ ἀνάρχῳ σου Πατρί, καὶ τῷ Ἁγίῳ σου Πνεύματι, νῦν καὶ ἀεί, καὶ.[208]

---

[198] εἰς ἄνεσιν Ren/Migne
[199] εἰς ἐμὲ Ren/Migne
[200] ἁγίασόν Ren/Migne
[201] προεγχίζοντα Ren
[202] ἀπορρίψης MS. Par., Thess.
[203] Cf. Psalm 50
[204] μηδὲ βδελύζῃ Thess.
[205] Cf. Psalm 50
[206] καταξιώθω Ren.
[207] ἀποδόκημος MS. Par.
[208] The Thessaloniki edition never abbreviates the ending of the Trintiarian formula.

Critical Text and Translation

2. Εὐχὴ μετὰ τὴν ἑτοιμασίαν τοῦ Ἁγίου Θυσιαστηρίου.

Δέσποτα Κύριε Ἰησοῦ Χριστὲ ὁ Θεὸς ἡμῶν· ὁ διὰ τῆς σωτηριώδους παρουσίας σου,

καὶ τῆς ἐλλάμψεως τοῦ παναγίου σου Πνεύματος, καταξιώσας[209] ἡμᾶς· τοὺς ταπεινοὺς[210] καὶ ἁμαρτώλους[211] καὶ[212] ἀναξίους δούλους σου, παραστῆναι τῷ ἁγίῳ σου θυσιαστηρίῳ

5 καὶ προσφέρειν καὶ λειτουργεῖν τοῖς ἀχράντοις Μυστηρίοις τῆς καινῆς σου διαθήκης. Αὐτὸς ζωοποιέ, καὶ τῶν[213] ἀγαθῶν χορηγέ, ποίησον μεθ'[214] ἡμῶν σημεῖον εἰς ἀγαθόν, καὶ ἀξίωσον ἡμᾶς ἐν καθαρῷ συνειδότι λατρεῦσαί σοι πάσας τὰς ἡμέρας[215] τῆς ζωῆς ἡμῶν,[216] καὶ ἐν ἁγιασμῷ ταύτην[217] τὴν θείαν προσενέγκειν σοι λειτουργίαν, εἰς ἄφεσιν ἁμαρτιῶν καὶ εἰς ἀπόλαυσιν τῆς μελλούσης μακαριότητος. Μνήσθητι Ἀγαθὲ Εὐέργετα Βασιλεῦ τῶν

10 ἰώνων, καὶ τῆς κτίσεως ἁπάσης Δημιουργέ, τῶν προσενεγκάντων καὶ δι' ὧν[218] προσήγαγον. Καὶ ἡμᾶς ἀκατακρίτους διαφύλαξον ἐν τῇ ἱερουργίᾳ τῶν θείων σου μυστηρίων.

Ὅτι ηὐλόγηται, καὶ ἡγίασται, καὶ δεδόξασται, τὸ πάντιμον καὶ μεγαλοπρεπὲς ἅγιον[219] ὄνομά σου, μετὰ τοῦ Πατρός, καὶ τοῦ ἁγίου Πνεύματος. Νῦν, καὶ.

3. Εὐχὴ τοῦ ἁγίου Εὐαγγελίου.

Εἰρήνη πᾶσιν.

Δέσποτα Κύριε Ἰησοῦ Χριστὲ ὁ Θεὸς ἡμῶν· ὁ τοῖς ἁγίοις σου μαθηταῖς καὶ ἱεροῖς σου ἀποστόλοις εἰπών, ὅτι πολλοὶ προφῆται καὶ δίκαιοι ἐπεθύμησαν ἰδεῖν, ἃ βλέπετε καὶ οὐκ

5 εἶδον, καὶ ἀκοῦσαι ἃ ἀκούετε καὶ οὐκ ἤκουσαν. Ὑμῶν[220] δὲ[221] μακάριοι οἱ ὀφθαλμοὶ ὅτι βλέπουσι· καὶ τὰ ὦτα ὑμῶν ὅτι ἀκούει.[222] Καὶ καταξιωθείημεν ἄρτι τοῦ ἀκοῦσαι καὶ ποιῆσαι τὰ ἅγιά σου Εὐαγγέλια, ταῖς λιταῖς τῶν ἱερῶν σου.

---

[209] καταξιώσας MS. Par.
[210] ταπε[ινοὺς] MS. Par.
[211] ἁμαρτώλ[ους] MS. Par.
[212] [καὶ] MS. Par.
[213] τῶν om. Ren/Migne
[214] μεθ' om. Thess.
[215] [ἡμέ]ρας MS. Par.
[216] ἡμ[ῶν] MS. Par.
[217] καὶ ἐν ἁγιασμῷ ταύτην σοι Ren/Migne.
[218] οὕς Thess.
[219] ἅγιον om. Thess.
[220] ἡμῶν Thess.
[221] γὰρ Ren/Migne.

The Liturgy of Saint Gregory the Theologian

Μνημόνευσον οὖν Δέσποτα καὶ νῦν πάντων τῶν ἐντειλαμένων ἡμῖν τοῖς[223] ἀναξίοις τοῦ
μνημονεύειν αὐτῶν, εἰς τὰς δεήσεις ἡμετέρας[224] καὶ τὰς αἰτήσεις, ἃς, ἀνβιβάζομέν σοι
10 Κύριε ὁ Θεὸς ἡμῶν. Τοὺς προτετελευτηκότας ἀνάπαυσον αὐτούς, τοὺς[225] κάμνοντας ἔρρωσον[226] αὐτούς.
Σὺ γὰρ εἶ ζωὴ ἡμῶν πάντων, καὶ σωτηρία ἡμῶν πάντων, καὶ ἐλπὶς ἡμῶν πάντων,[227] καὶ ἴασις ἡμῶν πάντων, καὶ ἀνάστασις οἰκεία πάντων ἡμῶν. Καὶ σοὶ τὴν δόξαν τιμὴν καὶ προσκύνησιν ἀναπέμπομεν, σὺν τῷ παντοκράτορί σου καὶ παντεπόπτῃ τέκοντι[228], καὶ τῷ παναγίῳ καὶ ζωαρχικῷ καὶ ὁμοουσίῳ σου Πνεύματι νῦν καὶ ἀεὶ, καὶ.[229]

4. Εὐχὴ τοῦ καταπετάσματος.

Οὐδεὶς ἄξιος τῶν συνδεδεμένων ταῖς σαρκικαῖς ἐπιθυμίαις καὶ ἡδοναῖς προσέρχεσθαι, ἢ προσεγγίζειν, ἢ λειτουργεῖν σοι βασιλεῦ τῆς δόξης. Τὸ γὰρ διακονεῖν σοι μέγα καὶ φοβερὸν καὶ αὐταῖς ταῖς ἐπουρανίαις δυνάμεσιν ἀπρόσιτον.[230] Ἀλλ' ὅμως, διὰ τὴν ἄφατον καὶ
5 ἄμετρόν[231] σου φιλανθρωπίαν, ἀτρέπτως καὶ ἀναλλοιώτως[232] γέγονας ἄνθρωπος, καὶ ἀρχιερεὺς ἡμῖν[233] ἐχρημάτισας, καὶ τῆς λειτουργικῆς ταύτης καὶ ἀναιμάκτου Θυσίας τὴν ἱερουργίαν παρέδωκας ἡμῖν ὡς Δεσπότης τῶν ἁπάντων. Σὺ γὰρ[234] εἶ δεσπόζεις τῶν ἐπουρανίων, καὶ τῶν[235] ἐπιγείων, καὶ τῶν καταχθονίων.[236] Ὁ ἐπὶ θρόνου Χερουβικοῦ ἐποχούμενος·[237] ὁ τῶν Σεραφὶμ Κύριος, καὶ βασιλεὺς τοῦ Ἰσραὴλ, ὁ μόνος ἅγιος καὶ ἐν

---

[222] Cf. the Gospel of Matthew 13:16
[223] τοῖς om. Ren/Migne.
[224] τὰς δεήσεις τὰς ἡμετέρας Thess.
[225] τοὺς om. Ren/Migne.
[226] τοὺς προτετελευτηκότας ἀνάπαυσον· τοὺς κάμνοντας ἔρρωσον Thess.|| ἔρρωσον MS. Par., Thess.
[227] καὶ σωτηρία ἡμῶν πάντων καὶ ἐλπὶς ἡμῶν πάντων om. Thess.
[228] σὺν τῷ ἀνάρχῳ σου πατρί Thess.
[229] Καὶ σοὶ τὴν δόξαν τιμὴν καὶ προσκύνησιν ἀναπέμπομεν, σὺν τῷ παντοκράτορί σου καὶ παντεπόπτῃ τέκοντι[229], καὶ τῷ παναγίῳ κ(αὶ) ζωαρχικῷ καὶ ὁμοουσίῳ σου Πν(εύματ)ι νῦν κ(αὶ) ἀεὶ, κ(αὶ).repetit MS. Par.
[230] ἀπρόσιτον om. Thess.
[231] ἀμέτρητόν σου Thess.
[232] ἀναλλοίως Ren/Migne.
[233] ἡμῶν Thess.
[234] Σὺ γὰρ μόνος Thess.
[235] τῶν om. Ren/Migne.
[236] καὶ τῶν καταχθονίων om. Thess.
[237] From ἐποχούμενος to ἐμοῦ the text is missing from the MS Paris, however, a reconstruction of the text was made by Renaudot and Migne (Ren (1847) I. pg. 88-89)

10 ἁγίοις ἀναπαυόμενος. Σὲ τοίνυν δυσωπῶ τὸν μόνον ἀγαθὸν καὶ εὐήκοον Θεὸν, ἐπίβλεψον ἐπ' ἐμὲ τὸν ἁμαρτωλὸν, καὶ ἀχρεῖον δοῦλόν σου· καὶ ἱκάνωσόν με τῇ δυνάμει τοῦ ἁγίου Πνεύμτος, ἐνδεδυμένον τὴν τῆς ἱερτείας χάριν, παραστῆναι τῇ ἁγίᾳ σου ταύτη τραπέζῃ καὶ ἱερουργῆσαι τὸ ἄχραντόν σου σῶμα καὶ τὸ τίμιόν σου αἷμα. Σοὶ γὰρ προσέρχομαι κλίνας τὸν ἐμαυτοῦ αὐχένα· καὶ δέομαί σου, μὴ ἀποστρέψῃς τὸ πρόσωπόν σου ἀπ' ἐμοῦ· μηδὲ
15 ἀποδοκιμάσῃς με ἐκ παίδων σου· ἀλλ' ἀξίωσόν με προσενεχθῆναί σοι τὰ Δῶρα ταῦτα, ὑπ' ἐμοῦ τοῦ ἁμαρτωλοῦ καὶ ἀναξίου δούλου σου.[238]

Σὺ γὰρ εἶ ὁ[239] ἁγιάζων καὶ ἁγιαζόμενος, προσφέρων τε καὶ προσφερόμενος, ὁ δεχόμενος καὶ δεκτός, ὁ διδοὺς καὶ διαδιδόμενος. Καὶ σοὶ τὴν[240] δόξαν ἀναπέμπομεν, μετὰ τοῦ Πατρός, καὶ

τοῦ ἁγίου Πνεύματος. Νῦν καὶ.[241]

5. Εὐχὴ[242] ἄλλη καταπετάσματος παρ' Αἰγυπτίοις.

Κύριε ὁ Θεὸς ἡμῶν, ὁ Παντοκράτωρ, ὁ ἐπιστάμενος τὸν νοῦν τῶν ἀνθρώπων, ὁ ἐτάζων καρδίας καὶ νεφρούς,[243] ὁ ἐμὲ τὸν ἀνάξιον καλέσας πρὸς τὴν σὴν λειτουργίαν ταύτην· μὴ βδελύξῃς[244] με· μηδὲ[245] τὸ πρόσωπόν[246] σου ἀποστρέψῃς ἀπ' ἐμοῦ. Ἀλλ' ἐξάλειψον

5 μου πάντα τὰ παραπτώματα· καὶ ἀπόπλυνόν μου τὸν ῥύπον τοῦ σώματος, καὶ τὸν σπίλον τῆς ψυχῆς, καὶ ὅλον με ἁγίασον. Ἵνα μὴ ἱκετεύω[247] σε δοῦναι ἄφεσιν ἄλλοις ἁμαρτιῶν, αὐτὸς ἀδόκημος γένωμαι. Ναὶ Κύριε μὴ ἀποστραφείς[248] με τεταπεινωμένον[249] καὶ κατησχυμμένον,[250] ἀλλ' ἐξαπόστειλόν μοι τὴν χάριν τοῦ ἁγίου σου Πνεύματος, καὶ ἀξίωσόν με παραστῆναι ἐπὶ τὸ ἅγιόν σου Θυσιαστήριον ἀκατακρίτως. Καὶ προσφέρειν

---

[238] δούλου σου τὰ Δῶρα ταῦτα Thess.
[239] ὁ om. Ren/Migne.
[240] τὴν om. Ren/Migne.
[241] Σὺ γὰρ εἶ ὁ προσφέρων, καὶ προφερόμενος, καὶ προσδεχόμενος, καὶ διαδιδόμενος, Χριστὲ ὁ Θεὸς ἡμῶν, καὶ σοι τὴν δόξαν ἀναπέμπομεν, σὺν τῷ ἀνάρχῳ σου Πατρὶ καὶ τῷ παναγίῳ καὶ ἀγαθῷ καὶ ζωοποιῷ Πνεύματι Thess.|| Νῦν καὶ om. Ren/Migne.
[242] The Anaphora of St. Gregory the Theologian begins here in the Kacmarcik Codex.
[243] Cf. Psalm 7:9.
[244] βδελύζῃ Thess.
[245] μὴ δὲ MS. Par.
[246] πρόσωπό Thess.
[247] ἱκετεύων MS. Par., Ren-Migne.
[248] [Ναὶ Κύριε μὴ ἀπος]τραφεὶς MS. Kac.|| ἀποστραφείην MS. Par., MS. Kac.|| ἀποστραφείς Migne/Thess.
[249] τεταπεινωμένος MS. Par., MS. Kac.
[250] κατησχυμμένος MS. Par., MS. Kac.|| κατησχυμένον Thess.

10 σοι τὴν²⁵¹ λογικὴν καὶ ἀναίμακτον προσφορὰν ταύτην μετὰ συνειδήσεως καθαρᾶς. Εἰς συγχώρησιν τῶν ἐμῶν ἁμαρτημάτων, καὶ τῶν παραπτωμάτων, καὶ εἰς ἄφεσιν τῶν τοῦ λαοῦ σου ἀγνοημάτων. Εἰς ἀνάπαυσιν καὶ ἀναψυχὴν τῶν προκεκοιμημένων πατέρων ἡμῶν καὶ ἀδελφῶν, καὶ εἰς στηριγμὸν παντὸς τοῦ λαοῦ σου, εἰς δόξαν σὴν τοῦ Πατρὸς, καὶ τοῦ Υἱοῦ, καὶ²⁵² τοῦ ἁγίου Πνεύματος. Νῦν καὶ.

6. Εὐχὴ τοῦ ἀσπασμοῦ.

Εἰρήνη πᾶσιν.²⁵³

Ὁ ὢν καὶ προὼν, καὶ διαμένων εἰς τοὺς αἰῶνας. Ὁ τῷ Πατρὶ συναΐδιος καὶ ὁμοούσιος καὶ

σύνθρονος καὶ συνδημιουργός. Ὁ διὰ μόνην ἀγαθότητα ἐκ τοῦ μὴ ὄντος εἰς τὸ εἶναι
5 παραγαγὼν²⁵⁴ τὸν ἄνθρωπον, καὶ θέμενος αὐτὸν ἐν παραδείσῳ τρυφῆς. Ἀπάτῃ δὲ τοῦ ἐχθροῦ καὶ παρακοῇ τῆς σῆς ἐντολῆς παραπεσόντα, ἀνακαινίσαι²⁵⁵ βουλόμενος καὶ πρὸς τὸ ἄρχαιον ἀναγαγεῖν ἀξίωμα. Οὐκ ἄγγελος, οὐκ ἀρχάγγελος, οὐ πατριάρχης, οὐ προφήτης²⁵⁶ τὴν ἡμῶν ἐνεχείρησας²⁵⁷ σωτηρίαν, ἀλλ᾽ αὐτὸς ἀτρέπτως σὰρξ γενόμενος καὶ ἐνηνθρώπησας.²⁵⁸ Κατὰ πάντα ὡμοιώθης²⁵⁹ ἡμῖν ἐκτὸς μόνης ἁμαρτίας.²⁶⁰ Μεσίτης ἡμῶν γέγονας²⁶¹ καὶ τοῦ Πατρὸς,
10 καὶ τὸ μεσότοιχον τοῦ φραγμοῦ· καὶ τὴν χρονίαν ἔχθραν καθελών.²⁶² Τὰ ἐπίγεια τοῖς ἐπουρανίοις συνῆψας, καὶ τὰ²⁶³ ἀμφότερα εἰς ἓν συνήγαγες, καὶ τὴν ἔνσαρκον ἐπλήρωσας οἰκονομίαν. Καὶ μέλλων σωματικῶς ἐλαύνειν²⁶⁴ εἰς οὐρανούς,²⁶⁵ θεϊκῶς τὰ πάντα πληρῶν, τοῖς ἁγίοις σου μαθηταῖς καὶ ἀποστόλοις ἔλεγες· εἰρήνην

---

²⁵¹ τὴν om. Ren/Migne.
²⁵² καὶ om. Ren/Migne.
²⁵³ Εἰρήνη πᾶσιν om MS. Καc.
²⁵⁴ παράγων Ren/Migne.
²⁵⁵ Wadi n' Natrun fragments begin here.
²⁵⁶ οὐκ ἀγγέλοις, οὐκ ἀρχαγγέλοις, οὐ πατριάρχαις, οὐ προφήταις Thess.
²⁵⁷ ἐνεχείρησε White.
²⁵⁸ ἐνανθρώπησας Thess., White.
²⁵⁹ ὁμοιώθης Ren/Migne.
²⁶⁰ τῆς ἁμαρτίας Ren/Migne, Thess.
²⁶¹ γενόμενος Ren/Migne, Thess.
²⁶² Cf. St. Paul's Episte to the Ephesians 2:14.
²⁶³ τὰ om. Thess.
²⁶⁴ [ἐλαύνειν] MS. Κac.
²⁶⁵ τοὺς οὐρανοὺς Ren/Migne, Thess.

ἀφίημι ὑμῖν, εἰρήνην τὴν ἐμὴν δίδωμι ὑμῖν.²⁶⁶ Ταύτην καὶ νῦν εἰρήνην ἡμῖν δώρησαι Δέσποτα. Χάρισαι²⁶⁷ παντὸς

15 ἀποκάθαρον²⁶⁸ μολύσματος, παντὸς δόλου καὶ πάσης κακίας καὶ πανουργίας καὶ τῆς θανατηφόρου μνησικακίας. Καὶ καταξίωσον ἡμᾶς, ἀσπάσασθαι ἀλλήλους²⁶⁹ ἐν φιλήματι ἁγίῳ,²⁷⁰ εἰς τὸ μετασχεῖν ἀκατακρίτως²⁷¹ τῆς ἀθανάτου καὶ ἐπουρανίου σου δωρεᾶς.

Χάριτι τῇ σῇ, τῆς εὐδοκίας²⁷² τοῦ Πατρὸς, καὶ ἐνεργείᾳ τοῦ παναγίου σου Πνεύματος.

Σὺ γὰρ εἶ ὁ χορηγὸς καὶ δοτὴρ πάντων τῶν ἀγαθῶν. Καὶ σοὶ τὴν δόξαν τὴν ἀίδιον
20 *δοξολογίαν ἀναπέμπομεν²⁷³ σὺν τῷ ἀνάρχῳ σου Πατρὶ, καὶ τῷ ἁγίῳ σου Πνεύματι, νῦν καὶ.²⁷⁴*

7. Εὐχὴ ἄλλη τοῦ ἀσπασμοῦ.²⁷⁵

Χριστὲ ὁ Θεὸς ἡμῶν, ἡ φοβερὰ καὶ ἀπερινόητος δύναμις τοῦ Θεοῦ καὶ Πατρός. Ὁ τοῦ φλογίνου θρόνου τῶν Χερουβὶμ ὑπερκαθήμενος, καὶ ὑπὸ πυρίνων δυνάμεων δωρυφορούμενος, καὶ πῦρ καταναλίσκον²⁷⁶ ὑπάρχων ὡς Θεός·²⁷⁷ καὶ διὰ τὴν σὴν ἄφατον

5 συγκατάβασιν καὶ φιλανθρωπίαν, μὴ φλέξας τῷ προσεγγισμῷ τὸν δολερὸν προδότην. Ἀλλὰ

φιλικὸν²⁷⁸ αὐτὸν ἀσπασάμενος ἀσπασμὸν,²⁷⁹ ἕλκων αὐτὸν εἰς μετάνοιαν, καὶ ἐπίγνωσιν τοῦ ἰδίου τολμήματος. Καταξίωσον ἡμᾶς Δέσποτα ἐπὶ τῆς φρικτῆς²⁸⁰ ταύτης ὥρας, ἐν ὁμονοίᾳ καὶ δίχα παντὸς ἐν δύο θυμοῦ, καὶ λειψάνου κακίας,

---

²⁶⁶ Cf. John 14:27.
²⁶⁷ χάρισαι om. Thess.
²⁶⁸ ἀποκάθαρος MS. Kac.‖ ἀπὸ καθαρῶς White.
²⁶⁹ ἀλλήλους om. Thess.
²⁷⁰ Cf. St. Paul's Epistle to the Romans 16:16.
²⁷¹ ἀκατακρήτως MS. Kac.
²⁷² εὐδοκίᾳ MS. Par.
²⁷³ ἐναπέμπομεν MS. Kac.‖ ἀναπέμπωμεν White.
²⁷⁴ ἀεὶ καὶ MS. Kac.‖ νῦν κ. εἰς τ. αἰω. ἀμήν White.‖ Wadi n' Natrun fragments break off here until the beginning of the Anaphora.
²⁷⁵ Thess omits this alternate prayer.
²⁷⁶ κατακαναλίσκον MS. Par.
²⁷⁷ Cf. Deutoronomy 4:24.
²⁷⁸ φηλικὸν MS. Kac.
²⁷⁹ ἀσπασμὸν om. Ren/Migne.
²⁸⁰ φρικτῆς om. MS. Kac.

ἀπολαβεῖν ἀλλήλους ἐν²⁸¹ ἁγίῳ φιλήματι. Καὶ μὴ κατακρίνῃς ἡμᾶς, ὑπὲρ μὴ ὁλοτελῶς²⁸² καὶ καθὼς ἀρέσαι τῇ σῇ ἀγαθότητι,

10 καθαρεύωμεν ἀπὸ πάσης τρυγὸς ἁμαρτίας, καὶ πονηρίας, καὶ τῆς θανατηφόρου μνησικακίας. Ἀλλ' αὐτὸς τῇ σῇ ἀφάτῳ καὶ ἀνεκδιηγήτῳ εὐσπλαγχνίᾳ, εἰδὼς τὸ πλάσμα ἡμῶν τὸ ἀσθενὲς καὶ κατώβρυθον,²⁸³ ἐξάλειψον πᾶσαν κηλίδα παραπτωμάτων ἡμῶν, ἵνα μὴ εἰς κρίμα ἢ εἰς κατάκριμα, ἡμῖν γένηται τὸ θεῖον τοῦτον μυστήριον.

Σὺ γὰρ εἶ ὁ δυνάμενος πᾶσαν ἀφιεῖν ἁμαρτίαν, καὶ ὑπερβαίνειν ἀδικίας καὶ ἀνομίας τῶν
15 ταλαιπωρῶν ἀνθρώπων, καθαρισμὸς τοῦ κόσμου παντὸς ὑπάρχων, καὶ σοὶ πρέπει ἡ παρὰ παντὸς συμφώνως δοξολογία τιμὴ καὶ προσκύνησις²⁸⁴, ἅμα τῷ ἀχράντῳ σου Πατρί, καὶ τῷ ζωοποιῷ σου Πνεύματι. Νῦν, καὶ.²⁸⁵

Part II: The Anaphora

1. Καὶ γίνεται ὁ ἀσπασμὸς²⁸⁶
Ὁ Διάκονος λέγει· Στῶμεν καλῶς.²⁸⁷
Ὁ Λαὸς λέγει· Ἔλεος εἰρήνης, θυσίαν αἰνέσεως.²⁸⁸
Ὁ Ἱερεὺς ἐκφωνήσει·²⁸⁹ Ἡ ἀγάπη τοῦ Θεοῦ καὶ²⁹⁰ Πατρός καὶ ἡ χάρις τοῦ μονογενοῦς
5 υἱοῦ Κυρίου δὲ καὶ Θεοῦ, καὶ σωτῆρος ἡμῶν Ἰησοῦ
Χριστοῦ καὶ ἡ κοινωνία καὶ ἡ δωρεὰ τοῦ ἁγίου Πνεύματος, εἴη²⁹¹ μετὰ
πάντων ὑμῶν.²⁹²
Ὁ Λαὸς λέγει· Καὶ μετὰ τοῦ πνεύμτός σου.²⁹³
Ὁ Ἱερεὺς λέγει·²⁹⁴ Ἄνω σχῶμεν²⁹⁵ τὰς καρδίας.

---

²⁸¹ ἐν MS. Par.
²⁸² ὁλογελῶς MS. Kac.
²⁸³ κατώβριθον MS. Kac.‖ κάτω βρίθον Ren/Migne.
²⁸⁴ σε MS. Kac.?
²⁸⁵ Νῦν κ. ἀεὶ κ. εἰς τ. αἰῶνας τ... MS. Kac.
²⁸⁶ Tit. κ MS. Par. Tit. [.......] MS. Kac.‖ The Thess edition inserts the dialogue surrounding the Creed from the Liturgy of St. John Chrysostom here.
²⁸⁷ Στῶμ(εν) καλῶς om. MS. Kac.
²⁸⁸ θυσ(ίαν) αἰ(νέσεως) om. MS. Kac., Ren/Migne., Thess.
²⁸⁹ Ὁ Ἱ(ερεὺς) ἐκφωνήσει om. White., MS. Kac., Thess.
²⁹⁰ καὶ om. Ren/Migne., Ger.
²⁹¹ ἔσαι White.
²⁹² ἡμῶν MS.Kac.
²⁹³ Κ(αὶ) μετ(ὰ) τοῦ πν(εύμτό)ς σου om. White., MS. Kac.

Critical Text and Translation

10 Ὁ Λαὸς λέγει· Ἔχομεν πρὸς τὸν Κύριον.²⁹⁶

Ὁ Ἱερεὺς λέγει·²⁹⁷ Εὐχαριστήσωμεν τῷ Κυρίῳ.²⁹⁸

Ὁ Λαὸς λέγει· Ἄξιον καὶ δίκαιον, ἄξιον καὶ δίκαιον, ἄξιον καὶ δίκαιον.²⁹⁹

2. Ἀρχὴ τῆς προσκομίδης.³⁰⁰

Ἀληθῶς³⁰¹ γὰρ³⁰² ἄξιόν ἐστιν καὶ δίκαιον σὲ αἰνεῖν, σὲ ὑμνεῖν,³⁰³ σὲ εὐλογεῖν, σὲ προσκυνεῖν, σὲ

δοξάζειν, τὸν μόνον ἀληθινὸν³⁰⁴ Θεὸν, τὸν φιλάνθρωπον, τὸν ἄφραστον,³⁰⁵ τὸν ἀόρατον, τὸν ἀχώρητον, τὸν ἄναρχον, τὸν αἰώνιον, τὸν ἄχρονον, τὸν ἀμέτρητον, τὸν ἄτρεπτον, τὸν

5 ἀπερινόητον, τὸν ποιητὴν τῶν ὅλων, τὸν λυτρωτὴν τῶν ἁπάντων, τὸν εὐϊλατεύοντα πάσαις ταῖς ἀνομίαις³⁰⁶ ἡμῶν, τὸν ἰώμενον πάσας τὰς νόσους ἡμῶν,³⁰⁷ τὸν λυτρούμενον ἐκ φθορᾶς τὴν ζωὴν ἡμῶν, τὸν στεφανοῦντα ἡμᾶς ἐν ἐλέει καὶ οἰκτιρμοῖς. Σὲ αἰνοῦσιν ἄγγελοι· σὲ

προσκυνοῦσιν ἀρχάγγελοι· σὲ ἀρχαὶ ὑμνοῦσι· σὲ κυριότητες ἀνακράζουσι· τὴν σὴν δόξαν

ἐξουσίαι ἀναγορεύουσι· σοὶ θρόνοι τὴν εὐφημίαν³⁰⁸ ἀναπέμπουσι, χιλίαι³⁰⁹ χιλιάδες σοὶ

10 παραστήκουσι·³¹⁰ καὶ μύριαι³¹¹ μυριάδες σοὶ τὴν λειτουργίαν³¹² προσάγουσι. Σὲ ὑμνεῖ τὰ ἀόρατα,³¹³ σὲ προσκυνεῖ τὰ φαινόμενα, πάντα ποιοῦντα τὸν λόγον σου Δέσποτα.

---

[294] Ὁ Ἱερεὺς λέγει om. MS. Par. MS. Kac., White., Ger.
[295] ὑμῶν White.
[296] Ἔχομ(εν) πρὸς τ(ὸν) Κ(ύριο)ν om. MS. Kac., White.
[297] Ὁ Ἱερεὺς λέγει om. MS. Par., MS. Kac., White.
[298] Ε[ὐ]αριστήσωμεν [τ]ῷ Κυρίῳ MS. Kac.
[299] Ἄξιον κ(αὶ) δίκ(αι)ον om. MS. Kac., White., Thess.|| On this page of the Anaphora, the Paris Manuscript indicates the responses of the people with the expected "Ὁ Λ(αὸς) λέγ(ει)" while the priest's parts are not marked with rubrics (I have added these for convenience), the priest lines are marked with capital letters in the margin. The last line is set up this way as well, however I have put the repetition of the ἄξιον καὶ δίκαιον into the people's response as there are numerous examples of triple responses in the liturgy, while the awkward transition from priest's part to the following prayer is unusual.
[300] Tit. om MS. Kac.|| Tit. προσκομίδης om. White.
[301] Ὁ Ἱερεὺς λέγει om. MS. Par., MS. Kac., White.|| Ἄξ[ιον] MS. Kac.
[302] γὰρ om. White
[303] σὲ ὑμνεῖν om. Ren/Migne., Thess.
[304] ἀλιθηνὸν MS. Kac.
[305] ἄφρα[στο]ν MS. Kac.
[306] πάσας τάς ἀνομίας Thess.
[307] Cf. Psalm 104.
[308] εὐφη[μί]αν MS. Kac.
[309] χ[ί]λια MS. Kac.

The Liturgy of Saint Gregory the Theologian

Ὁ Διάκονος λέγει· Οἱ καθήμενοι ἀνάστητε.[314]

Ὁ Ἱερεὺς λέγει·[315] Ὁ ὤν, Θεέ, Κύριε ἀληθινὲ ἐκ Θεοῦ ἀληθινοῦ· ὁ τοῦ Πατρὸς ἡμῖν ὑποδείξας τὸ φέγγος. Ὁ τοῦ ἁγίου Πνεύματος τὴν ἀληθῆ[316] γνῶσιν ἡμῖν χαρισάμενος. Ὁ τὸ
15 μέγα τοῦτο τῆς ζωῆς ἀναδείξας τὸ μυστήριον. Ὁ τὴν τῶν ἀσωμάτων τοῖς ἀνθρώποις χοροστασίαν πηξάμενος. Ὁ τὴν τῶν Σεραφὶμ τοῖς ἐπὶ γῆς παραδοὺς ὑμνῳδίαν.[317] Δέξαι μετὰ[318] τῶν ἀοράτων καὶ τὴν ἡμετέραν φωνήν. Σύναψον ἡμᾶς ταῖς ἐπουρανίαις δυνάμεσιν. Εἴπωμεν καὶ ἡμεῖς μετ' αὐτῶν πᾶσαν ἀτόπων[319] λογισμῶν[320] ἔννοιαν περιστείλαντες· βοήσωμεν ὥσπερ[321] ἐκεῖναι[322] ταῖς ἀσιγήτοις[323] ἀνακράζει[324] φωναῖς, ἀκαταπαύστοις
20 στόμασι τὸ σὸν μεγαλεῖον ὑμνήσωμεν.

3. The Pre-*Sanctus* and *Sanctus* Hymn

Ὁ Διάκονος λέγει·[325] Εἰς ἀνατολὰς βλέψατε.
Ὁ Ἱερεὺς λέγει·[326] Σοὶ γὰρ παραστήκει[327] κύκλῳ[328] τὰ Σεραφίμ, ἓξ πτέρυγες τῷ ἑνί, καὶ ἓξ πτέρυγες τῷ ἑνί.[329] Καὶ ταῖς μὲν δυσὶ[330] πτέρυξι κατακαλύπτουσι[331] τὰ πρόσωπα
5 ἑαυτῶν·[332] ταῖς δὲ δυσὶ τοὺς πόδας ἑαυτῶν· καὶ ταῖς[333] μὲν δυσὶ πετόμενα, καὶ ἐκέκραγον ἕτερον[334] πρὸς τὸν ἕτερον.

---

[310] παρεστήκασι Thess.
[311] [μ]ύρια MS. Kac.
[312] λιτουργίαν MS. Par., MS. Kac.
[313] ἀούρατα MS. Kac.
[314] Ὁ Διάκονος λέγει. [...] καθή[...] MS. Kac.
[315] Ὁ Ἱερεὺς λέγει om. MS. Par., MS. Kac.
[316] ἀλη MS. Kac.
[317] συμνῳδίαν MS. Kac.‖ ὑμνῳδίαν Thess.
[318] [με]τὰ MS. Kac.
[319] ἄτοπον Ren/Migne.
[320] λογισμῶν om. Ren/Migne.
[321] ἅπερ MS. Par., MS. Kac.
[322] ἐκείναι MS. Par.
[323] ἀσιγήτης MS. Kac.
[324] ἀνακράζοντες Thess.
[325] Ὁ Λαὸς λέγει MS. Par.
[326] Ὁ Ἱερεὺς λέγει om. MS. Par., MS. Kac.
[327] παρειστήκει MS. Par., MS. Kac.
[328] κύκλω MS. Par., MS. Kac.
[329] καὶ ἓξ πτέρυγες τῷ ἑνὶ om. Ren/Migne.
[330] [...]ὲν δυσ[ὶ] MS. Kac.
[331] κατακαλύπτει corr. MS. Par., MS. Kac.
[332] αὐτῶν MS. Kac.
[333] [της] MS. Kac.
[334] τὸν add. MS. Kac.

Ἐκφωνήσει.³³⁵

Τὸν ἐπινίκον ὕμνον τῶν σωτηριῶν ἡμῶν·³³⁶ μετὰ φωνῆς³³⁷ ἐνδόξου, λαμπρᾷ³³⁸ τῇ φωνῇ, ὑμνολογοῦντα³³⁹ ᾄδοντα³⁴⁰ βοῶντα³⁴¹ δοξολογοῦντα κεκραγότα³⁴² καὶ λέγοντα.

10 Ὁ Διάκονος λέγει· Πρόσχωμεν.³⁴³

Ὁ Λαὸς λέγει· Ἅγιος ἅγιος ἅγιος Κύριος σαβαώθ, πλήρης ὁ οὐρανός, κλ΄.

4. The Post-*Sanctus*

Ὁ Ἱερεὺς λέγει·³⁴⁴ Ἅγιος ἅγιος³⁴⁵ εἶ Κύριε καὶ πανάγιος. Ἐξαίρετόν³⁴⁶ σου τῆς οὐσίας τὸ φέγγος· ἄφραστός σου τῆς σοφίας ἡ δύναμις. Οὐδεὶς λόγος ἐκμετρήσει τῆς σῆς φιλανθρωπίας τὸ πέλαγος. Ἐποίησάς με ἄνθρωπον, ὡς φιλάνθρωπος· οὐκ αὐτὸς τῆς ἐμῆς
5 ἐπιδεὴς³⁴⁷ δουλείας, ἐγὼ δὲ μᾶλλον τῆς σῆς χρήζων³⁴⁸ δεσποτείας. Οὐκ ὄντα με δι' εὐσπλαγχνίαν παρήγαγες, οὐρανόν μοι πρὸς ὄροφον ἔστησας, γῆν μοι πρὸς βάσιν κατέπηξας. Δι' ἐμὲ θάλασσαν ἐχαλίνωσας, δι' ἐμὲ τὴν φύσιν τῶν ζώων ἀνέδειξας. Πάντα³⁴⁹ ὑπέταξας ὑποκάτω³⁵⁰ τῶν ποδῶν³⁵¹ μου·³⁵² οὐδ' ἕν³⁵³ τῶν³⁵⁴ τῆς σῆς φιλανθρωπίας ἐν ἐμοὶ³⁵⁵ πραγμάτων παρέλειπας.³⁵⁶

---

³³⁵ Ἐκφωνήσει om. MS. Καc., Thess.
³³⁶ ἡμ[ῶν] MS. Καc.
³³⁷ φ[ω]νῆς MS. Καc.
³³⁸ [λαμπρ]ᾷ MS. Καc.
³³⁹ φωνην MS. Καc.
³⁴⁰ [υμ]νολογουντα MS. Καc.
³⁴¹ [βωω]ντα MS. Καc.
³⁴² κραγοτα MS. Καc.
³⁴³ Πρόσχωμεν om. MS. Καc.
³⁴⁴ Ὁ Ἱερεὺς λέγει om. MS. Par., MS. Καc.
³⁴⁵ Ἅγιος, ἅγιος, ἅγιος Thess.
³⁴⁶ εξερετων MS. Καc.
³⁴⁷ ἐπιδεεῖ MS. Par., MS. Καc.
³⁴⁸ χρήζων Ger.
³⁴⁹ π[α]ντα MS. Καc.
³⁵⁰ ὑπὸ Ren/Migne.
³⁵¹ π[ο]δων MS. Καc.
³⁵² Cf. Ephesians 1:22.
³⁵³ ἕν MS. Par.‖ οὐδέν Thess.
³⁵⁴ των [της σης] MS. Καc.
³⁵⁵ ἐμὲ MS. Par.
³⁵⁶ π[α]ραλιπας MS. Καc.

10   Ὁ Λαὸς λέγει· Κύριε ἐλέησον.[357]
Ὁ Ἱερεὺς λέγει·[358] Σὺ ἔπλασάς με καὶ ἔθηκας ἐπ᾽ ἐμὲ[359] τὴν χεῖρά σου, τῆς σῆς ἐξουσίας ἐν ἐμοὶ τὴν εἰκόνα ὑπέγραψας, τοῦ λόγου τὸ δῶρον[360] ἐνέθηκας· εἰς τρυφήν[361] μοι τὸν παράδεισον ἤνοιξας· τῆς σῆς γνώσεως[362] τὴν διδασκαλίαν[363] παρέδωκας.[364] Ἔδειξάς με[365] τὸ δένδρον τῆς ζωῆς, μοι ξύλον ὑπέδειξας, τοῦ θανάτου τὸ κέντρον ἐγνώρισας. Ἑνός μοι φύτου τὴν ἀπόλαυσιν
15   ἀπηγόρευσας. Ἐξ αὐτοῦ μόνου οὖν εἶπάς μοι μὴ[366] φαγεῖν,[367] ἔφαγον ἐκ ὧν[368] τὸν νόμον ἠθέτησα· γνώμῃ τῆς ἐντολῆς παρημέλησα· ἐγὼ δὲ τοῦ θανάτου τὴν ἀπόφασιν ἥρπασα.
Ὁ Λαὸς λέγει· Κύριε ἐλέησον.[369]
Ὁ Ἱερεὺς λέγει·[370] Σὺ[371] μοί, ὦ Δέσποτα, τὴν τιμωρίαν μετέβαλες· ὡς ποιμὴν ἀγαθὸς εἰς[372] πλανώμενον[373] ἔδραμες. Ὡς Πατὴρ ἀληθινὸς ἐμοὶ τῷ πεπτωκότι συνήλγησας, πᾶσι
20   τοῖς πρὸς ζωὴν φαρμάκοις κατέδησας. Αὐτός μοι προφήτας[374] ἀπέστειλας· δι᾽ ἐμὲ τὸν νοσοῦντα, νόμον εἰς βοήθειαν ἔδωκας.[375] Αὐτός μοι τὰς[376] πρὸς ὑγίειαν[377] ᾧ παρανομηθείσας,[378] διηκόνησας· φῶς τοῖς πλανωμένοις[379] ἀνέτειλας· τοῖς[380]

---

[357] Κ(ύρι)ε ἐλέησον om. MS. Kac.
[358] Ὁ Ἱερεὺς λέγει om. MS. Par., MS. Kac.
[359] εμ[ε] MS. Kac.
[360] τὸ θεῖον δῶρον Thess.
[361] τρυφ[ην] MS. Kac.
[362] [γνω]σεως MS. Kac.
[363] διδ[ασ]καλιαν MS. Kac.
[364] παρεδωκα[ς] MS. Kac.
[365] μοι Thess.
[366] οὗ MS. Par., MS. Kac.
[367] φαγι MS. Kac.
[368] ἑκὼν MS. Par., Ger.‖ ἐκ ὧν om. Ren/Migne.
[369] Κύριε ἐλέησον om. MS. Kac.
[370] Ὁ Ἱερεὺς λέγει om. MS. Par., MS. Kac.
[371] Σὺ om. Ger.
[372] επι το MS. Kac.
[373] τὸ Ger.
[374] προφητα[ς] MS. Kac.
[375] ἔδωκας Thess.
[376] τὰ Ger.
[377] ὑγιεῖαν Ger.‖ ὑγιείαν Ren/Migne.
[378] παρανομηθεῖτοκας corr. MS. Par.‖ παρανομητης MS. Kac.‖ τὰς πρὸς ὑγίειαν ᾧ παρανομηθείσας om. Thess.
[379] πλανωμενος MS. Kac.
[380] τ in τοῖς added by a later hand in the MS. Par.

ἀγνοοῦσιν, ὁ ἀεὶ παρὼν ἐπεδήμησας.³⁸¹ Ἐπὶ³⁸² τὴν παρθενικὴν³⁸³ ἦλθες³⁸⁴ νηδύν, ὁ ἀχώρητος Θεὸς ὤν. Οὐχ ἁρπαγμὸν ἡγήσω τὸ εἶναι ἴσα Θεῷ, ἀλλ' ἑαυτὸν ἐκένωσας· μορφὴν δούλου
25 λαβών. Τὴν ἐμὴν³⁸⁵ ἐν σοι φύσιν³⁸⁶ ηὐλόγησας·³⁸⁷ ὑπὲρ ἐμοῦ τὸν νόμον ἐπλήρωσας·³⁸⁸ τοῦ πτώματός³⁸⁹ μου τὴν ἀνάστασιν ὑπηγόρευσας. Ἔδωκας τοῖς ὑπὸ τοῦ ᾅδου κρατουμένοις τὴν ἄφεσιν·³⁹⁰ τοῦ νόμου τὴν ἀρὰν ἀπεσόβησας.³⁹¹ Ἐν σαρκὶ τὴν ἁμαρτίαν κατήργησας·³⁹² τῆς σῆς ἐξουσίας³⁹³ μοι³⁹⁴ τὴν δυναστείαν³⁹⁵ ἐγνώρισας. Τυφλοῖς τὸ βλέπειν ἀπέδωκας· νεκροὺς ἐκ τάφων³⁹⁶ ἀνέστησας·³⁹⁷ ῥήματι τὴν φύσιν³⁹⁸
30 ἀνώρθωσας·³⁹⁹ τῆς σῆς εὐσπλαγχνίας⁴⁰⁰ μοι τὴν οἰκονομίαν⁴⁰¹ ὑπέδειξας· τῶν πονηρῶν τὴν⁴⁰² βίαν ὑπένεγκας.⁴⁰³ Τὸν νῶτόν⁴⁰⁴ σου δέδωκας εἰς μάστιγας,⁴⁰⁵ τὰς δὲ σιαγόνας σου ὑπέθηκας⁴⁰⁶ εἰς ῥαπίσματα· οὐκ ἀπέστρεψας⁴⁰⁷ δι' ἐμὲ τὸ πρόσωπόν σου ἀπὸ αἰσχύνης ἐμπτυσμάτων.⁴⁰⁸

Ὁ Λαὸς λέγει· Κύριε ἐλέησον.⁴⁰⁹

---

³⁸¹ Κύριε ἐλέησον MS. Par. (after ἀγνοοῦσιν) MS. Kac. (after ἐπεδήμησας).
³⁸² ε in ἐπὶ added by a later hand in the MS. Par.
³⁸³ παρθενηκην MS. Kac.
³⁸⁴ ηλ MS. Par.
³⁸⁵ [εμην] MS. Par.
³⁸⁶ φ[υ]σιν MS. Kac.
³⁸⁷ [ηυ]λογησας MS. Kac.
³⁸⁸ [επ]ληρωσας MS. Kac.
³⁸⁹ [πτωμα]τος MS. Kac.
³⁹⁰ αφ[ε]σιν MS. Kac.
³⁹¹ ἀπεσώβησας White.|| αποσωβησας MS. Kac.
³⁹² Κατηρ[γησ]ας MS Kac.
³⁹³ [εξουσιας] MS. Kac.
³⁹⁴ [μι] MS. Kac.
³⁹⁵ δυνάστειαν White.
³⁹⁶ τάφῶν MS. Par.
³⁹⁷ αν[εσ]τησας MS. Kac.
³⁹⁸ φυσις White.
³⁹⁹ ἀνόρθωσας White.
⁴⁰⁰ εὐ[σπλα]γχνίας White.
⁴⁰¹ ο[ίκονομιαν] White.
⁴⁰² [πονηρῶν τὴν] White.
⁴⁰³ ὑπήνεγκας MS. Par., MS. Kac., Thess.
⁴⁰⁴ [τὸν νῶτον] White.|| τ[ον νωτον] MS. Kac.
⁴⁰⁵ ε[ἰς μάστιγας] White.
⁴⁰⁶ υπηθηκας MS. Kac.
⁴⁰⁷ απεστριψας MS. Kac.
⁴⁰⁸ αἰσχύνη[ς εμ]πτυσμάτων White.|| Cf. Prophecy of Isaiah 50:6.
⁴⁰⁹ [Κύριε ἐλέησον] MS. Kac.

The Liturgy of Saint Gregory the Theologian

35   Ὁ Ἱερεὺς λέγει·⁴¹⁰ Ὡς πρόβατον ἐπὶ σφαγὴν ἦλθες, μέχρι σταυροῦ. Τὴν ἐμὴν κηδεμονίαν
ὑπέδειξας· τῷ σῷ τάφῳ τὴν ἐμὴν ἁμαρτίαν ἐνέκρωσας· εἰς οὐρανόν⁴¹¹ μοι⁴¹² τὴν ἐμὴν⁴¹³ ἀπαρχὴν ἀνεβίβασας·⁴¹⁴ τῆς σῆς ἀφίξεώς⁴¹⁵ μοι τὴν παρουσίαν⁴¹⁶ ἐμήνυσας·⁴¹⁷ ἐν ᾗ⁴¹⁸ μέλλεις ἔρχεσθαι⁴¹⁹ κρῖναι ζῶντας καὶ νεκρούς·⁴²⁰ καὶ ἀποδοῦναι ἑκάστῳ⁴²¹ κατὰ τὰ ἔργα αὐτοῦ.
40   Ὁ Λαὸς λέγει· Κατὰ τὸ ἔλεός σου⁴²² Κύριε. ⁴²³

5. The Consecration

Ὁ Ἱερεὺς λέγει·⁴²⁴ Ταύτης⁴²⁵ μου τῆς ἐλευθερίας προσφέρω⁴²⁶ σοι τὰ σύμβολα· τοῖς ῥήμασί⁴²⁷ σου ἐπιγράφω⁴²⁸ τὰ πράγματα.⁴²⁹ Σύ μοι τὴν μυστικὴν ταύτην⁴³⁰ λειτουργίαν⁴³¹ παρέδωκας τῆς⁴³² σῆς σαρκός, ἐν ἄρτῳ⁴³³ καὶ οἴνῳ⁴³⁴ τὴν μέθεξιν.⁴³⁵
5   Ὁ Λαὸς λέγει· Πιστεύομεν.⁴³⁶
Ὁ Ἱερεὺς λέγει·⁴³⁷ Τῇ γὰρ⁴³⁸ νυκτὶ ᾗ παρεδίδης⁴³⁹ αὐτὸς⁴⁴⁰ σευτόν, τῆς⁴⁴¹ σευτοῦ⁴⁴² ἐξουσίας.⁴⁴³

---

⁴¹⁰ Ὁ Ἱερεὺς λέγει om. MS. Par., MS. Kac., White.
⁴¹¹ οὐρανούς Thess.
⁴¹² μου MS. Par., MS. Kac., Ger.‖ μοι om. Ren/Migne., Thess.
⁴¹³ ἐμὴν MS. Par., MS. Kac., White., Ger.
⁴¹⁴ ἀνεβηβασας MS. Par., MS. Kac.‖ [ἀνε]βίβασας White.
⁴¹⁵ ἀφήξεως White.
⁴¹⁶ [μοι τὴν πα]ρουσίαν White.
⁴¹⁷ [παρουσιαν εμη]ν[υ]σας MS. Kac.
⁴¹⁸ [η] MS. Kac.
⁴¹⁹ [ἐν ᾗ μέλλεις ἔρ]χεσθαι White.
⁴²⁰ ζών[τας καὶ νεκ]ρούς White.
⁴²¹ ἀποδοῦ[ναι ἑκάστῳ] White.
⁴²² σου om. MS. Par.
⁴²³ κα[τὰ τὸ ἔλεός σου Κύριε] White.
⁴²⁴ Ὁ Ἱερεὺς λέγει om. MS. Par., MS. Kac., White.
⁴²⁵ αὐτός White.
⁴²⁶ μο[υ τῆς ἐλευθερίας προσφέ]ρω White.
⁴²⁷ σ[ύμβολα, τοῖς ῥήμασί] White.
⁴²⁸ [Ταυτη]ς μο[υ] της [ε]λ[ε]υθερ[ι]ας προσφ[ε]ρω σοι τα συμ[β]ολ[α] τοις ρημασι [σ]ου επιγραφω MS. Kac.
⁴²⁹ ἐπιγράφ[ω τὰ πράγματα] White.
⁴³⁰ ταύτην MS. Par.‖ μ[υστικὴν ταύτην] White.‖ ταύτην MS. Par.
⁴³¹ λειτουργίαν MS. Par., MS. Kac., White., Ger.‖ λιτουργίαν om. Ren/Migne. Thess.
⁴³² λειτουρ[γίαν παρέδωκας της] White.‖ From τῆς to ἐκέρασας the text is missing from the MS. Par. but can be reconstructed from the other manuscripts.
⁴³³ μι (μοι) add. MS. Kac., Ger.
⁴³⁴ σαρκὸ[ς ἐν ἄρτῳ καὶ οἴνῳ] White.‖ οινω παρεσχες add. MS. Kac., Ger.
⁴³⁵ μέθ[εξιν] White.
⁴³⁶ Πιστεύομεν om. MS.Kac., White.
⁴³⁷ Ὁ Ἱερεὺς λέγει om. MS. Par., MS. Kac., White.
⁴³⁸ γὰρ om. Thess.
⁴³⁹ παρεδίδου Thess.

Critical Text and Translation

Ὁ Λαὸς λέγει· Πιστεύομεν.[444]

Ὁ Ἱερεὺς λέγει·[445] Λαβὼν ἄρτον ἐν ταῖς ἁγίαις[446] καὶ ἀχράντοις καὶ ἀμωμήτοις[447] σου χερσίν, ἔνευσας ἄνω πρὸς[448] τὸν[449] ἴδιόν σου Πατέρα[450] Θεὸν ἡμῶν καὶ Θεὸν τῶν ὅλων·[451]

10   ηὐχαρίστησας, ηὐλόγησας, ἡγίασας, ἔκλασας, μετέδωκας τοῖς ἁγίοις σου μαθηταῖς[452] καὶ ἀποστόλοις[453] εἶπας.[454] Λάβετε[455] φάγετε τοῦτό[456] μου ἐστὶν[457] τὸ Σῶμα, τὸ ὑπὲρ ὑμῶν[458] καὶ πολλῶν κλώμενον, καὶ[459] διαδόμενον[460] εἰς

ἄφεσιν ἁμαρτιῶν·[461] τοῦτο ποιεῖτε εἰς τὴν ἐμὴν[462] ἀνάμνησιν. Ὡσαύτως[463] μετὰ τὸ δειπνῆσαι,[464] λαβὼν ποτήριον, καὶ ἐκέρασας αὐτὸ ἐκ γεννήματος[465] ἀμπέλου, καὶ ἐξ

15   ὕδατος[466] ηὐχαρίστησας, ηὐλόγησας,[467] ἡγίασας, μετέδωκας τοῖς ἁγίοις[468] σου[469] μαθηταῖς[470] καὶ ἀποστόλοις,[471] εἶπας· Πίετε[472] ἐξ αὐτοῦ[473] πάντες, τοῦτο μου

---

[440] [νυκτὶ ᾗ παρεδίδης αὐτὸς] White.
[441] τῇ Thess.
[442] εαυτου MS. Kac.
[443] τ[ῆς σεαυτοῦ ἐξουσίας] White.‖ ἐξουσίᾳ Thess.
[444] Πιστεύομεν om. MS. Kac., White.
[445] Ὁ Ἱερεὺς λέγει om. MS. Par., MS. Kac., White.
[446] [ἄρτον ἐν ταῖς ἁγίαις] White.
[447] [ἀχράντοις καὶ ἀμωμήτοις] White.
[448] [χερσιν, ἔνευσας ἄνω πρὸς] White.
[449] τὸν om. MS. Kac., Ren/Migne., Thess.
[450] [ἴδιόν σου Πατέρα] White.
[451] Θεὸν ἡμῶν καὶ Θεὸν τῶν ὅλων om. White.
[452] ηὐχαρίσ[τησας, ηὐλόγησας, ἡγίασας, ἔκλασας, μ]ετέδω[κας τοῖς ἁγίοις σου μ]αθηταῖς White.
[453] ἀποστόλοις om. White.
[454] [εἶπας] White.
[455] λαβετε MS. Kac.
[456] [Λάβετε φάγετε τοῦτ]ο White.
[457] [εστι]ν MS. Kac.‖ ἐστι Thess.
[458] [τὸ σῶμα, τὸ ὑπὲρ ὑ]μῶν White.
[459] πο[λλῶν κλώμενον, κ]αὶ White.
[460] διαδιδόμενον White., Thess.
[461] διαδιδό[μενον εἰς ἄφεσιν ἁ]μαρτιῶν White.
[462] [τοῦτο ποιεῖτε εἰς τὴν ἐ]μὴν White.
[463] ω[σα]υτος MS. Kac.
[464] [Ὡσαύτως μετὰ τὸ δει]πνῆσαι White.
[465] λα[βὼν ποτήριον, καὶ ἐκ]έρασ[ας αὐτὸ ἐκ γεννήματ]ος White.
[466] ἀμπέ[λου, καὶ ἐξ ὕδατος] White.
[467] [ηὐχαρίστησας, ηὐλόγη]σας White.
[468] ἡγί[ασας, μετέδωκας τοῖς ἁγί]οις White.
[469] τοῖς ἁγίοις [σεαυτοῦ] White.
[470] μαθήταις MS. Par.
[471] μαθηταῖς καὶ ἀποστόλοις σου Thess.
[472] Λάβετε πιετε MS. Kac.

ἐστὶν⁴⁷⁴ τὸ Αἷμα, τὸ τῆς καινῆς διαθήκης, τὸ ὑπὲρ ὑμῶν⁴⁷⁵ καὶ πολλῶν⁴⁷⁶ ἐκχυνόμενον εἰς ἄφεσιν ἁμαρτιῶν, τοῦτο ποιεῖτε εἰς τὴν ἐμὴν ἀνάμνησιν. Ὁσάκις γὰρ ἂν ἐσθίετε⁴⁷⁷ τὸν ἄρτον τοῦτον, πίνετε⁴⁷⁸ δὲ καὶ τὸ ποτήριον τοῦτο, τὸν ἐμὸν θάνατον καταγγέλλετε, καὶ τὴν ἐμὴν

20   ἀνάστασιν καὶ ἀνάληψιν⁴⁷⁹ ὁμολογεῖτε, ἄχρις οὗ ἂν ἔλθω.
Ὁ Λαὸς λέγει· Ἀμήν Ἀμήν Ἀμήν.⁴⁸⁰ Τὸν θάνατόν σου.⁴⁸¹

6. The *Epiklesis*

Ὁ Ἱερεὺς λέγει·⁴⁸² Ὥστε οὖν⁴⁸³ Δέσποτα μεμνημένοι τῆς ἐπὶ γῆς συγκαταβάσεως,

καὶ τοῦ ζωοποιοῦ θανάτου, καὶ τῆς τριημέρου σου ταφῆς, καὶ τῆς ἐκ νεκρῶν ἀναστάσεως, καὶ τῆς εἰς οὐρανοὺς ἀνόδου· καὶ τῆς ἐκ δεξιῶν τοῦ⁴⁸⁴ Πατρὸς καθέδρας,

5   καὶ τῆς μελλούσης ἀπ' οὐρανῶν δευτέρας καὶ φοβερᾶς καὶ ἐνδόξου σου παρουσίας. Ἐκφωνήσει.⁴⁸⁵

Τὰ σὰ ἐκ τῶν σῶν δώρων⁴⁸⁶ σοὶ προσφέροντες, κατὰ πάντα καὶ διὰ πάντα καὶ ἐν πᾶσιν.⁴⁸⁷
Ὁ Λαὸς λέγει· Σὲ αἰνοῦμεν, σὲ εὐλογοῦμεν.⁴⁸⁸

10   Ὁ Διάκονος λέγει· Κλίνατε Θεῷ⁴⁸⁹ μετὰ φόβου.⁴⁹⁰

---

[473] σεαυ[τοῦ εἶπας· Πίετε ἐξ αὐ]τοῦ White.
[474] ἐστι Thess.
[475] ημων MS. Kac.
[476] ἂν add. Ger.
[477] ἐσθίητε MS. Par.; ανεσθιητε MS. Kac.
[478] πίνητε MS. Par., MS. Kac.
[479] ἀνάληψιν om. Ren/Migne., Thess.
[480] Ἀμ(ήν). γ´ om. Thess.
[481] rubric (or possibly the response) in the MS. Kac., is illegible.
[482] Ὁ Ἱερεὺς λέγει om. MS. Par., MS. Kac.
[483] Ω[στε] ο[υν] MS. Kac.
[484] το MS. Kac.
[485] Ἐκφωνήσει om. MS. Kac.
[486] δωρον MS. Kac.
[487] There is an illegible note in the scholion.
[488] κτλ. Ger.
[489] Θεοῦ White.
[490] φόβου om. MS. Par.; [...]κλινα[...] MS. Kac.

Ὁ Ἱερεὺς λέγει ἐν ἑαυτῷ κλίνας·⁴⁹¹ Αὐτὸς, οὖν Δέσποτα τῇ σῇ φωνῇ τὰ προκείμενα
μεταποίησον· αὐτὸς παρὼν, τὴν μυστικὴν ταύτην⁴⁹² τὴν λειτουργίαν⁴⁹³ κατάρτισον· αὐτὸς ἡμῖν⁴⁹⁴ τῆς σῆς⁴⁹⁵ λατρείας τὴν μνήμην⁴⁹⁶ διάσωσον.⁴⁹⁷ Αὐτὸς τὸ Πνεῦμά σου τὸ πανάγιον κατάπεμψον.⁴⁹⁸ Ἵνα⁴⁹⁹ ἐπιφοίτησαν⁵⁰⁰ τῇ ἁγίᾳ καὶ ἀγαθῇ καὶ ἐνδόξῳ⁵⁰¹ αὐτοῦ

15 παρουσίᾳ, ἁγιάσῃ καὶ μεταποιήσῃ τὰ προκείμενα τίμια καὶ ἅγια Δῶρα ταῦτα, εἰς αὐτὸ τὸ Σῶμα καὶ τὸ Αἷμα τῆς ἡμετέρας ἀπολυτρώσεως.
Ὁ Διάκονος λέγει· Πρόσχωμεν.

Ὁ Λαὸς λέγει· Ἀμήν.⁵⁰²
Ὁ Ἱερεὺς ἐκφωνήσει·⁵⁰³ Καὶ ποιήσει⁵⁰⁴ τὸν μὲν ἄρτον τοῦτον γένηται⁵⁰⁵ εἰς τὸ⁵⁰⁶ ἅγιον

20 Σῶμά σου,⁵⁰⁷ τοῦ Κυρίου δὲ καὶ Θεοῦ καὶ σωτῆρος, καὶ παμβασιλέως ἡμῶν Ἰησοῦ Χριστοῦ, εἰς ἄφεσιν ἁμαρτιῶν, καὶ εἰς ζωὴν τὴν αἰώνιον τοῖς ἐξ αὐτοῦ μεταλαμβάνουσιν. Ὁ Λαὸς λέγει· Ἀμήν.⁵⁰⁸
Ὁ Ἱερεὺς λέγει·⁵⁰⁹ Τὸ⁵¹⁰ δὲ ποτήριον τοῦτο τὸ τίμιόν σου Αἷμα, τὸ τῆς καινῆς διαθήκης σου,⁵¹¹ τοῦ Κυρίου δὲ καὶ Θεοῦ καὶ σωτῆρος καὶ παμβασιλέως ἡμῶν Ἰησοῦ

---

[491] Ὁ Ἱερεὺς λέγει ἐν ἑαυτῷ κλίνας om. MS Κας.‖ κλῖνας MS. Par.‖ [κλινῶν] White.
[492] ταῦτην MS. Par.
[493] λειτουργίαν MS. Par., White.
[494] ημην MS. Κας.
[495] σ[η]ς MS. Κας.
[496] μνήσιν White.
[497] δυνάμωσον White.
[498] κα[ταπεμ]ψον MS. Κας.
[499] [ι]να MS. Κας.
[500] ἐπιφοιτήσαν MS. Par.‖ επιφι[τησ]αν MS. Κας.
[501] [τη αγια κε α]γαθη κε [ενδοξω] MS. Κας.
[502] Ὁ Λ(αὸς) λέγ(ει)· Πρόσχωμεν. Ὁ Δ(ιάκονος) λέγ(ει)· Ἀμήν. MS. Par., Ren/Migne., Thess.
[503] Ὁ Ἱερεὺς ἐκφωνήσει om. MS. Κας.‖ ἐκφωνήσει om. Thess.
[504] ποιήσῃ MS. Par., White.
[505] γεν[η]τε MS. Κας.‖ ἵνα γένηται Thess.
[506] τὸ om. Thess.
[507] σου σῶμα White.
[508] Ἀμήν om. White.
[509] [Ὁ Ἱερεὺς λέγει] MS. Κας.‖ Ὁ Ἱερεὺς λέγει om. MS. Par., MS., Κας., White.
[510] τα MS. Κας.
[511] σου om. White.

25 Χριστοῦ,⁵¹² εἰς ἄφεσιν ἁμαρτιῶν, καὶ εἰς ζωὴν τὴν⁵¹³ αἰώνιον τοῖς ἐξ αὐτοῦ μεταλαμβάνουσιν.
Ὁ Λαὸς λέγει· Ἀμήν.⁵¹⁴

7. The Intercessions

Ὁ Ἱερεὺς λέγει, καὶ ὁ Λαὸς ἀποκρίνεται τὸ Κύριε ἐλέησον.⁵¹⁵

Σὲ δυσωποῦμεν Χριστὲ ὁ Θεὸς ἡμῶν.
Τῆς ἐκκλησίας σου Κύριε τὴν κρηπῖδα⁵¹⁶ κατάπηξον.
5   Τῆς ἀγάπης ἡμῖν τὴν ὁμόνοιαν ῥίζωσον.
Τῆς πίστεως τὴν ἀλήθειαν αὔξησον.
Τῆς σῆς εὐσεβείας ἡμῖν τὴν ὁδὸν εὐθυτόμησον.
Τοὺς ποιμένας ὀχύρωσον.
Τοὺς ποιμαινομένους⁵¹⁷ ἀσφάλεισαι.⁵¹⁸
10 Δὸς τῷ κλήρῳ τὴν εὐκοσμίαν.
Τοῖς μοναχοῖς τὴν ἐγκράτειαν.⁵¹⁹
Τοῖς ἐν παρθενίᾳ τὸ σῶφρονον.⁵²⁰
Τοῖς ἐν σεμνῷ γάμῳ τὴν εὐζωΐαν.⁵²¹
Τοῖς ἐν μετανοίᾳ⁵²² τὸ ἔλεος.
15 Τοῖς πλουτοῦσι τὴν ἀγαθότητα.
Τοῖς πενομένοις τὴν ἐπικουρίαν.
Τοῖς πτωχοῖς⁵²³ τὴν⁵²⁴ βοήθειαν.

Τοὺς πρεσβύτας περίζωσον.⁵²⁵

---

⁵¹² "κ(αὶ) παμβ. is added in the margin by original or contemporary hand" White.
⁵¹³ τὴν om. MS. Kac.
⁵¹⁴ [Ὁ Λ(αὸς) λέγ(ει)· Ἀμήν] MS. Kac.
⁵¹⁵ τὸ Κύριε ἐλέησον MS. Kac.‖ ὁ Διάκονος: Τὰς δεήσεις Thess.
⁵¹⁶ κρηπῖδα Ren/Migne., Ger.
⁵¹⁷ ποιμενομένους Thess.
⁵¹⁸ ἀσφάλισαι Ren/Migne.
⁵¹⁹ [την οδον ευθυτομησον. Τους ποιμενας οχυρωσον. Τους ποιμαινομενους ασφαλισαι] Δ[ο]ς τω κληρ[ω] την ευκοσμιαν. Τ[οις] μοναχ[οις] την [εγκ]ρ[ατει]αν MS. Kac.
⁵²⁰ σωφρονεῖν Ren/Minge., Ger.
⁵²¹ [την] ευζ[ω]ιαν MS. Kac.
⁵²² [ν] [μ]ετανια MS. Kac.
⁵²³ π[τωχ]ις MS. Kac.
⁵²⁴ τον MS. Kac.

Τοὺς νέους σωφρόνησον.⁵²⁶
20   Τοὺς ἀπίστους ἐπίστρεψον.
Παῦσον τῆς ἐκκλησίας τὰ σχίσματα.⁵²⁷
Τῶν αἱρέσεων⁵²⁸ κατάλυσον τὰ φρυάγματα.
Πάντας ἡμᾶς πρὸς τὴν τῆς⁵²⁹ σῆς εὐσεβείας ὁμόνοιαν σύναψον.
Ὁ Λαὸς λέγει· Κύριε ἐλέησον.⁵³⁰
25   Ὁ Ἱερεὺς λέγει·⁵³¹ Μνήσθητι Κύριε τῆς εἰρήνης τῆς ἁγίας μόνης καθολικῆς καὶ ἀποστολικῆς σου ἐκκλησίας. Τῆς ἀπὸ περάτων, ἕως περάτων τῆς οἰκουμένης, καὶ τῶν ἐν αὐτῇ⁵³² ὀρθοδόξων ἐπισκόπων, τῶν ὀρθοτομησάντων τὸν λόγον τῆς ἀληθείας.
Ἐκφωνήσει.⁵³³
Ἐξαιρέτως⁵³⁴ τοῦ ἁγιωτάτου καὶ μακαριωτάτου ἀρχιερέως⁵³⁵ ἡμῶν Ἄββα ΔΔ´ Πάπα
30   καὶ πατριάρχου τῆς μεγαλοπόλεως Ἀλεξανδρείας.⁵³⁶ Καὶ ὑπὲρ τῶν περιόντων ἐπισκόπων, πρεσβυτέρων, διακόνων, ὑποδιακόνων,⁵³⁷ ἀναγνωστῶν,⁵³⁸ ψαλτῶν, ἐξορκιστῶν,⁵³⁹ μοναζόντων, ἀειπαρθένων, ἐγκρατῶν, χηρῶν, ὀρφανῶν, λαικῶν, καὶ ὑπὲρ παντὸς τοῦ πληρώματος, τῆς ἁγίας τοῦ Θεοῦ ἐκκλησίας τῶν πιστῶν.
Ὁ Λαὸς λέγει· Κύριε ἐλέησον.⁵⁴⁰
35   Ὁ Ἱερεὺς λέγει·⁵⁴¹ Μνήσθητι Κύριε τῶν εὐσεβῶς βασιλευσάντων.
Μνήσθητι Κύριε τῶν ἐν τῷ παλατίῳ⁵⁴² ἡμῶν ἀδελφῶν πιστῶν καὶ ὀρθοδόξων, καὶ παντὸς⁵⁴³ τοῦ⁵⁴⁴ στρατοπέδου.

---

[525] περ[ι]ζ[ωσ]ον MS. Kac.
[526] σωφρόνισον Ren/Migne., Ger.
[527] Παυσον τ[η]ς εκκλησιας [τ]α σχισματα MS. Kac.
[528] ηερεσεων MS. Kac.
[529] την την MS. Kac.
[530] [Κ(ύρι)ε ἐλέησον] MS. Kac.
[531] Ὁ Ἱερεὺς λέγει om. MS. Par., MS. Kac.
[532] αυτης MS. Kac.
[533] [ε]κφωνήσ[ει] MS. Par.‖ Ἐκφωνήσει om. MS. Kac., Thess.
[534] εξερ[ε]τως MS. Kac.
[535] αρχηερεως MS. Kac.
[536] Πάπα καὶ πατριάρχου τῆς μεγαλοπόλεως Ἀλεξανδρείας om. Thess.
[537] ὑποδιακόνων om. MS. Kac., Ren/Migne.
[538] ἀναγνώστων MS. Par.
[539] ἐπορκιστῶν MS. Par., MS. Kac.
[540] [Κύριε ἐλέησον] MS. Kac.
[541] Ὁ Ἱερεὺς λέγει om. MS. Par., MS. Kac.
[542] παλλατιω MS. Kac.

The Liturgy of Saint Gregory the Theologian

Μνήσθητι, Κύριε τῶν προσφερόντων τὰ τίμια[545] Δῶρα ταῦτα, καὶ[546] ὑπὲρ ὧν καὶ δι' ὧν προσεκόμισαν, καὶ μισθὸν οὐράνιον παράσχου πᾶσιν αὐτοῖς.[547]

40 Μνήσθητι Κύριε καὶ τῶν ἐν ὄρεσι· καὶ σπηλαίοις· καὶ ταῖς ὀπαῖς τῆς γῆς. Καὶ τῶν ἐν αἰχμαλωσίαις ὄντων ἀδελφῶν[548] ἡμῶν καὶ εἰρηνικὰς[549] ἀποκαταστάσεις[550] εἰς τὰ ἴδια χάρισαι.

Ὁ Διάκονος λέγει· Προσεύξασθε ὑπὲρ τῶν αἰχμαλώτων.

Ὁ Λαὸς λέγει. Κύριε ἐλέησον. Γ΄.[551]

45 Τότε κλίνει ὁ[552] Ἱερεὺς[553] τὴν ἑατοῦ κεφαλὴν λέγων καθ' ἑαυτὸν ἐν ἑαυτῷ[554] Μνήσθητι[555] Κύριε καὶ τῆς ἐμῆς ἀθλίας, καὶ ταλαιπώρου ψυχῆς, ταπεινώσεώς μου, καὶ συγχώρησόν[556] μοι πάντα τὰ ἐμὰ πλημμελήματα, καὶ ὅπου ἐπλεόνασεν ἡ ἁμαρτία, ὑπερπερίσσευσόν[557] σου τὴν χάριν, καὶ μὴ διὰ τὰς ἐμὰς ἁμαρτίας, καὶ τὴν βεβήλωσιν τῆς καρδίας μου, ὑστερήσῃς τὸν λαόν σου τῆς χάριτος τοῦ ἁγίου σου

50 Πνεύματος.[558]

Ὑψώσει τὴν κεφαλὴν καὶ ἐκφωνήσει[559]

Ὁ γὰρ Λαός[560] σου καὶ ἡ Ἐκκλησία σου ἱκετεύει σε, καὶ διά σοῦ καὶ σὺν σοὶ τὸν Πατέρα λέγουσα.

Ὁ Λαὸς λέγει· Ἐλέησον ἡμᾶς ὁ Θεὸς ὁ σωτὴρ ἡμῶν. Γ΄.[561]

---

[543] παντο MS. Kac.
[544] τοῦ om. MS. Kac.
[545] ἅγια Ren/Migne., Thess.
[546] καὶ om. MS. Kac.
[547] αυτης MS. Kac.
[548] αδ[ε]λφων MS. Kac.
[549] [κε ε]ρηνικας MS. Kac.
[550] εἰρ[ηνικ]ὰς ἀποκατασά[σει]ς White.
[551] Γ΄ om. Thess.; Although the mark following the "Lord, have mercy" here certainly looks like a capital gamma, indicating that the response should be repeated three times. The use of this gamma is inconsistent as in some other parts of the liturgy a threefold repetition is written out completely.
[552] ὁ om. Ren/Migne.
[553] ὁ τελετουργός Thess.
[554] [Ὁ Δ(ιάκονος) λέγ(ει)· Προσεύξασθε ὑπὲρ τῶν αἰχμαλώτων. Ὁ Λ(αὸς) λέγ(ει). Κ(ύρι)ε ἐλέησον. Γ΄. Τότε κλίνει ὁ Ἱ(ερεὺς) τὴν ἑατ(οῦ) κεφαλὴν λέγ(ων) καθ' ἑαυτὸν ἐν ἑαυτῷ] MS. Kac.
[555] Μ]νήσθητι White.
[556] κα[ὶ συ]γχώρησόν White.
[557] περίσσευσόν Ren/Migne., Thess.‖ [ηπερ]περισσευσον MS. Kac.
[558] καὶ μὴ διὰ τὰς ἐμὰς ἁμαρτίας, καὶ τὴν βεβήλωσιν τῆς καρδίας μου, ὑστερήσῃς τὸν λαόν σου τῆς χάριτος τοῦ ἁγίου σου Πνεύματος. om. Thess.
[559] [Ὑψώσει τὴν κεφαλὴν κ(αὶ) ἐκφωνήσει] MS. Kac.
[560] Ὁ γὰρ Λ]αός White.
[561] Ἐ]λέησον ἡμᾶς ὁ Θεὸς ὁ σ(ωτ)ὴρ ἡμῶν White.

Critical Text and Translation

55 Ὁ Ἱερεὺς λέγει· Ἐλέησον ἡμᾶς ὁ Θεὸς ὁ σωτὴρ ἡμῶν. Γ΄.
Ὁ Λαὸς λέγει· Κύριε ἐλέησον. Γ΄.
Ὁ Ἱερεὺς λέγει.[562] Μνήσθητι[563] Κύριε τοῦ ἀέρος καὶ τῶν καρπῶν τῆς γῆς.
Μνήσθητι Κύριε τῆς συμμέτρου ἀναβάσεως τῶν ποταμείων[564] ὑδάτων.
Μνήσθητι Κύριε τῶν ὑετῶν καὶ τῶν σπορίμων[565] τῆς γῆς.
60 Εὔφρανον[566] πάλιν καὶ ἀνακαίνισον τὸ πρόσωπον τῆς γῆς.
Τοὺς αὔλακας αὐτῆς μέθυσον πλήθυνον τὰ γενήματα[567] αὐτῆς. Παράστησον[568] ἡμῖν αὐτὰ[569] εἰς σπέρμα καὶ εἰς θερισμόν, καὶ νῦν εὐλογῶν εὐλόγησον, τὴν ζωὴν ἡμῶν οἰκονόμησον. Εὐλόγησον τὸν στέφανον τοῦ ἐνιαυτοῦ τῆς χρηστότητός σου.[570] Διὰ τοὺς πτωχοὺς τοῦ λαοῦ σου, διὰ τῆν χήραν[571] καὶ τὸν ὀρφανὸν, διὰ τὸν ξένον καὶ τὸν
65 προσήλυτον, καὶ δι' ἡμᾶς πάντας τοὺς ἐλπίζοντας ἐπί σοί,[572] καὶ ἐπικαλουμένους τὸ ὄνομά σου τὸ ἅγιον. Οἱ γὰρ ὀφθαλμοὶ πάντων εἴς σε ἐλπίζουσι, καὶ σὺ διδῶς τὴν τροφὴν αὐτῶν ἐν εὐκαιρίᾳ.[573] Ποίησον μεθ' ἡμῶν κατὰ τὴν ἀγαθότητά σου, ὁ διδοὺς[574] τροφὴν πάσι[575] σαρκί.[576] Πλήρωσον χαρᾶς καὶ εὐφροσύνης τὰς καρδίας ἡμῶν. Ἵνα ἐν παντὶ[577] πάντοτε πᾶσαν αὐτάρκειαν ἔχοντες, περισσεύσωμεν[578] εἰς πᾶν ἔργον ἀγαθὸν, τοῦ ποιεῖν
70 τὸ θέλημά σου τὸ ἅγιον.
Ὁ Λαὸς λέγει. Κύριε ἐλέησον.

Ὁ Ἱερεὺς λέγει,[579] καὶ ὁ Λαὸς ἀποκρίνεται τὸ Κύριε ἐλέησον.

---

[562] Ὁ Ἱερεὺς λέγει om. MS. Par., MS. Καc.
[563] Μ]νήσθητι White.
[564] ποτάμιων Thess.
[565] σπο[ρίμω]ν White.
[566] Ε]ὔφρανον White.
[567] γενήματα MS. Par.
[568] [ἐν ταῖς σταγόσιν αὐτῆς εὐφρανθήσετ ... λλούσα] MS. Par. in the margin.
[569] αὐτὸ MS. Par.
[570] Cf. Psalm 65.
[571] χ[ή]ραν MS. Par.
[572] σε Thess.
[573] Cf. Psalm 145.
[574] δίδως MS. Par.
[575] πᾶσι Thess.
[576] Cf. Psalm 136.
[577] πᾶσι Ren/Migne., Thess.
[578] περισσεύωμεν MS. Par., Thess., Ger.
[579] White om. preceding prayer.|| ὁ Διάκονος Thess.

The Liturgy of Saint Gregory the Theologian

  Χάρισαι[580] τῷ Λαῷ σου τὴν ὁμόνοιαν.

  Τῷ κόσμῳ τὴν εὐστάθειαν.

75 Τῷ ἀέρι τὴν εὐκρασίαν.

  Τοῖς νοσοῦσι[581] τὴν σωτηρίαν.

  Τοῖς δεομένοις τὴν ἀνάψυξιν.

  Τοῖς ἐν ἐξορίαις τὴν ἄνεσιν.

  Τοῖς ὀρφανοῖς τὴν βοήθειαν.

80 Ταῖς χηραῖς τὴν ἀντίληψιν.[582]

  Τοῖς θλιβομένοις ἐπάρκησον εἰς ἀγαθόν.[583]

  Τοὺς ἑστῶτας[584] ὀχύρωσον.[585]

  Τοὺς πεπτωκότας ἔγειρον.[586]

  Τοὺς ἑστηκότας[587] ἀσφάλισαι.[588]

85 Τῶν κεκοιμημένων μνήσθητι.

  Τῶν ἐν ὁμολογίᾳ τὰς πρεσβείας πρόσδεξαι.

  Τοὺς ἡμαρτηκότας[589] καὶ μετανοήσαντας συναρίθμησον μετὰ τῶν πιστῶν[590] σου.

  Τοὺς πιστοὺς συναρίθμησον μετὰ τῶν[591] μαρτύρων σου.[592]

  Μιμητὰς τοὺς παρόντας[593] ἐν τῷ τόπῳ τούτῳ τῶν ἀγγέλων κατάστησον.

90 Καὶ ἡμᾶς τῇ σῇ[594] Χάριτι πρὸς τὴν σὴν κεκλημένους[595] διακονίαν ἀναξίους ὄντας ὑπόδεξαι.[596]

  Ὁ Λαὸς λέγει· Κύριε ἐλέησον.

---

[580] Χ]άρισαι White.
[581] νοοῦσι Ger.
[582] χη[ραῖς τὴν ἀντίληψιν] White.
[583] Τοῖς θλιβ[ομένοις ἐπάρκησον εἰς] ἀγαθ[όν] White.‖ αγ[α]θον MS. Κας.
[584] εστωτ[ας] MS. Κας.‖ ἑστώτας MS. Par.
[585] Τοὺς ἑστῶτ[ας ὀχύρωσον]. White.
[586] Τοὺς πεπτω[κότας ἔγειρον] White.
[587] ἑστηκότας MS. Par.
[588] ἀσφάλεισαι MS. Par.
[589] Τοὺς ἡμαρ]τηκότας White.
[590] τοῖς πιστοῖς White.
[591] τῶν om. Ren/Migne., Thess.
[592] Τοὺς] πιστ[οὺς συναρίυμησον τοῖς] μαρτυσι σ[ου] White.
[593] Μι]μητ[άς, τοὺς παρόντας]. White.
[594] [σῇ] White.
[595] κε[κλη]μένους White.
[596] ὑπόδ[εξ]αι White.

Ὁ Ἱερεὺς λέγει·[597] Μνήσθητι[598] Κύριε καὶ τῆς πόλεως ἡμῶν[599] ταύτης, καὶ τῶν ἐν ὀρθοδόξῳ πίστει οἰκούντων ἐν αὐτῇ,[600] καὶ πάσης πόλεως καὶ χώρας σὺν παντὶ τῷ κόσμῳ[601] αὐτῶν. Καὶ ῥῦσαι[602] ἡμᾶς ἀπὸ λιμοῦ καὶ λοιμοῦ, σεισμοῦ καὶ καταποντισμοῦ, πυρός, καὶ ἀπὸ αἰχμαλωσίας βαρβάρων, καὶ ἀπὸ τῶν ἀλλοτρίων[603] μαχαιρῶν, καὶ ἐπαναστάσεως ἐχθρῶν τε καὶ αἱρετικῶν.

Ὁ Λαὸς λέγει· Κύριε ἐλέησον.[604]

Ὁ Ἱερεὺς λέγει·[605] Μνήσθητι Κύριε καὶ τῶν προλαβόντων ὁσίων[606] πατέρων ἡμῶν,[607] ὀρθοδόξων ἐπισκόπων,[608] καὶ πάντων τῶν ἀπ᾽ αἰῶνός σοι εὐαρεστησάντων,[609]

ἁγίων πατέρων, πατριαρχῶν, ἀποστόλων,[610] προφητῶν, κηρύκων,[611] εὐαγγελιστῶν, μαρτύρων, ὁμολογητῶν, καὶ παντὸς[612] πνεύματος δικαίου, ἐν πίστει Χριστοῦ τετελειωμένου.

Ἐκφωνήσει.[613]

Ἐξαιρέτως τῆς παναγίας ὑπερενδόξου ἀχράντου ὑπερευλογημένης δεσποίνης[614] ἡμῶν Θεοτόκου καὶ[615] ἀειπαρθένου Μαρίας.[616]

Τοῦ ἁγίου ἐνδόξου προφήτου προδρόμου βαπτιστοῦ καὶ μάρτυρος Ἰωάννου.

Τοῦ ἁγίου Στεφάνου τοῦ πρωτοδιακόνου καὶ πρωτομάρτυρος.

Καὶ τοῦ ἁγίου καὶ μακαρίου πατρὸς ἡμῶν Μάρκου[617] τοῦ ἀποστόλου καὶ εὐαγγελιστοῦ.

---

[597] Ὁ Ἱερεὺς λέγει om. MS. Par., MS. Kac., White.
[598] Μ]νήσθητι ˜White.
[599] [ἡ]μῶν White.‖ ἡμῶν om. Thess.
[600] [ἐν αὐ]τῇ White.‖ αυτης MS. Kac.
[601] κόσ[μῳ] White.
[602] ῥύσαι MS. Par.
[603] ἀλλοτρί[ων] White.
[604] Κύριε ἐλέησον om. White.
[605] Ὁ Ἱερεὺς λέγει om. MS. Par., MS. Kac., White.
[606] καὶ White.
[607] ἡ[μῶ]ν MS. Par.
[608] π[ρων ἡ]μῶν [ὀρ]θοδόξων ἐπ[ισκό]πων White.
[609] τῶ[ν ἀ]π᾽ [αἰῶνός] σοι εὐαρεστησάντων White.
[610] πατραρχῶ[ν, ἀπο]στόλων White.
[611] κηρ[ύκων] White.
[612] παντ[ὸς] White.
[613] Ἐκφωνήσει om. MS. Kac., White., Thess.
[614] δεσποίνας White.
[615] καὶ om. Thess.‖ κ[ε] White.
[616] In the Thess. there is a hymn added here.
[617] [Μάρκου] MS. Kac.

The Liturgy of Saint Gregory the Theologian

110 Καὶ τοῦ ἐν ἁγίοις πατρὸς[618] θεολόγου Γρηγορίου.[619]

Καὶ ὧν, ἐν τῇ σήμερον ἡμέρᾳ[620] τὴν ὑπόμνησιν ποιούμεθα[621] καὶ παντὸς χοροῦ τῶν

ἁγίων σου, Ὧν ταῖς εὐχαῖς καὶ πρεσβείαις[622] καὶ ἡμᾶς ἐλέησον καὶ σῶσον διὰ τὸ ὄνομά σου τὸ ἅγιον τὸ ἐπικληθὲν ἐφ' ἡμᾶς.

Ὁ Διάκονος λέγει[623] τὰ Δίπτυχα.[624]

115 Ὁ Ἱερεὺς λέγει ἐν ἑαυτῷ.[625]

Μνήσθητι[626] Κύριε τῶν προκεκοιμημένων ἐν τῇ ὀρθοδόξῳ[627] πίστει πατέρων ἡμῶν καὶ ἀδελφῶν, καὶ ἀνάπαυσον τὰς ψυχὰς αὐτῶν μετὰ ὁσίων, μετὰ δικαίων. Ἔκθρεψον[628] σύναψον εἰς τόπον χλόης, ἐπὶ ὕδατος ἀναπαύσεως ἐν παραδείσῳ τρυφῆς. Καὶ μετὰ τούτων[629] ὧν,[630] εἴπομεν τὰ ὀνόματα αὐτῶν.[631] Τότε μνημονεύει ζώντων καὶ νεκρῶν, καὶ

120 μετὰ δίπτυχα, ὁ Ἱερεὺς λέγει.[632] Μνήσθητι Κύριε ὧν, ἐμνήσθημεν, καὶ ὧν οὐκ ἐμνήσθημεν πιστῶν καὶ ὀρθοδόξων, μεθ' ὧν καὶ ἡμῖν σὺν αὐτοῖς, ὡς ἀγαθὸς καὶ φιλάνθρωπος Θεός.

Ὁ Λαὸς λέγει· Ἄνες ἄφες συγχώρησον.

8. The Closing Benediction

Ὁ Ἱερεὺς λέγει·[633] Σὺ γὰρ εἶ ὁ Θεὸς ἡμῶν ἐλεήμων. Ὁ μὴ βουλόμενος τὸν θάνατον τοῦ ἁμαρτωλοῦ ὡς τοῦ ἐπιστρέψαι καὶ ζῆν[634] αὐτόν.[635] Ὁ Θεὸς ἐπίσκεψον[636] ἡμᾶς ἐν τῷ σωτηρίῳ σου· ποίησον μεθ' ἡμῶν κατὰ τὴν ἐπιείκειάν σου, ὁ ποιῶν

---

[618] θεολόγου add. White.
[619] πατρὸς ἡμῶν Thess.
[620] [ἡμέρ]ᾳ White.
[621] ποιού[μεθ]α White.
[622] πρ[ε]σβιες MS. Kac.
[623] λέγει om. Thess.
[624] White notes that the rubric is effaced by the damp, but that it must be heavily abbreviated.
[625] Ὁ Ἱερεὺς λέγει ἐν ἑαυτῷ om. MS. Kac.; λέγει ἐν ἑαυτῷ om. Thess.
[626] Μ]νήσθητι White
[627] ὀρθοδόξῃ White.
[628] Ἔκθρεψον om. White.
[629] μετὰ τούτων om. White.
[630] σὺν ὧν White.
[631] αὐτῶν om. White.
[632] Τότε μνημονεύει ζώντων καὶ νεκρῶν, καὶ μετὰ δίπτυχα, ὁ Ἱερεὺς λέγει om. Thess.
[633] Ὁ Ἱερεὺς λέγει om. MS. Par., MS. Kac.
[634] τὸ Thess.; ζῆν Thess.

5   ὑπὲρ ἐκ περισσοῦ⁶³⁷ ὧν, αἰτούμεθα, ἢ νοοῦμεν.⁶³⁸ Ἵνα σου καὶ ἐν τούτῳ, καθὼς καὶ
ἐν παντὶ, δοξασθῇ⁶³⁹ καὶ ὑψωθῇ, καὶ ὑμνηθῇ, καὶ εὐλογηθῇ, καὶ ἁγιάσθῃ,⁶⁴⁰ τὸ πανάγιον καὶ ἔντιμον καὶ εὐλογημένον σου⁶⁴¹ ὄνομα ἅμα τῷ ἀχράντῳ σου Πατρὶ καὶ ἁγίῳ⁶⁴² Πνεύματι.

Part III: Post-Anaphora Prayers

Ὁ Λαὸς λέγει· Ὡς ἦν,⁶⁴³ καὶ ἔστι, καὶ ἔσται.
Ὁ Διάκονος λέγει· Κατέλθετε οἱ διάκονοι.⁶⁴⁴
Ὁ Ἱερεὺς λέγει· Εἰρήνη πᾶσιν.⁶⁴⁵
Ὁ Λαὸς λέγει· Καὶ τῷ πνεύματί σου.⁶⁴⁶

1. Προοίμιον τῆς κλάσεως⁶⁴⁷

Ἰησοῦ Χριστέ⁶⁴⁸ τὸ σωτήριον ὄνομα, ὁ τὰ θεῖα καὶ ἄχραντα καὶ ἐπουράνια ταῦτα μυστήρια διατυπώσας.⁶⁴⁹ Ὁ τοὺς μὲν ἱερεῖς ἐν τάξει ὑπηρετῶν στήσας, διὰ δὲ τῆς ἀοράτου σου δυνάμεως αὐτὰ μεταστοιχειώσας.⁶⁵⁰ Ὁ τοῖς καθαροῖς τῇ καρδίᾳ
5   ἐπιφαινόμενος καὶ τοῖς γνησίως⁶⁵¹ προσιοῦσι διὰ σεαυτοῦ παρέχοντος.⁶⁵²
Ὁ τότε εὐλογήσας, καὶ νῦν εὐλόγησον. Ἀμήν.⁶⁵³
Ὁ τότε ἁγιάσας, καὶ νῦν ἁγίασον. Ἀμήν.⁶⁵⁴

---

⁶³⁵ Cf. the Prophecy of Ezekiel 33:11.
⁶³⁶ επιστρεψον MS. Kac.‖ ἐπιστρέψαι Thess.‖ ἐπίσ[τρε]ψον MS. Par.
⁶³⁷ ὑπερεκπερισσοῦ Thess.
⁶³⁸ Cf. St. Paul's Epistle to the Ephesians 3:20.
⁶³⁹ δοξασθῇ MS. Par.
⁶⁴⁰ ἁγιασθῇ MS. Par.‖ αγια[σθη] MS. Kac.
⁶⁴¹ σου add. Ren/Migne.
⁶⁴² ἁγ[ίῳ] MS. Par.
⁶⁴³ ὅ[ς...] ἦν MS. Par.
⁶⁴⁴ Ὁ Διάκονος λέγει. Κατέλθετε οἱ διάκονοι. om. MS. Kac.
⁶⁴⁵ Ὁ Ἱερεὺς λέγει. Εἰρήνη πᾶσιν om. MS. Kac.
⁶⁴⁶ Ὁ Λαὸς λέγει. Καὶ τῷ πνεύματί σου om. MS. Kac.
⁶⁴⁷ Before the opening of the Προοίμιον τῆς κλάσεως is an almost illegible rubric in the MS. Kac. Although quite difficult to read, it does not seem to be a Greek word.
⁶⁴⁸ ὁ Ἱερεὺς λέγει. Ἰησοῦ Χριστέ Ren/Migne.
⁶⁴⁹ διατυπῶσας MS. Par.
⁶⁵⁰ μεταστοιλειώσας MS. Par.
⁶⁵¹ γνη[σ]ί[ως] MS. Par.
⁶⁵² παρέχων Thess.
⁶⁵³ Ἀμήν om. MS. Kac. Ren/Migne., Thess.

The Liturgy of Saint Gregory the Theologian

    Ὁ τότε κλάσας, καὶ νῦν διάθρεψον. Ἀμήν.[655]

    Ὁ τότε διαδοὺς τοῖς ἑαυτοῦ μαθηταῖς[656] καὶ ἀποστόλοις, καὶ νῦν Δέσποτα, διαδὸς ἡμῖν,

10   καὶ παντὶ τῷ λαῷ σου φιλάνθρωπε, παντοκράτωρ Κύριε ὁ Θεὸς ἡμῶν.

    Ὁ Διάκονος λέγει· Προσεύξασθε.[657]
    Ὁ Λαὸς λέγει· Κύριε ἐλέησον.[658]
    Ὁ Ἱερεὺς ἔγει· Εἰρήνη πᾶσιν.[659]

15   Ὁ Λαὸς λέγει· Καὶ τῷ πνεύμτί σου.[660]

2. Εὐχὴ τῆς κλάσεως.[661]

    Ὁ ὢν, ὁ ἦν, ὁ ἐλθών, καὶ πάλιν ἐρχόμενος, ὁ ἐν δεξιᾷ[662] τοῦ Πατρὸς καθήμενος· ὁ ἄρτος ὁ καταβὰς ἐκ τοῦ οὐρανοῦ, καὶ ζωὴν διδοὺς τῷ κόσμῳ·[663] ὁ μέγας ἀρχιερεὺς ὁ ἀρχηγός τῆς σωτηρίας ἡμῶν· τὸ[664] φῶς ἀληθινὸν, τὸ πρὸ πάντων αἰώνων. Ὃς ὢν

5   ἀπαύγασμα τῆς δόξης, καὶ χαρακτὴρ τῆς ὑποστάσεως αὐτοῦ τοῦ ἰδίου σου Πατρός.[665] Ὁ εὐδοκήσας καὶ καταξιώσας[666] κατελθεῖν ἐκ τῶν ὑψωμάτων τοῦ οὐρανοῦ, ἐκ κόλπων τοῦ ἀπροσίτου φωτὸς καὶ ἀληθινοῦ καὶ ἀοράτου[667] μόνου Πατρός. Σαρκωθεὶς δὲ ἐκ Πνεύματος Ἁγίου[668] καὶ ἐκ τῆς πανενδόξου ἀχράντου ἁγίας δεσποίνης ἡμῶν[669] Θεοτόκου καὶ ἀειπαρθένου Μαρίας, καὶ τελέως[670] ἐνανθρωπήσας· καὶ κατὰ[671] μετάστασιν, τὴν

10   ἀνθρωπότητα ἀναλλοιώσας, ἑνώσας ἑαυτῷ[672] καθ' ὑπόστασιν, ἀφράστως

---

[654] Ἀμὴν om. MS. Kac. Ren/Migne., Thess.
[655] Ἀμὴν om. MS. Kac. Ren/Migne., Thess.
[656] μαθήταις MS. Par.
[657] om. MS. Kac.
[658] om. MS. Kac.
[659] om. MS. Kac.
[660] om. MS. Kac.
[661] Before the opening of the Εὐχὴ τῆς κλάσεως is an almost illegible rubric in the MS. Kac. Although quite difficult to read, it does not seem to be a Greek word. MS. Kac. and Thess. do not include sections 2 and 3.
[662] δεξιᾷ MS. Par.
[663] Cf. the Gospel of John 6:51.
[664] . ὁ MS. Par.
[665] Cf. the Epistle of St. Paul to the Hebrews 1:3.
[666] καταξιώσας MS. Par.
[667] ἀ[ορά]του MS. Par.
[668] [ἁγ]ίου MS. Par. 11.
[669] ὑμῶν Ren/Migne.
[670] τελείως MS. Par.
[671] οὐκατὰ MS. Par.
[672] ἑαυτοῦ MS. Par.

καὶ ἀπερινοήτως, ἀτρέπτως δὲ καὶ ἀσυγχύτως, ψυχὴν ἔχουσαν λογικήν τε καὶ νοεράν. Οὕτως

προῆλθες ἐξ αὐτῆς θεανθρωπωθεὶς ὁμοούσιος τῷ[673] Πατρὶ κατὰ τὴν θεότητα, καὶ ὁμοούσιος ἡμῖν κατὰ τὴν ἀνθρωπότητα. Οὐ δύο πρόσωπα οὖν, οὐδὲ δύο μορφὰς ἤγουν, οὐδὲ ἐν δυσὶ φύσεσι γνωριζώμενος,[674] ἀλλ' εἷς Θεός, εἷς Κύριος, μία οὐσία μία
15 βασιλεία[675] μία δεσπότεια[676] μία ἐνέργεια μία ὑπόστασις μία θέλησις μία φύσις τοῦ Θεοῦ Λόγου σεσαρκωμένη καὶ προσκυνουμένη. Σταυρωθεὶς δὲ ἐπὶ[677] Ποντίου Πιλάτου καὶ ὁμολογήσας τὴν καλὴν ὁμολογίαν· παθὼν καὶ ταφεὶς καὶ ἀναστὰς τῇ τρίτῃ ἡμέρᾳ, καὶ ἀνελθὼν εἰς οὐρανοὺς καὶ καθίσας ἐν δεξιᾷ[678] τῆς μεγαλωσύνης τοῦ Πατρός, πατήσας τὸν θάνατον, καὶ τὸν ᾅδην σκυλεύσας, συντρίψας πύλας χαλκάς, καὶ μόχλους σιδηροὺς
20 υνεθλάσας,[679] καὶ τὸν αἰχμάλωτον Ἀδὰμ ἀνακαλεσάμενος ἐκ φθορᾶς, καὶ ἡμᾶς ἐλευθερώσας ἐκ τῆς τοῦ διαβόλου δουλείας.

Δι' ὃ δεόμεθα καὶ παρακαλοῦμέν σε φιλάνθρωπε ἀγαθὲ καταξίωσον ἡμᾶς ἐν καθαρᾷ καρδίᾳ τολμᾶν ἀφόβως, ἐπιβοᾶσθαι τὸν πάντων[680] δεσπότην ἐπουράνιον Θεὸν Πατέρα

ἅγιον καὶ λέγειν.

3. Εὐχὴ ἄλλη τῆς κλάσεως.

Σὺ γὰρ εἶ ὁ Λόγος τοῦ Πατρός, ὁ προαιώνιος Θεός, ὁ μέγας ἀρχιερεὺς ὁ ἐπὶ σωτηρίας τοῦ γένους τῶν ἀνθρώπων, σαρκωθεὶς καὶ ἐνανθρωπήσας, καὶ προσκαλεσάμενος
ἑαυτῷ ἐκ πάντων τῶν ἐθνῶν, γένος ἐκλεκτὸν[681] βασίλειον[682] ἱεράτευμα, ἔθνος ἅγιον, λαὸν
5 εἰς περιποίησιν. Δι' ὃ δεόμεθα καὶ παρακαλοῦμέν σε, φιλάνθρωπε ἀγαθὲ Κύριε, μὴ εἰς ἔλεγχον καὶ ὄνειδος, μὴ εἰς κρίμα, μηδὲ εἰς κατάκριμα τῶν ἡμετέρων

---

[673] τῷ om. Ren/Migne.
[674] γνωριζόμενος MS. Par.
[675] βασιλεία MS. Par.
[676] δεσποτεία MS. Par.
[677] ὑπὸ Ren/Migne.
[678] τῇ δεξιᾷ Ren/Migne.
[679] Cf. Psalm 107.
[680] πάν[τ]ων MS. Par.
[681] Cf. 1 Peter 2:9.
[682] βασιλεῖον MS. Par.

ἁμαρτιῶν, γενηθήτω ἡ θυσία αὐτή·[683] ὑπὲρ γὰρ τῶν ἀσθενειῶν ἡμῶν προσηνέγχαμεν·[684] ἀλλ' ὥσπερ τὰ πανάγιά σου τίμια Δῶρα ταῦτα· πάσης ἁγιωσύνης ἐμπλῆσαι κατηξίωσας, διὰ τῆς ἐπιφοιτήσεως τοῦ παναγίου σου Πνεύματος ἐπ' αὐτῶν. Οὕτως καὶ ἡμῶν τῶν ἁμαρτωλῶν δούλων σου, ἁγιάσαι
10 καταξίωσον τὰς ψυχάς, τὰ σώματα, τὰ πνεύματα, τὰς συνειδήσεις. Ὅπως πεφωτισμένη ψυχῇ, ἀνεπαισχύντῳ[685] προσώπῳ, καρδίᾳ καθαρᾷ, συνειδήσει ἀνυποκρίτῳ, ἡγιασμένοις[686] χείλεσιν, ἀγάπῃ τελείᾳ, ἐλπίδι ἀσφαλεῖ, τολμῶμεν μετὰ παρρησίας,[687] ἄνευ φόβου, λέγειν τὴν ἁγίαν προσευχήν, ἣν μετέδωκας τοῖς ἰδίοις τοῖς ἁγίοις σου[688] μαθηταῖς[689] καὶ ἱεροῖς σου[690] ἀποστόλοις, ὅταν προσεύχησθε,[691] οὕτως προσεύχεσθε ὑμεῖς. Πάτερ ἡμῶν, ὁ ἐν τοῖς
15 οὐρανοῖς.[692]

Ὁ Λαὸς λέγει· Ἁγιασθήτω τὸ ὄνομά σου.[693]

4. Εὐχὴ ἄλλη τῆς κλάσεως.

Εὐλογητὸς εἶ Χριστὲ ὁ Θεός ὁ Παντοκράτωρ ὁ λυτρωτὴς τῆς ἑαυτοῦ ἐκκλησίας· ὦ[694] Λόγε ὃν προνοοῦσιν αὐτόν, καὶ ἄνθρωπε ὃν προθεωροῦσιν αὐτόν. Ὁ διὰ τῆς ἀκαταλήπτου αὐτοῦ σαρκώσεως, ἑτοίμασας[695] ἡμῖν ἄρτον ἐπουράνιον, τοῦτο τὸ
5 σῶμά σου, ὃν ἔθου ἐμμυστήριον[696] καὶ πανάγιον ἐν τοῖς ἅπασιν. Ἐκέρασας ἡμῖν ποτήριον, ἐξ ἀμπέλου ἀληθείας, ἐκ θείας καὶ ἀχράντου σου πλευρᾶς. Ὁ καὶ μετὰ δεδωκέναι[697] τὸ πνεῦμα ἐκχέων ἐξ αὐτῆς αἷμα καὶ ὕδωρ, οἷς, ἁγιασμὸς τῷ κόσμῳ παντί. Κτῆσαι ἡμᾶς ἀγαθὲ Κύριε τοὺς ἀναξίους δούλους σου· ποίησον ἡμᾶς λαὸν

---

[683] αὔτη MS. Par.
[684] προσηνέγκαμεν MS. Par.
[685] ἀν'επ'αι'σχύντο MS. Par.
[686] ἡγιασμένοις MS. Par.
[687] παρρησίας MS. Par.
[688] σου om. Ren/Migne.
[689] μαθήταις Ms. Par.
[690] σου om. Ren/Migne.
[691] προσεύχεσθε MS. Par.
[692] Cf. the Gospels of Matthew 5:9.|| ὁ ἐν τοῖς οὐρανοῖς om. Ren/Migne.
[693] τὸ ὄνομά σου om. Ren/Migne.
[694] ὦ Ren/Migne.
[695] ἑτοιμάσας MS. Par.
[696] ἐν μυστήριον Ren/Migne., Thess.
[697] μετὰ τὸ δεδωκέναι MS. Κας., Thess.

περιούσιον βασίλειον⁶⁹⁸ ἱεράτευμα, ἔθνος ἅγιον. Ἁγίασον καὶ ἡμᾶς ὁ Θεός, ὥσπερ ἡγίασας τὰ
10 προκείμενα καὶ ἅγια Δῶρα ταῦτα, καὶ ἐποίησας αὐτὰ ἀόρατα ἐκ τῶν ὁρατῶν μυστήρια ὧν προνοοῦσιν αὐτά σοι Κύριε ὁ Θεὸς ὁ σωτὴρ ἡμῶν Ἰησοῦς Χριστός. Σὺ οὖν Κύριε διὰ τῆς πολλῆς σου εὐσπλαγχνίας, κατηξίωσας ἡμᾶς διὰ τοῦ βαπτίσματος γένεσθαι⁶⁹⁹ εἰς υἱοὺς καὶ κληρονόμους. Ἐδίδαξας ἡμᾶς τὸν τύπον τῆς προσευχῆς ὅς ἐστιν ἐμμυστήριος, τοῦ προσεύχεσθαι ἐν αὐτῇ⁷⁰⁰ τὸν ἄχραντόν σου Πατέρα. Σὺ οὖν καὶ νῦν Δέσποτα Κύριε
15 καταξίωσον ἡμᾶς, ἐν ἡγιασμένῃ⁷⁰¹ συνειδήσει, καὶ λογισμῷ ἀγαθῷ ὃν πρέπει τ...καὶ ἐν ...θε... πόθῳ,⁷⁰² καὶ παρρησίᾳ⁷⁰³ ἀγαθῇ τολμᾶν ἐπικαλεῖσθαι τὸν ἐν τοῖς οὐρανοῖς⁷⁰⁴ ἅγιον Θεὸν Πατέρα σου καὶ λέγειν.
Ὁ Λαὸς λέγει· Τὸ⁷⁰⁵ Πάτερ ἡμῶν.⁷⁰⁶
Καὶ μετὰ τὸ Πάτερ ἡμῶν.⁷⁰⁷

5. The Prayer following the Lord's Prayer

Ὁ Ἱερεὺς λέγει·⁷⁰⁸ Ναὶ Κύριε Κύριε ὁ δεδωκὼς ἡμῖν τὴν⁷⁰⁹ ἐξουσίαν τοῦ πατεῖν ἐπάνω ὄφεων καὶ σκορπιῶν, καὶ ἐπὶ πᾶσαν τὴν δύναμιν τοῦ ἐχθροῦ,⁷¹⁰ σύντριψον καὶ καθυπόταξον τὰς κεφαλὰς τῶν ἐχθρῶν ἡμῶν ὑπὸ τοὺς πόδας ἐν τάχει. Καὶ πᾶσαν τὴν
5 κακότεχνον αὐτῶν ἐπίνοιαν τὴν καθ' ἡμῶν διασκέδασον.
Ὅτι σὺ εἶ βασιλεὺς ἡμετέρων πάντων Χριστὲ ὁ Θεός⁷¹¹· καὶ σοὶ τὴν δόξαν καὶ τὴν εὐχαριστείαν, καὶ τὴν προσκύνησιν ἀναπέμπομεν, καθ' ἑκάστην⁷¹² ἡμέραν, σὺν τῷ ἀνάρχῳ σου Πατρί, καὶ τῷ ἁγίῳ Πνεύματι, νῦν.

---

⁶⁹⁸ [περιο]ύσιον βασι[λεῖ]ον MS. Par.
⁶⁹⁹ γενέσθαι MS. Par.
⁷⁰⁰ αὐτῆς MS. Kac.
⁷⁰¹ ἡγιασμένη MS. Par.
⁷⁰² τοῖς υἱοῖς, καὶ ἐν θεικῷ πόθῳ Ren/Migne.|| τελείοις καὶ ἐν θερμῷ πόθῳ Thess.
⁷⁰³ παρρησία MS. Par.
⁷⁰⁴ Thess. breaks off the prayer here and continues with the Lord's Prayer here.
⁷⁰⁵ τὸ om. Ren/Migne.
⁷⁰⁶ καὶ λέγειν Πάτερ ἡμῶν ὁ ἐν τοῖς οὐρανοῖς MS. Kac.
⁷⁰⁷ . Καὶ μετὰ τὸ Πάτερ ἡμῶν. om. MS. Kac.
⁷⁰⁸ Ὁ Ἱερεὺς λέγει om. MS. Kac., Ren/Migne.
⁷⁰⁹ τὴν om. Ren/Migne., Thess.
⁷¹⁰ Cf. the Gospel of Luke 10:19.
⁷¹¹ ὅτι σὺ εἶ Βασιλεὺς καὶ Σωτὴρ πάντων, Χριστὲ ὁ Θεὸς Thess.
⁷¹² ἑ[κάσ]την MS. Par.

The Liturgy of Saint Gregory the Theologian

6. Εὐχὴ τῆς κεφαλοκλισίας.[713]

   Ὁ Διάκονος λέγει· Τὰς κεφαλὰς[714] ὑμῶν.[715]

   Ὁ κλίνας οὐρανοὺς καὶ κατελθὼν[716] ἐπὶ τῆς γῆς, εἰς σωτηρίαν τοῦ γένους τῶν ἀνθρώπων. Ὁ τῆς σῆς χάριτος πᾶσαν ἐξαπλώσας τὴν εὐθηνίαν. Ὁ ποιῶν πάντα ὑπὲρ ἐκ
5 περισσοῦ,[717] ὧν, αἰτούμεθα ἢ νοοῦμεν. Φιλάνθρωπε ἀγαθέ, ἔκτεινόν σου τὴν χεῖρα[718] τὴν ἀόρατον[719] τὴν εὐλογημένην τὴν μεστὴν ἐλέους καὶ οἰκτιρμῶν. Καὶ εὐλογῶν εὐλόγησον τοὺς δούλους σου, καὶ καθάρισον αὐτοὺς ἀπὸ παντὸς μολυσμοῦ σαρκὸς καὶ πνεύματος. Καὶ ποίησον ἡμᾶς μετόχους καὶ συσσώμους γενέσθαι τῇ σῇ χάριτι. Ὅπως ἐν ἁγιότητι καὶ δικαιοσύνῃ σοὶ τὴν ἱκεσίαν προσάγοντες.[720]

10 *Καὶ σοὶ πρέπει πᾶσα δόξα, μεγαλοσύνη[721], κράτος τε καὶ ἐξουσία[722], ἅμα τῷ ἀχράντῳ*
   σου Πατρί, καὶ τῷ ἁγίῳ Πνεύματι, νῦν, καὶ.[723]

7. Εὐχὴ ἄλλη ὁμοίως.[724]

   Πρόσχες,[725] Κύριε Ἰησοῦ Χριστὲ ὁ Θεὸς ἡμῶν, ἐξ ἁγίου κατοικητηρίου σου,[726] καὶ ἀπὸ θρόνου δόξης[727] τῆς βασιλείας σου, καὶ ἐλθὲ εἰς τὸ ἁγιάσαι ἡμᾶς τοὺς ἐπικλίναντάς[728] σοι. Ὁ ἄνω τῷ Πατρὶ συγκαθήμενος, καὶ ὧδε ἡμῖν ἀοράτως[729] συνών. Καὶ καταξίωσον
5 τῇ κραταιᾷ σου χειρὶ μεταδοῦναι ἡμῖν τοῦ ἀχράντου σώματός σου, καὶ τοῦ τιμίου αἵματος,[730] καὶ δι' ἡμῶν[731] παντὶ τῷ λαῷ.

   Σὺ γὰρ, εἶ ὁ κλῶν, καὶ κλώμενος, καὶ ἄκλαστος· καὶ σοὶ τὴν δόξαν ἀναπέμομεν, σὺν τῷ σῷ[732] Πατρί, καὶ τῷ ἁγίῳ Πνεύματι, νῦν, καὶ.[733]

---

[713] Tit. Ὁ Ἱερεὺς ἀναγιγνώσκει τὴν Εὐχὴν τῆς Κεφαλοκλισίας Thess.
[714] [Τὰς κεφαλὰς] MS. Kac.
[715] ὑμῶν om. MS. Kac.|| Ὁ Διάκονος: Τὰς κεφαλὰς ἡμῶν τῷ Κυρίῳ κλίνωμεν Thess.
[716] καταβὰς Thess.
[717] ὑπερεκπερισσοῦ Thess.
[718] τὴν χεῖρα σου Thess.
[719] ὁρατὸν Thess.
[720] προσάγοντες ἀξίως μετάσχωμεν τῶν προκειμένων ἡμῖν ἀγαθῶν τοῦ ἀχράντου σώματός σου καὶ τιμίου αἵματός σου Thess.
[721] Καὶ Σὺ γὰρ προσκυνητὸς καὶ δεδοξασμένος ὑπάρχεις Thess.
[722] καὶ om. Ren/Migne.
[723] Ὁ Ἱερεύς: Πρόσχες Thess
[724] The rubrics of the MS- Kac. state that the following prayers are replaced with prayers from the Anaphora of St. Basil. The Anaphora of St. Gregory continues with the Σῶμα ἅγιον καὶ αἷμα τίμιον.
[725] μεγαλωσύνη MS. Par.
[726] τοῦ κατοικητηρίου σου Ren/Migne.
[727] δόξης om. Ren/Mign.
[728] ἐπικλινοντάς Thess.
[729] ἀόρατος MS. Par.
[730] καὶ τοῦ τιμίου αἵματος om. Ren/Migne.
[731] ὧν MS. Par.
[732] σῷ om. Ren/Migne.|| om. Thess.

Critical Text and Translation

Ὁ Διάκονος λέγει· Προσχῶμεν θεῷ μετὰ φόβου.[734]

8. Εὐχὴ τῆς ἐλευθερίας

    Εἰρήνη πᾶσιν.[735]

    Ὁ ἀμνὸς τοῦ Θεοῦ, ὁ αἴρων τὴν ἁμαρτίαν τοῦ κόσμου.[736] Ὁ τὸ πανάσπιλον αὐτοῦ αἷμα διαχύσας ἐπὶ τὴν τοῦ κόσμου ζωήν,[737] καὶ εἰς λύτρον καὶ ἀντάλλαγμα πάντων

5 ἑαυτὸν παρέδωκας, ἐκ θανάτου λυτρωσάμενος, ἐν ᾧ κατειχόμεθα· πεπραγμένοι ὑπὸ τὴν ἁμαρτίαν.[738] Ὁ τῶν φοβουμένων αὐτὸν ποιῶν τὸ θέλημα,[739] καὶ τῆς δεήσεως αὐτῶν εἰσακούσων,[740] καὶ σώζων αὐτούς· ὁ τοῦ δικαίου Ἰὼβ ἐπακούσας ἀνιστάμενος τὸ πρωῒ καὶ ὑπὲρ παιδίων φίλτρων θυσίας ποσαγαγὼν εἰπών.[741] Μήπως ἐνενόησαν υἱοί μου πονηρὰ ἐν τῇ καρδίᾳ αὐτῶν ἔναντι Θεοῦ.[742] Καὶ ἐμοῦ[743] τοῦ ἐλεεινοῦ καὶ ἁμαρτωλοῦ καὶ

10 χρείου σου δούλου ἱκετεύω[744] ὑπὲρ[745] τῶν σῶν οἰκετῶν, πατέρων μου καὶ ἀδελφῶν, καὶ ὑπὲρ τῆς ἐμῆς[746] ἀθλιότητος. Εὐμενεῖ προσώπῳ, καὶ γαληνῷ ὄμματι, ἔπιδε ἐφ' ἡμᾶς ἐν ταύτῃ τῇ ὥρᾳ. Καὶ πάρες οὖν ἡμῖν πᾶσαν ἀθετηρίαν, καὶ πᾶσαν παράβασιν, καὶ παρακοὴν νόμου, καὶ τῶν σῶν ἐντολῶν. Ἔτι δὲ καὶ πᾶσαν συνείδησιν, καὶ πᾶσαν ἐνθύμησιν, καὶ πάσαις πράξεσι, καὶ πάσαις κινήσεσι γεγονυίαις[747] ἐν ἑαυταῖς,[748]

15 ἡμερικῶς[749] τε καὶ νυκτερικῶς,[750] ἐπιδῆσαι καὶ κατακρατῆσαι κατὰ τῆς ψυχῆς. Καὶ ἀθώοσον[751] αὐτοὺς ἀπὸ πάσης συνειδήσεως πονηρῶν,[752] καὶ πάσης ἀκάρπου

---

[733] . καὶ om. Ren/Migne.´
[734] [Προσχῶμεν θεῷ μετὰ] MS. Par.
[735] Ὁ Λαός: Καί τῷ πνεύματί σου add. Thess.
[736] Cf. the Gospel of John 1:29.
[737] ζωὴν MS. Par.
[738] Cf. 1 Timothy 2:6.
[739] θ[έ]λημα MS. Par.
[740] εἰσακούσας Ren/Migne.
[741] προσαγαγὼν καὶ εἰπών Thess.
[742] Cf. Job 1:6.
[743] [ἐμοῦ] MS. Par.
[744] εἰκετεύω MS. Par.
[745] ἀχρείου σου δούλου, εἰσάκουσον, ἱκετεύοντος ὑπὲρ Thess.
[746] ἐμῆς om. MS. Par.
[747] γεγονυίαις MS. Par.15.
[748] αὐταῖς MS. Paris.|| ἑαυτοῖς Thess.
[749] ἡμερινῶς MS. Par.
[750] νυκτερινῶς MS. Par.|| νυχτερικῶς Thess.
[751] ἀθώωσον MS. Par., Thess.
[752] πονηρᾶς corr. MS. Par.

πράξεως, καὶ παντὸς λογισμοῦ πεπυρωμένου. Ἅτινα⁷⁵³ ἐστὶν βέβηλὰ⁷⁵⁴ παρὰ⁷⁵⁵ τὴν τῆς ψυχῆς καθαρότητα.⁷⁵⁶ Χάρισαι αὐτῶν τὴν τῶν ἁμαρτιῶν ἐπίγνωσιν, καὶ τελείως ἀπέχεσθαι ἀπ' αὐτῶν. Δώρησαι αὐτοῖς μετανοίας ἁγνότητος⁷⁵⁷ καὶ τὴν εἰς σε ἐπιστροφήν· σὺ γὰρ Δέσποτα

20 Κύριε ἐπτώχευσας ἑκουσίως ἐν τῷ σε σαρκωθῆναι διὰ τὴν τοῦ γένους ἡμῶν σωτηρίαν. Καὶ διέῤῥηξας⁷⁵⁸ τὸ καθ' ἡμῶν χειρόγραφον, διὰ τὴν ἐπὶ⁷⁵⁹ τοῦ σταυροῦ τῶν θείων σου παλάμων ἐφ' ἅπλωσιν.⁷⁶⁰ Φεῖσαι πάντων Δέσποτα φιλόψυχε, ὅτι τὰ σύμπαντα δοῦλα σά. Καὶ παρὰ σου ἡμέτερα ἀφετήρια, καὶ οὐδὲν τῶν ἐπιτηδευμάτων τῶν χειρῶν ἡμῶν. Δι' ὃ τὴν σὴν βασιλείαν δοξάζομεν καὶ ἀνυμνοῦμέν σε Χριστὲ ὁ Θεὸς ἡμῶν. Ἅτινα

25 ν....λου...ων....θόρων....Πάσαις⁷⁶¹ ἁμαρτίας⁷⁶² ἕως αἱρετικῶν καὶ ἐθνικῶν·⁷⁶³ ἔμπλησον ἡμᾶς τοῦ σοῦ φόβου, καὶ κατεύθυνον εἰς τὸ ἀγαθόν σου θέλημα.

Σὺ γὰρ, εἶ, ὁ θεὸς ἡμῶν, καὶ πρέπει σοι δόξα τιμὴ καὶ προσκύνησις.

9. Σῶμα καὶ αἷμα

Ὁ Διάκονος λέγει· Σῶμα καὶ αἷμα.⁷⁶⁴ Μετὰ φόβου θεοῦ πρόσχωμεν.⁷⁶⁵

Ὁ Ἱερεὺς ὑψοῖ τὸ σπουδικὸν⁷⁶⁶ καὶ ἐκφωνήσει. Τὰ ἅγια τοῖς ἁγίοις.

Ὁ Λαὸς λέγει· Κύριε ἐλέησον. Εἷς Πατὴρ ἅγιος, εἷς⁷⁶⁷ Υἱὸς ἅγιος, ἓν Πνεῦμα ἅγιον.⁷⁶⁸

5 Ἀμήν.

Ὁ Ἱερεὺς λέγει· Ὁ Κύριος μετὰ πάντων ὑμῶν.

Ὁ Λαὸς λέγει· Καὶ μετὰ τοῦ πνεύματός σου.

Ὁ Ἱερεὺς λέγει· Εὐλογητὸς Κύριος εἰς τοὺς αἰῶνας, Ἀμήν.

---

⁷⁵³ ἅτινα om. Ren/Migne.
⁷⁵⁴ ἅτινά [ἐσ]τιν βεβηλοῦ MS. Par.
⁷⁵⁵ παρὰ βεβηλὰ Ren/Migne.
⁷⁵⁶ [...]τα MS. Par.
⁷⁵⁷ ἁγνότητα Thess.
⁷⁵⁸ διέρρη[ξας] MS. Par.
⁷⁵⁹ διέρηξ[...]θ' ἡμῶν χειρό[...διὰ τὴν ἐπὶ MS. Par. The interpolated text is from the Renaudot edition.
⁷⁶⁰ ἐφάπλωσιν Ren/Migne., Thess.
⁷⁶¹ [πασῆς] MS. Par.
⁷⁶² ἡμέραις Ren/Migne.
⁷⁶³ [ἐ]θνικῶν MS. Par.

⁷⁶⁴ [Αἷμα] MS. Par.
⁷⁶⁵ Ὁ Ἱερεὺς λέγει. Σῶμα καὶ Αἷμα. Ὁ Δάκονος λέγει. Μετὰ φόβου Θεοῦ πρόσχωμεν Ren/Migne.
⁷⁶⁶ Δεσποτικὸν Ren/Migne.
⁷⁶⁷ [εἷς] MS. Par.
⁷⁶⁸ [ἅγ]ιον MS. Par.

Ὁ Λαὸς λέγει· Ἀμήν.
10   Ὁ Ἱερεὺς λέγει· Εἰρήνη πᾶσιν.
Ὁ Λαὸς λέγει· Καὶ τῷ πνεύματί σου.
Ὁ Ἱερεὺς λέγει· Σῶμα ἅγιον καὶ αἷμα τίμιον, ἀληθινὸν Ἰησοῦ Χριστοῦ υἱοῦ τοῦ Θεοῦ.[769]
Ἀμήν.
Ὁ Λαὸς λέγει· Ἀμήν.
15   Ὁ Ἱερεὺς λέγει·[770] Ἅγιον[771] τίμιον σῶμα καὶ αἷμα ἀληθινὸν Ἰησοῦ Χριστοῦ τοῦ Θεοῦ.
Ἀμήν.[772]
Ὁ Λαὸς λέγει· Ἀμήν.
Ὁ Ἱερεὺς λέγει·[773] Σῶμα καὶ αἷμα Ἐμμανουὴλ τοῦ Θεοῦ ἡμῶν, τοῦτό ἐστιν ἀληθῶς. Ἀμήν.
20   Ὁ Λαὸς λέγει· Ἀμήν.
Πιστεύω,[774] πιστεύω, πιστεύω, καὶ ὁμολογῶ ἕως ἐσχάτης ἀναπνοῆς. Ὅτι αὕτη[775] ἐστιν[776] ἡ σὰρξ ἡ ζωοποιὸς,[777] ἣν, ἔλαβες Χριστὲ ὁ Θεὸς ἡμῶν, ἐκ τῆς ἁγίας δεσποίνης ἡμῶν Θεοτόκου καὶ ἀειπαρθένου Μαρίας. Καὶ ἐποίησας αὐτὴν μίαν σὺν τῇ θεότητί σου, μὴ ἐν μίξει, μηδὲ ἐν φυρμῷ, μηδὲ ἐν ἀλλοιώσει. Καὶ ἐμαρτύρησας ἐπὶ Ποντίου Πιλάτου
25   τὴν καλὴν ὁμολογίαν, καὶ παρέδωκας[778] αὐτὴν ἡμῶν πάντων ἡμετέρων[779] ἐπὶ τοῦ ξύλου[780] τοῦ σταυροῦ τοῦ ἁγίου, ἐν τῷ θελήματί[781] σου. Ἀληθῶς πιστεύω, ὅτι θεότης σου, οὐδ' οὐ μηδέποτε χωρισθεῖσα ἐξ ἀνθρωπότητός σου, ἐν ἀτόμῳ, οὐδὲ ἐν ῥιπῇ ὀφθαλμοῦ.[782] Μετέδωκας αὐτὴν εἰς λύτρωσιν, καὶ εἰς ἄφεσιν ἁμαρτιῶν, καὶ εἰς ζωὴν τὴν αἰώνιον, τοῖς ἐξ αὐτῆς μεταλαμβάνουσι. Πιστεύω ὅτι αὕτη ἐστὶν ἀληθῶς, ἀμήν.
30   Ὁ Λαὸς λέγει· Ἀμήν.[783]

---

[769] [...]μα ἅγιο[ν καὶ] αἷ[...]τίμι[ον ... θι...] Ἰησοῦ Χριστοῦ ὑ[...]χθ[...]ἀμὴν MS. Par.
[770] Ὁ Ἱερεὺς λέγει om. MS. Par.
[771] [ἅγ]ιον MS. Par.
[772] Ren/Migne and Thess. edit this phrase to correspond to the first phrase.
[773] Ὁ Ἱερεὺς λέγει om. MS. Par.
[774] Ὁ Ἱερεὺς λέγει Ren/Migne.
[775] [ἀυτ]η MS. Par.
[776] ἐστι MS. Par.
[777] [ζω]οποιὸς MS. Par.
[778] [παράδωκας] MS. Κας.
[779] καὶ παρέδωκεν αὐτὴν ὑπὲρ ἡμῶν πάντων ...έρων Ren.; [καὶ παρέδωκας αὐ]τὴν [ἡ]μῶ[ν πά]ντων [ἡμε]τέρων MS. Par.
[780] καὶ παρέδωκας αὐτὴν ὑπὲρ ἡμῶν πάντων, αἴρων ἐπὶ τοῦ ζύλου MS. Κας.
[781] θελή[μα]τί MS. Par.
[782] ὀφ[θαλ]μοῦ MS. Par.
[783] Ὁ Λαὸς λέγει. Ἀμήν om. MS. Κας.

The Liturgy of Saint Gregory the Theologian

 Ὁ Διάκονος λέγει· Ἐν εἰρήνῃ καὶ ἀγάπῃ.[784]

 Ὁ Ἱερεὺς ἐκφωνήσει· Ἀκατάληπτε Θεέ Λόγε ἀχώρητε· ἀίδιε δέχου παρ' ἡμῶν τῶν ἁμαρτωλῶν ἐξ ἀναξίων χειλέων ὕμνον μετὰ τῶν ἄνω δυνάμεων.

 Σοὶ γὰρ πρέπει πᾶσα δόξα τιμὴ καὶ προσκύνησις, σὺν τῷ ἀνάρχῳ σου Πατρὶ,
35 *καὶ τῷ ζωοποιῷ σου Πνεύματι, εἰς πάντας τοὺς αἰῶνας τῶν αἰώνων. Ἀμήν.*[785]

 Ὁ Λαὸς λέγει ψαλμὸν ρ΄ν.[786]

 Ὁ Διάκονος λέγει· Συνάχθητε καὶ εἰσέλθετε οἱ διάκονοι μετ' εὐλαβείας.

10. Εὐχὴ εὐχαριστίας μετὰ τὴν μετάληψιν τῶν ἁγίων μυστηρίων.

 Ὁ Διάκονος λέγει· Ἐπὶ προσευχῆς στάθητε.

 Ὁ Ἱερεὺς λέγει· Εἰρήνη πᾶσιν.

 Ὁ Λαὸς λέγει· Καὶ τῷ πνεύματί σου.

5 Ὁ Διάκονος λέγει· Προσεύξασθε ὑπὲρ τῆς ἀξίας μεταλήψεως.

 Ὁ Λαὸς λέγει. Κύριε ἐλέησον.

 Ὁ Ἱερεὺς λέγει τὴν εὐχὴν ταύτην.[787]

 Εὐχαριστοῦμέν σοι Λόγε Θεοῦ ἀληθινέ, ὁ ἐκ τῆς οὐσίας τοῦ ἀνάρχου Πατρός. Ὅτι οὕτως ἠγάπησας ἡμᾶς καὶ ἔδωκας σεαυτὸν ὑπὲρ ἡμῶν ἐσφαγιάσθης.

10 Κεχάρισας[788] ἡμῖν διὰ τοῦ ἀχράντου σου σώματος, καὶ τοῦ τιμίου σου αἵματος, τὴν ἀπολύτρωσιν. Ὡς κατηξίωσας ἡμᾶς νῦν φιλάνθρωπε, ἵνα λάβωμεν ἐξ αὐτῶν εὐχαριστία.[789]

 Διὸ ἐξομολογοῦμέν σοι νῦν φιλάνθρωπε ἀγαθέ· καὶ σοὶ τὴν δόξαν καὶ τὴν τιμὴν καὶ τὴν προσκύνησιν διηνεκῶς ἀναπέμπομεν, σὺν τῷ ἀνάρχῳ σου Πατρὶ καὶ τῷ ἁγίῳ σου
15 *Πνεύματι, νῦν, καὶ.*[790]

11. Εὐχὴ τῆς κεφαλοκλισίας.[791]

 Ὁ Διάκονος λέγει· Τὰς κεφαλὰς ἡμῶν[792] τῷ Κυρίῳ κλίνατε.

---

[784] Ὁ Διάκονος λέγει. Ἐν εἰρήνῃ καὶ ἀγάπῃ om. MS. Kac.
[785] τῷ Πατρὶ καὶ τῷ ἁγίῳ Πνεύματι, ὁμοούσιε καὶ συναΐδιε White.|| This is the end of the Anaphora of St. Gregory in the MS. Kac.
[786] The Wadi n' Natrun fragments also prescribe Psalm ρλέ a hymn to the Trinity and an acrostic hymn to the Virgin Mary here.
[787] λέγει τὴν εὐχὴν ταύτην om. Thess.
[788] Κεχάρισαι MS. Par.|| Ἐχάρισας Thess.
[789] εὐχαριστίαν Thess.
[790] καὶ om. Ren/Migne.
[791] Tit. [τῆ]ς MS. Par. Tit. κεφαλοκλ[ισ]ίας MS. Par.|| Tit. Εὐχὴ τῆς κεφαλοκλισίας om. Thess.
[792] ὑμῶν MS. Par.

Ὁ ὤν, ὁ ἦν, ὁ ἐλθὼν εἰς τὸν κόσμον τοῦ φωτίσαι αὐτόν. Ὁ σαρκωθεὶς καὶ ἐνανθρωπήσας, καὶ σταυρωθεὶς δι' ἡμᾶς, καὶ παθὼν ἑκουσίως σαρκί, καὶ μείνας ἀπαθής, ὡς Θεός. Καὶ

5 ταφεὶς καὶ ἀναστὰς τῇ τρίτῃ ἡμέρᾳ καὶ ἀνελθὼν εἰς οὐρανούς, καὶ καθίσας ἐν δεξιᾷ[793] τῆς μεγαλωσύνης δόξης[794] τοῦ Πατρός· τό τε θεῖον καὶ ἅγιον καὶ ὁμοούσιον καὶ ὁμοδύναμον καὶ ὁμόδοξον καὶ συναΐδιον Πνεῦμα καταπέμψας ἐπὶ τοὺς ἁγίους σου μαθητάς καὶ ἀποστόλους, καὶ διὰ τούτου φωτίσας μὲν αὐτούς …τὴν ο..ουμ… Χριστέ, ὁ ἀληθινὸς θ…μ…[795] ….. καὶ Γαβριὴλ καὶ Ῥαφαήλ.[796]

10 Καὶ[797] τῶν[798] ἀγγέλων τετραμόρφων ζώων ἀσωμάτων· καὶ τῶν ἀγγέλων, καὶ τῶν εἰκοσιτεσσάρων πρεσβυτέρων. Τοῦ ἁγίου ἐνδόξου προφήτου προδρόμου βαπτιστοῦ καὶ μάρτυρος[799] Ἰωάννου. Τοῦ ἁγίου[800] Στεφάνου τοῦ πρωτοδιακόνου[801] καὶ πρωτομάρτυρος.[802] Τῶν θείων[803] ἱερῶν ἐνδόξων ἀποστόλων ἀθλοφόρων προφητῶν[804] καὶ καλλινίκων μαρτύρων. Καὶ τοῦ ἁγίου[805] καὶ μακαρίου πατρὸς ἡμῶν Μάρκου τοῦ ἀποστόλου καὶ

15 εὐαγγελιστοῦ.[806] Καὶ πάντων τῶν χόρων[807] τῶν ἁγίων[808] σου.

Καὶ σῶσον, καὶ ἐλέησον, καὶ εὐλόγησον, πάντα[809] χριστιανόν. Καὶ σοὶ τὴν δόξαν, καὶ τιμήν,[810] καὶ προσκύνησιν, σὺν τῷ ἀνάρχῳ σου Πατρί, καὶ τῷ ἁγίῳ Πνεύματι νῦν καὶ ἀεί, καὶ εἰς.[811]

Ἐν[812] εἰρήνῃ τοῦ Θεοῦ ἐτελειώθη ἡ θεία λειτουργία[813] ἡ ὡρισμένη τῷ ἐν ἁγίοις πατρὶ ἡμῶν θεολόγῳ Γρηγορίῳ.

---

[793] δεξιᾶ MS. Par.
[794] τῆς δόξης Ren/Migne., Thess.
[795] δι' αὐτῶν δὲ πᾶσαν τὴν οἰκουμένην Χριστέ, ὁ ἀληθινὸς θεὸς ἡμῶν Ren/Migne., Thess.|| The section dealing with the Holy Spirit as well as the illegible section is written in a smaller hand at the bottom of the page.
[796] [Ρα]φαήλ MS. Par.|| καὶ Γαβριὴλ καὶ Ῥαφαήλ om. Thess.
[797] [Κα]ὶ MS. Par.
[798] καὶ τῶν om. MS. Par. Ren/Migne., Thess.
[799] μαρτύρος MS. Par.
[800] ἅγιου MS. Par.
[801] πρoτοδιάκονου MS. Par.
[802] πρoτομαρτύρος MS. Par.
[803] θεῖων MS. Par.
[804] προφήτων MS. Par.
[805] ἅγιου MS. Par.
[806] εὐαγγελίστου MS. Par.
[807] τῶν χόρων om. Thess.
[808] ἅγιων MS. Par.
[809] πάντο MS. Par.
[810] τίμην MS. Par.
[811] νῦν καὶ ἀεί Ren/Migne.
[812] [Ἐν] MS. Par.
[813] λιτουργία MS. Par.

The Divine Liturgy of our Father among the Saints Gregory the Theologian

The Translation

Part I: Pre-anaphoral Prayers

1. The Prayer, which the Priest reads silently:
Master, Lord Jesus Christ, You who look upon us in mercy and compassion, who grant us, Your humble, sinful and unworthy servants the freedom to stand around Your Holy Altar, and to bring before You this fearful and bloodless sacrifice on behalf of our own sins and of the ignorances of Your people. For the remission and repose of our fathers and brothers, fallen asleep before us, and for the support of all Your people. Look upon me, Your useless servant, and wash away my errors by Your compassion. Purify my lips and my heart from

all defilement of flesh and spirit. Keep away from me every thought that is shameful and witless. Make me sufficient, by the power of Your Holy Spirit, for this Liturgy and accept me, through Your goodness, approaching Your Holy Altar. Be well pleased, Lord, that these gifts, about to be brought before You by our hands, become acceptable, coming down and helping my weaknesses. Do not cast me away from Your face, nor loathe me because of my unworthiness, but have mercy on me, O God, according to Your great mercy and, according to the depths of Your compassions, wash away my transgressions. So that I, coming into the presence of Your glory, may be deemed worthy of Your protection and the illumination of Your All Holy Spirit; and not become worthless, as a servant of sin, but, as Your servant, may I find grace and mercy and forgiveness of sins, in this present time and in the coming age. Yes Master, all-mighty, all-powerful Lord, hear my prayer.

For You are the One who accomplishes all things in all things; and we all seek aid and assistance from You in all things. For You are the lover of mankind, and You are praised, Jesus our God, with Your Father, who is without beginning, and Your Holy Spirit, now and ever.

2. The Prayer after the Preparation of the Holy Altar.
Master, Lord Jesus Christ our God, who, through Your saving presence and through the illumination of Your All Holy Spirit, deemed us, Your humble, sinful and unworthy servants, worthy to stand about Your Holy Altar, and to offer and perform the immaculate mysteries of Your New Covenant. Make Yourself, Life giver and giver of good things, a sign for good among us and deem us worthy, in pure understanding, to worship You all of the days of our life, and to offer unto You, in holiness, this Divine Liturgy, for the forgiveness of sins, and for the enjoyment of the coming blessedness.

Remember, Good One, Benefactor, King of the Ages and the Origin of all Creation, the ones offering and the ones on whose behalf they offered; and keep us uncondemned in the carrying out of Your Divine Mysteries.

For blessed and hallowed and glorified is Your all honorable and magnificent name, with the Father and the Holy Spirit, now, and.

3. The Prayer of the Holy Gospel
Peace be with all.
Master, Lord Jesus Christ our God, who said to Your holy Disciples and Apostles that many prophets and just men desired to see the things which you see, and did not, and to hear the things which you hear and did not; for your eyes are blessed because they see, and

The Liturgy of Saint Gregory the Theologian

your ears because they hear. May we now be made worthy of hearing and doing Your Holy Gospel through the prayers of Your priests. Therefore, Master, remember even now all of those who bade us, the unworthy, to remember them in our prayers and entreaties, which we send up to You, Lord, our God. Give rest to those fallen asleep before us; and grant good health to the sick.

> *For you are all of our life, salvation, hope, healing, and personal resurrection; and to You we send up glory, honor, and worship, together with Your all-powerful and all seeing begetter, and Your all-holy, life creating, and consubstantial Spirit, now and ever.*

4. The Prayer of the veil

None of those bound with the desires and pleasures of the flesh is worthy to approach and to come near or minister to You, King of Glory; for to serve You is great and fearful and unapproachable even to the Heavenly Powers themselves. Nevertheless, by Your ineffable and immeasurable love for mankind You became man immutably and unchangeably, You were called our high priest and, as Master of All, You gave to us the sacrifice of this Liturgy and of the bloodless sacrifice. For You alone are Master of all things in heaven and on the earth and below the earth, who sits upon the Cherubic throne, the Lord of the Seraphim and the King of Israel; who alone are Holy, and rests among the Holy. Therefore, I entreat You, the only good One, and the God who is willing to hear; look upon me, Your sinful and worthless servant, and make me sufficient, by the power of Your Holy Spirit, clothed in the grace of the priesthood, to stand around this, Your Holy Table, and to consecrate Your spotless Body and Your sacred Blood. For I come to You, bowing my neck; and I pray to You, do not turn Your face away from me; and do not reject me from among Your children; but make me, Your sinful and unworthy servant, worthy to bear to You these gifts.

> *For You are the one who makes holy and is made holy, who offers and the one who is being offered, accepts and is acceptable, the one who receives and is distributed; and to You we send up glory, with Your Father and the Holy Spirit, now and...*

5. Another prayer of the veil, according to the Egyptians.

Lord our God, the Pantokrator, who knows the secret hearts of men, who tests hearts and reins; who calls me, the unworthy one, towards this, Your Liturgy. Do not loathe me, nor turn Your face away from me, but wipe out all my transgressions and wash away the filth of my body and the blemish of my soul and hallow me completely. So that, while I beseech You to grant forgiveness of sins to others, I may not myself be rejected. Yes Lord, do not reject me, humbled and put to shame, but send down upon me the grace of Your Holy Spirit, and deem me worthy to stand at Your Holy Altar uncondemned, and to offer to You this rational and bloodless sacrifice, with a clean conscience, for the forgiveness of my sins and of my transgressions, and for the remission of the ingnorances of Your people, for the rest and respite for our fathers and brothers fallen asleep before us, and for the support of all Your people.

> *For Your glory, of the Father and the Son and the Holy Spirit, now and…*

6. The Prayer of the Greeting.
Peace be with all.
You who exist and preexist and remain unto the ages; who exist with, are consubstantial with, enthroned with and co-creator with the Father; who, through goodness alone, brought man from nothing into being, and set him in a garden of delight. Wishing to renew man, who fell away because of the deceit of the enemy and the disobedience of Your command, and to return him to his ancient honor; not an angel, nor an archangel, nor a patriarch, nor a prophet, but You Yourself brought our salvation to pass, having taken on flesh without hesitation and becoming man. In all things You became like us, except for sin alone. You became mediator between us and the Father, and You destroyed the middle wall of partition, and the long-lasting enmity. You joined the earthly with the heavenly, and You brought together the two into one and You filled the flesh with dispensation. And, being about to travel bodily into the heavens, filling all things full with divinity, You said to Your holy disciples and apostles: "Peace I send to you; My peace I give to you." Give us this peace even now, Master, and grant purification from all pollution, deceit, wickedness, villainy and death bringing malice, and deem us worthy to greet each other in a holy kiss, in order to partake uncondemned of Your immortal and heavenly gifts; by Your grace, through the goodwill of the Father and the action of the all-holy Spirit.

> *For You are the lord of the dance and the giver of all good things, and to You we send up the glory, the eternal doxology, with Your beginning less Father and with Your Holy Spirit, now and ever….*

7. An alternate prayer of the greeting.
Christ our God, the fearful and incomprehensible power of God the Father, who sits upon the fiery throne of the Cherubim, who is accompanied by the fiery powers, and are the consuming fire, beginning as God; and because of Your unutterable descent and love for man, do not burn up the wicked traitor by Your approach, but greeting him with a kiss of friendship, bring him to repentance and to the realization of his personal deeds. Deem us worthy,

Master, at this dreadful hour, in unity and without our entire soul split in two, and without a remnant of evil, to receive one another with a holy kiss. Do not condemn us completely, and as it pleases Your goodness, let us purify ourselves from every fruit of sin, of wickedness and of deadly malice. But, because of Your unutterable and ineffable compassion, our nature being visibly weak and heavily laden, wash away every stain of our transgressions, so that this divine mystery does not become a judgment or a condemnation for us.

For You are able to take away sin, and to pass over injustice and the lawless action of miserable man, and are the purification of the whole created world; and to You is due the doxology, honor and worship from all, with Your beginning less Father and Your life giving Spirit, now and...

Part II: The Anaphora

1. The Greeting takes place

The Deacon says: Let us stand well.
The People say: A mercy of peace; a sacrifice of praise.
The Priest says: The Love of God the Father, the grace of His only-begotten Son, our Lord and God and Savior Jesus Christ and the communion and the gift of the Holy Spirit, be with all of you.
The People say: And with your spirit.
The Priest says: Let us lift up (our) hearts.
The People say: We lift them up to the Lord.
The Priest says: Let us give thanks to the Lord.
The People say: It is worthy and proper, is worthy and proper, worthy and proper.

2. The Beginning of the Proskomide

Truly it is worthy and just to praise You, to hymn You, to worship You, to praise You, the one true God, the lover of mankind, the inexpressible, the invisible, the uncontainable, the beginning less, the eternal, the timeless, the immeasurable, the immovable, the unknowable; the Creator of all, the Redeemer of all, the One who has mercy on all our lawlessness, who heals all our ills, who ransoms our life from death; who crowns us in mercy and compassion. The angels praise You; the archangels worship You; the powers hymn You; the dominions lift up their voices to You; the principalities proclaim Your glory; the thrones send up songs of praise; a thousand thousands stand about You, and ten thousand ten thousands offer You the Liturgy. The invisible hymn You, the visible worship You, all things fulfill Your word, Master.

The Deacon says: Arise, you who are seated.

The Priest says: You who exist, Lord, true God from true God; who showed us the splendor of the Father; who granted us the true knowledge of the Holy Spirit; who revealed to us this great mystery of life; who fixed the chorus of the bodiless among men; who handed over the hymnody of the Seraphim to those upon the earth; accept our cry with that of the unseen. Join us to the heavenly powers, let us also speak together with them, setting aside every wicked and cunning thought, let us cry aloud just as they do, with never silent voices, let us hymn Your magnificence with mouths that will not cease.

3. The Pre-*Sanctus* and *Sanctus* Hymn

The Deacon says: Look unto the East.

The Priest says: For the Seraphim stand about You in a circle, one with six wings; and the other with six wings; and with two wings they hide their faces, and with two their feet; and with two they fly, and they cry each to the other:

He cries out

The victory hymn of our salvation, with a voice of glory, with a clear voice, hymning, calling out, glorifying, shouting and saying.

The Deacon says: Let us be attentive.

The People say: Holy, Holy, Holy, Lord of Sabaoth, the heavens are full … *and the rest.*

4. The *Post-Sanctus*

The Priest says: Holy, Holy are You, O Lord, and all-Holy. Exalted is the splendor of Your being; the power of Your wisdom is inexpressible. No word will measure out the ocean of Your love for man. You made me a man, as the lover of man. Though You Yourself were not in need of our servitude, but rather I in need of Your lordship, You created me from nothing, according to Your compassion; You set up the heavens for me as a roof; You planted the earth firmly for me, as a floor. For my sake You restrained the sea, for my sake You revealed the nature of living beings. You subjected all things underneath my feet, You omitted no part of Your love for man in me.

The People say: Lord, Have mercy.

The Priest says: You formed me and placed Your hand upon me. You marked upon me the image of Your authority. You placed within me the gift of speech. You opened Paradise for me as a delight. You gave me the teaching of Your knowledge. You showed me the tree of life and secretly showed me the wood (of the cross). You made known the sting of death. You forbade me the enjoyment of one plant: from this one alone You commanded me not to eat. I ate, through which I set aside the Law, knowingly I disregarded the command, I took up the sentence of death.

The Liturgy of Saint Gregory the Theologian

The People say: Lord, Have mercy.

The Priest says: You, O Master, changed the punishment for me, as Good Shepherd You ran after the wandering one, as true Father You shared my sorrow while I was suffering. You bound me up with all the medicines for life. You sent me prophets and, for my sake, the one who is sick, You set up the law as a help. You ministered to me, the disgracer of the law, those things that are for my health. You made the light rise up for those who wander. You, who are ever-present, lived among the ignorant. You came into the Virgin womb. You, the Uncontained One, although God, did not hold being equal with God something to be grasped, but emptied Yourself and, taking the form of a servant, blessed my nature in Yourself. You fulfilled the law on my behalf. You proclaimed my rising up after my fall. You granted release to those under the power of Hades. You drove away the curse of the law.

You abolished sin in the flesh. You made known to me the power of Your authority. You restored sight to the blind. You raised the dead from the graves. You set nature aright with a word. You made known to me the economy of Your compassion. You endured the violence of wicked men, You gave Your back to scourges, You submitted Your cheeks to blows; for my sake You did not turn Your face away from the shame of spittings.

The People say: Lord, Have mercy.

The Priest says: Like a sheep You went to the slaughter, You showed Your care for me, even to the cross. You put my sin to death in Your grave. You raised my sacrifice to heaven for me. You revealed to me the occasion of Your arrival, when You will come to judge the living and the dead and to render to each one according to his deeds.

The People say: According to Your mercy, O Lord.

5. The Consecration

The Priest says: I offer to You the symbols of my freedom, I inscribe the reality with Your words. You gave over to me this mystical Liturgy and the participation in Your Body through bread and wine.

The People say: We believe.

The Priest says: For, on the night on which You gave Yourself up, by Your own power.

The People say: We believe.

The Priest says: Taking bread in Your holy, undefiled and blameless hands, looking up toward Your own Father, our God, and the God of all; You gave thanks, blessed, hallowed, broke and gave a share of it to Your Holy disciples and apostles, saying:

"Take, eat; this is My Body, broken for you and for many, and distributed for the remission of sins. Do this in remembrance of me."

In the same way, after they had eaten, taking a cup and filling it with the fruit of the vine and with water, You gave thanks, blessed, hallowed, and gave a share of it to Your Holy disciples and apostles; saying:

"Drink of this all of you; this is my Blood of the new Covenant, poured out for you and for many for the remission of sins; do this in remembrance of me."

For whenever you eat this bread and drink this cup, you proclaim My death and confess My Ressurection and Ascension, until I come.

The People say: Amen, Amen, Amen. Your death.[814]

6. The Epiklesis

The Priest says: Therefore, Master, remembering Your descent upon the earth, Your life-giving death, Your three- day burial, Your Resurrection from the dead, Your ascent into the heavens, Your enthronement at the right hand of the Father and Your future second, awesome and glorious coming.

He cries out

Offering to You Your own gifts from Your own gifts, on behalf of all, and for all and in all.

The People say: We praise You, we bless You.

The Deacon says: Bow to God in awe.

The Priest says silently, bowing: Therefore, Master, transform the things lying before You with Your voice; complete this mystical Liturgy, being present here Yourself; preserve for us the memory of Your worship. Send down Your All-Holy Spirit, so that visiting, He may hallow and transform these precious and holy Gifts lying before You, by His holy, good and glorious presence, into the Body and Blood of our redemption.

The Deacon says: Let us be attentive.

The People say: Amen.

The Priest cries out: And He will make this bread to become Your Holy Body, of our Lord and God and Savior and King of all, Jesus Christ, for the remission of sins and for life eternal for those who partake of it.

The People say: Amen.

---

[814] This response usually continues: "Your death, Lord, we proclaim and we acknowledge Your Ressurection."

The Liturgy of Saint Gregory the Theologian

The Priest says: And this cup into the sacred Blood of the new Covenant, of our Lord and God and Savior and King of all, Jesus Christ, for remission of sins and life eternal for those who partake of it.
The People say: Amen.

7. The Intercessions
The Priest says the following and the People respond with: "Lord, Have Mercy"
We entreat You, Christ our God.
Lord, fix firmly the foundation of Your Church.
Root in us the unity of love.
Increase the truth of Faith.
Cut straight for us the path of Your piety.
Strengthen the shepherds.
Secure the flocks.
Grant good conduct to the clergy.
Grant temperance to the monastics.
Grant self-control to those in virginity.
Grant well-being to those in Holy Matrimony.
Grant mercy to those in repentance.
Grant kindness to the wealthy.
Grant aid to the poor.
Grant help to the beggars.
Gird round the old.
Moderate the young.
Turn around the unbelievers.
Cease the schisms of the Church.
Destroy the insolence of heresies.
Join all of us to the unity of Your piety.
The People say: Lord, Have Mercy.
The Priest says: Remember, Lord, the peace of Your One, Holy, Catholic and Apostolic Church, which is from one end of the inhabited earth to the other; and the Orthodox bishops in it, who teach the word of Truth.
He cries out
Especially for our most holy and blessed Father (name), Pope and Patriarch of the great city of Alexandria. For the current bishops, presbyters, deacons, subdeacons, readers,

chanters, exorcists, monks, ever-virgins, fasters, widows, orphans, the peoples, and for the entire fullness of the Holy Church of the faithful.

The People say: Lord, Have Mercy.

The Priest says: Remember, Lord, those ruling piously. Remember, Lord, our faithful and Orthodox brothers in the palace, and all those in the armed forces (lit: camps).

Remember, Lord, those offering these sacred gifts and on whose behalf and through whom they bring them, and grant all of them heavenly reward.

Remember also, Lord, those in the mountains, the caves and the holes of the earth; and our brothers in captivity, and grant them a peaceful return to their own homes.

The Deacon says: Pray on behalf of the captives.

The People say: Lord, Have Mercy. (Three times)

Then the Priest bows his head, saying to himself silently:

Remember also, Lord, my own wretched and miserable soul, my humble state, and forgive all my trespasses and wherever sin abounds, make Your grace abound there. Do not let Your people be in want of the grace of Your Holy Spirit because of my sin and the profanity of my heart.

He raises his head and cries out:

For Your people and Your church supplicate You, saying "Father" through You and with You.

The People say: Have mercy on us, O God, our Savior. (Three times)

The Priest says: Have mercy on us, O God, our Savior. (Three times)

The People say: Lord, Have Mercy (Three times)

The Priest says: Remember, Lord, the air and the fruits of the earth. Remember, Lord, the suitable ascent of the river water. Remember, Lord, the rains and the fields of the earth. Make glad again and renew the face of the earth.

Water its furrows, increase its bounty, furnish it for us for sowing and for harvesting, and now blessing them, bless us; administer our lives.

Bless the crown of the year of Your goodness for the poor among Your people, for the widow and the orphan, for the stranger and the sojourner and for all of us who hope in You, and call upon Your Holy Name. For the eyes of all look to You in hope, and You give them their food in due season. Do with us according to Your goodness, You who give food to all flesh. Fill our hearts with joy and gladness, so that in all things and at all times, having all things in sufficiency, we may abound in every good work, in order to do Your holy will.

The Liturgy of Saint Gregory the Theologian

The People say: Lord, Have Mercy.
The Priest says the following, and the People respond with "Lord, Have Mercy."
Grant unity to Your people.
Grant stability to the world.
Grand mildness to the air.
Grant salvation to the sick.
Grant relief to those in need.
Grant remission to those in exile.
Grant help to the orphan.
Grant aid to the widow.
Help those in distress to goodness.
Strengthen those standing.
Raise up those who have fallen.
Make safe those who have arisen.
Remember those who have fallen asleep.
Accept the prayers of those in faith.
Number the ones who have sinned and repented among Your faithful.
Number the faithful with Your Martyrs.
Establish those present in this place as imitators of the angels and receive us, though unworthy, called by Your grace into Your service.
The People say: Lord, Have Mercy.
The Priest says: Remember also, Lord, this our city, and those who dwell in it in the Orthodox faith; and every city and land with their entire order. Deliver us from famine and plague, earthquake and flood, fire and from captivity by barbarians and from foreign swords and from the uprisings of enemies and heretics.
The People say: Lord, Have Mercy.
The Priest says: Remember also, Lord, our Holy Fathers taken up before us, Orthodox bishops and all those pleasing to You through the ages: Holy Fathers, Patriarchs, Apostles, Prophets, Heralds, Evangelists, Martyrs, Confessors and every just spirit made perfect in the Faith of Christ.
He cries out:
Especially for our all-Holy, most glorious, pure, most blessed Lady, Theotokos and Ever Virgin Mary.
The Holy, glorious prophet, forerunner and Baptist John.
St. Stephen the protodeacon and protomartyr.
Our holy and blessed father Mark, apostle and evangelist.

Our father among the saints Gregory.

Those whose memory we celebrate on this day, and the whole choir of Your Saints, through whose prayers and intercessions, have mercy on us, and save us by Your Holy Name, which is invoked over us.

The Deacon recites the Diptychs
The Priest says silently:

Remember, Lord, our fathers and brothers fallen asleep before us in the Orthodox Faith, and give their souls rest with the blessed, with the just. Raise them up, join them and bring them together in Paradise, by the waters of rest, in a garden of delight, and with those whose names we will say.

Then he remembers the living and the dead, and after the Diptychs:
The Priest says: Remember, Lord, those who we remembered, as well as those we did not remember, faithful and Orthodox Christians, and with them remember also us, as a good and loving God.

The People say: Pardon, remit, forgive.

8. The Closing Benediction

The Priest says: For You are our merciful God, who does not wish the death of the sinner, but his repentance and life. O God, look upon us in Your deliverance; do with us according to Your leniency, who does exceedingly more than what we ask for, or can conceive of; so that, in this matter, just as in everything, Your all-Holy, precious and blessed name may be glorified, exalted, hymned, blessed and sanctified together with Your beginning less Father and Holy Spirit.

Part III: Post Anaphoral Prayers

The People say: As it was and is and will be.
The Deacon says: Deacons come forth.
The Priest says: Peace be with all.
The People say: And with your spirit.

1. Introduction to the Breaking

Jesus Christ, the saving name, who fashioned these divine, pure and heavenly mysteries; who established the priests among the ranks of Your servants; You transformed these

The Liturgy of Saint Gregory the Theologian

things by Your unseen power, who revealed them to the pure of heart and who hands himself over to those that approach lawfully.

You who blessed then, bless also now.

You who sanctified then, sanctify also now.

You who broke then, sustain also now.

You who gave it to Your disciples and apostles, give it also now to us, Master, and to all Your people, lover of man, all powerful Lord our God.

The Deacon says: Offer prayers.

The People say: Lord, Have Mercy.

The Priest says: Peace be with all.

The People say: And with your spirit.

2. The Prayer of the Breaking

You who are, and were, who came and is coming again; who is seated at the right hand of the Father; the bread who descended from heaven and gave life to the world; the great high priest, the beginning of our salvation; the true light who exists before the ages. Who is the effulgence of the glory, and the mark of the substance of Your personal Father. Who was well pleased and deemed it worthy to descend from the heights of heaven, from the bosom of the unapproachable light and of the one, true and invisible Father. You took flesh from the Holy Spirit, and from our all glorious, pure, holy Lady the Theotokos and Ever Virgin Mary and You became man perfectly. In this translation, You united humanity within Yourself, according to Your substance, immutably, inexpressibly, unknowably and unconfounded, having a rational and intelligent soul. You came out of this God-man union of one essence with the Father according to divinity and of one essence with us according to humanity.

You are not known in two faces, or rather not in two forms, nor in two natures; but one God, one Lord, one essence, one kingdom, one lordship, one energy, one nature, one will, one nature of God the Word, having taken on flesh and worshipped. You were crucified under Pontius Pilate, and You suffered the good confession; suffered and were buried and rose on the third day, and ascended into the heavens and were seated at the right hand of the magnificence of the Father. You trampled death underfoot and despoiled Hades; You crushed the gates of brass and broke the iron chains into pieces. You raised Adam out of perdition, who was held prisoner, and You freed us from servitude to the devil.

Critical Text and Translation

Therefore we pray to You and invoke You, good lover of man, deem us worthy, in purity of heart, to make bold to call the Lord of all, the heavenly God, Holy Father, and to say.

3. Another prayer of the breaking

You are the Word of the Father, the pre-eternal God, the great high-priest, who, for the salvation of the race of man, took flesh and became man, and called to himself from all peoples a chosen race, a royal priesthood, a holy nation, a people as a possesion. Therefore we pray to You and invoke You, Good One, lover of man, Lord: do not let this sacrifice become a shame or a reproach, nor a judgment or condemnation because of our sins. We sacrifice to You on behalf of our weaknesses, but, just as You deem it worthy to fill these, Your all-holy gifts with holiness, by the illumination of Your All-Holy Spirit upon it, so also deem it worthy to sanctify the souls, bodies, spirits and consciousnesses of Your sinful servants; so that, with illumined soul, shameless countenance, pure heart, a sincere conscience, hallowed lips, perfected love and secure faith, we may undertake, with licensce of speech, without fear, to say the holy prayer which You gave to Your own, Your holy disciples and Your divine apostles: "whenever you pray, to pray thus: Our Father, who art in heaven..."

The People say: Hallowed be thy name.

4. Another prayer of the breaking

Blessed are You, Christ God, the Pantokrator, redeemer of Your church; O Word, which they knew beforehand, O man, whom they saw beforehand. You, who, through Your incomprehensible flesh, prepares for us the heavenly bread, this, Your body, which You set up as the one (great) mystery and holy in all times. You mixed for us a cup from the vine of truth, from Your divine and immaculate side, from which You poured forth blood and water after You gave up Your spirit, through which the whole world is sanctified. Possess us, Good Lord, Your unworthy servants and make us a people set apart, a royal priesthood, a holy nation. Sanctify us also, O God, just as You sanctify these holy gifts laid out here, and as You made these mysteries for Yourself from tangible things, which they knew beforehand, Lord Jesus Christ, our God and Savior. Therefore, Lord, because of Your abundant mercy, You deemed us worthy to become sons and heirs through baptism. You taught us the form of prayer, which is mysterious, that we can pray with it to Your beginning less Father.

The Liturgy of Saint Gregory the Theologian

Therefore deem us worthy also now, Master, Lord with a hallowed conscience and with good reasoning, ...crux...[815] and noble boldness, dare to call upon Your Father, the holy God in heaven and to say.
The People say: The Our Father.
And After the "Our Father."

5. The Prayer following the Lord's Prayer
The Priest says: Yes Lord, Lord, who has given to us the power to tread upon serpents and scorpions and upon every power of the enemy, swiftly crush the heads of our enemies and subject them under our feet; and scatter to the winds every evil plan of theirs which is aimed against us.

> *For You are the King of us all, Christ our God, and to You we send up glory and thanks and adoration every day, with Your beginnignless Father and Holy Spirit, now ...*

6. The Prayer of the Bowing of the Head.
The Deacon says: Bow your heads to the Lord.
You who bent the heavens and descended upon the earth for the salvation of the race of men, who spread out every abundance of Your grace; who does all things far beyond that which we ask for, or conceive of, O Good One, Lover of man, extend Your unseen and blessed hand, full of mercy and compassion, and, You who blesses, bless Your servants and cleanse them from every defilement of flesh and spirit; and make us to become participants (in these mysteries) and of one body, by Your grace, so that we can offer You prayer in holiness and righteousness.

> *To You is due every glory, majesty, power and authority, together with Your beginning less Father and the Holy Spirit, now and...*

7. Another, similar prayer
Attend, Lord Jesus Christ from Your holy dwelling place, and from the glorious throne of Your kingdom; and come, for our sanctification, for those who bow down before You, You who are enthroned with the Father above, but are invisibly present here with us; and who deems it worthy to give us of Your spotless Body, by Your mighty hand, and through us to the whole people.

---

[815] The text is, according to the Renaudot edition translates to: "…which is proper for sons, and in fervent desire..."

Critical Text and Translation

8. The Prayer of Freedom

Peace be with all

O Lamb of God, who takes away the sin of the world, who shed Your completely spotless Blood for the life of the world as a ransom and as an exchange for all. You handed Yourself over in order to ransom us from death, in which we were bound, sold under sin. You who accomplish the will of those who fear You, hear their prayer and save them; You who heard the righteous Job: "rising up early and bringing forth sacrifices for the sake of his beloved children and saying: 'perhaps my sons considered evil things in their hearts before God.'"Hear me also, Your pitiful, sinful and unworthy servant, beseeching You on behalf of Your servants, my fathers and brothers, and on behalf of my own wretchedness. Grace us with Your face and with a tranquil eye, look upon us at this hour, and pardon us for every deviation, every disobedience of the law and of Your commandments; and more, bind every conscience and every desire, deed and turbulence within them, both during the day and at night, and rule over (our) soul. Absolve us from every complicity in evil things, from every unfruitful practice and from every inflamed thought, whatsoever is profane and contrary to the purity of the soul. Grant us the recognition of our sins, and to abstain completely from them. Grant them the repentance of purity and conversion to You. For You, Master, Lord, humbled Yourself willingly, in Your Incarnation, for the salvation of our race; You tore apart the handwriting against us, by stretching out Your divine hands upon the Cross. Spare us all, Master, who loves souls, for all things are Your servants and from You we have our beginning, the works of our hands are vain; therefore we glorify Your kingdom and we hymn You, Christ our God.

...crux...

because of every sin and of the heretics and gentiles.

Fill us with fear of You and direct us to Your good will.

For You are our God, and to You is due glory, honor and worship...

9. Body and Blood

The Deacon says: Body and Blood. With the fear of God, let us attend.

The Priest lifts up the Zealous piece (the Master's piece) and cries out:

The Holy things for the Holy!

The People say: Lord, Have Mercy; One Holy Father, One Holy Son, One Holy Spirit. Amen.

The Priest says: The Lord be with You.

The People say: And with your spirit.

The Priest says: Blessed is the Lord, unto the Ages. Amen.

The Liturgy of Saint Gregory the Theologian

The People say: Amen.
The Priest says: Peace be with all.
The People say: And with your spirit.
The Priest says: Truly the holy Body and precious Blood of Jesus Christ, the Son of God. Amen.
The People say: Amen.
The Priest says: The holy, precious Body and the true Blood of Jesus Christ the Son of God, Amen.
The People say: Amen.
The Priest says: The Body and Blood of Emmanuel, of our God, truly this is so. Amen.
The People say: Amen.
The Priest says: I believe, I believe, I believe and I confess until my last breath, that this is the life-giving flesh, which You took, Christ our God, from our holy Lady Theotokos and Ever Virgin Mary; and You made it one with Your divinity, neither in a mixture nor in a mingling nor in an alteration; and You bore witness under Pontius Pilate, the good confession, and You gave it over for all of us upon the wood of the Cross, according to Your will. Truly I believe that Your divinity was never divided from Your humanity, not in a moment, not in the twinkling of an eye. You gave it as a ransom, and as a remission of sins and for eternal life, for those who partake of it.
I believe that this is truly so. Amen.
The People say: Amen.
The Deacon says: In peace and love.
The Priest cries out:
Incomprehensible God, Word, uncontainable, eternal, accept from us sinners, from our unworthy lips, that which we hymn together with the heavenly powers.
> *For to You is due all glory, honor and worship, with Your beginning less Father and the life giving Spirit, unto all ages of ages. Amen.*

The People recite the 150th Psalm
The Deacon says: Be gathered together and approach with reverence O Deacons.

10. The Prayer after the Participation in the Holy Mysteries
The Deacon says: Stand for prayer.
The Priest says: Peace be with all.
The People say: And with your spirit.
The Deacon says: Offer prayers for the worthy participation.
The People say: Lord, Have Mercy.

The Priest says this prayer:
We thank You, true Word of God, who is of the substance of the beginning less Father, that You loved us so much and gave Yourself for us, and were sacrificed. You granted to us deliverance through Your spotless Body and sacred Blood, and that You have deemed us worthy now, lover of man, to partake in the Eucharist from them.

> *Therefore we now praise You, lover of man, and to You we ceaselessly send up glory, honor and worship, with Your beginning less Father and Your Holy Spirit, now and...*

11. The Prayer of the Bowing of the Head

The Deacon says: Bow your heads to the Lord.

You who are, who were, who came into the world to illumine it; who took flesh, became man and was crucified for us, and suffering willingly in the flesh, You remained passionless, as God; You were buried, rose on the third day, ascended into the heavens and were enthroned at the right hand of the great glory of the Father; You sent down upon Your holy disciples and apostles the divine, holy, consubstantial Spirit, equal to You in power and glory, who is equally eteranl with You, and through it You illumined them.

...crux...

Christ the true

...crux....

And Gabriel and Raphael.

the angels, the bodiless four formed creatures; and the angels, the twenty four elders; the holy, glorious prophet, forerunner Baptist and martyr John. St. Stephen the protodeacon and protomartyr; the divine, holy, glorious Apostles, the victorious prophets, the triumphant martyrs; our holy and blessed father Mark the apostle and evangelist; and the whole choir of Your saints.

Save, have mercy on and bless every Christian.

> *To You we offer glory, honor and worship; with Your beginning less Father and the Holy Spirit, now and ever, and unto...*

In the peace of God, the Divine Liturgy is completed, which was laid down by our Father among the Saints, the Theologian Gregory.

The Commentary

In this section, I will be taking a closer look at the text, and dealing in more detail with the questions posed in the Introduction. The Commentary will be divided into three parts: 1. The Pre-Anaphoral Rites; 2. The Anaphora; 3. The Post-Anaphoral Rites. Each of these sections will begin with a short description of the structure of the section as a whole. I will then proceed to look at each chapter (either an individual prayer or related group of prayers) in more detail.

The Commentary for each chapter will begin with an analysis of its Structure; following the Structure will be a discussion of the Function: what is the author trying to do in this section, this will lead to a better understanding of the anti-Arian function of each section; finally I will look at Intertextuality and Style: this will hopefully lead to a better understanding of the authorship, i.e. whether or not St. Gregory Nazianzus really is the author of this work. Though theological themes will be unavoidable, it is important, once again, to stress that this is primarily a literary discussion. For a theologically based Commentary see Alfred Gerhards Commentary of the Anaphora.

Commentary Part I: The Pre-Anaphora Rites

I. Pre-Anaphoral Rites

In this Commentary, the liturgy has been divided up into three sections: the pre-Anaphora, the post-Anaphora and the Anaphora itself. This triple division is based on the thematic focus of each section. The pre-Anaphora focuses on the ability and the permission needed by the priest and the people to approach the altar; the majority of the prayers in this section deal with purification, admittance and forgiveness. In the Anaphora itself the focus shifts from admittance and purification, since this is accomplished, to the hallowing and consecration of the Eucharistic gifts. In the final section the theme shifts again, back to purification, in light of the imminent reception of the Eucharist, and to thanksgiving following the reception of the Eucharist.

There is another possible point at which liturgical texts can be divided. Following the reading of the Gospel and the giving of the homily, the catechumens, those who are studying for Baptism, are dismissed from the Nave of the Church, to continue their instruction. The faithful, however, remain in the Nave for the remainder of the liturgy. The dismissal of the catechumens is commonly used as a dividing line in the liturgy. The division between the "liturgy of the catechumens" and the "liturgy of the faithful" is also marked by the transition between the reading of the lectionary and the beginning of the preparation of the Eucharist, therefore the two sections are also known as the "liturgy of the Word" and the "liturgy of the Eucharist."

The pre-Anaphoral section of the liturgy includes both the entire "liturgy of the Word" and the beginning of the "liturgy of the Eucharist." The thematic elements found in the pre-Anaphora are focused mainly on preparation. So, in the opening prayer of the liturgy, the priest prays that he be purified from his sins and that he be able to worthily approach the altar. Along with this "Prayer of Access" are several other types of prayers, such as the "Prayer of the Gospel" and the "Prayer of the Greeting."

I.1. Structure of the Pre-Anaphora

One of the first points of discussion must be where to end the pre-Anaphora and where to begin the Anaphora proper. As this liturgy must be considered a part of the West Syrian rite, even if a part of the Cappadocian/Constantinopolitan subfamily, the dividing line must be consistent with other Syrian liturgies. In Renaudot's *Liturgiarum Orientalium Collectio* the Syrian liturgies usually begin the Anaphora with the *oratio ante pacem*, the

The Liturgy of Saint Gregory the Theologian

"Prayer of the Greeting." In this Commentary, however, the dividing line will follow the precedent sent by the Commentary of Alfred Gerhards and begin the Anaphora with the *Sursum Corda* dialogue. The pre-Anaphora is divided into seven prayers, or rather, five prayers with two alternates.

1. Εὐχὴ ἥν ποιεῖ ὁ Ἱερεὺς καθ' ἑαυτὸν ἐν ἑαυτῷ: This, the first prayer of the Liturgy, sets the tone of the Liturgy, and serves as an introduction to the text; as well as being a "Prayer of Access" to the Altar.
2. Εὐχὴ μετὰ τὴν ἑτοιμασίαν τοῦ Ἁγίου Θυσιαστηρίου: In this prayer the officiating cleric justifies his role in the Liturgy, this prayer continues the themes started on in the first prayer.
3. Ἐυχὴ τοῦ ἁγίου Εὐαγγελίου: The prayer in which the proclamation of the Gospel is introduced.
4. Εὐχὴ τοῦ καταπετάσματος: The "Prayer of the Veil."
5. Εὐχὴ ἄλλη καταπετάσματος παρ' Αἰγυπτίοις: The alternate "Prayer of the Veil," which must have been added after the Liturgy was introduced into Egypt.
6. Εὐχὴ τοῦ ἀσπασμοῦ: The "Prayer of the Greeting," the kiss of peace, or the greeting is introduced by this prayer.
7. Εὐχὴ ἄλλη τοῦ ἀσπασμοῦ: The alternate prayer introducing the kiss of peace.

I.II. The Εὐχὴ ἥν ποιεῖ ὁ Ἱερεὺς καθ' ἑαυτὸν ἐν ἑαυτῷ

One of the major difficulties in researching the pre- and post-anaphoral rites of a liturgy is that there is no guarantee that the prayers are original to the liturgy. This difficulty presents itself immediately in our text as well. Hammerschmidt notes that the opening "Prayer of Access" in our liturgy has an almost exact correspondent in the Greek Liturgy of St. James: "Diese Oration fehlt im Koptischen wie im Syrischen, ist aber in der greichischen Jakobosliturgie des syrischen Ritus unter den Opferungsgebeten vorhanden."[816] In the following table the similarities between these two prayers can be seen (the differences have been underlined):

---

[816] Hammerschmidt (1957). pg. 80 "This prayer is missing in the Coptic and in the Syrian, but is found in the Syrian Liturgy of St. James among the Prayers of Offering."

Figure I.II.1: the differences between the "Prayer of Access" in the Liturgy of St. Gregory[817] and the "Opferungsgebet" in the Liturgy of St. James.[818]

The "Prayer of Access" in the Liturgy of St. Gregory the Theologian	The "Opferungsgebet" in the Greek Liturgy of St. James[819]
Ὁ ἐπισκεψάμενος ἡμᾶς ἐν ἐλέει καὶ οἰκτιρμοῖς, Δέσποτα Κύριε <u>Ἰησοῦ Χριστέ</u>, καὶ χαρισάμενος ἡμῖν παρρησίαν, τοῖς ταπεινοῖς καὶ ἁμαρτωλοῖς καὶ ἀναξίοις δούλοις σου παραστῆναι τῷ ἁγίῳ σου Θυσιαστηρίῳ καὶ προσφέρειν σοι τὴν φοβερὰν καὶ ἀναίμακτον Θυσίαν, ὑπὲρ τῶν ἡμετέρων ἁμαρτημάτων, καὶ τῶν τοῦ λαοῦ <u>σου</u> ἀγνοημάτων, <u>ἄνεσιν καὶ ἀνάπαυσιν τῶν προκοιμηθέντων πατέρων ἡμῶν καὶ ἀδελφῶν, καὶ στηριγμὸν παντὸς τοῦ λαοῦ σοῦ</u>. Ἐπίβλεψον ἐπ' ἐμὲ, τὸν ἀχρεῖον δοῦλόν σου, καὶ ἐξάλειψόν μου τὰ παραπτώματα, διὰ τὴν σὴν εὐσπλαγχνίαν. Καὶ καθάρισόν μου τὰ χείλη καὶ τὴν καρδίαν ἀπὸ παντὸς μολυσμοῦ σαρκός <u>τε</u> καὶ πνεύματος. Καὶ ἀπόστησον ἀπ' ἐμοῦ <u>πάντα</u> λογισμὸν αἰσχρόν τε καὶ ἀσύνετον. Καὶ ἱκάνωσόν με τῇ δυνάμει τοῦ ἁγίου σου Πνεύματος εἰς τὴν Λειτουργίαν ταύτην καὶ πρόσδεξαί με διὰ <u>τὴν σὴν</u> ἀγαθότητα προσεγγίζοντα τῷ ἁγίῳ σου Θυσιαστηρίῳ. <u>Καὶ</u> εὐδόκησον Κύριε δεκτὰ γενέσθαι τὰ <u>μέλλοντα</u> προσαγόμενά σοι Δῶρα, διὰ τῶν ἡμετέρων χειρῶν, συγκαταβαίνων ταῖς ἐμαῖς ἀσθενείαις. Καὶ μὴ ἀπορρίψης με ἀπὸ τοῦ προσώπου σου, <u>μὴ</u> βδελύξης <u>με,</u> τὴν ἐμὴν ἀναξιότητα, ἀλλ' ἐλέησόν με, <u>ὁ Θεὸς</u>, κατὰ τὸ μέγα ἔλεός σου, καὶ κατὰ τὸ πλῆθος τῶν οἰκτιρμῶν σου <u>ἐξάλειψον τὸ ἀνόμημά μου</u>. Ἵνα ἀκατακρίως προσελθὼν κατενώπιον τῆς δόξης σου, καταξιωθῶ	Ὁ ἐπισκεψάμενος ἡμᾶς ἐν ἐλέει καὶ οἰκτιρμοῖς δέσποτα κύριε καὶ χαρισάμενος παρρησίαν ἡμῖν τοῖς ταπεινοῖς καὶ ἁμαρτωλοῖς καὶ ἀναξίοις δούλοις σου παρεστάναι τῷ ἁγίῳ σου Θυσιαστηρίῳ καὶ προσφέρειν σοι τὴν φοβερὰν <u>ταύτην</u> καὶ ἀναίμακτον θυσίαν ὑπὲρ τῶν ἡμετέρων ἁμαρτημάτων καὶ τῶν τοῦ λαοῦ ἀγνοημάτων· ἐπίβλεψον ἐπ' ἐμὲ τὸν ἀχρεῖον δοῦλόν σου καὶ ἐξάλειψόν μου τὰ παραπτώματα διὰ τὴν σὴν εὐσπλαγχνίαν καὶ καθάρισόν μου τὰ χείλη καὶ τὴν καρδίαν ἀπὸ παντὸς μολυσμοῦ σαρκὸς καὶ πνεύματος καὶ ἀπόστησον ἀπ' ἐμοῦ πάντα λογισμὸν αἰσχρόν τε καὶ ἀσύνετον καὶ ἱκάνωσόν με τῇ δυνάμει τοῦ <u>παναγίου</u> σου πνεύματος εἰς τὴν λειτουργίαν ταύτην καὶ πρόσδεξαί με διὰ τὴν ἀγαθότητά σου προσεγγίζοντα τῷ ἁγίῳ σου θυσιαστηρίῳ καὶ εὐδόκησον Κύριε δεκτὰ γενέσθαι τὰ προσαγόμενά σοι <u>ταῦτα</u> Δῶρα διὰ τῶν ἡμετέρων χειρῶν συγκαταβαίνων ταῖς ἐμαῖς ἀσθενίαις καὶ μὴ ἀπορρίψης με ἀπὸ τοῦ προσώπου σου μηδὲ βδελύξῃ τὴν ἐμὴν ἀναξιότητα ἀλλ' ἐλέησόν με κατὰ τὸ μέγα ἔλεός σου καὶ κατὰ τὸ πλῆθος τῶν οἰκτιρμῶν σου <u>παρένεγκε τὰ ἀνομήματά μου</u> ἵνα ἀκατάκριτος προσελθὼν κατενώπιον τῆς δόξης σου καταξιωθῶ τῆς σκέπης <u>τοῦ μονογενοῦς σου υἱοῦ</u> καὶ τῆς ἐλλάμψεως τοῦ παναγίου Πνεύματος καὶ μὴ ὡς δοῦλος ἁμαρτίας ἀποδόκιμος γένωμαι ἀλλ' ὡς

---

[817] Cf. above pg. 59.
[818] For another comparison of these two texts see Hammerschmidt (1957). pg. 80-81
[819] Hammond and Brightman (1896). pg. 45; c.f also Mercier (1944). pp. 190-192

τῆς σκέπης <u>σου</u> καὶ τῆς ἐλλάμψεως τοῦ παναγίου σου Πνεύματος, καὶ μὴ ὡς δοῦλος ἁμαρτίας ἀποδόκιμος γένωμαι, ἀλλ' ὡς δοῦλος, ὅς εὕρω χάριν καὶ ἔλεος καὶ ἄφεσιν ἁμαρτιῶν, ἐν τῷ νῦν καὶ ἐν τῷ μέλλοντι αἰῶνι. Ναὶ Δέσποτα Παντόκρατορ, Παντοδύναμε Κύριε, <u>ἐπάκουσον</u> τῆς δεήσεώς μου. Σὺ γὰρ εἶ ὁ τὰ πάντα ἐνεργῶν ἐν πᾶσι καὶ τὴν παρὰ σου πάντες ἐπιζητοῦμεν ἐπὶ πᾶσι βοήθειάν τε καὶ ἀντίληψιν. <u>Ὅτι φιλάνθρωπος εἶ, καὶ δεδοξασμένος ὑπάρχεις, Ἰησοῦ ὁ Θεὸς ἡμῶν, σὺν τῷ ἀνάρχῳ σου Πατρί, καὶ τῷ Ἁγίῳ Πνεύματι, νῦν καὶ ἀεί...</u>	δοῦλος σὸς εὕρω χάριν καὶ ἔλεος καὶ ἄφεσιν ἁμαρτιῶν <u>ἐνώπιόν σου καὶ</u> ἐν τῷ νῦν καὶ ἐν τῷ μέλλοντι αἰῶνι· ναὶ δέσποτα παντοκράτορ παντοδύναμε Κύριε <u>εἰσάκουσον</u> τῆς δεήσεώς μου· σὺ γὰρ εἶ ὁ τὰ πάντα ἐνεργῶν ἐν πᾶσι καὶ τὴν παρὰ σου πάντες ἐπιζητοῦμεν ἐπὶ πᾶσι βοήθειάν τε καὶ ἀντίληψιν καὶ <u>τοῦ μονογενοῦς σου υἱοῦ καὶ τοῦ ἀγαθοῦ καὶ ζωοποιοῦ καὶ ὁμοουσίου Πνεύματος</u> νῦν καὶ εἰς τοὺς αἰῶνας τῶν αἰώνων

As can be seen in the comparison chart, the two prayers have only slight differences, the greatest differences being that the prayer is addressed to Christ in the Liturgy of St. Gregory and to the Father in the Liturgy of St. James. The St. Gregory version also adds a prayer for the departed, and the ekphoneseis vary. Hammerschmidt even postulates that many of the minor differences could be: "verschiedene Lesarten der Handschriften."[820] From this we can draw the conclusion that these prayers are related, they are so close in fact that one of these prayers seems to have been the template for the other, but which of these prayers came first? While Hammerschmidt admits: "Wo die Oration ihren ursprünglichen Sitz hatte, ist heute noch nicht festzustellen. Zu beachten ist aber, dass sie im monophysitischen Bereich nicht festzustellen ist."[821] He does seem to believe, however, that the prayer in the Liturgy of St. James is primary: "...so kann man in der Oration der gr Greglit doch sekundäre Züge erkennen, d.h. ihre Abhängigkeit von der griechischen Jakobosliturgie angedeutet finden."[822] What speaks for this theory is the argument of Theodor Schermann, that Liturgies, especially in the first four centuries of Church history, do not decrease in length but increase: "Es darf als ausgeschlossen gelten, dass in den ersten vier Jahrhunderten ene rückgängige Entwicklung in den Liturgien anzunehmen ist."[823] While it is true that the prayer in the Liturgy of St. Gregory is slightly longer, there does not seem to be a significant enough lenthening to make the claim without reservation. Ham-

---

[820] Hammerschmidt (1957). pg. 81 "Different readings of the manuscripts."
[821] Hammerschmidt (1957). pg. 82 "Wher the prayer has its original place cannot be determined today. Imprtant, however, is that it is not found in the Monophysite world."
[822] Hammerschmidt (1957). pg. 81 "Thus one can recognize secondary elements in the prayer of the Greek Liturgy of St. Gregory, that is, its dependence on the Greek Liturgy of St. James."
[823] Schermann (1920) (Cf. also Hammerschmidt (1957). pg. 82). "It can be considered impossible that a deletion is to be assumed (in prayers) in the first four centuries in liturgy."

merschmidt does offer another argument to augment this, he claims that: "die Oration der gr. Greglit ist zu einem an Christus gerichteten Gebet umgeschaffen."[824] There is one phrase in this prayer that seems to speak against this theory however: Σὺ γὰρ εἶ ὁ τὰ πάντα ἐνεργῶν ἐν πᾶσι. This phrase is also found in various other authors including St. Athnasius, St. Basil the Great, St. Marcellus the Theologian, as well as St. Epiphanius of Cyprus in works written against various sects of Arians. Such a weighted phrase being used in the prayer may point to an original anti-Arian stance of this prayer, which reflects the anti-Arian stance of the Liturgy of St. Gregory as a whole. Another issue is seen in the stylistic and functional intratextual links between the first and second prayers of the Liturgy of St. Gregory the Theologian, these links show that, even if adopted into the Liturgy of St. Gregory the Theologian from the Liturgy of St. James, this adoption and adaptation must have been done by the initial author.

The introductory function of this "Prayer of Access" seems also to be reflected, in a much abbreviated form, in the "Εὐχὴ τῶν Πιστῶν" of the Liturgy of St. Basil the Great, which serves an introductory function into the Liturgy of the Faithful (that is, the second part of the Liturgy), the points where this "Prayer of the Faithful" and the "Prayer of Access" in the Liturgy of St. Gregory the Theologian overlap are shown in the following table:

Figure I.II.2 Comparative Chart of this prayer in the Liturgy of St. Gregory the Theologian and the Liturgy of St. Basil the Great

Liturgy of St. Gregory Nazianzus	Liturgy of St. Basil the Great[825]
Ὁ ἐπισκεψάμενος ἡμᾶς ἐν ἐλέει καὶ οἰκτιρμοῖς, Δέσποτα Κύριε Ἰησοῦ Χριστέ, καὶ χαρισάμενος ἡμῖν παρρησίαν, τοῖς ταπεινοῖς καὶ ἁμαρτωλοῖς καὶ ἀναξίοις δούλοις σου παραστῆναι τῷ ἁγίῳ σου Θυσιαστηρίῳ καὶ προσφέρειν σοι τὴν φοβερὰν καὶ ἀναίμακτον Θυσίαν... Καὶ ἱκανωσόν με τῇ δυνάμει τοῦ ἁγίου σου Πνεύματος εἰς τὴν Λειτουργίαν ταύτην καὶ πρόσδεξαί με διὰ τὴν σὴν ἀγαθότητα προσεγγίζοντα τῷ ἁγίῳ σου Θυσιαστηρίῳ. Καὶ	Ὁ Θεός ὁ ἐπισκεψάμενος ἐν ἐλέει καὶ οἰκτιρμοῖς τὴν ταπείνωσιν ἡμῶν, ὁ στήσας ἡμᾶς τοὺς ταπεινοὺς καὶ ἁμαρτωλοὺς καὶ ἀναξίους δούλους σου κατενώπιον τῆς ἁγίας δόξης σου λειτουργεῖν τῷ ἁγίῳ σου Θυσιαστηρίῳ· σὺ ἐνίσχυσον ἡμᾶς τῇ δυνάμει τοῦ ἁγίου σου πνεύματος, εἰς τὴν διακονίαν ταύτην καὶ δὸς ἡμῖν λόγον ἐν ἀνοίξει τοῦ στόματος ἡμῶν εἰς τὸ ἐπικαλεῖσθαι τὴν χάριν τοῦ ἁγίου σου πνεύματος ἐπὶ τῶν μελλόντων

---

[824] Hammerschmidt (1957). pg. 82 "The prayer in the Liturgy of St. Gregory is reworked into one addressed to Christ."
[825] Hammond and Brightman (1896). pg. 317 and Trempelis (1982). pg. 167.

εὐδόκησον Κύριε δεκτὰ γενέσθαι τὰ μέλλοντα προσαγόμενά σοι Δῶρα, διὰ τῶν ἡμετέρων χειρῶν, συγκαταβαίνων ταῖς ἐμαῖς ἀσθενείαις.... Ἵνα ἀκατακρίως προσελθὼν κατενώπιον τῆς δόξης σου...	προτίθεσθαι δώρων.

As can be seen in the table, the two prayers share many of the same phrases and topics, though the prayer in the Liturgy of St. Basil is much shorter. The similarities are too great to attribute to mere coincidence. It seems then, that the these two prayers are also related. As we will see the Liturgy of St. Basil adopts a number of prayers directly from the Liturgy of St. Gregory, here, though, we see a prayer that is similar, but not identical, to explain this, we can postulate a model prayer, on which both of these ‚prayers of access' are based, and from which they take their stock phrases. It is possible that the model prayer was this "Opferungsgebet" from the Liturgy of St. James, however, in both St. Basil and St. Gregory, the prayers function as ‚prayers of Access' before the Entrance with the gifts, while in St. James the prayer functions as a Eucharistic prayer.

Unfortunately, we still cannot make a certain statement concerning the true origin of this prayer. While the anti-Arian phrasing and the commonalities with another "Prayer of Access" in the Liturgy of St. Basil point to the origins lying in the Liturgy of St. Gregory, it is undeniable that the Gregory text of the prayer is longer, which points to the origin in the Liturgy of St. James.

Problematic too, is that this Prayer is found again in the *Liturgia Praesanctificatorum* attributed to bishop Epiphanios of Salamis in Cyprus (320-403). This complicates matters, because Epiphanius wrote earlier than St. Gregory, putting this prayer in the running for the original prayer as well. The versions of the prayers in St. Gregory and in Epiphanius of Cyprus are shown in the following table:

The Commentary

Figure I.II.3: Comparative Chart of the ,'Prayer of Access'' in the Liturgy of St. Gregory the Theologian and the Liturgia Praesanctificatorum of Epiphanius of Cyprus.

The *"Prayer of Access"* of the Liturgy of St. Gregory the Theologian	In the *Liturgia Praesanctificatorum* of Epiphanius of Cyprus
Ὁ ἐπισκεψάμενος ἡμᾶς ἐν ἐλέει καὶ οἰκτιρμοῖς, Δέσποτα Κύριε <u>Ἰησοῦ Χριστέ</u>, καὶ χαρισάμενος ἡμῖν παρρησίαν, τοῖς ταπεινοῖς <u>καὶ ἁμαρτωλοῖς</u> καὶ ἀναξίοις δούλοις σου παραστῆναι τῷ ἁγίῳ σου Θυσιαστηρίῳ καὶ προσφέρειν σοι τὴν <u>φοβερὰν καὶ ἀναίμακτον Θυσίαν</u>, ὑπὲρ τῶν ἡμετέρων ἁμαρτημάτων, <u>καὶ τῶν τοῦ λαοῦ σου ἀγνοημάτων, ἄνεσιν καὶ ἀνάπαυσιν τῶν προκοιμηθέντων πατέρων ἡμῶν καὶ ἀδελφῶν, καὶ στηριγμὸν παντὸς τοῦ λαοῦ σοῦ.</u> Ἐπίβλεψον ἐπ' ἐμὲ, τὸν ἀχρεῖον δοῦλόν σου, καὶ ἐξάλειψόν μου τὰ παραπτώματα, διὰ τὴν σὴν εὐσπλαγχνίαν. Καὶ καθάρισόν μου τὰ χείλη καὶ τὴν καρδίαν ἀπὸ παντὸς μολυσμοῦ σαρκός τε καὶ πνεύματος. Καὶ <u>ἀπόστησον ἀπ' ἐμοῦ πάντα λογισμὸν αἰσχρόν τε καὶ ἀσύνετον</u>. Καὶ ἱκάνωσόν με τῇ δυνάμει τοῦ ἁγίου σου Πνεύματος εἰς τὴν Λειτουργίαν ταύτην καὶ πρόσδεξαί με διὰ τὴν σὴν ἀγαθότητα προσεγγίζοντα τῷ ἁγίῳ σου Θυσιαστηρίῳ. <u>Καὶ</u> εὐδόκησον Κύριε δεκτὰ γενέσθαι τὰ <u>μέλλοντα</u> προσαγόμενά σοι Δῶρα, διὰ τῶν ἡμετέρων χειρῶν, συγκαταβαίνων <u>ταῖς ἐμαῖς</u> ἀσθενείαις. Καὶ μὴ ἀπορρίψης με ἀπὸ τοῦ προσώπου σου, <u>μὴ βδελύξης με</u>, τὴν ἐμὴν ἀναξιότητα, ἀλλ' ἐλέησόν με, ὁ Θεός, κατὰ τὸ μέγα ἔλεός σου, <u>καὶ κατὰ τὸ πλῆθος τῶν οἰκτιρμῶν σου ἐξάλειψον τὸ ἀνόμημά μου</u>. Ἵνα ἀκατακρίως προσελθὼν κατενώπιον τῆς δόξης σου, <u>καταξιωθῶ τῆς σκέπης σου</u> καὶ τῆς ἐλλάμψεως τοῦ παναγίου σου Πνεύματος, καὶ μὴ ὡς δοῦλος ἁμαρτίας ἀποδόκιμος γένωμαι, <u>ἀλλ' ὡς δοῦλος, ὃς εὕρω χάριν καὶ ἔλεος καὶ ἄφεσιν ἁμαρτιῶν, ἐν τῷ νῦν καὶ ἐν τῷ μέλλοντι αἰῶνι</u>. Ναὶ Δέσποτα	Ὁ ἐπισκεψάμενος ἡμᾶς ἐν ἐλέει καὶ οἰκτιρμοῖς, Δέσποτα Κύριε καὶ χαρισάμενος ἡμῖν παρρησίαν τοῖς ταπεινοῖς καὶ ἀναξίοις δούλοις σου, παραστῆναι τῷ ἁγίῳ σου θυσιαστηρίῳ καὶ προσφέρειν σοι <u>τὴν λογικὴν ταύτην καὶ ἀναίμακτον λατρείαν</u> ὑπὲρ τῶν ἡμετέρων ἁμαρτημάτων, ἐπίβλεψον ἐπ' ἐμὲ τὸν ἀχρεῖον δοῦλόν σου καὶ ἐξάλειψόν μου τὰ παραπτώματα διὰ τὴν σὴν εὐσπλαγχνίαν καὶ καθάρισόν μου τὰ χείλη καὶ τὴν καρδίαν ἀπὸ παντὸς μολυσμοῦ σαρκὸς καὶ πνεύματος καὶ ἱκάνωσόν με τῇ δυνάμει τοῦ ἁγίου σου πνεύματος εἰς τὴν λειτουργίαν ταύτην. Καὶ πρόσδεξαί με διὰ τὴν ἀγαθότητά σου προσεγγίζοντα τῷ ἁγίῳ σου θυσιαστηρίῳ. Εὐδόκησον <u>δή</u>, Κύριε, δεκτὰ γενέσθα τὰ προσαγόμενά σοι Δῶρα <u>τοῦτα</u> διὰ τῶν ἡμετέρων χειρῶν, συγκαταβαίνων <u>ἡμῖν</u> ταῖς ἀσθενείαις. Καὶ μὴ ἀπορρίψης με ἀπὸ τοῦ προσώπου σου, <u>μηδὲ</u> βδελύξῃ τὴν ἐμὴν ἀναξιότητα, ἀλλ' ἐλέησόν με ὁ Θεὸς κατὰ τὸ μέγα ἔλεός σου <u>καὶ παρένεγκε τὰ ἀνομήματά μου, ἵνα ἀκατακρίτως προσελθὼν κατενώπιον καὶ παρένεγκε τὰ ἀνομήματά μου</u>, ἵνα ἀκατακρίτως προσελθὼν κατενώπιον τῆς δόξης σου, ἀξιωθῶ τῆς σκέπης τοῦ <u>μονογενοῦς σου υἱοῦ</u> καὶ μὴ ὡς δοῦλος ἁμαρτίας ἀδόκιμος γένωμαι. Ναί, δέσποτα παντοδύναμε κύριε, εἰσάκουσον τῆς δεήσεώς μου. Σὺ γὰρ εἶ ὁ πάντα ἐνεργῶν ἐν πᾶσι <u>καὶ τὴν παρὰ σοῦ πάντες ἐπιζητοῦμεν βοήθειαν.</u>

Παντόκρατορ, Παντοδύναμε Κύριε, ἐπάκουσον τῆς δεήσεώς μου. Σὺ γὰρ εἶ ὁ τὰ πάντα ἐνεργῶν ἐν πᾶσι καὶ τὴν παρὰ σου πάντες ἐπιζητοῦμεν ἐπὶ πᾶσι βοήθειάν τε καὶ ἀντίληψιν. Ὅτι φιλάνθρωπος εἶ, καὶ δεδοξασμένος ὑπάρχεις, Ἰησοῦ ὁ Θεὸς ἡμῶν, σὺν τῷ ἀνάρχῳ σου Πατρί, καὶ τῷ Ἁγίῳ Πνεύματι, νῦν καὶ ἀεί...	

While a number of phrases in used in the Liturgy of St .Gregory are missing in the Epiphanios text, the most striking difference is that, here too, the prayer is not directed to Christ. It would be logical to assume, since Epiphanius was active slightly earlier than Gregory the Theologian and since liturgical prayers addressed to Christ are unusual,[826] that the prayer to the Father is the primary prayer, and was adopted into the Liturgy of St. Gregory, and changed to conform to the style of the prayer. This interpretation does not bear further scrutiny. The first issue is that of the authorship of the *Liturgia Praesanctificatorum*. The earliest manuscript evidence of a Liturgy of the Presanctified Gifts is from the eigth century Barberini Codex.[827] Though this does not rule out an earlier date for this sort of text, that congregants would take elements of the Eucharist home with them or bring them to the sick without any sort of liturgical ritual,[828] makes a Byzantine ritual of this sort in the fourth century highly unlikely. It was only later, in the tenth through twelfth centuries, that the Presanctified Liturgies were ascribed to important figures of the ancient church, such as St. Basil the Great and Epiphanios of Cyprus.

1. *Structure:*

In the first section, beginning with ὁ ἐπισκεψάμενος ἡμας the prayer lays out the general purpose of the text: namely the culmination in the Eucharist. Two things are granted by Christ: παραστῆναι τῷ ἁγίῳ σου Θυσιαστηρίῳ and to προσφέρειν σοι τὴν φοβερὰν καὶ ἀναίμακτν Θυσίαν dependant on these two favors are three reasons for the offering of the Sacrifice: one offers (1) ὑπέρ...ἁμαρτημάτων, καὶ...ἀγνοημάτων; (2) ἄνεσιν καὶ ἀνάπαυσιν τῶν προλοιμηθέντων πατεέρων καὶ ἀδελφῶν; and finally (3) στηριγμὸν παντὸς τοῦ λαοῦ σου. In this way the entire Church receives benefit from the carrying out of this Liturgy; those present at the Liturgy, the departed members of the Church, and a generalized λαοῦ meant to cover all those who are not present at the Liturgy, but are still

---

[826] Despite the tradition of these prayers described by Gerhards, see above pg. 1-6.
[827] Swainson (1884). pg. xvii
[828] Justin. *First Apology* 65.

members of the Church. Interesting, though, is that these effects are not prayed for, but seem to constitute an automatic benefit of the Liturgy; the prayer is ultimately that Christ grants the congregants and the clergy the ability to carry out the Liturgy, out of which these automatic blessings flow.

In the second section we immediately see the generalization of the first section dissapear: the prayer changes from ὁ ἐπισκεψάμενος ἡμᾶς to ἐπίβλεψον ἐπ' ἐμὲ. It is now no longer the entire congregation that is the focus of this prayer, but the priest himself, who must entreat God for the worthiness to participate in the liturgy. This section of the prayer culminates in a very penitential quotation from the fiftieth Psalm: ἀλλ' ἐλέησόν με ὁ Θεὸς κατὰ τὸ μέγα ἔλεος σου, καὶ κατὰ τὸ πλῆθος τῶν οἰκτιρμῶν σου ἐξάλειψον τὸ ἀνόμημά μου. Seven requests of the priest, though actually imperatives serve to ensure his worthiness for the carrying out of the mystery. The first is a generalized plea for absolution; requests two and three serve to receive purification for the whole person of the priest, taking up the platonic threefold division of the person.[829] The remaining requests deal not, at least not directly, with the sinful nature of the priest, but rather his unworthiness in the face of such a mystery, therefore he asks that Christ: ἱκάνωσόν με τῇ δυνάμει τοῦ ἁγίου σου Πνεύματος εἰς τὴνΛειτουργίαν ταύτην. Following this series of requests, is laid out, parallel to the first section, three further requests which grow out of the actions done by Christ: (1) καταξιωθῶ τῆς σκέπης σου καὶ τῆς ἐλλάμψεως τοῦ παναγίου σου Πνεύματος; (2) μὴ...ἀποδόκημος γένωμαι; (3) εὕρω χάριν καὶ ἔλεος καὶ ἄφεσιν ἁμαρτιῶν. A final request to Christ finishes off the prayer: Ναὶ Δέσποτα Παντόκρατορ, Παντοδύναμε Κύριε, ἐπάκουσον τῆς δεήσεώς μου. Following the prayer is a closing benediction, in which the entire Trinity is mentioned for the first time in the Liturgy.

---

[829] Cf. Book IV of Plato's Republic

The Liturgy of Saint Gregory the Theologian

b. Figure I.II.4: The structure of the Introductory prayer

Part I: Function of the Liturgy	Part II: Purification of the Priest fo the Liturgy
1. Opening: General ὁ ἐπισκεψάμενος ἡμᾶς	*1. Opening:* Specific ἐπίβλεψον ἐπ' ἐμὲ
2. Dispensation granted to the general congregation by Christ. 　a. to stand about the Holy Altar 　b. to bring the Sacrifice	2. Requests of the priest for purification. 　a. washing away of errors 　b. purification of lips and heart 　c. that the mind be purified from wicked thoughts 　d. sufficiency for the coming Liturgy 　e. acceptance in the approach to the Altar 　e. acceptance of the Holy Gifts 　f. not to be cast away nor loathed because of unworthiness
3. Consequences of the Requests. 　a. help for **our** sins and those of the entire **people** 　b. repose for the departed 　c. support for whole people	3. Consequences of the Requests 　a. worthiness for protection and illumination 　b. not being worthless 　c. finding mercy and forgiveness
4. Final Request to be heard	
5. Closing Benediction	

2. Function:

As the Introductory Prayer, this text has the task to reflect the purpose of the entire text. The players in the text are introduced: Christ (line 1), the priest and people (line 2) and the Holy Spirit (line 10); the Holy Spirit is introduced, however, in a subordinate role,[830] always with the qualifier σου, linking the Holy Spirit inexorably with Christ, as the carrier out of Christ's Will. The third member of the Trinity, God the Father, is a non-entity in this prayer, only being mentioned in the closing benediction (line 22), and also carrying the qualifier σου; reflecting the subordinate role played by God the Father in this Liturgy. We see the focal point of this Liturgy already in the handling of the Trinity, the

---

[830] This is not to say, however, that the author of this Liturgy believed that Christ was a more important member of the Trinity than the Holy Spirit, or than the Father. We see in the use of the term homoousios to describe the relationship between Father and Son, that the author thought of them as equal members of the Trinity, and in the use of the term homoousios to describe the relationship between Son and Holy Spirit, that he thought of them too as equal. This is rather a literary devise to emphasize the divinity of the Son, to combat the Arians.

action takes place between the congregation (with its focal point in the priest) and Christ, whose Will is acted out by the Holy Spirit. This central aspect of Christ in the Liturgy can be attributed to a reaction against the theology of the Arians.

This prayer also serves as the "Prayer of Access" to the Altar; the celebrating clergy do not themselves have the authority to enter Altar area, or to celebrate the Liturgy. It is through this prayer that the priest receives from Christ the ability to offer Christ the bloodless sacrifice of the Liturgy.

1. (section I.1 lines 2-7) Ὁ ἐπισκεψάμενος ἡμᾶς ἐν ἐλέει καὶ οἰκτιρμοῖς, Δέσποτα, Κύριε Ἰησοῦ Χριστέ, καὶ χαρισάμενος ἡμῖν παρρησίαν, τοῖς ταπεινοῖς καὶ ἁμαρτωλοῖς καὶ ἀναξίοις δούλοις σου παραστῆναι τῷ ἁγίῳ σου θυσιαστηρίῳ, καὶ προσφέρειν σοι τὴν φοβερὰν καὶ ἀναίμακτον Θυσίαν, ὑπὲρ τῶν ἡμετέρων ἁμαρτημάτων, καὶ τῶν τοῦ λαοῦ σου ἀγνοημάτων, ἄνεσιν καὶ ἀνάπαυσιν τῶν προκοιμηθέντων πατέρων ἡμῶν καὶ ἀδελφῶν, καὶ στηριγμὸν παντὸς τοῦ λαοῦ σου.

The very first phrase of line one sets the tone for the entire Liturgy, ἐπισκεψάμενος, "overlooking," sets two stages for the action in the text, the first is the level of Divinity, the one doing the looking. This is the level where Christ is. The second level is ours, the earthly realm, onto which Christ looks. The word ἐπισκεψάμενος also serves to underscore the central role that Christ plays in the Liturgy: the one who oversees, the ἐπίσκοπος, the bishop, is the one who celebrates the Liturgy. This word, then, serves to set Christ up as the high priest of the church, who ist he actual celebrant of this Liturgy. Christ is also immediately set up as God, and is addressed with titles befitting his divinity: Δέσποτα and Κύριε. The stark division between Christ and ‚us,' the ταπεινοῖς καὶ ἁμαρτωλοῖς καὶ ἀναξίοις δούλοις is softened, however, by Christ not looking upon us in judgement; but with ἐλέει καὶ οἰκτιρμοῖς, with mercy and compassion. This mercy and compassion serve to bridge the gap between the two levels, bringing "us" and Christ closer together, making him more present in the Liturgy. It also serves to begin a journey within this prayer, the reader begins far removed from the divinity of Christ, but gradually grows closer to him as the prayer proceeds; this makes the prayer a microcosm of the Liturgy itself.[831] The requests made of Christ then also serve to bridge the gap between the heavenly and the earthly. The priest states that Christ gives the congregation the ability to παραστῆναι τῷ ἁγίῳ σου

---

[831] Unlike in Western theology, there is no one point in the Liturgy in which the Eucharistic elements are no longer bread and wind, but the Body and Blood of Christ; it is the journey through the Liturgy which hallows the elements, bringing the worshipper on a journey to heaven, this journey is made, in a shortened form, in this prayer as well.

Θυσιαστηρίῳ, this exact phrase is used only in this prayer,[832] however the verb: παραστῆναι is used of the angels in the Book of Job (1:6),[833] who stand about the Lord: Καὶ ὡς ἐγένετο ἡ ἡμέρα αὕτη, καὶ ἰδοὺ ἦλθον οἱ ἄγγελοι τοῦ θεοῦ παραστῆναι ἐνώπιον τοῦ κυρίου.[834] The congregants are to become like the angels in this passage, to come and stand about the Lord, that is, the holy altar. Antoher stock liturgical phrase προσφέρειν σοι τὴν φοβερὰν καὶ ἀναίμακτον Θυσίαν, found in the Liturgy of St. Basil the Great and in the *Libellus de consecratione eucharistica* of Marcus Eugenicus, is used to show that, in the carrying out of the Liturgy, one approaches Christ, breaking down the separation between the two levels, the earthly and the heavenly. The use of the term Θυσίαν rather than λατρείαν, the term used in the *Liturgia Praesanctificatorum,* points to an Old Testament element in this prayer, explored further in the commentary on the second prayer.

The divinity of Christ is further emphasized in the qualifying σου, which accompanies the two mentions of the Θυσιαστήριον, the Altar Table in lines 3 and 11, and the use of the word: λαός in lines 4 and 6. Such phrasing is not unusual, especially in the context of a Liturgy, however, the σου usually refers to God the Father, rather than to Christ as it does here. In the first prayer of the Greek Egyptian Liturgy of St. Basil, the priest reads: Σῶσον τὸν λαόν σου, ὃν περιεποήσω διὰ τοῦ αἵματος τοῦ Χριστοῦ σου[835] and εἰς τὸ ἅγιον καὶ ὑπερουράνιον, καὶ νοερόν σου Θυσιαστήριον.[836] By transferring the ownership of the people and the Altar from God the Father to Christ, the author establishes Christ as equal in power to God the Father.

2. (section I.1 lines 7-16) Ἐπίβλεψον ἐπ' ἐμὲ τὸν ἀχρεῖον δοῦλόν σου καὶ ἐξάλειψόν μου τὰ παραπτώματα, διὰ τὴν σὴν εὐσπλαγχνίαν. Καὶ καθάρισόν μου τὰ χείλη καὶ τὴν καρδίαν ἀπὸ παντὸς μολυσμοῦ σαρκός τε καὶ πνεύματος. Καὶ ἀπόστησον ἀπ' ἐμοῦ πάντα λογισμὸν αἰσχρόν τε καὶ ἀσύνετον. Καὶ ἱκάνωσόν με τῇ δυνάμει τοῦ ἁγίου σου Πνεύματος εἰς τὴν Λειτουργίαν ταύτην καὶ πρόσδεξαί με διὰ τὴν σὴν ἀγαθότητα, προσεγγίζοντα τῷ ἁγίῳ σου Θυσιαστηρίῳ. Καὶ εὐδόκησον Κύριε δεκτὰ γενέσθαι τὰ μέλλοντα προσαγόμενά σοι Δῶρα, διὰ τῶν ἡμετέρων χειρῶν, συγκαταβαίνων ταῖς ἐμαῖς ἀσθενείαις. Καὶ μὴ ἀπορρίψῃς με ἀπὸ τοῦ προσώπου σου, μὴ βδελύξῃς με τὴν ἐμὴν ἀναξιότητα, ἀλλ' ἐλέησόν με, ὁ Θεὸς κατὰ τὸ μέγα ἔλεος σου, καὶ κατὰ τὸ πλῆθος τῶν οἰκτιρμῶν σου ἐξάλειψον τὸ ἀνόμημά μου.

---

[832] And, of course, in the prayer found in the *Liturgia Praesanctificatorum* of Epiphanius of Cypurs.
[833] Among numerous other passages in Scripture and the Church Fathers where the verb is used, such as Gregory of Nazianzus, St. Basil the Great, Origen, Athanasius etc…
[834] Job 1:6: "One day the angels came to present themselves before the Lord." (NIV)
[835] Renaudot (1847). I. pg. 57 "Save Your people, which You have saved through the blood of Your Christ."
[836] Renaudot. (1847). I. pg. 61 "To Your divine, heavenly and spiritual altar."

The Commentary

This section, in which the priest begs Christ for the purification he requires to carry out the Divine Liturgy, further emphasizes the divinity of Christ. It is to Him, to whom the priest must turn. Like the first part of the prayer, this section begins with the establishment of two levels; this is done with a quotation from the Psalms: Ἐπίβλεψον ἐπ' ἐμὲ[837] since Christ looks favorably upon the priest, He must be in a position of authority over him, the distance between Christ and the priest is here not as pronounced, however, as it was in the first section of the prayer, since the priest is no longer one of the: ταπεινοῖς καὶ ἁμαρτωλοῖς καὶ ἀναξίοις δούλοις, but now only ἀχρεῖον. The pleas for purification, for the physical cleansing from the μολυσμοῦ σαρκός τε καὶ πνεύματος[838] and the mental cleansing from the: λογισμὸν αἰσχρόν τε καὶ ἀσύνετον[839] which only Christ can fulfill, through the power of the Holy Spirit, who carries out his will: καὶ ἱκάνωσόν με, τῇ δυνάμει τοῦ ἁγίου σου Πνεύματος, serve to continue pushing those participating in this Liturgy into the heavenly realm which is its ultimate goal. It is only through Christ that one is worthy enough to bring Christ the offering through which the blessings, mentioned in the first section of the prayer, are received. Christ becomes then the means and the end of this Liturgy.

The requests here are not requests, however, they are a list of imperatives: ἐπίβλεψον ... ἐξάλειψόν ... καθάρισόν ... ἀπόστησον ... ἱκάνωσόν ... πρόσδεξαί ... εὐδόκησον ... μὴ ἀπορρίψῃς ... μὴ βδελύξῃς ... ἐλέησόν ... ἐξάλειψον. This conversational style brings the priest even closer to Christ by emphasizing his presence among the congregants, we hear, so to speak, one half of a conversation, once again bridging the gap between divinity and the "useless servants."

These requests, these imperatives, culminate in a quotation from the quintessential text of penitence and purification, the fiftieth Psalm. This Psalm becomes extremely popular in liturgical services, especially in the Byzantine penitential services, such as Great Compline, and in the Paraklesis to the Theotokos; but also in more general services such as Orthros and even in the Divine Liturgy of St. John Chrysostom, in which the priest recites the fiftieth Psalm while preparing for the Great Entrance. The extremely penitential nature of this Psalm seems out of place for the joyous nature of a Liturgy, but penitence is an im-

---

[837] Cf. Psalm 85:16; as well as Psalm 118.
[838] This phrase is a common one, used numerous times, for example, by St. Basil the Great in his work: *De baptismo libri duo*; and in the *Stromata* of Athanasius of Alexandria, It also finds its place in liturgical language, not only in this Liturgy, but in the Liturgy of St. Basil as well. The phrase originates in the New Testament, in the Second Epistle of St. Paul to the Corinthians 7:2. Alhough the phrase was used often and in various types of theological contexts, the liturgcial (and that of baptism) context also emphasises the role of the Church as hospital, and as ort for the healing of both soul and body.
[839] Though the λογισμὸν αἰσχρόν are often described in theological writings; such as Cyril of Alexandria and John Chrysostom. The added ἀσύνετον seems to be unique to this Liturgy.

portant part of a "Prayer of Access," especially in the context of the Old Testament temple sacrifice, the context suggested by the Θυσίαν. Penitence was so important for the High Priest when he entered the Holy of Holies because of the dire consequences which he would earn if he entered unworthily.

3. (section I.1 lines 16-20): Ἵνα ἀκατακρίως προσελθὼν κατενώπιον τῆς δόξης σου, καταξιωθῶ τῆς σκέπης σου καὶ τῆς ἐλλάμψεως τοῦ παναγίου σου Πνεύματος, καὶ μὴ ὡς δοῦλος ἁμαρτίας ἀποδόκιμος γένωμαι, ἀλλ,' ὡς δοῦλος, ὅς εὕρω χάριν καὶ ἔλεος καὶ ἄφεσιν ἁμαρτιῶν, ἐν τῷ νῦν καὶ ἐν τῷ μέλλοντι αἰῶνι. Ναὶ Δέσποτα Παντόκρατορ, Παντοδύναμε Κύριε, ἐπάκουσον τῆς δεήσεώς μου.

Finally the reader moves closer (προσελθὼν), along with the officiating priest, to the goal of the prayer: the κατενώπιον τῆς δόξης σου, a phrase which is unique to this Liturgy, entrance into Christ's presence in the heavenly realm. The numerous requests are showing their effect and one is now ready to begin the Liturgy. This attained position must be maintained, however, if the Liturgy is to be carried out successfully, therefore three more requests are made of Christ, through which the priest hopes to remain on course into this heavenly level.

The first request once again reminds the reader that Christ is still, even once reaching this level, above the worshipper, he asks for Christ's protection as well as illumination by the Holy Spirit. The other two requests are similar: that the priest receive absolution from sins and offenses, and not become an ἀποδόκιμος δοῦλος. He has finally broken out of this and become a servant of God (i.e. Christ) rather than the servant of ἁμαρτιάς as he was at the beginning of the prayer, and prays that this remain so, and that he receve grace and mercy "in this, and in the coming age" from now on he is to be servant of Christ, and as this servant can carry out the sacrament of the Divine Liturgy.

The final sentence of this section, and of the prayer proper, is a final appeal to Christ to hear this prayer. This last appeal brings a note of desperation and a ray of hope into the prayer, this is a quotation from the Book of Ruth: 13:17: ἐπάκουσον τῆς δεήσεώς μου καὶ ἰλάσθητι τῷ κλήρῳ σου καὶ στρέψον τὸ πένθος ἡμῶν εἰς εὐωχίαν ἵνα ζῶντες ὑμνῶμέν σου τὸ ὄνομα κύριε καὶ μὴ ἀφανίσῃς στόμα αἰνούντων σοι.[840] Here Mardochai prays desperately for the salvation of his people. This same mix of hope and desperation should be felt by the congregants at the end of this prayer, the journey has begun, a journey with the goal of the Eucharist and ultimately Salvation, but which can only be completed with the help

---

[840] "Hear my prayer and have mercy on Your inheritance, turn our sorrow into joy, so that living we may hymn Your name, Lord, and may You not destroy the mouths of those praising You."

of God. All the requests for Christ aid and for purification are once more reiterated in this last prayer. Again the divinity of Christ is emphasized, by using several epithets: Δέσποτα Παντόκρατορ and Παντοδύναμε Κύριε.

4. (section I.1 lines 21-23) Σὺ γὰρ εἶ ὁ τὰ πάντα ἐνεργῶν ἐν πᾶσι, καὶ τὴν παρὰ σου πάντες ἐπιζητοῦμεν ἐπὶ πᾶσι βοήθειάν τε καὶ ἀντίληψιν. Ὅτι φιλάνθρωπος εἶ, καὶ δεδοξασμένος ὑπάρχεις Ἰησοῦ ὁ Θεὸς ἡμῶν, σὺν τῷ ἀνάρχῳ σου Πατρί, καὶ τῷ Ἁγίῳ Πνεύματι, νῦν καὶ ἀεί, καὶ...

Following the prayer proper is a closing benediction with the first reference to the Trinity in the work. Though the Structure of this benediction seems standard, there are several things that stand out.

Christ is referred to as the one who τὰ πάντα ἐνεργῶν ἐν πᾶσι. This is a slightly altered quotation of Paul's First Letter to the Corinthians 12: 6: καὶ διαιρέσεις ἐνεργημάτων εἰσιν, καὶ ὁ αὐτὸς Θεὸς ὁ ἐνεργῶν τὰ πάντα ἐν πᾶσιν.[841] This phrase becomes extremely important in anti-Arian polemical literature. Athanasius of Alexandria uses it in his works: *Contra Sabellianos* and *Dialogi duo contra Macedonianos*; by Basil the Great in *Adversus Eunomium*; by Marcellus the Theologian in *De Incarnatione et contra Arianos*. In the *Panarion* of Epiphanius of Cyprus, this quotation is used to establish the close tie between Christ and the Holy Spirit, especially in their effect on the congregation of Christians, and so to denounce Macedonianism. As an anti-Arian phrase, this fits in well with the function of the prayer as a whole, making it likely that the prayer is original to this, very anti-Arian, liturgy. This is also one of the phrases which show that the liturgy itself is directed against the Arians rather than the Monophysites, as suggested by Jungmann.

Following this, the author writes: καὶ τὴν παρὰ σου πάντες ἐπιζητοῦμεν ἐπὶ πᾶσι βοήθειάν τε καὶ ἀντίληψιν, this is a slight alteration on the usual stock phrases used in these benedictions such as: καὶ σοι τὴν δόξαν, τιμὴν καὶ προσκύνησιν ἀναπέμπομεν[842] or Ὅτι ηὐλόγηται καὶ ἡγίασται καὶ δεδόξασται τὸ πάντιμον καὶ μεγαλοπρεπὲς ἅγιον ὄνομα σου.[843] This continues the trend in this prayer, to establish Christ's divininty, and then personalize the relationship between Christ and the worshipper. Christ is the Creator, but one still goes to him for "aid and assistance in all things." It is this personalization, so prevalent in this prayer, which makes me doubtful of Jungmann's theory that this Liturgy was written in the sixth century, and must be interpreted in light of the Monophysite controversy

---

[841] Corinthians 12:6: "There are different kinds of working, but in all of them and in everyone it is the same God at work." (NIV)
[842] From the Εὐχὴ τοῦ ἁγίου Εὐαγγελίου
[843] From the Εὐχὴ μετὰ τὴν ἑτοιμασίαν τοῦ Ἁγίου Θυσιαστηρίου.

rather than the Arian controversy. Though the divinity of Christ, His majesty and power are all emphasized, but so is his connection to the average Christian, his mercy and his compassion on them.

Finally, at the very end of the prayer is the first mention in the Liturgy of the Trinity. This is possibly the most delicate moment in this first prayer. So far the author has been able to emphasize Christ's divinity by avoiding God the Father;[844] in order to keep Christ's divinity in focus, even while bringing up God the Father, the source of the Trinity, the author sets the other members of the Trinity in relation to Christ: σὺν τῷ ἀνάρχῳ σου Πατρί, καὶ τῷ Ἁγίῳ σου Πνεύματι.[845] He also expressly states Christ's divinity for the first time: Ἰησοῦ ὁ Θεὸς ἡμῶν, but, as usual, adds a qualifier that emphasizes his connection with humanity, he is not only God, he is the φιλάνθρωπος God.

I.III. The Prayer after the Preparation of the Holy Altar

Eusebe Renaudot remarks on the similarities between this prayer and a prayer in the Coptic Liturgy of St. Basil,[846] there are, however, no prayer in the Greek, Coptic or Syrian liturgical families that could serve this prayer as a template.[847] Since there is also no alternate for this prayer in the manuscripts, we can conclude that this prayer was written by the original author of this text. The numerous links between this and the previous prayer, which will be the focus of this investigation, show too that the previous prayer must have been adopted into the Liturgy (if not original to this Liturgy) at the time of its origin.

1. Structure

---

[844] while the Holy Spirit has been mentioned twice in the prayer, God the Father is not mentioned at all
[845] That the invocation of the Trinity in the *ekphonesis* is set up in this way is certainly not unique to this liturgy, (see for example the Dismissal prayers of the Memorial Service) and there is a long tradition of prayers addressed to Christ in the Liturgy, the *ekphoneseis* of which are usually set up in this manner. In an anti-Arian context such as this, however, this 'normal' *ekphonesis* receives new meaning. It is also interesting to note that certain prayers addressed to Christ do not have this Structure, for example the Prayer of Thanksgiving after Communion attributed to St. Basil has the following Trinitarian formula: σὺν τῷ Πατρὶ καὶ τῷ Ἁγίῳ Πνεύματι (with Your Father and the Holy Spirit).
[846] Renaudot (1847). I. pg. 280. Hammerschidt, however, downplays these similarities: "...was bezüglich der Stellung innerhalb der vorbereitenden Gebete stimmt, aber nicht in bezug auf den Text. Und gerade der Text ist ja das Entscheidende, wenn auch die Stellung innerhalb der Liturgie manchen Aufschluss geben kann. Die Oratio der kopt Baslit ... zeigt einen ähnlichen Aufbau, ist aber doch inhaltlich und in der Wortwahl ... sehr verschieden" Hammerschmidt (1957). pg. 83 "This is true in respect to its place in the prayers of preparation, but not in respect to the text itself. It is the text that is important, even if its place in the liturgy can lead to various conclusions. The prayer of the Coptic Liturgy of St. Basil has a similar structure, but is different in content and style."
[847] Hammerschmidt (1957). pg. 83

The Commentary

This second prayer is divided into three, functionally different sections. The first part of the prayer begins with the direct address of Christ: Δέσποτα Κύριε Ἰησοῦ Χριστὲ ὁ Θεὸς ἡμῶν this opens a description of how Christ has worked within the community: through his παρουσία and the ἐλλάμψεως τοῦ παναγίου...Πνεύματος and he has καταξιώσας ἡμᾶς "deemed us worthy," of two different aspects of the liturgical rite: 1. to stand about the Holy Altar; and 2. to minister the ἀχράντοις Μυστηρίοις τῆς καινῆς σου διαθήκης. Between the descriptions of how Christ functions in the community and what he brings to pass, the author underlines who is being affected by Christ: ἡμᾶς, τοὺς ταπεινοὺς καὶ ἁμαρτώλους καὶ ἀναξίους δούλοις.

The second opening of the prayer is a second address of Christ: Αὐτὸς ζωοποιὲ, καὶ τῶν ἀγαθῶν χορηγὲ. This section of the prayer consists of two sets of requests, based on the verbs: ποίησον and ἀξίωσον. Following the requests themselves, the author discusses how these requests, if granted, will affect the worshippers.

The third section opened by a third address of Christ: Ἀγαθε, Εὐέργετα, Βασιλεῦ τῶν αἰώνων, καὶ τῆς κτίσεως ἁπάσης Δημιουργὲ. Here we see another two sets of requests, based around the verbs: Μνήσθητι and διαφύλαξον.

Finally, closing the prayer is the Trinitarian benediction. The normal, expected, Trinitarian formula: Father, Son and Holy Spirit, There is no direct mention of the Son, but a row of descriptive verbs: ηὐλόγηται, καὶ ἡγίασται, καὶ δεδόξασται which qualify the name of Christ.

The structure of this prayer can also be seen in the following Table:

The Liturgy of Saint Gregory the Theologian

Table I.III.1 The Structure of the Prayer after the Preparation of the Holy Altar.[848]

Part I	Part II	Part III
1. Opening: Δέσποτα Κύριε Ἰησοῦ Χριστὲ ὁ Θεὸς ἡμῶν	1. Second Opening: Αὐτὸς ζωοποιὲ, καὶ τῶν ἀγαθῶν χορηγὲ.	1. Third Opening: Ἀγαθὲ Εὐέργετα Βασιλεῦ τῶν αἰώνων, καὶ τῆς κτίσεως ἁπάσης Δημιουργέ
2. Means by which Christ effects the congregation: διὰ τῆς σωτηριώδους παρουσίας σου, καὶ τῆς ἐλλάμψεως τοῦ παναγίου σου Πνεύματος	2. First Request: ποίησον μεθ' ἡμῶν σημεῖον εἰς ἀγαθόν.	2. First Reqest: Μνήσθητι...τῶν προσενεγκάντων καὶ δι' ὧν προσήγαγον.
3. Who is being effected: ἡμᾶς... τοὺς ταπεινοὺς καὶ ἁμαρτωλοὺς καὶ ἀναξίους δούλους σου	3. Second Request: ἀξίωσον ἡμᾶς a. ἐν καθαρῷ συνειδότι λατρεῦσαί σοι πάσας τὰς ἡμέρας τῆς ζωῆς ἡμῶν b. καὶ ἐν ἁγιασμῷ ταύτην τὴν θείαν προσενέγκειν σοι λειτουργίαν	3. Second Request: καὶ ἡμᾶς ἀκατακρίτους διαφύλαξον ἐν τῇ ἱερουργίᾳ τῶν θείων σου μυστηρίων.
4.. Effect of Christ on the Congregation: ὁ...καταξιώσας ἡμᾶς... παραστῆναι τῷ ἁγίῳ σου Θυσιαστηρίῳ καὶ προσφέρειν καὶ λειτουργεῖν τοῖς ἀχράντοις Μυστηρίοις τῆς καινῆς σου διαθήκης	4. Effect of the Requests: εἰς ἄφεσιν ἁμαρτῶν καὶ εἰς ἀπόλαυσιν τῆς μελλούσης μακαριότητος.	
4. Closing Benediction: a. Christ: Ὅτι ηὐλόγηται, καὶ ἡγίασται, καὶ δεδόξασται, το πάντιμον καὶ μεγαλοπρεπὲς ἅγιον ὄνομά σου. b. Remainder of the Trinity: μετὰ τοῦ Πατρὸς καὶ τοῦ ἁγίου Πνεύματος		

---

[848] Cf. also Hammerschmidt (1957). pg. 83

The Commentary

2. Function:[849]

1. (section I.2 lines 2-5): Δέσποτα Κύριε Ἰησοῦ Χριστὲ ὁ Θεὸς ἡμῶν· ὁ, διὰ τῆς σωτηριώδους παρουσίας σου, καὶ τῆς ἐλλάμψεως τοῦ παναγίου Πνεύματος, καταξιώσας ἡμᾶς· τοὺς ταπεινοὺς καὶ ἁμαρτωλοὺς καὶ ἀναξίους δούλους σου, παραστῆναι τῷ ἁγίῳ σου θυσιαστηρίῳ καὶ προσφέρειν καὶ λειτουργεῖν τοῖς ἀχράντοις Μυστηρίοις τῆς καινῆς σου διαθήκης.

This prayer is introduced by an initial direct address of Christ, this type of introduction becomes standard in the prayers of the pre-anaphora (with the exception of the "Prayer of the Veil"). The vocatives used here immediately connect the second prayer back to the one preceeding it. The phrase centers around the name of Christ Ἰησοῦ Χριστέ, the focus of the Liturgy, which becomes the focus of this introductory phrase. The preceeding epithets: Δέσποτα and Κύριε, take up the phrasing of the direct address which begins the first prayer, while the following epithen: ὁ θεὸς ἡμῶν takes up the phrasing from the closing. This intratextual link between these two prayers sets up several others which connect the two prayers closely with one another, these can be seen in the following table.

Table I.III.2: The Intratextual links between Prayer I and Prayer II

Prayer I	Prayer II
1. (line 22): Δέσποτα Κύριε Ἰησοῦ Χριστέ 2. (line 48): Ἰησοῦ ὁ Θεὸς ἡμῶν	1. (line 51): Δέσποτα Κύριε Ἰησοῦ Χριστὲ ὁ Θεὸς ἡμῶν
3. (line 40): Ἵνα ἀκατακρίτως προσελθὼν κατενώπιον τῆς δόξης σου, καταξιωθῶ τῆς σκέπης σου, καὶ τῆς ἐλλάμψεως τοῦ παναγίου σου Πνεύματος	2. (lines 51-52): διὰ τῆς σωτηριώδους παρουσίας σου, καὶ τῆς ἐλλάμψεως τοῦ παναγίου σου Πνεύματος, καταξιώσας
4. (lines 23-25): ἡμᾶς... τοῖς ταπεινοῖς καὶ ἁμαρτωλοῖς καὶ ἀναξίοις δούλοις σου, παραστῆναι τῷ ἁγίῳ σου Θυσιαστηρίῳ, καὶ προσφέρειν σοι τὴν φοβερὰν καὶ ἀναίμακτον Θυσίαν, ὑπὲρ τῶν ἡμετέρων ἁμαρτημάτων	3. (lines 53-55): ἡμᾶς, τοὺς ταπεινοὺς καὶ ἁμαρτώλους καὶ ἀναξίους δούλους σου, παραστῆναι τῷ ἁγίῳ σου Θυσιαστηρίῳ, καὶ προσφέρειν καὶ λειτουργεῖν τοῖς ἀχράντοις Μυστηρίοις τῆς καινῆς σου διαθήκης.

---

[849] Between the first prayer, which functions as a "Prayer of Access" and the second, the Prayer after the Preparation of the Holy Altar, there must be a series of rites through which the clergy prepare the Altar for the coming ceremony. Unfortunately, none of the manuscripts give any information as to what these rites may have entailed. It is safe to assume, that by the fourteenth century, when these manuscripts were written, the rites had conformed (at least in Egypt) to those of the other Coptic liturgies (i.e. the liturgies of Sts. Basil and Mark).

As we see in this table, the majority of the first section of the prayer is linked to the preceeding one. This prayer can, then, be interpreted as a continuation, or a fulfillment of the first prayer.

The first two prayers of the Liturgy act, then, as unit which surrounds the "preparation of the Altar." Through first prayer, the "Prayer of Access," the officiating priests receive permission to approach the Altar. This second section functions as a conclusion to the "'Prayer of Access," readying the participants to launch into the remainder of the Liturgy. This difference is shown in the moods used by the two prayers. In the second prayer, the author uses the verb: καταξιώσας in line 2; this is opposed to the verb: καταξιωθῶ in line 18 of the first prayer. In the second prayer the journey is complete, one is present in the *parousia* of Christ and receives the enlightenment of the Holy Spirit, one is deemed worthy to "stand about the Holy Altar, and to offer and minister the spotless Mysteries of Your New Covenant," the goals expressed, but not fulfilled, in the καταξιωθῶ of the first prayer. This fulfilled journey transforms the "useless, sinfull and unworthy servants" from lines 2-3 of the first prayer into the ministering servants of Christ.

Interesting too in this context is the choice of terminology when discussing the Eucharist. In the first prayer, the Eucharist is termed the φοβερὰν καὶ ἀναίμακτον Θυσίαν while, in the second prayer, the term used is the ἀχράντοις Μυστηρίοις τῆς καινῆς σου διαθήκης. Both of these terms are widely used in describing the Eucharist. The use of the term Θυσία in the first prayer, does call to mind the Old Testament Temple worship. In the second prayer, though, the connection between the Eucharist and the New Testament is not only alluded to, but explicitly stated as the: ἀχράντοις Μυστηρίοις τῆς καινῆς σου διαθήκης. In this double take on the Eucharist we see another way in which these prayers play on one another: we have seen how the journey to the *parousia*, the presence of Christ, begun in the first prayer continues and is fulfilled in the second, with this variation in Eucharistic terms we see another journey undertaken by the congregation, from the sinful life outside the Liturgy to the perfected state in which the Liturgy can be undertaken; exemplified as the journey from the Old to the New Testaments, from the Fall of Adam to the birth of Christ and the beginning of His salvific *parousia*.

The functional elements seen here are similar to those seen in the first prayer (as the majority of this section of the second prayer consists of quotations from the first prayer this is hardly surprising). 1. The direct address of Christ as Δέσποτα, Κύριε, and Θέος. 2. The use of the qualifier σου when discussing the Altar: σου Θυσιαστηρίῳ, and the New Testament: τῆς καινῆς σου διαθήκης, by which Christ is declared as the God of the New Testament, as He will be declared the God of the Old Testament. 3. That "we:" ἡμᾶς, who are ταπεινοὺς καὶ ἁμαρτώλους καὶ ἀναξίους δούλους are perfected, or, at least, made worthy, of this Liturgy through the *parousia* of Christ.

2. (section I.2 lines 6-9) Ἀυτὸς ζωοποιὲ, καὶ τῶν ἀγαθῶν χορηγὲ,[850] ποίησον μεθ' ἡμῶν σημεῖον εἰς ἀγαθόν καὶ ἀξίωσον ἡμᾶς ἐν καθαρῷ συνειδότι λατρεῦσαί σοι πάσας τὰς ἡμέρας τῆς ζωῆς ἡμῶν, καὶ ἐν ἁγιασμῷ ταύτην τὴν θείαν προσενέγκειν σοι λειτουργίαν, εἰς ἄφεσιν ἁμαρτιῶν, καὶ εἰς ἀπόλαυσιν τῆς μελλούσης μακαριότητος.

Opening this section with a second group of vocatives creates a renewed opening to this prayer, allowing the focus tochange. While the first section of this prayer serves as a completion of the first prayer; this second section, however, presents a list of requests 1. that Christ make himself a sign for the good, 2. that He deem "us" worthy to worship Him in purity all the days of ‚our' lives; and 3. that He deem "us" worthy to perform this Liturgy in holiness. The concern here is no longer the attainment of the higher level which was the goal of the journey in the first prayer and the first section of this second prayer, rather the focus has become retaining this level, and not only in the context of the Liturgy, but throughout the life of the worshippers.

The author uses the first request to stress the reality of the *parousia* of Christ among the congregants. Up to this point in the text the contact between the congregants and Christ has been qualified by the presence of the Holy Spirit, who works the will of Christ among the congregation. This go-between is no longer necessary, and Christ can work His will Himself.

The second request projects the effect of the Liturgy into the whole life of the worshipper, the goal is not to be made worthy for just this service, but to retain this holiness through the rest of one's life. The worthiness attained through the upward journey is not only meant for the here and now, but must continue until one has reached εἰς ἀπόλαυσιν τῆς μελλούσης μακαριότητος.

In the third request the author returns to the 'here and now' of the Liturgy, and asks to be able to offer this Liturgy in holiness. This is another phrase that shows that the journey is completed, the servants that were unworthy, sinful, etc.. are now able to take part in the Liturgy in "holiness," a drastic change in position for these servants, undergone through the *parousia* of Christ and the "sign for the good" requested above. It is in this holiness, acheived for and in this Liturgy, that the congregation receives the forgiveness of sins and the ἀπόλαυσιν τῆς μελλούσης μακαριότητος promised as consequences of these requests.

---

[850] A similar epithet of Christ is found in the Apostolic Constitutions. Cf. Bouyer (1989). pg. 90.

The Liturgy of Saint Gregory the Theologian

3. (section I.2 lines 9-12) Μνήσθητι Ἀγαθὲ Εὐέργετα Βασιλεῦ τῶν αἰώνων, καὶ τῆς κτίσεως ἁπάσης Δημιουργὲ, τῶν προσενεγκάντων, καὶ δι' ὧν προσήγαον. Καὶ ἡμᾶς ἀκατακρίτους διαξύλαξον ἐν τῇ ἱερουργίᾳ τῶν θεῖον σου μυστηρίων.

Once again a string of vocatives reopens the prayer, again with a slightly different purpose. The first request is an extremely loaded one, and one that looks forward to the Anaphora (more specifically to the remebrances in the Anaphora) Μνήσθητι is a word used almost exclusively (this is the only instance outside of the Anaphora that it is used, though he related μνημόνευσον is found in the "Prayer of the Holy Gospel.") in the context of those remembrances, in which the various members of the Church and the whole world are prayed for. Why, then, is this type of prayer used so far removed from its proper position in the Anaphora? The answer may lie in the string of vocatives that follow the opening of the request: Ἀγαθὲ: Good One, Εὐέργετα: Benefactor, Βασιλεῦ τῶν αἰώνων: King of the Ages, and τῆς κτίσεως ἁπάσης Δημιουργὲ: Source of all Creation. These vocatives, all addressed to Christ, serve to underscore His divinity. Two: Βασιλεῦ and Δημιουργὲ serve to underscore the majesty of His divinity, while two: Ἀγαθὲ[851] and Εὐέργετα serve to underscore His love for man. The clear declaration of divinity in this series of epithets stands in stark contrast to the simple: Μνήσθητι Κύριε which introduces each of the remembrences in the Anaphora. That this Μνήσθητι Κύριε still refers to Christ can be forgotten in the lengthy series of commemorations. This first Μνήσθητι, with its strongly worded vocatives, may, then, be meant to be remembered during the similar constructions of the commemorations, and serve to bring the anti Arian purpose of this Liturgy into the Anaphora as well.

The requests in this section seem almost out of place. In the last section they were meant to keep the congregation in the *parousia* of Christ, which they had finally reached. Here, though the prayer is for remembrance and protection (διαξφύλαξον ἐν τῇ ἱερουργίᾳ τῶν θεῖον σου Μυστηρίων). These requests serve to remind those participating in the Liturgy that the Eucharist is a dangerous thing, when not participated in worthily (cf. I Corinthians 11:27); it is then not enough to have arrived at the parousia of Christ, one must then participate in it in "holiness" and "uncondemned."

4. (section I.2 lines 13-14) Ὅτι ηὐλόγηται, καὶ ἡγίασται, καὶ δεδόξασται, τὸ πάντιμον καὶ μεγαλοπρεπὲς ἅγιον ὄνομά σου, μετὰ τοῦ Πατρὸς, καὶ τοῦ ἁγίου Πνεύματος. Νῦν, καὶ.

Interesting in this Benediction is that the other members of the Trinity are here mentioned without a direct link or subordination to Christ. Such subordination as is usual in the

---

[851] Cf. Mark 10:18 for Good in reference to God.

Liturgy so far seems almost to be unecceseary here however, the closing Benediction revolves around the πάντιμον καὶ μεγαλοπρεπὲς ἅγιον ὄνομά of Christ, which alone is worthy of blessing, hallowing and glorification. The rest of the members of the Trinity seem to be added as an afterthought. In this way the author still emphasizes Christ over the other members of the Trinity, even without the direct link.

I.IV. The Prayer of the Holy Gospel

Before discussing the structure of this prayer, it should be noted that the location of this prayer within the liturgy is unique. In Syrian liturgies, as well as in the offshoot branch of this liturgy, the Cappadocian Liturgy, the prayer of the Gospel comes before the 'Prayer of Access' to the Altar. In the (Byzantine) Liturgy of St. Basil, one of our few extant Cappadocian Liturgies, the 'Prayer of Access' is seen in the: ΕΥΧΗ ΤΩΝ ΠΙΣΤΩΝ,[852] which the priest recites after the Gospel reading, before the Entrance with the Gifts. Of similar Structure is the Liturgy of St. John Chrysostom. Here the 'Prayer of Access', the ΕΥΧΗ ΤΩΝ ΠΙΣΤΩΝ is also found after the reading of the Holy Gospel. In the Liturgy of St. Gregory the Theologian, however, the expected placement of the Prayer of the Holy Gospel is not fulfilled, and it occurs after the "Prayer of Access." This reversal of the prayers seems to occur in analogy to the other Egyptian Liturgies. We see this same Structure in the (Greek Egyptian) Liturgy of St. Mark; in which the 'Prayer of Access' is the first prayer recited by the priest.[853] The prayer[854] of the Gospel is placed much later in the Liturgy, before rituals surrounding the kiss of peace.

Such an alteration of the Liturgy of St. Gregory throws new light onto its use in Egypt. In the modern Coptic Church only the Anaphora is in use, and is spliced into the larger body of the standard Coptic Liturgy, the Manuscript of the Kacmarcik Codex as well as the Wadi n' Natrun fragments seem to conform to this type of usage, as they contain only the Anaphora of the Liturgy of St. Gregory (along with the Anaphora of St. Basil). The anomaly is the Paris Codex 325, which includes the entire text of the Liturgy. If this text was altered to conform to Egyptian practices, then we must agree with the explanation of Gerhards and White, who suggest that the Liturgy of St. Gregory was celebrated in Greek on special occasions in the monasteries, but we must go even further than this, the

---

[852] The commonalities between this prayer and the 'Prayer of Access' in the Liturgy of St. Gregory were discussed in the first chapter of the commentary, see pp. 168.
[853] Renaudot (1847). I. pp. 1-2. We see from the use of similar language and themes as are used in the Prayers of Access in the other Liturgies, that this is a prayer of the same type.
[854] Or, rather, the rituals leading up to the reading of the Gospel: Cf. Renaudot (1847). I. pg. 125.

Liturgy was celebrated in Greek, and in full (not only the Anaphora) up until at least the fourteenth century.

If the Structure of our Liturgy has been altered to conform to the Egyptian standard, then we must investigate another question: was the prayer of the Gospel merely moved from its position before the "Prayer of Access," or was it removed, and replaced by another prayer, the prayer which is now in this liturgy? The introduction of a new prayer is certainly a possibility, it was a common practice to adopt and adapt other prayers. The problem is, however, that there does not seem to be any indication that there ever was an alternate Prayer of the Gospel. There are several prayers in the liturgy, which seem to be secondarily added, but all these are already noted as alternate prayers in the manuscript.[855] In the (Byzantine) Liturgy of St. Basil, however, we find a prayer, which may prove to be the replaced original prayer:

> Ἔλλαμψον ἐν ταῖς καρδίαις ἡμῶν φιλάνθρωπε Δέσποτα,
> τὸ τῆς σῆς θεογνωσίας ἀκήρατον φῶς, καὶ τοὺς τῆς διανοίας
> ἡμῶν ὀφθαλμοὺς διάνοιξον εἰς τὴν τῶν εὐαγγελικῶν σου κηρυγ-
> μάτων κατανόησιν. Ἔνθες ἡμῖν καὶ τὸν τῶν μακαρίων σου ἐν-
> τολῶν φόβον, ἵνα, τὰς σαρκικὰς ἐπιθυμίας πάσας καταπατήσαν-
> τες, πνευματικὴν πολιτείαν μετέλθωμεν, πάντα τὰ πρὸς εὐαρέ-
> στησιν τὴν σὴν καὶ φρονοῦντες καὶ πράττοντες. Σὺ γὰρ εἶ ὁ φω-
> τισμὸς τῶν ψυχῶν καὶ τῶν σωμάτων ἡμῶν, Χριστὲ ὁ Θεός, καὶ
> σοὶ τὴν δόξαν ἀναπέμπομεν σὺν τῷ ἀνάρχῳ σου Πατρὶ καὶ τῷ
> παναγίῳ καὶ ἀγαθῷ, καὶ ζωοποιῷ σου Πνεύματι, νῦν καὶ ἀεὶ καὶ
> εἰς τοὺς αἰῶνας τῶν αἰώνων. Ἀμήν.[856]

It is not unusual to see prayers addressed to Christ in liturgical texts, and the Prayer of the Holy Gospel seems one of the most logical prayers within the Liturgy to address to

---

[855] Another problem presents itself, when did this reworking of the Liturgy take place? A certain date *ante quem* is the fourteenth century and the publication of the Paris Manuscript. A certain date *post quem* does not exist, however, and we must content ourselves with assuming the reworking of the Greek text to have been made around the same time as the adoption of the Liturgy in Egypt and the translation of the text into Coptic.

[856] *Ieratikon* (1982). pg. 164 and Trempelis (1982). pg. 53 "Shine in our hearts, Master, the lover of man, the unsullied light of Your divine knowledge, and open the eyes of our understanding for the contemplation of the proclaiming of Your Gospel. Place within us also fear of Your blessed commandments, so that, conquering every desire of the flesh we may become spiritual citizens, thinking and doing all the things for Your pleasure. For You are the enlightener of our souls and bodies, Christ God, and to You we send up glory, with Your beginningless Father and Your all-holy, good and lifegiving Spirrit, now and ever and to the ages of ages. Amen."

Christ. There are, however, few prayers in the (Byzantine) Liturgy of St. Basil directed to Christ. The majority of these prayers, for example: the Prayer before the Great Entrance and the Prayer before the distribution of Holy Communion, are taken directly from the Liturgy of St. Gregory. It would be a very great coincidence that another prayer addressed to Christ is from a different source than the only other prayers written in this style in the entire text.

Since it is likely, then, that the prayer from the Liturgy of St. Basil is the original prayer from the Liturgy of St. Gregory, we will analyze both prayers.

1. Structure of the original prayer

This prayer is divided into three sections. The first section is built around three imperatives, two of which deal with opening the perception of the worshipper to the Gospel: ἔλλαμψον and διάνοιξον. Each of these imperatives opens a way in which Christ should prepare the worshipper to hear the Gospel, through ἔλλαμψον a request is made for the enlightenment of the heart of the worshipper with the τὸ τῆς σῆς θεογνωσίας ἀκήρατον φῶς. After the heart, it is the "eyes of our mind," which must be prepared for the reading of the Gospel, with the imperative: διάνοιξον. The third imperative: ἔνθες, requests that Christ ‚instill' ἡμῖν καὶ τὸν τῶν μακαρίων σου ἐντολῶν φόβον, this is only possible once the worshipper has been prepared and enlightened by the first two imperatives.

The second section of this prayer is subordinate to the first section, introduced by the subordinating conjunction ἵνα, and consists of the result for the worshipper that occur through the enlightenment with the θεογνωσίας and the opening of the "eyes of the mind" and through the instilling of the φόβον, which are given to the worshipper in the first section. This result is the ability to: πνευματικὴν πολιτείαν μετέλθωμεν. Along with this main result are two others, subordinated to the main result by being expressed as participles: 1. τὰς σαρκικὰς ἐπιθυμίας πάσας καταπατήσαντες and 2. πάντα τὰ πρὸς εὐαρέστησιν τὴν σὴν καὶ φρονοῦντες καὶ πράττοντες.

The final section is opened by a phrase that refers back to the beginning of the prayer: Σὺ γὰρ εἶ ὁ φωτισμὸς τῶν ψυχῶν καὶ τῶν σωμάτων ἡμῶν. Christ becomes the "enlightener" by fulfilling the requests made in the first section. This is followed by the rest of the *Ekphonesis* and the Trinitarian formula. The structure of this prayer is also illustrated in the following table.

Figure I.IV.1: the Sturcture of the Original Prayer of the Holy Gospel.

The Original Prayer of the Holy Gospel
Part I Series of Imperatives 1. First request: ἔλλαμψον ἐν ταῖς καρδίαις ἡμῶν, φιλάνθρωπε Δέσποτα, τὸ τῆς σῆς θεογνωσίας ἀκήρατον φῶς 2. Second request: καὶ τοὺς τῆς διανοίας ἡμῶν διάνοιξον ὀφθαλμοὺς εἰς τὴν τῶν εὐαγγελικῶν σου κηρυγμάτων κατανόησον. 3. Third request, can only occur after the worshipper is prepared by the fulfillment of the first two requests: ἔνθες ἡμῖν καὶ τὸν τῶν μακαρίων σου ἐντολῶν φόβον

Part II (subordinate to Part I, introduced by ἵνα)
Results of the Imperatives
  1. Main result: ἵνα...πνευματικὴν πολιτείαν μετέλθωμεν
  2. First secondary result (expressed as a participle): τὰς σαρκικὰς ἐπιθυμίας πάσας καταπατήσαντες
  3. Second secondary result (expressed as a participle): πάντα τὰ πρὸς εὐαρέστησιν τὴν σὴν καὶ φρονοῦντες καὶ πράττοντες.

Part III
Ekphonesis
  1. Reference back to the beginning of the Prayer: σὺ γὰρ εἶ ὁ φωτισμὸς τῶν ψυχῶν καὶ τῶν σωμάτων ἡμῶν, Χριστὲ ὁ Θεός
  2. Offering of glory to Christ: καὶ σοὶ τὴν δόξαν ἀναπέμπομεν
  3. Trinitarian Formula: σὺν τῷ ἀνάρχῳ σου Πατρὶ καὶ τῷ παναγίῳ καὶ ἀγαθῷ καὶ ζωοποιῷ σου Πνεύματι
  4. Closing: νῦν καὶ ἀεὶ καὶ εἰς τοὺς αἰῶνας τῶν αἰώνων. Ἀμήν.

II. The Secondary Prayer of the Holy Gospel

If we are to establish this prayer as secondary, then we must establish, or at least discuss, a paradigm by which it was adopted into the Liturgy. It is not unusual for prayers to be taken from other sources into Liturgies. This same prayer is found in the Coptic Liturgy of St. Mark.[857] That this is not the original prayer and was adopted into the Liturgy of St.

---

[857] Hammond and Brightman (1896). pg. 155. Hammerschmidt also mentions that this prayer is found in the Egyptian Liturgy of St. Basil as well. Hammerschmidt (1957). pg. 84; Cf. also Day (1972). pg. 84.

The Commentary

Gregory late, is shown by the use of the term *homoousios* in the context of the Holy Spirit in the *ekphonesis*. We have discussed that the Syrian and Egyptian Liturgies often use this term in relation to the Holy Spirit in the *ekphonesis*, and that this is not usually done in this liturgy. The author seems to use the term homoousios only within the body of the prayer itself as part of his anti-Arian agenda. We see an example of this in the first prayer of this liturgy, which, as we discussed above, may have been taken from the Greek Liturgy of St. James. In the ‚original' St. James version the term homoousios is used in the *ekphonesis*, but is abandoned in the Liturgy of St. Gregory. It is possible that the clerics who adapted the Liturgy of St. Gregory felt that the lengthy and complicated Prayer of the Gospel was out of place in the context of an Egyptian Liturgy and replaced it with this shorter, simpler prayer. This is possible because the Prayer of the Gospel in the Egyptian Liturgy is one of the prayers in the pre-Anaphora addressed to Christ, which means that it could be adopted into the Liturgy of St. Gregory easily, since it fits in with the theme of the rest of the Liturgy.

This prayer begins with a vocative: Δέσποτα Κύριε Ἰησοῦ Χριστὲ ὁ Θεὸς ἡμῶν. The most important section of this prayer is composed around a quotation from the Gospel of Scripture:[858] ὅτι πολλοὶ προφῆται καὶ δίκαιοι ἐπεθύμησαν ἰδεῖν, ἃ βλέπετε καὶ οὐκ εἶδον, καὶ ἀκοῦσαι ἃ ἀκούετε, καὶ οὐκ ἤκουσαν. Ὑμῶν γὰρ μακάριοι οἱ ὀφθαλμοὶ ὅτι βλέπουσι· καὶ τὰ ὦτα ὑμῶν ὅτι ἀκούει. The quotation, and its purpose in preparing the listeners for the proclamation of the Holy Gospel is rounded out by the request: καταξιωθείημεν...ἀκοῦσαι...ποιῆσαι τὰ ἅγια σου Εὐαγγέλια, ταῖς λιταῖς τῶν ἱερῶν σου.

Following this first section is one built around three imperatives: Μνημόνευσον, ἀνάπαυσον and ἔρρωσον. This is followed by the final section, the *ekphonesis*; this begins with a series of descriptions of Christ, He is the: ζωή, σωτηρία, ἐλπὶς, ἴασις and ἀνάστασις. Following this description is the usual καὶ σοι τὴν δόξαν τιμήν καὶ προσκύνησιν ἀναπέμπομεν followed by the invocation of the Holy Trinity. Interesting to note, though, is that the two prayers have very similar *ekphoneseis*:

Figure I.IV.2: the Ekphonesis of the Prayer of the Gospel.

Ekphonesis in the Liturgy of St. Gregory	**Ekphonesis in the Liturgy of St. Basil**
1.*Description of Christ*: Σὺ γὰρ εἶ ζωὴ ἡμῶν πάντων, καὶ σωτηρία ἡμῶν πάντων, καὶ ἐλπὶς ἡμῶν πάντων, καὶ ἴασις ἡμῶν πάντων, καὶ ἀνάστασις	1. *Description of Christ*: Σὺ γὰρ εἶ ὁ φωτισμὸς τῶν ψυχῶν καὶ τῶν σωμάτων ἡμῶν, Χριστὲ ὁ Θεός

---

[858] 1 Peter 1:10

οἰκεία πάντων ἡμῶν.	
2. Offering: Καὶ σοὶ τὴν δόξαν τιμὴν καὶ προσκύνησιν ἀναπέμπομεν	2. Offering: καὶ σοὶ τὴν δόξαν ἀναπέμπομεν
3. The Father: σὺν τῷ παντοκράτορί σου καὶ παντεπόπτῃ τέκοντι	3. The Father: σὺν τῷ ἀνάρχῳ σου Πατρὶ
4. The Holy Spirit: καὶ τῷ παναγίῳ καὶ ζωαρχικῷ καὶ ὁμοουσίῳ σου Πνεύματι νῦν καὶ ἀεί, καὶ.	4. The Holy Spirit: καὶ τῷ παναγίῳ καὶ ἀγαθῷ, καὶ ζωοποιῷ σου Πνεύματι, νῦν καὶ ἀεὶ καὶ εἰς τοὺς αἰῶνας τῶν αἰώνων. Ἀμήν.

The Structure of this secondary prayer is seen in the following Table:

Figure I.IV.3: the Sturcture of the Secondary Prayer of the Holy Gospel.[859]

The Secondary Prayer of the Holy Gospel

1. The Main Idea of the Prayer.
   a. Opening: Δέσποτα Κύριε Ἰησοῦ Χριστὲ ὁ Θεὸς ἡμῶν· ὁ τοῖς ἁγίοις σου μαθηταῖς καὶ ἱεροῖς σου ἀποστόλοις εἰπών
   b. Quotation from Matthew: ὅτι πολλοὶ προφῆται καὶ δίκαιοι ἐπεθύμησαν ἰδεῖν, ἃ βλέπετε καὶ οὐκ εἶδον, καὶ ἀκοῦσαι ἃ ἀκούετε καὶ οὐκ ἤκουσαν. Ὑμῶν γὰρ μακάριοι οἱ ὀφθαλμοὶ ὅτι βλέπουσι· καὶ τὰ ὦτα ὑμῶν, ὅτι ἀκούει.
   c. First request: Καὶ καταξιωθείημεν ἄρτι τοῦ ἀκοῦσαι καὶ ποιῆσαι τὰ ἅγιά σου Εὐαγγέλια, ταῖς λιταῖς τῶν ἱερῶν σου.

2. Series of Requests.
   a. Remembrance of others: Μνημόνευσον οὖν Δέσποτα καὶ νῦν, πάντων τῶν ἐντειλαμένων ἡμῖν τοῖς ἀναξίοις τοῦ μνημονεύειν αὐτῶν, εἰς τὰς δεήσεις ἡμετέρας καὶ τὰς αἰτήσεις, ἃς, ἀναβιβάζομέν σοι Κύριε ὁ Θεὸς ἡμῶν.
   b. For the Deceased: Τοὺς προτετελευτηκότας ἀνάπαυσον αὐτούς
   c. For the Sich: τοὺς κάμνοντας, ἔρρωσον αὐτούς.

---

[859] Section I.3 lines 1-15.

> 3. *Ekphonesis*
>   a. *Description of Christ*: Σὺ γὰρ εἶ ζωὴ ἡμῶν πάντων, καὶ σωτηρία ἡμῶν πάντων, καὶ ἐλπὶς ἡμῶν πάντων, καὶ ἴασις ἡμῶν πάντων, καὶ ἀνάστασις οἰκεία πάντων ἡμῶν.
>   b. Offering: Καὶ σοι τὴν δόξαν τιμὴν καὶ προσκύνησιν ἀναπέμπομεν
>   c. The Father: σὺν τῷ παντοκράτορί σου καὶ παντεπόπτῃ τέκοντι...
>   d. The Holy Spirit: καὶ τῷ παναγίῳ καὶ ζωαρχικῷ καὶ ὁμοουσίῳ σου Πνεύματι νῦν καὶ ἀεί, καὶ.

2. Function
I. The original Prayer:[860]

1. (lines 1-4) Ἔλλαμψον ἐν ταῖς καρδίαις ἡμῶν, φιλάνθρωπε Δέσποτα, τὸ τῆς σῆς θεογνωσίας ἀκήρατον φῶς, καὶ τοὺς τῆς διανοίας ἡμῶν ὀφθαλμοὺς διάνοιξον εἰς τὴν τῶν εὐαγγελικῶν σου κηρυγμάτων κατανόησιν.

Beginning the prayer with the imperative ἔλλαμψον is interesting, it breaks this prayer out of the paradigm of the prayers seen so far, since it begins with an imperative rather than with an invocation of Christ. In doing so the purpose of this prayer is made clear. While the goal of the first two prayers was to ascend to Christ and receive the purification necessary to carry out the Liturgy, here the goal is the illumination to understand the Gospel lesson: εἰς τὴν τῶν εὐαγγελικῶν σου κηρυγμάτων κατανόησιν. This illumination is imparted by the φιλάνθρωπε Δέσποτα, who, we find out later in the prayer is Jesus Christ;[861] this vocative once again unites two aspects of Christ, the majesty of His divinity and His love for humanity.

That it is Christ who imparts this illumination, this τὸ τῆς σῆς θεογνωσίας ἀκήρατον φῶς is striking. As we saw in the first and second prayer of the Liturgy, it is the Holy Spirit who usually imparts illlumination: καὶ τῆς ἐλλάμψεως τοῦ παναγίου σου Πνεύματος. How, then, is it that this same illumination now comes from Christ? By transferring to Christ this 'function' of the Holy Spirit, the author underscores Christ's place in the Trinity and His function and presence among His congregation. It is this transference of divine function to Christ that makes the anti-Arian stance strong here. Not only is the Gospel reading about Christ, it is also understood only if Christ allows it. Note too, the empha-

---

[860] The text and line numbering is taken from the Liturgy of St. Basil. *Ieratikon* (1982). pg. 164
[861] In the *ekphonesis* of this prayer in the Liturgy of St. Basil there is a direct address: Χριστὲ ὁ Θεός. In my postulated original version of this prayer, however, it is possible to discern that Christ is meant as the addressee because each Person in the Trinitarian formula in the *ekphonesis* is mentioned with their relationship to Christ, with the qualifying σου. The use, in the main part of the prayer, of the epithet Δέσποτα, an epithet which is specific to Christ, is used, which is changed in the Liturgy of St. James to the more general Κύριε.

sis placed on the connection between Christ and the "divine knowledge," like the Altar in the Prayers of Access, the "divine knowledge" belongs solely to Christ, and it is the purpose of the Prayer to partake in it, this Prayer of the Gospel, then, functions, in a certain sense, like the Prayers of Access, the difference being the goal is no longer the Altar, but the "divine knowledge" of the Gospel.

2. (lines 4-7) Ἔνθες ἡμῖν καὶ τὸν τῶν μακαρίων σου ἐντολῶν φόβον, ἵνα τὰς σαρκικὰς ἐπιθυμίας πάσας καταπατήσαντες, πνευματικὴν πολιτείαν μετέλθωμεν, πάντα τὰ πρὸς εὐαρέστησιν τὴν σὴν καὶ φρονοῦντες καὶ πράττοντες.

The third request, built around the imperative ἔνθες, is constructed parallel to the first two requests. Rather than illumination, however, it is fear that is requested here. Fear of the commandments, which are placed here on an equal footing with the "divine knowledge," discussed above, since they have the same source: Christ: μακαρίων σου ἐντολῶν. These commandments are not the Law of the Old Testament, but the commandments of Christ in the New.[862] The result of these requests, which is presented in the ἵνα phrase, comes about from two sources then, not only from illumination, but from morality as well.[863]

What, then, are the results of the illumination and the obedience to the commandments? A state of being, which seems almost Manichaean in its intent, in which the temptations of the flesh are overcome and one can focus on living the spiritual life.[864] The final part of this section describes what this spiritual life entails: πάντα τὰ πρὸς εὐαρέστησιν τὴν σὴν καὶ φρονοῦντες καὶ πράττοντες. This becomes, then, a circular prayer, what is asked of Christ in the first section, illumination and fear of the commandments, becomes that which is lived in the spiritual life: "thinking and doing that which pleases You." With this circular Structure of the prayer the author sets up Christ as the linchpin of the life of the worshipper, the goal of which is to do Christ's will in deed and thought, by requesting of Christ the abilitiy to do it.

3. (lines 7-12) Σὺ γὰρ εἶ ὁ φωτισμὸς τῶν ψυχῶν καὶ τῶν σωμάτων ἡμῶν, Χριστὲ ὁ Θεός, καὶ σοὶ τὴν δόξαν ἀναπέμπομεν, σὺν τῷ ἀνάρχῳ σου Πατρὶ καὶ τῷ παναγίῳ καὶ ἀγαθῷ, καὶ ζωοποιῷ σου Πνεύματι, νῦν καὶ ἀεὶ καὶ εἰς τοὺς αἰῶνας τῶν αἰώνων. Ἀμήν.

---

[862] This sets up Christ, once again, as the God of the New Testament.
[863] Illumination and morality is often seem as the basis of Eastern Christianity, known as orthodoxia and orthopraxia.
[864] I do not wish to imply that the author of this Liturgy came under any influence from the Manichaeans or the Gnostics, it is interesting to note, however, that the evil of the flesh as opposed to the goodness of the soul is emphasized here.

The Commentary

By addressing Christ as the "enlightener" the author returns to the beginning of the prayer, finishing the thought. The request was made of Christ to "shine within our hearts," and through the carrying out of this request He becomes the "enlightener." The author also references the beginning of the prayer in naming Christ the enlightener of both souls and bodies. This returns the readers attention to the dual aspect of humanity: the body (referring back to the shining within the heart) and the soul (opening the eyes of the mind).

II. The secondary Prayer:
1. (section I.3 lines 2-7) Δέσποτα, Κύριε Ἰησοῦ Χριστὲ ὁ Θεὸς ἡμῶν· ὁ τοῖς ἁγίοις σου μαθηταῖς καὶ ἱεροῖς σου ἀποστόλοις εἰπών, ὅτι πολλοὶ προφῆται καὶ δίκαιοι ἐπεθύμησαν ἰδεῖν, ἃ βλέπετε καὶ οὐκ εἶδον, καὶ ἀκοῦσαι ἃ ἀκούετε καὶ οὐκ ἤκουσαν. Ὑμῶν γὰρ μακάριοι οἱ ὀφθαλμοὶ ὅτι βλέπουσι· καὶ τὰ ὦτα ὑμῶν ὅτι ἀκούει. Καὶ καταξιωθείημεν ἄρτι τοῦ ἀκοῦσαι καὶ ποιῆσαι τὰ ἅγιά σου Εὐαγγέλια, ταῖς λιταῖς τῶν ἱερῶν σου.

Alhough this prayer is, like the other prayers of the Liturgy, addressed to Christ, this is the only feature that seems to tie it with the other prayers. As mentioned above, the majority of the Prayer consists of a quotation from the Gospel of Matthew, with only a short request for the ability to hear and carry out the Holy Gospel following it. Such a long quotation is unusual in this Liturgy, the author of which seems to prefer shorter quotations which are built into the text of the prayer.[865] The quotation is a slight reworking of the verses Matthew 13:16-17 and of 1 Peter 1:10. This quotation is in the context of the parables of Christ, in the following verse He begins the parable of the sower, this provides an excellent introduction to the Gospel reading, the verses that introduce the words of Christ in the Gospel (the parables) are used to introduce the more general word of Christ, Gospel itself.

2. (section I.3 lines 8-11): Μνημόνευσον οὖν Δέσποτα καὶ νῦν, πάντων τῶν ἐντειλαμένων ἡμῖν τοῖς ἀναξίοις τοῦ μνημονεύειν αὐτῶν, εἰς τὰς δεήσεις ἡμετέρας καὶ τὰς αἰτήσεις, ἃς, ἀναβιβάζομέν σοι Κύριε ὁ Θεὸς ἡμῶν. Τοὺς προτετελευτηκότας, ἀνάπαυσον αὐτούς, τοὺς κάμνοντας ἔρρωσον αὐτούς.

Though the requests in this section of the Prayer are taken from the Prayer of the Gospel in the Coptic Liturgy of St. Mark, they seem out of place. They have nothing to do with the Gospel reading as such, and the prayers for the dead and the sick seem to more usual for petitions in the Anaphora than in a prayer for the Gospel. This part of the prayer seems almost to be a paraphrased set of petitions tacked on to the end of the Prayer of the Gospel, rather than part of the Prayer of the Gospel proper. While there are no petitions

---
[865] Cf. the quotation from Psalm 50 in the first Prayer.

The Liturgy of Saint Gregory the Theologian

preceeding the Gospel reading in the Egyptian rite,[866] there is a set of petitions in the Liturgy of St. James that preceed the Gospel, these petitions do not, however, include requests like those found in this prayer. It is, therefore, impossible to say whether there was such a set of petitions in the Liturgy of St. Gregory, and whether this second section of this prayer is a paraphrasing of it. It seems, though, that these requests do not belong in a Prayer of the Gospel, and may have some other source.

3. (section I.3 lines 12-15) Σὺ γὰρ εἶ ζωὴ ἡμῶν πάντων, καὶ σωτηρία ἡμῶν πάντων, καὶ ἐλπὶς ἡμῶν πάντων, καὶ ἴασις ἡμῶν πάντων, καὶ ἀνάστασις οἰκεία πάντων ἡμῶν. Καὶ σοι τὴν δόξαν τιμὴν καὶ προσκύνησιν ἀναπέμπομεν, σὺν τῷ παντοκράτορί σου καὶ παντεπόπτῃ τέκοντι, καὶ τῷ παναγίῳ καὶ ζωαρχικῷ καὶ ὁμοουσίῳ σου Πνεύματι νῦν καὶ ἀεί, καὶ.

The *ekphonesis* begins with a series of descriptions of Christ. A series of five descriptors are used: "the life of us all, the salvation of us all, the hope of us all, the healing of us all and the personal ressurection of us all." These descriptors form a chiasm in which the temporal and eternal are juxtaposed: life and eternal life (ressurection), as are salvation and its consequence: healing, this chiasm is built surrounding hope. Thus the author continues the thought of the prayer, that Christ is both the goal and the means toward this goal.

Of great interest is the invocation of the Trinity. Once again the other members of the Trinity are discussed according to their relationship with Christ. Here, though, the emphasis on the relationship between Christ and the Father is taken to its extreme. The author avoids using the standard Πατὴρ, instead opting to use a term that to my knowledge is used in this manner in no other liturgical work: τῷ παντοκράτορί σου τέκοντι.[867] Why, though, would the author use this phrase, rather than the more standard phrasing of the *ekphonesis*? The term Father implies authority, therefore even with the qualifying ‚σου,' in the previous Ekphoneseis, the authority of the Father over the Son is implied. The term ‚begetter' does not have this same implication, and the author uses this somewhat awkward phrasing in order to deemphasize the authority of the Father, building up the divinity of Christ.

With the end of the *ekphonesis* comes one of the most startling statements in the Liturgy thus far: καὶ ὁμοουσίῳ σου Πνεύματι. This is the first time that the term homoousios is used in the liturgy, and it is interesting to note that this first use is in reference to the Holy Spirit rather than the Son. While this use of the term homoousios is a mark that this prayer was adapted into the liturgy at a later date, the term still builds on the overall theme

---

[866] Hammond and Brightman (1896). pg. 155-156; Cf. also Cuming (1990). pp. 11-13.
[867] the verb τίκτω when referring to a mother means to give birth, but when referring to a male means to beget, thus this reference to the Father is as the ‚all-powerful begetter' of Christ.

of the liturgy, anti-Arianism. The author is able to attack both the Arians and the Macedonians with this one statement, because the term homoousios comes before the Holy Spirit, the worshippers who hear it can first associate it in their minds with Christ, as the term is used in the Nicene Creed, and so attacks the Arian position on Christ; then, with the actual association with the Holy Spirit, the Macedonian position is also attacked.

I.V. The Prayer of the Veil[868]

There are a number of prayers in the Liturgy of St. Gregory that have alternates. Here we see the first example of such a prayer, the Εὐχὴ τοῦ καταπετάσματος and the Εὐχὴ τοῦ καταπετάσματος παρ' Αἰγυπτίοις. In his Commentary on the Coptic Ananphora of St. Gregory, Hammerschmidt only discusses the second prayer, since this is the prayer used in the Coptic translation.[869] As to the origin of this second prayer, he says: "Der stärkste Beweis für seine ursprüngliche Nichtzugehörigkeit zur Greglit. ist aber, dass es als einziges Gebet dieser Liturgie an Gott Vater gerichtet ist."[870] That this prayer is not addressed to Christ shows that it was not only adopted into the Liturgy from another source, but at a later date as well. The first prayer of the Liturgy is most likely adopted from the Liturgy of St. James, but by the original author of the Liturgy of St. Gregory, as it is rewritten to Christ. Since the Εὐχὴ τοῦ καταπετάσματος παρ' Αἰγυπτίοις is not rewritten to fit this scheme, it must be adopted later, after the anti-Arian nature of the Liturgy was no longer recognized as its most important aspect. The title of the prayer also show us the origin of the Prayer, it must be of Egyptian origin, strange though, is that the prayer is found in none of the other Egyptian Liturgies. Hammerschmidt shows the Egyptian origin in the use of

---

[868] The purpose of a Prayer of the Veil is explained by Hammerschmidt: "Diese Abtrennung geschieht entweder durch die Ikonostase (Bilderwand) oder auch – besonders in älterer Zeit, in den nestorianischen Kirche aber auch heute noch – durch einen Vorhang, wobei der Gedanke zugrunde liegt, das Heiligtum den Blicken zu entziehen. Unsere Oration hat daher ihren Namen, weil sie nicht beim Altare, sondern nur innerhalb des durch den Vorhang abgetrennten Heiligtums beim Vorhang selbst gesprochen wurde." That it is the curtain of the Altar that is meant and not the veils placed over the Gifts is argued in footnote 25 of Hammerschmidt (1957). pg. 85-86. "The separation occurs either through the Iconostasis (the icon screen) or also – especially in ancient times, but still today in the Nestorian church – through a curtain, the background idea of which is to shield the Sanctuary fron view. Our prayer takes this name because it is not said at the Altar, but only within the Sanctuary itself, divided off by the veil." Much of this prayer is missing from the Paris Manuscript, the text is found in the edition of Renaudot.
[869] Hammerschmidt (1957). pg 85
[870] Hammerschmidt (1957). pg 92 "The strongest proof that this is originally not a part of the Liturgy of St. Gregory is, however, that it is the only prayer of the liturgy that is addressed to God the Father."

the term: ἀναψυχὴν.[871] This prayer was, then, adopted into the Liturgy of St. Gregory from an older (according to Hammerschmidt) Egyptian source. The question remains, however: why was this prayer adopted into the Liturgy of St. Gregory? The answer postulated by Hammerschmidt is that the prayer was: "ihr später, als man für sie eine Oratio veli benötigte, vorgesetzt wurde."[872] He also speculates, in a footnote, that this may be a sign that the Liturgy of St. Gregory did not have an original Prayer of the Veil. This explanation is not entirely satisfying, as the Paris Manuscript contains another Prayer of the Veil.

This first Prayer of the Veil is addressed to Christ and since the strongest argument for the secondary nature of the Prayer of the Veil among the Egyptians was that it is addressed to the Father, we cannot dismiss this Prayer as such. It is possible that this Prayer too was adopted from another source. This Prayer has an exact correspondance in the the Byzantine Liturgies of St. Basil and St. John Chrysostom of the ninth century.[873] Here the text is used as the Prayer before the Great Entrance. If, as Hammerschmidt postulates, the Liturgy of St. Gregory did not have an original Prayer of the Veil, then it is possible that the Prayer was adopted from the Byzantine Liturgy of St. Basil. This seems an unlikely scenario, however. Unlike the Egyptian and Syrian Liturgies, the Pre-Anaphora of the Byzantine Liturgies of St. Basil and St. John Chrysostom do not have many prayers addressed to Christ, we have already discussed one of the only other prayers in this section, the Prayer of the Gospel. It is, then, unlikely that the origin of a prayer addressed to Christ lies in a Liturgy in which this is a rarity, rather than in a Liturgy in which it is the rule. The second reason lies in how the Prayer is used in the respective Liturgies. In the Byzantine Liturgies this prayer is used as the Prayer of the Great Entrance, while in the Liturgy of St. Gregory, it functions as the preparatory prayer for the Anaphora.[874] There are, however,

---

[871] Hammerschmidt (1957). pg. 90-91. In this section he lays out the various places where this term is used, from which one can discern its Egyptian origin: "Es ist allgemein anerkannt, dass Ausdrücke wie refrigerium, refrigerii sedes, refrigerare, requies aeterna, auch die Bezeichnung des Grabes als 'Hauses der Ewigkeit' ägyptischen Ursprunges sind." "It is generally accept that expressions like *refrigerium, refrigerii sedes, refrigerare, requies aeterna* and calling the grave the 'House of Eternity' are of Egyptian origin." Hammerschmidt goes on to give various examples of how this term is used in Egyptian prayers and how it spreads to other Liturgical families (his example is the Syrian Liturgy of Timothei Alexandrini and Severi Antiocheni). The other, more telling example he gives is a fragmen: "altkoptischer Liturgie" which uses this term.
[872] Hammerschmidt (1957). pg. 90 "put forth later, as one needed an *Oratio Veli* for it (the Liturgy)."
[873] Hammond and Brightman (1896). pg. 318; Hammerschmidt (1957). pg. 89 footnote 32, he notes too that there are other places where the Byzantine rite and the Greek/Egyptian rite coincide. This prayer is also found in the Liturgy of the Armenians (Cf. Hammond and Brightman (1896). pg. 430). I find it highly unlikely, however, that this is the origin of the prayer, since the Armenian Liturgy (the Soorp Baradak) came under heavy Byzantine influence (note that the Monogenes Hymn of Justinian is also found in the Armenian Liturgy Cf. Hammond and Brightman (1896). pg. 421).
[874] Hammerschmidt counts it as part of the Anaphora, while Gerhards does not.

certain small differences between the version of the prayer in the Liturgy of St. Gregory and the version in the Liturgy of St. Basil:

Table I.V.1: the differences between the Liturgy of St. Gregory and St. Basil

The Liturgy of St. Gregory the Theologian	The Liturgy of St. Basil[875]
Οὐδεὶς ἄξιος τῶν συνδεδεμένων ταῖς σαρκικαῖς ἐπιθυμίαις καὶ ἡδοναῖς προσέρχεσθαι, ἢ προσεγγίζειν, ἢ λειτουργεῖν σοι βασιλεῦ τῆς δόξης. Τὸ γὰρ διακονεῖν σοι μέγα καὶ φοβερὸν καὶ αὐταῖς ταῖς ἐπουρανίαις δυνάμεσιν <u>ἀπρόσιτον</u>. Ἀλλ᾽ ὅμως, διὰ τὴν ἄφατον καὶ ἄμετρόν σου φιλανθρωπίαν, ἀτρέπτως καὶ ἀναλλοιώτως γέγονας ἄνθρωπος, καὶ ἀρχιερεὺς ἡμῖν ἐχρημάτισας, καὶ τῆς λειτουργικῆς ταύτης καὶ ἀναιμάκτου Θυσίας τὴν ἱερουργίαν παρέδωκας ἡμῖν ὡς Δεσπότης τῶν ἁπάντων. Σὺ γὰρ εἶ δεσπόζεις τῶν ἐπουρανίων, καὶ τῶν ἐπιγείων, καὶ τῶν <u>καταχθονίων</u>, ὁ ἐπὶ θρόνου Χερουβικοῦ ἐποχούμενος. Ὁ τῶν Σεραφὶμ Κύριος, καὶ βασιλεὺς τοῦ Ἰσραήλ, ὁ μόνος ἅγιος, καὶ ἐν ἁγίοις ἀναπαυόμενος. Σὲ τοίνυν δυσωπῶ τὸν μόνον ἀγαθὸν καὶ εὐήκοον <u>Θεὸν</u>, ἐπίβλεψον ἐπ᾽ ἐμὲ τὸν ἁμαρτωλόν, καὶ ἀχρεῖον δοῦλόν σου· καὶ ἱκάνωσόν με τῇ δυνάμει τοῦ ἁγίου Πνεύματος, ἐνδεδυμένον τὴν τῆς ἱερατείας χάριν, παραστῆναι τῇ ἁγίᾳ σου ταύτῃ τραπέζῃ καὶ ἱερουργῆσαι τὸ ἄχραντόν σου σῶμα καὶ τὸ τίμιόν <u>σου</u> αἷμα. Σοὶ γὰρ προσέρχομαι κλίνας τὸν ἐμαυτοῦ αὐχένα· καὶ δέομαί σου, μὴ ἀποστρέψῃς τὸ πρόσωπόν σου ἀπ᾽ ἐμοῦ· μηδὲ ἀποδοκιμάσῃς με ἐκ παίδων σου· ἀλλ᾽ ἀξίωσόν <u>με προσενεχθῆναί σοι τὰ Δῶρα ταῦτα, ὑπ᾽ ἐμοῦ τοῦ ἁμαρτωλοῦ καὶ ἀναξίου δούλου σου</u>. Σὺ γὰρ εἶ ὁ ἁγιάζων καὶ ἁγιαζόμενος, προσφέρων τε καὶ	Οὐδεὶς ἄξιος τῶν συνδεδεμένων ταῖς σαρκικαῖς ἐπιθυμίαις καὶ ἡδοναῖς προσέρχεσθαι ἢ προσεγγίζειν ἢ λειτουργεῖν σοι, βασιλεῦ τῆς δόξης. Τὸ γὰρ διακονεῖν σοι μέγα καὶ φοβερὸν καὶ αὐταῖς ταῖς ἐπουρανίαις δυνάμεσιν. Ἀλλ᾽ ὅμως, διὰ τὴν ἄφατον καὶ ἄμετρόν σου φιλανθρωπίαν, ἀτρέπτως καὶ ἀναλλοιώτως γέγονας ἄνθρωπος, καὶ ἀρχιερεὺς ἡμῖν ἐχρημάτισας, καὶ τῆς λειτουργικῆς ταύτης καὶ ἀναιμάκτου Θυσίας τὴν ἱερουργίαν παρέδωκας ἡμῖν, ὡς Δεσπότης τῶν ἁπάντων. Σὺ γὰρ <u>μόνος, Κύριε ὁ Θεὸς ἡμῶν</u>, δεσπόζεις τῶν ἐπουρανίων καὶ τῶν ἐπιγείων, ὁ ἐπὶ θρόνου Χερουβικοῦ ἐποχούμενος, ὁ τῶν Σεραφεὶμ Κύριος καὶ βασιλεὺς τοῦ Ἰσραήλ, ὁ μόνος ἅγιος καὶ ἐν ἁγίοις ἀναπαυόμενος. Σὲ τοίνυν δυσωπῶ, τὸν μόνον ἀγαθόν, καὶ εὐήκοον· ἐπίβλεψον ἐπ᾽ ἐμὲ τὸν ἁμαρτωλὸν καὶ ἀχρεῖον δοῦλόν σου <u>καὶ καθάρισόν μου τὴν ψυχὴν καὶ τὴν καρδίαν ἀπὸ συνειδήσεως πονηρᾶς</u>· καὶ ἱκάνωσόν με τῇ δυνάμει τοῦ ἁγίου Πνεύματος, ἐνδεδυμένον τὴν τῆς ἱερατείας χάριν, παραστῆναι τῇ ἁγίᾳ σου ταύτῃ τραπέζῃ καὶ ἱερουργῆσαι τὸ <u>ἅγιον καὶ</u> ἄχραντόν σου Σῶμα καὶ τὸ τίμιόν Αἷμα. Σοὶ γὰρ προσέρχομαι, κλίνας τὸν ἐμαυτοῦ αὐχένα, καὶ δέομαί σου· μὴ ἀποστρέψῃς τὸ πρόσωπόν σου ἀπ᾽ ἐμοῦ, μηδὲ ἀποδοκιμάσῃς με ἐκ παίδων σου, <u>ἀλλ᾽ ἀξίωσον προσενεχθῆναί σοι ὑπ᾽ ἐμοῦ τοῦ ἁμαρτωλοῦ καὶ ἀναξίου δούλου σου</u>

---

[875] Holy Cross (1985). pp. 13-14. Cf. also Hammond and Brightman (1986). pg. 318 and Trempelis (1982). pg. 71

προσφερόμενος, ὁ δεχόμενος καὶ δεκτός, ὁ διδοὺς καὶ διαδιδόμενος. Καὶ σοὶ τὴν δόξαν ἀναπέμπομεν, μετὰ τοῦ Πατρὸς καὶ τοῦ ἁγίου Πνεύματος. Νῦν καὶ.	τὰ Δῶρα ταῦτα. Σὺ γὰρ εἶ ὁ προσφέρων καὶ προσφερόμενος καὶ προσδεχόμενος καὶ διαδιδόμενος, Χριστὲ ὁ Θεὸς ἡμῶν, καὶ σοὶ τὴν δόξαν ἀναπέμπομεν, σὺν τῷ ἀνάρχῳ σου Πατρὶ καὶ τῷ παναγίῳ καὶ ἀγαθῷ καὶ ζωοποιῷ σου Πνεύματι, νῦν καὶ ἀεὶ καὶ εἰς τοὺς αἰῶνας τῶν αἰωνων. Ἀμήν.

The function of this Prayer can be determined in the phrasing of the request: ἐπίβλεψον ἐπ᾽ ἐμὲ τὸν ἁμαρτωλὸν, καὶ ἀχρεῖον δοῦλόν σου καὶ καθάρισόν μου τὴν ψυχὴν καὶ τὴν καρδίαν ἀπὸ συνειδήσεως πονηρᾶς· καὶ ἱκάνωσόν με τῇ δυνάμει τοῦ Ἁγίου σου Πνεύματος, ἐνδεδυμένον τὴν τῆς ἱερατείας χάριν, παραστῆναι τῇ ἁγίᾳ σου ταύτῃ τραπέζῃ καὶ ἱερουργῆσαι τὸ ἅγιον καὶ ἄχραντόν σου Σῶμα καὶ τὸ τίμιον Αἷμα. The priest prays for the ability to stand before the Altar and to "celebrate the mystery of Your holy and pure Body and Your precious Blood" This prepares the celebrant, not for the Entrance with the Gifts, but for the coming prayers and rituals surrounding the hallowing of the Gifts in the Anaphora. We must conclude, then, that this Prayer is not only written in the correct style to be original in the Liturgy of St. Gregory, but stands in its proper place there as well; this Prayer was, then, not adopted by the Liturgy of St. Gregory, but rather by the Liturgy of St. Basil.

This returns us to the question: why was the alternate Prayer of the Veil adopted into the Liturgy, especially since the Liturgy already posesses a Prayer of the Veil? Hammerschmidt, as mentioned above, demonstrates that the secondary Prayer of the Veil is of Egyptian origin, it is possible, then, that this Prayer was added to the Liturgy as it was translated into Coptic, and was subsequently added into the Greet text as an alternate.[876]

1. Structure
The Prayer begins with a strong statement of the holiness of God by describing the unworthiness of man before Christ, and continues by expanding this to include the "heavenly powers." Following this statement is a series of phrases that describe 1. the Incarnation; 2. Christ's place in the Liturgy and 3. Christ's lordship. These are followed by three requests, two requests for purification surround a request for the ability to take part in the Anaphora. Finally the *ekphonesis* begins with a number of descriptive phrases that deal with the di-

---

[876] Unfortunately, this is impossible to prove, as we do not possess any Greek manuscripts earlier than the fourteenth century.

chotomy of Christ's place in the Liturgy, and finishes with the Trinitarian formula. The Structure of this prayer is also shown in the following table:

Table I.V.2: The Prayer of the Veil[877]

The Prayer of the Veil
1. Opening of the Prayer I. The Unworthiness of Man to come before Christ: Οὐδεὶς ἄξιος τῶν συνδεδεμένων ταῖς σαρκικαῖς ἐπιθυμίαις καὶ ἡδοναῖς προσέρχεσθαι, ἢ προσεγγίζειν, ἢ λειτουργεῖν σοι βασιλεῦ τῆς δόξης. II. The Unworthiness of even the heavenly powers before Christ: Τὸ γὰρ διακονεῖν σοι μέγα καὶ φοβερὸν καὶ αὐταῖς ταῖς ἐπουρανίαις δυνάμεσιν ἀπρόσιτον.
2. Phrases describing Christ I. Christ's Incarnation: Ἀλλ' ὅμως, διὰ τὴν ἄφατον καὶ ἀμέτρητόν σου φιλανθρωπίαν, ἀτρέπτως καὶ ἀναλλοιώτως γέγονας ἄνθρωπος, II. Christ's place in the Liturgy: καὶ ἀρχιερεὺς ἡμῶν ἐχρημάτισας, καὶ τῆς λειτουργικῆς ταύτης καὶ ἀναιμάκτου Θυσίας τὴν ἱερουργίαν παρέδωκας ἡμῖν, ὡς δεσπότης τῶν ἁπάντων. III. Christ's lordship: a. Σὺ γὰρ εἶ δεσπόζεις τῶν ἐπουρανίων, καὶ τῶν ἐπιγείων, καὶ τῶν καταχθονίων. b. Ὁ ἐπὶ θρόνου Χερουβικοῦ ἐποχούμενος· c. ὁ τῶν Σεραφεὶμ Κύριος, καὶ βασιλεὺς τοῦ Ἰσραήλ, d. ὁ μόνος ἅγιος καὶ ἐν ἁγίοις ἀναπαυόμενος.

---

[877] Section I.4 lines 1-19.

The Liturgy of Saint Gregory the Theologian

3. Requests

I. Request for purification:
Σὲ τοίνυν δυσωπῶ τὸν μόνον ἀγαθὸν καὶ εὐήκοον Θεὸν, ἐπίβλεψον ἐπ' ἐμὲ τὸν ἁμαρτωλὸν, καὶ ἀχρεῖον δοῦλον σου·

II. Request for the worthy participation in the Anaphora:
καὶ ἱκάνωσόν με τῇ δυνάμει τοῦ Ἁγίου σου Πνεύματος, ἐνδεδυμένον τὴν τῆς ἱερατείας χάριν, παραστῆναι τῇ ἁγίᾳ σου ταύτῃ τραπέζῃ καὶ ἱερουργῆσαι τὸ ἅγιον καὶ ἄχραντόν σου σῶμα καὶ τὸ τίμιον αἷμα.

III. Bowing of one's head, request for purification and acceptance:
Σοὶ γὰρ προσέρχομαι, κλίνας τὸν ἐμαυτοῦ αὐχένα· καὶ δέομαί σου, μὴ ἀποστρέψῃς τὸ πρόσωπόν σου ἀπ' ἐμοῦ· μηδὲ ἀποδοκιμάσῃς με ἐκ παίδων σου· ἀλλ' ἀξίωσον προσενεχθῆναι σοι τὰ Δῶρα ταῦτα, ὑπ' ἐμοῦ τοῦ ἁμαρτωλοῦ καὶ ἀναξίου δούλου σου.

4. *Ekphonesis*

I. The dichotomy of Christ in the Liturgy:
a. Σὺ γὰρ εἶ ὁ ἁγιάζων καὶ ἁγιαζόμενος,
b. προσφέρων τε καὶ προσφερόμενος,
c. ὁ δεχόμενος καὶ δεκτός,
d. ὁ διδοὺς καὶ διαδιδόμενος.

II. Trinitarian formula and closing Benediction
Καὶ σοὶ τὴν δόξαν ἀναπέμπομεν, μετὰ τοῦ Πατρὸς, καὶ τοῦ ἁγίου Πνεύματος. Νῦν καὶ.

2. Function
1. (section I.4 lines 2-4): Οὐδεὶς ἄξιος τῶν συνδεδεμένων ταῖς σαρκικαῖς ἐπιθυμίαις καὶ ἡδοναῖς προσέρχεσθαι, ἢ προσεγγίζειν, ἢ λειτουργεῖν σοι βασιλεῦ τῆς δόξης. Τὸ γὰρ διακονεῖν σοι μέγα καὶ φοβερὸν καὶ αὐταῖς ταῖς ἐπουρανίαις δυνάμεσιν ἀπρόσιτον.

    This opening serves a double purpose in the prayer: 1. It introduces the topic of the prayer, purification, and serves to explain why this purification is necessary; 2. once again it underscores the power and the divinity of Christ.

The Commentary

The purpose of the Prayer of the Veil is the preparation of the priest for the coming Anaphora, this opening illustrates this purpose in a string of infinitives: the priest is prepared in this prayer to προσέρχεσθαι, to προσεγγίζειν and to λειτουργεῖν. Why, though, is preparation necessary? This is answered in the first two words of the prayer, purification must be sought because Οὐδεὶς ἄξιος, no one is worthy of carrying this out, this is qualified, however, it is those: τῶν συνδεδεμένων ταῖς σαρκικαῖς ἐπιθυμίαις καὶ ἡδοναῖς who are unworthy. This is the purpose of the prayer, to free the priest from his subservience to the pleasures of the flesh, to give him *apatheia*, a concept striven for in late Greek philosphy as well. This unworthiness is further emphasized by the juxtaposed vocative which describes Chrst: βασιλεῦ τῆς δόξης.

The other purpose of this opening is to emphasize the divinity of Christ. The only vocative in this section, discussed above, is instrumental in this. The juxtoposition, which emphasizes the uworthiness of the priest, also emphasizes the power of Christ, calling him the "king of glory." The aspect that truly underlines the anti-Arian nature of this prayer follows in the next sentence: Τὸ γὰρ διακονεῖν σοι μέγα καὶ φοβερὸν καὶ αὐταῖς ταῖς ἐπουρανίαις δυνάμεσιν ἀπρόσιτον. This sentence seems uneccesary, the prayer already establishes the need for purification, why then this extra declaration of superiority? The Arian view of Christ is that He is the first created being, that He was created in order to facilitate the creation of the world for man. This makes Christ, in a certain sense, one of the heavenly powers. By using this phrase the author very deliberately places Christ not only above the priest serving at the Liturgy, but also above the angelic powers of heaven, underscoring His place as God.

2. (section I.4 lines 4-10): Ἀλλ' ὅμως, διὰ τὴν ἄφατον καὶ ἄμετρόν σου φιλανθρωπίαν, ἀτρέπτως καὶ ἀναλλοιώτως γέγονας ἄνθρωπος, καὶ ἀρχιερεὺς ἡμῖν ἐχρημάτισας, καὶ τῆς λειτουργικῆς ταύτης καὶ ἀναιμάκτου Θυσίας τὴν ἱερουργίαν παρέδωκας ἡμῖν ὡς Δεσπότης τῶν ἁπάντων. Σὺ γὰρ εἶ δεσπόζεις τῶν ἐπουρανίων, καὶ τῶν ἐπιγείων, καὶ τῶν καταχθονίων. Ὁ ἐπὶ θρόνου Χερουβικοῦ ἐποχούμενος· ὁ τῶν Σεραφὶμ Κύριος, καὶ βασιλεὺς τοῦ Ἰσραήλ, ὁ μόνος ἅγιος καὶ ἐν ἁγίοις ἀναπαυόμενος.

In this section the author continues the thought of the last section, emphasizing the divinity of Christ in a list of descriptive phrases. As discussed in the first prayer, however, the author is a proponent of anti-Arian theology, not of Monophysite theology, the author must preserve the delicate balance of Nicene Christology, in order to do this the author needs to deal with Christ's human nature as well as His divine nature, so that the anti-Arian polemic not progress to the other extreme. Therefore in the first sentence of this section the author juxtaposes the human nature of Christ: γέγονας ἄνθρωπος and his divine nature: ὡς Δεσπότης τῶν ἁπάντων. In earlier prayers the author shows the human nature of Christ by always mollifying direct statements of divinity by emphasizing His love for man as well. This tendence is continued here in the author's statement on the Incarnation, which Christ undergoes: διὰ τὴν ἄφατον καὶ ἄμετρόν σου φιλανθρωπίαν. The author uses the juxtaposition between humanity and divinity which he sets up not only to emphasize the Christological position of the Nicenes, but to explain Christ's place in the Liturgy as well: as man he is the "High Priest:" ἀρχιερεὺς ἡμῖν ἐχρημάτισας. "High Priest" as a title for Christ is one that is used often in Christian literature and iconography.[878] This title reinforces the central role of Christ in the Liturgy by equating Christ first with the high priest of the Old Testament Temple as well as with the bishop, who celebrates the Liturgy,[879] as "High Priest," then, Christ bridges the Old and New Testaments. As God Christ is also the source and purpose of the Liturgy: τῆς λειτουργικῆς ταύτης καὶ ἀναιμάκτου Θυσίας τὴν ἱερουργίαν παρέδωκας ἡμῖν. The source in that He hands over the form of the Liturgy to "us," and the purpose in that He hands over the bloodless sacrifice, in the form of His Body and Blood.

Following this exposition on the Incarnation the author continues his emphasis of the divinity of Christ, this list begins by describing the dominion Christ has over the cosmos: Σὺ γὰρ εἶ δεσπόζεις τῶν ἐπουρανίων καὶ τῶν ἐπιγείων, καὶ τῶν καταχθονίων. In this statement the verb δεσπόζεις is used to refer back to the last sentence, the description of Christ's divine nature: Δεσπότης τῶν ἁπάντων. Interesting is that a similar phrase occurs in an early Christian novel, the *Acta Xanthippe et Polyxenae*: σὺ γὰρ βασιλεὺς ζωῆς καὶ θανάτου, ὡς ἤκουσα, καὶ σὺ δεσπόζεις τῶν ἐπουρανίων καὶ ἐπιγείων καὶ καταχθονίων[880] here the phrase is part of a prayer that Xanthippe makes to the ‚God of Paul' right before her baptism. When looking at the various influences that the author lists on this work, we see numerous other Apocryphal Acts and other early Christian hagiographical literature, but no liturgical works.[881] Though the purpose of these two Christian genres is different, the audience is the same,[882] perhaps it is this common audience that accounts for the similar language we see here.

---

[878] Christ the High Priest is often depicted iconographically in the vestments of a bishop.
[879] Only the bishop has the authority to celebrate the Eucharist, the priests only celebrate on the sufferance of the bishop, who gives them the antimitsion, which has the signature of the bishop on it and grants them the blessing of the bishop to celebrate the Eucharist.
[880] Cf. *Acta Xanthippae et Polyxenae*. Section 20 line 24. "For You are the king of life and of death, as I heard, and You rule the heavenly and the earthly and those below the earth."
[881] James (1893). pg. 43-58
[882] James (1893). pg. 54

The Commentary

What follows expounds on this dominion. In the first two He is the lord of the ἐπουρανίων: ὁ ἐπὶ θρόνου Χερουβικοῦ ἐποχούμενος· ὁ τῶν Σεραφὶμ Κύριος, here two of the ranks of angels stand for all of the angelic powers.[883] The ἐπιγείων, are represented in the phrase: βασιλεὺς τοῦ Ἰσραὴλ. Israel is, in a Christian context, the Church. The final of the three divisions of the cosmos, the καταχθονίων, which one would expect to find next in this series, is not mentioned. Instead, the author returns to the ἐπουρανίων by saying that Christ is: ὁ μόνος ἅγιος, καὶ ἐν ἁγίοις ἀναπαυόμενος.[884] The anti-Arian and anti-Pneumatomachian nature of this phrase is confirmed by Athanasius who uses it in his work *contra Macedonianos*.[885] The author marks Christ as the Master of the Cosmos in two ways: the first time the author divides all of Creation into three ‚geographical' locations the heavenly, the earthly, and the cthonic; this time the author divides Creation into the different members of the Church: 1. the angelic powers, 2. the Church militant on earth (Israel) and 3. the Church triumphant in heaven (ἐν ἁγίοις).

3. (section I.4 lines 10-13): Σὲ τοίνυν δυσωπῶ τὸν μόνον ἀγαθόν καὶ εὐήκοον Θεόν, ἐπίβλεψον ἐπ' ἐμὲ τὸν ἁμαρτωλὸν, καὶ ἀχρεῖον δοῦλόν σου· καὶ ἱκάνωσόν με τῇ δυνάμει τοῦ ἁγίου Πνεύματος, ἐνδεδυμένον τὴν τῆς ἱερατείας χάριν, παραστῆναι τῇ ἁγίᾳ σου ταύτῃ τραπέζῃ καὶ ἱερουργῆσαι τὸ ἄχραντόν σου σῶμα καὶ τὸ τίμιόν σου αἷμα.

The author has now moved on to the part of the prayer in which the priest requests purification for the Anaphora.[886] This section begins by looking back to the one preceeding it, here Christ is called: τὸν μόνον ἀγαθόν, καὶ εὐήκοον Θεὸν that Christ is the one who "alone" is good connects with the idea of Him being the one who ‚alone' is holy. The request for purification begins with another intratextual connection: ἐπίβλεψον ἐπ' ἐμὲ τὸν ἁμαρτωλὸν καὶ ἀχρεῖον δοῦλόν σου connecting back to the beginning of the private prayer of the priest in the first prayer of the Liturgy: ἐπίβλεψον ἐπ' ἐμὲ, τὸν ἀχρεῖον δοῦλόν σου. This intratextual connection exists because both of these prayers have the same purpose, to purify the priest, and to empower him for the coming ritual. The prayer continues with another quotation from the first prayer: καὶ ἱκάνωσόν με τῇ δυνάμει τοῦ ἁγίου Πνεύματος.[887] Since these two prayers share the same purpose their Structure follows the same pattern from now on. In the first prayer the priest requests: καὶ ἱκάνωσόν με τῇ δυνάμει τοῦ ἁγίου

---

[883] Cf. the final prayer of the Liturgy, in which the other ranks of angels are also discussed along with the Cherubim and the Seraphim.
[884] A similar phrase also found in the Prophet Isaiah 57:15.
[885] Cf. Athanasius. *Dialogi duo contra Macedonianos*. Volume 28 page 1305 line 16.
[886] Note that each of the remaining sections begins with a form of 'σου.' Connecting each of these sections together.
[887] Cf. section I.1 lines 10 ff.

Πνεύματος εἰς τὴν Λειτουργίαν ταύτην καὶ πρόσδεξαί με διὰ τὴν σὴν ἀγαθότητα, προσεγγίζοντα τῷ ἁγίῳ σου Θυσιαστηρίῳ· καὶ εὐδόκησον Κύριε δεκτὰ γενέσθαι τὰ μέλλοντα προσαγόμενά σοι Δῶρα. First the priest asks for the ability to stand about the Altar, and only then for the ability to offer the gifts. This prayer is set up similarly, first the priest asks to for the grace to stand about the holy table and then for the grace to offer the Body and Blood, the "gifts" mentioned in the first prayer: ἐνδεδυμένον τὴν τῆς ἱερατείας χάριν, παραστῆναι τῇ ἁγίᾳ σου ταύτῃ τραπέζῃ, καὶ ἱερούργησαι τὸ ἄχραντόν σου Σῶμα καὶ τὸ τίμιόν σου Αἷμα.

4. (section I.4 lines 13-16): Σοὶ γὰρ προσέρχομαι κλίνας τὸν ἐμαυτοῦ αὐχένα· καὶ δέομαί σου, μὴ ἀποστρέψῃς τὸ πρόσωπόν σου ἀπ' ἐμοῦ· μηδὲ ἀποδοκιμάσῃς με ἐκ παίδων σου· ἀλλ' ἀξίωσόν με προσενέχθηναί σοι τὰ Δῶρα ταῦτα, ὑπ' ἐμοῦ τοῦ ἁμαρτωλοῦ καὶ ἀναξίου δούλου σου.

Before continuing with the requests for purification, the author makes another intra-textual reference, this time not back to the first prayer, but forward to the post-Anaphoral prayers, the "Prayer of the Bowing of the Head."[888] The remainder of this prayer is spoken: κλίνας τὸν ἐμαυτοῦ αὐχένα. The bowing of the head is a symbol of subservience, of humility, the proper state for a priest asking for purification.

After this short interlude, which underlines the proper, penitent, state the priest should be in, the author returns to the structure of a prayer of purification we saw in the first prayer. Like in the first prayer the author continues on to request that Christ not reject him: μὴ ἀποστρέψῃς τὸ πρόσωπόν σου ἀπ' ἐμοῦ· μηδὲ ἀποδοκιμάσῃς με ἐκ παίδων σου this corresponds to: καὶ μὴ ἀπορρίψῃς με ἀπὸ τοῦ προσώπου σου, μὴ βδελύξῃς, με τὴν ἐμὴν ἀναξιότητα[889] in the first prayer, where the priest also asks not to be removed from the face of Christ. The first prayer goes on to ask for mercy, quoting from Psalm 50: ἀλλ' ἐλέησόν με ὁ Θεὸς κατὰ τὸ μέγα ἔλεός σου, καὶ κατὰ τὸ πλῆθος τῶν οἰκτιρμῶν σου, ἐξάλειψον τὸ ἀνόμημά μου.[890] In the "Prayer of the Veil," however, it is not only purification that is sought, but worthiness, the worthiness to participate in the Anaphora: ἀλλ' ἀξίωσόν με προσενέχθηναί σοι τὰ Δῶρα ταῦτα, ὑπ' ἐμοῦ τοῦ ἁμαρτωλοῦ καὶ ἀναξίου δούλου σου. The prayer proper, before the *ekphonesis*, ends on a profound note, however. One is still a "sinful and unworthy servant," even after all of the purification prayed for.

---

[888] It is not the phrasing that is referenced, but the fact that these prayers are said while bowing the head, note too that the *ekphonesis* of the alternate "Prayer of the Bowing of the Head" is set up similarly to the *Ekphonesis* of this Prayer of the Veil, built around the dichotomy of Christ's place in the Liturgy.
[889] Cf. section I.1 line 14.
[890] Cf. section I.1 line 15-16.

This underscores what is said at the beginning of the prayer, no one is worthy to minister to Christ, and it is only through Christ that this worthiness is gained.

5. (section I.4 lines 17-19): Σὺ γὰρ εἶ ὁ ἁγιάζων καὶ ἁγιαζόμενος, προσφέρων τε καὶ προσφερόμενος, ὁ δεχόμενος καὶ δεκτός, ὁ διδοὺς καὶ διαδιδόμενος. Καὶ σοὶ τὴν δόξαν ἀναπέμπομεν, μετὰ τοῦ Πατρός, καὶ τοῦ ἁγίου Πνεύματος. Νῦν καὶ.

The *ekphonesis* of this prayer emphasizes the point made by the author in the second section of this prayer: the dichotomy of Christ, his human and divine natures, and their place in the Liturgy. The author does this in a string of participles: Christ is the one who "...hallows and is hallowed, the one who offers and is offered, the one who accepts and is accepted, who receives and is distributed..." this all points to Christ's role in the Liturgy as the Eucharist and His place as the "High Priest" who carries out the Liturgy.

I.VI. The Other Prayer of the Veil among the Egyptians.

While this prayer cannot be considered original to the Liturgy of St. Gregory, nevertheless, this prayer became part of the Liturgy, and must therefore be discussed. This prayer marks the beginning of the Coptic Liturgy of St. Gregory, we will be briefly discussing how the Coptic text differs from the Greek text, in this Hammerschmidt's commentary will be indispensable. This will not be necessary for this prayer, however, since, though there are numerous differences between the Coptic and the Greek text this particular prayer is identical in its Coptic and Greek versions.[891]

1. Structure[892]

Like many prayers in this liturgy, this one begins with a direct address, unlike the majority of the prayers in this Liturgy, however, it is not a direct address of Christ, but a more general address of God. Following this initial address are three descriptive phrases which serve to define how God works within the context of this prayer. Following these descriptions are two sets of requests, in the first set of requests, the priest asks for purification, this section ends with a descrition of how this purification will allow the priest to fulfill his function in the Anaphora. The second set of requestst emphasizes and completes the thought of the purification requested in the first set, in the context of the Anaphora, it too culminates in describing the result of these requests. The structure of this prayer is also shown in the following table:

---
[891] Hammerschmidt (1957). pg. 85
[892] Cf. also Hammerschmidt (1957). pg. 87 for another exposition of the structure of this prayer.

The Liturgy of Saint Gregory the Theologian

Table I.VI.1: The Other Prayer of the Veil among the Egyptians[893].

The Other Prayer of the Veil among the Egyptians
1. Direct address of God as Lord and Pantokrator: Κύριε ὁ Θεὸς ἡμῶν, ὁ Παντοκράτωρ

2. Phrases which describe God:
  I.   Omniscience
       ὁ ἐπιστάμενος τὸν νοῦν τῶν ἀνθρώπων
  II. Judge of men
       ὁ ἐτάζων καρδίας καὶ νεφροὺς
  III. Origin of the liturgical function of the priest
       ὁ ἐμὲ τὸν ἀνάξιον καλέσας πρὸς τὴν σὴν λειτουργίαν ταύτην

3. First set of requests: Purification of soul and body
  I.   not to be turned away
       μὴ βδελύξῃς με· μηδὲ τὸ πρόσωπόν σου ἀποστρέψῃς ἀπ' ἐμοῦ.
  II. the wiping out of transgressions
       Ἀλλ' ἐξάλειψόν μου πάντα τὰ παραπτώματα
  III. the washing of body and soul
       καὶ ἀπόπλυνόν μου τὸν ῥύπον τοῦ σώματος, καὶ τὸν σπῖλον τῆς ψυχῆς
  IV. the receiving of holiness
       καὶ ὅλον με ἁγίασον.
      a. Result of the first set of requests: that the priest not be rejected.
          Ἵνα μὴ ἱκετεύων σε δοῦναι ἄφεσιν ἄλλοις ἁμαρτιῶν, αὐτὸς ἀδόκημος γένωμαι.

4. Second set of requests: Purification and the grace to participate in the Anaphora   I.   not to be rejected

---

[893] Section I.5 lines 1-14.

Ναὶ Κύριε μὴ ἀποστραφείης με τεταπεινωμένον καὶ κατῃσχυμμένον

II. the grace of the Holy Spirit

ἀλλ' ἐξαπόστειλόν μοι τὴν χάριν τοῦ ἁγίου σου Πνεύματος

III. worthiness to stand about the Altar and to offer sacrifice

καὶ ἀξίωσόν με παραστῆναι ἐπὶ τὸ ἅγιόν σου Θυσιαστήριον ἀκατακρίτως. Καὶ προσφέρειν σοι τὴν λογικὴν καὶ ἀναίμακτον προσφορὰν ταύτην μετὰ συνειδήσεως καθαρᾶς.

   a. Result of the Liturgy when undertaken in purity:

      i. forgiveness of sins

Εἰς συγχώρησιν τῶν ἐμῶν ἁμαρτημάτων καὶ τῶν παραπτωμάτων, καὶ εἰς ἄφεσιν τῶν τοῦ λαοῦ σου ἀγνοημάτων.

      ii. rest for those fallen asleep

Εἰς ἀνάπαυσιν καὶ ἀναψυχὴν τῶν προκεκοιμημένων πατέρων ἡμῶν καὶ ἀδελφῶν

      iii. support for the people

καὶ εἰς στηριγμὸν παντὸς τοῦ λαοῦ σου.

5. *Ekphonesis* and the Trinitarian formula:

Εἰς δόξαν σὴν τοῦ Πατρὸς, καὶ τοῦ Υἱοῦ, καὶ τοῦ ἁγίου Πνεύματος. Νῦν καὶ.

2. Function

1. (section I.5 lines 2-3): Κύριε ὁ Θεὸς ἡμῶν, ὁ Παντοκράτωρ, ὁ ἐπιστάμενος τὸν νοῦν τῶν ἀνθρώπων, ὁ ἐτάζων καρδίας καὶ νεφροὺς, ὁ ἐμὲ τὸν ἀνάξιον καλέσας πρὸς τὴν σὴν λειτουργίαν ταύτην·

This section introduces the subject in this prayer: Κύριε ὁ Θεὸς ἡμῶν. Before describing what the ‚Lord our God does, however, the author gives four descriptive phrases. He is 1. "Pantokrator," 2. "the one who knows the inner hearts of men;" 3. "who tests the hearts and reins,"[894] and 4. "who calls me, the unworthy, to this Your Liturgy." Each of these four phrases describe a different aspect of God's divinity: 1. power, God is the Pantokrator, the all-powerful; 2. knowledge, God is all-knowing, He can see the ‚inner hearts'

---

[894] In ancient Greek philosophy and medicine, the heart and the kidneys were thought to be the seat of the soul (Crivellato and Ribatti. (2007). passim). Another possible seat of the soul was the 'phren,' the diaphragm. This phrase too is Biblical in origin: Cf. Jeremiah 17:10; Psalm 26:2; Psalm 7:9; Jeremiah 11:20.

of men and therefore knows about them what no-one else can; 3. judgment, this is a natural consequence of the first two descriptions, because God is all-powerful and all-knowing, He is able to ‚test' humanity; 4. liturgical function: it is God who ‚calls' the priest to the Liturgy, and who, as we will see in the rest of this prayer,[895] empowers him to carry it out.

According to Hammerschmidt, it is the second and fourth of these descriptions that are important, he calls the fact that God is all-knowing: "(eine) Eigenschaft, die für die kommende Bitte besonders wichtig ist..."[896] I believe, though, that Hammerschmidt overlooks the importance of the term "Pantokrator" here. In section four, the priest confesses his unworthiness to be a part of the Liturgy,[897] God is able to recognize the unworthiness of the priest, and to judge him as unworthy, but these attributes only allow God a passive role, only by also being Pantokrator can God bypass this unworthiness and call the priest to minister at the Liturgy. It is then not only the knowledge that is important in this prayer, but the ability of God to act on that knowledge and to make the priest worth, which make the Liturgy possible.

2. (section I.5 lines 4-10): μὴ βδελύξῃς με· μηδὲ τὸ πρόσωπόν σου ἀποστρέψῃς ἀπ' ἐμοῦ. Ἀλλ' ἐξάλειψόν μου πάντα τὰ παραπτώματα· καὶ ἀπόπλυνόν μου τὸν ῥύπον τοῦ σώματος, καὶ τὸν σπῖλον τῆς ψυχῆς, καὶ ὅλον με ἁγίασον. Ἵνα μὴ ἱκετεύων σε δοῦναι ἄφεσιν ἄλλοις ἁμαρτιῶν αὐτὸς ἀδόκιμος γένωμαι. Ναὶ Κύριε μὴ ἀποστραφείης με τεταπεινωμένον καὶ κατησχυμμένον, ἀλλ' ἐξαπόστειλόν μοι τὴν χάριν τοῦ ἁγίου σου Πνεύματος, καὶ ἀξιωσόν με παραστῆναι ἐπὶ τὸ ἅγιόν σου Θυσιαστήριον ἀκατακρίτως. Καὶ προσφέρειν σοι τὴν λογικὴν καὶ ἀναίμακτον προσφοφὰν ταύτην μετὰ συνειδήσεως καθαρᾶς.

As request for purification in the first "Prayer of the Vei" is structured in a similar manner to the request for purification in the "Prayer of Access" at the beginning of the Liturgy, so we see a similar Structure here as well. In both of these sections the prayers for purification begin with the priest recognizing his own unworthiness in this prayer: ἐμὲ τὸν ἀνάξιον and in the first "Prayer of the Veil:" ἐπίβλεψον ἐπ' ἐμὲ τὸν ἁμαρτωλὸν καὶ ἀχρεῖον δοῦλον σου however, the order of the requests is changed, as illustrated in the following table:

---

[895] As well as in the previous prayer.
[896] Hammerschmidt (1957). pg. 87 "A quality which is especially important for the coming requests."
[897] Hammerschmidt (1957). pg. 86

Table I.VI.2: *Differences in the request for purification:* [898]

The Prayer of the Veil	The Prayer of the Veil among the Egyptians
1. Request for empowerment and grace from the Holy Spirit. 2. The ability to stand about the ‚Holy Table' and to offer the ‚spotless Body and the sacred Blood.' 3. Request not to be rejected. 4. Request for worthiness (purification).	1. Request not to be rejected (corresponds to part three in the first prayer). 2. Request for purification and holiness (corresponds to part four in the first prayer). 3. The request that the Holy Spirit be sent down upon the priest (corresponds to part one of the first prayer). 4. The ability to stand about the ‚Holy Altar' and to bring forth the offering (corresponds to part two from the first prayer).

This correspondence of content in the two Prayers of the Veil can be explained using the description of the second prayer by Hammerschmidt: "Das Gebet der Greglit ist ein typisches Vorbereitungsgebet, wie es so oft am Beginn liturgischer Handlungen zu finden ist."[899] Even if the various parts that make up this prayer are in a different order each one contains the necessary elements for this type of prayer.

Hammerschmidt discusses another intersting problem that comes up in this prayer: how to understand the term λογικὴν in the phrase τὴν λογικὴν καὶ ἀναίμακτον προσφοφὰν ταύτην.[900] He concludes that this term must be translated by the word ‚geistig:' "...in der

---

[898] Hammerschmidt divides the "Bitte um Heiligung zum heiligen Dienst" "the request for sanctification fort he sacred service" into three parts: "negativ: ...(verwirf mich nicht...),...(wende dein Antlitz nicht von mir ab...)" "negative: ...(do not cast me away)...(do not turn Your face away from me)" and "positiv: ...(wasche ab...), ...(reinige mich...)" "positive...(wash away)...(purify me)" and the "Bitte um Herabsendung des heiligen Geistes zum würdigen Vollzug der Eucharistiefeier." "Prayer for the sending down of the Holy Spirit for the worthy celebration of the Eucharist." Hammerschmidt (1957 pg. 87
[899] Hammerschmidt (1957). pg. 89 "The prayer of the Liturgy of St. Gregory is a typical prayer of preparation, like it is so often found at the beginning of liturgical action."
[900] See Hammerschmidt (1957). pg. 88-89

griechischen Sakralsprache bedeutet λογικός "geistig"und "göttlich", wofür in der lateinischen spiritalis eintrat."[901] That the term "spiritual" rather than "rational" is better is also argued by Hammerschmidt:[902] "Im Neuen Testament werden λογικός und πνευματικός nebeneinander gebraucht, so dass λογικὴ θυσία = πνευματικὴ θυσία "Opfer im Geist" bedeutet."[903] This term is also widely used in Liturgy, and it seems especialy in the Egyptian Liturgies, so for example the Coptic Liturgy of St. Mark has: "...AND OFFER thee this SACRIFICE, HOLY REASONABLE SPIRITUAL and unbloody..."[904] This helps to confirm this second Liturgy of the Veil as secondary, and seems to substantiate Hammerschmidt's claim that this prayer is of Egyptian origin.[905]

3. (section I.5 lines 10-13) Εἰς συγχώρησιν τῶν ἐμῶν ἁμαρτημάτων, καὶ τῶν παραπτωμάτων, καὶ εἰς ἄφεσιν τῶν τοῦ λαοῦ σου ἀγνοημάτων. Εἰς ἀνάπαυσιν καὶ ἀναψυχὴν τῶν προκεκοιμημένων πατέρων ἡμῶν καὶ ἀδελφῶν, καὶ εἰς στηριγμὸν παντὸς τοῦ λαοῦ σου,

This section discusses the purpose of the Liturgy, described by Hammerschmidt as: "Zweck: 1. Nachlassung der Sünden des Priesters 2. Nachlassung der Sünden des Volkes 3. Ruhe den verstorbenen Vätern und Brüdern 4. Erbauung des ganzen Volkes..."[906] This describes the effect on the Liturgy on the Church, but not on the entire Church as described in the previous Prayer, the Liturgy is not efficacious for the heavenly, but for the human part of the Church, the priest (or bishop), the congregation (the people) and for those fallen asleep.

---

[901] Hammerschmidt (1957). pg. 88, Footnote 28 "in the Greek sacred language λογικός means 'spiritual' and 'divine' for which Latin *spiritalis* is used."
[902] After discussing how this term is used in pre-Christian sacrificial language.
[903] Hammerschmidt (1957). pg. 88 "In the New Testament λογικός and πνευματικός are used interchangeably, so that λογικὴ Θυσία = πνευματικὴ Θυσία, means spiritual sacrifice."
[904] Hammond and Brightmann (1896). pg. 163
[905] This is not to say, however, that this phrase comes up exclusively in Egyptian Liturgies, we see the same phrase in the *Testamenta XII Patriarcharum*: Προσφέρουσι δὲ Κυρίῳ ὀσμὴν εὐωδίας λογικήν, καὶ ἀναίμακτον προσφοράν. *Testamentum* 3 chapter 3 section 6 line 2. "They bear to the Lord a spiritual fragrance and a bloodless sacrifice."
[906] Hammerschmidt (1957). pg. 87 "Purpose: 1. Forgiveness of the sins of the priest. 2. Forgiveness of the sins of the people. 3. Peace for the fathers and brothers who have died. 4. The building up of the entire people."

4. (lines 121-122): εἰς δόξαν σὴν τοῦ Πατρὸς, καὶ τοῦ Υἱοῦ, καὶ τοῦ ἁγίου Πνεύματος. Νῦν καὶ.

In the *ekphonesis* glory is offered to the Trinity.[907] Interesting is the invocation of the Trinity, here we do not see the Christ centered invocations we have seen so far, this, more than anything else shows that this prayer is not addressed to Christ. Up to this point the only vocatives: Κύριε ὁ Θεὸς ἡμῶν...Παντοκράτωρ... Κύριε do not specify who is being addressed. In this *ekphonesis* it seems that it is the Trinity as such that is being invoked, rather than any specific member of the Trinity. The priest does pray, though, to have sent upon him the χάριν τοῦ ἁγίου <u>σου</u> Πνεύματος. The σου implies that this prayer is, in fact, addressed to a specific member of the Trinity. We can discover which member of the Trinity is meant by looking at parallels in other Ekphoniseis, such as in the Liturgy of St. Basil, the majority of the prayers in the pre-Anaphora are addressed to God the Father, and in the *ekphoneseis* the same focus on the Trinity is found, for example: Ὅτι πρέπει σοι πᾶσα δόξα, τιμὴ καὶ προσκύνησις, τῷ Πατρὶ καὶ τῷ Υἱῷ καὶ τῷ Ἁγίῳ Πνεύματι, νῦν καὶ ἀεὶ καὶ εἰς τοὺς αἰῶνας τῶν αἰώνων.[908] It seems then, that this prayer is addressed to God the Father, rather than to the Trinity as a whole, and certainly not to Christ.

I.VII. The Prayer of the Greeting[909]

The Greek term: ἀσπασμός, which I have tranlsated as "greeting," is the *terminus technicus* in the Greek (and Coptic) liturgy for the kiss of peace.[910] The kiss of peace as a ritual was practiced by the Early Christians, the ritual is already mentioned in the New Testament: Romans 16:16,[911] I Corinthians 16:20,[912] II Corinthians 13:12,[913] I Thessalonians 5:26[914] and I Peter 5:14.[915] Other Early Church writers also dealt with this kiss of peace such as St. Augustine, Origen, St. John Chrysostom and Pseudo-Dionysius among others.

---

[907] Ibid.
[908] "For to You is due all glory, honor and worship to the Father and the Son and the Holy Spirit, now and ever and to the ages of ages."
[909] Though the Coptic translation of this prayer is very similar, like the Prayer of the Veil, there are some differences which are noted by Hammerschmidt on pg. 94 of his commentary, the most important differences are two phrases in the Greek which are not in the Coptic translation: ὁ τῷ πατρὶ συναΐδιος καὶ ὁμοούσιος, καὶ σύνθρονος καὶ συνδημιουργός and χάρισαι παντὸς ἀποκάθαρον μολύσματος, παντὸς δόλου καὶ πάσης κακίας, καὶ πανουργίας καὶ τῆς θανατηφόρου μνησικακίας.
[910] Cf. Hammerschmidt (1957). pg. 92
[911] ἀσπάσασθε ἀλλήλους ἐν φιλήματι ἁγίῳ "Greet one another with a holy kiss."
[912] same as above.
[913] ἀσπάσασθε ἀλλήλους ἐν ἁγίῳ φιλήματι "Greet one another with a holy kiss."
[914] ἀσπάσασθε τοὺς ἀδελφοὺς ἐν φιλήματι ἁγίῳ "Greet all the brothers with a holy kiss."
[915] ἀσπάσασθε ἀλλήλους ἐν φιλήματι ἀγάπης "Greet one another with a kiss of love."

Another good proof for the antiquity of this ritual is its the widespread in various liturgical families. The prayer in the Liturgy of St. Gregory corresponds to the prayer following the singing of the *Agnus Dei* in the Tridentine Mass: Domine Jesu Christe, qui dixisti Apostolis tuis: Pacem relinquo vobis, pacem meam do vobis: ne respicias peccata mea, sed fidem Ecclesiae tuae, eamque secundum voluntatem tuam pacificare et coadunare digneris: Qui vivis et regnas Deus per omnia saecula saeculorum. Amen.[916] Here one can also see the difference between the ritual in the East and the West, in the East the kiss of peace is exchanged before the Anaphora begins, while in the West the kiss of peace is exchanged near the reception of Communion. In the Byzantine Liturgies, the kiss of peace is exchanged following the exclamation: ἀγαπήσωμεν ἀλλήλους, ἵνα ἐν ὁμονοίᾳ ὁμολογήσωμεν[917] made by the deacon. The kiss of peace was also used in other liturgical rites, outside of the Liturgy proper, the new bishop, for example, was greeted with a "kiss of peace, just as in Justin's account in reference to the newly baptized"[918] We see then, how central the kiss of peace was, and is, in the liturgical life of the Church.

In the Liturgy of St. Gregory we see that, like the "Prayer of the Veil," there is an alternate prayer offered for the "Prayer of the Greeting." The question presents itself, then: which of these two prayers is original to the Liturgy and which is secondary. In Hammerschmidt's commentary, he quotes H. Engberding, that: "später aufgenommene Gebete vor den älteren stehen,"[919] we have already seen, however, that this is not always true. The second of the "Prayers of the Veil" is certainly not original to this Liturgy, and it is not in the first place. This tendence cannot always be followed then, and I must agree with Hammerschmidt who says that, while it is not possible to say without doubt which prayer is original, it is more likely that the author wrote the first prayer,[920] although both prayers are addressed to Christ.[921] I believe that the first prayer is the original and the second is the one that was adapted for two main reasons: the christology of the two prayers and the Structure. Especially in the beginning of the first prayer, where the author discusses the nature

---

[916] Missale Romanum (1922). Pg. 303. Note that this prayer in the Roman Liturgy has the same quotation, John 14:27, as this, first "Prayer of the Greeting." "Lord Jesus Christ, who said to Your Apostles: 'peace I leave with you, my peace I give to you: do not regard my sins, but the faith of Your church, You will have deemed it worthy to pacify and bring them into one: who lives and reigns as Lord for all ages of ages. Amen."
[917] "Let us love one another, so that in oneness we may confess."
[918] Jungmann (1959). pg. 66
[919] Hammerschmidt (1957). pg. 98 "prayers adopted later stand before older ones."
[920] Hamerschmidt (1957). pg. 98
[921] The fact that both of these prayers are addressed to the Son shows that whichever of these prayers was adopted into the Liturgy was adopted early and adapted to fit the scheme of the Liturgy, unlike the Prayer of the Veil among the Egyptians, which was still addressed to the Father.

of Christ, we see a christology that is in line with that of the Cappadocian Fathers and of the Nicene Creed. While the divinity of Christ and the Incarnation are stressed in both prayers, this christology is a more central aspect of the first prayer. In fact, the first prayer is only recognizable as a "Prayer of the Greeting" at the end of the prayer,[922] in the quotation of John 14:27. This quotation seems oddly out of place in the prayer, it is even placed in the wrong context: it is placed just preceeding the Ascension, but in John this passage comes before the arrest and crucifixion. There are only two explanations for this: 1. that the author made a mistake or 2. that this prayer is a composite of two, patched together to make a "Prayer of the Greeting."

That this is merely a mistake seems unlikely. The author has an otherwise extensive knowledge of Scripture, and such a blatant mistake would be odd. The second option seems more likely, the christological theme would work better as the first prayer of the Anaphora, wich often deals with the history of salvation.[923] It may be that later authors added a new Prayer to replace what they thought to be an oddly set up Prayer of the Greeting. Hammerschmidt too believes that this prayer may be original to this Liturgy.[924] He notes too that the Coptic manuscripts attribute this prayer either to St. Gregory the Theologian or to St. Severus,[925] he rules out St. Severus as a possibility however, since this would place the dating of the prayer into the Monophysite controversy, and there is no trace of Monophysite theology in this prayer, instead the theology fits perfectly into the anti-Arian stance of St. Gregory.[926] Hammerschmidt offers the possible authorship of this prayer as a reason that the Anaphora, which he assumes is not written by St. Gregory, is called the Anaphora of St. Gregory, he postulates that the "Prayer of the Greeting of St. Gregory" may have lent its author to the rest of the Anaphora.[927] I tend to disagree with this premise. While the Coptic manuscripts may attribute this prayer to St. Gregory, the Greek manuscripts do not, and not only the Anaphora, but the entire Liturgy is attributed to St. Gregory. That the authorship of the enitire anaphora is taken by analogy from one prayer seems to be already a stretch, but that the entire Liturgy takes its authorship from one prayer is highly unlikely. Hammerschmidt, though, believes that the traditional authors attributed to

---

[922] Hammerschmidt claims that the history of salvation presented in the Prayer is the "Grund derer um den würdingen Empfang und die würdigen Weitergabe des Friedenskusses gebeten wird..." (Pg. 93).
[923] A possible explanation for this prayer is that the author wrote several prayers of the Anaphora to one of which he added a quotation that allowed him to use it as the ‚Prayer of the Greeting.' Another explanation, offered by Hammerschmidt, is that the author added the christological section of this prayer onto an already existing "Prayer of the Greeting." pg. 96
[924] Hammerschmidt (1957). pg. 95-96
[925] Ibid.
[926] Ibid.
[927] Ibid.

the Liturgies are certainly not the actual authors,[928] in the meantime, however, it has been proven that, for example, the Liturgies of St. Basil and St. John Chrysostom were, in part, written by the traditional authors.[929] Though it may not be possible to prove that St. Gregory was the author of this whole Litrugy, it is conceivable, seeing the christology presented, that he wrote a number, or even most, of the prayers within the Liturgy.

1. Structure

This prayer can be divided into six major sections, including the *ekphonesis*. In the first section, the author discusses the divinity of Christ, he does so by dealing with 1. the nature of His existence; 2. His relationship with the Father and 3. His role as Creator.

In the second section the author moves on to discussing Christ's role in Salvation, the central statement of this section is: τῆν ἡμῶν ἐνεχείρησας σωτηρίαν. The author explains why this salvation comes to pass using a participial phrase: βουλόμενος dependant on this participle are two infinitives: ἀνακαινίσαι and ἀναγαγεῖν. At the end of this section, the author describes how Christ brings the salvation He wills to pass, in the Incarnation: ἀτρέπτως σὰρξ γενόμενος καὶ ἐνηνθρώπησας.

The third section is, to a great extent, a continuation of the description of how Christ brings salvation to pass. Here the author, in a list of four phrases, gives a step by step description of what Christ did, following the Incarnation, to bring about salvation: 1. mediating between God the Father and humanity; 2. destroying the "middle wall of partition;" 3. joining the ‚earthly with the heavenly;' and, finally, 4. filling the ‚flesh with dispensation.'

The fourth section culminates in the quotation from John 14:27: εἰρήνην ἀφιημι ὑμῖν, εἰρήνην τὴν ἐμὴν δίδωμι ὑμῖν.[930] Odd, however, is the context in which this quotation is placed. As one would expect in a prayer that spans the Incarnation and Salvation (Christ's life and Ressurection), the prayer ends in the Ascension into Heaven, shortly before which, the author claims that Christ says this. This quotation is, however, from before Christ's arrest and execution, we will discuss why this quotation is out of place in the next section of this commentary.

In the same way as the third section builds off of the second, the fifth section builds off of the fourth. The peace mentioned in the fourth section preface the requests in the fifth. Three requests: peace, purification and worthiness to exchange the holy kiss, are followed by the effects of these requests, if fulfilled: the ability to partake in the Eucharist.

---

[928] c.f Hammerschmidt (1961). pg. 10
[929] Cf. *Oxford Dictionary of Byzantium* (1991)
[930] "Peace I leave with you, my peace I give to you."

The Commentary

The *ekphonesis* is written in the style which we have become accustomed to: 1. epitheta of Christ; 2. the sending up of glory to Christ and 3. the Trinitarian formula.

Table I.VII.1: The structure of The Prayer of the Greeting[931]

The Prayer of the Veil

1. Section One: description of the divinity of Christ:
 	
    I.   The nature of Christ's existence:
            i. ὁ ὢν
            ii. καὶ προὼν
            iii. καὶ διαμένων εἰς τοὺς αἰῶνας.
    II.   His relationship with the Father: Ὁ τῷ Πατρὶ...
            i. συναΐδιος
            ii. καὶ ὁμοούσιος
            iii. καὶ σύνθρονος
            iv. καὶ συνδημιουργός.
    III.   His role as Creator:
            i. Ὁ διὰ μόνην ἀγαθότητα ἐκ τοῦ μὴ ὄντος εἰς τὸ εἶναι παραγαγὼν τὸν ἄνθρωπων, καὶ θέμενος αὐτὸν ἐν παραδείσῳ τρυφῆς.

2. Section Two: Christ's role in Salvation.
 	
    I.   Why Christ brought salvation to pass:
        a. ἀνακαινίσαι βουλόμενος, καὶ πρὸς τὸ ἀρχαῖον ἀναγαγεῖν ἀξίωμα.
            i. History of the Fall: Ἀπάτῃ δὲ τοῦ ἐχθροῦ καὶ παρακοῇ τῆς σῆς ἐντολῆς παραπεσόντα... (dependent on the previous statement, but is placed before it in the text).
    II.   Main statement of this section: Christ himself brings our salvation to pass:
        a. οὐκ ἄγγελος, οὐκ ἀρχάγγελος, οὐ πατριάρχης, οὐ προφήτης τὴν ἡμῶν ἐνεχείρησας σωτηρίαν

---

[931] Cf. section I.6 lines 1-21.

The Liturgy of Saint Gregory the Theologian

	III.	How Christ brought salvation to pass:
	a.	ἀλλ' αὐτὸς ἀτρέπτως σὰρξ γενόμενος καὶ ἐνηνθρώπησας. Κατὰ πάντα ὡμοιώθης ἡμῖν ἐκτὸς μόνης ἁμαρτίας.

3. Section Three: (continues thought from above) step by step history of salvation:

    I.   Mediation:
Μεσίτης ἡμῶν γέγονας καὶ τοῦ Πατρὸς

    II.   Destroyer of the wall of partition between humanity and God, and of the enmity between humanity and God:
καὶ τὸ μεσότοιχον τοῦ φραγμοῦ· καὶ τὴν χρονίαν ἔχθραν καθελών.

    III.   Joiner of the heavenly and the earthly:
Τὰ ἐπίγεια τοῖς ἐπουρανίοις συνῆψας, καὶ τὰ ἀμφότερα εἰς ἓν συνήγαγες

    IV.   Filling of the flesh with dispensation:
καὶ τὴν ἔνσαρκον ἐπλήρωσας οἰκονομίαν.

4. Section Four: Completion of salvation and transition to the kiss of peace.

    I.   Completion of salvation in the Ascension into Heaven:
Καὶ μέλλων σωματικῶς ἐλαύνειν εἰς οὐρανούς, θεικῶς τὰ πάντα πληρῶν

    II.   Transition to the quotation:
τοῖς ἁγίοις σου μαθήταις καὶ ἀποστόλοις ἔλεγες·

    III.   Quotation from John 14:27:
εἰρήνην ἀφίημι ὑμῖν, εἰρήνην τὴν ἐμὴν δίδωμι ὑμῖν.

5. Section Five: Requests and the consequeces of those requests.

    I.   Requests:
        a.   For peace:
Ταύτην καὶ νῦν εἰρήνην ἡμῖν δώρησαι Δέσποτα.
        b.   For purification:
Χάρισαι
            i. from pollution

        παντὸς ἀποκάθαρον μολύσματος

      ii. deceit

        παντὸς δόλου

      iii. wickedness

        καὶ πάσης κακίας

      iv. villainy

        καὶ πανουργίας

      v. death bringing malice

        καὶ τῆς θανατηφόρου μνησικακίας.

    c. For worthiness in the exchange of the holy kiss:

      Καὶ καταξίωσον ἡμᾶς, ἀσπάσασθαι ἀλλήλους ἐν φιλήματι ἁγίῳ

II. Consequensce of the Requests

    εἰς τὸ μετασχεῖν ἀκατακρίτως τῆς ἀθανάτου καὶ ἐπουρανίου σου δωρεᾶς.

    a. the means by which these consequences are achieved:

      Χάριτι τῇ σῇ, εὐδοκίᾳ τοῦ Πατρὸς, καὶ ἐνεργείᾳ τοῦ παναγίου σου Πνεύματος.

6. Section Six: the *Ekphonesis*.

    I. Epitheta of Christ:

      a. Lord of the Dance.

        Σὺ γὰρ εἶ ὁ χορηγὸς

      b. Giver of Good things.

        καὶ δοτὴρ πάντων τῶν ἀγαθῶν.

    II. Glory sent up to Christ:

      Καὶ σοὶ τὴν δόξαν τὴν ἀίδιον δοξολογίαν ἀναπέμπομεν

    III. The Trinitarian formula:

      σὺν τῷ ἀνάρχῳ σου Πατρὶ καὶ τῷ ἁγίῳ σου Πνεύματι, νῦν καὶ ἀεί.

2. Function

1. (section I.6 lines 3-5): Ὁ ὢν καὶ προὼν, καὶ διαμένων εἰς τοὺς αἰῶνας. Ὁ τῷ Πατρὶ συναΐδιος καὶ ὁμοούσιος καὶ σύνθρονος καὶ συνδημιουργός. Ὁ διὰ μόνην ἀγαθότητα ἐκ

τοῦ μὴ ὄντος εἰς τὸ εἶναι παραγαγὼν τὸν ἄνθρωπων, καὶ θέμενος αὐτὸν ἐν παραδείσῳ τρυφῆς.

The purpose of the first part of this prayer is made clear in the very first sentence, the christological statment made is strongly anti-Arian.[932] The first sentence focuses on the eternal nature of Christ's existence, He is the one who "exists, who preexists, and who exists unto the ages." This type of introduction (one which stresses eterity) to a prayer occurs several more times in this Liturgy. In the beginning of the Anaphora the author writes: ὁ ὢν, Θεὲ, Κύριε,[933] the Prayer of the Breaking begins: ὁ ὢν, ὁ ἦν, ὁ ἐλθών καὶ πάλιν ερχόμενος,[934] and the Prayer of Freedom begins: ὁ ὢν, ὁ ἦν, ὁ ἐλθὼν εἰς τὸν κόσμον τοῦ φωτίσαι αὐτὸν.[935] The numerous times that such an introduction is used, shows that the eternity of Christ, and thus His divinity, is one of the ideas that the author wishes to convey, it is also a strong indication that the same author wrote these prayers, and that it is therefore these prayers, rather than their alternates (if any) that are original to this Liturgy.[936] Important to note too is that the term ὁ ὢν shows that the author Christ as the God of the Old Testament, this term is the Greek translation of Yahweh, the name of God revealed to Moses in the burning bush.[937] This term is also found in Byzantine (and other Eastern) Iconography, the Icons of Christ have a cross inscribed in the halo, within this cross this term is inscribed, allowing Christ to be identified as such, and identifies Him as the God of the Old Testament.

Perhaps more imporant than ὁ ὢν in the anti-Arian stance here is the term: καὶ προών. The Arians contested the divinity of Christ by claiming that Christ was a created being, that is, that there was a time when the Son did not exist. This phrase cuts at this central statement of Arian theology. If Christ pre-exists, that is, has always existed, then there was never a time when the Son did not exist, and therefore He is not a creation, but, as the author goes on to say, the Creator. There remains one aspect of the eternal existence of Christ that the author discusses, that He will "remain unto the ages." This aspect is the least powerful of the three in the anti-Arian polemic of this section.

Following the discussion of Christ's eternal nature, the author turns to describing Christ's divinity in relationship to the Father. This is unusual, in that the author has, up to this point, shied away from emphasizing this relationship, the Father is not even mentioned

---

[932] Cf. Hammerschmidt (1957). pg. 94
[933] Section II.2 line 13
[934] Section III.2 line2.
[935] Section III.11 line 3.
[936] With the exception of the "Prayer of the Breaking."
[937] Exodus 3:1-22

outside of the Ekphoneseis in the first few prayers, so that a focus on the Father's divinity does not obscure the purpose of the work, the emphasis of Christ. Here though, this relationship does not obscure Christ, but serves to reinforce His divinity. The author uses four terms to outline this relationship: συναίδιος καὶ ὁμοούσιος καὶ σύνθρονος καὶ συνδημιουργός, immediately noticable is that three of the terms are built in the same way, συν- with a following term, here –eternal, -throned and –creator. This type of wordplay becomes popular in Byzantine hymnography, especially when the relationship between Christ and the Father is being emphasized, for example in the Ressurectional Apolytikion of the Plagial of the First Tone: τὸν συνάναρχον Λόγον Πατρὶ καὶ Πνεύματι.

The fourth term: ὁμοούσιος is unusual in a Liturgy. Here, though, the term fits into the anti-Arian, Nicene christology underscored in this section. Interestingly, a similar phrase is used by Gelasius of Cyzicus in his work *Historia eccesiastica*: ἐκ τοῦ ἀεὶ ὄντος ἀληθινοῦ θεοῦ καὶ πατρός, συνάναρχος τῷ πατρί, συναΐδιος τῷ πατρί, συμβασιλεύων ἀεὶ τῷ πατρί, ὁμοούσιος τῷ πατρί, ἰσοδύναμος τῷ πατρί, συνδημιουργὸς τῷ πατρί.[938] In this work, Gelasius, a fifth century author from Bithynia, shows that the Nicene Fathers were not Monophysites. The similarity may be explained in that Gelasius of Cyzicus was familiar with this Liturgy, this would be further proof of a Byzantine reception of this Liturgy.

The final part of this section describes Christ as the Creator of humanity and the one who set them in a "garden of delight." Along with setting Christ up as Creator, referring back to the συνδημιουργός above, this section shows that this prayer may originally have been a prayer from the Anaphora, the phrase:[939] ἐκ τοῦ μὴ ὄντος εἰς τὸ εἶναι παραγαγὼν τὸν ἄνθρωπων corresponds almost exactly to a phrase from the prayer before the singing of the *Sanctus* Hymn in the Liturgy of St. John Chrysostom: Σὺ ἐκ τοῦ μὴ ὄντος εἰς τὸ εἶναι ἡμᾶς παρήγαγες[940] in the Anaphora of the Liturgy of St. Basil[941] too is the Creation of humanity discussed: πλάσας γὰρ τὸν ἄνθρωπον, χοῦν λαβὼν ἀπὸ τῆς γῆς ... τέθεικας αὐτὸν ἐν τῷ Παραδείσῳ τῆς τρυφῆς which corresponds to the final phrase of this section: καὶ θέμενος αὐτὸν ἐν παραδείσῳ τρυφῆς. These exact correspondences indicate that this was originally meant to be a part of the Anaphora, and not, as Hammershcmidt postulates, the

---

[938] Gelasius Cyzicnus. *Historia Ecclesiastica*. Book 2 chapter 15 section 3 line 7 "coeternal with the Father, reign eternally with the Father, consubstantial with the Father, of the same strength with the Father, co-creator with the Father."
[939] The Prayers of the Kiss of Peace in most of the major Liturgies do not contain such histories of salvation, Cf. the Liturgies of St. James (Greek and Syrian; Hammond and Brightmann (1896). Pp. 43 and 83 respectively) and the Coptic Liturgy of St. Mark (Hammond and Brighmann (1896). Pg. 162-163).
[940] Trempelis (1982). pg. 103 "You brought us into being out of nothing."
[941] Hamond and Brightman (1896). pg. 324 and Trempelis (1982). pg. 179-180 "for You created humanity, taking dust from the earth...You placed him in the Paradise of delight."

The Liturgy of Saint Gregory the Theologian

means by which Christ allows the kiss of peace to be exchanged.[942] Further substantiation of this theory is provided in the content of the next section.

2. (Section I.6 lines 5-9): Ἀπάτῃ δὲ τοῦ ἐχθροῦ καὶ παρακοῇ τῆς σῆς ἐντολῆς παραπεσόντα, ἀνακαινίσαι βουλόμενος καὶ πρὸς τὸ ἄρχαιον ἀναγαγεῖν ἀξίωμα. οὐκ ἄγγελος, Οὐκ ἀρχάγγελος, οὐ πατριάρχης, οὐ προφήτης τὴν ἡμῶν ἐνεχείρησας σωτηρίαν, ἀλλ' αὐτὸς ἀτρέπτως σὰρξ γενόμενος καὶ ἐνηνθρώπησας. Κατὰ πάντα ὡμοιώθης ἡμῖν ἐκτὸς μόνης ἁμαρτίας.

This section deals with the fall and salvation of humanity. Interesting is that the fall is glossed over, there is no mention of Adam and Eve, of the serpent, of the tree of the knowledge of good and evil. The history of the fall is summarized in two phrases, as being "deceived by the enemy" and in "disobedience of your commandment" these corresponds to a phrase from the Anaphora of St. Basil: καὶ τῇ ἀπάτῃ τοῦ ὄφεως[943] this shows, once again, the possible origin of this prayer in the Anaphora. The focus here is on Christ, however, and this requires that the Prayer focus more on salvation, in which Christ plays a far greater role than on the fall. The author goes so far as to present salvation as the will of Christ, as if the rest of the Trinity played no part in bringing salvation about: βουλόμενος it is Christ who wills salvation "to renew ... and to return him to his ancient worthiness," this centrality of Christ in salvation is further emphasized in the following phrase: οὐκ ἄγγελος, οὐκ ἀρχάγγελος, οὐ πατριάρχης, οὐ προφήτης τὴν ἡμῶν ἐνεχείρησας σωτηρίαν. This is an important christological point, which underscores the Nicene emphasis of Christ as God, the author shows that no power in heaven, "not an angel, nor an archangel" nor on earth, "not a patriarch, or a prophet" was involved in bringing about salvation, since these would not have been able to, and it was only in the Incarnation that salvation was achieved: ἀλλ' αὐτὸς ἀτρέπτως σὰρξ γενόμενος καὶ ἐνηνθρώπησας. The author's discussion of the Incarnation is also important in refuting the claim that this Liturgy was a late Monophysite liturgy.[944] It is not the Incarnation as such that shows it is not Monophysite, rather it is the last phrase of this section: κατὰ πάντα ὡμοιώθης ἡμῖν ἐκτὸς μόνης ἁμαρτίας. The Monophysite teaching is that Christ had no human nature, only a divine nature, since the author describes Christ as becoming in "all things like us, except for sin alone" he cannot be a Monophysite, because this shows Christ as true man, as well as the true God he was described as above.

---

[942] Hammerschmidt (1957). Pg. 93
[943] Hammond and Brightman (1896). pg. 324 and Trempelis (1982). pg. 180 "and through the deceit of the serpent."
[944] Bouyer (1989). pg. 357

3. (Section I.6 lines 9-12): Μεσίτης ἡμῶν γέγονας καὶ τοῦ Πατρὸς, καὶ τὸ μεσότοιχον τοῦ φραγμοῦ, καὶ τὴν χρονίαν ἔχθραν καθελών. Τὰ ἐπίγεια τοῖς ἐπουρανίοις συνῆψας, καὶ τὰ ἀμφότερα εἰς ἓν συνήγαγες, καὶ τὴν ἔνσαρκον ἐπλήρωσας οἰκονομίαν.

In this section the author discusses the steps of salvation. As Hammerschmidt notes,[945] much is taken from Ephesians 2: 14. Hammerschmidt also notes that: "Hier ist an eine Versöhnung des ganzen Kosmos mit Gott gedacht, wobei der Bezug auf Eph 2 wiederum offensichtlich ist. Der Gedanke, dass auch die unvernünftige Kreatur durch den Sündenfall mitbetroffen wurde, ist ja auf Grund der Paulusbriefe nicht ungewöhnlich, vgl. Röm 8, 22."[946] Is seems to be the inclusion of "peace" in Ephesians 2:14 which leads Hammerschmidt to believe that this was meant as a "Prayer of the Greeting:" "vor ein älteres, schon vorhandenes Friedensgebet gesetzt."[947] The connection with peace in this section is, perhaps, the reason that this Anaphoral prayer could be added on, to another prayer and then used as the "Prayer of the Greeting."

The way in which salvation takes place in this prayer is through the reunification of God and man. The author has stated that Christ wished to return humanity to its original state, the state enjoyed in the "garden of delight." In order to do this Christ: Τὰ ἐπίγεια τοῖς ἐπουρανίοις συνῆψας, καὶ τὰ ἀμφότερα εἰς ἓν συνήγαγες, καὶ τὴν ἔνσαρκον ἐπλήρωσας οἰκονομίαν each of these steps brings humanity closer together to God, until they are one. This is reminiscent of the idea of *Theosis* as espoused by Gregory of Nyssa, that salvation consists of "becoming divine by grace"[948] this *Theosis*, becoming like God, is made possible through the unification brought about by Christ.

4. (Section I.6 lines 12-14): Καὶ μέλλων σωματικῶς ἐλαύνειν εἰς οὐρανοὺς, θεικῶς τὰ πάντα πληρῶν, τοῖς ἁγίοις σου μαθηταῖς καὶ ἀποστόλοις ἔλεγες· εἰρήνην ἀφίημι ὑμῖν, εἰρήνην τὴν ἐμὴν δίδωμι ὑμῖν.

Hammerschmidt comments on the term θεικῶς and its contrast with σωματικῶς: "obwohl Christus nach seiner Gottheit alles zu jeder Zeit – also auch zur Zeit seiner leiblichen Himmelfahrt – erfüllt, ist er leiblich – um das Heilswerk zu vollenden – in den Him-

---

[945] Hammerschmidt (1957). pg. 93
[946] "Here the idea is the reconciliation of the entire cosmos with God, and the allusion to Eph. 2. Is clear. The idea that even the unintelligent creatures were affected in the fall is not unusual based on the letters of Paul, Cf. Romans 8:22."
[947] Hammerschmidt (1957). pg. 96 "placed before an older, already present 'Prayer of the Peace.'"
[948] Cf. McGuckin (2006)

mel aufgefahren. Wenn man diesen Text so auffasst, ergibt sich eine staunenswerte theologische Prägnanz, die eine wohl ausgewogene Christologie verrät."[949]

The author also uses this section to lay out the culmination of salvation in the end of Christ's Incarnation, the Ascension into Heaven. "Filling all things with divinity" also refers back to the history of salvation presented in the last section, especially the final: τὴν ἔνσαρκον ἐπλήρωσας οἰκονομίαν. The discussion of the Incarnation is also the final part of the first prayer. This first part was added onto a second, pre-existing,[950] "Prayer of the Greeting." The second prayer begins with a quotation from John 14:27. The problem, as we mentioned above, is that the prayer puts this quotation in the context of the Ascension. In the Gospel, however, this quotation is part of a longer exposition on the "Promise of the Holy Spirit" as the editors of the New Revised Standard Version title this section, this section comes before even the betrayal of Christ by Judas, so long before the Ascension into Heaven. Such a problem in the prayer, as we discussed above, points to a knitting together of two different prayers, in this case the transition from an Anaphoral prayer to a "Prayer of the Greeting." This knitting together also points to this prayer as primary, it is unlikely that a new prayer, most of which does not fit into the scheme of a "Prayer of the Greeting," would be written to replace, or stand as an alternate to one that is written in the style of a traditional "Prayer of the Greeting."

5. (Section I.6 lines 14-18): Ταύτην καὶ νῦν εἰρήνην ἡμῖν δώρησαι Δέσποτα. Χάρισαι παντὸς ἀποκάθαρον μολύσματος, παντὸς δόλου καὶ πάσης κακίας καὶ πανουργίας καὶ τῆς θανατηφόρου μνησικακίας. Καὶ καταξίωσον ἡμᾶς, ἀσπάσασθαι ἀλλήλους ἐν φιλήματι ἁγίῳ, εἰς τὸ μετασχεῖν ἀκατακρίτως τῆς ἀθανάτου καὶ ἐπουρανίου σου δωρεᾶς. Χάριτι τῇ σῇ, εὐδοκίᾳ τοῦ Πατρὸς, καὶ ἐνεργείᾳ τοῦ παναγίου σου Πνεύματος.

The prayer continues in a series of requests for purification. In the "Prayer of the Greeting" one must ask for purification in order to be worthy enough to "greet one another in a holy kiss." We see a similar theme in the "Prayer of the Greeting" in the Syrian Liturgy of St. James:[951]

> O God of all and Lord, account these our unworthy selves worthy of this salvation, o thou lover of men, that pure of ALL GUILE AND all HYPOCRISY we may greet one another WITH A KISS HOLY and divine, being united

---

[949] Hammerschmidt (1957). pg. 93-94 "Although Christ fills all things at all times – so even at the time of His bodily Ascension, he ascended bodily in order to complete salvation. When one interprets this text in this way, it shows an astonishing theological fullness, that shows a well developed Christology."

[950] According to Hammerschmidt, see above.

[951] And in the alternate "Prayer of the Greeting," which we will see in the following section.

with the bond of love and peace: through our Lord God and Saviour Jesus Christ thine only Son our Lord through whom and with whom to thee is fitting flory and honour and dominion with thy Spirit allholy and good and adorable and lifegiving and consubstatial with thee now and ever and world without end[952]

The similarities between this "Prayer of the Greeting," and the second section of the prayer in the Liturgy of St. Gregory are striking: 1. request for purification, 2. quotation from Romans 16:16 "greet one another with a holy kiss," 3. *ekphonesis*. This Structure, then, shows a typical form of the "Prayer of the Greeting."

Purity is asked for, however, not only for the worthy participation in the kiss of peace, but also for the worthy participation in the ἀθανάτου καὶ ἐπουρανίου σου δωρεᾶς. This request seems out of place, and is not found in Syrian or Greek Liturgy of St. James. We do find mention of the Eucharist in the "Prayer of the Greeting" of the Coptic Liturgy of St. Mark: "...Vouchsafe us therefore, o our master, with a pure heart and a soul full of grace to STAND before thee AND OFFER thee this SACRIFICE, HOLY REASONABLE SPIRITUAL and unbloody, for pardon of our trespasses AND forgiveness of THE ERRORS of thy PEOPLE..."[953] This may be, then, typical of Egyptian Prayers of the Greeting, confirming Hammerschmidt's theory that this was a pre-existing Egyptian prayer which was added to the first part of the prayer.[954]

Extremely interesting is the final phrase of this section: Χάριτι τῇ σῇ εὐδοκίᾳ τοῦ Πατρός, καὶ ἐνεργείᾳ τοῦ παναγίου σου Πνεύματος. This phrase bears the hallmarks of an *ekphonesis*, or part of an *ekphonesis*. While the usual sending up of glory, which begins an *ekphonesis*, is omitted, the Trinitarian formula is here presented. This is odd, since the prayer has a complete *ekphonesis* following this section, and it is highly unusual that a prayer has two. This seems to be further proof of the division of the prayer into two parts.
6. (Section I.6 lines 19-21): Σὺ γὰρ εἶ ὁ χορηγὸς καὶ δοτὴρ πάντων τῶν ἀγαθῶν. Καὶ σοὶ τὴν δόξαν ἀίδιον δοξολογίαν ἀναπέμπομεν σὺν τῷ ἀνάρχῳ σου Πατρί, καὶ τῷ ἁγίῳ σου Πνεύματι, νῦν καὶ ἀεὶ.

---

[952] Hammond and Brightmann (1986). Pg. 83. Note the mention of the Holy Spirit as "consubstantial with thee" in this 'Monophysite' Liturgy. Cf. also Day (1972). pg. 178.
[953] Hammond and Brightmann (1896). pg. 163
[954] This does not mean that the author was from Egypt, or even that the author was the one who put these two prayers together. Another problem is that this second part of the prayer is addressed to the Son as well, while the Prayer of the Greeting in the Coptic Liturgy of St. Mark, for example, is addressed to the Father. I believe this is because the model for the second part of this prayer was re-written to conform to the first part of the prayer.

Here we see the *ekphonesis* proper of this prayer. This *ekphonesis* is unremarkable insofar as it is made up of the usual elements: 1. epitheta of Christ; 2. sending up of glory and doxology and 3. Trinitarian formula with common epithets of the Father "beginning less" and of the Holy Spirit. Of the two epithets of Christ, the first is very interesting: ὁ χορηγὸς. This stands out because it is an unusual way of describing Christ. In 2 Peter 1:1-11, the verb ἐπιχορήγω is used of those who supply, but not of Christ, here this sense of "supplying" is transferred to Christ, as supplier, which is then supported by the second epithet "giver of good things." This epithet is also used in the *Apostolic Constitution* of Hippolytus.[955]

Where, though, did this *ekphonesis* come from? We have seen that the *ekphonesis* of the second prayer become incorporated into the main text. One possibility is that this is the *ekphonesis* of the first prayer is used as the *ekphonesis* for the entire prayer. A second possibility is that the person who united these two prayers wrote an entirely new *ekphonesis*. A third possibility is that this is an *ekphonesis* from another, unknown prayer, which is used here.

I.VIII. The alternate Prayer of the Greeting[956]

1. Structure.

This, second, Prayer of the Greeting is divided into three sections. The first section concerns the nature of Christ. The section begins with a direct address of Christ: Χριστὲ ὁ Θεὸς ἡμῶν, following this vocative are four phrases that underscore Christ's divine power:

---

[955] Bouyer (1986). pg. 90

[956] The Greek and Coptic texts do not vary as much in this prayer as in the previous prayer: Hammerschmidt notes on pg. 98 of his commentary that the only difference is: "Nur die Schlussformel weicht etwas von dem koptischen Text ab." The *ekphonesis* in the Coptic text is prefaced by a short dialogue between priest, people and deacon (Hammerschmidt translation lines 42-44 pg. 19): "Der Diakon spricht: Betet für vollkommenen Frieden und Liebe und den heiligen Friedenskuss (Plur.) der Apostel. Das Volk spricht: Herr, erbarme dich. Der Priester spricht…" This dialogue is not seen in the Greek text of the prayer. In the *ekphonesis* itself the Coptic text has a slightly different ending (Hammerschmidt translation lines 46-47): "…der Ruhm, die Ehre, die Herrlichkeit (eigentl.: Grösse) (und) die Anbetung (προσκύνησις), mit deinem guten (ἀγαθός) Vater und dem lebenspendenden und dir wesensgleichen (ὁμοούσιος) heiligen Geist (πνεῦμα) jetzt und zu aller Zeit und bis zur Ewigkeit aller Ewigkeiten. Amen." This is opposed to the ending of the *Ekphonesis* in the Greek text: καὶ σοὶ πρέπει ἡ παρὰ παντὸς συμφώνως δοξολογία τιμὴ καὶ προσκύνησις ἅμα τῷ ἀχράντῳ σου Πατρὶ καὶ τῷ ζωοποιῷ σου Πνεύματι. Νῦν, καὶ.' The final difference between the Coptic and Greek texts is following the *Ekphonesis*, where the Coptic text adds an exclamation of the deacon (Hammerschmidt translation lines 48-49. Pg. 21): "Der Diakon spricht: Grüsst einander mit heiligem Kuss. [Der Diakon spricht:] Herr, erbarme dich. Herr, erbarme dich. Herr, erbarme dich. Ja, Herr, der du bist Jesus Christus, der Sohn Gottes, erhöre uns und erbarme dich unser."

The Commentary

1. the first phrase discusses the relationship between Christ and the Father, He is the φοβερὰ καὶ ἀπερινόητος δύναμις τοῦ Θεοῦ καὶ Πατρός. In the following two phrases, Christ is described in terms of fire, and in terms of the angelic powers 2. Christ sits on the: φλογίνου θρόνου τῶν Χερουβὶμ and 3. Christ is accompanied by the πυρίνων δυνάμεων. In the last phrase, the author continues describing Christ in terms of fire, but returns to His divine nature 4. Christ "exists as God," as the "consuming fire."

The second section of the prayer is the longest, and it is in this section that the purpose of the prayer, the preparation for the "holy kiss" culminates. This section consists of a list of six requests for mercy, purification and for the worthy participation in the "holy kiss" and in the Eucharist. These requests are introduced by the reason because of which Christ will grant these requests: διὰ τὴν σὴν ἄφατον συγκατάβασιν καὶ φιλανθρωπίαν. Following this introduction, the author launches immediately into the list of requests, in this list there are two types of requests, negative and positive, the list is made in a pattern of one negative request followed by two positive. The list culminates in the effect that these prayers have: ἵνα μὴ εἰς κρίμα ἢ εἰς κατάκριμα, ἡμῖν γένηται τὸ θεῖον τοῦτον μυστήριον.

The final section of this prayer is the *ekphonesis*. This *ekphonesis* falls into the standard we have seen so far. Three sections make up this *ekphonesis*: 1. the descriptions of Christ; 2. the sending up of worship and doxology and 3. the Trinitarian formula.

A more detailed description of the Structure of this prayer is given in the following table:

Table I.VIII.1: the structure of the Alternate Prayer of the Greeting[957]

The Alternate Prayer of the Greeting

1. Section One: Christ's divine nature.
    I. Opening: Direct address of Christ.
        Χριστὲ ὁ Θεὸς ἡμῶν
    II. List of four descriptive phrases about Christ:
        a. relationship between Christ and God the Father
            ἡ φοβερὰ καὶ ἀπερινόητος δύναμις τοῦ Θεοῦ καὶ Πατρός.
        b. Christ who sits on the fiery throne of the Cherubim
            Ὁ τοῦ φλογίνου θρόνου τῶν Χερουβὶμ ὑπερκαθήμενος

---

[957] Section I.7 lines 1-17.

   c. Christ who is accompanied by the fiery powers
    καὶ ὑπὸ πυρίνων δυνάμεων δωρυφορούμενος
   d. Christ who is the burning fire, who exists as God
    καὶ πῦρ καταναλίσκον ὑπάρχων ὡς Θεός·

---

2. Section Two: Requests for mercy, purification and worthy participation in the ‚holy kiss.'
 I. Introduction to the requests: for what reason Christ will answer the requests
  καὶ διὰ τὴν σὴν ἄφατον συγκατάβασιν καὶ φιλανθρωπίαν
 II. List of six requests
   a. not to burn up the ‚wicked traitor' (negative request)
    μὴ φλέξας τῷ προσεγγισμῷ τὸν δολερὸν προδότην.
   b. to bring self realization (positive request)
    ἑλκῶν αὐτὸν εἰς μετάνοιαν, καὶ ἐπίγνωσιν τοῦ ἰδίου τολμήματος.
    i. how this self-realization is accomplished, through a ‚holy kiss' from Christ
     Ἀλλὰ φιλικὸν αὐτὸν ἀσπασάμενος ἀσμπασμόν,
   c. worthiness for the ‚holy kiss' (positive request)
    Καταξίωσον ἡμᾶς Δέσποτα, ἐπὶ τῆς φρικτῆς ταύτης ὥρας, ἐν ὁμονοίᾳ καὶ δίχα παντὸς ἐν δύο θυμοῦ, καὶ λειψάνου κακίας, ἀπολαβεῖν ἀλλήλους ἐν ἁγίῳ φιλήματι.
   d. Not to condemn ‚us' completely (negative request)
    Καὶ μὴ κατακρίνῃς ἡμᾶς, ὑπὲρ μὴ ὁλοτελῶς
   e. purification (positive request)
    καὶ καθὼς ἀρέσαι τῇ σῇ ἀγαθότητι, καθαρεύωμεν ἀπὸ
    i. from ‚every fruit of sin'
     τρυγὸς ἁμαρτίας
    ii. from wickedness
     καὶ πονηρίας
    iii. from deadly malice
     καὶ τῆς θανατηφόρου μνησικακίας.
   f. wash away ‚every stain of our transgressions' (positive request)
    ἐξάλειψον πᾶσαν κηλίδα παραπτωμάτων ἡμῶν
    i. why Christ washes away these trangsressions
     1. because of His compassion
      Ἀλλ' αὐτὸς τῇ σῇ ἀφάτῳ καὶ ἀνεκδιηγήτῳ εὐσπλαγχνίᾳ
     2. because of our weakness

The Commentary

> εἰδὼς τὸ πλάσμα ἡμῶν τὸ ἀσθενὲς καὶ κατώβρυθον

IV. Conclusion to the requests: what are the results of this purification.

> ἵνα μὴ εἰς κρίμα ἢ εἰς κατάκριμα, ἡμῖν γένηται τὸ θεῖον μυστήριον.

3. Section Three: *ekphonesis*.
    I. Epitheta of Christ
        a. who takes away sin
> Σὺ γὰρ εἶ ὁ δυνάμενος πᾶσαν ἀφιεῖν ἁμαρτίαν

        b. who passes over injustice
> καὶ ὑπερβαίνειν ἀδικίας καὶ ἀνομίας τῶν ταλαιπωρῶν ἀνθρώπων

        c. who purifies the whole world
> καθαρισμὸς τοῦ κόσμου παντὸς ὑπάρχων

    II. glory and doxology that is due to Christ
> καὶ σοὶ πρέπει ἡ παρὰ παντὸς συμφώνως δοξολογία τιμὴ καὶ προσκύνησις

    III. Trinitarian formula
> ἅμα τῷ ἀχράντῳ σου Πατρὶ, καὶ τῷ ζωοποιῷ σου Πνεύματι. Νῦν, καὶ.

2. Function

1. (Section I.7 lines 2-4): Χριστὲ ὁ Θεὸς ἡμῶν, ἡ φοβερὰ καὶ ἀπερινόητος δύναμις τοῦ Θεοῦ καὶ Πατρὸς. Ὁ τοῦ φλογίνου θρόνου τῶν Χερουβὶμ ὑπερκαθήμενος, καὶ ὑπὸ πυρίνων δυνάμεων δωρυφορούμενος, καὶ πῦρ καταναλίσκον ὑπάρχων ὡς Θεός,

This prayer is probably the secondary of the two Prayers of the Greeting. Hammerschmidt even postulates that: "Unwarscheinlich ist, dass der Kompilator oder Verfasser der Liturgie selbst zwei Gebete verfasst hat. Vielleicht hat er aber auch das zweite bereits vorgefunden und in die Liturgie – zur Auswahl – eingefügt."[958] The question though, if Hammerschmidt is correct and the author takes this second prayer from another source, is: why is this prayer addressed to Christ? One possibility is that the prayer was not originally addressed to Christ, but was rewritten by the author to conform to this Liturgy, like the author adapts the first prayer from the Greek Liturgy of St. James. That this prayer was adapted early would also explain why this prayer is addressed to Christ, while prayers add-

---

[958] Hammerschmidt (1957). pg. 98 "It is unlikely that the compiler or author of this liturgy wrote two prayers himself. Perhaps he added the second, preexisting, prayer into the liturgy – for variety."

ed later, such as the second "Prayer of the Veil," do not bother with this adaptation and are addressed to the Father. Another possibility is that this prayer was already addressed to Christ when adopted into this Liturgy. We see in other Egyptian liturgies, such as the Liturgy of St. Mark, that the "Prayer of the Greeting" is addressed to the Father,[959] the same is true for many other Eastern Liturgies, such as both the Syrian and Greek Liturgies of St. James.[960] There is another liturgical tradition, however, in which the "Prayer of the Greeting" is addressed to Christ, in the Tridentine Masss. Although this is a different liturgical tradition, this does show that there is a possibility of having such a prayer addressed to Christ outside the special context of this particular Liturgy. The third option is that this prayer was added by a later cleric, who thought that the first prayer was not sufficient, and that a new Prayer of the Greeting was required.

This prayer begins with a direct address of Christ: Χριστὲ ὁ Θεὸς ἡμῶν, this is not unusual, and so far the majority of the prayers have had a vocative at or near the beginning of the text. What is unusual is what follows: ἡ φοβερὰ καὶ ἀπερινόητος δύναμις τοῦ Θεοῦ καὶ Πατρὸς, that the author describes Christ according to His relationship with the Father. What is out of the ordinary is that Christ is presented subordinate to the Father as the "power of the Father," the author of the Liturgy has stayed away from such subordination so far, and this more than anything shows that this prayer is not original to this Liturgy.

Following this is a list of three further descriptions of Christ, these are very striking because each of them deals describes Christ in terms of fire. He sits upon "the fiery throne of the Cherubim" He is accompanied by "the fiery powers" and He exists as God, as the "consuming fire." God is often shown as fire in Scripture, the angel of God appeared to Moses as a burning bush,[961] the Holy Spirit descended on the apostles as tongues of fire,[962] this biblical imagery is adopted here, and it is used to emphasize the power and glory of Christ.

2. (Section I.7 lines 4-13): καὶ διὰ τὴν σὴν ἄφατον συγκατάβασιν καὶ φιλανθρωπίαν, μὴ φλέξας τῷ προσεγγισμῷ τὸν δολερὸν προδότην. Ἀλλὰ φιλικὸν αὐτὸν ἀσπασάμενος ἀσπασμόν, ἑλκὼν αὐτὸν εἰς μετάνοιαν, καὶ ἐπίγνωσιν τοῦ ἰδίου τολμήματος. Καταξίωσον ἡμᾶς Δέσποτα ἐπὶ τῆς φρικτῆς ταύτης ὥρας, ἐν ὁμονοίᾳ καὶ δίχα παντὸς ἐν δύο θυμοῦ, καὶ λειψάνου κακίας, ἀπολαβεῖν ἀλλήλους ἐν ἁγίῳ φιλήματι. Καὶ μὴ κατακρίνῃς ἡμᾶς, ὑπὲρ μὴ ὁλοτελῶς καὶ καθὼς ἀρέσαι τῇ σῇ ἀγαθότητι, καθαρεύωμεν ἀπὸ πάσης τρυγὸς

---

[959] Cf. Hammond and Brightmann (1896). pg. 123
[960] Cf. Hammond and Brightmann (1896). pp. 43 and 83
[961] Exodus 3: 1-22
[962] Acts 2: 1-31

ἁμαρτίας, καὶ πονηρίας, καὶ τῆς θανατηφόρου μνησικακίας. Ἀλλ' αὐτὸς τῇ σῇ ἀφάτῳ καὶ ἀνεκδιηγήτῳ εὐσπλαγχνίᾳ, εἰδὼς τὸ πλάσμα ἡμῶν τὸ ἀσθενὲς καὶ κατώβρυθον, ἐξάλειψον πᾶσαν κηλίδα παραπτωμάτων ἡμῶν, ἵνα μὴ εἰς κρίμα ἢ εἰς κατάκριμα, ἡμῖν γένηται τὸ θεῖον τοῦτον μυστήριον.

This section focuses on purification. That the majority of this prayer focuses on this purification shows that this was written solely as a "Prayer of the Greeting," unlike the first prayer. The goal of this purification is twofold: ἀπολαβεῖν ἀλλήλους ἐν ἁγίῳ φιλήματι and ἵνα μὴ εἰς κρίμα ἢ εἰς κατάκριμα, ἡμῖν γένηται τὸ θεῖον τοῦτον μυστήριον the kiss of peace and the Eucharist. Here we see another possible link to the Egyptian origin of this prayer, as we saw in the last section, it is the Egyptian Liturgies that deal with the Eucharist as well as the kiss of peace.

Since we have seen a number of purification prayers in this liturgy before, there is no need to go over the prayer in detail. There are, however, a number of phrases which bear a closer look. The author is able to phrase much of the prayer in terms referring to kissing. The phrase: τὸν δολερὸν προδότην is part of the first request not to be turned away, it refers to the kiss Judas gave to Christ when betraying him in the Garden of Gethsemane.[963] In this way the author connects the request of purification with an example of giving a "kiss of peace" unworthily. After dealing with the consequences of a kiss given unworthily, the author deals with the consequences of a worthy kiss: φιλικὸν αὐτὸν ἀσπασάμενος ἀσπασμὸν after asking Christ not to turn away from him, the priest asks Him to greet him "with a kiss of friendship" this kiss, unlike that of Judas is worthy, and brings not destruction, but revelation: "bring him to repentance and to the realization of his personal deeds" and this revelation leads to salvation. An interesting aspect of a worthy kiss of peace is unity: ἐν ὁμονοίᾳ καὶ δίχα παντὸς ἐν δύο θυμοῦ unity is an important part of Christianity, this is illustrated in Ephesians 4:5-6. Here the author shows that unity makes the difference between giving the kiss of peace worthily or unworthily. The final phrase of interest here is: τῆς θανατηφόρου μνησικακίας. This is rather rare, the only other prayer seems to be the first "Prayer of the Greeting" in this Liturgy. This, along with the fact that it is addressed to Christ, and the stress on the divine power of Christ in fire, seems to affirm Hammerschmidt's postulation that this prayer was added to the Liturgy by the original author as an alternate, and adapted to fit the christology of this Liturgy.

3. (Section I.7 lines 14-17): Σὺ γὰρ εἶ ὁ δυνάμενος πᾶσαν ἀφιεῖν ἁμαρτίαν, καὶ ὑπερβαίνειν ἀδικίας καὶ ἀνομίας τῶν ταλαιπωρῶν ἀνθρώπων, καθαρισμὸς τοῦ κόσμου παντὸς

---

[963] Cf. Matthew 26: 47-50

ὑπάρχων, καὶ σοὶ πρέπει ἡ παρὰ παντὸς συμφώνως δοξολογία τιμὴ καὶ προσκύνησις, ἅμα τῷ ἀχράντῳ σου Πατρὶ, καὶ τῷ ζωοποιῷ σου Πνεύματι. Νῦν, καὶ.

The *ekphonesis* of this prayer follows the same Structure as that of the last prayer. Interesting to note, however, is the continuation of the aspect of purification in the *ekphonesis*. The initial epitheta of Christ are: ὁ δυνάμενος πᾶσαν ἀφιεῖν ἁμαρτίαν, καὶ ὑπερβαίνειν ἀδικίας καὶ ἀνομίας τῶν ταλαιπωρῶν ἀνθρώπων, καθαρισμὸς τοῦ κόσμου παντὸς ὑπάρχων each one of these stresses the role of Christ as the purifier from sin. This is unusual in that the *ekphonesis* does not always continue the thought of the main prayer, but we have seen this same phenomenon in the original "Prayer of the Gospel," in which the *ekphonesis* begins by stressing Christ as the illuminator, following a prayer in which illumination is prayed for.

Commentary Part II: The Anaphora

II.I. Introduction

The Anaphora comprises perhaps the most important part of the liturgy, and has consequently received the lion's share of scholarly attention. It is in during the Anaphora that the Eucharistic elements are consecrated and prepared to be consumed by the congregation. Despite variations in the specific structure, all liturgical families of the Eastern Church have certain elements in common in the Anaphora: the Sursum Corda dialogue, in which the celebrant, deacon and people are involved in a dialogue that echoes the Jewish meal prayers; the Sanctus, with its introductory and concluding prayers; the Consecration, in which the words of Christ at the last Supper are repeated; the *epiklesis*, in which the Holy Spirit is entreated to descend on the Eucharistic elements and transform them; various commemorations of the saints, the living, the dead; and an ending doxology before moving on to the post-Anaphora and the distribution of the Eucharist.

Table II.I.1: The general Structure of an Anaphora.

The Anaphora
1. The Sursum Corda Dialogue
2. The Pre-Sanctus Prayer
3. The Post-Sanctus Prayer
4. The Consecration
5. The Epiklesis
6. The Commemorations
7. The Final Doxology

The commonalities found in the Eastern, or as Jungmann terms it, the Oriental Liturgy, are due to its "correspondence to the primitive *eucharistia* of the ancient Christians ..."[964] The only major difference he sees between this primitive form and the Anaphorae found in the Oriental liturgies involves the *epiklesis*:

> In each Mass, according to Christ's institution, there are two points where the divine omnipotence is conjoined to the action of the priest, thus causing a supernatural effect: the Consecration and the communion. Hence it is very natural that in the priest's prayer some acknowledgement should be made of the fact that here God Himself has to act...This petition we may call *epiclesis*, an invocation of God by which that effect is solicited. If the petition concerns the Consecration we call it a Consecration-*epiclesis*, if the communion, a communion-*epiclesis*.[965]

He goes on to explain how the *epiklesis* can assist in identifying the family of origin of the liturgy: "The homeland of the solemn and elaborate *epiclesis*...is the Syrian (or Syro-Byantine) liturgical region. Here it must have become customary towards the end of the fourth century (not earlier) to insert such a prayer in the place of a more ancient formula."[966] This, more elaborate formula asks God to not only send down His Holy Spirit to change the gifts, but to send the Holy Spirit upon the worshippers as well.[967]

The Anaphora fulfills an important function for scholars of liturgical history as well, in preserving original sections of the text with a minimum of change. Since this section of the liturgy is so integral and holy, it is, as explained above, the part of the liturgy

---

[964] Jungman (1959). pg. 218
[965] Ibid.
[966] Jungman (1959). pg. 219
[967] Jungman (1959). pp. 218-219; see also the Anaphora of the Liturgy of St. Basil.

that tends to contain the oldest prayers, since later editors, copyists and clerics are less likely to change a prayer in the Anaphora than a prayer from another part of the Liturgy. Consequently, the Anaphorae of the various liturgies have received the majority of the scholarly attention, and the Liturgy of St. Gregory is no exception. Both commentaries, that of Hammerschmidt and that of Gerhards, focus on the Anaphora. It is, therefore, not necessary to spend a great amount of time on the theology presented; instead the focus of this commentary will be on the literary format, especially to understand how the functionalization seen so far is continued and adapted to fit the Anaphora.

This change is exemplified in the use of the term *homoousios*, in both the preceding and following sections; the term is used as an epithet of Christ and the Holy Spirit. This epithet serves both to make a theological point, that both Christ and the Holy Spirit are, in fact, God, and serves the anti-Arian function; by using this term, the Arians and Pneumatomachians are excluded from worshipping in this liturgy without making any overt attack on them. The Arians and Pneumatomachians are excluded because they cannot themselves acknowledge Christ or the Holy Spirit as God; it is not an outside force of persecution that bars them from participation, but their own beliefs.[968] Our expectation would be, then, that the author would use this term in the Anaphora as well, since the important place of the Anaphora in the liturgy would make this more effective, as the interest and attention of the worshipper is kept by the succession of important prayers and petitions. This expectation, however, is never fulfilled; *homoousios* is not used once in the Anaphora. This seeming lack of utilization can, perhaps, be attributed to a hesitancy on the part of the author to so blatantly functionalize a section of the liturgy that was otherwise treated with such reverence and conservatism.

This is not to say, however, that the author abandons his agenda entirely during the Anaphora. The author continues with the "Christusanrede," which is, especially in the Anaphora, almost unheard of.[969] He also continues more subtly in attributing to Christ the function and action usually attributed to other members of the Trinity. This transference is noticeable, for example in the *epiklesis*. One of the ways in which the date and place of origin of a liturgy can be determined is in the form of the *epiklesis*. There are numerous forms of this *epiklesis*, as described by Jungman: "With regard to the wording the epiclesis can be formulated in many ways: simply that God may bring about the effect; or that He

---

[968] Cf. Newman (2014). Pg. 2
[969] There are examples of other Anaphorae in which prayers are addressed to Christ, but none in which He is the sole recipient of all prayers. It is also far more common to find prayers outside of the Anaphor addressed to Christ than it is within the Anaphora.

send His Holy Spirit over the gifts or into the souls of the recipients..."[970] It is the "Syro-Byzantine" liturgy of the late fourth century, which shows the more developed, more complicated epiklesis that asks God to send down His Holy Spirit. What we know of the Liturgy of St. Gregory places it directly into this time frame and location, but the author plays with this paradigm, it is not God the Father who is asked to send down the Holy Spirit, but Christ:

> Therefore, Master, transform the things lying before You with Your voice; complete this mystical Liturgy, being present Yourself; preserve for us the memory of Your worship. Send down Your All-Holy Spirit, so that visiting, He may hallow and transform these precious and holy Gifts lying before You, by His holy, good and glorious presence, into the Body and Blood of our redemption.

Although this prayer could refer to God the Father, since nowhere is it explicitly stated that it is Christ who is being addressed, the phrases: ... being present Yourself... and ... preserve for us the memory of Your worship... show that it is, in fact, Christ who is being addressed; the relationship of the liturgy and Christ has been discussed on numerous occasions in the text. The ambiguity of the text may be attributed to the normal practice of directing this prayer to God the Father. The author puts Christ in the place usually reserved for God the Father, as the sender of the Holy Spirit.[971]

The Anaphora of the Liturgy of St. Gregory is especially interesting, since, as is shown by Gerhards and Hammerschmidt, the text includes elements of Egyptian, Syrian and Byzantine influence. Although these are well documented by these two authors, they are important enough to warrant another discussion.

The Structure of the Anaphora is similar to that described above, the Structure of the *eucharistia* of the primitive Church, as it is termed by Jungman.

1. The Anaphora opens with a blessing of the priest and the Sursum Corda dialogue.

2. Following the Sursum Corda dialogue is the Ἀρχὴ τῆς προσκομίδης, which consists of two prayers divided by a command by the deacon for those seated to stand. It seems possible, according to the title of the prayer, that this is where the Anapho-

---

[970] Jungman (1959). pg. 218
[971] Making Christ send the Holy Spirit seems reminiscent of the filioque clause which was inserted into the Creed at the Third Council of Toledo (589), which too was meant to combat the Arians, in this case the Visigothic invaders.

ra proper begins, I have chosen to include the *Sursum Corda* dialogue, however, and follow the precedent set in Gerhard's text.

3. The central section of the Anaphora, and the section in which the Eucharistic gifts are prepared, spans the five chapters: the pre-Sanctus prayer; the Sanctus, the hymn of the Angels transitions to the Consecration; the Consecration, in which the Consecration in the Synoptic Gospels[972] are echoed; finally the *epiklesis* finishes this section of the Anaphora; it is in the *epiklesis* that the priest prays that the Holy Spirit be sent down upon the gifts prepared in the previous chapters.

4. Though the previous section is the most important, since it is in that section that the Eucharist is prepared, the majority of the Anaphora is taken up by the various remembrances. These take two general forms: 1. either the remembrances begin with the command: μνήσθητι or 2. the remembrances are in the form of a series of petitions. These remembrances cycle through every possible aspect of both the church and everyday life, dealing with the living, the dead, the saints, as well as the proper rising of the river water and other matters that would be of concern to the ordinary layman.

5. Closing the Anaphora is a benediction, which transitions to the prayer of the breaking and the distribution of the Eucharist.

II.II. The Sursum Corda.

This dialogue is found, in slightly different forms, in every extant, complete liturgical text and it is, unlike many of the other sections held in common in more than one liturgy,[973] almost always found in the same place, as the opening of the preface to the Anaphora.[974] The universal nature of this dialogue suggests that this was already a widespread phrase in the early Christian Church. The origin of these phrases seems to be in Scripture; a similar phrase is found in one of the books of the Major Prophets, Lamentations. In Lamentations 3:41, which reads: ἀναλάβωμεν καρδίας ἡμῶν ἐπὶ χειρῶν πρὸς ὑψηλὸν ἐν οὐρανῷ.[975] The Greek of the *Sursum Corda,* however, has ἄνω σχῶμεν rather than ἀναλάβωμεν. The other command given by the priest: "let us give thanks to the Lord" has

---

[972] Cf. Matthew 26:26; Mark 14:22 Luke 22:19 and 1 Corinthians 11:24-25.
[973] Such as the *Sanctus* and the *Gloria*.
[974] *Oxford Dictionary of the Christian Church*, 3rd edition (ed. F. L. Cross & E. A. Livingstone), p.1561. Oxford University Press, 1997.
[975] "Let us raise up our hearts upon our hands towards the heights in heaven."

numerous parallels in Scripture, in which exhortations are made to give thanks to God, for example in Psalm 107:1.[976]

Some differences do exist in the formulation of this dialogue, and even the Coptic translation of the Liturgy of St. Gregory does not conform exactly to the Greek original. In the first exclamation of the Deacon, for example, the Greek text has merely: Στῶμεν καλῶς[977] while the Coptic text has a much longer Deacon's part: ΣΤΩΜΕΝ ΚΑΛΩΣ: ΣΤΩΜΕΝ ΕΥΛΑΒΩΣ: ΣΤΩΜΕΝ ΕΚΤΕΝΩΣ: ΣΤΩΜΕΝ ΕΝ ΕΙΡΗΝΗ: ΣΤΩΜΕΝ ΜΕΤΑ ΦΟΒΟΥ ΘΕΟΥ: ΚΑΙ ΤΡΟΜΟΥ ΚΑΙ ΚΑΤΑΝΥΞΕΩΣ. ΠΡΟΣΦΕΡΕΙΝ ΚΑΤΑ ΤΡΟΠΟΝ: ΣΤΑΘΗΤΕ: ΕΙΣ ΑΝΑΤΟΛΑΣ ΒΛΕΨΑΤΕ: ΠΡΟΣΧΩΜΕΝ[978] Other differences occur in the *Sursum Corda* itself, which in the Greek text is: Ἄνω σχῶμεν τὰς καρδίας[979] while the Coptic text adopts the form used in the Liturgy of St. Mark: ΑΝΩ ΥΜΩΝ ΤΑΣ ΚΑΡΔΙΑΣ.[980] The Coptic text also moves the final exclamation of the priest in the *Sursum Corda* dialogue of this liturgy: Ἄξιον καὶ δίκαιον, ἄξιον καὶ δίκαιον to the beginning of the following prayer.[981]

Already the *Apostolic Constitutions* one of the earliest liturgical texts, of the late third or early fourth century,[982] uses this dialogue as an introduction to the Anaphora: Ἡ χάρις τοῦ παντοκράτορος Θεοῦ καὶ ἡ ἀγάπη τοῦ κύριου ἡμῶν Ἰησοῦ Χριστοῦ καὶ ἡ κοινωνία τοῦ ἁγίου Πνεύματος ἔστω μετὰ πάντων ὑμῶν...Καὶ μετὰ τοῦ πνεύματος σοῦ...Ἄνω τὸν νοῦν...Ἔχομεν πρὸς τὸν Κύριον...Εὐχαριστήσωμεν τῷ Κυρίῳ...Ἄξιον καὶ δίκαιον.[983] The structure of the *Sursum Corda* dialogue in the *Apostolic Constitutions* is the same as that found in the other liturgies: three phrases exclaimed by the priest followed by the response by the people. The difference lies what is being raised up to God. As the name implies, the usual liturgical term, at least in the Byzantine and Roman liturgical families, is not νοῦς, but καρδία. We must consider, then, if it is possible that not the heart, but the soul, was originally raised to God, as there is a clear distinction between *nous* and

---

[976] The Scriptural instances are adopted into the liturgy via the Passover ritual. Cf. Bouyer (1989). pg. 91 ff.
[977] "Let us stand well"
[978] Hammerschmidt (1957). pg. 20. A great percentage of Coptic liturgical text keeps the original Greek phrasing rather than translate it, as is the case here. "Let us stand well, let us stand in awe, let us stand with fervor, let us stand in peace, with trembling and stupefaction. To offer according to custom: stand: look unto the east: let us attend."
[979] Hammond and Brightman (1896). pg. 125 "let us lift up (our) hearts."
[980] Hammerschmidt (1957). pg. 22; Cf. Day (1972). pg. 89 and Cuming (1990). pg. 20 footnote 7. "upward with the hearts"
[981] Cf. Hammond and Brightman (1896). pg. 22
[982] Bradshaw (2002). pp. 85-87
[983] Hammond and Brightman (1896). pg. 14 "The grace of the all powerful God and the love of our lord Jesus Christ and the communion of the Holy Spirit be with all of you...and with your spirit...upward with the soul...we lift it up to the Lord...let us thank the Lord...it is worthy and just."

The Liturgy of Saint Gregory the Theologian

kardia in liturgical language.[984] This seems to be borne out by the *Sursum Corda* dialogue found in other liturgies. In another Syrian rite liturgy, that of the Nestorian "Church of the East,"[985] it is not the heart that is raised to God, but the mind: "The grace of our Lord Jesus Christ and the love of God the Father, and the felloiwiship of the Holy Ghost be with us all now and ever and world without end...Lift up your minds...Unto thee, o God of Abraham and of Isaac and of Israel o glorious king."[986] In the *Soorp Baradack* as well, the liturgy of the Armenian Apostolic Church, the same νοῦς is lifted up: "The grace, the love and the divine sanctifying power of the Father and the Son and the Holy Ghost be with you and with all...The doors, the doors, with all wisdom and caution lift up your minds with divine fear...We lift them up unto thee, o Lord almighty."[987] It is difficult to come to a conclusion from these liturgies, as they include a West Syrian, an East Syrian and a Syro-Byzantine rite liturgy. The theological background of the various liturgies is also different, as one of them was written before even the Arian controversy broke out, one of them belongs to the Nestorian Church and the third belongs to a non-Chalcedonian "Monophysite" Church.

Opposed to the liturgies that use νοῦς in the Sursum Corda are the liturgies that use καρδία, which are in the clear majority. Here too we see a distribution over various rites and in various theological families. In the non-Chalcedonian Churches it is the Egyptian rite that uses this term, as is seen in the Greek and Coptic Anaphoras of St. Mark: Ὁ Κύριος μετὰ πάντων...Ἄνω ἡμῶν τὰς καρδίας...Εὐχαριστήσωμεν τῷ Κυρίῳ.[988] In the Syro-Byzantine family, we see the Liturgy of St. Basil and the Liturgy of St. John Chrysostom, both with an identical *Sursum Corda* dialogue: Ἡ χάρις τοῦ Κυρίου ἡμῶν Ἰησοῦ Χριστοῦ καὶ ἡ ἀγάπη τοῦ Θεοῦ καὶ Πατρὸς καὶ ἡ κοινωνία τοῦ ἁγίου Πνεύματος εἴη μετὰ πάντων ἡμῶν...Ἄνω σχῶμεν τὰς καρδίας...Εὐχαριστήσωμεν τῷ Κυρίῳ.[989] Another member of the Syro-Byzantine family, the Liturgy of St. Gregory, has a similar phrasing to that of the Liturgies of St. Basil and St. John Chrysostom: Ἡ ἀγάπη τοῦ Θεοῦ καὶ Πατρός καὶ ἡ χάρις τοῦ μονογενοῦς υἱοῦ, Κυρίου δὲ καὶ Θεοῦ, καὶ σωτῆρος ἡμῶν Ἰησοῦ Χριστοῦ· καὶ ἡ

---

[984] See, for example, the quotation from Psalm 7:9 in the Εὐχὴ ἀλλὴ καταπέτασματος παρ' Αἰγυπτίοις in which Go dis described as the one who: ἐπιστάμενος τὸν νοῦν τῶν ἀνθρώπων as well as the one who: ἐτάζων καρδίας καὶ νεφροὺς.
[985] i.e. the East Syrian Rite
[986] Hammond and Brightman (1896). pg. 283
[987] Hammond and Brightman (1896). pg. 435
[988] Hammond and Brightman (1896). pp. 125 and Cuming (1990). pg. 20 footnote 7, the Coptic version of this is found in Hammond and Brightman (1896). pg 164 as well as in Day (1972). pg. 89. "The Lord be with all ...upward with our hearts...let us give thanks to the Lord."
[989] Hammond and Brightman (1896) pg. 321 and Trempelis (1982). pp. 96 and 173. "The grace of our Lord Jesus Christ and the love of God and Father and the communion of the Holy Spirit be with all of us...let us lift up (our) hearts...let us give thanks to the Lord."

δωρεὰ τοῦ ἁγίου Πνεύματος εἴη μετὰ πάντων ὑμῶν...Ἄνω σχῶμεν τὰς καρδίας...Εὐχαριστήσωμεν τῷ Κυρίῳ.[990] In the Western rite too, this phrasing is used: Per omnia saecula saeculorum...Dominus vobiscum...Sursum corda...Gratias agamus Domino Deo nostro.[991]

Another group of liturgies seems to build a middle ground between the liturgies discussed above, and the text we see in the Liturgy of St. Gregory. These liturgies include, again, liturgies of both Chalcedonian and non-Chalcedonian churches, and a variety of liturgical rites. In the Greek Liturgy of St. James: Ἄνω σχῶμεν τὸν νοῦν καὶ τὰς καρδίας.[992] A similar phrasing is found in the Syrian Anaphora of St. James: "The minds and hearts of all of us be on high...They are with the Lord our God."[993]

Following the rule that liturgical prayer is not abbreviated, but added to,[994] we must conclude that the shortest blessing of the priest: Ὁ Κύριος μετὰ πάντων found in the Greek and Coptic Liturgy of St. Mark represents the original form of this blessing, which was then expanded into the various forms seen above. The *Sursum Corda* itself must also follow this rule, it must be either the νοῦς or the καρδία that was used originally, the other term introduced in confusion between the mind and the heart. The origin of this phrase, however, is discussed by Louis Bouyer who notes that, while Semitic in origin, the "invitation *Sursum Corda – Habemus ad Dominum*...seems to be a properly Christian creation."[995] The final command of the priest, to give thanks, is, however, part of the Jewish meal ritual: "...is textually the Jewish formula that preceeds the three *berakoth* at the end of the meal. We must be even more specific and emphasize that it is the formula that was to be used for a meal of less than ten people, that is a group which did not form the minimum required for Synagogue worship."[996] The Semitic origin of this dialogue explains the two forms found in the various liturgies. The heart, though the original term in the dialogue, had only a "physiological meaning for the Greeks and Latins"[997] and the term was replaced in many of the Greek liturgies to νοῦς that it would make more sense to the worshippers, since to them it was the νοῦς that was the seat of the soul.

---

[990] See below pg. 253.
[991] *Missale Romanum* (1922). pg. 292. "For all ages of ages...The Lord be with you all...lift up the hearts...lit us give thanks to the Lord our God."
[992] Hammond and Brightman (1896). pp. 49-50 and Mercier (1944). pp. 196-198. "let us lift up soul and hearts."
[993] Hammond and Brightman (1896). pp. 84 and Day (1972). pg. 180.
[994] Schermann (1920)
[995] Bouyer (1989). pg. 181
[996] Bouyer (1989). pp. 181-182
[997] Bouyer (1989). pg. 181

The Liturgy of Saint Gregory the Theologian

1. Structure

The structure of the *Sursum Corda* in the Liturgy of St. Gregory follows the established pattern followed in the majority of other liturgies as well. This structure consists of a number of phrases exclaimed by the priest or deacon, followed by their respective responses by the people. In the Liturgy of St. Gregory, the priest has five exclamations, which begin with an exhortation Στῶμεν καλῶς, followed by a blessing and two other exhortations.

To the first exhortation, the people respond: Ἔλεος εἰρήνης, θυσίαν αἰνέσεως. A phrase through which the purpose of the coming section is identified and celebrated. The blessing of the priest receives the customary response to blessings; Καὶ μετὰ τοῦ πνεύματος σου, including the celebrant in the blessing he has just given: the celebrant does not bless himself πάντων ὑμῶν because he is blessing in his office as a priest, representing on earth Christ at the heavenly Altar, but as a human he too is in need of blessing, and the return of the blessing by the people includes him in the love, grace and communion of the Holy Trinity he has just blessed the people with. The responses following the last two exhortations are affirmations of either doing the action commanded: Ἔχομεν πρὸς τὸν Κύριον, the people respond to the command to raise up their hearts, or of the necessity of performing this action it is Ἄξιον καὶ δίκαιον to give thanks to God. The structure of the Sursum Corda can also be seen in the following table:

Figure I.II.1: The structure of the Sursum Corda dialogue.[998]

The *Sursum Corda* Dialogue	
Couplet I: Exhortation by the deacon and response by the people.	Ὁ Διάκονος λέγει· Στῶμεν καλῶς Ὁ Λαὸς λέγει· Ἔλεος εἰρήνης, θυσίαν αἰνέσεως.
Couplet II: Blessing by the priest and response by the people.	Ὁ Ἰερεὺς λέγει· Ἡ ἀγάπη τοῦ Θεοῦ καὶ Πατρός καὶ ἡ χάρις τοῦ μονογενοῦς υἱοῦ Κυρίου δὲ καὶ Θεοῦ, καὶ σωτῆρος ἡμῶν Ἰησοῦ Χριστοῦ καὶ ἡ κοινωνία καὶ ἡ δωρεά

---

[998] Cf. Section II.1 lines 1-12.

	τοῦ ἁγίου Πνεύματος, εἴη μετὰ πάντων ὑμῶν. Ὁ Λαὸς λέγει· Καὶ μετὰ τοῦ πνεύματός σου.
Couplet III: Exhortation by the priest and affirmation of the people.	Ὁ Ἱερεὺς λέγει· Ἄνω σχῶμεν τὰς καρδίας. Ὁ Λαὸς λέγει· Ἔχομεν πρὸς τὸν Κύριον.
Triplet I: Exhortation by the priest, affirmation by the people.	Ὁ Ἱερεὺς λέγει· Εὐχαριστήσωμεν τῷ Κυρίῳ Ὁ Λαὸς λέγει· Ἄξιον καὶ δίκαιον, ἄξιον καὶ δίκαιον, ἄξιον καὶ δίκαιον

2. Function

This section does little to further the anti-Arian purpose of the text as a whole. It fits, rather, into the category of elements that must be present in a liturgy; therefore the Trinitarian blessing given by the priest is not altered into a more Christ centered formula, but remains in the expected style and form. The ambiguous phrasing: Ἔχομεν πρὸς τὸν Κύριον in the people's response does allow the established "Christusanrede" to continue its work. Since it is never specified that the Lord in questions is God the Father rather than Christ, the worshipper should automatically connect this usage of Κύριος with the previous usages, all of which referred to Christ. This section, then, even if not specifically advancing the propagandistic agenda of the rest of the work, does nothing to hinder it.

The style of the *Sursum Corda* in the Liturgy of St. Gregory also provides the first hint in the Anaphora of what liturgical family this text belongs to. In the Egyptian liturgies, the blessing of the priest is rather simple: Ὁ Κύριος μετὰ πάντων, this stands in marked contrast to the lengthy blessings of the Syrian and Syro-Byzantine rites.[999] The blessing found in the liturgy of St. Gregory corresponds most closely to the Syrian model, especially in the invocation of God the Father before Christ[1000] and the use of not only κοινωνία but δωρεὰ in the invocation of the Holy Spirit. In the *Sursum Corda* itself, however, the Liturgy of St. Gregory shows itself to have more in common with the Syro-Byzantine liturgies, since it is only the καρδία which is lifted, and not τὸν νοῦν καὶ τὰς καρδίας. This connection with both the Syrian and Syro-Byzantine families is borne out by the research

---

[999] the liturgies of Sts. James, Basil and John Chrysostom.
[1000] Which is reversed in the Syro-Byzantine liturgies of Sts. Basil and John Chrysosotom.

done by Hammerschmidt and Gerhards, who both remark on the Syrian and Byzantine nature of the Anaphora.[1001] It also lends credence to the Cappadocian origin of this liturgy, since the Cappadocian liturgy forms part of the larger West Syrian rite, but also forms the basis of the Byzantine rite in the Liturgy of St. Basil.

II.III. The Ἀρχὴ τῆς προσκομίδης

Following the *Sursum Corda* dialogue begins the first prayer of the Anaphora, the "Opening of the *Proskomede*." This type of prayer is found in almost every liturgy. It functions not only as the opening of the Anaphora, but as a transition from the thanks given to God at the end of the *Sursum Corda* to the Pre-Sanctus prayer. As such, these prayers tend to begin in the same way, by reflecting the response of the people, Ἄξιον καὶ δίκαιον, in the preceding dialogue. In the Byzantine Liturgy of St. Basil, however, the author does not begin with this expected style, but with a discussion of the nature of God the Father: Ὁ ὢν Δέσποτα Κύριε Θεὲ Πατὴρ παντοκράτωρ προσκυνητὲ ἄξιον ὡς ἀληθῶς καὶ δίκαιον καὶ πρέπον τῇ μεγαλοπρεπείᾳ τῆς ἁγιωσύνης σου σὲ αἰνεῖν σὲ ὑμνεῖν σὲ εὐλογεῖν σε προσκυνεῖν.[1002] This does not, however, replace the normal tradition, but is an expansion upon it, and the author returns to the normal phrasing following this opening: Ἄξιον καὶ δίκαιον σὲ ὑμνεῖν σοὶ εὐχαριστεῖν σε προσκυνεῖν[1003] as it is found in the Syro-Byzantine Liturgy of St. John Chrysostom, a typical form of this prayer.

The prayer also tends to close in the same way, at least in the Syro-Byzantine liturgies, with a description of the honor paid to God by the angels, once again reflecting the upward journey so important in Eastern theology; moving from earthly to heavenly worship. This is also where the The Ἀρχὴ τῆς προσκομίδης sets up the *Sanctus* hymn that follows it, becoming the pre-Sanctus prayer. While each liturgy formulates the final part of this prayer in different ways, there is a general Structure used in all the liturgies, shown in the following excerpt from the Greek- Syrian Liturgy of St. James: ἄγγελοι ἀρχάγγελοι θρόνοι κυριότητες ἀρχαί τε καὶ ἀξαπτέρυγα σεραφὶμ ἃ ταῖς μὲν δυσὶ πτέρυξι κατακαλύπτει τὰ πρόσωπα ἑαυτῶν, ταῖς δὲ δυσὶ τοὺς πόδας καὶ ταῖς δυσὶν ἱπτάμενα κέκραγεν ἕτερος

[1001] Cf. for example Hammerschmidt (1957). pp. 176-177
[1002] Hammond and Brightman (1896). pp. 321-322 and Trempelis (1982). pp. 173-174. "You are He who is, Sovereign Lord God, almighty and to be worshipped. It is thus truly right, just and befitting the greatness of Your holiness, that we praise You, sing to You, bless You, adore You, give thanks to You, glorify You..." Karahalios (1993). pg. 20.
[1003] Hammond and Brightman (1896). pp. 321-322 and Trempelis (1982). pg. 101. "It is worthy and just to hymn You, to thank You, to worship You."

πρὸς τὸν ἕτερον ἀκαταπαύστοις στόμασιν, ἀσιγήτοις δοξολογίαις.[1004] The elements involved are the various ranks of the angels: the angels, archangels, thrones, dominions, principalities, power, seraphim and cherubim. These angels are each described as participating in worship in various ways. The Seraphim, since they are considered the rank of angel that sings the *Sanctus* in the vision of Isaiah,[1005] receive the greatest attention in this list, their physical description is given: six wings; as well as their habits: they cover their feet with two wings, their faces with two wings and they fly with two wings, they also cry to one another and eternally sing the *Sanctus* hymn. The prayer then transitions with a final exclamation of the priest and the *Sanctus* hymn is sung.

The Egyptian liturgies are set up in a slightly different manner, as exemplified in the Liturgy of the Coptic Jacobites and the Greek-Egyptian Liturgy of St. Mark. The opening of the prayer is the same, echoing the ending of the *Sursum Corda* dialogue, but this does not transition into the Sanctus hymn, rather the ending discusses the worship of the Eucharist: "...this reasonable sacrifice and this unbloody service which all nations offer unto thee from the rising of the sun unto the gowing down of the same and from the north to the south, for thy name is great, o Lord, among the Gentiles and in every place incensce is offered unto thine holy name and a purified sacrifice..."[1006] Following this is a series of Intercessions, and only after these are completed do we find what was the conclusion of the Ἀρχὴ τῆς προσκομίδης, the *Sanctus* hymn The interposition of the Intercessions between the opening and closing of this prayer in the Egyptian rite is another indication that the Liturgy of St. Gregory cannot belong to the Egyptian family, since the Intercessions in this liturgy are only made after the Epiklesis.

In the Liturgy of St. Gregory we see an almost unique form of this prayer.[1007] Instead of one prayer, as we have seen in the Syro-Byzantine liturgies, or a disruption by a

---

[1004] "Angels, archangels, thrones, dominions, powers and the six winged Seraphim, with two wings they hide their faces, with two their feet and flying with two they cry out each to the other with unceasing voices, the unsilenced doxologies."

[1005] Isaiah 6:3 and Revelation 4:8.

[1006] Hammond and Brightman (1896). pg. 165 we see the origin of this prayer in the Greek text, as well as that the intercessions follow the *Sursum Corda* in Cuming (1990). pp. 21 ff. Day (1972). pg. 89 has a different prayer.

[1007] The unique nature of these prayers in the Liturgy of St. Gregory is reflected in the Coptic translation, which is almost an exact reflection of the Greek, there are only two exceptions. When dealing with the orders of angels and how they give glory to God the Coptic text has: "…Du bist es, dem die Engel lobsingen, indem dich die Erzengel anbeten, du bist es, den die Mächte preisen, indem dir die Herrschaften singen." (Hammerschmidt's translation, Hammerschmidt (1957) pg. 25). This puts the glory of the angels and the powers in a subservient position to that of the archangels and the dominions. These are kept separate in the Greek: Σὲ αἰνοῦσιν ἄγγελοι· σὲ προσκυνοῦσιν ἀρχάγγελοι· σὲ ἀρχαὶ ὑμνοῦσι· σὲ κυριότητες ἀνακράζουσι· τὴν σὴν δόξαν ἐξουσίαι ἀναγορεύουσι.

long string of Intercessions, as in the Egyptian liturgies, the Liturgy of St. Gregory has two prayers of the priest, punctuated by an exclamation by the deacon: Οἱ καθήμενοι ἀνάστητε. It does not seem, however, that this is the original Structure of this section of the Anaphora.

The first of the prayers is set up in the form seen in most other liturgies, beginning with the affirmation of the *Sursum Corda*: Ἀληθῶς γὰρ ἄξιόν ἐστιν καὶ δίκαιον σὲ αἰνεῖν, σὲ ὑμνεῖν, σὲ εὐλογεῖν, σὲ προσκυνεῖν, σὲ δοξάζειν, τὸν μόνον ἀληθινὸν Θεόν. The second mirrors the unique beginning found in the Liturgy of St. Basil: Ὁ ὢν, Θεὲ, Κύριε ἀληθινὲ ἐκ Θεοῦ ἀληθινοῦ. A possible explanation for why this liturgy has two prayers here instead of one is that there was originally only one prayer, to which a second one was added later. Problematic is that both of these prayers are in use in the text of the liturgy, while other examples of prayers which have been added later show one prayer as the main prayer, while the others are presented as alternates. In the case of the "Prayer of the Greeting," for example, there is the Εὐχὴ τοῦ ἀσπασμοῦ as well as an Εὐχὴ ἄλλη τοῦ ἀσπασμοῦ. It may be that the presence of both of these prayers in the main text of the liturgy occurs here in analogy to the text of the Liturgy of St. Mark, in which the *Sanctus* hymn and the text of the Ἀρχὴ τῆς προσκομίδης are separated by the numerous Intercessions. This separation in the Alexandrian liturgy accustoms the editors of the liturgy to a lengthy text here, or even leads them to expect this Structure, leading them to keep both prayers in the main text of the liturgy.

Since only one of these prayers is orignal to the liturgy this begs the question, which one is original and which one is the secondary prayer? The first clue is found in the theory that newer prayers are inserted before the older prayers.[1008] According to this theory, then, it is the prayer beginning: Ὁ ὢν, Θεὲ, Κύριε ἀληθινὲ ἐκ Θεοῦ ἀληθινοῦ that is the original, and the prayer beginning: Ἀληθῶς γὰρ ἄξιόν ἐστιν that is secondary. This theory has not always been borne out in this liturgy, as seen, for example, in the Εὐχὴ τοῦ καταπετάσματος. The alternate, second prayer, is certainly a later addition, as it is identified as the Εὐχὴ τοῦ καταπετάσματος παρ' Αἰγυπτίοις, which, as the liturgy originates outside of Egypt, shows that it must be a later addition, in this case, however, the theory seems to be substantiated. As the second prayer opens analogously to that in the Liturgy of St. Basil:

[1008] Hammerschmidt (1957). pg. 98

The Commentary

Figure II.III.1: The "Beginning of the Proskomede" in the Liturgies of St. Gregory and St. Basil

1. The Liturgy of St. Basil[1009]	2. The Liturgy of St. Gregory the Theologian[1010]
<u>Ὁ ὢν Δέσποτα Κύριε Θεὲ Πατὴρ παντοκράτωρ</u> προσκυνητὲ ἄξιον ὡς ἀληθῶς καὶ δίκαιον καὶ πρέπον τῇ μεγαλοπρεπείᾳ τῆς ἁγιωσύνης σου σὲ αἰνεῖν σὲ ὑμνεῖν σὲ εὐλογεῖν σὲ προσκυνεῖν σοὶ εὐχαριστεῖν σὲ δοξάζειν τὸν μόνον ὄντως ὄντα Θεὸν καὶ σοὶ προσφέρειν ἐν καρδίᾳ...ἄναρχε ἀόρατε ἀκατάληπτε ἀπερίγραπτε ἀναλλοίωτε, <u>ὁ πατὴρ τοῦ κυρίου ἡμῶν Ἰησοῦ Χριστοῦ τοῦ μεγάλου Θεοῦ καὶ σωτῆρος τῆς ἐλπίδος ἡμῶν</u>...τὸ φῶς τὸ ἀληθινὸν παρ' <u>οὗ τὸ Πνεῦμα τὸ ἅγιον ἐξαφάνη</u>, τὸ τῆς ἀληθείας πνεῦμα, τὸ τῆς υἱοθεσίας χάρισμα, ὁ ἀρραβὼν τῆς μελλούσης κληρονομίας, ἡ ἀπαρχὴ τῶν αἰωνίων ἀγαθῶν, ἡ ζωοποιὸς δύναμις, ἡ πηγὴ τοῦ ἁγιασμοῦ παρ' <u>οὗ πᾶσα κτίσις λογική τε καὶ νοερὰ δυναμουμένη σοὶ λατρεύει καὶ σοὶ τὴν ἀΐδιον ἀναπέμπει</u>	<u>Ὁ ὢν, Θεέ, Κύριε ἀληθινὲ ἐκ Θεοῦ ἀληθινοῦ· ὁ τοῦ Πατρὸς ἡμῖν ὑποδείξας τὸ φέγγος. Ὁ τοῦ ἁγίου Πνεύματος τὴν ἀληθῆ γνῶσιν ἡμῖν χαρισάμενος. Ὁ τὸ μέγα τοῦτο τῆς ζωῆς ἀναδείξας τὸ μυστήριον. Ὁ τὴν τῶν ἀσωμάτων τοῖς ἀν(θρώπ)οις χοροστασίαν πηξάμενος. Ὁ τὴν τῶν Σεραφὶμ τοῖς ἐπὶ γῆς παραδοὺς ὑμνῳδίαν. Δέξαι μετὰ τῶν ἀοράτων καὶ τὴν ἡμετέραν φωνήν. Σύναψον ἡμᾶς ταῖς ἐπουρανίαις δυνάμεσιν.</u> Εἴπωμεν καὶ ἡμεῖς μετ' αὐτῶν πᾶσαν ἄτοπον λογισμῶν ἔννοιαν <u>περιστείλαντες· βοήσωμεν ὥσπερ ἐκεῖναι, ταῖς ἀσιγήτοις ἀνακράζει φωναῖς, ἀκαταπαύστοις στόμασι τὸ σὸν μεγαλεῖον ὑμνήσωμεν.</u>

[1009] Hammond and Brightman (1896). pp. 321-322 and Trempelis (1902). pp. 173-179. "You are He who is, Sovereign Lord God, almighty and to be worshipped. It is truly right, just and befitting the greatness of Your holiness, that we praise You, sing to You, bless You, adore You, give thanks to You, glorify You, as the only true God; that with reprentant hearts and in the spirit of humility we offer You this our spiritual worship...eternal, invisible, beyond comprehending or describing, unchanging the Father of our Lord Jesus Christ, the great God and Savior, the object of our hope...the true Light. Through Him the Holy Spirit was made manifest, the Spirit of Truth, the gift of adoption, the foretaste of the future inheritance, the first fruits of eternal blessings, the life-giving power, the fountainhead of holiness. Empowered by Him every rational and intelligent being sings ceaselessly of Your glory, for all serve You. It is You the Angels and the Archangels adore, the Thrones and Dominions, the Principalities, the Virtues, the Powers and the Cherubim of many eyes. It is You the Seraphim encircle, each with six wings: with the two they cover their faces, with the two their feet, and flying with two, they cry out to one another with ceaseless voices, in perpetual praise." Karahalios (1993). pg. 20-21.

[1010] Cf. Section II.2 lines 13-20.

δοξολογίαν ὅτι τὰ σύμπαντα δοῦλα σά· σὲ γὰρ αἰνοῦσιν ἄγγελοι ἀρχάγγελοι θρόνοι κυριότητες ἀρχαὶ ἐξουσίαι δυνάμεις καὶ τὰ πολυόμματα χερουβείμ, σοὶ παρίστανται κύκλῳ τὰ σεραφείμ, ἓξ πτέρυγες τῷ ἑνὶ...	

The similar content and style of the two prayers, especially in the opening, show that one depends on the other and, since the prayers adopted by the Liturgy of St. Basil tend to be adopted wholesale, while the author of the Liturgy of St. Gregory adapts the borrowed prayers to fit the specific style of his liturgy, it seems that the origin lies in the Liturgy of St. Basil.[1011] This uniquely styled opening to the prayer was then later replaced with another prayer, which opens in a way that conforms more to the style seen both in the Egyptian liturgies and in the majority of other liturgical traditions. Although it is possible that this first prayer is the original and that the second prayer is a later insertion, it seems illogical that a standard prayer would be replaced later by one with unique style. That the first prayer is as a later addition is also seen in the alliterated phrase in reference to Christ's nature: τὸν ἄφραστον, τὸν ἀόρατον, τὸν ἀχώρητον, τὸν ἄναρχον, τὸν αἰώνιον, τὸν ἄχρονον, τὸν ἀμέτρητον, τὸν ἄτρεπτον, τὸν ἀπερινόητον corresponds to an alliterated phrase in the Liturgy of St. Basil in reference to the nature of God the Father: ἄναρχε ἀόρατε ἀκατάληπτε ἀπερίγραπτε ἀναλλοίωτε. Although the accusatives of the Liturgy of St. Basil have been changed to vocatives to conform to the dialogue style, the similar alliteration is striking and suggests that the author of the replacement prayer recognized the prayer as being influenced by that in the Liturgy of St. Basil and kept an aspect of that style.

1. Structure

As noted above, this prayer is, in fact, two prayers that are connected by an exclamation of the Deacon.

I. Prayer I

The first of the two prayers, written in the same style as is found in the majority of other liturgies, can be divided into three main parts. In the first section of the prayer the

---

[1011] This further strengthens the notion that the Liturgy of St. Gregory was in use in the Constantinopolitan/Cappadocian area before its introduction into Egypt.

author underscores the final final exchange in the *Sursum Corda* dialogue: Εὐχαριστήσωμεν τῷ Κυρίῳ...Ἄξιον καὶ δίκαιον, ἄξιον καὶ δίκαιον, ἄξιον καὶ δίκαιον. This is done by opening the prayer using the same wording as the response: Ἀληθῶς γὰρ ἄξιόν ἐστιν. In the prayer, however, the discussion does not end with the thanks that it is worthy to give to God, but that it is also worthy and just to praise, hymn, worship and praise as well: καὶ δίκαιον σὲ αἰνεῖν, σὲ ὑμνεῖν, σὲ εὐλογεῖν, σὲ προσκυνεῖν, σὲ δοξάζειν. Following the opening of the prayer through this intratextual link with the *Sursum Corda*, another section opens in which the nature of God is discussed.

The second section of the prayer begins in direct succesion to the opening, in fact within the same sentence: σὲ προσκυνεῖν, σὲ δοξάζειν τὸν μόνον ἀληθινόν Θεὸν. This second section deals with the nature of God[1012] in a series of seventeen phrases. These phrases fall into two categories, eight of these phrases fall into the first and nine into the second, the second category of phrases is surrounded by the first two of which fall before and six after. The second category of phrases are all an associated by alliterated, each phrase beginning with an alpha. This, as was mentioned above, creates an intertextual link with the Byzantine liturgy of St. Basil, in which there is an alliterated series of phrases is used to describe God the Father. This alliteration also forms an intratextual link with prayers in the liturgy of St. Gregory, specifically with the Εὐχὴ τοῦ ἀσπασμοῦ: ὁ τῷ Πατρὶ συναίδιος, καὶ ὁμοούσιος, καὶ σύνθρονος καὶ συνδημιουργός as well as in the final prayer of the liturgy, the Εὐχὴ τῆς κεφαλοκλισίας: καὶ ὁμοούσιον, καὶ ὁμοδύναμον, καὶ ὁμόδοξον in this way, the author of this later prayer is able to link his text with the liturgy into which it is inserted.

The final section of this prayer is the discussion of the various types of angels and in what type of worship they are involved in. The entire σαβαώθ, the entire angelic host is described: ἄγγελοι...ἀρχάγγελοι...ἀρχαὶ...κυριότητες...ἐξουσίαι... θρόνοι. Following the string of specific angels is a discussion of the angelic worship in a more general sense: χίλιαι χιλιάδες...μύριαι μυριάδες...ἀόρατα...φαινόμενα. The expected ending conclusion of this prayer is not found here, however, as the discussion of the Seraphim and the *Sanctus* hymn follows only after the second prayer in this series.

[1012] The author fits the style of this prayer into the larger style of the liturgy by never mentioning what member of the Trinity is being discussed here, it may be God the Father, as is the usual case in the counterparts of this prayer in other liturgies, because the author never indicates it, the reader can assume that it is Christ being discussed here, as in the rest of the liturgy.

The Liturgy of Saint Gregory the Theologian

Figure II.III..2: The structure of the first prayer in the Ἀρχὴ τῆς προσκομίδης[1013]

The first of the prayers in the Ἀρχὴ τῆς προσκομίδης
1. Opening of the prayer: I. Intratextual link with the *Sursum Corda* dialogue: Ἀληθῶς γὰρ ἄξιον ἐστιν καὶ δίκαιον II. Transition to other types of worship due to God: σὲ αἰνεῖν, σὲ ὑμνεῖν, σὲ εὐλογεῖν, σὲ προσκυνεῖν, σὲ δοξάζειν
2. Discussion of the nature of God: I. Two descriptive phrases in category 1: 1. τὸν μόνον ἀληθινὸν Θεὸν 2. τὸν φιλάνθρωπον II. Nine descriptive phrases in category 2: 1. τὸν ἄφραστον 2. τὸν ἀόρατον 3. τὸν ἀχώρητον 4. τὸν ἄναρχον 5. τὸν αἰώνιον 6. τὸν ἄχρονον 7. τὸν ἀμέτρητον 8. τὸν ἄτρεπτον 9. τὸν ἀπερινόητον III. The remaining six phrases in category 1: 1. τὸν ποιητὴν τῶν ὅλων 2. τὸν λυτρωτὴν τῶν ἁπάντων 3. τὸν εὐιλατεύοντα πάσαις ταῖς ἀνομίαις ἡμῶν 4. τὸν ἰώμενον πάσας τὰς νόσους ἡμῶν 5. τὸν λυτρούμενον ἐκ φθορᾶς τὴν ζωὴν ἡμῶν 6. τὸν στεφανοῦντα ἡμᾶς ἐν ἐλέει καὶ οἰκτιρμοῖς
3. Discussion of the worship of the heavenly powers: I. The worship of the specific types of angels: 1. Σὲ αἰνοῦσιν ἄγγελοι· 2. σὲ προσκυνοῦσιν ἀρχάγγελοι· 3. σὲ ἀρχαὶ ὑμνοῦσι· 4. σὲ κυριότητες ἀνακράζουσι· 5. τὴν σὴν δόξαν ἐξουσίαι ἀναγορεύσουσι· 6. σοὶ θρόνοι τὴν εὐφημίαν ἀναπέμπουσι

[1013] Cf. Section II.2 lines 1-12.

> II. More general discussion of worship: 1. χιλίαι χιλιάδες σοὶ παραστήκουσι· 2. καὶ μύριαι μυριάδες σοὶ τὴν λειτουργίαν προσάγουσι. 3. Σὲ ὑμνεῖ τὰ ἀόρατα 4. σὲ προσκυνεῖ τὰ φαινόμενα
>
> III. Ending to the section and this prayer: πάντα ποιοῦντα τὸν λόγον σου Δέσποτα.

II. Prayer 2.

Unlike the previous prayer, the second, original prayer, is divided into only two sections. The first part is a discussion of Christ's nature. The second section does discuss the worship of the heavenly powers, as we saw above, however the way in which the heavenly powers are portrayed does not conform to the usual discussion found in the majority of liturgies, but, in a series of requests, focuses on worship of humanity being joined to that of the heavenly powers.

The discussion of Christ's nature, and in the case of this prayer we know that it is Christ as opposed to the other members of the Trinity: Κύριε ἀληθινὲ ἐκ Θεοῦ ἀληθινοῦ. In eight descriptive phrases, the author discusses this nature. The first six discuss the nature of Christ as such, and His role as mediator between God and man as well as describing Christ's role in history. The final two descriptive phrases of the series serve as a transition from the discussion of Christ's nature to the discussion of the human and angelic worship: ὁ τὴν τῶν ἀσωμάτων τοῖς ἀνθρώποις χοροστασίαν πηξάμενος. Ὁ τὴν τῶν Σεραφὶμ τοῖς ἐπὶ γῆς παραδοὺς ὑμνῳδίαν.

In the second section of the prayer, the priest makes two requests that Christ make the worship of the angelic powers and that of humans to be equal. These are followed by hortatory subjunctives by which the priest exhorts the people in the congregation to purify themselves and to join their worship with those heavenly powers.

Table II.III.3: The structure of the second prayer in the Ἀρχὴ τῆς προσκομίδης[1014]

The second of the prayers in the Ἀρχὴ τῆς προσκομίδης
1. Discussion of Christ's nature

[1014] Cf. Section II.2 lines 13-20.

> I. Pure discussion of Christ's nature: 1. Ὁ ὤν 2. Θεὲ 3. Κύριε ἀληθινὲ ἐκ Θεοῦ ἀληθινοῦ
>
> II. Discussion of Christ's role in history: 1. ὁ τοῦ ἁγίου Πνεύματος τὴν ἀληθῆ γνῶσιν ἡμῖν χαρισάμενος. 2. Ὁ τὸ μέγα τοῦτο τῆς ζωῆς ἀναδείξας τὸ μυστήριον.
>
> III. Transition to the discussion of the angelic powers: 1. Ὁ τὴν τῶν ἀσωμάτων τοῖς ἀνθρώποις χοροστασίαν πηξάμενος. 2. Ὁ τὴν τῶν Σεραφὶμ τοῖς ἐπὶ γῆς παραδοὺς ὑμνῳδίαν.

> 2. Association between mortal and heavenly worship:
>
> I. Requests that human and angelic worship be made equal: 1. Δέξαι μετὰ τῶν ἀοράτων καὶ τὴν ἡμετέραν φωνήν. 2. Σύναψον ἡμᾶς ταῖς ἐπουρανίαις δυνάμεσιν.
>
> II. Exhortation to join human worship to angelic worship: 1. Εἴπωμεν καὶ ἡμεῖς μετ' αὐτῶν 2. πᾶσαν ἀτόπων λογισμῶν ἔννοιαν περιστείλαντες· 3. βοήσωμεν ὥσπερ ἐκεῖναι 4. ταῖς ἀσιγήτοις ἀνακράζει φωναῖς 5. ἀκαταπαύστοις στόμασι τὸ σὸν μεγαλεῖον ὑμνήσωμεν.

2. Function

The clarity of the functionalization that has characterized the text up to the Anaphora does not come across quite as strongly in this section. This can be explained in the same way as the fact that the term ὁμοούσιος is not used in the Anaphora. The Anaphora would not be an appropriate place for such blatant propaganda. This is not to say, however, that there is none, but that it is presented in a more subtle form than in the previous or subsequent sections.

I. the first prayer.
1. (Section II.2 lines 1-2): Ἀληθῶς γὰρ ἄξιόν ἐστιν καὶ δίκαιον σὲ αἰνεῖν, σὲ ὑμνεῖν, σὲ εὐλογεῖν, σὲ προσκυνεῖν, σὲ δοξάζειν

This opening does not play any specific role in function of the text, rather the author here takes up the phrasing of the opening of this prayer in various other liturgies. Χριστὲ ὁ Θεὸς ἡμῶν is also missing in the discussion of God's nature that follows this opening. In fact, Christ's name is entirely missing from this prayer.

The Commentary

2. (Section II.2 lines 2-5): τὸν μόνον ἀληθινὸν Θεὸν, τὸν φιλάνθρωπον, τὸν ἄφραστον, τὸν ἀόρατον, τὸν ἀχώρητον, τὸν ἄναρχον, τὸν αἰώνιον, τὸν ἄχρονον, τὸν ἀμέτρητον, τὸν ἄτρεπτον, τὸν ἀπερινόητον

As mentioned above, the name of Christ is never mentioned in this prayer, but neither is the name of any other member of the Trinity. The location of this prayer within the Christ centered text of this liturgy, however, allows the worshippers to assume that the object of this prayer is Christ. The allitorated list of epithets, discussed above, works similarly, the worshipper assumes Christ is the object, since no other member of the Trinity is specified.

3. (Section II.2 lines 5-7): τὸν ποιητὴν τῶν ὅλων, τὸν λυτρωτὴν τῶν ἁπάντων, τὸν εὐιλατεύοντα πάσαις ταῖς ἀνομίαις ἡμῶν, τὸν ἰώμενον πᾶσας νόσους ἡμῶν, τὸν λυτρούμενον ἐκ φορᾶς τὴν ζωὴν ἡμῶν, τὸν στεφανοῦντα ἡμᾶς ἐν ἐλέει καὶ οἰκτιρμοῖς.

Longer phrases follow the previous section, again referring to an unspecified member of the Trinity. These progress through the history of salvation in an almost chrnonological order. The author begins his descriptions with God as the Creator τὸν ποιητὴν τῶν ὅλων in this way not only setting God in a position of authority over creation, but also underscoring the close relationship humanity has with God: in creating humankind He has the first interaction with humanity. It is important to note, however, that it is not only humanity that is the focus here, while humanity becomes the central player in this section of the prayer, through the description of salvation, it is here still all creation that is being discussed. The subsequent description: τὸν λυτρωτὴν τῶν ἁπάντων takes a large step forward in the history of salvation, passing over the Old Testament and taking up again following the Incarnation, The next three descriptions: τὸν εὐιλατεύοντα πάσαις ταῖς ἀνομίαις ἡμῶν· τὸν ἰώμενον πᾶσας νόσους ἡμῶν· τὸν λυτρούμενον ἐκ φορᾶς τὴν ζωὴν ἡμῶν do not discuss any specific moment in the history of salvation, but offer a general explanation of both how humanity fell, putting it in terms of criminal behavior, sickness, and danger; and how God forgave, healed and saved humanity respectively. The author also reuses λυτρούμενον, looking back to God's function as ‚Savior' as perhaps His most important function, in terms of humanity.

This section is styled chronologically and goes through the history of salvation. This, along with the deliberate ambiguity of the prayer points not only to a connection with the Liturgy of St. Basil, but seems to indicate a deliberate connection with the Liturgy of St. Gregory as well, showing that this is not a prayer taken from another liturgy and inserted into the Liturgy of St. Gregory, but a prayer written specifically for this liturgy.

4. (Section II.2 lines 7-11): Σὲ αἰνοῦσιν ἄγγελοι· σὲ προσκυνοῦσιν ἀρχάγγελοι· σὲ ἀρχαὶ ὑμνοῦσι· σὲ κυριότητες ἀνακράζουσι· τὴν σὴν δόξαν ἐξουσίαι ἀναγορεύουσι· σοὶ θρόνοι τὴν εὐφημίαν ἀναπέμπουσι, χίλιαι χιλιάδες σοὶ παραστήκουσι· καὶ μύριαι μυριάδες σοὶ τὴν λειτουργίαν προσάγουσι. Σὲ ὑμνεῖ τὰ ἀόρατα, σὲ προσκυνεῖ τὰ φαινόμενα, πάντα ποιοῦντα τὸν λόγον σου Δέσποτα.

The purpose of this entire prayer is finally seen in the very end: πάντα ποιοῦντα τὸν λόγον σου Δέσποτα This phrase creates a ring composition with the opening: Ἀληθῶς γὰρ ἄξιόν ἐστιν, καὶ δίκαιον σὲ αἰνεῖν, σὲ ὑμνεῖν, σὲ εὐλογεῖν, σὲ προσκυνεῖν, σὲ δοξάζειν The rightness of worshipping God is affirmed by the statement that all things do so. The purpose of this prayer is, then, to illustrate the importance of this worship and to underscore the worsip of the various parts of creation. This prayer does not only enompass the worship of angels, as is the focus of the majority of this final section, nor is it only the worship of the visible, terrestrial world, that of humanity, discussed in the second section of the prayer, that is important. Both have their appointed place, and both must be understood in reference to God, who receives the worship and to whom it is "fitting and right" to do so.

5. (Section II.2 line 12): Ὁ Διάκονος λέγει· Οἱ καθήμενοι ἀνάστητε.

This exclamation of the deacon forms a separation between the first prayer and the second prayer. The deacon commands the people to stand, but this seems odd, why would the deacon command the people to stand for the second prayer and not for the first? The position of this exclamation gives us another clue as to which of the prayers is original, and which is inserted. Since it is illogical to stand for one of these prayer and not the other, the position seems to be left over from a time before the insertion of the first prayer into the liturgy. when the second prayer was the only prayer, before which the congregation would have to stand.

II. The second prayer.
1. (Section II.2 lines 13-16): Ὁ ὤν, Θεέ, Κύριε ἀληθινὲ ἐκ Θεοῦ ἀληθινοῦ· ὁ τοῦ Πατρὸς ἡμῖν ὑποδείξας τὸ φέγγος. Ὁ τοῦ ἁγίου Πνεύματος τὴν ἀληθῆ γνῶσιν ἡμῖν χαρισάμενος. Ὁ τὸ μέγα τοῦτο τῆς ζωῆς ἀναδείξας τὸ μυστήριον. Ὁ τὴν τῶν ἀσωμάτων τοῖς ἀνθρώποις χοροστασίαν πηξάμενος. Ὁ τὴν τῶν Σεραφὶμ τοῖς ἐπὶ γῆς παραδοὺς ὑμνῳδίαν,

This section opens with the Greek translation of the name of God in the Old Testament: Ὁ ὤν, though this does not, as we saw in the first prayer, necessarily mean that Christ is being addressed, since His name is not explicitly stated, this is the title written in the halo of Icons of Christ since at least the sixth century.[1015] This title is also used as an intratextual connection with other prayers in this liturgy, so, for example the Εὐχὴ τῆς κεφαλοκλισίας at the very end of the liturgy, which begins: Ὁ ὤν, ὁ ἦν, ὁ ἐλθὼν εἰς τὸν κόσμον τοῦ φωτίσαι αὐτόν this intratextuality between prayers is quite common in the Liturgy of St. Gregory, as is seen in numerous other links between prayers in the liturgy. While this does imply that the prayer was an original part of the liturgy, it does not prove it, as the prior prayer too was linked with other prayers in the liturgy. Other evidence, as presented above, shows that it is the second prayer that is original, which means that the intratextuality here is to underscore that Christ ist he God of the Old Testament as well as of the New, while the intratextuality in the first prayer is used to justify its place in the text.

Following this opening is an intertextual reference, an almost exact quotation from the Nicene Creed: Κύριε ἀληθινὲ ἐκ Θεοῦ ἀληθινοῦ.[1016] In this way the author not only makes clear that it is Christ being discussed here, which is confirmed by the subsequent: ὁ τοῦ Πατρὸς ἡμῖν ὑποδείξας τὸ φέγγος. Ὁ τοῦ ἁγίου Πνεύματος τὴν ἀληθῆ γνῶσιν ἡμῖν χαρισάμενος in which the author names the other two members of the Trinity. In this way, the author builds up the divine nature of Christ not only by identifying Him with the name of the God of the Old Testament, but by referring to the Nicene Creed through which he can both underscore this reality as well as remind the worshippers of the canons of the Council and the defeat of the Arians.

The two following phrases do not only show that it is Christ who is the subject of this prayer, they also describe part of the relationship between the members of Trinity in relation to Christ. The relationship between Christ and the Father is discussed in terms of salvation, interestingly Christ is not described as being equal, or even superior to the Father, as is implied in other prayers of the liturgy, where the Father is discussed only in terms of the Son Πατρός σου, here, however, Christ is the conduit of the φέγγος, the splendour, of the Father. The same image of Christ as mediator between humanity and the rest of the Trinity is presented in the next phrase as well, in which it is Christ who "...granted us the true knowledge of the Holy Spirit..." This seems to be in opposition to other instances in which the relationship between Christ and the Holy Spirit is discussed, in which the author seems to come close to the theological position espoused by other adversaries of the Arians: the *filioque*. This dichotomy results from the different purposes of the two sections. Here, the author focuses not on Christ's place in the Trinity, but on His interaction with humanity. Here the focus is on Christ and how He bring together the heavenly and the

---

[1015] Such as the Icon of Christ kept at the St. Catherine's Monastery on Mt. Sinai from the sixth century.
[1016] "true Lord from true God" Corresponding to: Θεὸν ἀληθινὸν ἐκ Θεοῦ ἀληθινοῦ "true God from true God." (Hammond and Brightman (1896) pg. 383).

earthly. In these two instances it is the divine that is brought together with the earthly, shortly after, however, it is the angelic powers that are united with humanity.

Between the discussion of the divine and angelic powers, is an intriguing phrase: ὁ τὸ μέγα τοῦτο τῆς ζωῆς ἀναδείξας τὸ μυστήριον. Not only does Christ give humanity knowledge and experience of the heavenly, both divine and angelic, he also, as Creator (as ὁ ὤν) the one who creates life and a consciousness within humans, the one who, quite literally, "...reveals...the great mystery of life..." The author also creates a counterpoint between γνῶσις and μυστήριον between knowledge and mystery. The author is not claiming that one can receive true knowlege of God through Christ, but that life remains a mystery, he uses the term mystery to tie in the great mystery that is the Eucharist, setting Christ up in this one section as both Creator and Redeemer.

The author then returns to the link between heaven and earth: ὁ τὴν τῶν ἀσωμάτων τοῖς ἀνθρώποις χοροστασίαν πηξάμενος. Ὁ τὴν τῶν Σεραφὶμ τοῖς ἐπὶ γῆς παραδοὺς ὑμνῳδίαν the link discussed here is not between the divine and human, but between the angelic and human. This completes the link that Christ builds between the heavenly and earthly, itself an interesting propagandistic point. Usually the link between the heavenly and the earthly is the Holy Spirit, hence the phrase: to the Father, in the Son, through the Holy Spirit, when discussing prayer. This is, once more, an example of the author shifting aspects and functions of the other members of the Trinity to Christ, in this case it is not the power or majesty of God the Father that is translated to Christ, but the closeness of the Holy Spirit to humanity that the author uses to remind the worshippers of Christ's relationship with them. This does not only have an anti-Arian function, but serves to drive the narrative of the liurgy forward as well. The author needs to progress to the worship of the Seraphim in the *Sanctus* hymn, but he does so in a way that continues to emphasize the connection of the heavenly and the earthly through Christ, who unifies the worship of τῶν ἀσωμάτων generally and τῶν Σεραφὶμ specifically with that of humanity.

2. (Section II.2 lines 16-20): Δέξαι μετὰ τῶν ἀοράτων καὶ τὴν ἡμετέραν φωνήν. Σύναψον ἡμᾶς ταῖς ἐπουρανίαις δυνάμεσιν. Εἴπωμεν καὶ ἡμεῖς μετ' αὐτῶν πᾶσαν ἀτόπων λογισμῶν ἔννοιαν περιστείλαντες· βοήσωμεν ὥσπερ ἐκεῖναι ταῖς ἀσιγήτοις ἀνακράζει φωναῖς, ἀκαταπαύστοις στόμασι τὸ σὸν μεγαλεῖον ὑμνήσωμεν.

In this final section of this prayer the author continues in the broad focus established in the last section, the unification of worship between the heavenly and the earthly. However, the author changes the way in which he does this, he no longer relies on statements on the nature of Christ's relationship with humanity, but uses requests to create the same visual. Christ is not only He who τὴν τῶν ἀσωμάτων τοῖς ἀνθρώποις χοροστασίαν πηξάμενος. He is also the one who is asked to join the φωνὴν of humanity with that of the bodiless, and then to join, not only the worship, but their very selves. The final phrases of the prayer are both an underscoring of what has come before: βοήσωμεν ὥσπερ ἐκεῖναι, ταῖς ἀσιγήτοις ἀνακράζει φωναῖς, ἀκαταπαύστοις στόμασι τὸ σὸν μεγαλεῖον ὑμνήσωμεν, humans and angels sing their worship with one voice "with never silent voices, let us hymn Your magnificence with mouths that will not cease..." This also transitions to the beginning of the pre-*Sanctus* prayer, in which similar phrasing is used to describe the worship of the Seraphim: "...with a voice of glory, with a clear voice, hymning, calling out, glorifying, shouting and saying..."

II.IV. The Pre-*Sanctus* Prayer and the *Sanctus* hymn

The section which is here termed the Pre-*Sanctus* prayer is separated from the previous prayers in a separation of convenience. The theme of angelic worship shared in physically by humanity was, after all, a major part of the two preceeding prayers. The separation is made here for two reasons, partly because the preceeding two prayers are termed the Ἀρχὴ τῆς προσκμίδης in the manuscript, and, while the pre-*Sanctus* does not have its own title in the manuscript, is in this way kept separate from the *Sanctus*; it is possible, however to interpret the first prayer in the series as the Ἀρχὴ τῆς προσκμίδης, and the second as the Pre-*Sanctus*, using the command of the deacon to rise as the transition marker. There is, however, a second exclamation of the deacon: Εἰς ἀνατολὰς βλέψατε which separates the pre-*Sanctus* proper from the preceeding prayers. These exclamations may be of later origin, but they show a progression, the worshippers are commanded to stand first, and then to look unto the East, the direction of prayer. It is possible, that these two commands were originally together, but that when the first prayer was inserted, the editors broke up the two, a hypothesis that would leave the original prayer still separate from the pre-*Sanctus*.

The pre-Sanctus, as it is found here:[1017]

Σοὶ γὰρ παραστήκει κύκλῳ τὰ Σεραφίμ, ἓξ πτέρυγες τῷ ἑνί, καὶ ἓξ πτέρυγες τῷ ἑνί. Καὶ ταῖς μὲν δυσὶ πτέρυξι κατακαλύπτουσι τὰ πρόσωπα ἑαυτῶν· ταῖς δὲ δυσὶ τοὺς πόδας ἑαυτῶν· καὶ ταῖς μὲν δυσὶ πετόμενα, καὶ ἐκέκραγον ἕτερον πρὸς τὸν ἕτερον...Τὸν ἐπινίκον ὕμνον τῶν σωτηριῶν ἡμῶν· μετὰ

[1017] There is only one slight difference between the Greek and Coptic texts of this prayer is that the Coptic texts add the Cherubim to the angels that stand around the throne of God: ΝΙΧΕΡΟΥΒΙΜ ΝΕΜ ΝΙΣΕΡΑΦΙΜ (Hammerschmidt (1957). pg. 26).

φωνῆς ἐνδόξου, λαμπρᾷ τῇ φωνῇ, ὑμνολογοῦντα, ᾄδοντα βοῶντα δοξολογοῦντα κεκραγότα καὶ λέγοντα.

is found in slightly altered forms in every liturgy. In the majority of these liturgies, however, the pre-*Sanctus* forms a direct part of what is here the Ἀρχὴ τῆς προσκμίδης, without an intervening exclamation of the deacon. So, for example, we see in the Anaphora of St. James in the Syrian "Jacobite" liturgy: "...and the seraphim with six wing and with two of their wings they veil their face and with twain their feet and with twain they do fly one to another, with unceasing voices and unhushed theologies, a hymn of victory crying and shouting and saying..."[1018] It is in the Egyptian liturgical family that a breakup of the various prayers preceeding the *Sanctus*. Following the Intercessions that divide the *Sursum Corda* and the Sanctus, the deacon exclaims: Εἰς ἀνατολὰς βλέψατε,[1019] the same exclamation made by the deacon in the Liturgy of St. Gregory. Following this is the pre-*Sanctus*, which shows several similarities with that in the Liturgy of St. Gregory, many of these similarities can be attributed to the universal nature of the *Sanctus* and its associated prayers. One phrase which is striking, however, shows a focus in the Coptic Liturgy of St. Mark on the co-worship of the angelic and the human: "...But with all them that hallow thee, receive our hallowing, o Lord, at our hands also, praising thee with them and saying..."[1020] The focus on co-worship is not an exclusively Egyptian motif, however, in the Byzantine tradition, for example, the Cherubic hymn during the Great Entrance claims: Οἱ τὰ χερουβὶμ μυστικῶς εἰκκονίζοντες καὶ τῇ ζωοποιῷ τριάδι τὸν τρισάγιον ὕμνον προσᾴδοντες πᾶσαν τὴν βιωτικὴν ἀποθώμεθα μέριμναν[1021] In this hymn the worshippers stand with and in place of the Cherubim, just as in the pre-Sanctus, the worshippers stand in place of and with the Seraphim.

The *Sanctus* itself is nearly identical in everly liturgical tradition, in the Latin text: Sanctus, Sanctus, Sanctus Dominus Deus Sabaoth Pleni sunt caeli et terra gloria tua. Hosanna in excelsis. Benedictus qui venit in nomine Domini. Hosanna in excelsis.[1022] The Greek text is as follows: Ἅγιος ἅγιος ἅγιος Κύριος σαβαώθ πλήρης ὁ οὐρανὸς καὶ ἡ γῆ τῆς

[1018] Hammond and Brightman (1896), pg. 86 and Day (1972). pg. 180.
[1019] Hammond and Brightman (1896). pg. 175 and Cuming (1990). pg. 36.
[1020] Ibid.
[1021] Hammond and Brightman (1896). pg. 377 "Representing the Cherubim mystically and singing the Trisagion hymn to the life giving Trinity, let us set aside all cares of life."
[1022] The Tridentine Mass (2004). pg. 324 "Holy, holy, holy God Sabaoth, full are the heavens and the earth with Your glory. Hosannah in the hightest. Blessed is he who comes in the name of the Lord. Hosannah in the highest."

δόξης σου ὡσαννὰ ἐν τοῖς ὑψίστοις εὐλογημένος ὁ ἐρχόμενος ἐν ὀνόματι Κυρίου ὡσαννὰ ἐν τοῖς ὑψίστοις...[1023] The origin of this hymn is in the Prophecy of Isaiah 6:3:

> In the year that King Uzziah died, I saw the Lord, high and exalted, seated on a throne; and the train of his robe filled the temple. ² Above him were seraphim, each with six wings: With two wings they covered their faces, with two they covered their feet, and with two they were flying. ³ And they were calling to one another: "Holy, holy, holy is the LORD Almighty; the whole earth is full of his glory." ⁴ At the sound of their voices the doorposts and thresholds shook and the temple was filled with smoke.[1024]

This hymn was not only adopted into the Christian liturgy, but into the Jewish ritual as well:

> Even today at the beginning of the Synagogue service there is a vestige of the reading that was once here in the beginning. It ist he *Qaddish* pryer which was the original conclusion of the *targum* i.e. the paraphrastic Aramaic translation that followed the ritual Hebrew reading of the Holy Scriptures....all join ithe Sheliach sibbur in chanting the Qadushah Holy Holy Holy is JHWH of Hosts; the whole earth is full of his glory...[1025]

The use of this hymn in the Jewish meal prayers and liturgical cycle would explain why it was adopted wholesale by every liturgical tradition, as it would have been adopted in the first few centuries of the church, perhaps as early as 200 A.D.[1026] This hymn, then, becomes part of the ommon inheritance that the early Christians took from the Jewish ritual, which was then adopted into every form of Christian liturgical worship. A similar situation to that seem above in the *Sursum Corda*, a section of the Jewish meal ritual, which too was adopted by the very earliest Christians and so spread into every Christian liturgical tradition.

[1023] Hammond and Brightman (1986). pg. 324 "Holy, holy, holy, Lord Sabaoth, full are heaven and earth with Your glory, hosanna in the heights, blessed is he who comes in the name of the Lord, hosanna in the heights."
[1024] Isaiah 6:1-4 (NIV text)
[1025] Bouyer (1989). pg. 62. The Hebrew for this prayer is: "Kadosh Kadosh Kadosh Adonai Tz'vaot Melo Kol Haaretz Kevodo."
[1026] Pinson (2009). pp. 64-65

The Liturgy of Saint Gregory the Theologian

1. Structure

The pre-*Sanctus* and *Sanctus* hymn are set up in what seems to be a dialogue style, as was seen above in the *Sursum Corda* dialogue. The deacon speaks twice, the priest speaks once and the people have one hymn, the *Sanctus* itself. This is where the similarities end, however, this is not a dialogue, the deacon and priest do not set up the response of the people, rather the priest and people take turns in their prayer while the deacon gives directions.

The section begins with an exclamation by the deacon: Εἰς ἀνατολὰς βλέψατε. This command, that the congregation should turn to the east is a call to prayer. Following this exclamation is the pre-Sanctus prayer itself, a continuation and conclusion to the preceeding section, prayed by the priest. This prayer is divided into two parts, the first is a physical description of the Seraphim who stand around the throne of God. The Seraphim have: ἕξ πτέρυγες τῷ ἑνί, καὶ ἓξ πτέρυγες τῷ ἑνὶ. These six wings are used to cover their faces, feet and to fly. The second part of the prayer ist he final transition to the *Sanctus* hymn by describing the way in which the Seraphim worship: Τὸν ἐπινίκον ὕμνον τῶν σωτηριῶν ἡμῶν· μετὰ φωνῆς ἐνδόξου, λαμπρᾷ τῇ φωνῇ, ὑμνολογοῦντα ᾄδοντα βοῶντα δοξολογοῦντα κεκραγότα καὶ λέγοντα. This exclamation is followed by a command of the deacon, who calls the people in the congregation to attention by exclaiming: Προσχῶμεν. After which the people chant the Sanctus hymn: Ἅγιος ἅγιος ἅγιος Κύριος σαβαώθ, πλήρης ὁ οὐρανός, (κλ΄). This section concludes in the singing of the hymn and the post-*Sanctus* begins. The Structure of the section can also be seen in the following table:

Table II.IV.1: The Structure of the pre-Sanctus and the Sanctus hymn.[1027]

The Structure of the pre-*Sanctus* and the *Sanctus* hymn.	
1. The exclamation of the deacon that opens the section:	Εἰς ἀνατολὰς βλέψατε
2. The main part of the section is the prayer of the priest in which the physical attributes and their worship are described.	1. Σοὶ γὰρ παραστήκει κύκλῳ τὰ Σεραφίμ, ἓξ πτέρυγες τῷ ἑνί, καὶ ἓξ πτέρυγες τῷ ἑνί. Καὶ ταῖς μὲν δυσὶ πτέρυξι κατακαλύπτουσι τὰ πρόσωπα ἑαυτῶν· ταῖς δὲ δυσὶ τοὺς πόδας ἑαυτῶν· καὶ ταῖς μὲν δυσὶ πετόμενα, καὶ ἐκέκραγον ἕτερον πρὸς τὸν ἕτερον. 2. Τὸν ἐπινίκον ὕμνον τῶν σωτηριῶν ἡμῶν· μετὰ φωνῆς ἐνδόξου, λαμπρᾷ τῇ φωνῇ, ὑμνολογοῦντα ᾄδοντα βοῶντα δοξολογοῦντα κεκραγότα καὶ λέγοντα.
3. The second exclamation of the deacon by which he prepares for the *Sanctus* hymn.	Πρόσχωμεν
4. The Sanctus hymn is chanted by the people, completing this section.	Ἅγιος ἅγιος ἅγιος Κύριος σαβαώθ, πλήρης ὁ οὐρανός, (κλ΄).

[1027] Cf. Section II.3 lines 1-11

The Liturgy of Saint Gregory the Theologian

2. Function

The universal nature of the pre-*Sanctus* and *Sanctus* hymn, the fact that this prayer and hymn, or ones almost identical to them are found in almost every liturgy, belies the fact that this prayer is used to further the anti-Arian function of the liturgy. In this way, this section is analogous to the *Sursum Corda* dialogue. These are included in the text because they are necessary in the genre of liturgy rather than because they promote the underlying function of this liturgy. This may explain why the name of Christ name is not once mentioned in this section, as it is not in the following post-*Sanctus* section.

Despite the lack of programmed functionalization in this section, its place in this liturgy, and even the fact that it does not contain the name of a member of the Trinity, helps to further that in the rest of the liturgy. The parallelization of the Seraphim worshipping on one side and humans worshipping in the same way on the other fulfills the intratextual link built in the second prayer in the Ἀρχὴ τῆς προσκομίδης in which this same parallelization is discussed, in which humans and angels worship Christ together.

II.V. The post-*Sanctus* prayers

Following the singing of the *Sanctus* hymn is a series of four prayers, separated from one another by the people's response: Κύριε, ἐλέησον. The Coptic translation of this series of prayers is almost identcal to the Greek original, with a few variations that must have cropped up in the translation process.[1028] This series of prayers provides a lengthy transition from the *Sanctus* hymn to the Consecration. In the Liturgy of St. Gregory this is done by focusing on a different aspect of the history of salvation in each of the prayers in this section,[1029] The author of this liturgy does not only look forward to the Consecration however, he also looks back to the *Sanctus* prayer by beginning the series with an opening that reflects the language of the Sanctus hymn: Ἅγιος ἅγιος εἶ Κύριε καὶ πανάγιος.

[1028] I will not go over every difference between the two texts, as they are all minor, and can be seen in Hammerschmidt. The 'Lord Have Mercy' that separates the first and second prayer (Hammerschmidt (1957). pg. 30). Another, greater difference is seen in line 121 of the Coptic text, which Hammerschmidt translates as: "Als ein wahrhaftes Licht bist du denen aufgegangen, die verirrt haben und unwissend sind." (Hammerschmdit (1957) pg. 31). This corresponds to the Greek: φῶς τοῖς πλανωμένοις ἀνέτειλας. The opening of the next section, the Consecration: ... Ταύτης μου τῆς ἐλευθερίας προσφέρω σοι τὰ σύμβολα, τοῖς ῥήμασί σου ἐπιγράφω τὰ πράγματα. Σύ μοι τὴν μυστικὴν ταύτην λειτουργίαν παρέδωκας τῆς σῆς σαρκός, ἐν ἄρτῳ καὶ οἴνῳ τὴν μέθεξιν... is placed by Hammerschmidt into the post-*Sanctus* (Hammerschmidt (1957). pg. 35). The other minor changes can be seen in Hammerschmidt (1957). pp. 27-35.

[1029] See the Function section below for a more complete discussion of this.

The Commentary

This opening is another hint at the origins of this liturgy. Gerhards and Hammerschmidt both comment on the Syro-Byzantine nature of the post-*Sanctus* prayers.[1030] The Egyptian liturgies, such as the Greek and Coptic Liturgies of St. Mark open the post-Sanctus prayers by discussing not the holiness of God, but the glory of God: "Truly heaven and earth are full of thine Holy Glory through thine onlybegotten Son our Lord and God and our Saviour and the king of us all Jesus Christ. Fill this also, thy sacrifice, o Lord, with the blessing that is from thee, through the descent upon it of thine Holy Spirit, and in blessing bless..."[1031] A nearly identical text is found in the Greek Liturgy of St. Mark:

Πλήρης γάρ ἐστιν ὡς ἀληθῶς ὁ οὐρανὸς καὶ ἡ γῆ τῆς ἁγίας σου δόξης διὰ τῆς ἐπιφανείας τοῦ κυρίου καὶ θεοῦ καὶ σωτῆρος ἡμῶν Ἰησοῦ Χριστοῦ· πλήρωσον ὁ Θεὸς καὶ ταύτην τὴν θυσίαν τῆς παρὰ σοῦ εὐλογίας διὰ τῆς ἐπιφοιτήσεως τοῦ παναγίου σου πνεύματος· ὅτι αὐτὸς ὁ κύριος καὶ θεὸς καὶ παμβασιλεὺς ἡμῶν Ἰησοῦς ὁ χριστὸς τῇ νυκτὶ ᾗ παρεδίδου ἑαυτόν ὑπὲρ τῶν ἁμαρτιῶν ἡμῶν...[1032]

Where the Liturgy of St. Gregory forcuses the post-*Sanctus* prayers on the historical, leading up to the Last Supper and its liturgical example for the Consecration of the gifts, the Egyptian prayer focuses on the mystical filling of the world generally and the gifts specifically by divinity.

The Syro-Byzantine liturgies begin the post-*Sanctus* with a reference back to the *Sanctus* itself. This is usually done through the double or triple repetition of the: Ἅγιος, in the Liturgy of St. Gregory, however, this is done with a double repetition: Ἅγιος ἅγιος εἶ Κύριε καὶ πανάγιος. Similar openings are seen in other Syro-Byzantine liturgies, such as the Liturgy of St. Basil: Ἅγιος εἶ ὡς ἀληθῶς καὶ πανάγιος καὶ οὐκ ἔστιν μέτρον τῆς μεγαλοπρεπείας.[1033] Though the Liturgy of St. Basil does not use a double repetition of Ἅγιος other similarities unite these two liturgies, there is only one member of the Trinity being discussed, and the term πανάγιος is used in a nearly identical fashion, to underscore the holiness of that individual member of the Trinity. In other Syro-Byzantine liturgies,

---

[1030] Hammerschmidt (1957). pp. 175-176
[1031] From the Liturgy of the Egyptian Jacobites including the Anaphora of St. Mark. (Hammond and Brightman (1896). pg. 176).
[1032] Hammond and Brightman (1896). pg 132 and Cuming (1990). pp. 39-40. "Truly heaven and earth are full of Your divine glory, through the splendor of our Lord and God and Savior Jesus Christ. O God, fill also this sacrifice with Your blessing, through the enlightenment of Your all-holy Spirit. For our Lord and God and king of us all Jesus Christ Himself, on the night on which He handed himselof over for our sins..."
[1033] Hammond and Brightman (1896). pg. 324 and Trempelis (1982). pg. 179. "Truly You are holy and all holy and there is no measure of Your majesty."

such as the Liturgy of St. James the opening takes on a slightly different form: Ἅγιος εἶ, Βασιλεῦ τῶν αἰώνων καὶ πάσης ἁγιωσύνης κύριος καὶ δοτήρ ἅγιος καὶ ὁ μονογενής σου υἱὸς ὁ κύριος ἡμῶν Ἰησοῦς Χριστὸς δι' οὗ τὰ πάντα ἐποίησας, ἅγιον δὲ καὶ τὸ πνεῦμά σου τὸ πανάγιον τὸ ἐρευνῶν τὰ πάντα καὶ τὰ βάθη σου τοῦ Θεοῦ.[1034] In this liturgy the repetition of Ἅγιος is used to discuss each of the members of the Trinity in succession, rather than only one, and it is only after this discussion that the author moves on to a short overview of the history of salvation. A similar opening is found in the Liturgy of St. John Chrysostom: Ἅγιος εἶ καὶ πανάγιος καὶ ὁ μονογενής σου υἱὸς καὶ τὸ πνεῦμά σου τὸ ἅγιον.[1035] These slightly alternate forms of the opening point to a difference in the sub-families within the Syro-Byzantine (or West Syrian) liturgical family. The liturgies that can be called properly Syrian, that belong to the churches of Antioch and Jerusalem, tend to discuss the entire Trinity in the opening of this prayer, even the earliest of these, the Apostolic Constitutions, shows a tendence in this direction, though only two members of the Trinity are mentioned here: Ἅγιος γὰρ εἶ ὡς ἀληθῶς καὶ πανάγιος, ὕψιστος καὶ ὑπερυψούμενος εἰς τοὺς αἰῶνας. ἅγιος δὲ καὶ ὁ μονογενής σου υἱὸς ὁ κύριος ἡμῶν καὶ θεὸς Ἰησοῦς ὁ Χριστὸς.[1036] Once again, the Liturgies of St. Basil and St. Gregory the Theologian prove their common origin in the Cappadocian/Constantiniopolitan liturgical sub-family of the Syrian rite. Both of these liturgies discuss only one of the members of the Trinity rather than the Triity as a whole. Perhaps it is the spatial separation between the opening ἅγιος which describes God the Father and the repetition of the term in the description of Christ in the Apostolic Constitutions that leads to the two different forms of the opening. The Cappadocian/Constantinopolitan liturgies pick up on only the first of the uses of Ἅγιος while the other Syrian liturgies pick up on the use of ἅγιος with another member of the Trintiy, prompting the use of the term with the entire Trinity rather than with only one or two of the members.

The content the post-*Sanctus* prayers in the Liturgy of St. Gregory the Theologian mirrors the Syro-Byzantine liturgies as well. In these liturgies, the history of salvation, from Creation through the history of the Old Testament, the Incarnation and leading into the Last Supper dialogue and the Consecration is presented. This is seen in the Liturgy of

---

[1034] Hammond and Brightman (1896). pg. 51 and Mercier (1944). pg. 200. "You are holy, king of the ages and the lord and provider of all, holy too is Your onlybegotten Son, our Lord Jesus Christ, through whom all things were made and holy is Your all-holy Spirit who reveals all things and Your depths O God."
[1035] Hammond and Brightman (1896) pg. 324 and Trempelis (1982). pg. 106. "You are holy and all holy, as is Your onlybegotten Son and Your Holy Spirit."
[1036] Hammond and Brightman (1896). pg. 19. "For You are truly holy and all holy, most exalted and highest to all ages, holy too is Your onlybegotten Son, our Lord and God and Savior Jesus Christ."

the Syrian Jacobites:[1037] "For holy art thou all-sovereign almighty terrible good, of fellowfeeling and especially as touching thy creature: who madest man out of the earth and gavest him delight in paradise..." Here the author begins with the Creation, but not of the universe, he begins with the second story of Creation found in Genesis Chapter two, in which humanity is not the last created creature, but the first, and then placed in the Garden of Eden. The section continues: "but when he transgressed thy commandment and fell thou didst not pass him by nor forsake him, o good, but didst chasten him as an exceeding merciful father: thou calledst him by the law, thou didst lead him by the prophets..." In this short section the author discusses the fall of Adam and Eve, the expulsion from Paradise and the entire spiritual history of Israel recounted in the Old Testament.[1038] The author completes the post-Sanctus with the discussion of the Incarnation: "...and last of all didst send thine onlybegotten Son into the world that he might renew thine image: who, when he had come down and been incarnate of the Holy Ghost and of the holy mother of God and evervirgin Mary and conversed with men and done all things for the redemption of our race..." In this short section, a mere eleven lines of text, the author is able to convey the entire history of salvation. In the Greek Liturgy of St. John Chrysostom we see a similar situation, a short prayer in which the author attempts to portray this same theme: ἅγιος εἶ καὶ πανάγιος καὶ μεγαλοπρεπὴς ἡ δόξα σου ὃς τὸν κόσμον σου οὕτως ἠγάπησας ὥστε τὸν υἱόν σου τὸν μονογενῆ ἵνα πᾶς ὁ πιστεύων εἰς αὐτὸν μὴ ἀπόληται ἀλλ' ἔχῃ ζωὴν αἰώνιον.[1039] This text, though discussing the same theme as the Liturgy of St. James, does not go into the same specifics. The same them is found in the Liturgy of St. Gregory, here, however, the section is lengthy, comprising the four individual prayers discussed at the beginning of this section. One of the very few other liturgies in which there is such a lengthy post-*Sanctus* is in the Greek Liturgy of St. Basil. In the Liturgy of St. Basil the same themes are discussed. Creation of the world;[1040] and the Creation of humanity.[1041] These are the same themes found in the first prayer in the St. Gregory text:

> Ἐποίησάς με ἄνθρωπον, ὡς φιλάνθρωπος· οὐκ αὐτὸς τῆς ἐμῆς ἐπιδεὴς δουλείας, ἐγὼ δὲ μᾶλλον τῆς σῆς χρῄζων δεσποτείας. Οὐκ ὄντα με δι' εὐσπλαγχνίαν παρήγαγες, οὐρανόν μοι πρὸς ὄροφον ἔστησας, γῆν μοι πρὸς βάσιν κατέπηξας.

[1037] The Syrian translation of the Greek Liturgy of St, James. Hammond and Brightman (1896). pg. 86
[1038] The spiritual history i.e. the prophetic and Messianic teachings of the Old Testament, rather than the physical history of Israel, i.e. the Judges and the Kings.
[1039] Hammond and Brightman (1896). pg. 324 and Trempelis (1982). pp. 106-107. "You are holy and all holy and majestic is Your glory, since You have loved Your world so much thatYou gave Your onlybegotten Son, that all who believe in Him shall not perish, but will have life eternal."
[1040] Cf. Hammond and Brightman (1896). pg. 324 and Trempelis (1982). pg. 179
[1041] Cf. Ibid and Trempelis (1982). pp. 179-180.

Δι' ἐμὲ θάλασσαν ἐχαλίνωσας· δι' ἐμὲ τὴν φύσιν τῶν ζώων ἀνέδειξας. Πάντα ὑπέταξας ὑποκάτω τῶν ποδῶν μου· οὐδ' ἓν τῶν τῆς σῆς φιλανθρωπίας ἐν ἐμοὶ πραγμάτων παρέλειπας[1042]

Though both the prayers discuss the creation of both humanity and the cosmos as a whole, which we have not seen in the other liturgies, the Liturgy of St. Gregory puts a far greater emphasis on it. This emphasis can be explained through two propagandistic aspects of the Liturgy of St. Gregory. Christ is referred to in a number of the prayers of the Liturgy as ὁ ὤν, as the God of the Old Testament and therefore the Creator. By doing so, the author underscores Christ's divinity in the manner he has done so in a number of other prayers, by assigning to Christ the authority or function of another member of the Trinity. The function of Creator also puts Christ into a closer relationship with the humans whom He creates, the very cosmos is created by Christ specifically for humanity. This creates a relationship of love and dependance between Christ and humanity that does not include the other members of the Trinity.

The following table illustrates the similarities between the post-Sanctus prayers of the Liturgy of St. Basil and the Liturgy of St. Gregory.

[1042] Section II.4 lines 4-9.

The Commentary

Figure II.V.1: the post-Sanctus prayers in the Liturgies of Sts. Basil[1043] and Gregory the Theologian.[1044]

The Thematic Element presented.	The Liturgy of St. Gregory the Theologian.	The Liturgy of St. Basil.[1045]
1. Creation of the cosmos and of humanity.	Prayer I: Ἐποίησάς με ἄνθρωπον, ὡς φιλάνθρωπος· οὐκ αὐτὸς τῆς ἐμῆς ἐπιδεὴς δουλείας, ἐγὼ δὲ μᾶλλον τῆς σῆς χρῄζων δεσποτείας. Οὐκ ὄντα με δι' εὐσπλαγχνίαν παρήγαγες, οὐρανόν μοι πρὸς ὄροφον ἔστησας, γῆν μοι πρὸς βάσιν κατέπηξας. Δι' ἐμὲ θάλασσαν ἐχαλίνωσας, δι' ἐμὲ τὴν φύσιν τῶν ζώων ἀνέδειξας.	καὶ ὅσιος ἐν πᾶσιν τοῖς ἔργοις σου ὅτι ἐν δικαιοσύνῃ καὶ κρίσει ἀληθινῇ πάντα ἐπήγασες ἡμῖν...πλάσας γὰρ τὸν ἄνθρωπον, χοῦν λαβὼν ἀπὸ τῆς γῆς, καὶ εἰκόνι τῇ σῇ ὁ Θεὸς τιμήσας

[1043] Hammond and Brightman (1896). pp. 324-326 and Trempelis (1982). pp. 179-181

[1044] Cf. Section II.4 lines 4-39.

[1045] "You are holy in all Your works, for with righteousness and true judgment You have ordered all things for us. For having made man by taking dust from the earth, and having honored him with Your own image, O God, You placed him in a garden of delight, promising him eternal life and the enjoyment of everlasting blessings in the observance of Your commandments. But when he disobeyed You, the true God who had created him, and was led astray by the deception of the serpent becoming subject to death through his own transgressions, You, O God, in Your righteous judgment, expelled him from paradise into this world, returning him to the earth from which he was taken, yet providing for him the salvation of regeneration in Your Christ. For You did not forever reject Your creature whom You made, O Good One, nor did You forget the work of Your hands, but because of Your tender compassion, You visited him in various ways: You sent forth prophets; You performed mighty works by Your saints who in every generation have pleased You. You spoke to us by the mouth of Your servants the prophets, announcing to us the salvation which was to come; You gave us the law to help us; You appointed angels as guardians. And when the fullness of time had come, You spoke to us through Your Son Himself, through whom You created the ages. He, being the splendor of Your glory and the image of Your being, upholding all things by the word of His power, thought it not robbery to be equal with You, God and Father. But, being God before all ages, He appeared on earth and lived with humankind. Becoming incarnate from a holy Virgin, He emptied Himself, taking the form of a servant, conforming to the body of our lowliness, that He might change us in the likeness of the image of His glory. For, since through man sin came into the world and through sin death, it pleased Your only begotten Son, who is in Your bosom, God and Father, born of a woman, the holy Theotokos and ever virgin Mary; born under the law, to condemn sin in His flesh, so that those who died in Adam may be brought to life in Him, Your Christ. He lived in this world, and gave us precepts of salvation. Releasing us from the delusions of idolatry, He guided us to the sure knowledge of You, the true God and Father. He acquired us for Himself, as His chosen people, a royal priesthood, a holy nation. Having cleansed us by water and sanctified us with the Holy Spirit, He gave Himself as ransom to death in which we were held captive, sold under sin. Descending into Hades through the cross, that He might fill all things with Himself, He loosed the bonds of death. He rose on the third day, having opened a path for all flesh to the resurrection from the dead, since it was not possible that the Author of life would be dominated by corruption. So He became the first fruits of those who have fallen asleep, the first born of the dead, that He might be Himself the first in all things. Ascending into heaven, He sat at the right hand of Your majesty on high and He will come to render to each according to His works. As memorials of His saving passion, He has left us these gifts which we have set forth before You according to His commands... (Vaporis (1988).).

		Πάντα ὑπέταξας ὑποκάτω τῶν ποδῶν μου· οὐδ' ἓν τῶν τῆς σῆς φιλαν(θρωπ)ίας ἐν ἐμοὶ πραγμάτων παρέλειπας.	
2.	The Placement of humanity in Paradise and the fall of humanity.	Prayer II: εἰς τρυφήν μοι τὸν παράδεισον ἤνοιξας· τῆς σῆς γνώσεως τὴν διδασκαλίαν παρέδωκας. Ἔδειξάς με τὸ δένδρον τῆς ζωῆς, μοι ξύλον ὑπέδειξας, τοῦ θανάτου τὸ κέντρον ἐγνώρισας. Ἑνός μοι φυτοῦ τὴν ἀπόλαυσιν ἀπηγόρευσας. Ἐξ αὐτοῦ μόνου οὖν εἶπάς μοι μὴ φαγεῖν, ἔφαγον ἐκ ὧν τὸν νόμον ἠθέτησα· γνώμῃ τῆς ἐντολῆς παρημέλησα· ἐγὼ δὲ τοῦ θανάτου τὴν ἀπόφασιν ἥρπασα.	τέθεικας αὐτὸν ἐν παραδείσῳ τῆς τρυφῆς ἀθανασίαν ζωῆς καὶ ἀπόλαυσιν αἰωνίων ἀγαθῶν ἐν τῇ τηρήσει τῶν ἐντολῶν σου ἐπαγγειλάμενος αὐτῷ· ἀλλὰ παρακούσαντα σοῦ τοῦ ἀληθινοῦ Θεοῦ τοῦ κτίσαντος αὐτὸν καὶ τῇ ἀπάτῃ τοῦ ὄφεως ὑπαχθέντα νεκρωθέντα τε αὐτὸν τοῖς οἰκείοις αὐτοῦ παραπτώμασιν ἐξωρίσας αὐτὸν ἐν τῇ δικαιοκρισίᾳ σου ὁ Θεὸς ἐκ τοῦ παραδείσου εἰς τὸν κόσμον τοῦτον καὶ ἀπέστρψας αὐτοὶ εἰς τὴν γῆν ἐξ ἧς ἐλήφθη οἰκονομῶν αὐτῷ τὴν ἐκ παλιγγενεσίας σωτηρίαν τὴν ἐν αὐτῷ τῷ Χριστῷ σου·
3.	The history of Salvation up to the Crucifixion.	Prayer III: ὡς ποιμὴν ἀγαθὸς εἰς πλανώμενον ἔδραμες. Ὡς Πατὴρ ἀληθινὸς ἐμοὶ τῷ πεπτωκότι συνήλγησας, πᾶσι τοῖς πρὸς ζωὴν φαρμάκοις κατέδησας. Αὐτός μοι προφήτας ἀπέστειλας· δι' ἐμὲ τὸν νοσοῦντα, νόμον εἰς βοήθειαν ἔδοκας. Αὐτός μοι τὰς πρὸς ὑγιείαν ὦ παρανομηθείσας, διηκόνησας· φῶς τοῖς πλανωμένοις ἀνέτειλας· τοῖς	οὐ γὰρ ἀπεστράφης τὸ πλάσμα σου εἰς τέλος ὃ ἐποίησας ἀγαθέ οὐδὲ ἐπελάθου ἔργου χειρῶν σου, ἀλλ' ἐπεσκέψω πολυτρόπως διὰ σπλάγχνα ἐλέους σου, Προφήτας ἐξαπέστειλας, ἐποίησας δυνάμεις διὰ τῶν ἁγίων σου τῶν καθ' ἑκάστην γενεὰν καὶ γενεὰν εὐαρεστησάντων σοι, ἐλάλησας ἡμῖν διὰ στόματος τῶν δούλων σου τῶν προφητῶν προκαταγγέλλων ἡμῖν τὴν μέλλουσαν ἔσεσθαι σωτηρίαν, νόμον ἔδωκας εἰς βοήθειαν, ἀγγέλους

ἀγνοοῦσιν, ὁ ἀεὶ παρὼν ἐπεδήμησας. Ἐπὶ τὴν παρθενικὴν ἦλθες νηδύν, ὁ ἀχώρητος Θεὸς ὤν. Οὐχ ἁρπαγμὸν ἡγήσω τὸ εἶναι ἴσα Θεῷ, ἀλλ᾽ ἑαυτὸν ἐκένωσας· μορφὴν δούλου λαβών. Τὴν ἐμὴν ἐν σοι φύσιν ηὐλόγησας· ὑπὲρ ἐμοῦ τὸν νόμον ἐπλήρωσας· τοῦ πτώματός μου τὴν ἀνάστασιν ὑπηγόρευσας. Ἔδωκας τοῖς ὑπὸ τοῦ ᾅδου κρατουμένοις τὴν ἄφεσιν· τοῦ νόμου τὴν ἀρὰν ἀπεσόβησας. Ἐν σαρκὶ τὴν ἁμαρτίαν κατήργησας· τῆς σῆς ἐξουσίας μοι τὴν δυναστείαν ἐγνώρισας. Τυφλοῖς τὸ βλέπειν ἀπέδωκας· νεκροὺς ἐκ τάφων ἀνέστησας· ῥήματι τὴν φύσιν ἀνώρθωσας· τῆς σῆς εὐσπλαγχνίας μοι τὴν οἰκονομίαν ὑπέδειξας· τῶν πονηρῶν τὴν βίαν ὑπένεγκας. Τὸν νῶτόν σου δέδωκας εἰς μάστιγας, τὰς δὲ σιαγόνας σου ὑπέθηκας εἰς ῥαπίσματα· οὐκ ἀπέστρεψας δι᾽ ἐμὲ τὸ πρόσωπόν σου ἀπὸ αἰσχύνης ἐμπτυσμάτων.	ἐπέστησας φύλακας· ὅτε δὲ ἦλθεν τὸ πλήρωμα τῶν καιρῶν ἐλάλησας ἡμῖν ἐν αὐτῷ τῷ υἱῷ σου δι᾽ οὗ καὶ τοὺς αἰῶνας ἐποίησας, ὅς ὢν ἀπαύγασμα τῆς δόξης καὶ χαρακτὴρ τῆς ὑποστάσεώς σου φέρων τε τὰ πάντα τῷ ῥήματι τῆς δυνάμεως αὐτοῦ οὐχ ἁρπαγμὸν ἡγήσατο τὸ εἶναι ἴσα σοὶ τῷ Θεῷ καὶ Πατρὶ ἀλλὰ Θεὸς ὢν προαιώνιος ἐπὶ τῆς γῆς ὤφθη καὶ τοῖς ἀνθρώποις συνανεστράφη καὶ ἐκ παρθένου ἁγίας σαρκωθεὶς ἐκένωσεν ἑαυτὸν μορφὴν δούλου λαβών, σύμμορφος γενόμενος τῷ σώματι τῆς ταπεινώσεως ἡμῶν ἵνα ἡμᾶς συμμόρφους ποιήσῃ τῆς εἰκόνος τῆς δόξης αὐτοῦ· ἐπειδὴ γὰρ δι᾽ ἀνθρώπου ἡ ἁμαρτία εἰσῆλθεν εἰς τὸν κόσμον καὶ διὰ τῆς ἁμαρτίας ὁ θάνατος, ηὐδόκησεν ὁ μονογενής σου υἱός ὁ ὢν ἐν τοῖς κόλποις σοῦ τοῦ Θεοῦ καὶ Πατρός, γενόμενος ἐκ γυναικός τῆς ἁγίας θεοτόκου καὶ ἀειπαρθένου Μαρίας, γενόμενος ὑπὸ νόμον, κατακρῖναι τὴν ἁμαρτίαν ἐν τῇ σαρκὶ αὐτοῦ ἵνα οἱ ἐν τῷ Ἀδὰμ ἀποθνήσκοντες ζωοποιηθῶσιν ἐν αὐτῷ τῷ χριστῷ σου· καὶ ἐμπολιτευσάμενος τῷ κόσμῳ τούτῳ, δοὺς προστάγματα σωτηρίας, ἀποστήσας ἡμᾶς τῆς πλάνης τῶν εἰδώλων, προσήγαγεν τῇ ἐπιγνώσει σοῦ τοῦ ἀληθινοῦ Θεοῦ καὶ Πατρός κτησάμενος ἡμᾶς ἑαυτῷ λαὸν περιούσιον, βασίλειον ἱεράτευμα, ἔθνος ἅγιον,

The Liturgy of Saint Gregory the Theologian

| 4. The Crucifixion and foreshadowing of the Parousia. | Prayer IV: Ὡς πρόβατον ἐπὶ σφαγὴν ἦλθες, μέχρι σταυροῦ. Τὴν ἐμὴν κηδεμονίαν ὑπέδειξας· τῷ σῷ τάφῳ τὴν ἐμὴν ἁμαρτίαν ἐνέκρωσας· εἰς οὐρανόν μοι τὴν ἐμὴν ἀπαρχὴν ἀνεβίβασας· τῆς σῆς ἀφίξεώς μοι τὴν παρουσίαν ἐμήνυσας· ἐν ᾗ μέλλεις ἔρχεσθαι κρῖναι ζῶντας καὶ νεκρούς· καὶ ἀποδοῦναι ἑκάστῳ κατὰ τὰ ἔργα αὐτοῦ. | καὶ καθαρίσας ἡμᾶς ἐν ὕδατι καὶ ἁγιάσας τῷ Πνεύματι τῷ ἁγίῳ ἔδωκεν ἑαυτόν ἀντάλλαγμα τῷ θανάτῳ ἐν ᾧ κατειχόμεθα πεπραμένοι ὑπὸ τῆς ἁμαρτίας καὶ κατελθὼν διὰ τοῦ σταυροῦ εἰς τόν ᾅδην ἵνα πληρώσῃ ἑαυτῷ τὰ πάντα ἔλυσεν τὰς ὠδῖνας τοῦ θανάτου καὶ ἀναστὰς τῇ τρίτῃ ἡμέρᾳ καὶ ὁδοποιήσας πάσῃ σαρκὶ τὴν ἐκ νεκρῶν ἀνάστασιν καθότι οὐκ ἦν δυνατὸν κρατεῖσθαι ὑπὸ τῆς φθορᾶς τὸν ἀρχηγὸν τῆς ζωῆς ἐγένετο ἀπαρχὴ τῶν κεκοιμημένων, πρωτότοκος ἐκ τῶν νεκρῶν ἵνα ᾖ αὐτὸς τὰ πάντα ἐν πᾶσιν πρωτεύων καὶ ἀνελθὼν εἰς τοὺς οὐρανούς ἐκάθισεν ἐν δεξιᾷ τῆς μεγαλωσύνης ἐν ὑψηλοῖς ὃς καὶ ἥξει ἀποδοῦναι ἑκάστῳ κατὰ τὰ ἔργα αὐτοῦ· κατέλιπεν δὲ ἡμῖν ὑπομνήματα τοῦ σωτηρίου αὐτοῦ πάθους ταῦτα, ἃ προτεθείκαμεν, κατὰ τὰς αὐτοῦ ἐντολάς |

    Although the phrasing is different in these two liturgies, both include discussions of themes that are not commonly found in the post-*Sanctus* prayer such as the creation of the cosmos and the foreshadowing of the *Parousia*. Generally, the post-*Sanctus* is a prayer that leads into the Consecration, therefore the prayer usually discusses the Incarnation and leads into the Last Supper dialogue. The similarities shown here underscore, once again, the relationship between these two liturgies, and show that thir common origin in the Cappadocian/Constantinopolitan liturgical family of the larger West Syrian rite.

    The post-*Sanctus* prayer in the Liturgy of St. Gregory the Theologian can be considered a microcosm of the liturgy as a whole, as it contains a summation of the christological theology presented in the rest of the text. This has proven important in the debate surrounding the origin of the text, as the christological theology expressed in this section parallels that of St. Gregory the Theologian. The specifics of this christology need not be discussed here, as the exact parallels have been worked out by Sanchez Caro.[1046] we have seen examples of this christology throughout the work already: Christ is expressed as the Creator, and as the Redeemer, He receives various other attributes that are usually associated with other members of the Trinity. Because of these similarities: "Baumstark was inclined to take their attributions seriously,[1047] for this eucharist undeniably evokes the formulas of prayers to Christ which abound in the sermons and poems of Gregory."[1048] Bouyer, though admitting to an influence by St. Gregory doubts his authorship: "For our part, we would be of the opinion that it must have been composed by a reader of his work, molded by his christocentric piety and filled with the memory of his expressions."[1049] Bouyer gives no reason for his reservations, but may hang together with his categorization of this liturgy as a "late Syrian Anaphora,"[1050] as we have discussed above, however, other internal evidence points to the fourth century and the Cappadocian/Constantinopolitan rite as a point the origin, which does substatiate Baumstark's idea.

1. Structure[1051]

The post-*Sanctus* prayer is, to a certain extent, is a misnomer, as the section stretches over four prayers, each one separated by a response by the people: Κύριε ἐλέησον. The first of these prayers begins: Ἅγιος ἅγιος εἶ Κύριε καὶ πανάγιος, which connects these prayers back to the *Sanctus* hymn itself. Following this introduction to the section are three phrases that deal with Christ's nature: Ἐξαίρετόν σου τῆς οὐσίας τὸ φέγγος· ἄφραστός σου τῆς σοφίας ἡ δύναμις. Οὐδεὶς λόγος ἐκμετρήσει τῆς σῆς φιλανθρωπίας τὸ πέλαγος. The discussion of Christ's nature is not central here, but a description of Christ as Creator, and then in His role as Redeemer. Christ is immediately introduced as the Creator: Ἐποίησάς με ἄνθρωπον, ὡς φιλάνθρωπος which is followed up immediately by explaining Christ's relationship with humans: οὐκ αὐτὸς τῆς ἐμῆς ἐπιδεὴς δουλείας, ἐγὼ δὲ μᾶλλον τῆς σῆς χρῄζων δεσποτείας. It is only at this point that the author comes to the central point of this first prayer, the Creation of humanity in the context of the Creation of humanity.

[1046] See above in the introduction.
[1047] The attribution of this liturgy to St. Gregory the Theologian.
[1048] Bouyer (1989). pg. 357
[1049] Ibid.
[1050] Ibid.
[1051] Since there is already a table in which the structure of this section is discussed, there will not be another in this discussion.

The second prayer continues with the theme of Creation, then shifts to the fall of humanity. The prayer opens with four phrases that describe the way in which Christ sets humanity apart from the other created beings: Σὺ ἔπλασάς με καὶ ἔθηκας ἐπ' ἐμὲ τὴν χεῖρά σου, τῆς σῆς ἐξουσίας ἐν ἐμοὶ τὴν εἰκόνα ὑπέγραψας, τοῦ λόγου τὸ δῶρον ἐνέθηκας. This is followed by three phrases which discuss the placement of humans in Paradise: εἰς τρυφήν μοι τὸν παράδεισον ἤνοιξας· τῆς σῆς γνώσεως τὴν διδασκαλίαν παρέδωκας· Ἔδιξάς με τὸ δένδρον τῆς ζωῆς, μοι ξύλον ὑπέδειξας. By mentioning the tree of life, the author is able to segway into a discussion of how humanity fell: τοῦ θανάτου τὸ κέντρον ἐγνώρισας. Ἑνός μοὶ φύτου τὴν ἀπόλαυσιν ἀπηγόρευσας·. Ἐξ αὐτοῦ μόνου οὖν εἰπάς μοι μὴ φαγεῖν, ἔφαγον ἐκ ὧν τὸν νόμον ἠθέτησα· γνώμῃ τῆς ἐντολῆς παρημέλησα· ἐγὼ δὲ τοῦ θανάτου τὴν ἀπόφασιν ἥρπασα.

The third prayer is the longest of the four, it moves on from the fall of humanity to the discussion of Christ's involvement in human affairs before the Incarnation and from the Incarnation to the Crucifixion. In seven phrases, the Old Testament aspect of Christ: ὤ ὤν, is laid out. Juxtaposed to the Old Testament Christ is the Incarnation and Christ of the New Testament. Over a series of eleven phrases the author discusses his theology of the Incarnation. The Christ of the New Testament is described in the last eight phrases of this prayer, in which the life of Christ is summarized: the specific miracles τυφλοῖς τὸ βλέπειν ἀπέδωκας· νεκροὺς ἐκ τάφων ἀνέστησας; as well as the more general salvific work of Christ's Incarnation: ῥήματι τὴν φύσιν ἀνώρθωσας· τῆς σῆς εὐσπλαγχνίας μοι τὴν οἰκονομίαν ὑπέδειξας. The final four phrases of this prayer are used to transition from Christ's life to the Crucifixion: τῶν πονηρῶν τὴν βίαν ὑπένεγκας. Τὸν νῶτόν σου δέδωκας εἰς μάστιγας, τὰς δὲ σιαγόνας σου ὑπέθηκας εἰς ῥαπίσματα· οὐκ ἀπέστρεψας δι' ἐμὲ τὸ πρόσωπόν σου ἀπὸ αἰσχύνης ἐμπτυσμάτων.

Following the lengthy description of Christ's salvific work in His Incarnation is a short concluding prayer in which Christ's salvific work as God in His Crucifixion, His Ressurection and the Parousia is discussed in four separate phrases, each of which is devoted to a different aspect of Christ's action as God.

2. Function

It is the stylization of this section as a dialogue, which functions as the main vector of anti-Arian theology in this section. The dialogue style brings Christ into an intimate relationship with the worshipper, even while discussing Christ's divinity. The christology presented in this section is especially interesting, as it parallels almost exactly that of St. Gregory. \

The Commentary

1. (Section II.4 lines 2-4): Ἅγιος ἅγιος εἶ Κύριε καὶ πανάγιος. Ἐξαίρετόν σου τῆς οὐσίας τὸ φέγγος· ἄφραστός σου τῆς σοφίας ἡ δύναμις. Οὐδεὶς λόγος ἐκμετρήσει τῆς σῆς φιλανθρωπίας τὸ πέλαγος.

The opening of the post-*Sanctus* reflects the wording of the *Sanctus* itself, as is the norm for liturgies of the West Syrian rite. Following this opening, the author does not immediately proceed to a discussion of the creation, as is seen in the Liturgy of St. Basil.[1052] Instead, the author discusses various aspects of Christ's divinity which falls into the same scheme as we have seen throughout the liturgy, the author begins with the exaltation of Christ: "...Exalted is the splendor of Your being; the power of Your wisdom is inexpressible..." The choice of words here looks back to the Neoplatonic philosophy which marks the theology of the Cappadocians.[1053] οὐσία is a term used throughout the works of St. Gregory, as well as the other Cappadocian Fathers and Origen, along with the term *hypostasis*, in order to combat the Arians.[1054] These terms were used to define the relationship of the members of the Trinity with one another, *ousia* as the essence of the Trinity, as one God; *hypostasis* as the individual persons that are part of this *ousia*. Interestingly, the author only uses the term ousia in reference to Christ, rather than *hypostasis*, in this way, the author referrs also to the Nicene Creed, in which Christ is referred to in terms of the *ousia* of the Father: ὁμοούσιον τῷ Πατρί. Once again an aspect of the Father is transferred to the Son, though declared of the same essence as the Father in the Creed, it is still within the context of the relationship with the Father. Here, however, the description is not made in terms of a relationship, but only in terms of Christ. This use reflects several other points within this liturgy, and creates another intratextual link in the work, between the post-*Sanctus* prayer, the "Prayer of the Greeting" and the "Prayer of the Bowing of the Head."

The second of these phrases discusses the wisdom of Christ, the σοφία. This epithet, one which is also used in Platonic philosophy,[1055] of Christ is only used one in the entire liturgy, in this place. The term may be used here as an intermediate stage between the divinity presented by the term "ousia" and the connection with humanity: τῆς σῆς φιλανθρωπίας. *Sophia* is an aspect of divinity, one which binds humanity with God, and one which St. Gregory the Theologian discusses: "How can he be ignorant of anything that is, when he is Wisdom, the maker of the worlds, who brings all things to fulfilment and recreates all things, who is the end of all that has come into being?"[1056] This aspect of

---

[1052] Hammond and Brightman (1896). pg. 324
[1053] For a discussion of the Platonic philosophy in the Cappadocian Fathers, see, for example, Callahan (1958).
[1054] McGrath (1998). pg. 22
[1055] See Matthews (1991).
[1056] Gregory Nazianzen *Orationes*, 30.15.

Christ, as the personification of knowledge, is an important aspect of Eastern Theology, and is celebrated in the Church of Hagia Sophia, constructed first by Constantine and later rebuilt by Emperor Justinian.

The final phrase in this series completes the transition from the divine nature of Christ toward the human: Οὐδεὶς λόγος ἐκμετρήσει τῆς σῆς φιλανθρωπίας τὸ πέλαγος. This phrase also acts as a transition from the discussion of Christ to the discussion of the Creation. The phrasing here may also be meant ironically: "...No word will measure out the ocean of Your love for man..." is followed by a lengthy section in which this love is spelled out in the description of Creation, the History of Salvation and the *Parousia*.

2. (Section II.4 lines 4-9): Ἐποίησάς με ἄνθρωπον, ὡς φιλάνθρωπος· οὐκ αὐτὸς τῆς ἐμῆς ἐπιδεὴς δουλείας, ἐγὼ δὲ μᾶλλον τῆς σῆς χρῄζων δεσποτείας. Οὐκ ὄντα με δι' εὐσπλαγχνίαν παρήγαγες, οὐρανόν μοι πρὸς ὄροφον ἔστησας, γῆν μοι πρὸς βάσιν κατέπηξας. Δι' ἐμὲ θάλασσαν ἐχαλίνωσας, δι' ἐμὲ τὴν φύσιν τῶν ζῴων ἀνέδειξας. Πάντα ὑπέταξας ὑποκάτω τῶν ποδῶν μου· οὐδ' ἓν τῶν τῆς σῆς φιλανθρωπίας ἐν ἐμοὶ πραγμάτων παρέλειπας.

The opening of this section sets the tone, the focus is on the creation of humanity. Before continuing, however, the author first fulfills what was said before: Οὐδεὶς λόγος ἐκμετρήσει τῆς σῆς φιλανθρωπίας τὸ πέλαγος... is fulfilled in ...Ἐποίησάς με ἄνθρωπον, ὡς φιλάν(θρωπ)ος... this also plays into the ironic aspect discussed above, the love of Christ, which the author first declares as immeasurable is then defined, Christ's love for man is expressed by His creation of man.

The focus on humanity's creation continues in the following two phrases, first the author discusses the reason which brought humanity into being. The author does not do this through a simple statement of fact, rather he begins with a statement of *apophatic* theology, a system of theology in which a negative statement is made, rather than a positive statement, this was the favorite form of theology of many of the early Eastern theologians, including the Cappadocian fathers.[1057] In this case the apophatic theology is found in the phrase: οὐκ αὐτὸς τῆς ἐμῆς ἐπιδεὴς δουλείας it was not in order to create servants that humanity was brought into being, the reason humanity is created in a number of creation myths. This *apophatic* theology is then qualified by a statement of *cataphatic* theology: ἐγὼ δὲ μᾶλλον τῆς σῆς χρῄζων δεσποτείας, the reason for creation is transferred from Christ to humanity, as the author has transferred epitheta and attributes from other members of the Trinity to Christ. It is because of the need of humanity for God that humanity is

---

[1057] Lossky (1997). pg. 81

created, this is the immesurable φιλάνθρωπια discussed above by the author. By making the reason for creating humanity dependant on both on the love of Christ for man and the need of man for Christ, the author inexorably links the two, underscoring Christ's central position in the liturgy. Forming a couplet with <u>why</u> humanity is created is <u>how</u>: δι' εὐσπλαγχνίαν. It is through the "compassion" of Christ, who recognizes the need of humanity for God's lordship and brings it to pass.

The reason how and why humanity is brought into being completes the initial discussion of the creation of humanity, a discussion taken up again in the second prayer of this series. Here the author interrupts with a discussion of the other elements of creation: 1. the heaven; 2. the earth; 3. the ocean; 4. living creatures. The author remains, however, in the context of the relationship between Christ and humanity, all these things are created for humanity: "...for me...for my sake... You subjected all things underneath my feet..." as part of the compassion which He showed in the creation of humanity itself and showing that the relationship between Christ and humanity transcends the relationship between Christ and the rest of creation, as all other things were created for the benefit of humanity rather than out of compassion for other created beings. It seems strange that the author interrupts his discussion of humanity's creation. In this way the author is able to reference both the first and second chapter of Genesis, in which the order of Creation is described differently. Like the second chapter of Genesis, the liturgy presents an anthropocentric view of creation in which humanity is the first created creature, for which all else is created, like Adam is the first created in Genesis 2 (after the earth and heaven are made), and then placed in paradise created for him.[1058] In this prayer, it is the second chapter of Genesis that provides the context of creation, the sole use of this context is interrupted by the reopening of the discussion of humanity's creation in the following prayer. This reopening places the creation of the rest of creation once again before the creation of humanity, echoing the order in which the first chapter of Genesis is written. This is emphasized in this prayer by the phrase: πάντα ὑπέταξας ὑποκάτω τῶν ποδῶν μου and in the following chapter by the phrase: τῆς σῆς ἐξουσίας ἐν ἐμοὶ τὴν εἰκόνα ὑπέγραψας, both of which reflect Genesis 1:26-27: By using imagery from both chapters 1 and 2 of Genesis, the author is able to project a theology of creation that rests on the relationship between Christ and humanity, an anthropocentric view of creation in which humantiy is at the same time the cause for and the crown of creation.

[1058] Genesis 2: 6-8

The Liturgy of Saint Gregory the Theologian

3. (Section II.4 lines 11-13): Σὺ ἔπλασάς με καὶ ἔθηκας ἐπ' ἐμὲ τὴν χεῖρά σου, τῆς σῆς ἐξουσίας ἐν ἐμοὶ τὴν εἰκόνα ὑπέγραψας, τοῦ λόγου τὸ δῶρον ἐνέθηκας· εἰς τρυφήν μοι τὸν παράδεισον ἤνοιξας·

The beginning of this prayer reflects the content of the previous prayer. Here the author continues the description of creation. Here again, despite the single image of being created in the image of God that evokes the first chapter of Genesis, the focus is on the second. Humanity is created by the hand of God, rather than by the spoken word. Rational thought: τοῦ λόγου τὸ δῶρον must be placed into humanity, as life is breathed into humanity in Genesis 2:7. Finally, humanity is placed into a paradise of delight, into Eden. Here again, however, what seems to be the sole use of Genesis 2 is weakened by imagery taken from Genesis 1. Not only is τὴν εἰκόνα used in reference to creation, a reference to the image of God, which humanity is in Genesis 1, but the rational thought gifted to humantiy is the τοῦ λόγου τὸ δῶρον. Logos is not only rational thought, but the spoken word, the means by which creation is accomplished in Genesis 1. The logos could also refer to Christ himself, another reference to the image of God in which humantiy is made, and a foreshadowing of the Incarnation and Crucifixion of Christ, in which He gives Himself as a gift for the salvation of His creation.

4. (Section II.4 lines 13-16): τῆς σῆς γνώσεως τὴν διδασκαλίαν παρέδωκας. Ἔδειξάς με τὸ δένδρον τῆς ζωῆς, μοι ξύλον ὑπέδειξας, τοῦ θανάτου τὸ κέντρον ἐγνώρισας. Ἑνός μοι φύτου τὴν ἀπόλαυσιν ἀπηγόρευσας. Ἐξ αὐτοῦ μόνου οὖν εἰπάς μοι μὴ φαγεῖν, ἔφαγον ἐκ ὧν τὸν νόμον ἠθέτησα· γνώμῃ τῆς ἐντολῆς παρημέλησα· ἐγὼ δὲ τοῦ θανάτου τὴν ἀπόφασιν ἥρπασα.

The second half of this prayer transitions from the creation of humanity to his experiences in Paradise and the ultimate fall from grace. The experiences in Paradise are summed up in two phrases: τῆς σῆς γνώσεως τὴν διδασκαλίαν παρέδωκας. Ἔδειξάς με τὸ δένδρον τῆς ζωῆς, μοι ξύλον ὑπέδειξας. These phrases present a historical perspective, looking back on what life was like in the Paradise of Eden, in which humanity enjoyed both a personal knowledge of God and eternal life, but they also look forward, to the renewed Paradise made possible by Christ's Incarnation, Crucifixion and Ressurection. The author does this in the phrase μοι ξύλον ὑπέδειξας a foreshadowing that the tree of life in this prayer represents not only the tree of life in the Garden of Eden, but the cross, the true tree of life. This foreshadowing of redemption serves several purposes, it reminds the worshippers in the congregation of their relationship with Christ, not only as Creator, as is established thus far in these prayers, but as Redeemer as well. It also foreshadows the ending of this set of prayers even before the fall of humantiy is brought up.

The Commentary

The discussion of the fall is, to a great extent, a summary of the story in Genesis, though it is personalized. Rather than Adam and Eve, it is I who is the transgressor of the law, who eats of the fruit. It is not unusual for a liturgical text not use Adam and Eve's nam in this context, but the intense personalization is unique to this text, and is used by the author to strengthen the relationship between Christ and humanity already established. The author is, in a certain sense, saying: "Despite what I have done to Christ, see what He will do for me." This culminates in the ending of this prayer: γνώμῃ τῆς ἐντολῆς παρημέλησα· ἐγὼ δὲ τοῦ θανάτου τὴν ἀπόφασιν ἥρπασα, it is not Christ, angry over the insult done to Him, who expells humanity from Paradise and sets up death as a punishment, it is humanity who cuts itself off from Christ who condemns itself and receives as death as a consequence of its action.

5. (Section II.4 lines 18-22): Σὺ μοί, ὦ Δέσποτα, τὴν τιμωρίαν μετέβαλες· ὡς ποιμὴν ἀγαθὸς εἰς πλανώμενον ἔδραμες. Ὡς Πατὴρ ἀληθινὸς ἐμοὶ τῷ πεπτωκότι συνήλγησας, πᾶσι τοῖς πρὸς ζωὴν φαρμάκοις κατέδησας. Αὐτός μοι προφήτας ἀπέστειλας· δι' ἐμὲ τὸν νοσοῦντα, νόμον εἰς βοήθειαν ἔδοκας. Αὐτός μοι τὰς πρὸς ὑγιείαν ὦ παρανομηθεῖσας, διηκόνησας·

In these post-*Sanctus* prayers, the author wishes to present the relationship between humantiy and Christ as deeply personal, but also as dependant. In creating humantiy Christ recognized first the need that humanity has for God, and in doing so also recognizes the other needs humantiy has, and fulfills those needs. Here humanity is in perhaps even more desparate need, having "...taken up the sentences of death..." through the actions in the Garden of Eden, and Christ immediately fulfills this need: Σὺ μοί, ὦ Δέσποτα, τὴν τιμωρίαν μετέβαλες. The close proximity of Σὺ and μοὶ show, stylistically, the closeness which the author is attempting to convey, but Christ is mentioned first, again showing the dependance of the human on Him. This relationship is again taken up in another phrase of this prayer: ὡς Πατὴρ ἀληθινὸς ἐμοὶ τῷ πεπτωκότι συνήλγησας. Here again the epithet for Christ, "true Father" is placed in direct proximity to "me" and the relationship is based here on sympathy, Christ suffers with his creation, which foreshadows His suffering for His creation in the Crucifixion, since it is death that humantiy suffers due to the fall. The very epithet used here of Christ works in the propagandistic scheme set up in the liturgy as a whole and in these prayers specifically. He is termed the "true Father," implying both authority over His creation, and an intimate knowledge of and relationship with it; it also fits into the established paradigm of transferring epitheta from God the Father to Christ.

In this prayer, the working of Christ in the Old Testament is described, both generally: ὡς ποιμὴν ἀγαθὸς εἰς πλανώμενον ἔδραμες...Αὐτός μοι τὰς πρὸς ὑγιείαν ὦ παρανομηθείσας, διηκόνησας;[1059] as well as in specific instaces: 1. the sending of the prophets; and 2: the establishment of the Ten Commandments. It is especially interesting to note the relative brevity in the description of Christ's actions in the Old Testament when compared to the following sections of the prayer, which describe Christ's actions in the New Testament. Though the author does show the action taken by Christ in the Old Testament, he wishes to focus on parts of Scripture in which Christ is physically present on earth, on the tangible relationship enjoyed by humanity and Christ during that time, as a foreshadowing of the tangible relationship that will be enjoyed with Him in Paradise.

6. (Section II.4 lines 22-25): φῶς τοῖς πλανωμένοις ἀνέτειλας· τοῖς ἀγνοοῦσιν, ὁ ἀεὶ παρὼν ἐπεδήμησας. Ἐπὶ τὴν παρθενικὴν ἦλθες νηδύν, ὁ ἀχώρητος Θεὸς ὤν. Οὐχ ἁρπαγμὸν ἡγήσω τὸ εἶναι ἴσα Θεῷ, ἀλλ' ἑαυτὸν ἐκένωσας· μορφὴν δούλου λαβών. Τὴν ἐμὴν ἐν σοι φύσιν ηὐλόγησας·

Here we see the transition from the discussion of the Old Testament to the New: φῶς τοῖς πλανωμένοις ἀνέτειλας can be interpreted as beloging to either, and, by referring to both provides a bridge between the two. The light for those who wander can refer to the pillar of fire that led the Hebrews to safety while fleeing from Egypt;[1060] as well as to the *Nunc Dimittis* prayer of St. Simeon, in which salvation is described as a "light of revelation to the Gentiles."[1061] The author begins with the Incarnation: ἐπὶ τὴν παρθενικὴν ἦλθες νηδύν. This entire section is similar in structure to the corresponding passage in the Byzantine Liturgy of St. Basil: οὐχ ἁρπαγμὸν ἡγήσατο τὸ εἶναι ἴσα σοὶ τῷ Θεῷ καὶ Πατρὶ ἀλλὰ Θεὸς ὢν προαιώνιος ἐπὶ τῆς γῆς ὤφθη καὶ τοῖς ἀνθρώποις συνανεστράφη καὶ ἐκ παρθένου ἁγίας σαρκωθεὶς ἐκένωσεν ἑαυτὸν μορφὴν δούλου λαβών.[1062] This seems to be another instance which shows the interdependance of these two texts. This phrase does not seem to fit into the established pattern of the Liturgy of St. Gregory so far, the author has on a number of occasions gone out of his way not to make a comparison between Christ and God the Father, and in this set of prayers has not even mentioned God the Father. It seems strange then, that all of a sudden the author would subordinate Christ to God the Father in this manner. This does, however, move the relationship between Christ and humanity forward, since, by subordinating Himself to God the Father, He takes the form of a human. This change of form allows for a closer relationship than before, and makes it possible for

---

[1059] Note again the close proximity of Ἀυτός and μοι.
[1060] Exodus 13
[1061] Luke 2:29-32
[1062] Hammond and Brightman (1896). pp. 325-326 and Trempelis (1982). pg. 180. "He did not consider to be equal to You, God and Father, a thing to be grasped, but being God from eternity, He was seen on earth and dwelt among men, and taking flesh from the holy virgin, He emptied Himself, taking the form of a slave."

Christ to heal the sickness, as the medical allusions above suggest, that was contracted during the fall: τὴν ἐμὴν ἐν σοι φύσιν ηὐλόγησας. As a human Christ is able to resanctify humanity, it was not just the Crucifixion and Ressurection that were necessary for salvation then, according to the author, but Christ's very life, which makes humanity holy again.

7. (Section II.4 lines 25-30): ὑπὲρ ἐμοῦ τὸν νόμον ἐπλήρωσας· τοῦ πτώματός μου τὴν ἀνάστασιν ὑπηγόρευσας. Ἔδωκας τοῖς ὑπὸ τοῦ ᾅδου κρατουμένοις τὴν ἄφεσιν· τοῦ νόμου τὴν ἀρὰν ἀπεσόβησας. Ἐν σαρκὶ τὴν ἁμαρτίαν κατήργησας· τῆς σῆς ἐξουσίας μοι τὴν δυναστείαν ἐγνώρισας. Τυφλοῖς τὸ βλέπειν ἀπέδωκας· νεκροὺς ἐκ τάφων ἀνέστησας· ῥήματι τὴν φύσιν ἀνώρθωσας· τῆς σῆς εὐσπλαγχνίας μοι τὴν οἰκονομίαν ὑπέδειξας·

This section of the prayer reflects section 5. Here the various works of Christ during His life on earth, which lead to the salvation of humantiy, are recounted. As before, there are both general statements: τοῦ πτώματός μου τὴν ἀνάστασιν ὑπηγόρευσας as well as instances which refer to specific miracles: τυφλοῖς τὸ βλέπειν ἀπέδωκας.

8. (Section II.4 lines 30-33): τῶν πονηρῶν τὴν βίαν ὑπένεγκας. Τὸν νῶτόν σου δέδωκας εἰς μάστιγας· τὰς δὲ σιαγόνας σου ὑπέθηκας εἰς ῥαπίσματα· οὐκ ἀπέστρεψας δι' ἐμὲ τὸ πρόσωπόν σου ἀπὸ αἰσχύνης ἐμπτυσμάτων.

This section parallels a previous section of the prayer. In section four, the author paraphrases Genesis 2 and describes the fall of humanity from Paradise. Here, the final part of Christ's life, leading up to the Crucifixion, is described: 1. suffering because of wicked men; 2. scourging; 3. being struck on the cheek; 4. spittings in the face. This section underscores the humility of Christ established by the text adapted from the Liturgy of St. Basil, God Himself suffered these things to make possible the triumph to come.

9. (Section II.4 lines 35-39): Ὡς πρόβατον ἐπὶ σφαγὴν ἦλθες, μέχρι σταυροῦ. Τὴν ἐμὴν κηδεμονίαν ὑπέδειξας· τῷ σῷ τάφῳ τὴν ἐμὴν ἁμαρτίαν ἐνέκρωσας· εἰς οὐρανόν μοι τὴν ἐμὴν ἀπαρχὴν ἀνεβίβασας· τῆς σῆς ἀφίξεώς μοι τὴν παρουσίαν ἐμήνυσας· ἐν ᾗ μέλλεις ἔρχεσθαι κρῖναι ζῶντας καὶ νεκροὺς· καὶ ἀποδοῦναι ἑκάστῳ κατὰ τὰ ἔργα αὐτοῦ.

In this final section the author continues the previous section stylistically, by summarizing the life of Christ. Here the humiliation suffered by Christ is completed in the Crucifixion and overcome in the Ressurection. Christ is once again depicted as the God on whom humanity is entirely reliant: καὶ ἀποδοῦναι ἑκάστῳ κατὰ τὰ ἔργα αὐτοῦ. This section is unique in this prayer as well in that it combines Scriptural revelation from the Gospels, the Acts of the Apostles and Revelations, with a quotation from the Nicene Creed:

κρῖναι ζῶντας καὶ νεκροὺς[1063] which points the worshipper once agian to the anti-Arian nature of this liturgy.

II.VI. The Consecration[1064]

In the post-*Sanctus*, the author has laid out the entirety of the history of salvation, but an important part is missing, namely the institution of the Eucharist in the Last Supper dialogue. The author must, then, break from the linear description of the events in salvation and backtrack to before the Crucifixion to continue with the next section of the liturgy, the Consecration. This is an unusual Structure. The Egyptian liturgies have an entirely different approach to the post-*Sanctus* which discusses the fullness of the cosmos with God, and uses this fulness as a parallel to the fulness of the gifts with God, rather than focusing on the history of salvation, and is thus able to transition to the Consecration:

> ...Fill this also thy sacrifice, o Lord, with the blessing that is from thee, through the descent upon it of thine Holy Spirit, and in blessing bless...and in purifying purify...these thy precious gifts which have been set before thy face, this bread and cup...For thine onlybeggoten Son our Lord and God and our Saviour and the king of us all Jesus Christ in the same night in which He gave Himself...took bread...[1065]

The transition is not seamless, however, as the author was forced to depart from the mystical, and from wording that reflects the epiklesis, to the historical. The Greek Syrian Liturgy of St. James, however, is set up to avoid such a break. This liturgy has a post-*Sanctus* written in the same style as that of the Liturgy of St. Gregory, what we determined above to be the style that marks the West Syrian rite, an historical description of Salvation, from Creation on. The Liturgy of St. James does not discuss this entire history, however, using the narrative to lead into the Consecration.

> μέλλων δὲ τὸν ἑκούσιον καὶ ζωοποιὸν διὰ σαυροῦ θάνατον ὁ ἀναμάρτητος ὑπὲρ ἡμῶν τῶν ἁμαρτωλῶν καταδέχεσθαι, ἐν τῇ νυκτὶ ᾗ παρεδίδοτο,

---

[1063] "to judge the living and the dead"
[1064] A large section of this prayer is missing in the Paris Manuscript, but can be reconstructed from the Kacmarcik Codex and the Wadi n' Natrun fragments.
[1065] Hammond and Brightman (1896). pg 176

μᾶλλον δὲ ἑαυτὸν παρεδίδου, ὑπὲρ τῆς τοῦ κόσμου ζωῆς καὶ σωτηρίας...λαβὼν τὸν ἄρτον[1066]

Another Liturgy of the West Syrian rite that avoids the abrupt backtracking found in the Liturgy of St. Gregory is the Byzantine Liturgy of St. John Chrysostom. The author of this Liturgy does conform to the historical exposition found in the other West Syrian liturgies, but, according to his own genius for summation, is able to describe the history of salvation in a few words.[1067] There is only one other liturgy in the West Syrian rite, in which the same backtracking is necessary, the Byzantine Liturgy of St. Basil. In this liturgy too the author discusses the historical progression of salvation.[1068] This continues as it does in the Liturgy of St. Gregory, with the Crucifixion, the Ressurection, the Ascension into Heaven and finally the *Parousia*, until, finally, the author must backtrack to before the Crucifixion in order to discuss the Last Supper dialogue and the Consecration.[1069] This is, then, another feature which the Liturgies of Sts. Basil and Gregory hold in common against the other early liturgies that make up the West Syrian rite, showing again their common origin in the Cappadiocian/Constantinopolitan subfamily of this larger branch.

Where this feature comes from is a difficult question to answer. It may be that there are other, non extant, Cappadocian/Constantinopolitan liturgies on which these authors base their works, however as we do not have these for comparison, we must proceed as if this feature origniates in one of these two liturgies and is adopted into the other. The possiblilty that this originates in the Liturgy of St. Gregory is supported by the fact that the continuation of the history of salvation to its conclusion fits into the attempt by the author to establish the relationship between Christ and humanity dependant on Christ as God. This same continuation need not necessarily be used as the driving force behind an agenda, however, but merely to bring the circle of salvation to a close, Christ begins as God, becomes a human through the Incarnation and ends as both God and man in the *Parousia*. The stylistic borrowings from the Liturgy of St. Basil into the Liturgy of St. Gregory in this section, such as the idea of Christ not deeming "equality with God something to be grasped"[1070] also support the origin of this prayer style in the Liturgy of St. Basil.

[1066] Hammond and Brightman (1896). pg. 51 and Mercier (1944). pp. 200-204. "being about to (undergo) the willing and life giving death on the cross, which He suffered for us sinners, on the night on which He was given up, or gave Himself up, for the life of the world...taking up the bread."
[1067] Hammond and Brightman (1896). pg. 324 and 327 and Trempelis (1982). pp. 106-107.
[1068] Hammond and Brightman (1896). pp, 324-326 and Trempelis (1982). pg. 179-180.
[1069] Hammond and Brightman (1896). pg. 327.
[1070] Post-Sanctus Prayer line 247

The Liturgy of Saint Gregory the Theologian

1. Structure

The author of every liturgy constructs the Consecration in a slightly different way, and the author of the Liturgy of St. Gregory is no different.[1071] Even the Coptic translation takes some licensce, it is not in the prayer itself, however, that the changes are found, rather they are in the responses of the people and of the Deacon. The same holds true for the *epiklesis* as well.[1072] Despite these differences, however, the structure of the Consecration is generally the same, that of the Liturgy of St. Gregory is shown in the following table:[1073]

Table II.VI.1: The structure of the Consecration.[1074]

Section	The Liturgy of St. Gregory
Part I: The Introduction	Ταύτης μου τῆς ἐλευθερίας προσφέρω σοι τὰ σύμβολα· τοῖς ῥήμασί σου ἐπιγράφω τὰ πράγματα. Σύ μοι τὴν μυστικὴν ταύτην λειτουργίαν παρέδωκας τῆς σῆς σαρκός, ἐν ἄρτῳ καὶ οἴνῳ τὴν μέθεξιν.
Part II: The placement in time.	Τῇ γὰρ νυκτὶ ᾗ παρεδίδης αὐτὸς σευτόν, τῆς σευτοῦ ἐξουσίας.
Part IV: Action with the bread.	Λαβὼν ἄρτον ἐν ταῖς ἁγίαις καὶ ἀχράντοις καὶ ἀμωμήτοις σου χερσίν, ἔνευσας ἄνω πρὸς τὸν ἴδιόν σου Πατέρα Θεὸν ἡμῶν καὶ Θεὸν τῶν ὅλων· ηὐχαρίστησας, ηὐλόγησας, ἡγίασας, ἔκλασας, μετέδωκας τοῖς ἁγίοις σου μαθηταῖς καὶ ἀποστόλοις εἶπας·
Part V: Quotation from the Last Supper, blessing the bread.	Λάβετε φάγετε τοῦτό μου ἐστὶν τὸ Σῶμα, τὸ ὑπὲρ ὑμῶν καὶ πολλῶν κλώμενον, καὶ διαδόμενον εἰς ἄφεσιν ἁμαρτιῶν· τοῦτο ποιεῖτε εἰς τὴν ἐμὴν ἀνάμνησιν.
Part VI: Action with the Wine.	Ὡσαύτως μετὰ τὸ δειπνῆσαι, λαβὼν ποτήριον, καὶ ἐκέρασας αὐτὸ ἐκ γεννήματος ἀμπέλου, καὶ ἐξ ὕδατος ηὐχαρίστησας, ηὐλόγησας, ἡγίασας, μετέδωκας τοῖς ἁγίοις σου μαθηταῖς κ(αὶ)

[1071] It is these peculiarities that will be the focus of the Function section below.
[1072] As these differences do not change the meaning of the text, I will not list out every difference here. Instead, Cf. Hammerschmidt (1957). pp. 34-43
[1073] For comparison see the Consecration prayers in the other liturgies of the West Syrian and Alexandrian families such as the Byzantine Liturgy of St. Basil (Hammond and Brightman (1986). pp. 327-328 and Trempelis (1982). pp. 181-182); The Greek Syrian Liturgy of St. James (Hammond and Brightman (1986). pp. 51-52 and Mercier (1944). pp. 200-204); and the Greek Egyptian Liturgy of St. Mark (Hammond and Brightman (1986). pp. 132-133 and Cuming (1990). pp. 39-44).
[1074] Section II.5 lines 1-21.

	ἀποστόλοις, εἶπας·
Part VII: Quotation from the Last Supper, blessing the wine.	Πίετε ἐξ αὐτοῦ πάντες, τοῦτο μου ἐστὶν τὸ Αἷμα, τὸ τῆς καινῆς διαθήκης, τὸ ὑπὲρ ὑμῶν καὶ πολλῶν ἐκχυνόμενον εἰς ἄφεσιν ἁμαρτιῶν, τοῦτο ποιεῖτε εἰς τὴν ἐμὴν ἀνάμνησιν.
Part VIII: Conclusion to the Consecration.	Ὁσάκις γὰρ ἂν ἐσθίετε τὸν ἄρτον τοῦτον, πίνετε δὲ καὶ τὸ ποτήριον τοῦτο, τὸν ἐμὸν θάνατον καταγγέλλετε, καὶ τὴν ἐμὴν ἀνάστασιν καὶ ἀνάληψιν ὁμολογεῖτε, ἄχρις οὗ ἂν ἔλθω.

2. Function

As seen in the table above, the general structure of the Consecration is the same in all of these major liturgies. There are a few differences in the various texts, however The Liturgy of St. Gregory and the Liturgy of St. Basil, for example, keep the phrase: τοῦτο ποιεῖτε εἰς τὴν ἐμὴν ἀνάμνησιν as part of the Consecration of the wine, while the Liturgy of St. James and the Liturgy of St. Mark break this section from the Consecration using a response of the people: Ἀμήν[1075] and add it to the conclusion that separates the Consecration from the beggining of the epiklesis.

Since the majority of this prayer is of a common origin, there is no need to discuss each aspect in detail, as we have done with the majority of the other prayers of the liturgy. There are, however, several differences between the Liturgy of St. Gregory and the other liturgies that would be of interest to discuss. The entire passage is marked by the distinct style of the Liturgy of St. Gregory, that is, it is written in the form of "Christusanrede:" ηὐχαρίστησας, ηὐλόγησας, ἡγίασας, μετέδωκας τοῖς ἁγίοις σου μαθηταῖς καὶ ἀποστόλοις, εἶπας, rather than the normal, third person historical description found in the other liturgies. This change of style, as it has done throughout the liturgy, underscores the personal relationship between Christ and those in the congregation, with all of humanity. Such a style, which mimics that of a dialogue, in the part of the liturgy which recalls a historical event in the life of Christ, helps the congregation to participate in this Consecration, to participate in the life of Christ, rather than to merely hear about it.

There is one section of the Consecration in the Liturgy of St. Gregory that has no correspondence in any other liturgy, the introduction: Ταύτης μου τῆς ἐλευθερίας προσφέρω σοι τὰ σύμβολα· τοῖς ῥήμασί σου ἐπιγράφω τὰ πράγματα. Σύ μοι τὴν μυστικὴν ταύτην λειτουργίαν παρέδωκας τῆς σῆς σαρκός, ἐν ἄρτῳ καὶ οἴνῳ τὴν μέθεξιν. In the other

---

[1075] Hammond and Brightman (1896). pg. 52 and 133

liturgies the opening of the Consecration is used to set up the historical timeframe in which the Consecration takes place, setting up the time of the Consecration as shortly before the end of Christ's life. The opening in the Liturgy of St. Gregory, however, does not reflect the remembrance of the historical event found in the other liturgies, but the mystical participation in the historical event. This is shown in the juxtaposition of σύμβολα and πράγματα, the symbols of the Eucharist, the ἄρτῳ καὶ οἴνῳ, become reality for the worshippers, not just through the ῥήμασί of the Consecration, but through the mystical participation in the entire liturgy: τὴν μυστικὴν ταύτην λειτουργίαν, though this is the general Eastern view of the Eucharist, that the participation in the reality of the Eucharist is accomplished through the participation in the liturgy, this is especially true in this Liturgy, in which the "Christusanrede" creates an even more personal and immediate participation for the worshipper.

II.VII. The *Epiklesis*

Following the Consecration almost every liturgy contains an *epiklesis*, in which the Holy Spirit is called down upon the bread and wine and asked to transform them into the Body and Blood of Christ. This prayer type, which seems almost standard, originates in the West Syrian rite, and was adopted not only into the various subfamilies that make it up, such as the Byzantine liturgies, but into the other rites, which were heavily influenced by the West Syrian: "...Another prayer of a very definite type, but which actually is scarcely found in its fulness elsewhere but in the West Syrian rite and the rites influenced by it: the 'epiclesis,' i.e. an invocation petitioning the descendt of the Holy Spirit to consecrate the bread and wine..."[1076] Though the description here of the *epiklesis* as an invocation of the Holy Spirit is accurate in that this is what it becomes, the earliest *epikleseis* were not necessarily directed at the Holy Spirit, as Bouyer himself points out: "This epiclesis, however, even when we see it already directed to the Holy Spirit, began by being merely a development added to the conclusion of the anamnesis..."[1077] This attribution to the West Syrian helps to substantiate the claim that the Liturgy of St. Gregory is not an Alexandrian liturgy, but belongs to the West Syrian rite. The original form of the Alexandrian anaphora, as laid out by Bouyer, does not include an *epiklesis*:

1.) initial act of thanksgiving; 2) first prayer recalling sacrifice; 3) copious intercessions and commemorations ending with a prayer for the acceptance of the

---

[1076] Bouyer (1989). pg. 143
[1077] Bouyer (1989). pg. 219

sacrifice; 4) resumption of the thanksgiving, leading up to the *Sanctus*; 5) a new prayer petitioning fort he acceptance of the sacrifice with a formal invocation for the consecration of the elements; 6) the Consecration; 7) the anamnesis; 8) a last invocation that the sacrifice offered be accepted, and more precisely that it have ist effects of grace in us, and 9) the final doxology.[1078]

Despite the original lack of an *epiklesis* in the Alexandrian rite, one was added under the influence of the West Syrian rite.[1079] In the Coptic translation of the Alexandrian liturgy of St. Mark, for example, an *epiklesis* is added following the Consecration:

Have mercy upon us, o God the Father almighty, and send down from thine holy height...the Paraclete thine Holy Spirit...upon us thy servants and upon these thy precious gifts which have been set before thee, upon this bread and upon this cup that they may be hallowed and changed...and that he may make this bread the holy body of Christ...and this cup also his precious blood of the new Testament...even of our Lord and our God and our Saviour and the king of us all Jesus Christ...:[1080]

The adoption of the *epiklesis* into the Alexandrian rite must have occurred relatively early, however, as the anaphora of the Ethiopian liturgy, shows an *epiklesis* as well: "We beseech thee that thou wouldest send thine Holy Spirit on the oblation of this church..."[1081]

Although the theological interpretation of the prayers has not been a priority in this Commentary, the *epiklesis* is of such theological importance, that a short discussion of the theological background would be in order. A point of contention arose between the Eastern and Western Churches is the precise time when the Eucharistic elements are transformed from bread and wine into the Body and Blood of Christ, in the West, the moment of change is at the Consecration, in the East, however, it was the descent of the Holy Spirit at the *epiklesis* that was put forward as the moment of change.[1082] As stated by Bouyer,[1083] however, this is not a binding theological dogma, but an explanation of convenience, as there is no individual point within the liturgy at which the elements are transformed, but that the liturgy as a whole is the means by which this is done. The liturgy, then, becomes a ladder by which the congregation climbs to heaven and can there participate in the heaven-

---
[1078] Ibid.
[1079] Bouyer (1989). pg. 143
[1080] Hamond and Brightman (1896). pg. 179
[1081] Hamond and Brightman (1896). pg. 190
[1082] Bouyer (1989) pg. 7
[1083] Ibid.

ly liturgy celebrated by Christ. Such upward motion, from the earth to the heaven, is a theme touched upon on a number of occasions in the Liturgy of St. Gregory, for example in the opening "Prayer of Access."

Despite the imagery of ascent implicit in the Eastern liturgy, the majority of the *epikleseis* center on the prayer that the Holy Spirit descend. In the Liturgy of St. Basil, for example, the priest prays that: σὲ παρακαλοῦμεν ἅγιε ἁγίων εὐδοκίᾳ τῆς σῆς ἀγαθότητος ἐλθεῖν τὸ Πνεῦμα σου τὸ Πανάγιον ἐφ' ἡμᾶς καὶ ἐπὶ τὰ προκείμενα Δῶρα ταῦτα.[1084] Through this descent the congregation is able to participate in two more Scriptural events, the Annunciation to Mary and Pentecost. By manifesting the bread and wine into the Body and Blood, the Holy Spirit reopens the Incarnation, allowing the congregants to meet Christ face to face.[1085] In the same way, the Holy Spirit reenacts what occured on Pentecost by descending on the congregants, as He descended on the apostles in the upper room.[1086] In perhaps the most sacred part of the liturgy, then, both the birth of Christ and the birth of the Church are celebrated and through this both the mystical action of the Holy Spirit in the transformation of the gifts and the historical action of God in the history of salvation are linked.

1. Structure

As we saw in the discussion of the Consecration there is a standard Structure to the *epiklesis*. The *epiklesis* begins with a transitional prayer,[1087] which finishes the discussion of the history of salvation in the post-*Sanctus* and the Consecration and set up for the remainder of the prayer:

> Now also, o God the Father almighty, showing the death of thine onlybegotten Son our Lord and God and our Saviour and the king of us all Jesus Christ, confessing his holy resurrection and his ascension into the heavens and his session at thy right hand, o Father, looking for his second advent, coming from the heavens, fearful and glorious at the end of this wolrd, wherein he cometh to judge the world in righteousness and to render to every man according to his works whether it be good or bad.[1088]

[1084] Hammond and Brightman (1896). pg. 329 and Trempelis (1982). pg. 183. "We pray You, holy of holies, in the favor of Your goodness, to send down Your all Holy Spirit upon us and upon these gifts laid out."
[1085] Hieromonk Gregorios (2012). 240-242
[1086] Acts 2:1-31
[1087] This transitional prayer is called the *Anamnesis* and is usually considered a separate part of the Anaphora, I include it here as part of the *epiklesis* because of the dependance of the *Anamnesis* on the following *epiklesis*, both stylistically and content wise.
[1088] Hammond and Brightman (1896). pg. 178

The Commentary

The above quotation, taken from the Coptic anaphora of St. Mark, is a good example of the universal nature of this opening prayer. In the West Syrian liturgies the post-*Sanctus* and the Consecration describe the entirety of history, from creation to the *Parousia*, for which this prayer provides a good conlusion. In the Egyptian liturgies, however, it is not history, but the mystical presence of God in the cosmos which is discussed, and it is only in this prayer that the historical acts of God are discribed as well.

In the Liturgy of St. Greogry the Theologian there is an interjection by the priest before the *epiklesis* continues with the prayer in which the Spirit is invoked: Τὰ σὰ ἐκ τῶν σῶν δώρων σοὶ προσφέροντες, κατὰ πάντα καὶ διὰ πάντα καὶ ἐν πᾶσιν. This seems to be reflected in a similar phrase found in the Copitc Liturgy of St. Mark: "Before thine Holy Glory we have set thine own gifts of thine own, o our holy Father."[1089] This phrase is not found, however, in the Greek original of this anaphora, and must be a later interpolation.[1090] Under what influence, however, does this enter into the Egyptian rite? The West Syrian rite, which had such a heavy influence over the Egyptian rite, seems a logical place to begin, but here too this phrase is missing from the Greek Liturgy of St. James.[1091] A phrase nearly identical to that found in the Liturgy of St. Gregory is found in the Byzantine Liturgy of St. Basil: τὰ σὰ ἐκ τῶν σῶν σοὶ προσφέροντες κατὰ πάντα καὶ διὰ πάντα.[1092] Here we see another commonatlity that underscores the common, Cappadocian/Constantinopolitan origin of both these liturgies, since it is unlikely that the phrase was adopted into the Egyptian rite, as we saw in the Coptic anaphora of St. Mark, and from there converted back into a form more similar to the original when added into the Liturgy of St. Gregory.

Following the response to this interjection: Σὲ αἰνοῦμεν, σὲ εὐλογοῦμεν,[1093] the *epiklesis* continues with a prayer in which God the Father[1094] is asked to send down the Holy Spirit upon the gifts. This prayer is followed by a series of exclaimed petitions by the priest, responded to by the people with Ἀμὴν, in which the exact working of the Holy Spirit on the gifts is described, so in the Byzantine Liturgy of St. Basil: τὸν μὲν ἄρτον τοῦτον αὐτὸ τὸ τίμιον σῶμα τοῦ κύριου καὶ θεοῦ καὶ σωτῆρος ἡμῶν Ἰησοῦ Χριστοῦ...ἀμήν...τὸ δὲ

[1089] Ibid.
[1090] Cf. Hammond and Brightman (1896). pp. 133-134
[1091] Cf. Hammond and Brightman (1896). pp. 53-54
[1092] Hammond and Brightman (1896). pg. 329. "Your own of Your own we offer to You, on behalf of all and for all."
[1093] As well as an exclamation of the deacon: Κλίνατε Θεῷ μετὰ φόβου in the case of the Liturgy of St. Gregory.
[1094] Except in the Liturgy of St. Gregory, in which it is Christ who is addressed.

ποτήριον τοῦτο αὐτὸ τὸ τίμιον αἷμα τοῦ κυρίου καὶ θεοῦ καὶ σωτῆρος ἡμῶν Ἰησοῦ Χριστοῦ...ἀμὴν...τὸ ἐκχυθὲν ὑπὲρ τῆς τοῦ κόσμου ζωῆς...ἀμὴν.[1095]

Each liturgical author is able to work within this standard structure and write unique prayers that reflects the theological context of the rest of their liturgies. A good example of this is seen in the Liturgies of St. Basil and St. Gregory, in which the introduction is nearly identical, both directed at Christ and both discussing the history of salvation with almost identical vocabulary, this shows, once again, the connection the two liturgies share, and this may be another prayer adapted into the Liturgy of St. Basil from the Liturgy of St. Gregory. Despite these similarities, the prayer of invocation of the Holy Spirit itself is quite different, showing the different purposes of the two authors.

[1095] Hammond and Brightman (1896). pg. 330 and Trempelis (1982). pg. 183. "This bread the precious Body of our Lord and God and savior Jesus Christ, Amen. And this cup itself, the precious Blood of our Lord and God and savior Jesus Christ, Amen. Poured out for the life of the world, Amen."

The Commentary

Table II.VII.1: Comparative Chart of the epikleseis in the Liturgy of St. Gregory and the Liturgy of St. Basil.

Structure	1. Liturgy of St. Gregory.[1096]	2. Byzantine Liturgy of St. Basil.[1097]
I. Introductory prayer:	Ὥστε οὖν Δέσποτα μεμνημένοι τῆς ἐπὶ γῆς συγκαταβάσεως, καὶ τοῦ ζωοποιοῦ θανάτου, καὶ τῆς τριημέρου σου ταφῆς, καὶ τῆς ἐκ νεκρῶν ἀναστάσεως, καὶ τῆς εἰς οὐρανοὺς ἀνόδου· καὶ τῆς ἐκ δεξιῶν τοῦ Πατρὸς καθέδρας, καὶ τῆς μελλούσης ἀπ' οὐρανῶν δευτέρας καὶ φοβερᾶς καὶ ἐνδόξου σου παρουσίας.	Μεμνημένοι οὖν δέσποτα καὶ ἡμεῖς τῶν σωτηρίων αὐτοῦ παθημάτων, τοῦ ζωοποιοῦ σταυροῦ, τῆς τριημέρου ταφῆς, τῆς ἐκ νεκρῶν ἀναστάσεως, τῆς εἰς οὐρανοὺς ἀνόδου, τῆς ἐκ δεξιῶν σοῦ τοῦ Θεοῦ καὶ Πατρὸς καθέδρας καὶ τῆς ἐνδόξου καὶ φοβερᾶς δευτέρας αὐτοῦ παρουσίας.
II. The exclamation of the priest and the responses:	Τὰ σὰ ἐκ τῶν σῶν δῶρων σοὶ προσφέροντες, κατὰ πάντα καὶ διὰ πάντα καὶ ἐν πᾶσιν. ὁ Λαὸς λέγει· Σὲ αἰνοῦμεν, σὲ εὐλογοῦμεν. ὁ Διάκονος λέγει· Κλίνατε Θεῷ μετὰ φόβου. .	Τὰ σὰ ἐκ τῶν σῶν σοὶ προσφέροντες κατὰ πάντα καὶ διὰ πάντα...Σὲ ὑμνοῦμεν σὲ εὐλογοῦμεν σοὶ εὐχαριστοῦμεν Κύριε καὶ δεόμεθα σου ὁ θεὸς ἡμῶν.

[1096] Cf. Section II.6 lines 1-27
[1097] Hammond and Brightman (1896). pp. 328-330 and Trempelis (1982). pp. 182-184.
"Therefore, Master, we also, remembering His saving passion and life giving cross, His three; day burial and resurrection from the dead, His ascension into heaven, and enthronement at Your right hand, God and Father, and His glorious and awesome second coming.
Priest: We offer to You these gifts from Your own gifts in all and for all.
People: We praise You, we bless You, we give thanks to You, and we pray to You, Lord our God.
Priest: Therefore, most holy Master, we also, Your sinful and unworthy servants, whom You have made worthy to serve at Your holy altar, not because of our own righteousness (for we have not done anything good upon the earth), but because of Your mercy and compassion, which You have so richly poured upon us, we dare to approach Your holy altar, and bring forth the symbols of the holy Body and Blood of Your Christ. We pray to You and call upon You, O Holy of Holies, that by the favor of Your goodness, Your Holy Spirit may come upon us and upon the gifts here presented, to bless, sanctify, and make this bread to be the precious Body of our Lord and God and Savior Jesus Christ.
(He blesses the holy Bread.)
Deacon: Amen.
Priest: And this cup to be the precious Blood of our Lord and God and Savior Jesus Christ.
(He blesses the holy Cup.)
Deacon: Amen.
(He blesses them both.)
Priest: Shed for the life and salvation of the world.
Deacon: Amen. Amen. Amen.**Priest:** And unite us all to one another who become partakers of the one Bread and the Cup in the communion of the one Holy Spirit. Grant that none of us may partake of the holy Body and Blood of Your Christ to judgment or condemnation; but, that we may find mercy and grace with all the saints who through the ages have pleased You: forefathers, fathers, patriarchs, prophets, apostles, preachers, evangelists, martyrs, confessors, teachers, and every righteous spirit made perfect in faith." (Vaporis (1988).).

The Liturgy of Saint Gregory the Theologian

III. Prayer of the Invocation of the Holy Spirit:	Αὐτὸς, οὖν Δέσποτα τῇ σῇ φωνῇ τὰ προκείμενα μεταποίησον· αὐτὸς παρών, τὴν μυστικὴν ταύτην λειτουργίαν κατάρτισον· αὐτὸς ἡμῖν τῆς σῆς λατρείας τὴν μνήμην διάσωσον. Αὐτὸς τὸ Πνεῦμά σου τὸ πανάγιον κατάπεμψον. Ἵνα ἐπιφοίτησαν τῇ ἁγίᾳ καὶ ἀγαθῇ καὶ ἐνδόξῳ αὐτοῦ παρουσίᾳ ἁγιάσῃ καὶ μεταποιήσῃ τὰ προκείμενα τίμια καὶ ἅγια Δῶρα ταῦτα, εἰς αὐτὸ τὸ Σῶμα καὶ τὸ Αἷμα τῆς ἡμετέρας ἀπολυτρώσεως. ὁ Διάκονος λέγει· Προσχῶμεν. ὁ Λαὸς λέγει· Ἀμὴν.	Διὰ τοῦτο δέσποτα πανάγιε καὶ ἡμεῖς οἱ ἁμαρτωλοὶ καὶ ἀνάξιοι δοῦλοί σου οἱ καταξιωθέντες λειτουργεῖν τῷ ἁγίῳ σου θυσιαστηρίῳ, οὐ διὰ τὰς δικαιοσύνας ἡμῶν· οὐ γὰρ ἐποιήσαμέν τι ἀγαθὸν ἐπὶ τῆς γῆς· ἀλλὰ διὰ τὰ ἐλέη σου καὶ τοὺς οἰκτιρμούς σου οὓς ἐξέχεας πλουσίως ἐφ᾽ ἡμᾶς θαρροῦντες προσεγγίζομεν τῷ ἁγίῳ σου θυσιαστηρίῳ καὶ προθέντες τὰ ἀντίτυπα τοῦ ἁγίου σώματος καὶ αἵματος τοῦ χριστοῦ σου σοῦ δεόμεθα καὶ σὲ παρακαλοῦμεν ἅγιε ἁγίων εὐδοκίᾳ τῆς σῆς ἀγαθότητος ἐλθεῖν τὸ Πνεῦμά σου τὸ Πανάγιον ἐφ᾽ ἡμᾶς καὶ ἐπὶ τὰ προκείμενα Δῶρα ταῦτα καὶ εὐλογῆσαι αὐτὰ καὶ ἁγιάσαι καὶ ἀναδεῖξαι
IV. The series of petitions of the priest:	Καὶ ποιήσει τὸν μὲν ἄρτον τοῦτον γένηται εἰς τὸ ἅγιον Σῶμά σου, τοῦ Κυρίου δὲ καὶ Θεοῦ καὶ σωτῆρος, καὶ παμβασιλέως ἡμῶν Ἰησοῦ Χριστοῦ, εἰς ἄφεσιν ἁμαρτιῶν, καὶ εἰς ζωὴν τὴν αἰώνιον τοῖς ἐξ αὐτοῦ μεταλαμβάνουσιν. Ἀμὴν. Τὸ δὲ ποτήριον τοῦτο τὸ τίμιόν σου Αἷμα, τὸ τῆς καινῆς διαθήκης σου, τοῦ Κυρίου δὲ καὶ Θεοῦ καὶ σωτῆρος καὶ παμβασιλεώς ἡμῶν Ἰησοῦ Χριστοῦ, εἰς ἄφεσιν ἁμαρτιῶν, καὶ εἰς ζωὴν τὴν αἰώνιον τοῖς ἐξ αὐτοῦ μεταλαμβάνουσιν. Ἀμὴν.	τὸν μὲν ἄρτον τοῦτον αὐτὸ τὸ τίμιον σῶμα τοῦ κυρίου καὶ θεοῦ καὶ σωτῆρος ἡμῶν Ἰησοῦ Χριστοῦ...ἀμήν...τὸ δὲ ποτήριον τοῦτο αὐτὸ τὸ τίμιον αἷμα τοῦ κυρίου καὶ θεοῦ καὶ σωτῆρος ἡμῶν Ἰησοῦ Χριστοῦ...ἀμήν...τὸ ἐκχυθὲν ὑπὲρ τῆς τοῦ κόσμου ζωῆς...ἀμήν.

V. Conclusion:	None	ἡμᾶς δὲ πάντας τοὺς ἐκ τοῦ ἑνὸς ἄρτου καὶ τοῦ ποτηρίου μετέχοντας ἑνῶσαι ἀλλήλοις εἰς ἑνὸς Πνεύματος ἁγίου κοινωνίαν καὶ μηδένα ἡμῶν εἰς κρίμα ἢ εἰς κατάκριμα ποιῆσαι μετασχεῖν τοῦ ἁγίου σώματος καὶ αἵματος τοῦ χριστοῦ σου ἀλλ' ἵνα εὕρωμεν ἔλεον καὶ χάριν μετὰ πάντων τῶν ἁγίων τῶν ἀπ' αἰῶνός σοι εὐαρεστησάντων προπατόρων πατέρων πατριαρχῶν προφητῶν ἀποστόλων κηρύκων εὐαγγελιστῶν μαρτύρων ὁμολογητῶν διδασκάλων καὶ παντὸς πνεύματος δικαίου ἐν πίστει τετελειωμένων.

2. Function

In the last section we began discussing the way in which an author is able to convey his purpose despite liturgical convention. This can be seen in the prayer of the invocation of the Holy Spirit. Despite the similar liturgical function of this prayer in both the Liturgy of St. Gregory and the Liturgy of St. Basil, to enable the descent of the Holy Spirit upon the Eucharistic elements, each liturgy has quite a different functional element. In the Liturgy of St. Basil the style points to the author creating a "Prayer of Access:" ἡμεῖς οἱ ἁμαρτωλοὶ καὶ ἀνάξιοι δοῦλοί σου, by using terms such as "sinful" and "unworthy" in reference to those ministering the liturgy, the author reflects the concept discussed in the post-*Sanctus* of the Liturgy of St. Gregory, that humanity is in need of God's lordship. It is through this lordship that humanity becomes: οἱ καταξιωθέντες λειτουργεῖν τῷ ἁγίῳ σου θυσιαστηρίῳ. This "Prayer of Access" is one in a series, praying for the worthiness to participate in the important actions of the liturgy, the entrance with the gifts, the epiklesis, the Eucharist.

In the Liturgy of St. Gregory, however, this prayer is not a "Prayer of Access" but the most overt attempt at propaganda in the Anaphora. The function here is once again based on the "Christusanrede" seen throughout the liturgy. By directing this prayer to Christ, the author once again tranfers an attribute of another member of the Trinity to Christ, in this case it is the position of source of the Trinity. In the other *epikleseis*, the Father is asked to send down the Holy Spirit, but here it is Christ who is addressed. This seems at first to be a small matter, part of the overall style of the "Christusanrede" found in the rest of the liturgy, this though, also plays on Christ's promise to his disciples that He would send the Holy Spirit down upon them after His death.[1098] By addressing the *epiklesis* to Christ, and evoking this Gospel passage, the author is able to connect this text back to the Gospel reading as well as to the post-*Sanctus* and forward to the Eucharist, to all those things Christ taught.

Though the addressing of the *epiklesis* to Christ does not imply that the Holy Spirit proceeds eternally from the Son, which goes against the description of the Trinity in the Nicene Creed, the theological statement with the greatest influence on and most often quoted in this text: καὶ εἰς τὸ Πνεῦμα τὸ ἅγιον τὸ κύριον τὸ ζωοποιὸν τὸ ἐκ τοῦ Πατρὸς ἐκπορευόμενον.[1099] This passage could be misunderstood to have the same theoloigcal meaning as became the standard in the Creed of the Western Church: filioque procedit. This theological position was adopted in the West originally for the same reason the Holy Spirit is sent down upon the gifts by Christ in this liturgy, to combat the Arians. The Nicene Christians in Spain added the phrase to the Creed at the Third Council of Toledo (589) in order to combat the Arianism of the Visigothic invaders.

II.VIII. The Intercessions[1100]

Following the *epiklesis* in the Liturgy of St. Gregory is a long section of intercessions and rememberances. In these rememberances every possible need of the worshipper is prayed for, from the salvation of their ancestors to the proper inundation of the Nile. A long section of intercessions is another of the universal aspects of the anaphora. The position of the rememberances confirms, once again, the place of the Liturgy of St. Gregory in one of the subfamilies of the West Syrian rite, rather than in the Alexandrian rite.[1101] In the Alexandrian rite, such as the Liturgy of St. Mark, the intercessions are placed between the *Sursum Corda* dialogue and the *Sanctus* hymn[1102] instead of following the epiklesis, as in West Syrian rite, for example in the Liturgy of St. James and in the Liturgy of St. Basil.[1103]

[1098] John 14:26-27
[1099] Hammond and Brightman (1896). pg. 43. "and the Holy Spirit, the lord, the life giver, who proceeds from the Father"
[1100] The majority of the Intercessions have been rewritten in the Coptic translation, as such it is not vital that the differences be shown here. Major differences include the interpolation of repetitions of the prayers of the priest by the deacon; the prayer for a temperate climate is divided into several parts each used during a different time of the year. (Hammerschmidt (1957). pg. 42-61
[1101] Cf. Hammerschmidt (1957). pg. 175-176
[1102] Hammond and Brightman (1896). pp. 126-132
[1103] Hammond and Brightman (1896). pp. 54-58 and 330-337

The Commentary

1. Structure

In the Liturgy of St. Gregory there are two types of intercessions, the majority of the intercessions begin with: Μνήσθητι and are written as an individual prayer, responded to by the people with: Κύριε ἐλέησον. There are two longer sections of intercessions which do not fit into this first type, but consist of a series of short petitions each of which is responded to by the people with: Κύριε ἐλέησον. The first of these two longer sets of petitions begins the series of intercessions and deals mostly with the those directly involved with the church, while the second set of such petitions, positioned in the middle of the series of intercessions, deals with the entire cosmos.

The two series of petitions are used to open and to strenghten the reopening of the intercessions, each of the sections of the intercessions adopts the theme in the respective petitions that open the section. The first section discussing the human world of the church and politics, while the second section broadens the discussion to include the rest of the cosmos, especially the natural world.

Table I.VIII.1 The Intercessions in the Liturgy of St. Gregory.[1104]

Section one of the Intercessions
I. This section begins with a series of petitions. These petitions pray for: the church; the unity of love; the truth of Faith; the path of piety; the shepherds; the flock; the clergy; the monastics; the virgins; those in marriage; the repentant; the wealthy; the poor; the begars; the old; the young; the unbelievers and the unity of the Church.
II. In the first intercession, the priest prays for the unity of the Church and the hierarchs of the Church.
III. The second intercession prays specifically for the Patriarch of Alexandria and then in a series for all of the various orders of the Church.
IV. The third intercession prays for the civil authority, both for the court in the palace as

---

[1104] Cf. Section II.7 lines 1-123.

well as for the military.

V. The fourth intercession prays for the specific congregation, for those bringing the gifts for the Eucharist.

VI. The fifth intercession broadens the discussion from the specific congregation to the larger congregation of monastics and, though it does not seem to fit the thematic established, to the release of the captives.

VII. The final intercession is for the priest himself, that he not be considered unworthy to administer the Sacrament. Following this last intercession is a transitional section made up of an exclamation of the priest: Ὁ γὰρ Λαός σου καὶ ἡ Ἐκκλησία σου ἱκετεύει σε, καὶ διά σοῦ καὶ σύν σοι τὸν Πατέρα, λέγουσα and several responses by the people: Ἐλέησον ἡμᾶς ὁ Θ(εὸ)ς ὁ σ(ωτ)ὴρ ἡμῶν and Κύριε ἐλέησον.

Section two of the Intercessions

I. In the first intercession of this series, the priest prays for proper seasons, as well as the proper inundation, allowing for the physical prosperity of the people: Πλήρωσον χαρᾶς καὶ εὐφροσύνης τὰς καρδίας ἡμῶν. Ἵνα ἐν παντὶ πάντοτε πᾶσαν αὐτάρκειαν ἔχοντες, περισσεύσωμεν εἰς πᾶν ἔργον ἀγαθὸν, τοῦ ποιεῖν τὸ θέλημά σου τὸ ἅγιον.

II. The second place in this series of intercessions is given to the second series of petitions, which pray for: unity; stability; the air; the sick; those in need; those in exile; the orphans; the widows; for those in distress; for strength; for those who have fallen; for those who are rising; for those who have fallen asleep; for those who confess; for those who are repentant; for recognition among the martyrs; for the ability to

III. In the third place, but the only the second intercession, the priest prays for the physical protection of the Orthodox faithful both of that specific community as well as all of the Orthodox.

IV. The third intercession asks for the salvation of the various types of saints who have fallen asleep: ἁγίων πατέρων, πατριαρχῶν, ἀποστόλων, προφητῶν, κηρύκων, εὐαγγελιστῶν, μαρτύρων, ὁμολογητῶν, καὶ παντὸς πνεύματος δικαίου.

V. The fourth intercession remembers several of the saints important to the liturgy specifically as well as to the Egyptian Church in general, among others: the Virgin Mary; John the Baptist; St. Stephen the first martyr; St. Mark the Evangelist and St. Gregory the Theologian.

VI. Following the reading of the Diptychs ist he fifth intercession, in which those who have fallen asleep and are not saints. Following this is a second reading of the Diptychs, specifically the living and the dead.

VII. In the sixth and final intercession, the priest makes a generic prayer for all things that may have been left out during the intercessions: Μνήσθητι, Κύριε, ὧν ἐμνήσθημεν, καὶ ὧν οὐκ ἐμνήσθημεν πιστῶν καὶ ὀρθοδόξων, μεθ' ὧν καὶ ἡμῖν σὺν αὐτοῖς, ὡς ἀγαθός καὶ φιλάνθρωπος Θεός.

2. Function

These intercessions, although in the position expected of a Syrian liturgy, do fall under the influence of the Alexandrian intercessory formulae. This is seen in several places, for example in the prayer for the hierarchs, in which the Pope and Patriarch of Alexandria is commemmorated; in the prayer for the natural world, the priest prays for the: τῆς συμμέτρου ἀναβάσεως τῶν ποταμείων ὑδάτων, a consideration of vital importance in Egpyt, which was dependant on the proper inundation of the Nile for its prosperity, but of much lesser importance in Syria and Cappadocia; in the commemoration of the saints St. Mark the Evangelist, through whose efforts the Church in Egypt was created, is commemmorated. Despite the Egyptian influence, the Syrian flavor of the intercessions still comes to the fore, for example in the commemoration of the saints, in which St. Stephen, the protomartyr, is remembered. Although he is recognized as a saint in Egypt, he belongs geographically to the Syrian world and it is in the commemorations of the saints in Liturgy of St. James that we see St. Stephen commemorated and described in the same way as he is in the Liturgy of St. Gregory: τῶν ἁγίων προφητῶν πατριαρχῶν δικαίων· τοῦ ἁγίου Στεφάνου τοῦ προτοδιακόνου καὶ πρωτομάρτυρος.[1105]

One of the intercessions: Μνήσθητι, Κύριε τῶν ἐν τῷ παλατίῳ ἡμῶν ἀδελφῶν πιστῶν, καὶ ὀρθοδόξων, καὶ παντὸς τοῦ στρατοπέδου,[1106] is of great interest because it corresponds closely to one of the Interecssions in the Liturgy of St. Basil: Μνήσθητι Κύριε πάσης ἀρχῆς καὶ ἐξουσίας καὶ τῶν ἐν παλατίῳ ἀδελφῶν ἡμῶν καὶ παντὸς τοῦ στρατοπέδου.[1107] This correspondence is another indication of the origin of the Liturgy of St. Gregory in Constantinople, like the Liturgy of St. Basil, this text prays for the well being of the Emperor and the Roman army situated in Constantinople.

The nature of this section creates difficulty in the anti-Arian function, since the focus of the section is not on Christ, but on the people, places and things being commemorated. There is one section which does advance the angenda seen so far, the transitional section between the two major sets of intercessions: .

Ὑψώσει τὴν κεφαλὴν κ(αὶ) ἐκφωνήσει.
Ὁ γὰρ Λαός σου καὶ ἡ Ἐκκλησία σου ἱκετεύει σε, καὶ διά σοῦ καὶ σύν σοι τὸν Πατέρα λέγουσα.
Ὁ Λαὸς λέγει· Ἐλέησον ἡμᾶς ὁ Θεὸς ὁ σωτὴρ ἡμῶν. Γ΄.
Ὁ Ἱερεὺς λέγει· Ἐλέησον ἡμᾶς ὁ Θεὸς ὁ σωτὴρ ἡμῶν. Γ΄.
Ὁ Λαὸς λέγει· Κύριε ἐλέησον. Γ΄.

Here again we see the attribution to Christ of various elements that would usually be attributed to God the Father, it is Christ's people and Christ's Church. This transference seems to come to a head in the phrase: καὶ διά σοῦ καὶ σύν σοι τὸν Πατέρα, λέγουσα, which does not actually call Christ "Father," the author almost seems to tease the worshippers with this and is able to combine three ideas in this one phrase. First the author looks forward to the recitation of the Lord's Prayer in the post-Anaphora, and reminds the worshippers that it was Christ that instituted this prayer. Second, the author reminds that Christ

---

[1105] "the holy prophets and just patriarchs; St. Stephen the first deacon and the first martyr."
[1106] Lines 355-356
[1107] Hammond and Brightman (1896). pg. 333 and Trempelis (1982). pg. 186. "Remember, Lord, every leader and commander and our brothers in the palace and all those in the army camp."

is the mediator between humanity and God the Father and that He is the only way to get to the Father.[1108] Thirdly, the author is able to both underscore Christ's role in the Trinity, since God the Father is His Father, and at the same time plays on Christ's role in Creation as the "Father" of humanity, since the worshippers could not help but associate Πατέρα, with Christ, since He is the only person of the Triniy addressed in this liturgy.

II.IX. The Final Benediction

The Anaphora closes with a final benediction. This is not an uncommon way for the anaphora to finish. Parallels to this benediction are found in the other liturgy of the Cappadocian/Constantinopolitan rite, the Liturgy of St. Basil: Καὶ δὸς ἡμῖν ἐν ἑνὶ στόματι καὶ μιᾷ καρδίᾳ δοξάζειν καὶ ἀνυμνεῖν τὸ πάντιμον καὶ μεγαλοπρεπὲς ὄνομά σου τοῦ Πατρὸς καὶ τοῦ Υἱοῦ καὶ τοῦ ἁγίου Πνεύματος νῦν καὶ ἀεὶ καὶ εἰς τοὺς αἰῶνας τῶν αἰώνων.[1109] This is not a feature that is limited to this subfamily, however, as a similar benediction is found in the Syrian Liturgy of St. James.[1110] These closing benedictions seem to be an offshoot of the commemorations that form the bulk of the ending of the anaphora, however, even in liturgical families that close the anaphora with the epiklesis, such as the Alexandrian Liturgy of St. Mark, a benediction marks the transition of the anaphora to the post anaphora.[1111]

1. Structure.[1112]

The closing benediction of the anaphora in the Liturgy of St. Gregory begins, as many of the prayers in this Liturgy do, with a direct address of Christ: Σὺ γὰρ εἶ ὁ Θεὸς ἡμῶν, ἐλεήμων, which is qualified by a descriptive phrase discussing Christ's compassion: ὁ μὴ βουλόμενος τὸν θάνατον τοῦ ἁμαρτωλοῦ ὡς τοῦ ἐπιστρέψαι καὶ ζῆν αὐτόν.

At this point the prayer reopens, with a second address of Christ: Ὁ Θεὸς, this newly opened section also focuses on the compassion of Christ for humanity: ὁ ποιῶν ὑπὲρ ἐκ περισσοῦ ὧν αἰτούμεθα, ἢ νοοῦμεν. The focus on compassion in this section is under-

---

[1108] John 13:6

[1109] Hammond and Brightman (1896). pg. 337 and Trempelis (1982). pg. 124. "And grant to us, that in one voice and one heart to glorify and hymn Your all precious and glorious name, of the Father and Son and the Holy Spirit, now and ever and to the ages of ages."

[1110] Cf. Hammond and Brightman (1896). pg. 58 and Mercier (1944). pg. 222.

[1111] Cf. Hammond and Brightman (1896). pg. 134 and Cuming (1990). pg. 49 footnote 12.

[1112] Since this is so short of a section, a table describing the structure is not needed. The Coptic translation of this section is, other than the addition of several responses that belong to the beginning of the post-Anaphora in the Greek text, identical to that of the Greek original. (Hammerschmidt (1957). pg. 62-63). Cf. pp. 117-118.

scored by two imperatives: ἐπίσκεψον ἡμᾶς ἐν τῷ σωτηρίῳ σου· ποίησον μεθ' ἡμῶν κατὰ τὴν ἐπιείκειάν σου, a style reminiscent of the opening of the 50th Psalm.[1113] The compassion with which Christ deals with humanity is then used by the author to tranisition to the final Trinitarian formula, the compassion of Christ leads to the glorification of the name of Christ, as well as the remainder of the Trinity: Ἵνα σου καὶ ἐν τούτῳ, καθὼς καὶ ἐν παντὶ, δοξάσθη καὶ ὑψωθῇ καὶ ὑμνηθῇ, καὶ εὐλογηθῇ, καὶ ἁγιάσθη, τὸ πανάγιον καὶ ἔντιμον καὶ εὐλογημένον σου ὄνομα ἅμα τῷ ἀχράντῳ σου Πατρὶ καὶ ἁγίῳ Πνεύματι.

2. Function

In this closing benediction we see a prayer structure common to the Liturgy of St. Gregory, but only seen here in the anaphora. We see again, the propagandistic elements seen in the rest of the liturgy: 1. the direct address of the prayer to Christ establishes a direct connection between the worshipper and Christ; 2. the mixture of discussing Christ's power and compassion underscores Christ's divinity as well as His connection with the worshippers; 3. any doubt as to the focus of the prayer is removed through the concentration on the name of Christ which is not only "all-Holy, precious and blessed" but also "glorified, exalted, hymned, blessed and sanctified" 4. the final Trinitarian formula shows the common transference of focus and attributes from the other members of the Trinity.

Commentary Part III: Post-Anaphoral Rites

III.I. Structure

Beginning after the final doxology of the Anaphora are the post-Anaphoral rites. This section of the Liturgy contains some of the most important prayers in the Liturgy, such as those of the Breaking and Communion and the Lord's Prayer. This section is, however, largely forgotten, and this study is, to my knowledge, the first that deals with the Greek text of the Post-Anaphora,[1114] this is unfortunate, as this section is, theologically, perhaps even more important than the Anaphora, as the final preparations of the Eucharist, as well as its distribution amongst the faithful occur here. The difficulty in dealing with the post-Anaphoral rites of a Liturgy is the same as that which plagues the pre-Anaphora, un-

---

[1113] Psalm 50 1:1
[1114] There are some notes on these prayers in the Renaudot text, as well as some comments in the Migne, but no thorough investigation has been made. The Coptic text of this part of the Liturgy was included in the Hammerschmidt commentary, however, and will be vital fort his investigation.

certainty of the origin of the prayers, since clerics were often ready to substitute prayers in a Liturgy with others that suited them better. That is not to say, however, that the prayers we see here are not original, before assuming that possibility we must have some compelling evidence. This problem is not as prevalent in the Anaphora, where clerics were less willing to tamper.

The post-Anaphora consists of ten sections (or rather eight sections with several alternates) leading up to the distribution of the Eucharist, and two prayers following the Eucharist leading up to the dismissal of the congregation.

1. From the End of the Anaphora to the Eucharist
    a. The Προοίμιον τῆς κλάσεως: a short prayer which introduces the Prayer of the Breaking which follows.
    b. The Εὐχὴ τῆς κλάσεως: this prayer is read before the breaking of the Eucharistic bread into sections, this prayer also serves to introduce the Lord's Prayer, which is then recited by the congregation.
    c. Two alternates for the Εὐχὴ τῆς κλάσεως.
    d. A short prayer following the recitation of the Lord's Prayer, which discusses the power granted to Christians over the power of evil.
    e. The Εὐχὴ τῆς κεφαλοκλισίας: this and its alternate (continuation?) seem to have a similar function to the Prayer of Access we saw at the beginning of the Liturgy; this set prepares for participation in the Eucharist, where the previous prepares for participation in the preparation of the Eucharist.
    f. The Εὐχὴ τῆς ἐλευθερίας: is a prayer of purification for a more worthy participation in the Eucharist.
    g. Though not strictly a prayer (it is, rather, a number of prayers as well as a dialogue between clergy and congregation), the section I have called the Σῶμα καὶ αἷμα consists of a dialogue in which the final preparations for the Eucharist are made, and a statement of faith is made as to what is occuring in the Eucharist.
2. From the Eucharist to the Dismissal
    a. The Εὐχὴ εὐχαριστίας μετὰ τὴν μετάληψιν τῶν ἁγίων μυστηρίων marks the end of the Euchist, and gives thanks for the ability to participate in it.
    b. The Εὐχὴ τῆς κεφαλοκλισίας is the final prayer of the Liturgy, it summarizes the theological points made in the Liturgy and then dismisses the congregation in peace.

III.II. The "Introduction to the Breaking"[1115]

Before the :Introduction to the Breaking" begins, there is a short dialogue between the congregation, the priest and the deacon. This dialogue, or a similar dialogue, occurs in the other major Liturgies used in Egypt as well. in the Greek-Egyptian Liturgy of St. Basil: Ὁ Λαὸς λέγει. Ὥσπερ ἦν. Ὁ Διάκονος λέγει. Κατέλθετε οἱ διάκονοι. Ὁ Ἱερεὺς λέγει. Εἰρήνη πᾶσιν.[1116] as well as in the Greek-Egyptian Liturgy of St. Mark: Ὁ Λαός. Ὥσπερ ἦν καὶ ἔστιν. Ὁ Ἱερεύς. Εἰρήνη πᾶσιν. Ὁ Διάκονος. Προσεύξασθε.[1117] This dialogue serves as a bridge from the Anaphora to the Prayers of the Breaking. The dialogue between clergy and laity serves to refocus the attention of the congregation that may have wandered during the long prayers of the Anaphora. There are a number of actions that accompany the dialogue: 1. the priest turning and blessing the people while he says "peace be with all;" 2. the deacons process, following the command: "come down o ye deacons." This movement also serve to refocus any flagging attentions in the congregation.

The Byzantine rite, as well as the Greek-Syrian rite, has a similar transition from the Anaphora to the Breaking and Communion. Both of these rites (have a set of petitions following the doxologies that mark the end of the Anaphora.[1118]

The actual "Introduction to the Breaking" presents an interesting problem. Hammerschmidt notes that while the Greek Egyptian Liturgy of St. Basil has a prayer like this,[1119] as does the Coptic version of the Liturgy of St. Mark, the Greek Liturgy of St.

[1115] The text of this prayer in the Coptic Liturgy, though to a great extent identical to the Greek, has a different beginning, this is seen in Hammerschmidt's edition, the translation of which reads: "Der Priester spricht: Unser Herr, unser Erlöser (σωτήρ), guter (ἀγαθός) Menschenliebender, Lebenspenderer unserer Seelen (ψυχή), Gott der sich selbst für uns dahin gegeben hat, uns zu retten wegen unserer Sünden, der durch das Vielsein seines Erbarmens die Feinschaft der (=mit den) Menschen (nachgelassen hat) zunicht gemacht hat, der Einziggeborene (μονογενής) Gott, der im Schosse seines Vaters ruht." (Hammerschmidt (1957). Pg. 63.) "The priest says: Our Lord, our savior, good lover of man, life giver to our souls. God who gave Himself for us to save us because of our sins, who because of the extent of His mercy, put aside the enmity with mankind, the onlybegotten God who rests in the bosom of His Father." The remainder of the prayer are almost identical in the two versions, with several small exceptions laid out by Hammerschmidt: "...stimmt wieder im Griechischen mit dem Koptischem mit Ausnahme zweier kleiner Zusätze im Koptischen in 333 [of his Coptic edition] ... (**heilige** Jünger und **heilige** Apostel), des Zusatzes φιλάνθρωπε und des Fehlens des 'unser' bei 'Herr' im griechischen Text desselben Satzes überein." Hammerschmidt (1957). pg. 149

[1116] Renaudot (1847). I pg. 71. "The people say: Just as it was. The deacon says: Come down O deacons. The priest says: Peace be with all."

[1117] Renaudot (1847). I pg. 142. "The people say: As it was and is. The priest says: Peace be with all. The deacon says: Pray!"

[1118] For the Liturgy of St. James see Hammond and Brightman (1896). pg. 48.) For the Liturgy of St. Basil see Ieratikon1987 (2007). pg. 183.

[1119] See Hammerschmidt (1957). pg. 150 and Renaudot (1847). I. pg. 71-72.

The Commentary

Mark does not.[1120] This leads him to contradict Hannssens, who claims that the presence of such an introduction in the Liturgies of St. Basil and St. Gregory must mean that it is an ancient practice in Egyptian Liturgies.[1121] Hammerschmidt contradicts this by pointing out that the Greek version of the Liturgy of St. Mark is, in fact, older than the Coptic translation, and that the evidence of this prayer in the Coptic tranlsation must be attributed to influence from these other Liturgies.[1122] The lack of an introductory prayer in this position in the Liturgy of St. Mark then indicates that it is not an Egyptian practice (Hammerschmidt makes a distinction between the Coptic rite: "d.h. der Liturgien, die in der koptischer Sprache vorhanden sind" and the Egyptian rite as a whole).[1123]

The question we must strive to answer then is: where does this prayer come from? The prayer contains nothing that gives it away as not original to this Liturgy, especially since the prayer in this Liturgy is addressed to Christ, while the corresponding prayer in the Liturgy of St. Basil is not.[1124] If, then, this prayer is original to the Liturgy of St. Gregory this may help us in narrowing down its place of origin. Unfortunately, this type of prayer seems to be rather rare, Hammerschmidt has established that it is not of Egyptian origin, we can also determine that the Byzantine Liturgies of St. Basil and St. John Chrysostom[1125] do not have such a prayer, neither does the Greek-Syrian Liturgy of St. James.[1126] If we further our search, we see that there is also no corresponding prayer in the Syrian Jacobite Liturgy (that is, the Syrian Liturgy of St. James).[1127] There are, however, numerous other Liturgies in the Syrian family,[1128] although I have not been able to collect all of the texts, the earliest ones (the Anaphora of the Twelve Apostles, the Liturgy of St. James etc...) do not have a corresponding prayer. Neither do the Armenian Soorp Baradack,[1129] or even in the Nestorian Liturgies of Persia.[1130]

[1120] Hammerschmidt (1957). pg. 150
[1121] Hanssens (1930-31). III. 487
[1122] Hammerschmidt (1957). pg. 150
[1123] Ibid.
[1124] We saw in the pre-Anaphora that prayers which are added later are often not changed to be addressed to Christ, while those that are original, even if the author takes them from another source, are rewritten.
[1125] Cf. Hammond and Brightmann (1896). pp. 307-359
[1126] Cf. Hammond and Brightmann (1896). pp. 33-48 and Mercier (1944). pp. 222-224.
[1127] Cf. Hammond and Brightmann (1896). pp. 70-110 and Day (1972). pp. 186-188.
[1128] Including a Syrian Liturgy of St. Gregory the Theologian, which seems to have very little in comon with the Greek-Egyptian Liturgy of the same name. Cf. Renaudot (1847) II. For more information on the Syrian Anaphoras, see the series *Anaphorae Syriacae*.
[1129] Cf. Hammond and Brightmann (1896). pp. 412-457
[1130] Cf. Hammond and Brightmann (1896). pp. 248-305, the Anaphora of Sts. Adda and Mari.

The Liturgy of Saint Gregory the Theologian

There seem to be two ways of explaining the fact that such an introductory prayer crops up in only two places: the Greek Egyptian Liturgies of St. Gregory and St. Basil.[1131] There may be a Liturgy which provided the necessary example that either I have not been able to find, or the prayers of which outside of the Anaphora dissapeared in favor of the prayers of a more standard Liturgy. The other possibility is that this prayer is an innovation by the author of the Liturgy of St. Gregory, added as a way to underscore his purpose, as an anti-Arian polemic work, and the prayers in the Liturgy of St. Basil and the Coptic translations were added in analogy to it.

1. Structure

Like most of the prayers we discussed in the Pre-Anaphora, this prayer begins with a direct address of Christ: Ἰησοῦ Χριστέ. This direct address is followed by an epithet: τὸ σωτήριον ὄνομα. This introduction is followed by a series of Christ's deeds. 1. Christ establishes the Eucharist; 2. Christ establishes the rank of the priests, who carry out the Eucharist; 3. Christ transforms the bread and wine into His Body and Blood (during the Anaphora); 4. Christ hands Himself over, in the form of the Eucharist, to those who receive it worthily.

Following this short history of the Eucharist, the priest makes four requests of Christ: 1. Christ is asked to bless; 2. to sanctify; 3. to break; 4. and to give. This prayer is also interesting in that it does not have end in an *ekphonesis*, but in another dialogue. This may be because this is not a prayer in and of itself, but serves to introduce the next prayer, the "Prayer of the Breaking." The structure of this section can also be seen in the following table:

Figure III.II.1: The Structure of the "Introduction to the Breaking."[1132]

The "Introduction to the Breaking"
I. Bridging Dialogue, begins the last section of the Liturgy, the Post-Anaphora.   a. Ὁ Λαὸς λέγει· Ὡς ἦν, καὶ ἐστι, καὶ ἔσται.   b. Ὁ Διάκονος λέγει· Κατέλθετε οἱ διάκονοι.   c. Ὁ Ἱερεὺς λέγει· Εἰρήνη πᾶσιν.   d. Ὁ Λαὸς λέγει· Καὶ τῷ πνεύματι σου.

[1131] And from there the various Coptic Liturgies.
[1132] Cf. Section III.1 lines 1-15, Cf. also Hammerschmidt (1957). pg. 148

The Commentary

II. The Opening: Direct address of Christ: Ἰησοῦ Χριστέ τὸ σωτήριον ὄνομα

II. Part I. The history of the Eucharist
   a. Fashioner of this mystery: ὁ τὰ θεῖα καὶ ἄχραντα καὶ ἐπουράνια ταῦτα μυστήρια διατυπώσας.
   b. Founder of the priesthood: Ὁ τοὺς μὲν ἱερεῖς ἐν τάξει ὑπηρετῶν στήσας
   c. Transformer of the Eucharistic elements: διὰ δὲ τῆς ἀοράτου σου δυνάμεως αὐτὰ μεταστοιχειώσας.
   d. Access granted to those who approach worthily: Ὁ τοῖς καθαροῖς τῇ καρδίᾳ ἐπιφαινόμενος καὶ τοῖς γνησίως προσιοῦσι διὰ σεαυτοῦ παρέχοντος.

III. Part II. Requests made of Christ
   e. Bless: Ὁ τότε εὐλογήσας, καὶ νῦν εὐλόγησον. Ἀμὴν.
   f. Sanctify: Ὁ τότε ἁγιάσας, καὶ νῦν ἁγίασον. Ἀμὴν.
   g. Break: Ὁ τότε κλάσας, καὶ νῦν διάθρεψον. Ἀμὴν.
   h. Give: Ὁ τότε διαδοὺς τοῖς ἑαυτοῦ μαθηταῖς καὶ ἀποστόλοις, καὶ νῦν Δέσποτα διαδὸς ἡμῖν, καὶ παντὶ τῷ λαῷ σου φιλάνθρωπε, παντοκράτορ Κύριε ὁ Θεὸς ἡμῶν.

III. Ending Dialogue.
   a. *Ὁ Διάκονος λέγει·* Προσεύξασθε.
   b. *Ὁ Λαὸς λέγει·* Κύριε ἐλέησον.
   c. *Ὁ Ἱερεὺς λέγει·* Εἰρήνη πᾶσιν.
   d. *Ὁ Λαὸς λέγει·* Καὶ τῷ πνεύματί σου.

2. Function

Before looking at the text itself, we should note that the "manual purpose," of this text is laid out in Hammerschmidt's Commentary.[1133] Here he lays out the *actiones manuales* which the priest performs while the prayer is being read. It is important to note, however, that these actions are based on the Coptic rite and the Coptic text, and may not be entirely transferable the Greek text, which, as we have discussed, is probably not originally from Egypt, and therefore the Coptic rites are not original to it.

1. (Section III.1 lines 2-5): Ἰησοῦ Χριστέ, τὸ σωτήριον ὄνομα, ὁ τὰ θεῖα καὶ ἄχραντα καὶ ἐπουράνια ταῦτα μυστήρια διατυπώσας. Ὁ τοὺς μὲν ἱερεῖς ἐν τάξει ὑπηρετῶν στήσας, διὰ δὲ τῆς ἀοράτου σου δυνάμεως αὐτὰ μεταστοιχειώσας. Ὁ τοῖς καθαροῖς τῇ καρδίᾳ ἐπιφαινόμενος, καὶ τοῖς γνησίως προσιοῦσι διὰ σεαυτοῦ παρέχοντος.

The majority of the first section of this prayer is devoted to a list of deeds, the origin of which is made clear in the first phrase of the prayer: Ἰησοῦ Χριστέ, τὸ σωτήριον ὄνομα. By making this clear at the very beginning of the prayer, the author underscores, as we will see, the place of Christ in the Liturgy as both author and celebrant.

In the list of deeds that follows this opening, Christ is portrayed as author of the Liturgy. Each deed describes a step in the history of the Eucharist, from its origin at the Last Supper to the present celebration. 1. The first phrase deals with the establishment of the Eucharist: τὰ θεῖα καὶ ἄχραντα καὶ ἐπουράνια ταῦτα μυστήρια διατυπώσας, this refers to the first Eucharist, its prototype, the Last Supper, where Christ, "fashioned" the form of the Eucharist by his fourfold action. 2. In the second phrase: τοὺς μὲν ἱερεῖς ἐν τάξει ὑπηρετῶν στήσας, we learn that Christ sets certain people apart as His servants, this ensures the continuation of the Eucharist after He is no longer present on earth. This phrase is qualified, however, by the following. 3. Here we see that, though Christ establishes the priesthood to carry out the mystery of the Eucharist, it is still Christ that changes the Eucharistic elements: διὰ δὲ τῆς ἀοράτου σου δυνάμεως αὐτὰ μεταστοιχειώσας. By setting this prayer up in this way, the author establishes a type of symbiosis between priest and Christ in the Liturgy, neither can carry out the Eucharist without the other.[1134] Christ is put in the higher position, however, and, so to speak, uses the priest as His instrument.[1135] 4.

[1133] Cf. Hammerschmidt (1957). pp. 150-151

[1134] Here the audience for this liturgy is set out, the more important audience is the clergy, whose symbiotic relationship with Christ in the liturgy is shown here. The theological opinion of the clergy would have more weight in a theological controversy such as the Arian controversy. Despite the focus on the clergy, the author does not ignore the laity, and by addressing every prayer of the liturgy to Christ, he ensures that the message is made clear to the laity as well.

[1135] This is made more clear in the next section of this prayer.

The Commentary

After describing the relationship between priest and Christ in the Liturgy, the author moves on to the final step in the history of the Eucharist, the reception of the Eucharist by the congregation: Ὁ τοῖς καθαροῖς τῇ καρδίᾳ ἐπιφαινόμενος, καὶ τοῖς γνησίως προσιοῦσι διὰ σεαυτοῦ παρέχοντος. In this section we see why there have been such numerous prayers of purification. Chris is "revealed" and ‚hands Himself over' in the Eucharist, but only to those who are "pure of heart" and who approach "lawfully." The author does not go quite as far in this as St. Paul does,[1136] there is no threat of condemnation for those who recieve, but we see here that it only benefits those who receive it worthily.

This section establishes Christ as the fashioner of the Eucharist, and describes the history of the Eucharist from its beginning at the Last Supper to the present celebration. In the next section, the author shows that Christ in not only the origin of the Liturgy, but plays an active role in its carrying out.

2. (Section III.1 lines 6-11): Ὁ τότε εὐλογήσας, καὶ νῦν εὐλόγησον. Ἀμὴν. Ὁ τότε ἁγιάσας, καὶ νῦν ἁγίασον. Ἀμὴν. Ὁ τότε κλάσας, καὶ νῦν διάθρεψον. Ἀμὴν. Ὁ τότε διαδοὺς τοῖς ἑαυτοῦ μαθηταῖς καὶ ἀποστόλοις, καὶ νῦν Δέσποτα, διαδὸς ἡμῖν, καὶ παντὶ τῷ λαῷ σου φιλάνθρωπε, παντόκρατορ, Κύριε ὁ Θεὸς ἡμῶν.

This section focuses on the fourfold action of Christ at the Last Supper: 1. blessing, 2. sanctifying, 3. breaking and 4. giving. The author uses this in order to illustrate two points, the continuity of the Eucharist, and the place of Christ within the Liturgy. By juxtaposing the two temporal words: τότε and νῦν the author bridges the historical gap between the Last Supper and the present celebration of the Eucharist. By doing so the author emphasizes the connection between the Last Supper and each subsequent Eucharist. He also continues the thought begun in the last section, that the priest is an instrument of Christ. It is not the priest who blesses, hallows, breaks and gives out the Eucharist, it is Christ. By obscuring the priest's role in favor of Christ, the author reaffirms the place of Christ as the High Priest.

The dichotomy in this prayer, that Christ is both the origin and the one that carries out the Liturgy, shows Christ as both God, the origin of the Liturgy, and as man, the High Priest who carries it out. This is a duality leads to the conclusionthat the purpose of this prayer is to affirm the Nicene Christology, and as such is an original part of this Liturgy, and not a later addition.

[1136] Cf. I Corinthians 11: 23-26

III.III. The "Prayer of the Breaking"[1137]

What makes this prayer stand out from the rest of the prayers of the Liturgy is that there is no request made in the prayer itself. Only in the *ekphonesis* does the priest make the request of the prayer known, the ability to take part in the Lord's Prayer.[1138] This "Prayer of the Breaking" lays out the nature of Christ's existence, the Incarnation, the Crucifixion, the Resurrection, the destruction of Hades and the redemption of humanity. Problematic is that much of the prayer seems to deal with a non-Chalcedonian view of Christ, which, as Hammerschmidt points out,[1139] may place the text in the incorrect Christological controversy to be original to this Liturgy. Hammerschmidt proves, however, that what seems to be the use of Monophysite language in this prayer may be an adoption of the language used by Cyril of Alexandria.[1140] Whether or not this is to be taken as a directly Monophysite prayer, however, the theological language is, to a great extent, outside of that normally used in the Liturgy.[1141] We do see, however, numerous instances in which the divinity of Christ is emphasized, which brings us back to the theological discussion shared by the rest of the Liturgy.

Hammerschmidt also points to the fact that this prayer is not used in the Coptic Liturgy to show that this prayer is not original to the Liturgy.[1142] Although there is a possibility that this prayer was added to the Liturgy following its translation into Coptic, Hammerschmidt has suggested before that the author may have added alternate prayers for "abwechslung,"[1143] the possibility of more than one prayer for the same function does exist, and it would be logical that the Coptic translators would pick one of the prayers to use in their standard Liturgy.

It is not only the theological problems, nor the lack of a corresponding Prayer in the Coptic translation that brings me to share Hammerschmidt's view, that this is not an original Prayer, it is the awkward fit of this prayer within the Liturgy. The purpose of the "Prayer of the Breaking" is to: 1. introduce the Lord's Prayer and 2. to make final prepara-

---

[1137] That is first "Prayer of the Breaking."
[1138] Hammerschmidt notes that this *ekphonesis* is not organically a part of the prayer, and may have been tacked on at the end to tie it in with its liturgical function, to introduce the Lord's Prayer. (pg. 157).
[1139] Hammerschmidt (1957). pg. 162
[1140] Hammerschmidt (1957). pp. 157-162. Since Hammerschmidt lays this out so well in his commentary, there is no need for me to repeat it here, though I will come back to his arguments later in this commentary. Suffice it to say that there are several phrases in the Greek, sufficient to repeat here is the cornerstone of his argument, the phrase: μία φύσις τοῦ θεοῦ λόγου σεσαρκωμένη. (pg. 161).
[1141] Hammerschmidt (1957). pg. 162
[1142] Hammerschmidt (1957). pg. 162-163
[1143] Hammerschmidt (1957). pg. 96

tions for the Eucharist.[1144] As we mentioned above, none of these purposes are addressed in the Prayer, which focuses entirely on the theological. Although the purpose of this work is the propagation of a theological viewpoint and the marginalization of those who do not share it, this has always been done by the author in the context of the prayers of the Liturgy, that is, the prayers have a dual purpose, both to underscore Nicene theology and to carry out their proper function within the Liturgy. This prayer does not carry out its function and is thus stylistically different from the other prayers. The other stylistic issue is with the *ekphonesis*, which seems, as we said above, tacked on to the end of the Liturgy, up to this point, and especially in the pre-Anaphora, the *ekphoneseis* have continued or completed the thought presented in the prayer. It is this atypical style that shows, when weighted with the partially Monophysite theology and the lack of Coptic evidence, that this is not an original prayer.

The question, then, becomes, where did this prayer come from? Hammerschmidt offers no possibilities, other than saying that none of the manuscripts of the Coptic Liturgy of St. Gregory contain this prayer. No prayer like this is present in the other Greek-Egyptian Liturgies, whose "Prayers of the Breaking" are all geared towards the recitation of the Lord's Prayer and the reception of the Eucharist. H. Engberding offered one possibility when he noted that, although he could not find any exact parallels to the text, the Anaphora of John of Bosra, which reads: unus Filius, unus Christus, una persona, una natura, sive suppositum Verbi incarnati,[1145] an interesting parallel to the οὐ δύο πρόσωπα οὖν, οὐδὲ δύο μορφὰς ἤγουν, οὐδὲ ἐν δυσὶ φύσεσι γνωριζώμενος, ἀλλ᾽ εἷς Θεός, εἷς Κύριος, μία οὐσία...μία φύσις τοῦ Θεοῦ Λόγου σεσαρκωμένη καὶ προσκυνουμένη found in our text. This led H. Engberding to assume either that the Anaphora of John of Bosra was influenced by the Liturgy of St. Gregory, or that the prayers in both of these texts came from the same source.[1146] Since we cannot be sure when this prayer was introduced into the Liturgy, and therefore cannot speculate as to whether it could have had any influence on the Anaphora of St. John of Bosra or not. The other suggestion, however, that both these prayers are based on a third prayer, which reflects an "apollinaristisch-

---

[1144] Preparation for the Eucharist in the sense of spiritual preparation, the manual actions of the priest occur at a different point, after the Elevation: "Das griechische und koptische Gebet trägt eigentlich nur mit Rücksicht auf seine Stellung innerhalb der Liturgie diesen Namen, da es mit der fractio selbst nichts mehr zu tun hat." (Hammerschmidt (1957). pg. 152) "The Greek and Coptic prayer is only named so because of its place in the liturgy as it has nothing to do with the fraction itself."
[1145] Renaudot (1847). II. pg. 423 "one Son, one Christ, one person, one nature that is set beneath the incarnate Word."
[1146] Engberding (1953). pg. 729

monotheletischer Vorstellung"[1147] seems, barring any forthcoming information, to be the best explanation. Although describing the prayer as "Monothelite" may be exaggerated, it may be more accurate to say Monothelite leanings, this would explain what seems to be this conciliatory theology, emphasizing both the Incarnation and the unity of Christ. Another possibility why this prayer contains what seems to be contradictory theology is in the context of the Coptic Church, which must be identified not as a Monophysite Church, but rather a Miaphysite Church. It is the seemingly slight difference in these theologies[1148] that accounts for this seeming contradiction. Especially interesting is the Structure of the prayer, which, in parts, parallels the Nicene Creed as well as the *Monogens Hymn* of Justinian. This similarity also gives us a date *post quem* for this prayer, the Hymn of Justinian as well as the Monophysite/Miaphysite and Monothelite controversies stem from the middle of the sixth century, while our Liturgy belongs in the fourth, proving definitively that this prayer cannot be part of the original Liturgy.

1. Structure

This Prayer, like the majority of the other Prayers in the Liturgy, begins with a direct address of Christ. The remainder of the Prayer consists of twenty one descriptive phrases that can be broadly categorized into three sections, each of which deals in some way with the Incarnation. The first section consists of seven phrases that underscore Christ's divinity: he is called, among other things, the "bread who descended from heaven and gave life to the world" and "the great high priest."

The second section, beginning with Σαρκωθεὶς deals with the theology of the Incarnation. This theological exposition builds the largest section of this prayer. This section consists of only four phrases, but each of these phrases is longer and more complicated than those of the first and third sections. This section contains the majority of the difficult theology that does not fit into the Christological controversy which the rest of the Liturgy deals with.

The final section, beginning with Σταυρωθείς deals with the remainder of the history of salvation, once again the style shifts to numerous (nine), short descriptive phrases. These deal with the Crucifixion, Ressurection, the destruction of Hades and the redemption of Adam. A more complete structural analysis is given in the following table:

[1147] Hammerschmidt (1957). pg. 163; footnote 253
[1148] The Monophysites believe that Christ had no human nature, while the Miaphysites believe that this human nature existed, but that the divine and human natures were combined in the one *physis*.

The Commentary

Figure III.III.1: The structure of the "Prayer of the Breaking."[1149]

The "Prayer of the Breaking"
Opening: ὁ ὤν, ὁ ἦν, ὁ ἐλθών, καὶ πάλιν ἐρχόμενος,

1. Part I. Christ's Divinity and introduction to the Incarnation: seven descriptive phrases.
 	
    a. ὁ ἐν δεξιᾷ τοῦ Πατρὸς καθήμενος·
 	
    b. ὁ ἄρτος ὁ καταβὰς ἐκ τοῦ οὐρανοῦ, καὶ ζωὴν διδοὺς τῷ κόσμῳ·
 	
    c. ὁ μέγας ἀρχιερεύς
 	
    d. ὁ ἀρχηγός τῆς σωτηρίας ἡμῶν·
 	
    e. τὸ φῶς ἀληθινὸν, τὸ πρὸ πάντων αἰώνων.
 	
    f. Ὅς ὢν ἀπαύγασμα τῆς δόξης, καὶ χαρακτὴρ τῆς ὑποστάσεως αὐτοῦ τοῦ ἰδίου σου Πατρός.
 	
    g. Ὁ εὐδοκήσας καὶ καταξιώσας κατελθεῖν ἐκ τῶν ὑψωμάτων τοῦ οὐρανοῦ, ἐκ κόλπων τοῦ ἀπροσίτου φοτὸς καὶ ἀληθινοῦ καὶ ἀοράτου μόνου Πατρός.

2. Part II. The theology of the Incarnation: four descriptive phrases.
 	
    a. Σαρκωθεὶς δὲ ἐκ Πνεύματος Ἁγίου καὶ ἐκ τῆς πανενδόξου ἀχράντου ἁγίας δεσποίνης ἡμῶν Θεοτόκου καὶ ἀειπαρθένου Μαρίας, καὶ τελέως ἐνανθρωπήσας·
 	
    b. καὶ κατὰ μετάστασιν, τὴν ἀνθρωπότητα ἀναλλοιώσας, ἑνώσας ἑαυτῷ καθ' ὑπόστασιν, ἀφράστως καὶ ἀπερινοήτως, ἀτρέπτως δὲ καὶ ἀσυγχύτως, ψυχὴν

[1149] Cf. Section III.2 lines 1-24. For the structure of this prayer, Cf. also Hammerschmidt (1957). pp. 152-153

ἔχουσαν λογικήν τε καὶ νοεράν.

c. Οὕτως προῆλθες ἐξ αὐτῆς θεανθρωπωθεὶς ὁμοούσιος τῷ Πατρὶ κατὰ τὴν θεότητα, καὶ ὁμοούσιος ἡμῖν κατὰ τὴν ἀνθρωπότητα.

d. Οὐ δύο πρόσωπα οὖν, οὐδὲ δύο μορφὰς ἤγουν, οὐδὲ ἐν δυσί φύσεσι γνωριζώμενος, ἀλλ᾽ εἷς Θεός, εἷς Κύριος, μία οὐσία μία βασιλεία μία δεσπότεια μία ἐνέργεια μία ὑπόστασις μία θέλησις μία φύσις τοῦ Θεοῦ Λόγου σεσαρκωμένη καὶ προσκυνουμένη.

3. Part III. The history of salvation: nine descriptive phrases.

a. Σταυρωθεὶς δὲ ἐπὶ Ποντίου Πιλάτου καὶ ὁμολογήσας τὴν καλὴν ὁμολογίαν·

b. παθὼν καὶ ταφεὶς καὶ ἀναστὰς τῇ τρίτῃ ἡμέρᾳ, καὶ ἀνελθὼν εἰς οὐρανούς

c. καὶ καθίσας ἐν τῇ δεξιᾷ τῆς μεγαλωσύνης τοῦ Πατρός,

d. πατήσας τὸν θάνατον,

e. καὶ τὸν ᾅδην σκυλεύσας,

f. συντρίψας πύλας χαλκάς, καὶ μόχλους σιδηροὺς συνεθλάσας,

g. καὶ τὸν αἰχμάλωτον Ἀδὰμ ἀνακαλεσάμενος ἐκ φθορᾶς,

h. καὶ ἡμᾶς ἐλευθερώσας ἐκ τῆς τοῦ διαβόλου δουλείας.

4. Part IV. The *ekphonesis*.

a. Δι᾽ ὃ δεόμεθα καὶ παρακαλοῦμεν σε φιλάνθρωπε ἀγαθέ καταξίωσον ἡμᾶς ἐν καθαρᾷ καρδίᾳ τολμᾶν ἀφόβως, ἐπιβοᾶσθαι τὸν πάντων δεσπότην ἐπουράνιον Θεόν, Πατέρα ἅγιον καὶ λέγειν.

The Commentary

2. Function

In this part of the Commentary, building on that which Hammerschmidt has already written, we will be focusing in on two things, firstly: the addition of Miaphysitism into the mix of possible theological origins; and secondly: the parallels in structure and word choice between this prayer and the Nicene Creed and the *Monogens Hymn* of Justinian.

1. (Section III.2 line 2): ὁ ὤν, ὁ ἦν, ὁ ἐλθών, καὶ πάλιν ἐρχόμενος,

Beginning this prayer with this phrase is telling, we have seen similar phrasing in the first "Prayer of the Greeting:" Ὁ ὤν, καὶ προών, καὶ διαμένων εἰς τοὺς αἰῶνας. Although the opening of this prayer is structured differently to reflect a different purpose, it seems that the author of this prayer decided to give his prayer the air of authenticity by choosing to emulate the opening of one of the prayers original to this Liturgy, this is seen too in the phrases that follow the opening, both deal with Christ's closeness to the Father, in the "Prayer of the Breaking:" ὁ ἐν δεξίᾳ τοῦ Πατρὸς καθήμενος, and in the ‚Prayer of the Greeting:' ὁ τῷ Πατρὶ συναΐδιος καὶ ὁμοούσιος καὶ σύνθρονος καὶ συνδημιουργός. Like the opening, this first statement of Christ is not identical in these prayers, but the similarity of the paralleled passages leaves little doubt that the "Prayer of the Breaking" is meant to remind the listener of the "Prayer of the Greeting." The choice of this prayer as a model is a deliberate one: both prayers deal with the Incarnation and its effects, the history of Salvation. The history of Salvation presented in the "Prayer of the Greeting," however, follows the theology of the Nicene fathers closely, while this prayer shows influence from the Monophysite/Miaphysite or Monothelite theology. The author attempts to hang his prayer onto the Nicene model presented by modelling much of his structure and language on that found in the Nicene Creed. It seems then that, though this prayer was certainly not originally a part of the Liturgy of St. Gregory, the prayer was deliberately modelled after a prayer that was, in order that it gain acceptance as an authentic part of this Liturgy.

2. (Section III.2 line 2): ὁ ἐν δεξίᾳ τοῦ Πατρὸς καθήμενος·

This phrase serves, in part, to again connect the "Prayer of the Breaking" with its model the "Prayer of the Greeting" in the mind of the listener. The phrase also serves as the beginning of a ring composition, ending with the phrase: καὶ καθίσας ἐν τῇ δεξίᾳ τῆς μεγαλωσύνης τοῦ Πατρός. This ring composition is central to the argument of the prayer, that, though Christ became man, His humanity was, in a certain sense, a brief interlude of His divinity. Christ begins the prayer sitting at the right hand of the Father, and, following the Incarnation, the Crucifixion and the Ressurection, Christ ascends and sits once more at His usual place at the right hand of the Father, as though nothing happened in between.

Underscoring this emphasis of the divinity is what follows the ring composition, it is only here that we learn the purpose of the Incarnation: the destruction of Hades and the Salvation of mortals. By listing this after the closing of the ring composition, when Christ is seated next to the Father once more, the author asserts that it is Christ *as God* who destroyed Hades, otherwise the author would have put the description of the destruction of Death following the phrase: καὶ ὁμολογήσας τὴν καλὴν ὁμολογίαν, since the rest of the history of Salvation is presented in chronological order.

3. (Section III.2 lines 3-4): ὁ ἄρτος ὁ καταβὰς ἐκ τοῦ οὐρανοῦ, καὶ ζωὴν διδοὺς τῷ κόσμῳ· ὁ μέγας ἀρχιερεύς ὁ ἀρχηγὸς τῆς σωτηρίας ἡμῶν· τὸ φῶς ἀληθινόν, τὸ πρὸ πάντων αἰώνων.

These four phrases are a microcosm of the entire prayer. We see all the themes of this prayer: the Incarnation, the history of salvation and the preexistence of Christ as God, all touched on. This section is also interesting because it is the only part of the prayer that deals with the Eucharist; the first description of Christ's nature is not that He is the "Logos" as He is later termed in this prayer, but as the ἄρτος, the "bread." The focus of the prayer as a whole, however, is on the theology of the Incarnation, and no mention is made of the Eucharist in the only place one may expect it, the discussion of Salvation at the end of the prayer. This lack of discussion of the Eucharist, outside of this section, is important in showing what the purpose of the prayer is. The preparation for the Eucharist is one of the two major themes of this type of prayer, so if the Eucharist is relegated to such a minor section of the prayer, this cannot be an original "Prayer of the Breaking." This phrase, however, has an interesting parallel in the Greek-Syrian Liturgy of St. James, which shows, in the priest's private prayer before receiving the Eucharist: Δέσποτα Χριστέ, ὁ Θεὸς ἡμῶν, ὁ οὐράνιος ἄρτος, ἡ τροφὴ τοῦ παντὸς κόσμου,[1150] both of these phrases describe Christ as "bread" one as still "heavenly" and the other as having descended from heaven; both phrases also describe the effects of this "bread" on the universe, either as its food, or as its life. Despite some differences, it seems that the author of this prayer was aware enough of the purpose of a "Prayer of the Breaking" to adapt a phrase from a Eucharistic prayer.

The lynchpin of this section is the phrase: ὁ μέγας ἀρχιερεύς, which ties together the first phrase, describing Christ as the "bread" and the third and fourth, which describe him as the "origin of Salvation" and the "true light" respectively. The intent of the author is to tie together his later exposition on Salvation: πατήσας τὸν θάνατον, καὶ τὸν ἅδην

[1150] "Master Christ our God, the heavenly bread, the food of the entire world."

σκυλεύσας, συντρίψας πύλας χαλκάς, καὶ μόχλους σιδηροὺς συνθλάσας, καὶ τὸν αἰχμάλωτον Ἀδὰμ ἀνακαλεσάμενος ἐκ φθορᾶς, καὶ ἡμᾶς ἐλευθερώσας ἐκ τῆς τοῦ διαβόλου δουλείας, which is here exemplified in His description of Christ as the "origin of our salvation" together with Christ's place in the Eucharist. Christ as the "bread" He is also the one who "gives life to the whole world." Salvation, then is manifested through the "bread" of the Eucharist. We see too that Christ is presented as both the offering, the "bread" and the offerer, the "great high priest." That the author of this prayer uses a theme that comes up so often in this Liturgy supports the contention made above, that the author wrote this prayer specifically for this Liturgy, and put effort into linking it with themes and style found in other parts of the text.

The ring composition that marks this prayer is also reflected in this microcosm, the prayer as a whole begins with Christ at the right hand of God, and this section begins with an affirmation of this, Christ is the "bread that descends from heaven." The closing bracket returns Christ to the realm of heaven as the "true light that existed before the ages." Here it seems as though Christ never leaves the heavenly sphere, even during the Incarnation. This emphasis of the divine over the human is characteristic of the rest of this prayer, the human is subsumed in the divine. Miaphysitism is much more compatible with the phraseology found in this prayer, which emphasizes both the humanity of Christ and the unity of Christ's nature.

4. (Section III.2 lines 4-5): Ὃς ὢν ἀπαύγασμα τῆς δόξης, καὶ χαρακτὴρ τῆς ὑποστάσεως αὐτοῦ τοῦ ἰδίου σου Πατρός.

The author begins discussing the nature of Christ here. This section is an adaptation from Paul's Epistle to the Hebrews 1:3: "He is the reflection of God's glory and the exact imprint of God's very being." The author has to rewrite this section to fit in with the dialogue style of the rest of the prayer. The dependance of the Son on the Father described in this section is unusual in this Liturgy. The anti-Arian stance of this Liturgy makes such statements rare, the author of the Liturgy tends not even to mention the Father unless it is absolutely necessary.[1151] That the author of this prayer makes such a statement is another reason we can see that this prayer is a later addition to the Liturgy rather than an original part of it.

This section discusses the relationship between the Father and the Son in the Trinity, while the rest of the prayer deals with the theology of Christ's natures and the Incarna-

---

[1151] Note above in the opening prayer of the Liturgy. The Father is not even mentioned in this prayer until the *ekphonesis* and the obligatory mention of the Father in the Trinitarian formula.

tion. The author is using two models for his prayer: the section of the Nicene Creed that deals with Christ and the *Monogens Hymn* of Justinian, both of which begin with Christ's relationship with the Father. The *Monogens Hymn* begins: Ὁ μονογενὴς Υἱὸς καὶ Λόγος τοῦ Θεοῦ ἀθάνατος ὑπάρχων[1152] and the section of the Creed begins: Καὶ εἰς ἕνα Κύριον, Ἰησοῦν Χριστόν, τὸν Υἱὸν τοῦ Θεοῦ τὸν μονογενῆ, τὸν ἐκ τοῦ Πατρὸς γεννηθέντα πρὸ πάντων τῶν αἰώνων. Φῶς ἐκ φωτός, Θεὸν ἀληθινὸν ἐκ Θεοῦ ἀληθινοῦ γεννηθέντα, οὐ ποιηθέντα, ὁμοούσιον τῷ Πατρί, δι' οὗ τὰ πάντα ἐγένετο.[1153] A phrase from the last section already established a link with this part of the Nicene Creed: τὸ φῶς ἀληθινόν, τὸ πρὸ πάντων αἰώνων with Φῶς ἐκ φωτός. Though the author does not base this section directly on either of these texts, it is the following sections that show a greater dependance on the other two texts.

5. (Section III.2 lines 5-7): Ὁ εὐδοκήσας καὶ καταξιώσας κατελθεῖν ἐκ τῶν ὑψωμάτων τοῦ οὐρανοῦ, ἐκ κόλπων τοῦ ἀπροσίτου φωτὸς καὶ ἀληθινοῦ καὶ ἀοράτου μόνου Πατρός.

The author shows, again, that this prayer is not original by breaking out of the established pattern of the Liturgy. Though this section is about Christ, who deems it worthy to descend from heaven, the emphasis seems to be on the Father, on whom Christ is dependant. This dependance belies the anti-Arian purpose of the rest of the Liturgy. We also see a greater correspondence with the vocabulary used in the Nicene Creed. Christ deems it worthy: κατελθεῖν ἐκ τῶν ὑψωμάτων τοῦ οὐρανοῦ, corresponding to: κατελθόντα ἐκ τῶν οὐρανῶν.[1154] While both the Nicene Creed and the *Monogens Hymn* give the reason why Christ decides to become Incarnate: τὸν δι' ἡμᾶς τοὺς ἀνθρώπους καὶ διὰ τὴν ἡμετέραν σωτηρίαν[1155] in the Nicene Creed and: καὶ καταδεξάμενος διὰ τὴν ἡμετέραν σωτηρίαν[1156] in the *Monogens Hymn*, this background is failing in the prayer, which only discusses Salvation in two places.

6. (Section III.2 lines 7-9): Σαρκωθεὶς δὲ ἐκ Πνεύματος Ἁγίου, καὶ ἐκ τῆς πανενδόξου ἀχράντου ἁγίας δεσποίνης ἡμῶν Θεοτόκου καὶ ἀειπαρθένου Μαρίας, καὶ τελέως ἐνανθρωπήσας·

[1152] Hammond and Brightman (1896). pg. 33. "Only begotten Son and Word of God, existing immortal."
[1153] Hammond and Brightman (1896). pp. 42-43. "And in one Lord, Jesus Christ, the Son of God the only begotten, begotten of the Father before all of the ages. Light from light, true God from true God, begotten not made, consubstantial with the Fatherm, through whom all was made."
[1154] "Coming down from heaven."
[1155] "Who for us humans and for our salvation."
[1156] "and accepting, for our salvation"

The Commentary

These lines open the second, largest and most important section of the prayer, in which the author lays out his theological interpretation of the Incarnation. This can be seen by a shift in style. In the surrounding two sections the author uses numerous short phrases, while this section is broken up into three long sentences.

This section is especially interesting because of the similarity it bears both the Nicene Creed and the *Monogens Hymn* of Justinian, and seems to be, in fact, a quotation that mixes the two texts together, though the Nicene Creed proves to be the more important of the two model texts. The author begins with the verb: σαρκωθείς, which corresponds to the participle: σαρκωθέντα in the Nicene Creed. Using this verb, the author makes clear his intention to discuss the Incarnation, and connects himself to the Nicene Creed and the nearly universally accepted authority it bears.[1157] The prayer continues: ἐκ Πνεύματος Ἁγίου καὶ...Μαρίας... καὶ... ἐνανθρωπήσας, continuing the close adaptation of the text of the Nicene Creed: ἐκ Πνεύματος Ἁγίου καὶ Μαρίας τῆς Παρθένου καὶ ἐνανθρωπήσαντα.[1158] The greatest difference is that a second person sg. aorist verb is used in the prayer while a participle is used in the Nicene Creed, and this is accounted for by the difference in style, as the prayer is written in a dialogue form with Christ, conforming to the rest of the Liturgy.

The other major difference is the treatment of the Virgin Mary in this prayer. She is called the πανενδόξου ἀχράντου ἁγίας δεσποίνης ἡμῶν Θεοτόκου καὶ ἀειπαρθένου Μαρίας. A row of epithets like these are common for the Virgin Mary, especially during the Remembrences following the Epiklesis, so in the Greek-Syrian Liturgy of St. James: ἐξαιρέτως τῆς παναγίας καὶ ὑπερευλογημένης, ἀχράντου δεσποίνης ἡμῶν Θεοτόκου καὶ ἀειπαρθένου Μαρίας.[1159] This type of epithet is not seen in the Nicene Creed, which does not even use the title: Θεοτόκος. A similar construction is found, however, in the *Monogens Hymn* of Justinian, where we see the following in reference to the Incarnation: σαρκωθῆναι ἐκ τῆς ἁγίας Θεοτόκου καὶ ἀειπαρθένου Μαρίας,[1160] the similarity between the formulations are not to be overlooked, and it seems that the extra titles the Virgin Mary is given in the prayer serve to underscore the importance placed on the Incarnation by the author. This connection to the *Monogens Hymn* is further borne out in the final phrase of this section: καὶ τελέως ἐνανθρωπήσας. The term: ἐνανθρωπήσας corresponds to the phrasing of the *Monogenes Hymn*, the problem lies in the τελέως which, while there is no exact

---

[1157] It also connects his prayer more closely with the rest of the Liturgy, which reflects almost exclusively the theological standpoints of the Nicene Creed.
[1158] "from the Holy Spirit and the virgin Mary and became man"
[1159] Hammond and Brightman (1896). pg. 46 and Mercier (1944). pg. 214. "Remembering our holy and blessed, pure lady the Theotokos and ever virgin Mary."
[1160] "taking flesh from the holy Theotokos and ever virgin Mary"

correspondence, seems to reflect the ἀτρέπτως. It seems then, that the author chose to comment on the Hymn of Justinian and on the Nicene Creed by taking the phrasing used and changing it to reflect his own theological position.

7. (Section III.2 lines 9-11): καὶ κατὰ μετάστασιν, τὴν ἀνθρωπότητα ἀναλλοιώσας, ἑνώσας ἑαυτῷ καθ᾽ ὑπόστασιν, ἀφράστως καὶ ἀπερινοήτως, ἀτρέπτως δὲ καὶ ἀσυγχύτως, ψυχὴν ἔχουσαν λογικήν τε καὶ νοεράν.

In this section the author continues his discussion of the Incarnation, dealing especially with its mystery, it is: ἀφράστως καὶ ἀπερινοήτως and the moment of the "God-man making" as it is termed in the next section. This section continues in the theological vein of the τελέως ἐνανθρωπήσας and culminates in Christ having a ψυχὴν that is λογικήν τε καὶ νοεράν. Describing Christ's soul in this way underscores His human nature, as a "rational soul" is an aspect of humanity given. If this were a Monophysite prayer such a statement could not be made, nor could the author write that Christ "united humanity" within Himself.

Interesting too is the choice of the word: ἀσυγχύτως. A Monophysite prayer would shy away from such a term, because it is used in both the Council of Chalcedon and the Third Council of Constantinople (680-681) to argue for a dual nature of Christ, both human and divine, and this is incompatible with Monophysite theology.

8. (Section III.2 lines 11-13): οὕτως προῆλθες ἐξ αὐτῆς θεανθρωπωθεὶς ὁμοούσιος τῷ Πατρὶ κατὰ τὴν θεότητα, καὶ ὁμοούσιος ἡμῖν κατὰ τὴν ἀνθρωπότητα.

The word: θεανθρωπωθείς interests us here, this cannot be a word used by the Monophysites, and this word alone seems to prove that this prayer cannot be interpreted in light of Monophysite theology.

The second part of this section further removes the Monophysites as a possible origin for this prayer. This is a quotation from the Council of Chalcedon, which condemned the Monophysites.[1161] It seems unlikely that a Monophysite author would use quotations from the very Council which condemned his beliefs in order to prove them. We can also see here that the use of this quotation is very important to the author, since the use of the term homoousios is rare in liturgical writing, so in order to break with the traditional avoidance of that term the author must find the theology imparted by this phrase of utmost importance.

[1161] Percival (1971). pg. 264

The Commentary

9. (Section III.2 lines 13-16): Οὐ δύο πρόσωπα οὖν, οὐδὲ δύο μορφὰς ἤγουν, οὐδὲ ἐν δυσὶ φύσεσι γνωριζώμενος, ἀλλ' εἷς Θεός, εἷς Κύριος, μία οὐσία μία βασιλεία μία δεσπότεια μία ἐνέργεια μία ὑπόστασις μία θέλησις μία φύσις τοῦ Θεοῦ Λόγου σεσαρκωμένη καὶ προσκυνουμένη.

This is a section that causes great confusion. There has, up to this point, not been any one statement that offers Monophysite theology, quite the opposite in fact, as can be seen in the quotation from the Council of Chalcedon and in the strengthening of ἀτρέπτως ἐνανθρωπήσας[1162] in the *Monogenes Hymn* to: τελέως ἐνανθρωπήσας. In this section the text shifts to a theological position which focuses entirely on the unity of Christ's natures: οὐδὲ ἐν δυσὶ φύσεσι γνωριζώμενος. The repetition of: εἷς and μία serve to underscore this unity. This is a complete turn about in the theology: μία φύσις τοῦ Θεοῦ Λόγου σεσαρκωμένη καὶ προσκυνουμένη even contradicting the contention made by the author before that Christ was endowed with a ‚rational and intelligent soul' during the Incarnation, here Christ is the Word of God made flesh, not as a human, but as a covering over of His divinity.

This is also the only section of this prayer from which one could interpret the text as Monothelite in origin. It is the use of the term: μία θέλησις which leads to that conclusion, however, this term is used in a long list, all of which are set up in the same way: μία οὐσία, μία βασιλεία, μία δεσπότεια, etc. These terms serve to emphasize the unity of Christ's natures, rather than giving a point of compromise which both the Chalcedonian and Monophysite Christians would agree to, which was the purpose of Monothelitism.

How, then, to explain this dichotomy? One possibility is that this section of the prayer is a still later addition to this prayer, which was itself a later addition to the Liturgy. The majority of this section seems to be a quotation from St. Cyril.[1163] It is possible that a later cleric, who believed that the two natures of Christ were too dominant in this prayer added this quotation to lend more weight to Christ's unity and thus maintain the balance of Miaphysitism. It is also possible that the author himself added this quotation for this same reason. What is sure, however, is that the author was not a Monophysite, this has been proven by the earlier statements of this prayer. That he was a Monothelite seems unlikely based only on one phrase. The theology does, however, fit into the Miaphysite style, and we must decide that the author was a Miaphysite theologian, who added this prayer into the Liturgy of St. Gregory sometime in the sixth century, following the writing of the *Monogenes Hymn* of Justinian.

[1162] "unchangedly becoming man"
[1163] McGuckin (2004). pg. 140

The Liturgy of Saint Gregory the Theologian

10. (Section III.2 lines 16-21): Σταυρωθεὶς δὲ ἐπὶ Ποντίου Πιλάτου καὶ ὁμολογήσας τὴν καλὴν ὁμολογίαν· παθὼν καὶ ταφεὶς καὶ ἀναστας τῇ τρίτῃ ἡμέρα, καὶ ἀνελθὼν εἰς οὐρανοὺς καὶ καθίσας ἐν τῇ δεξίᾳ τῆς μεγαλωσύνης τοῦ Πατρός, πατήσας τὸν θάνατον, καὶ τὸν ᾅδην σκυλεύσας, συντρίψας πύλας χαλκάς, καὶ μόχλους σιδηροὺς συνεθλάσας, καὶ τὸν αἰχμάλωτον Ἀδὰμ ἀνακαλεσάμενος ἐκ φθορᾶς, καὶ ἡμᾶς ἐλευθερώσας ἐκ τῆς τοῦ διαβόλου δουλείας.

Having completed the theological discussion of the Incarnation, the author now returns to the history of Salvation, and to the style he abandoned for the central section of the prayer: numerous short phrases. He also returns here to the format of the Nicene Creed. The author paraphrases the Nicene Creed in the first half of this section: Σταυρωθεὶς δὲ ἐπὶ Ποντίου Πιλάτου καὶ ὁμολογήσας τὴν καλὴν ὁμολογίαν· παθὼν καὶ ταφεὶς καὶ ἀναστας τῇ τρίτῃ ἡμέρα καὶ ἀνελθὼν εἰς οὐρανούς, καὶ καθίσας ἐν τῇ δεξίᾳ τῆς μεγαλωσύνης τοῦ Πατρός, which corresponds to: Σταυρωθέντα τε ὑπὲρ ἡμῶν ἐπὶ Ποντίου Πιλάτου καὶ παθόντα καὶ ταφέντα. Καὶ ἀναστάντα τῇ τρίτῃ ἡμέρᾳ κατὰ τὰς Γραφάς. Καὶ ἀνελθόντα εἰς τοὺς οὐρανοὺς καὶ καθεζόμενον ἐκ δεξιῶν τοῦ Πατρός.[1164]

Although there are slight differences in phrasing, these sections are virtually identical. The following phrases, which describe Christ's destruction of death, are, however, not found in the Nicene Creed, however. We must once again turn to the *Monogenes Hymn* of Justinian for not only a a summarized version of this section of the Nicene Creed: σταυρωθείς τε Χριστὲ ὁ Θεός.[1165] but a description of Christ's destruction of death: θανάτῳ θάνατον πατήσας,[1166] an almost direct correspondence with: πατήσας τὸν θάνατον in the "Prayer of the Breaking." The description in the "Prayer of the Breaking" is more in depth, however, once again showing that the author is not content in just paraphrasing the *Monogenes Hymn*, but feels the need to outdo Justinian.

The Structure of the majority of the prayer, then, is a combination of the Nicene Creed and the Hymn of Justinian. The Nicene Creed being used to bolster the authority of the prayer, and the Hymn of Justinian being used as a source as well as a foundation to build on.

The author places his discussion of Christ's destruction of death in the incorrect chronological place. This should be between the Crucifixion and the Ressurection, but has been moved to after the Ascenscion into Heaven. Since the rest of the history of Salvation is written out chronologically, this must be done deliberately and the question then be-

---

[1164] "and being crucified for us under Pontius Pilate and suffering and was buried. Rising on the third day according to the Writings. Ascending to the heavens and sitting at the right hand of the Father."
[1165] "and You were crucified, Christ God"
[1166] "and by death You destroyed death"

comes: why did the author move this section to after the Ascension? One possibility is that the author wanted to keep the sections taken from the Nicene Creed together and the sections from the *Monogenes Hymn* together, and did not wish to confuse his readers by intertwining the two sources. What seems a more likely reason, however, is that the author wished to underscore that Christ destroyed death as God, not as a human, and therefore put the description of this destruction after Christ ascended to Heaven.

11. (Section III.2 lines 22-24): Δι' ὃ δεόμεθα καὶ παρακαλοῦμέν σε φιλάνθρωπε ἀγαθέ καταξίωσον ἡμᾶς ἐν καθαρᾷ καρδίᾳ τολμᾶν ἀφόβως, ἐπιβοᾶσθαι τὸν πάντων δεσπότην ἐπουράνιον Θεὸν Πατέρα ἅγιον, καὶ λέγειν.

Although Hammerschmidt tends to disgard this *ekphonesis*, claiming that it was not an original part of the prayer, not being an organic outgrowth of the rest of the text;[1167] this does not seem entirely convincing. The "Prayer of the Breaking" has two functions: 1. to make final preparations for the Eucharist; and 2. to introduce the recitation of the Lord's Prayer. Although these functions are not fulfilled in this prayer, the author does touch on the Eucharistic element in calling Christ the "bread." It is possible that this *ekphonesis* was tacked on in the same way by the author, not to entirely fulfill the function of a "Prayer of the Breaking," but to legitimize its insertion into the Liturgy by at least looking like one. This would also explain the seeming awkward introduction of the Lord's Prayer, if someone later took the time to add an *ekphonesis*, why leave such an abrupt transition. There is also an inherant awkwardness in this *ekphonesis*, being the transition from a prayer addressed to Christ to one addressed to the Father. This prayer, by having several places where the Father is mentioned, does prepare the reader for a following prayer addressed to a different member of the Trinity.

While there is no doubting the awkwardness of this *ekphonesis*, the awkwardness does not necessarily derive from being added later, but is inherant in the double purpose of the prayer as both a theological second Creed as well as a "Prayer of the Breaking."

III.IV. The "Other Prayer of the Breaking"[1168]

Like the first "Prayer of the Breaking" in the Greek text, the second is not usually found in the Coptic tranlsation.[1169] This discrepancy leads Hammerschmidt to conclude

---

[1167] Hammerschmidt (1896). pg. 154-155
[1168] The second "Prayer of the Breaking" of three in this Liturgy.
[1169] Though Hammerschmndt points out that the Oxford Manuscript (Hunt. 403) of the Coptic Liturgy of St. Gregory does contain this prayer. Hammerschmidt (1957). pg. 163

that this prayer too is not original to the Liturgy of St. Gregory, but also a later addition to the text: "Das zweite Brechungsgebet der gr Greglit dürfte auch noch der vor monophysitischen Zeit angehören und ist vielleicht auch erst nach der Entstehung der Greglit eingesetzt worden. Es ist ja unwahrscheinlich, dass eine Liturgie von vornherein zwei verschiedene Gebete für ein und denselben Zweck aufweist."[1170] That the prayer only occurs once in the Coptic translations does not necessarily mean that it was not there in the Greek initially, there are a number of prayers in the Post-Anaphora section of this Liturgy that have no correspondance in the Coptic text, and it would be logical for the Coptic translators to choose only one of the "Prayers of the Breaking" in order to standardize the text for use in the Coptic language. To claim too, that the prayer must be later because there would not be two prayers for the same purpose is not entirely founded, as Hammerschmidt has himself postulated two prayers added by the author in order to provide "abwechslung."[1171] Although we cannot reach a conclusion, whether or not the second prayer was composed by the original author of this Liturgy, we can make a diachronic conclusion about the order in which this Liturgy was put together, while adopting Hammerschmidt's claim that the third prayer is the original prayer incorporated into the Liturgy by the author. We must conclude that the second "Prayer of the Breaking" predates the first. A number of factors come together to lead us to this conclusion: 1. the complete lack of a Coptic translation of the first prayer compared to the existence of a Coptic translation of the second prayer in at least one manuscript. 2. The placement of the prayers also indicates that the first prayer is later than the second prayer. We have discussed before that, generally speaking, prayers are found in reverse chronological order in a text, that is, youngest first.[1172] 3. Internal evidence also suggests that the first prayer was added later than the second. The first prayer, as we discussed above, fulfills the function of a "Prayer of the Breaking" only in the broadest sense,[1173] this begs the question: why was this third prayer inserted into the Liturgy here? One reason may be as an extention of the second prayer, which begins with a short section on the Incarnation and Salvation, the topics which dominate the first prayer.

[1170] Hammerschmidt (1957). pg. 163; see also Hanssens (1930-1931) III. pg. 493. "The second Prayer of the Breaking of the Liturgy of St. Gregory may belong to the premonophysite time and was perhaps even added just after the creation of the Liturgy of St. Gregory. It is unlikely, that a liturgy has two different prayers for the same reason."
[1171] Hammerschmidt (1957). pg. 96. "variety"
[1172] Hammerschmidt (1957). pg. 98
[1173] By briefly mentioning the Eucharist in the body of the prayer and the Lord's Prayer only in an *ekphonesis* with a dubious origin.

It is the preoccupation with the Incarnation and Salvation shown in both of these prayers that make them so unique. Generally, a "Prayer of the Breaking" falls into the *genre* of purification prayer, focusing on the purification of the individual rather than making theological statements. The only exception seems to be the beginning of each prayer, where the power of God is expressed, by, for example, giving a description of the various ranks of angels that surround the throne of God. Why then, do these two prayers bring up the topic of the Incarnation? It is in answering this question that we finish the diachronic analysis of these prayers: the third ‚Prayer of the Breaking' in the Liturgy of St. Gregory has only one phrase that deals with the Incarnation: ὦ Λόγε, ὃν προνοοῦσιν αὐτὸν, καὶ ἄνθρωπε ὃν προθεωροῦσιν αὐτόν, this statement concerning the two natures of Christ, made by the author of the Liturgy, is taken and developed by the author of the second prayer, and is then taken and further refined by the author of the first prayer.

1. Structure

This prayer is divided into two sections, the first begins with a direct address of Christ: Σὺ γὰρ εἶ ὁ Λόγος τοῦ Πατρός, ὁ πραιώνιος Θεός and deals with the theology of the Incarnation and the Salvation of humanity. The second section begins with a renewed address of Christ: φιλάνθρωπε ἀγαθέ, Κύριε and switches topics, becoming a prayer of purification for the Eucharist and the recitation of the Lord's Prayer.

Part I of this prayer can be subdivided into three smaller sections: 1. the establishment of the Christ's divine function; 2. the Incarnation; and 3. Christ's selection of the elect, who are the Church, and thus His human function.

Part II of this prayer, which covers the majority of the text, turns the prayer into a prayer of purification, changing topics to the Eucharist and the Lord's Prayer, the topics normally discussed in a "Prayer of the Breaking." This section begins with a request for Christ, that the Eucharist not become "a condemnation," this is the first mention of the Eucharist in this prayer, this first request is completed with a qualification, Christ is asked not to condemn the participant in the Eucharist because "we offer on behalf of our weakness." Following this first request, the author describes how Christ should deal with those coming to receive the Eucharist. It is in this second section that the author deals both with the Eucharist, which the author uses as a template, Christ should hallow the communicant as He hallows the gifts they receive. This hallowing is then used to prepare for the Lord's Prayer, which rounds out the remainder of the prayer. The structure of this prayer can also be seen in the following table.

The Liturgy of Saint Gregory the Theologian

Table III.IV.1 The Structure of the alternate "Prayer of the Breaking."[1174]

The Alternate "Prayer of the Breaking"
Part I: Incarnation and Salvation. 1. Opening Invocation: Σὺ γὰρ εἶ ὁ Λόγος τοῦ Πατρός, ὁ πραιώνιος Θεός, ὁ μέγας ἀρχιερεὺς 2. Incarnation: ὁ ἐπὶ σωτηρίας τοῦ γένους τῶν ἀνθρώπων, σαρκωθεὶς καὶ ἐνανθρωπήσας, 3. Salvation of the ‚Elect:' καὶ προσκαλεσάμενος ἑαυτῷ ἐκ πάντων τῶν ἐθνῶν, γένος ἐκλεκτὸν βασίλειον ἱεράτευμα, ἔθνος ἅγιον, λαὸν εἰς περιποίησιν.
Part II: Prayer of Purification. 1. Reopening of the Prayer: Δι' ὃ δεόμεθα καὶ παρακαλοῦμέν σε, φιλάνθρωπε ἀγαθέ Κύριε, 2. Switch to a prayer of purification: μὴ εἰς ἔλεγχον καὶ ὄνειδος, μὴ εἰς κρίμα, μηδὲ εἰς κατάκριμα τῶν ἡμετέρων ἁμαρτιῶν, γενηθήτω ἡ θυσία αὐτή· 3. Justification for the purification: ὑπὲρ γὰρ τῶν ἀσθενειῶν ἡμῶν προσηνέγχαμεν· 4. Template how Christ should sanctify the communicants: ἀλλ' ὥσπερ τὰ πανάγιά σου τίμια Δῶρα ταῦτα· πάσης ἁγιωσύνης ἐμπλῆσαι κατηξίωσας, διὰ τῆς ἐπιφοιτήσεως τοῦ παναγίου σου Πνεύματος ἐπ' αὐτῶν. Οὕτως καὶ ἡμῶν τῶν ἁμαρτωλῶν δούλων σου, ἁγιάσαι καταξίωσον τὰς ψυχάς, τὰ σώματα, τὰ πνεύματα, τὰς συνειδήσεις, 5. Consequence of the purification: Ὅπως πεφωτισμένῃ ψυχῇ, ἀνεπαισχύντῳ προσώπῳ, καρδίᾳ καθαρᾷ, συνειδήσει ἀνυποκρίτῳ, ἡγιασμαμένοις χείλεσιν, ἀγάπῃ τελείᾳ, ἐλπίδι ἀσφαλεῖ, τολμῶμεν μετὰ παρρησίας, ἄνευ φόβου, λέγειν τὴν ἁγίαν

[1174] Cf. Section III.3 lines 1-16.

> προσευχήν, ἥν μετέδωκας τοῖς ἰδίοις τοῖς ἁγίοις σου μαθηταῖς καὶ ἱεροῖς σου ἀποστόλοις, ὅταν προσεύχησθε, οὕτως προσεύχεσθε ὑμεῖς. Πάτερ ἡμῶν, ὁ ἐν τοῖς οὐρανοῖς.

2. Function

1. (Section III.3 lines 2-5): Σὺ γὰρ εἶ ὁ Λόγος τοῦ Πατρός, ὁ προαιώνιος Θεός, ὁ μέγας ἀρχιερεὺς ὁ ἐπὶ σωτηρίας τοῦ γένους τῶν ἀνθρώπων, σαρκωθεὶς καὶ ἐνανθρωπήσας, καὶ προσκαλεσάμενος ἑαυτῷ ἐκ πάντων τῶν ἐθνῶν, γένος ἐκλεκτὸν βασίλειον ἱεράτευμα, ἔθνος ἅγιον, λαὸν εἰς περιποίησιν.

Like the majority of prayers in this liturgy, the opening of the prayer is a direct address of Christ. Unusually, however, it is not a short, one or two word phrase, but a long, involved, row of descriptve phrases. What truly makes this opening stand out, however, is that it begins with: Σὺ γὰρ εἶ, this formula is otherwise never seen at the beginning of prayers in this Liturgy, but is a common way of opening the *ekphonesis*, both in this Liturgy and in others.[1175] From the wording of this opening, then, it seems that this prayer has its origin in the *ekphonesis* of another prayer. Unfortunately it has proved impossible locate the prayer which the author of this prayer uses as a template. As we will see, however, the ending of this prayer is reminiscent of the "Prayer of the Breaking" found in the Greek-Syrian Liturgy of St. James, this commonality makes it likely that the opening of this prayer too has its origin in the Greek-Syrian rite.

Following the direct address, where we would expect the Trinitarian formula in an *ekphonesis*, the author begins a short discussion of the Incarnation. Such a discussion of the Incarnation is unusual in such a Prayer, and, as we discussed above, this discussion may hold the key as to the diachronic Structure of the three "Prayers of the Breaking." Unlike the long, problematic,[1176] theological discussion in the first prayer, this prayer has only a few words dealing with the Incarnation: ὁ ἐπὶ σωτηρίας τοῦ γένους τῶν ἀνθρώπων σαρκωθεὶς καὶ ἐνανθρωπήσας. In this section, however, the author is able to make statements about: 1. the origin of the Incarnation, that is, which person of the Trinity was the driving force behind the Incarnation. In this prayer it is Christ, as opposed to the first prayer, in which the Father is outshines the Son. This focus on Christ makes the true origin of this prayer more difficult to pinpoint, as it is in line with the focus of the rest of the Liturgy, where the first prayer had several major differences. 2. The purpose of the Incarnation,

---

[1175] See, for example, the *ekphonesis* of the ‚Prayer of the Gospel' in the Liturgy of St. Basil. This begins: Σὺ γὰρ εἶ ὁ εὐαγγελισμὸς καὶ φωτισμός. "For You are the good news and enlightenment,"
[1176] In that it is difficult to pinpoint exactly what theology of the Incarnation is being expounded in it.

which the author describes as: ἐπὶ σωτηρίας τοῦ γένους τῶν ἀνθρώπων, here the author also takes up the language of the Nicene Creed, which is retained through the rest of the discussion of the Incarnation: Τὸν δι' ἡμᾶς τοὺς ἀνθρώπους καὶ διὰ τὴν ἡμετέραν σωτηρίαν...σαρκωθέντα...ἐνανθρωπήσαντα.[1177] That this too is meant to evoke the Nicene Creed is doubtful however, and this may just be the author using the normal theological terms associated with the Incarnation, unlike the first prayer, in which the parallels to the Nicene Creed stand out. 3. Finally, the author comes to the actual theological discussion of the Incarnation, which he does in only two words: σαρκωθεὶς καὶ ἐνανθρωπήσας, by using these two words the author shows that he is not espousing Monophysite, Miaphysite or Monothelite theologies, since Christ both takes flesh and becomes man; nor does he profess the diaphysite leanings of the Nestorians, since no mention of made of a division between the divine and human natures of Christ. The language used in the Nicene Creed in this prayer seems to place this prayer before the Christological controversies concerning the relationship between the natures of Christ, giving weight to the idea that this prayer was added either by the author of the liturgy himself, or shortly after.

Following this section on the Incarnation, the author turns to the salvation of humanity: καὶ προσκαλεσάμενος ἑαυτῷ ἐκ πάντων τῶν ἐθνῶν, γένος ἐκλεκτὸν, βασίλειον ἱεράτευμα, ἔθνος ἅγιον, λαὸν εἰς περιποίησιν. The author presents us with a bit of a dichotomy here, since he has already stated that Christ underwent the Incarnation for the "salvation of the race of man." If Christ's purpose in the Incarnation was to save all of humanity, why then does He call to himself a group of "elect?" The calling to Himself of the "royal priesthood" and "holy nation" is the establishment of the Church. Similar phrasing can be seen in the Byzantine Liturgy of St. Basil: κτησάμενος ἡμᾶς ἑαυτῷ λαὸν περιούσιον, βασίλειον ἱεράτευμα, ἔθνος ἅγιον.[1178] In the Liturgy of St. Basil, this phrase is not found in the "Prayer of the Breaking," but in the prayer following the *Sanctus*, where it is used in the context of the salvation of humanity, the connection of this section with the salvific work of Christ is further emphasized by this phrase.

2. (Section III.3 lines 5-7): Δι' ὃ δεόμεθα καὶ παρακαλοῦμέν σε, φιλάνθρωπε ἀγαθέ Κύριε μὴ εἰς ἔλεγχον καὶ ὄνειδος, μὴ εἰς κρίμα, μηδὲ εἰς κατάκριμα τῶν ἡμετέρων ἁμαρτιῶν, γενηθήτω ἡ θυσία αὕτη· ὑπὲρ γὰρ τῶν ἀσθενειῶν ἡμῶν προσηνέγκαμεν·

With the second address of Christ: Φιλάνθρωπε ἀγαθέ, Κύριε, the author reopens the prayer, this time with a new aim, turning the prayer from an exposition of the Incarna-

---

[1177] "Who for us, for mankind, and for our salvation...taking flesh...becoming man."
[1178] Hammond and Brightman (1896). pg. 326. "consecrating us for Himself a chosen people, a royal priesthood, a divine nation."

tion into a prayer for purification. Following this transformation, the author explains why such a prayer is necessary while preparing for communion: "...that this sacrifice not become a condemnation..." The problem is a difficult one, one should not partake of the Eucharist unworthily, as the Christian Church in Corinth was warned of by St. Paul, but one can never be truly worthy to receive the Eucharist, so he asks that God forgive the sins of those who are sacrificing for them to be forgiven.

3. (Section III.3 lines 7-10): ἀλλ' ὥσπερ τὰ πανάγιά σου τίμια Δῶρα ταῦτα πάσης ἁγιωσύνης ἐμπλῆσαι κατηξίωσας, διὰ τῆς ἐπιφοιτήσεως τοῦ παναγίου σου Πνεύματος ἐπ' αὐτῶν. Οὕτως καὶ ἡμῶν τῶν ἁμαρτωλῶν δούλων σου, ἁγιάσαι καταξίωσον τὰς ψυχάς, τὰ σώματα, τὰ πνεύματα, τὰς συνειδήσεις.

Here the author changes focus, he no longer fears condemnation for his unworthiness, but asks for transformation. This section is reminiscent of the "Prayer of the *epiklesis*" in the Byzantine liturgy of St. Basil: καὶ σὲ παρακαλοῦμεν, Ἅγιε Ἁγίων, εὐδοκίᾳ τῆς σῆς ἀγαθότητος, ἐλθεῖν τὸ Πνεῦμά σου τὸ Ἅγιον ἐφ' ἡμᾶς, καὶ ἐπὶ τὰ προκείμενα Δῶρα ταῦτα, καὶ εὐλογῆσαι αὐτά, καὶ ἁγιάσαι, καὶ ἀναδεῖξαι.[1179] In both of these sections, the sanctification of the worshipper is linked with the transformation of the Eucharistic elements, through the Holy Spirit: 1. ἐλθεῖν τὸ Πνεῦμά σου τὸ Ἅγιον ἐφ' ἡμᾶς and 2. διὰ τῆς ἐπιφοιτήσεως τοῦ παναγίου σου Πνεύματος. This formula seems, then, to originate in the West Syrian and Byzantine liturgical families. While the phrase in this prayer does not correspond exactly to this Byzantine formulation, by using the elements of this phrase: the descent of the Holy Spirit; the transformation of the gifts and the sanctification of the worshipper, the author forms an intertextual connection between his prayer and the "Prayer of the *epiklesis*." Such an intertextual connection is warranted here, because through it the author links his prayer with another preparatory prayer and can so legitimize the prepartory function of his own prayer. Interesting, though, is that the author does not leave the Byzantine formula as is, but adapts it. The transformation of the Gifts can then be used as a template, (ὥσπερ τὰ πανάγιά σου τίμια Δῶρα ταῦτα) for the transformation of the recipient from a sinful being into a being that is entirely: τὰς ψυχάς, τὰ σώματα, τὰ πνεύματα, τὰς συνειδήσεις, made worthy to receive the Eucharist.

4. (Section III.3 lines 10-15): Ὅπως πεφωτισμένῃ ψυχῇ, ἀνεπαισχύντῳ προσώπῳ, καρδίᾳ καθαρᾷ, συνειδήσει ἀνυποκρίτῳ, ἡγιασμαμένοις χείλεσιν, ἀγάπῃ τελείᾳ, ἐλπίδι ἀσφαλεῖ,

---

[1179] Hammond and Brightman (1896). pg. 329 and Trempelis (1982). pg. 183. "And we pray to You, Holy of Holies, in the mercy of Your goodness, to lead Your Spirit, the Holy one, upon us and upon these gifts laid out, bless them, hallow them and make them manifest."

τολμῶμεν μετὰ παρρησιας, ἄνευ φόβου, λέγειν τὴν ἁγίαν προσευχήν, ἥν μετέδωκας τοῖς ἰδίοις τοῖς ἁγίοις σου μαθηταῖς καὶ ἱεροῖς σου ἀποστόλοις, ὅταν προσεύχησθε, οὕτως προσεύχεσθε ὑμεῖς. Πάτερ ἡμῶν, ὁ ἐν τοῖς οὐρανοῖς.

This section concludes this prayer, it also introduces the prayer which follows the "Prayer of the Breaking," the Lord's Prayer. In this section the author fulfills the dual function of the "Prayer of the Breaking" by praying for worthiness both in receiving the Eucharist and in praying the Lord's Prayer, this shows that this prayer was written as a "Prayer of the Breaking" even if the author focuses on the theology of the Incarnation as well. This is as opposed to the first "Prayer of the Breaking" which shows itself as not original to the Liturgy because, while there was a request for worthiness to pray the Lord's Prayer, the Eucharist, while touched upon, did not receive the proper attention necessary in a "Prayer of the Breaking."

The majority of the rest of this section consists of how the worshipper hopes to be able to pray the Lord's Prayer: πεφωτισμένῃ ψυχῇ, ἀνεπαισχύντῳ προσώπῳ, καρδίᾳ καθαρᾷ, συνειδήσει ἀνυποκρίτῳ, ἡγιασμαμένοις χείλεσιν, ἀγάπῃ τελείᾳ, ἐλπίδι ἀσφαλεῖ, τολμῶμεν μετὰ παρρησιας, ἄνευ φόβου, while slightly longer than normal, this row of parallels the normal formula and the language of purification found in the "Prayers of the Breaking" in a number of Liturgies.[1180] What is unusual here is the teleological ending to the prayer: ἥν μετέδωκας τοῖς ἰδίοις τοῖς ἁγίοις σου μαθηταῖς καὶ ἱεροῖς σου ἀποστόλοις, ὅταν προσεύχησθε, οὕτως προσεύχεσθε ὑμεῖς. Πάτερ ἡμῶν, ὁ ἐν τοῖς οὐρανοῖς. Because the "Prayer of the Breaking" introduces a prayer addressed to the Father, it is often accompanied by epithets describing the Father, as we see in the third "Prayer of the Breaking" in the Egyptian Liturgy of St. Basil: ἐπιβοᾶσθαι τὸν πάντων δεσπότην ἐπουράνιον Θεὸν πατερὰ ἅγιον, καὶ λέγειν.[1181] The author of this prayer, however, was able to use the fact that Christ taught the prayer to his disciples and apostles to return the focus of the prayer to Christ and away from the Father. This focus on Christ has two possible explanations. 1. The author whished to give his prayer a greater sense of authenticity or 2. this is an origi-

---

[1180] In the Greek-Syrian Liturgy of St. James, for example, we see: μετὰ παρρησίας, ἀκατακρίτως, ἐν καθαρᾷ καρδίᾳ, ψυχῇ πεφωτισμένῃ, ἀνεπαίσχυντῳ προσώπῳ, ἡγιασμένοις χείλεσι. In the Byzantine Liturgy of St. Basil we see: μετὰ παρρησίας, ἀκατακρίτως. "with frankness, uncondemned, in a pure heart, with an enlightened soul, shameless countenance, hallowed lips." The Egyptian Liturgy of St. Basil, like the Liturgy of St. Gregory contains three different prayers; the first one is taken from the Byzantine Liturgy of St. Basil, the second prayer contains the expected: ἐν καθαρᾷ καρδιᾳ, ψυχῇ πεφβτισμένῃ, τολμῶμεν μετὰ παρρησίας, the third prayer is unique in that it has very little of this formula: τολμῶμεν ἀφόβως. This formula is found in the Liturgy of St. Mark as well, but in this Liturgy it is adopted verbatim from the Liturgy of St. James, which supports Hammerschmidt's contention that the "Prayer of the Breaking" is not an original Egyptian prayer, but an import from the Syrian (and it seems Byzantine) rites.

[1181] Renaudot (1847). I. pg. 74. "to call upon the Master of all, the heavenly God, the holy Father and to say."

nal "Prayer of the Breaking" of this Liturgy. The majority of internal evidence thus far, especially the progression of the theological discussion from one prayer to another within this Liturgy, suggests, however, that this is not the original prayer.

III.V. The Second "Other Prayer of the Breaking"[1182]

This, final text in the series of "Prayers of the Breaking," is the only one of the three that is also found in the Coptic translation of this Liturgy. While the majority of the text is identical, Hammerschmidt points out three instances where the texts differ:[1183] 1. In lines 7-8 of the Greek text, instead of ποίησον ἡμᾶς λαὸν περιούσιον, βασίλειον ἱεράτευμα, ἔθνος ἅγιον, the Coptic text has (in the translation of Hammerschmidt pg. 67): "Erschaffe uns dir zu einem versammelten Volk, einem Königreich, Priestertum und heiligen Geschlecht."[1184] 2. In lines 10-11 of the Greek text, instead of: κατηξίωσας ἡμᾶς διὰ τοῦ βαπτίσματος γενέσθαι εἰς υἱοὺς καὶ κληρονόμους. The Coptic text reads (in the translation of Hammerschmidt pg. 67): "Denn du hast uns alle wegen deiner zahlreichen Barmherzigkeiten der Sohnschaft durch die heiligen Taufe würdig gemacht."[1185] 3. The final inconsistency is on line 15 of the Greek text, instead of: ἅγιον Θεόν, Πατέρα σου, the Coptic text reads (in the translation of Hammerschmidt on pg. 67): "Gott, deinen heiligen Vater..."[1186] These inconsistencies can be easily explained away as flaws in the translation rather than any revision in the text itself.

Renaudot and Hammerschmidt recognize a problem in the Greek text. Hammerschmidt points out that the phrase: ὃν προνοοῦσιν αὐτὸν, καὶ ἄνθρωπε, ὃν προθεωροῦσιν αὐτόν is "etwas umständlich"[1187] since the Alexandrian Greeks would[1188] have written this: λόγε ὃν νοοῦσιν, ἄνθρωπε ὃν θεωροῦσιν.[1189] Following this line of reasoning, Renaudot comes to the conclusion that this section was added into the Greek text secondarily.[1190] Hammerschmidtm takes a further step and proposes that this section was adopted into the Greek text following the Coptic translation: "Könnte es in diesem Fall nicht so sein, dass man sich an die koptische Konstruktion anschloss? ETOYEPNOIN

[1182] The third "Prayer of the Breaking."
[1183] Hammerschmidt (1957). pg. 156
[1184] "Make us for Yourself into a united people, one kingdom, a priesthood and a holy nation."
[1185] "For You have made us worthy, because of Your great mercy, for sonship through Holy Baptism."
[1186] "God, Your holy Father."
[1187] Hammerschmidt (1957). pg. 153. "somewhat awkward"
[1188] Or rather, should have.
[1189] Hammerschmidt (1957). pg. 153
[1190] Renaudot (1847). I. pg. 289

MMO? ist doch sehr auffällig (freilich müsste man dann annehmen, der Einschub sei in dem griechischen Text erst dann erfolgt als der koptische ihn bereits hatte)."[1191] Although an interesting theory, it is not entirely convincing. While the Greek and Coptic are very similar, it would be highly unusual, as Hammerschmidt admits, for the Greek text to be influenced by the Coptic, and it is much more likely that the Coptic is a faithful representation of the Greek. The focus of the argument presented by Renaudot and Hammerschmidt, that this text would be different in the tradition of the Alexandrian Greeks, only holds up under the assumption that this text does, in fact, have its origin in Alexandria. We have seen, however, in multiple places in this Liturgy, that the text has its origin in the Syrian rite, or, more specifically, in Cappadocia. We have also seen that the author of this Liturgy is either St. Gregory himself, or someone who attempts to simulate his style. The style of the Greek is, then, not the usual Alexandrian style, but an Atticistic Greek, in which both terms: προνοέω, which is usually found in the middle voice, just as it is presented here, and προθεωρέω are commonly used.[1192]

1. Structure

This prayer begins with an invocation of Christ, who is called, among other epithets, *Pantokrator*. The remainder of the prayer can be roughly divided into three sections: 1. the section dealing with the Eucharist; 2. the section dealing with the Lord's Prayer and 3. a transition from this prayer to the, following, Lord's Prayer.

The first portion of this prayer deals with the Eucharist. We can further subdivide it into two parts, the first which introduces first the Body, and then the Blood, and a second section, which discusses the calling forth and sanctification of the "elect." The second portion of this prayer is contingent on the Eucharist, through which humanity becomes worthy of adoption to sonship and to pray the Lord's Prayer. Contingent upon this section is the last, in which the priest transitions from the "Prayer of the Breaking" to the Lord's Prayer by begging for worthiness. The Structure of the prayer is then: Christ deems humanity worthy of partaking in the Eucharis, <u>therefore</u> humanity is able to pray the Lord's Prayer, <u>therefore</u> the congregants do so, while asking not to be condemned for this bold action. The Structure can also be seen in the following table:

[1191] Hammerschmidt (1957). pg. 153. "Could it not be in this case that one linked oneself to the Coptic translation?...is quite conspicuous (certainly one must assume that the introduction happened in the Greek after the Coptic translation already had it)."
[1192] Cf. the definitions in the Liddell and Scott.

The Commentary

Table III.V.1: the Structure of the second Εὐχὴ ἀλλὴ τῆς Κλάσεως.[1193]

The Second Alternate "Prayer of the Breaking"

Part I: The opening Invocation.
 	
1. The Core of the Invocation and the direct address of Christ: Εὐλογητὸς εἶ Χριστὲ ὁ Θεός
2. A row of four epitheta and theological expositions of Christ's nature.
    a. ὁ Παντοκράτωρ
    b. ὁ λυτρώτης τῆς ἑαυτοῦ ἐκκλησίας
    c. ὦ Λόγε ὃν προνοοῦσιν αὐτὸν
    d. καὶ ἄνθρωπε ὃν προθεωροῦσιν αὐτόν.

Part II: The exposition on the Eucharist.
 	
1. The Preparation of the Eucharist for the Church, first the establishment of the Body and then of the Blood.
    a. Ὁ διὰ τῆς ἀκαταλήπτου αὐτοῦ σαρκώσεως, ἑτοίμασας ἡμῖν ἄρτον ἐπουράνιον, τοῦτο τὸ σῶμά σου, ὃν ἔθου ἐμμυστήριον καὶ πανάγιον ἐν τοῖς ἅπασιν.
    b. Ἐκέρασας ἡμῖν ποτήριον, ἐξ ἀμπέλου ἀληθείας, ἐκ θείας καὶ ἀχράντου σου πλευρᾶς. Ὁ καὶ μετὰ δεδωκέναι τὸ πνεῦμα ἐκχέων ἐξ αὐτῆς αἷμα καὶ ὕδωρ, οἷς, ἁγιασμὸς τῷ κόσμῳ παντί.
2. The calling forth of the ‚Elect' as the Church: Κτῆσαι ἡμᾶς ἀγαθὲ Κύριε τοὺς ἀναξίους δούλους σου· ποίησον ἡμᾶς λαὸν περιούσιον βασίλειον ἱεράτευμα, ἔθνος ἅγιον.
3. A request to be sanctified as the gifts are sanctified, and a final prayer for the changing of the gifts: Ἁγίασον καὶ ἡμᾶς ὁ Θεός, ὥσπερ ἡγίασας τὰ προκείμενα καὶ ἅγια Δῶρα ταῦτα, καὶ ἐποίησας αὐτὰ ἀόρατα ἐκ τῶν ὁρατῶν μυστήρια ὧν προνοοῦσιν αὐτά σοι Κύριε ὁ Θεὸς ὁ σωτὴρ ἡμῶν Ἰησοῦς Χριστός.

[1193] Cf. Section III.3 lines 1-18. For another description of the layout of this prayer see: Hammerschmidt (1957). pg. 152-153

Part III: The introduction to the Lord's Prayer.

1. The elevation to the status of sons and heirs through the Eucharist: Σὺ οὖν Κύριε διὰ τῆς πολλῆς σου εὐσπλαγχνίας, κατηξίωσας ἡμᾶς διὰ τοῦ βαπτίσματος γένεσθαι εἰς υἱοὺς καὶ κληρονόμους.
2. The teaching of the Lord's Prayer to the apostles: Ἐδίδαξας ἡμᾶς τὸν τύπον τῆς προσευχῆς ὅς ἐστὶν ἐμμυστήριος, τοῦ προσεύχεσθαι ἐν αὐτῇ τὸν ἄχραντόν σου Πατέρα.

Part IV: The transition to the Lord's Prayer.

1. Request that, through the teaching of Christ and through the Eucharist, the worshippers may pray the Lord's Prayer without condemnation: Σὺ οὖν καὶ νῦν Δέσποτα Κύριε καταξίωσον ἡμᾶς, ἐν ἁγιασμένῃ συνειδήσει, καὶ λογισμῷ ἀγαθῷ ὃν πρέπει τοῖς υἱοις καὶ ἐν θεικῷ πόθῳ,[1194] καὶ παρρησίᾳ ἀγαθῇ τολμᾶν ἐπικαλεῖσθαι τὸν ἐν τοῖς οὐρανοῖς ἅγιον Θεόν Πατέρα σου καὶ λέγειν.

2. Function
1. (Section III.4 lines 2-3): Εὐλογητὸς εἶ Χριστὲ ὁ Θεός ὁ Παντοκράτωρ ὁ λυτρώτης τῆς ἑαυτοῦ ἐκκλησίας· ὦ Λόγε ὃν προνοοῦσιν αὐτόν, καὶ ἄνθρωπε, ὃν προθεωροῦσιν αὐτόν.

    The first aspect of this prayer that strikes the reader is the opening invocation, since, while it does follow the standard of direct addresses of Christ, it is structured differently than most other prayers in this Liturgy. We have seen a number of ways in which the author begins his prayers: 1. usually he begins with a stock phrase such as Δέσποτα, Κύριε, Ἰησοῦ Χριστὲ, and continues his discussion from that point; 2. when the theological message of the prayer outweighs the need to underscore Christ's place as God, the author begins with a short summation of the topic of the prayer, as we saw in the Οὐδεὶς ἄξιος of the "Prayer of the Veil."[1195] While this prayer falls under the first category of opening, this

---

[1194] as reconstructed by Renaudot.
[1195] Section I.4 line 2.

seems to be the only time the phrase "Blessed are you, Christ our God," is used in the Liturgy, certainly the only time it is used as an opening.

The phrase: ὁ λυτρώτης τῆς ἑαυτοῦ ἐκκλησίας is the first textual evidence that this prayer was written by the original author of the Liturgy. This phrase foreshadows the discussion of the calling forth and hallowing of the Church from among the nations in the second portion of this prayer. Such foreshadowing and intratextual allusion are a hallmark of this author.[1196]

The final two phrases of this portion of the Liturgy: ὦ Λόγε ὃν προνοοῦσιν αὐτὸν, καὶ ἄνθρωπε ὃν προθεωροῦσιν αὐτόν are difficult to understand. Fortunately, Hammerschmidt and Renaudot both speculate as to the meaning of the text:

> Der Sinn der Stelle ist: Christus als Logos, als Wort Gottes kann nur mit dem Geist erfasst werden, seiner menschlichen Natur hingegen ist er auch für das sinnliche Auge sichtbar. Nach Renaudot[1197] haben verschiedene orientalische Kommentatoren die Stelle so ausgelegt, dass di Apostel Christus mit den leiblichen Augen nur nach seiner menschlichen Natur sehen konnten und die Gottheit nur mit den Augen des Geistes erfassten. Ebenso sollen die Christen beim Empfang der Eucharistie, wenn sie mit den leiblichen Augen blosses Brot und Wein wahrnehmen, mit dem inneren Auge des Glaubens die Gottheit Christi erfassen, die unter den Gestalten von Brot und Wein verborgen liegt.[1198]

Hammerschmidt goes on to say that this is a proof for the "Glauben an die Realpräsenz in der ägyptischen Kirche"[1199] This does not necessarily have to be interpreted in the context of Egyptian theology, especially if the phrasing does not fit the Greek used in Alexandria, since this fits into the larger world of eastern theology as well. As such, these phrases can be another example showing that the prayer was written either by Gregory himself, or by an author attempting to pass himself off as Gregory.

[1196] Such as the intratextual link in the use of the term homoousios in the "Prayer of the Veil" and the "Prayer of the Bowing of the Head."

[1197] Cf. Renaudot (1847) I. pg. 289

[1198] Hammerschmidt (1957). pg. 153. "The sense here is: Christ as the Logos, as the Word of God can only be grasped using the spirit, with His human nature, however, He is also visible to the eye of the senses. Following Renaudot, various oriental commentators have laid out the text, that the Apostles could only see Christ according to His human nature with their eyers and only His godhead with the eyes of the spirit. In the same way the Christian should, when receiving the Eucharist, when they see only bread and wine with the bodily eyes, understand the godhead of Christ with their spiritual eyes, which are hidden in the form of the bread and wine."

[1199] Ibid. "Belief in the real presence in the Egyptian Church."

It is these two phrases that lay the foundation for the increasing focus on the Incarnation in the two subsequently added prayers. Here though, the Incarnation is not the focus of the prayer, but serves rather to underscore the true purpose of such a prayer, the preparation for the Eucharist.

2. (Section III.4 lines 3-5): Ὁ διὰ τῆς ἀκαταλήπτου αὐτοῦ σαρκώσεως, ἑτοίμασας ἡμῖν ἄρτον ἐπουράνιον, τοῦτο τὸ σῶμα σου, ὃν ἔθου ἐμμυστήριον καὶ πανάγιον ἐν τοῖς ἅπασιν.

This section establishes the focus of the prayer, on the Eucharist. If we accept the explanation that Hammerschmit provides for the previous section, we can also interpret this as a continuation of this thought. What was hinted at in the last section, that the true Body of Christ is to be seen in the mundane form of the bread, is here explicitly stated. This is also done by a clever substitution, by using the demonstrative τοῦτο when discussing the Body of Christ, the author emphasizes the presence of this Body as the true reality of what is seen when looking at the bread, one can imagine the priest gesturing toward the bread while he says these words, further emphasizing the connection between the Body and the bread.

The mystery of the transformation of the bread into the Body of Christ is termed ἐμμυστήριον by the author,[1200] a term which he uses again while discussing the Lord's Prayer: τύπον τῆς προσευχῆς ὅς ἐστὶν ἐμμυστήριος, by using this same term, the author links the mystery of the Eucharist with the recitation of the Lord's Prayer, in a certain sense equating the two as an inseprable part of the Christian identity.

3. (Section III.4 lines 5-7): Ἐκέρασας ἡμῖν ποτήριον, ἐξ ἀμπέλου ἀληθείας, ἐκ θείας καὶ ἀχράντου σου πλευρᾶς. Ὁ καὶ μετὰ δεδωκέναι τὸ πνεῦμα ἐκχέων ἐξ αὐτῆς αἷμα καὶ ὕδωρ, οἷς ἁγιασμὸς τῷ κόσμῳ παντί.

In this section the author underscores the reality of the presence of Christ's Blood as the wine by purposely confusing the origin of what fills the cup: ἐξ ἀμπέλου ἀληθείας, ἐκ θείας καὶ ἀχράντου σου πλευρᾶς. We cannot be sure if the cup is filled for us from the vine, or from "Your sacred and spotless sides." The following phrase: ὁ καὶ μετὰ δεδωκέναι τὸ πνεῦμα ἐκχέων ἐξ αὐτῆς αἷμα καὶ ὕδωρ, οἷς ἁγιασμὸς τῷ κόσμῳ παντί, is not only a short phrase describing the salvation of humanity through the Cross, but again underscores the "true presence" of Christ in the Eucharist, wine and water flowed from the

---

[1200] The author also terms the transformation: καὶ πανάγιον ἐν τοῖς ἅπασιν, this term "all holy in all things," which seems to mean (and Hammerschmidt agrees, Cf. Hammerschmidt (1957) pg. 153): "the holiest of the holy."

side of Christ when he was stabbed by the Roman soldier, wine and water are also the elements used in the preparation of the Eucharist.

The final phrase of this section: οἷς ἁγιασμὸς τῷ κόσμῳ παντί foreshadows the following section, which deals with the selection and calling forth of the Church. While this section promises that the Blood of Christ, shed on the Cross, is meant for the salvation of the whole world, by which creation is meant, the next section discusses what part of humanity receives salvation, that is, the "elect."

4. (Section III.4 lines 8-9): Κτῆσαι ἡμᾶς ἀγαθὲ Κύριε, τοὺς ἀναξίους δούλους σου· ποίησον ἡμᾶς λαὸν περιούσιον, βασίλειον ἱεράτευμα, ἔθνος ἅγιον.

The author continues his discussion of salvation here. It is no longer the entire world that is saved, however, but a request is made to transform "us" into a λαὸν περιούσιον, βασίλειον ἱεράτευμα, ἔθνος ἅγιον. The author makes a distinction then, between the potential salvation, which is "for the entire cosmos" and actual salvation, which works among "us." This discussion is, then, the calling forth of the Church.

The author of the second "Prayer of the Breaking" did not only continue and expand upon the theological exposition on the Incarnation, he also makes an intertextual link with the original prayer by taking specific phrases and topics found in the rest of the prayer. This section corresponds to: καὶ προσκαλεσάμενος ἑαυτῷ ἐκ πάντων τῶν ἐθνῶν, γένος ἐκλεκτὸν, βασίλειον ἱεράτευμα, ἔθνος ἅγιον, λαὸν εἰς περιποίησιν in the second prayer, which shows the emphasis on the Church in salvation even more strongly than this section does. That there is a larger connection between the two prayers, other than the exposition on the Incarnation, suggests that the author of the second prayer meant to replace the third prayer with one that would have been recognizeable for a congregation used to the third prayer, showing that the second prayer was not only meant as a theological discussion in the form of a prayer, but to be used liturgically, perhaps even as an alternate.

The use of: κτησάμενος ἡμᾶς ἑατῷ λαὸν περιούσιον, βασίλειον ἱεράτευμα, ἔθνος ἅγιον[1201] in the Liturgy of St. Basil, brings up the question: is there an intertextual connection between these two prayers, and if so, which Liturgy has the allusion and which is being alluded to? We have seen a number of other places where these two Liturgies coincide, thus far the Liturgy of St. Basil has adopted more from Liturgy of St. Gregory.[1202] It seems, however, that there is no need to assume any intertextual connection here, since Liturgy often makes use of stock phrases, it is quite possible that two authors would use

---

[1201] Hammond and Brightman (1896). pg. 404. "acquiring us for Himself as a people set apart, a royal priesthood, a holy nation."
[1202] The 'Prayer of the Veil,' for example.

almost identical phrases in similar contexts without one of them necessarily making a direct connection with the other.

5. (Section III.4 lines 9-11): Ἁγίασον καὶ ἡμᾶς ὁ Θεός, ὥσπερ ἡγίασας τὰ προκείμενα καὶ ἅγια Δῶρα ταῦτα, καὶ ἐποίησας αὐτὰ ἀόρατα ἐκ τῶν ὁρατῶν μυστήρια ὧν προνοοῦσιν αὐτά σοι Κύριε ὁ Θεὸς ὁ σωτὴρ ἡμῶν Ἰησοῦς Χριστός.

Here we see another theme taken up by the author of the previous prayer, the sanctification of the congregant in the same way that the gifts are sanctified. This section corresponds to the: ἀλλ᾽ ὥσπερ τὰ πανάγιά σου τίμια Δῶρα ταῦτα πάσης ἁγιωσύνης ἐμπλῆσαι κατηξίωσας, διὰ τῆς ἐπιφοιτήσεως τοῦ παναγίου σου Πνεύματος ἐπ᾽ αὐτῶν. Οὕτως καὶ ἡμῶν τῶν ἁμαρτωλῶν δούλων σου, ἁγιάσαι καταξίωσον τὰς ψυχάς, τὰ σώματα, τὰς συνειδήσεις of the previous prayer. Two differences stand out between these two texts. Interesting to note is that the author of this prayer does not mention the working of the Holy Spirit in the transformation of the gifts for the Eucharist, while the author of the secondary prayer does, following the form of an *epiklesis*. This discrepancy may be the result of the differing purposes of these two texts. This text fits into the purpose of the work as a whole, to underscore the role of Christ in the Trinity and to combat the Arians, this is often done by emphasizing Christ to the exclusion of other members of the Trinity.[1203] The second prayer, however, follows through with the de-emphasis of the Father, but does not do the same with the Spirit.

The theological significance of the following section: καὶ ἐποίησας αὐτὰ ἀόρατα ἐκ τῶν ὁρατῶν is explained by Hammerschmidt:

> Der Sinn ist nach dem Gesagten ziemlich klar: Brot und Wein sind die Opfergaben, die mit den Sinnen (des Gesichts) wahrgenommen werden können. Nach der Wandlung (gleichgültig nun, ob diese nach koptischer Auffassung durch den Einsetzungsbericht, durch die Epiklese oder aber auch durch beide zusammen vollzogen sind) ist unter den Opfergaben Christus mit seinem verklärten Leib gegenwärtig. Diese Tatsache kann aber nur mehr mit den Augen des Glaubens wahgenommen werden, ist also für das leibliche Auge unfassbar.[1204]

[1203] Though the Holy Spirit is less often excluded than the Father, since this Liturgy is meant to combat the Arian oftshoots, such as the Macedonians as well.

[1204] Hammerschmidt (1957). pg. 155. "The sense is, following what is said, quite clear: bread and wine are the offering that can be comprehended with the senses (of the face). After the transformation (whether this is done, following the Coptic belief, through the Consecration, through the *epiklesis*, or through both together) Christ is made present among the offerings. This can only be understood with the eyes of faith, and is invisible to the bodily eye."

The Commentary

Hammerschmidt's interpretation is literal and departs from the ability of the communicant to see the bread and wine and not see the Body and Blood. While this interpretation picks up on the idea presented at the very beginning of this prayer, which discusses the Incarnation in terms of humans being able to perceive Christ as Logos and as man. The phrase can, however, also simply be interpreted as "heavenly from earthly," as the phrase "the visible and invisible" is used in the Creed to describe the creation of the heavenly and earthly parts of Creation. Calling the bread "earthly" also hinges on the Eucharist as an offering of all creation. The sense of the passage may be the same using both interpretations, it is where the ability of humanity to see comes in that changes, the interpretation of Hammerschmidt it is the ability to see the bread and wine, in the second interpretation it is the ability to see the earthly vs. the inability to see the heavenly.

It is possible that both of these interpretations must be used to truly understand this portion of the text, this would explain the section that follows: μυστήρια, ὧν προνοοῦσιν, the term μυστήρια means both mystery, since it is impossible for humans to know how the bread and wine become the body and blood, and sacrament, which supports the interpretation of "heavenly and earthly" and its implications of a sacrifice of all creation. The term: προνοοῦσιν is a direct quote from the beginning of this prayer, which discusses the ability of humans to perceive Christ as Logos, supporting the contention that the "invisible from the visible" deals directly with the ability of humans to perceive.

The final part of this section: αὐτά σοι, Κύριε ὁ Θεός, ὁ σωτὴρ ἡμῶν Ἰησοῦς Χριστός is also difficult to interpret. It seems, however, that the αὐτά is the object of the ἐποίησας from the line above, the whole line being interpreted as: "and make these things unseen from seen, make them a mystery, which they perceived beforehand, make them for You, Lord our God, our Savior Jesus Christ." Christ is the end and means of the liturgical worship. Here Christ is portrayed as the High Priest, He offers the gifts. He is also God, therefore He offers them to Himself, and is the one who transforms them into the Body and Blood, the invisible from the visible.

6. (Section III.4 lines 11-13): Σὺ οὖν Κύριε διὰ τῆς πολλῆς σου εὐσπλαγχνίας, κατηξίωσας ἡμᾶς διὰ τοῦ βαπτίσματος γενέσθαι εἰς υἱοὺς καὶ κληρονόμους.

Here the prayer switches its focus from the Eucharist to the Lord's Prayer. The image of adoption used to show the connection of worshipper to God, through which the worshipper attains the worthiness to recite the Lord's Prayer. In the next section, the recitation of the prayer is said to be: πρέπει τοῖς υἱοῖς.[1205] It is interesting, though, the focus is here

---

[1205] Reconstructed so by Renaudot/Migne.

on the sacrament of Baptism, rather than the Eucharist. The context of the prayer calls for a focus on the Eucharist, however, and there seems to be no other "Prayer of the Breaking" in which a sacrament other thant the Eucharist is mentioned. Perhaps the author is using the sacrament of Baptism to allude to the Eucharist, Baptism is, after all, the prerequisite for receiving the Eucharist, and it is at their Baptism that the newly baptized recieves the Eucharist for the first time. The author may have written the prayer in this way that the transition from the Eucharist to the Lord's Prayer, and, while directly speaking about neither, alludes to both. To the Eucharist through the sacrament of Baptism and to the Lord's Prayer by an intratextual allusion to a later part of the prayer.

7. (Section III.4 lines 13-14): Ἐδίδαξας ἡμᾶς τὸν τύπον τῆς προσευχῆς ὅς ἐστιν ἐμμυστήριος, τοῦ προσεύχεσθαι ἐν αὐτῇ τὸν ἄχραντόν σου Πατέρα.

The word ἐμμυστήριος here was already used by the author while discussing the Eucharist: τοῦτο τὸ σῶμά σου, ὃν ἔθου ἐμμυστήριον. The double use of this word links the discussion of the Eucharist with that of the Lord's Prayer, marking the recitation of the Lord's Prayer as a sacrament, a mystery. This section also discusses Christ teaching "us" the Lord's Prayer in order to be able to pray to the Father. This is another section which shows the connection between this, original, prayer, and the second prayer, which discusses Christ teaching the prayer to His apostles and disciples. This focus on Christ serves to curb the presence of the Father in this prayer, and is unique to this Liturgy. The author wishes to keep to the overall theme, underscoring Christ as God, and he does so by emphasizing Him over the other members of the Trinity, especially the Father. So even in a transition to a prayer directed entirely to the Father, Christ role must be defined and defended.

8. (Section III.4 lines 14-17): Σὺ οὖν καὶ νῦν Δέσποτα Κύριε καταξίωσον ἡμᾶς, ἐν ἡγιασμένῃ συνειδήσει, καὶ λογισμῷ ἀγαθῷ ὃν πρέπει τ...καὶ ἐν θε...πόθῳ[1206] καὶ παρρησίᾳ ἀγαθῇ τολμᾶν ἐπικαλεῖσθαι τὸν ἐν τοῖς οὐρανοῖς ἅγιον Θεόν Πατέρα σου καὶ λέγειν.

The focus on Christ, in spite of transitioning to a prayer directed solely to the Father, is continued here. It is Christ who deems worthy to recite the prayer, and the prayer is directed to Πατέρα σου rather than to just the Πατέρα. Other than this discrepancy, the transitional part of this prayer looks much like in other "Prayers of the Breaking." The congregants ask to be deemed worthy of reciting the prayer, and to be able to do so in purity, this is expressed in row of descriptions: ἐν ἡγιασμένῃ συνειδήσει, καὶ λογισμῷ ἀγαθῷ,...ἐν θεικῷ πόθῳ καὶ παρρησίᾳ ἀγαθῇ this is necessary because calling upon God

---

[1206] τοῖς υἱοῖς, καὶ ἐν θεικῷ πόθῳ is interpolated by Ren/Migne.

the Father directly is not something to be done lightly, the congregants "dare," τολμᾶν, to do this only at this point in the Liturgy, because they have finally reached a state of purity through the various "Prayers of Access" and of purification that have been recited thus far. This is expressed by the author through another intratextual allusion. The πάντα λογισμὸν αἰσχρόν τε καὶ ἀσύνετον, which the priest prayed to be turned away from him in the first prayer of this Liturgy is now turned into a λογισμῷ ἀγαθῷ, the wickedness of the fallen world has been turned into holiness during the course of the Liturgy, and the worshippers are worthy now of both the Lord's Prayer and to participate in the Eucharist.

III.VI. The Prayer following the Lord's Prayer

Following the recitation of the Lord's Prayer, a number of liturgies insert another prayer before moving on. This prayer seems to originate in the Syrian rite, and to enter from there into the Egyptian family of liturgies. In the Syrian Liturgy of St. James, for example, the following prayer is found:

> Yea, o Lord our God, lead us not into temptation which we are not able to bear but make with the temptation also a way of escape that we may be able to bear it, and deliver us from evil: by Christ Jesus our Lord through whom and with whom to thee is fitting glory and honour and dominion with thy Spirit allholy and good and adorable and lifegiving and consubstantial with thee now and ever and world without end[1207]

This prayer, as we see, consists of the last two phrases from the Lord's Prayer "lead us not into temptation" and "deliver us from evil" interspersed with additional requests for relief from temptation and followed by an *ekphonesis*. A similar prayer is found in the Coptic Liturgy of St. Mark:

> Yea, we beseech thee, o Lord our God, lead none of us into temptation which we are not able to bear by reason of our weakness but with the temptation give us also the way of escape that we may be able to quench all the fiery kindled darts of the enemy, and deliver us from the evil one and his works: in Christ our Lord through whom *and the rest.*[1208]

[1207] Hammond and Brightman (1896). pg. 100 and Day (1972). pg. 189.
[1208] Hammond and Brightman (1896). pg. 182

There can be no doubt that these two prayers are related, as the Egyptian version is nearly identical to the Syrian, with only a few phrases, such as "that we may be able to quench all the fiery kindled darts of the enemy" that separate the two.

While the Greek Liturgies of the Syrian and Egyptian rites also have similar prayers,[1209] it seems that the Byzantine Liturgies of Sts. Basil and Chrysostom (in the ninth century) did not, but did share a similar *ekphonesis*: ὅτι σοῦ ἐστιν ἡ βασιλεία καὶ ἡ δύναμις καὶ ἡ δόξα τοῦ Πατρὸς καὶ τοῦ Υἱοῦ καὶ τοῦ ἁγίου Πνεύματος νῦν καὶ ἀεὶ καὶ εἰς τοὺς αἰῶνας τῶν αἰώνων.[1210] Since this *ekphonesis* is so similiar to the *ekphoneseis* we see in this post-Lord's Prayer prayer, and since the Byzantine rite is so well documented, without this prayer, we can postulate that this prayer was inserted between the Lord's Prayer and the *ekphonesis* secondarily.

The Greek Liturgy of St. Gregory contains a prayer of this type, but that does not seem to be derivative of the prayer found in the Syrian Liturgy of St. James, as it neither quotes the last two phrases of the Lord's Prayer nor asks for temptation to be transformed. This could lead to the conclusion that this liturgy is an independant liturgy of the Syrian rite. The structure of this prayer in the Greek text of the Liturgy of St. Gregory, however, does not conform to the standard of the Syrian rite, as can be seen in a comparison with the text of the Syrian Liturgy of St. Gregory:

> Ita, mansuete, ne adducas super nos tentationem eam cuius pondus ferre non possimus, sed per misericordiam tuam paternam corripe adoratores tuos, Domine, et libera et eripe nos a malo et a viribus ei subiectis, quoniam tuum est imperium et tu es rex saeculorum, et tibi gloriam referimus et unigenito Filio tuo et Spiritui Sancto, nunc.[1211]

When looking at other Syrian liturgies we often see the same Structure, for example the *Liturgia Minor Sancti Jacobi*: Domine, ne inducas nos in tentationem, etc. et referemus tibi gloriam et gratiarum actionem et unigenito.[1212]

[1209] Including the quotation of the last two phrases of the Lord's Prayer, the prayer for relief from temptation and the *ekphonesis*.

[1210] Hammond and Brightman (1896). pg. 392. "For Yours is the kingdom and the power and the glory of the Father and the Son and the Holy Spirit now and ever and to the ages of ages."

[1211] Anaphorae Syriacae (1941). pp. 149, 151. "Therefore, tame, and do not give to us temptation, which we cannot bear, but on account of Your fatherly mercy, gather up those who adore You, Lord, and deliver and save us from evil and from men who wish to subject us. For Yours is the power and You are the king of ages, and to You we send up glory and to Your onlybegotten Son and to the Holy Spirit, now."

[1212] Renaudot (1847) 2. pg. 131. "Lord do not lead us into temptation, etc…and we send up to You glory and thanksgiving as wells as to Your onlybegotten."

The Commentary

The differences between this prayer in the Liturgy of St. Gregory and in the other Liturgies can be explained another way. An extended version of the ending of the prayer from the Greek-Egyptian Liturgy of St. Mark seems to be inserted into the Liturgy of St. Gregory.

Table 6.1: The similarities between the Liturgies of Sts. Gregory and Mark.

1. The Liturgy of St. Gregory the Theologian[1213]	2. The Liturgy of St. Mark[1214]
Ναὶ, Κύριε Κύριε <u>ὁ δεδωκὼς ἡμῖν τὴν ἐξουσίαν τοῦ πατεῖν ἐπάνω ὄφεων καὶ σκορπιῶν, καὶ ἐπὶ πᾶσαν τὴν δύναμιν τοῦ ἐχθροῦ</u>, σύντριψον καὶ καθυπόταξον τὰς κεφαλὰς τῶν ἐχθρῶν ἡμῶν ὑπὸ τοὺς πόδας ἐν τάχει. Καὶ πᾶσαν τὴν κακότεχνον αὐτῶν ἐπίνοιαν, τὴν καθ' ἡμῶν διασκέδασον.	Σὺ γὰρ ἔδωκας ἡμῖν ἐξουσίαν πατεῖν ἐπάνω ὄφεων καὶ σκορπίων, καὶ ἐπὶ πᾶσαν τὴν δύναμιν τοῦ ἐχθροῦ.

We must conclude, then, that the Greek text of this prayer was inserted into the Liturgy of St. Gregory secondarily, following the model of the Liturgy of St. Mark. This conclusion is supported by the fact that, while this prayer does appear in the Coptic translation of the Liturgy, it does not seem to be the same prayer. Unfortunately the prayer is only extant in fragments, but only one of these fragments could have come from the Greek text. The text, according to Hammerschmidt is: "Der Priester spricht: Ja, Herr, Herr...Du, Herr...Herr, Herr..."[1215] The first "Yes, Lord, Lord..." may reflect the opening of the Greek text, but this is the only place in the text where the word Κύριε is used. From the few words remaining in the Coptic text then, we can conclude that the Coptic and Greek texts of these prayers do not contain the same prayers, since the "Yes, Lord, Lord..." beginning seems to be a standard opening to this prayer, used in a number of Liturgies. Since we have seen that the Coptic and Greek texts tend to correspond closely, this discrepancy, coupled with the similarity between the prayer in the Liturgy of St. Gregory and the text in the Lit-

---

[1213] Section III.5 lines 1-8.
[1214] Hammond and Brightman (1896). pg. 136 and Cuming (1990). pg. 50.
[1215] "The priest says: Yes, Lord, Lord...You, Lord...Lord, Lord."

urgy of St. Mark makes it very likely that this prayer was originally not part of this Liturgy.[1216] This has an important consequence for finding the origin of this liturgy, since the majority of Syrian and Egyptian liturgies contain this prayer, the fact that this liturgy does not is a strong indication that it belongs to the family of liturgies that does not contain this prayer, the Byzantine family.

1. Structure

This prayer is divided into three parts. The first part is built around the usual direct address of Christ, which is expanded with the quotation from the Liturgy of St. Mark. The second section refers back to the first, this time requesting that Christ fulfill the description of Him given in the first section. Finally the priest gives the usual, though slightly modified, *ekphonesis*. The Structure can also be seen in the following table:

Figure I.VI.1: the structure of the Prayer following the Lord's Prayer.[1217]

The Prayer following the Lord's Prayer

1. Opening and the direct address of Christ:
   a. The Direct Address: Ναὶ Κύριε Κύριε
 	
   b. The extension of the direct address: ὁ δεδωκὼς ἡμῖν τὴν ἐξουσίαν τοῦ πατεῖν ἐπάνω ὄφεων καὶ σκορπιῶν, καὶ ἐπὶ πᾶσαν τὴν δύναμιν τοῦ ἐχθροῦ,

2. Request that Christ fulfill His description from above:
   a. That the "enemy" be subjected: σύντριψον καὶ καθυπόταξον τὰς κεφαλὰς τῶν ἐχθρῶν ἡμῶν ὑπὸ τοὺς πόδας ἐν τάχει.
 	
   b. That the enemy's plans be thwarted: Καὶ πᾶσαν τὴν κακότεχνον αὐτῶν ἐπίνοιαν, τὴν καθ' ἡμῶν διασκέδασον.

[1216] We must also conclude that the addition of the prayer into the Greek text must have been rather late, and must have occured well after the translation of the Greek text into Coptic. This may even be an instance in which the Coptic translation influenced the original Greek text, and the text was added to standardize the Greek text as an Egyptian Liturgy, after the Coptic text had already been so changed.
[1217] Cf. Section III.5 lines 1-8.

> 3. The *ekphonesis*:
>   a. Second direct address of Christ: Ὅτι σὺ εἶ βασιλεὺς ἡμετέρων πάντων Χριστὲ ὁ Θεός·
>   b. The "sending up" to Christ: καὶ σοι τὴν δόξαν καὶ τὴν εὐχαριστείαν, καὶ τὴν προσκύνησιν ἀναπέμπομεν, καθ' ἑκάστην ἡμέραν,
>   c. The Trinitarian formula: σὺν τῷ ἀνάρχῳ σου Πατρί καὶ τῷ ἁγίῳ Πνεύματι, νῦν.

2. Function

1. (Section III.5 lines 2-5): Ναὶ Κύριε Κύριε, ὁ δεδωκὼς ἡμῖν τὴν ἐξουσίαν τοῦ πατεῖν ἐπάνω ὄφεων καὶ σκορπιῶν, καὶ ἐπὶ πᾶσαν τὴν δύναμιν τοῦ ἐχθροῦ, σύντριψον καὶ καθυπόταξον τὰς κεφαλὰς τῶν ἐχθρῶν ἡμῶν ὑπὸ τοὺς πόδας ἐν τάχει. Καὶ πᾶσαν τὴν κακότεχνον αὐτῶν ἐπίνοιαν, τὴν καθ' ἡμῶν διασκέδασον.

This section begins with the "Yes, Lord," which we have seen begins this type of prayer in most Liturgies. Following this opening is a quotation from the Gospel of Luke 10:19. This section is also a quotation from the final part of the corresponding prayer in the Greek-Egyptian Liturgy of St. Mark.

The prayer continues with an appeal to Christ to fulfill the description given of Him by the priest in the first part of the prayer. He is describes as the one who makes it possible to tread upon the enemy, and here the priest prays that Christ truly do this. This is also a reference to Romans 16:20.

The final portion of this section asks Christ to "scatter to the winds every evil plan of theirs which is aimed against us." If we continue the interpretation of this text in light of this prayer in other Egyptian and Syrian Liturgies, the "evil plan" can be equated with the: "...give us also the way of escape that we may be able to quench all the fiery kindled darts of the enemy, and deliver us from the evil one and his works..." in the Coptic Liturgy of St. Mark.[1218] This is further an allusion to Ephesians 6:16. We see from this as well, that the text in this Liturgy is compiled from this prayer in various other Liturgies, and certainly not original to this text.

[1218] Hammond and Brightman (1896). pg. 182 a similar prayer is found in Day (1972). pg. 96: "We also pray you, O good Father, lover of goodness, that we may not be led into temptation nor become subject to the dominion of sin, but that we may be delivered from all evil. Rebuke the devil who tempts us and may all occasions of sin be removed from us, through your holy power. *(Aloud:)* Through Jesus Christ our Lord."

2. (Section III.5 lines 6-8): Ὅτι σὺ εἶ βασιλεὺς ἡμετέρων πάντων Χριστὲ ὁ Θεός· καὶ σοι τὴν δόξαν καὶ τὴν εὐχαριστείαν, καὶ τὴν προσκύνησιν ἀναπέμπομεν, καθ᾽ ἑκάστην ἡμέραν, σὺν τῷ ἀνάρχῳ σου Πατρί, καὶ τῷ ἁγίῳ Πνεύματι, νῦν.

The *ekphonesis* of this prayer shows its origin in the Syrian Liturgy of St. James. Both begin the *ekphonesis* with an invocation of Christ. The Liturgy of St. James begins: "...by Christ Jesus our Lord..."[1219] The Liturgy of St. Gregory reopens the prayer: Ὅτι σὺ εἶ βασιλεὺς ἡμετέρων πάντων Χριστὲ ὁ Θεός. This reworking of the Syrian form is to be expected in this Liturgy, we have seen a similar reworking on a number of occasions, where prayers from other sources are adapted to fit into the framework of the Liturgy of St. Gregory.

The *ekphonesis* still maintains the semblance of the other *ekphoneseis*, especially that of the Syrian Liturgy of St. James, which shares a number of features with this Liturgy: here Christ is addressed as "king." That the Trinity also has the "glory" is reflected in this text as well, in which "glory" is one of the offerings sent up to Christ. The greatest difference is that offerings are sent up Christ, rather than just being a list of things belonging to the Trinity. Secondly, what is being sent up differs from the standard, not only, "kingdom," "power" and "glory," but δόξαν καὶ τὴν εὐχαριστείαν, καὶ τὴν προσκύνησιν. A similar formulation is also seen in the Syrian Liturgy of St. James: "by Christ Jesus our Lord through whom and with whom to thee is fitting glory and honour and dominion with thy Spirit..."[1220]

The Trinitarian formula also differs from the standard text of this *ekphonesis*. The genitive construction: τοῦ Πατρὸς καὶ τοῦ Υἱοῦ καὶ τοῦ ἁγίου Πνεύματος is replaced by a dative prepositional phrase: σὺν τῷ ἀνάρχῳ σου Πατρί, καὶ τῷ ἁγίῳ Πνεύματι. The third member of the Trinity, Christ, is missing from this formula, since Christ is emphasized at the beginning of the *ekphonesis* leaving him out of the Trinitarian forumla serves to underscore His importance in the Liturgy.

III.VII. The "Prayer of the Bowing of the Head"

This prayer is something of a problem, since the text is found only in the Greek, and not in the Coptic translation, the Coptic liturgy jumps from the Lord's Prayer immediately to the preparation and reception of the Eucharist.[1221] One possibility for this discrepancy is that this prayer would be contained within the *crux* from lines 348-351. This does

---

[1219] Hammond and Brightman (1896). pg. 100 and Day (1972). pg. 189
[1220] Hammond and Brightman (1896). pg. 100 and Day (1972). pg. 189
[1221] Cf. Hammerschmidt (1957). pg. 69

not seem to be the case, however, as the lines in Hammerschmidt's text are not long enough to contain the amount of text in the *crux* that would be necessary for this prayer, especially since the first line at least must correspond to the "Prayer following the Lord's Prayer." The lack of this prayer in the Coptic text is puzzling, since both the Greek-Egyptian and the Coptic liturgical families have a "Prayer of the Bowing of the Head" here.[1222]

When dealing with a prayer that is in the Greek, but not in the Coptic text, the first question we must answer is: was the prayer added secondarily to the Greek? Since, however, this prayer seems to be present in the Egyptian liturgical families, we must look outside of Egypt for examples of Liturgies without a "Prayer of the Bowing of the Head" where this prayer is lacking, and the influence of which could account for the Liturgy of St. Gregory originally not having this prayer. Looking first to the Syrian liturgies, we see that these liturgies too have such a prayer in the same place, both the Syrian liturgies and the Greek-Syrian liturgies. In the Syrian Liturgy of St. James we see, for example:

> To thee thy servants bow down their heads awaiting the rich mercies which come from thee. Send, o Lord, the rich blessings which come from thee and sanctify our souls and bodies and spirits that we may be worthy to partake of the body and blood of Christ our Saviour: by the grace and mercies and love toward mankind of Christ Jesus our Lord with whome thou art blessed and glorified in heaven and on earth with thy Spirit all-holy and good and adorable and lifegiving and consubstantial with thee now and ever and world without end.[1223]

The same prayer in the Syrian Liturgy of St. Gregory reads as follows:

> Tibi igitur et ante te supplicatur haereditas tua, Domine, et a serenitate tua poscit indulgentiam debitorum suorum et remissionem omnium transgressionum suarum. ‚Sanctifica' omnes nos ‚in veritate' tua; lustra cogitationes servorum tuorum; custodi oves gregis tui ut eucharistiam hanc spiritualem mereatur sine labe et macula recipere, dum per eam absumis tu potius omne genus iniquitatis et reliquias eorum quae a nobis inique gesta sunt, per gratiam et per misericordiam et per philanthropiam unigeniti Filii tui, quocum tibi con-

---

[1222] Cf. Hammond and Brightman (1896). pp. 137 and 183
[1223] Hammond and Brightman (1896). pg. 100-101 and Day (1972). pg. 189.

venit gloria et honor et potestas cum Spiritu tuo sanctissimo et bono et vivificanti tibique consubstantiali, nunc.[1224]

We see then that the Syrian rite cannot serve as a model for a Liturgy that does not contain a "Prayer of the Bowing of the Head." We see too, that the Byzantine rite cannot serve as an example either. As both the Liturgies of St. Basil and of St. John Chrysostom have such a prayer, so we see in the Liturgy of St. Basil.

The Liturgy of the Armenians, which is also part of the Byzantine liturgical family also has a prayer of this type, one that interests us, as it is not addressed to the Father, but to the Holy Spirit:

> Holy Ghost which art the fountain of life and the spring of mercy, have mercy on this people which bowed down adoreth thy godhead: keep them entire and stamp upon their hearts the posture of their bodies for the inheritance and possession of good things to come...Through Jesus Christ our Lord with whom to thee, o Holy Ghost, and the Father almighty glory dominion and honour is fitting now and ever and world without end. Amen.[1225]

This type of prayer is, then, common in most liturgical families, and, since the Liturgy of St. Gregory is not an original Egyptian prayer, but one that was introduced into Egypt from the West Syrian i.e Cappadocian rite, it is almost certain that the the prayer is original to the Greek text. The question as to why is there no corresponding prayer in the Coptic text, remains however, and must be answered.

A possible answer is seen in the Egyptian rite. We have noted that all three major liturgies of the Egyptian rite in Greek contain such a prayer, as does the Coptic Liturgy of St. Mark. There is, however, some indication that this prayer may not be original to the Coptic rite, but may have been a later addition.

There are two alternate prayers of the "Bowing of the Head" in the Coptic Liturgy of St. Mark, the first, which opens: "To thee, o Lord, we bow our minds and our bodily

---

[1224] *Anaphorae Syriacae* (1940). 1 pg. 141. "Therefore Your dependants supplicate You, to You and before You, Lord, and ask forgiveness of their debts and remission of all their sins from Your serenity. 'Sanctify' all of us 'in Your truth;' purify the thoughts of Your servants, whatch over the sheep of Your flock so that it deserve to receive the spiritual eucharist, without blemish and stain. While, on their behalf, You annihilate every type of iniquity and You leave behind those who intend injustice against us, through the grace and mercy and the love of man of Your onlybegotten Son, together with whom to You is befitting glory, honor and power together with Your most holy Spirit, who is good and life-giving and consubstantial with You, now."
[1225] Hammond and Brightman (1896). pp. 446-447

necks acknowledging thy sovereignty and confessing our servitude and asking also for what is expedient for each one of us..."[1226] This opening does show that this is a "Prayer of the Bowing of the Head," the title of the prayer, however, shows that it is a borrowed prayer, as it is called "A prayer before the receiving of the mysteries, of John of Bostra, to the Father"[1227] The Anaphora of St. John of Bostra is a Syrian Liturgy, which suggests that the Coptic "Prayer of the Bowing of the Head" is, again, an element of the Syrian rite which was introduced into the Egyptian liturgical family. The alternate "Prayer of the Bowing of the Head" in the Coptic Liturgy of St. Mark, which is most likely the original prayer, since it is the last in the series, is not written in the style which we find in other prayers of this type:

> *A prayer of Absolution to the Father*
> Master Lord God almighty, the healer of our souls and our bodies and our spirits, thou who saidst unto Peter by the mouth of thine onlybegotten Son our Lord and our God and our Saviour Jesus Christ Thou art Peter: upon this rock I will build my Church and the gates of Hell prevail not against it: I will give unto thee the keys of the kingdom of Heaven: what things thou shalt bind on earth shall be bound in heaven and what things thou shalt loose on earth shall be loosed in heaven: let thy servants therefore, o master, my fathers and my brethren and mine own infirmity be absolved out of my mouth and through thin Holy Spirit, o God good and lover of ma, who takest away the sin of the world. Be ready to receive the repentance of thy servants for a light of knowledge unto forgiveness of sins: for thou art merciful and gracious, thou art long suffering and abundant in thy goodness and truth. But if we have sinned against thee whether in word or in deeds, pardon, forgive us, as a God good and a lover of man. Absolve us [and absolve all thy people *here he mentions whom he will*] from all sins and from all curses and from all denials and from all false oaths and from all intercourse with the heretics and the heathen. Bestow on us, o our master, understanding and power that we may utterly free from every evil ork of the adversary, and grant us at all times to do thy goodpleasure: write our name with the choir of thy saints in the kindom of heaven: in Christ Jesus our Lord through whom *and the rest*.[1228]

[1226] Hammond and Brightman (1896). pg. 183
[1227] Ibid.
[1228] Hammond and Brightman (1896). pg. 183-184 and Day (1972). pg. 96.

The Liturgy of Saint Gregory the Theologian

The first, and most striking, difference is that this prayer never discusses bowing the head. We saw above that almost every prayer of this type either begins, or in some way acknowledges that the worshippers are bowing their heads ὑποκεκλικότας σοι τὰς ἑαυτῶν κεφαλὰς,[1229] bending their necks or in another position of worshipful supplication, from which this type of prayer takes its name. The content of this prayer shows that it corresponds rather to the "Prayer of Freedom" in the Liturgy of St. Gregory rather than a "Prayer of the Bowing of the Head." Both prayers contain long quotations from Scripture: this prayer has a quotation from the Gospels: "Thou art Peter: upon this rock I will build my Church and the gates of Hell prevail not against it: I will give unto thee the keys of the kingdom of Heaven: what things thou shalt bind on earth shall be bound in heaven and what things thou shalt loose on earth shall be loosed in heaven"[1230] while the "Prayer of Freedom" in the Liturgy of St. Gregory the Theologian has a long quotation from the Book of Job. The "Prayers of the Bowing of the Head," do not contain such long, direct quotations, but content themselves with allusion. More telling is that these prayers are each the last prayers of absolution and purification before the distribution of the Eucharist in their respective liturgies. We can conclude then, that this prayer was reinvented to serve as a "Prayer of the Bowing of the Head."

If, then, both prayers in the Coptic Liturgy of St. Mark are either not original to the liturgy or reinvented to serve in this capacity, we must conclude that the Coptic Liturgy of St. Mark did not originally have a "Prayer of the Bowing of the Head," and if not, then it is possible that this type of prayer, too was an import into the Egyptian Liturgy from the Syrian or Byzantine families. That the Greek Liturgy of St. Gregory has such a prayer, while the Coptic translation does not, can be explained using two different scenarios: either the prayer is original to the Greek Liturgy and was then abandoned in the Coptic text, in order to make it correspond to the Egyptian norm;[1231] or this prayer was added secondarily to the Greek text after the adoption of this type of prayer in the Egyptian rite. There is, however, no reason to conclude that this prayer is not original to the liturgy, several of the later interpolated prayers we have seen are either not addressed to Christ, or betray a theology not consistent with the rest of the liturgy. As neither of these are true in the case of this prayer, we must conclude that the prayer is original to this Liturgy and, while the other Greek-Egyptian Liturgies, this is a further proof that this Liturgy is not originally an Egyptian

---

[1229] As is found in the Liturgy of St. Basil, Hammond and Brightman (1896). pp. 340-341. "bending down their own heads to You."
[1230] Hammond and Brightman (1896). pg. 183-184 and Day (1972). pg. 96.
[1231] Which means that the Coptic translation was made before the adoption of this type of prayer in the Egyptian rite.

Liturgy, but an import from the Syrian/Cappadocian rites. It is even possible that the Egyptian liturgical family adopted this type of prayer under the influence of the Greek Liturgy of St. Gregory.

1. Structure

The prayer opens with a direct address of Christ, in this prayer we see a slightly modified form, however, as the opening of the prayer must also discuss the bowing that gives the prayer its name. The prayer is divided into two sections: the first discusses Christ in three descriptive phrases; the second section is also subdivided into three, each subsection is built around an imperative, each one furthering the relationship between Christ and the congregation. The prayer is finished with the *ekphonesis*.

Section one of the prayer revolves around the person of Christ, in three subsections. In the first subsection Christ is the one who "bends the heavens" and who brings salvation to the "race of humanity." In the second, Christ is the one who extends His grace to those for who He brought salvation in the first subsection. In the final subsection of this first part, Christ is described as the one who does everything more than for who He brought salvation in the first subsection can imagine.

The second part of this prayer begins with a reopening of the prayer, with a renewed invocation of Christ. Following the reopening of the prayer, the priest makes four requests, each framed as an imperative: 1. that Christ stretches forth his hand; 2. that Christ bless His "slaves;" 3. that Christ purify these "slaves" from "every stain of flesh and spirit;" 4. that Christ make the "slaves" into "participants and of one body." This string of imperatives is followed by the result of the action taken by Christ introduced by: ὅπως. The structure of the prayer can also be seen in the following table:

The Liturgy of Saint Gregory the Theologian

Figure III.VII.1: Structure of the "Prayer of the Bowing of the Head."[1232]

The "Prayer of the Bowing of the Head"
Part I: Discussion of the person of Christ. 1. Christ as the origin of the Incarnation and the salvation of humanity: Ὁ κλίνας οὐρανοὺς καὶ κατελθὼν ἐπὶ τῆς γῆς, εἰς σωτηρίαν τοῦ γένους τῶν ἀνθρώπων. 2. Christ as the origin of grace: Ὁ τῆς σῆς χάριτος πᾶσαν ἐξαπλώσας τὴν εὐθηνίαν. 3. Christ as the giver of good things: Ὁ ποιῶν πάντα ὑπὲρ ἐκ περισσοῦ, ὧν, αἰτούμεθα ἢ νοοῦμεν.

Part II: Requests made of Christ, using imperatives.
 	
1. Reopening of the Prayer: Φιλάνθρωπε ἀγαθέ,
 	
2. That Christ stretches forth His hand: ἔκτεινόν σου τὴν χεῖρα
    Three epithets are used to describe the ‚hand' of Chrit.
        I. Unseen: τὴν ἀόρατον
        II. Blessed: τὴν εὐλογημένην
        III. Full of mercy and compassion: τὴν μεστὴν ἐλέους καὶ οἰκτιρμῶν.
 	
3. That Christ bless His "slaves:" Καὶ εὐλογῶν εὐλόγησον τοὺς δούλους σου,
 	
4. That Christ cleanse His "slaves:" καὶ καθάρισον αὐτοὺς ἀπὸ παντὸς μολυσμοῦ σαρκὸς καὶ πνεύματος.
 	
5. That Christ transform "us:" Καὶ ποίησον ἡμᾶς μετόχους καὶ συσσώμους γενέσθαι τῇ σῇ χάριτι,

---

[1232] Section III.6 lines 1-11.

> 6. Consequence of this transformation: Ὅπως ἐν ἁγιότητι καὶ δικαιοσύνῃ σοι τὴν ἱκεσίαν προσάγοντες.

> Part III: the *ekphonesis*
>
> 1. Worship due to Christ: Καὶ σοι πρέπει πᾶσα δόξα, μεγαλοσύνη, κράτος τε καὶ ἐξουσία,
>
> 2. Trinitarian formula: ἅμα τῷ ἀχράντῳ σου Πατρὶ, καὶ τῷ ἁγίῳ Πνεύματι, νῦν, καὶ.

2. Function

1. (Section III.6 lines 3-5): Ὁ κλίνας οὐρανοὺς καὶ κατελθὼν ἐπὶ τῆς γῆς, εἰς σωτηρίαν τοῦ γένους τῶν ἀνθρώπων. Ὁ τῆς σῆς χάριτος πᾶσαν ἐξαπλώσας τὴν εὐθηνίαν. Ὁ ποιῶν πάντα ὑπὲρ ἐκ περισσοῦ, ὧν, αἰτούμεθα ἢ νοοῦμεν·

Although this section is structurally divided into three parts, I have decided to discuss them all at once since they are not only related in content, but form a continuous flow of content, that culminates in the final salvation of man, the goal stated at the beginning of the prayer: εἰς σωτηρίαν τοῦ γένους τῶν ἀνθρώπων. The movement of the content from goal to fulfillment is a style we have seen before in this liturgy, for example in the second prayer of the pre-Anaphora. The rising trend in the content (of both these prayers) show the debt the author owes the Neoplatonic school of philosophy, the philosophers of which[1233] often speak in terms of ascending levels of consciousness. This, again, speaks for the authorship of Gregory the Theologian, since he was educated in the Neoplatonic tradition and had extensive contact with other, Christian, authors who were also educated in this tradition: St. Basil the Great and St. Gregory of Nyssa. While an interesting indication of authorship, the Neoplatonic tradition becomes too important in Eastern Christian theology to use as a proof.

The "Prayer of the Bowing of the Head" usually begins with, or has close to the beginning, the phrase from which the prayer takes its name: "have mercy on this people which bowed down adoreth thy godhead."[1234] Such a direct statement is, however, missing in the Liturgy of St. Gregory, instead a description of Christ is given: Ὁ κλίνας οὐρανοὺς. The author keeps true to the form of the prayer by using the proper terminology: κλίνας,

---
[1233] Cf. for example *On Beauty* by Plotinus.
[1234] From the *Soorp Baradak*. Hammond and Brightman (1896). pg. 446

making the prayer still recognizable and usable as a "Prayer of the Bowing of the Head." The focus of the prayer is shifted, however, from the human worshipper who bows his head to Christ to Christ, who bows the heavens. We have seen a similar shift of focus on numerous occasions in this Liturgy when dealing with the Trinity. Attributes or items usually associated either with the Father or with the Holy Spirit are associated with Christ in order to deemphasize the other members of the Trinity and emphasize the divinity of the Son. Here the central role played by humanity in this prayer is taken away in order to keep the emphasis of the Liturgy on Christ, it also allows the author to continue the discussion of the Incarnation begun in the "Prayer of the Breaking."

The focus of the Incarnation is also shifted, where the Liturgy of St. Basil, for example, has the driving impulse of the Incarnation as the Father, who sends Christ into the world to work salvation,[1235] the Liturgy of St. Gregory has the entire plan of salvation attributed to Christ: it is He who changes the nature of Creation, "bends the heavens," and makes it possible for the Incarnation to take place. It is also Christ who: κατελθὼν ἐπὶ τῆς γῆς. He is not sent by God the Father, but takes the entirety of man's salvation: εἰς σωτηρίαν τοῦ γένους τῶν ἀνθρώπων upon Himself. This discussion of the Incarnation serves a very important purpose in the intent of the author for this Liturgy: it continues the anti-Arian emphasis of Christ over the other members of the Trinity which excludes the Arians from salvation and from participation in this Eucharistic celebration. If Christ plays the role that is set for Him by God the Father, then it is not ultimately necessary for Him to be divine. If, as is suggested in this Liturgy, however, it is Christ who is the origin of the Incarnation and of salvation, then the Arians deny salvation itself by denying the divinity of Christ. Following the theology of the Incarnation presented here, Christ cannot be anything but divine, if He plays such a central role, and denying this divinity robs Christ of the power to do that which the author attributes to Him.

In the second part of this section: ὁ τῆς σῆς χάριτος πᾶσαν ἐξαπλώσας τὴν εὐθηνίαν the content progresses from the goal: salvation, toward the fulfillment of that goal. The progression is, however, also a chronological one, moving from a discussion of the Incarnation to Christ's ministry on earth: ὁ τῆς σῆς χάριτος πᾶσαν ἐξαπλώσας τὴν εὐθηνίαν. The "grace" spoken of here may refer to the salvation brought about by the Incarnation, or to the various miracles performed by Christ during His lifetime, or, more likely, both.

The same chronological and thematic progression noted above is also seen between the second and third parts of this section. The verb of the third part is a participle that is no

---

[1235] Ὅτε δὲ ἦλθε τὸ πλήρωμα τῶν καιρῶν, ἐλάλησας ἡμῖν ἐν αὐτῷ τῷ Υἱῷ σου. "When the fullness of time came, You spoke to us in Your Son himself." Vaporis ed. (1988). pg 26 (Cf. also Hammond and Brightman (1896). pg. 324-325).

longer in the aorist: κλίνας...ἐξαπλώσας, but in the present: ποιῶν. By using the continuous action implicit in the present participle the author is able to lead the reader (or listener) to two slightly different interpretations that contrast with the completed actions implicit in the aorist participles: 1. that Christ has acted in His Church throughout its history; and 2. that Christ continues to act in His Church in the present as well. This chronological progression leads, then, from the Incarnation to the present, but also ties in the future in the discussion of salvation. That Christ does πάντα ὑπὲρ ἐκ περισσοῦ, ὧν αἰτούμεθα ἢ νοοῦμεν, once again underscores the divinity of Christ, since He knows what is needed better than those who actually need it. This phrase also links this prayer with the "Prayer of the Breaking" original to the Liturgy, both of these prayers use the verb νοέω in reference either to Christ or to the actions of Christ throughout history.

2. (Section III.6 lines 5-9): Φιλάνθρωπε ἀγαθέ, ἔκτεινόν σου τὴν χεῖρα τὴν ἀόρατον τὴν εὐλογημένην τὴν μεστὴν ἐλέους καὶ οἰκτιρμῶν. Καὶ εὐλογῶν εὐλόγησον τοὺς δούλους σου, καὶ καθάρισον αὐτοὺς ἀπὸ παντὸς μολυσμοῦ σαρκὸς καὶ πνεύματος. Καὶ ποίησον ἡμᾶς μετόχους καὶ συσσώμους γένεσθαι τῇ σῇ χάριτι, Ὅπως ἐν ἁγιότητι καὶ δικαιοσύνῃ σοι τὴν ἱκεσίαν προσάγοντες.

Although the second section has a markedly different content, indicated by the reopening of the prayer in a second direct address of Christ, the structure continues with the chronological and logical progression we discussed in the first section: following the extension of Christ's hand He is asked to bless His "slaves," this is a logical progression since the proper position for blessing is with the hand extended. After the blessing Christ is asked to purify the "slaves," the phrase here: ἀπὸ παντὸς μολυσμοῦ σαρκὸς καὶ πνεύματος, has been used often before in this and other liturgies. In the final request the priest asks Christ to transform the congregation into participants. The progression we have discussed is made clear here (though the progression from stretching out the hand and giving a blessing is explainable, the progression from blessing to purifying is less clear) the key is in the term used in describing the congregation when asking for blessing and for purification they are referred to as: "Your slaves," however, after the request for purification, they are referred to merely as: "us" this implies that the purification was and needed to be completed before Christ transforms them into participants. Central to the transformation of the congregants is τῇ σῇ χάριτι, while this is a theological statement, that it is by "grace" that Christ transforms His people and bring salvation, it is also a intratextual allusion to the first section of the prayer, where Christ is described as the one who: ὁ τῆς σῆς χάριτος πᾶσαν ἐξαπλώσας. This, hypothetical, description of God's Grace is then contextualized and made concrete in the second section.

The structure of the final request transitions the string of imperatives into their result. Usually the result in such a structure is access for the congregants to the Eucharist, here, however, the congregant does not receive anything from Christ, but permission to bring their prayers to Christ.

3. (Section III.6 lines 10-11): Καὶ σοι πρέπει πᾶσα δόξα, μεγαλοσύνη, κράτος τε καὶ ἐξουσία, ἅμα τῷ -ἀχράντῳ σου Πατρὶ, καὶ τῷ ἁγίῳ Πνεύματι, νῦν, καὶ.

The final section of this prayer is the *ekphonesis*. Unlike the standard *ekphoneseis* of this liturgy, and of most liturgies, the text does not specify to who the glory etc... is due to, usually an *ekphonesis* will include the specific name of the member of the Trinity to whom the prayer is directed. Here, however, the only indication is the word: σοι, which, based on the rest of the prayer, must be Christ. The rest of the *ekphonesis* is fairly standard, using the stock phrases commonly found in the endings of prayers and in the Trinitarian formula.

III.VIII. Another, similar, Prayer

The Liturgy of St. Gregory has a second prayer that acts as a "Prayer of the Bowing of the Head." This is not in itself surprising, as the Coptic Liturgy of St. Mark also has two of these prayers.[1236] What is unusual, is that this prayer corresponds almost exactly to a prayer found in the Byzantine Liturgy of St. Basil.[1237]

[1236] Cf. Hammond and Brightman (1896). pg. 341
[1237] Hammerschmidt, for example, claims that the prayer in the Liturgy of St. Gregory shows a: "Fortentwicklung" of the Byzantine Liturgy (pg. 167, footnote 271).

The Commentary

Figure III.VIII.1: Comparison of the texts of this prayer in the Liturgies of St. Basil and of St. Gregory.

In the Liturgy of St. Basil[1238]	In the Liturgy of St. Gregory
Πρόσχες Κύριε Ἰησοῦ Χριστέ ὁ Θεὸς ἡμῶν ἐξ ἁγίου κατοικητηρίου σου καὶ ἀπὸ θρόνου δόξης τῆς βασιλείας σου καὶ ἐλθὲ εἰς τὸ ἁγιάσαι ἡμᾶς ὁ ἄνω τῷ Πατρὶ συγκαθήμενος καὶ ᾧδε ἡμῖν ἀοράτως συνών καὶ καταξίωσον τῇ κραταιᾷ σου χειρὶ μεταδοῦναι ἡμῖν τοῦ ἀχράντου σώματός σου, καὶ τοῦ τιμίου αἵματος, καὶ δι' ἡμῶν παντὶ τῷ Λαῷ.	Πρόσχες, Κύριε Ἰησοῦ Χριστὲ ὁ Θεὸς ἡμῶν, ἐξ ἁγίου κατοικητηρίου σου, καὶ ἀπὸ θρόνου δόξης τῆς βασιλείας σου, καὶ ἔλθε εἰς τὸ ἁγιάσαι ἡμᾶς <u>τοὺς ἐπικλίναντάς σοι</u>. Ὁ ἄνω τῷ Πατρὶ συγκαθήμενος, καὶ ᾧδε ἡμῖν ἀοράτως συνών. Καὶ καταξίωσον τῇ κραταιᾷ σου χειρὶ μεταδοῦναι ἡμῖν τοῦ ἀχράντου σώματός σου, καὶ τοῦ τιμίου αἵματος, καὶ δι' ἡμῶν παντὶ τῷ λαῷ. <u>Σὺ γὰρ εἶ ὁ κλῶν, καὶ κλώμενος, καὶ ἄκλαστος· καὶ σοὶ τὴν δόξαν ἀναπέμομεν, σὺν τῷ σῷ Πατρί, καὶ τῷ ἁγίῳ Πνεύματι, νῦν, καὶ.</u>

As we see in the table, the prayers are, with two exceptions, virtually identical. The underlined differences are an addition of the phrase: τοὺς ἐπικλίναντάς σου in the main body of the prayer and the addition of an *ekphonesis* to conclude the prayer. This leads us to a number of questions about this prayer that must be answered: 1. does this prayer have its origin in the Liturgy of St. Gregory or in the Liturgy of St. Basil? 2. Is the prayer in the proper place in the Liturgy of St. Gregory? 3. What do these conclusions say about the origin of the Liturgy of St. Gregory?

In the Byzantine Liturgy of St. Basil there are very few prayers directed to Christ, they are almost exclusively directed to God the Father. We have discussed the "Prayer of the Veil" and the possibility that the "Prayer of the Gospel" found in the Liturgy of St. Basil has its origin in the Liturgy of St. Gregory as well. Since we have established a pattern of adoption from the Liturgy of St. Gregory to the Liturgy of St. Basil, this would be the logical conclusion. We have, however, discussed before, that it is unusual for Litugical texts to get longer.[1239] The addition of an *ekphonesis* and the phrase: τοὺς ἐπικλίναντάς σοι

[1238] Hammond and Brightman (1896). pg. 129 and Trempelis (1982). pg. 129
[1239] Scherman (1920).

suggest, then that it does originate in the Liturgy of St. Basil. It is far more likely, however, that this prayer is an original part of the Liturgy of St. Gregory, and was adopted by the Litugy of St. Basil. The addition of the phrase: τοὺς ἐπικλίναντάς σοι as well as the *ekphonesis*[1240] can be explained as an attempt to adapt this prayer into a "Prayer of the Bowing of the Head" by later editors who were no longer aware of the origin of the Liturgy and wished to conform the liturgy to the Egyptian rite. By explaining the differences seen in the Liturgies of St. Gregory and St. Basil in this way, we see that the prayer must have its origin in the Liturgy of St. Gregory.

That this prayer has its origin in the Liturgy of St. Gregory has some important implications in determining its origin. The Liturgy of St. Gregory cannot be considered an Egyptian liturgy. This type of prayer does not come up in the Syrian rite proper either, and this, along with the adoption of several prayers from this liturgy into the Liturgy of St. Basil, is a strong argument for placing this liturgy in the subdivision of the Syrian rite in Cappadocia, that the Liturgy of St. Gregory has its origin in the same liturgical family as the Liturgy of St. Basil.

1. Structure.

This prayer can be divided into four parts, the first and third are built around imperatives, while the second discusses the dual nature of Christ, the final section is the *ekphonesis*, which may be a secondary addition to the prayer. The first section of the prayer, in fact, the prayer itself begins with an imperative: Πρόσχες, following this first imperative is the direct address of Christ: Κύριε Ἰησοῦ Χριστὲ ὁ Θεὸς ἡμῶν, which we see in the majority of the prayers in this Liturgy. This section contains one other imperative: ἔλθε. Following this first section is a brief discussion of Christ's dual nature: τῷ Πατρὶ συγκαθήμενος...ἡμῖν ἀοράτως συνών. The final section of the main text of the prayer is built around another imperative: .καταξίωσον, which is elaborated upon with an infinitive phrase: μεταδοῦναι ἡμῖν. In the *ekphonesis* we see three subsctions, one which discusses the person of Christ, one which describes the various types of worship due to Christ and a third which contains the Trinitarian formula. The structure of this prayer can also be seen in the following table.

[1240] Note that the *ekphonesis* in this prayer has a similar structure to that of the "Prayer of the Bowing of the Head."

The Commentary

Figure III.VIII.2: The structue of the other "Prayer of the Bowing of the Head:"[1241]

The other "Prayer of the Bowing of the Head"

Part I: Section is built around two imperatives.

1. That Christ look down from heaven onto the congregation: Πρόσχες, Κύριε Ἰησοῦ Χριστὲ ὁ Θεὸς ἡμῶν, ἐξ ἁγίου κατοικητηρίου σου, καὶ ἀπὸ θρόνου δόξης τῆς βασιλείας σου,

2. That Christ come Himself down to the congregation: καὶ ἐλθὲ εἰς τὸ ἁγιάσαι ἡμᾶς τοὺς ἐπικλίναντάς σοι.

Part II: A section that discusses Christ's dual nature.

1. Christ's place with the Father: Ὁ ἄνω τῷ Πατρὶ συγκαθήμενος,

2. Christ's place among the congregation: καὶ ὧδε ἡμῖν ἀοράτως συνών.

Part III: A second section built around an imperative.

1. That Christ deem "it" worthy: Καὶ καταξίωσον τῇ κραταιᾷ σου χειρί

2. Following the imperative is an infinitive phrase describing what Christ should deem it worthy to do: μεταδοῦναι ἡμῖν τοῦ ἀχράντου σώματός σου, καὶ τοῦ τιμίου αἵματος, καὶ δι' ἡμῶν παντὶ τῷ λαῷ.

Part IV: The *Ekphonesis*.

1. A brief description of the dichotomy of the person of Christ: Σὺ γὰρ, εἶ ὁ κλῶν,

---

[1241] Cf. Section III.7 lines 1-9.

> καὶ κλώμενος, καὶ ἄκλαστος·
>
> 2. The type of worship sent up to Christ: καὶ σοι τὴν δόξαν ἀναπέμομεν,
>
> 3. The Trinitarian formula: σὺν τῷ σῷ Πατρί, καὶ τῷ ἁγίῳ Πνεύματι, νῦν, καὶ.

2. Function

1. (Section III.7 lines 2-3): Πρόσχες, Κύριε Ἰησοῦ Χριστὲ ὁ Θεὸς ἡμῶν, ἐξ ἁγίου κατοικητηρίου σου καὶ ἀπὸ θρόνου δόξης τῆς βασιλείας σου,

The two imperatives in the first part of this prayer: Πρόσχες and ἔλθε are marked by a dichotomy, movement and stasis, Christ is both asked to look down upon the congregation and to come down and visit them Himself. This underscores again the duality of His nature, as God He is asked to watch over the Church and as man He is asked to join the congregation and to participate in the Eucharist as the "great high priest." Of special interest as well is the σου, which identifies the: κατοικητηρίου and the βασιλεία as belonging to Christ, rather than to the Father or the Holy Spirit. This is a strategy that we have seen employed by the author on numerous occasions throughout the Liturgy.

2. (Section III.7 line 3-4): καὶ ἔλθε εἰς τὸ ἁγιάσαι ἡμᾶς τοὺς ἐπικλίναντάς σοι.

This imperative brings movement into the Prayer. This movement, with its resulting hallowing of the congregation, is the opposite of the movement the author has presented so far. The author has often discussed the rising up of the congregation toward Christ, receiving their hallowing through this rising up toward the holy. This ἔλθε can be interpreted doubly 1. as describing the Incarnation and 2. as describing the Eucharist. As the Incarnation it is the descent of Christ onto the earth and His life as a human that hallows. The imperative is present tense, however, putting it in the context of the present Liturgy and of the Eucharist, though the usual convention is to pray to the Holy Spirit to descend and hallow the congregation and the gifts, there have been numerous attributes of both the Father and the Holy Spirit that the author has put onto Christ. The Eucharistic interpretation also links this request of Christ with the request that follows at the end of the prayer, which asks Christ to distribute the Eucharist to "us."

3. (Section III.7 line 4) Ὁ ἄνω τῷ Πατρὶ συγκαθήμενος, καὶ ὧδε ἡμῖν ἀοράτως συνών·

This short break in the requests makes a strong theological statement, again with a double interpretation. The dual nature of Christ, as divine, with the Father, and human, on earth with "us." The use of the term: ἀοράτως suggests that it is the Eucharist that is being discussed, as Christ is not seen in human form directly, but indirectly in the form of the bread and wine and not the Incarnation.

4. (Section III.7 lines 4-6): καὶ καταξίωσον τῇ κραταιᾷ σου χειρί, μεταδοῦναι ἡμῖν τοῦ ἀχράντου σώματός σου, καὶ τοῦ τιμίου αἵματος, καὶ δι' ἡμῶν παντὶ τῷ λαῷ.

The final imperative introduces the ultimate purpose of this prayer, a preparatory prayer for the Eucharist. The final phrase: καὶ δι' ἡμῶν παντὶ τῷ λαῷ. If "we" refers to the entire Christian people, then who is left that is to receive the Eucharist. If "we" refers only to the congregation in the Church building, then other Christians will receive the Eucharist in other Churches and have no need to have it distributed to them. "We" could then be interpreted as the clergy, through whose prayers the Eucharist is sanctified, and who receive the Eucharist before the rest of the congregation. This prayer is, then, a private prayer of the priest, who prays first to receive the Eucharist himself and then to become an instrument to distribute the Eucharist to the people of the congregation.

5. (Section III.7 lines 7-9): Σὺ γὰρ, εἶ ὁ κλῶν, καὶ κλώμενος, καὶ ἄκλαστος· καὶ σοι τὴν δόξαν ἀναπέμομεν, σὺν τῷ σῷ Πατρί, καὶ τῷ ἁγίῳ Πνεύματι, νῦν, καὶ.

The *ekphonesis* of this prayer contains the elements we have seen in the majority of the other *ekphoneseis* of this Liturgy: 1. a short descriptive section about Christ; 2. a section of worship sent up to Christ and 3. a Trinitarian formula. What stands out in this *ekphonesis* is the description of Christ. We have seen a similar formulation in the 'Prayer of the Veil,' before the Anaphora, in which the duality of Christ's nature is discussed using contradictory statements. This section also plays into the Eucharistic theme of this prayer, the bread for the Eucharist, the Body of Christ, is broken into pieces, but Christ remains whole and the process can be repeated at the next Liturgy.

III.IX. The "Prayer of Freedom"

The "Prayer of Freedom" marks the transition to prayers which directly prepare for the Eucharist. This is the longest of the prayers in the Post-Anaphora and one of the longest prayers in the liturgy. Perhaps the length of the prayer is indicative of the important place this prayer holds in the progress of the liturgy. This prayer fits well into the genre of "Prayer of Access." Similar prayers are found in several liturgical tradition, especially in the Byzantine Liturgy of St. Basil and the Greek-Syrian Liturgy of St. James. Such prayers are not found, however, in the so-called Monophysite Liturgies, such as the Coptic Liturgy of St. Mark and the Syrian Liturgy of St. James, or even in the Armenian *Soorp Baradak*.[1242] The lack of such a prayer in the Monophysite liturgies also answers the question: why is this prayer missing in the Coptic translation of the Liturgy of St. Gregory? Generally in answering this question we must analyze two possiblities, either that the prayer was original to the liturgy and disappeared in the translation process, or that there was no prayer there originally and that one was added under the influence of another liturgy after the translations had been made. Though it is possible that a prayer was added later to the Greek Liturgy of St. Gregory, these borrowings tend to be versions of an already existing prayer, adapted to fit into the Christological format of the rest of the liturgy.[1243] There does not seem, however, to be a prayer in any other liturgy in which a prayer that could serve as a template exists. The conclusion must then be, that this prayer is original to the Liturgy, and was removed during the translation process to conform it to the Coptic rite. This adds another piece to the mounting evidence that this Liturgy is not Egyptian in origin, but belongs to the West Syrian/Cappadocian rite. In exploring the prayers in the Liturgy of St. Basil and the Liturgy of St. James that are similar to the "Prayer of Freedom," we can further investigate the origin of this Liturgy.

In the Byzantine Liturgy of St. Basil, a short prayer follows the Breaking of the bread: Μελίζεται καὶ διαμερίζεται ὁ Ἀμνὸς τοῦ Θεοῦ, ὁ μελιζόμενος καὶ μὴ διαιρούμενος· ὁ πάντοτε ἐσθιόμενος, καὶ μηδέποτε δαπανώμενος, ἀλλὰ τοὺς μετέχοντας ἁγιάζων.[1244] There are numerous differences between the two prayers, the most obvious being the length of the prayer in the Liturgy of St. Gregory. Other differences are in the placement of the two prayers, in the Liturgy of St. Basil, this prayer is found following the proclamation: τὰ ἅγια τοῖς ἁγίοις,[1245] while the prayer in the Liturgy of St. Gregory is placed before this proclamation and the true opening of the Eucharist. Despite these differenes, a phrase that is found near the beginning of both points to a possible connection: ὁ Ἀμνὸς τοῦ Θεοῦ, this is by no means a rare phrase in a liturgical context,[1246] however, the phrase is found in very few other of the other major Eastern liturgies, in the Greek or Syrian Liturgies of St. James, nor in the Coptic or Greek Liturgies of St. Mark. Since few other liturgies, and no

---

[1242] Cf. Hammond and Brightman (1896). pp. 184;101 and 447 respectively.
[1243] The first Prayer of the Liturgy is a good example of this, other prayers are adopted without even an adaptation, such as the secondary "Prayer of the Veil."
[1244] *Ieratikon* (1987). pg. 186 and Trempelis (1982). pg. 217. "broken and shared out is the lamb of God, who is broken and not divided up, who is always eaten and never consumed, but hallowing those who partake."
[1245] "The holy things for the holy."
[1246] See, for example, the text of the *Gloria* in both the Roman and Byzantine traditions, and of the *Agnus Dei* in the Roman rite.

other Eastern Liturgies contain this phrase, the fact that it appears in both liturgies cannot be attributed to standard liturgical phraseology, nor can one attribute this to mere coincidence, seeing the numerous other points of congruence between the two liturgies.

Left to be explained is what ramifications a point of congruence between these two Liturgies would have. The first problem to be explained is: why do these two prayers belong to different sections of the Liturgy, if they are related? It is possible that the prayer was moved in the Liturgy of St. Gregory to conform it to the Egyptian norm (that is, the Coptic Liturgy of St. Mark), which has no prayer until the: Σωμα αγιον.[1247]

Another possibility is found in the similarities between this prayer and a prayer from the Greek-Syrian Liturgy of St. James.[1248] Though this prayer is much shorter than the one in the Liturgy of St. James, it does stand in the position in the text. Interesting is that this prayer in the is also directed to Christ, rather than to the Father. Though this seems to support the relationship between the two prayers, we must not forget that there is a tradition of prayers to Christ in the Liturgy, and that the prayer in the Liturgy of St. James falls into this tradition, while the prayer in the Liturgy of St. Gregory stands in the Christological agenda of the rest of the text. The greatest similarity between the two prayers lies in quotations from Scripture that are near the beginning of each. In the Liturgy of St. James we see: σὺ γὰρ εἶπας δέσποτα Ἅγιοι ἔσεσθε ὅτι ἐγὼ ἅγιος ἐμί.[1249] While in the Liturgy of St. Gregory: Ὁ τοῦ δικαίου Ἰὼβ ἐπακούσας ἀνιστάμενος υἱοί μου πονηρὰ ἐν τῇ καρδίᾳ αὐτῶν ἔναντι Θεοῦ. While a quotation from Scripture is by no means out of place in a Liturgy, the way that these two quotations are situated within the prayer is unusual. The majority of Scriptural quotations and allusions in a Liturgy are not introduced, but flow within the text of the prayers, it is only with quotations of great importance, such as the Consecration: ἔδωκεν τοῖς ἁγίοις αὐτοῦ μαθηταῖς καὶ ἀποστόλοις εἰπών· Λάβετε φάγετε· τοῦτο μου ἐστὶν τὸ Σῶμα,[1250] that one sees a break within the text in order to introduce a quotation, this suggests that it is the Scriptural reference that forms the center of the argument in each of these prayers. Interesting too is that both Scriptural quotations deal with being holy, coming at the problem from two different angles. The prayer in the Liturgy of St. James gives an instruction to be holy like Christ is holy, while the prayer in the Liturgy of St. Gregory discusses the problems with not being holy. Holiness plays an important part in this prayer because of its function as an Eucharistic prayer, a state of holiness has been

---

[1247] Hammond and Brightmann (1896). pg. 184
[1248] Hammond and Brightman (1896). pg. 61 and Mercier (1944). pg. 220.
[1249] Hammond and Brightman (1896). pg. 61 and Mercier (1944). pg. 220. "For You said, Lord, be holy as I am holy."
[1250] Cf. Hammond and Brightman (1896). pg. 328. "Gave it to His holy disciples and apostles saying: take eat, this is my Body."

The Liturgy of Saint Gregory the Theologian

achieved in preparation for the Eucharist that must be maintained in this prayer and during the entire preparation of the Eucharistic elements. We have, up to this point, only discussed the Greek-Egyptian Liturgies in passing, this is because the Greek Liturgy of St. Mark adopts the prayer used in the Greek Liturgy of St. James with few changes, it is possible, then, that the Egyptian rite does not have a prayer here originally, and that it is only under influence of the Syrian and Byzantine rites that a prayer is introduced here.

Interesting to note is that a similar prayer is seen in the western, Tridentine rite, the *Agnus Dei*.[1251] This prayer contains the same elements we have discussed: the identification of Christ as the "Lamb of God;" as we saw in the Liturgy of St. James, this prayer is addressed to Christ, an expression of the this tradition discussed in the Commentary by Gerhardts; this prayer also shows a quotation from Scripture: Pacem relinquo vobis, pacem do vobis. This quotation is introduced as those in the Liturgies of St. James and St. Gregory. The prayer in the Roman rite also conforms very closely to the structure found in the Liturgy of St. Gregory. Both begin with a discussion of the person of Christ, then transition to a series of petitions, and culminate in a short *ekphonesis*. I do not believe, however, that these commonalities point to an influence of one of these Liturgies on the other, rather this seems to be an expression of the influence of the Eastern rite on the Western.

Using the congruence of the extraordinary elements of the prayer in the Liturgy of St. Gregory and its counterparts in the Liturgies of St. Basil and of St. James, we can conclude that this prayer comes out of the same tradition as these two prayers. Which of these prayers provide a direct correlation is impossible to say, however, it does support placing this Liturgy within the context of the Cappadocian liturgical family, as an ofshoot of the Syrian rite.

1. Structure.

As discussed above, this is the longest prayers in the Post-Anaphora and one of the longest prayers in the entire Liturgy, this prayer consists of three parts: 1. the first, shorter, section of the body of text is comprised of four phrases, each of which discusses the person of Christ, each introduced with: ὁ. It is in this section that the introduced quotation of Scripture is found. Following a transitional: καὶ ἐμοῦ, τοῦ ἐλεεινοῦ καὶ ἁμαρτωλοῦ καὶ ἀχρείου σου δούλου ἱκετεύω ὑπὲρ τῶν σῶν οἰκετῶν, πατέρων μου καὶ ἀδελφῶν, καὶ ὑπὲρ τῆς ἐμῆς ἀθλιότητος, follows a second, longer, section consisting of nine subsections. Each of these subsections is built around an imperative, and continues the thought of the one before, building the requests from recognition to salvation: εὐμενεῖ προσώπῳ ... ἔπιδε ἐφ' ἡμᾶς... παρὲς οὖν ἡμῖν ... ἐπιδῆσαι ... κατακρατῆσαι ... ἀθῳοσον ... χάρισαι ... δώρησαι ...

[1251] *Missale Romanum* (1922). pg. 303

The Commentary

φεῖσαι ... ἔμπλησον. Inserted between the eighth and ninth imperatives is a sentence that discusses the Incarnation of Christ and the Salvation of humanity that results from it and from the crucifixion, between the ninth and tenth imperatives is a second insertion, which discusses the nature of humanity in comparison with God. The final section of the prayer is the *ekphonesis*, the *ekphonesis* of this prayer is highly unusual for this Liturgy, and contains very few of the usual elements, the discussion of Christ's nature and even Christ's name is missing, as is the Trinitarian formula which usually stands at the end of the *ekphonesis*. The structure of this prayer can also be seen in the following table:

Table III.IX.1: The Structure of the "Prayer of Freedom."[1252]

The "Prayer of Freedom"
Part I: Discussion of Christ's person and actions. 1. Christ as the "Lamb of God:" Ὁ ἀμνὸς τοῦ Θεοῦ, ὁ αἴρων τὴν ἁμαρτίαν τοῦ κόσμου. 2. Christ as the savior of humanity through the shedding of His blood: Ὁ τὸ πανάσπιλον αὐτοῦ αἷμα διαχύσας ἐπὶ τὴν τοῦ κόσμου ζωήν, καὶ εἰς λύτρον καὶ ἀντάλλαγμα πάντων ἑαυτὸν παρέδωκας, ἐκ θανάτου λυτρωσάμενος, ἐν ᾧ κατειχόμεθα· πεπραγμένοι ὑπὸ τὴν ἁμαρτίαν. 3. Christ as the one who fulfills the requests of those who "fear Him:" Ὁ τῶν φοβουμένων αὐτὸν ποιῶν τὸ θέλημα, καὶ τῆς δεήσεως αὐτῶν εἰσακούσων, καὶ σώζων αὐτούς· 4. The quotation from the Book of Job: ὁ τοῦ δικαίου Ἰὼβ ἐπακούσας ἀνιστάμενος τὸ πρωὶ καὶ ὑπὲρ παιδίων φίλτρων θυσίας προσαγαγὼν εἰπών. Μήπως ἐνενόησαν υἱοί μου πονηρὰ ἐν τῇ καρδίᾳ αὐτῶν ἔναντι Θεοῦ.
Part II (a): Transition from the discussion of Christ to the list of imperatives.

[1252] Cf. Section III.8 lines 1-27.

The Liturgy of Saint Gregory the Theologian

1. prayer for the Church commuity and for the priest himself: Καὶ ἐμοῦ τοῦ ἐλεεινοῦ καὶ ἁμαρτωλοῦ καὶ ἀχρείου σου δούλου ἱκετεύω ὑπὲρ τῶν σῶν οἰκετῶν, πατέρων μου καὶ ἀδελφῶν, καὶ ὑπὲρ τῆς ἐμῆς ἀθλιότητος.

Part II (b): List of imperatives, Christ is asked to:

1. Grace "us:" Εὐμενεῖ προσώπῳ, καὶ γαληνῷ ὄμματι,

2. Look upon "us:" ἔπιδε ἐφ' ἡμᾶς ἐν ταύτῃ τῇ ὥρᾳ.

3. Pardon "us:" Καὶ παρὲς οὖν ἡμῖν πᾶσαν ἀθετηρίαν, καὶ πᾶσαν παράβασιν, καὶ παρακοὴν νόμου, καὶ τῶν σῶν ἐντολῶν.

4. Bind: Ἔτι δὲ καὶ πᾶσαν συνείδησιν, καὶ πᾶσαν ἐνθύμησιν, καὶ πάσαις πράξεσι, καὶ πάσαις κινήσεσι γεγονυίαις ἐν ἑαυταῖς, ἡμερικῶς, τε καὶ νυκτερικῶς ἐπιδῆσαι

5. Prevail: καὶ κατακρατῆσαι κατὰ τῆς ψυχῆς.

6. Absolve: Καὶ ἀθώοσον αὐτοὺς ἀπὸ πάσης συνειδήσεως πονηρῶν, καὶ πάσης ἀκάρπου πράξεως, καὶ παντὸς λογισμοῦ πεπυρωμένου. Ἅτινα ἐστιν παρὰ βεβηλὰ παρὰ τὴν τῆς ψυχῆς καθαρότητα.

7. Grant: Χάρισαι αὐτῶν τὴν τῶν ἁμαρτιῶν ἐπίγνωσιν, καὶ τελείως ἀπέχεσθαι ἀπ' αὐτῶν.

8. Grant: Δώρησαι αὐτοῖς μετανοίας ἁγνότητος καὶ τὴν εἰς σὲ ἐπιστροφήν·

9. Spare all of "us:" Φεῖσαι πάντων Δέσποτα φιλόψυχε, ὅτι τὰ σύμπαντα δοῦλα σά·

10. Fill ‚us:' ἔμπλησον ἡμᾶς τοῦ σοῦ φόβου, καὶ κατεύθυνον εἰς τὸ ἀγαθόν σου θέλημα.

Part II (c): The two inserted extrapolations.

1. Between the eighth and ninth imperatives: discusses the Incarnation, as well as salvation and redemption through the cross: σὺ γὰρ Δέσποτα Κύριε ἐπτώχευσας ἑκουσίως ἐν τῷ σε σαρκωθῆναι, διὰ τὴν τοῦ γένους ἡμῶν σωτηρίαν. Καὶ διέρρηξας τὸ καθ' ἡμῶν χειρόγραφον, διὰ τὴν ἐπὶ τοῦ σταυροῦ τῶν θείων σου παλάμων ἐφ' ἅπλωσιν.

2. Between the ninth and tenth imperatives: discusses the nature of man and the futility of humanity when not working with God, there is a *crux* in the text here which makes interpretation of the second half nearly impossible: Καὶ παρά σου ἡμέτερα ἀφετήρια, καὶ οὐδὲν τῶν ἐπιτηδευμάτων τῶν χειρῶν ἡμῶν. Δι' ὃ τὴν σὴν βασιλείαν δοξάζομεν καὶ ἀνυμνοῦμέν σε Χριστὲ ὁ Θεὸς ἡμῶν. Ἅτινα ν...λου...ων...θόρων... Πάσαις ἁμαρτίας ἕως αἱρετικῶν καὶ ἐθνικῶν·

Part III: The *ekphonesis*

1. The *ekphonesis* begins with a direct address of Christ, addressed as ‚God' and finishes with the worship due to Him: Σὺ γὰρ, εἶ, ὁ Θεὸς ἡμῶν, καὶ πρέπει σοι δόξα τιμὴ καὶ προσκύνησις.

2. Function
1. (Section III.8 line 3): ὁ ἀμνὸς τοῦ Θεοῦ, ὁ αἴρων τὴν ἁμαρτίαν τοῦ κόσμου·

This opening conforms to a style we have seen on numerous occasions throughout this Liturgy, by opening the prayer with a direct address of Christ the author leaves no doubt in the congregations mind as to who the focus of this Liturgy is. This also serves to refocus the attention of the congregation, by addressing each prayer to Christ so explicitly, the shock value is taken full advantage of. In this way the attentions of the members of the congregation, which may have been wandering during the long prayers of the priest, are refocused at the beginning of each new prayer.

What stands out in this opening is the way that Christ is addressed: ὁ ἀμνὸς τοῦ Θεοῦ. While this is a common epithet of Christ, both in Liturgy and Scripture, the use of this epithet breaks the standard relationship paradigm of the Trinity, as presented in this

Liturgy, generally it is the other members of the Trinity who are described in terms of their relationship with Christ. The author is much more likely to refer to the Father or the Holy Spirit, and even aspects belonging to the Father or to the Holy Spirit, in reference to Christ: σου, than he is to put Christ in a seemingly suberservient position to another member of the Trinity. This would undermine the propagandistic point the author focuses on, Christ as God. In this instance, however, the seeming subservience implied by the phrase is offset by the second part of the epithet: ὁ αἴρων τὴν ἁμαρτίαν τοῦ κόσμου. Already in Scripture, it is attested that only God can take away sin.[1253] Since the two parts of the phrase are almost always seen together, they form a unit in the mind of the worshippers, underscoring rather than undermining the idea of Christ's divinity.

2. (Section III.8 lines 3-6): Ὁ τὸ πανάσπιλον αὐτοῦ αἷμα διαχύσας ἐπὶ τὴν τοῦ κόσμου ζωήν, καὶ εἰς λύτρον καὶ ἀντάλλαγμα πάντων ἑαυτὸν παρέδωκας, ἐκ θανάτου λυτρωσάμενος, ἐν ᾧ κατειχόμεθα· πεπραγμένοι ὑπὸ τὴν ἁμαρτίαν.

The sections following the opening are meant to underscore its function, describing now how Christ operates as God. This section details how Christ: αἴρων τὴν ἁμαρτίαν τοῦ κόσμου by shedding His πανάσπιλον...αἷμα. The link back to the first section is made by the phrase: ἐπὶ τὴν τοῦ κόσμου ζωήν, the repetition of the word κόσμου shows that the taking away of the sin, begun in the opening, is completed in the shedding of blood, detailed in this section.

The remainder of the section is found, in a slightly different form, in the Liturgy of St. Basil, in the prayer before the Consecration: καὶ καθαρίσας ἐν ὕδατι, καὶ ἁγιάσας τῷ Πνεύματι τῷ ἁγίῳ, ἔδωκεν ἑαυτὸν ἀντάλλαγμα τῷ θανάτῳ, ἐν ᾧ κατειχόμεθα, πεπραγμένοι ὑπὸ τὴν ἁμαρτίαν.[1254] The similarities are both in the description of Christ as who hands himself over to death as an ἀντάλλαγμα, as well as in the description of the catalyst for this: in the Liturgy of St. Basil it is: ἐν ὕδατι and in the Liturgy of St. Gregory it is the πανάσπιλον blood. Though different elements, it is their purity and the purity they impart that act as a catalyst for salvation, and which look forward to the transition of the prayer in the Liturgy of St. Gregory into a prayer of purification for the Eucharist. Two points differ in the two text, in the Liturgy of St. Gregory the verb is in the second person singular, creating a dialogue style with Christ present throughout the text; in the Liturgy of St. Basil, the verb is in the third person singular, describing what Christ has done. The second point

---

[1253] Cf. the story of the paralitic in Mark 2: 1-12
[1254] Hammond and Brightman (1896). pp. 326-327 and Trempelis (1982). pg. 181. "Cleansing in water and hallowing through the Holy Spirit, He gave Himself over as a ransom to death, in which we were held captive, having been sold under sin."

concerns what is done before Christ gives himself as a ransom for death. In the Liturgy of St. Gregory, it is after the shedding of His blood, while in the Liturgy of St. Basil, it is following the sanctification through water and the spirit, a reference to Christ's direction on receiving Salvation to Nicodemus in the Gospel of John.[1255]

That the two liturgies interacted has been seen in the number of prayers in the Liturgy of St. Basil that were adopted from the Liturgy of St. Gregory. Here, however, the opposite seems to be the case, a place where the author of the Liturgy of St. Gregory uses intertexutuality to refer to a prayer in the Liturgy of St. Basil. The instances in which the Liturgy of St. Basil adopts from the Liturgy of St. Gregory have been entire prayers rather than small snippets from prayers, and usually remain in the style they were written in, that is, in the dialogue style and directed to Christ, here we see a portion of text in a third person style, part of a longer prayer addressed to the Father. We have seen intertextual allusion involving adaptation of prayers from other sources in the Liturgy of St. Gregory already, the opening prayer of the liturgy, for example, was most likely adapted from the Greek-Syrian Liturgy of St. James. After having established the vector of movement of this text, we must investigate too, why this text portion was chosen by the author of the liturgy to fit here.

The "Prayer of Freedom" is the last prayer before the direct preparation of the Eucharistic elements and their distribution, the proximity to the Eucharist, as well as the transformation of the text into a prayer of purification in the second section, links this prayer inseprably with the Eucharist. By intertextually linking this part of the prayer, which is introduced by the shedding of Christ's blood, with a prayer that introduces the hallowing of the Eucharistic elements underscores the presence of Christ in the Eucharist and the reality of the wine as the blood of Christ. The author also alludes to this part of the Liturgy of St. Basil because of its connection to Baptism. The link between Baptism, the sacrament through which a Christian gains access to the Eucharist, and the Eucharist, through which the world, according to the author, recieves salvation: ἐπὶ τὴν τοῦ κόσμου ζωὴν. We see this in another prayer in the Liturgy of St. Gregory as well, in the "Prayer of the Breaking,"[1256] which plays with the "adoption to sonship" through Baptism, and the preparation for receiving the Eucharist. By alluding to this text, then, which discusses purification through Baptism, the author of the Liturgy of St. Gregory is able to link the shedding of Christ's blood with the Eucharist, and the Eucharist with Baptism.

[1255] Cf. the Gospel of John 3:1-13
[1256] All three of these prayers discuss this imagery.

3. (Section III.8 lines 6-7): Ὁ τῶν φοβουμένων αὐτὸν ποιῶν τὸ θέλημα, καὶ τῆς δεήσεως αὐτῶν εἰσακούσων, καὶ σώζων αὐτούς·

This section continues to underscore the function of the opening, to define Christ as God. Rather than continuing with the discussion of how Christ deals with the world as a whole: ἐπὶ τὴν τοῦ κόσμου ζωήν, the author turns to discussing how Christ deals with the individual Christians: τῶν φοβουμένων αὐτόν. This is discussed in three ways: Christ 1. does their will; 2. listens to their prayer and 3. saves them. The author seems to set this up with two goals in mind: 1. to progress from least to most important: the doing of one's will by Christ is contingent on Him hearing the prayer, but the most important prayer that one can have is to receive salvation, therefore salvation is set at the end of the list. 2. The Structure shows the spiritual benefit of prayer, salvation, and the temporal benefit, the carrying out of the will of the one making the prayer, surround the catalyst, being heard by Christ.

4. (Section III.8 lines 7-11): ὁ τοῦ δικαίου Ἰὼβ ἐπακούσας ἀνιστάμενος τὸ πρωὶ καὶ ὑπὲρ παιδίων φίλτρων θυσίας προσαγαγὼν εἰπών. Μήπως ἐνενόησαν υἱοί μου πονηρὰ ἐν τῇ καρδίᾳ αὐτῶν ἔναντι Θεοῦ. Καὶ ἐμοῦ τοῦ ἐλεεινοῦ καὶ ἁμαρτωλοῦ, καὶ ἀχρείου σου δούλου, ἱκετεύω ὑπὲρ τῶν σῶν οἰκετῶν, πατέρων μου καὶ ἀδελφῶν, καὶ ὑπὲρ τῆς ἐμῆς ἀθλιότητος.

The author finishes the progression to the specific here, having dealt with Christ's relationship with the whole world, and with Christians in general, here he discusses how Christ deals with the prayer of an individual. The choice of Job is made in order to continue the though expressed in the preceeding section: τῶν φοβουμένων αὐτόν are the ones whose prayers are heard, and who is a better example of fearing God than Job?[1257]

The author is also very deliberate in his use of an Old Testament example. There are New Testament examples of righteous figures the author could have put in this place, but he chooses an Old Testament figure to underscore Christ as the God of the Old Testament as well as the New.

This section is also important for the progression of this prayer, the author has now completed his discussion of how Christ functions as God with the various levels of His creation, and wishes to continue to the ‚purification' section of this prayer. He does so by choosing a quotation in which a righteous man prays for the imperfections and sins of his sons. The author is able to transfer this example to himself in the next section: ἱκετεύω ὑπὲρ τῶν σῶν οἰκετῶν, πατέρων μου καὶ ἀδελφῶν, καὶ ὑπὲρ τῆς ἐμῆς ἀθλιότητος. Just as

---

[1257] Cf. the numerous troubles he endures without losing his faith in the Book of Job.

Job prays for his sons, the priest prays for his fathers and brothers, but unlike Job, the priest must also pray for himself, because he has not attained the worthines that Job had, transitioning the prayer into the list of imperatives that constitute a prayer of purification to reach the level of worthiness needed to receive the Eucharist.

5. (Section III.8 lines 11-19, 22 and 25-26): Εὐμενεῖ προσώπῳ καὶ γαληνῷ ὄμματι, ἔπιδε ἐφ' ἡμᾶς ἐν ταύτῃ τῇ ὥρᾳ. Καὶ παρὲς οὖν ἡμῖν πᾶσαν ἀθετηρίαν, καὶ πᾶσαν παράβασιν, καὶ παρακοὴν νόμου, καὶ τῶν σῶν ἐντολῶν. Ἔτι δὲ καὶ πᾶσαν συνείδησιν, καὶ πᾶσαν ἐνθύμησιν, καὶ πάσαις πράξεσι, καὶ πάσαις κινήσεσι γεγωνυίαις ἐν ἑαυταῖς, ἡμερικῶς τε καὶ νυκτερικῶς ἐπιδῆσαι καὶ κατακρατῆσαι κατὰ τῆς ψυχῆς. Καὶ ἀθώοσον αὐτοὺς ἀπὸ πάσης συνειδήσεως πονηρῶν, καὶ πάσης ἀκάρπου πράξεως, καὶ παντὸς λογισμοῦ πεπυρωμένου. Ἅτινα ἐστὶν βεβηλὰ παρὰ τὴν τῆς ψυχῆς καθαρότητα. Χάρισαι αὐτῶν τὴν τῶν ἁμαρτιῶν ἐπίγνωσιν, καὶ τελείως ἀπέχεσθαι ἀπ' αὐτῶν. Δώρησαι αὐτοῖς μετανοίας ἀγνότητος καὶ τὴν εἰς σὲ ἐπιστροφήν...Φεῖσαι πάντων, Δέσποτα φιλόψυχε ὅτι τὰ σύμπαντα δοῦλα σά... ἔμπλησον ἡμᾶς τοῦ σοῦ φόβου, καὶ κατεύθυνον εἰς τὸ ἀγαθόν σου θέλημα.

Following the transition from the discussion of Christ's nature and His relationship with the world, with Christians as a whole and with an individual, to prayer of purification, are a list of requests, expressed as imperatives. This list of imperatives, like the list of ways Christ interacts with Christinans as a whole earlier in the prayer, progresses and culminates in the final imperative, in which Christ is asked to fill ἡμᾶς τοῦ σοῦ φόβου, connecting the prayer purification back to the τῶν φοβουμένων αὐτὸν who receive salvation.

Over the course of these prayers, these imperatives, the author moves the discussion upward from the profane to the holy,[1258] the upward journey begins first with the descent of Christ to the level of the worshipper, another allusion to the Incarnation, He is asked to Εὐμενεῖ προσώπῳ καὶ γαληνῷ ὄμματι, and to ἔπιδε...ἐν ταύτῃ τῇ ὥρᾳ. Without this acceptance and the willingness of Christ to look upon and initiate the contact with the worshipper the entire process of salvation is impossible.

The author's purpose in this text is to underscore Christ's place as God, and God cannot remain at this lower level, therefore the author begins the upward journey of the individual along with Christ, first Christ is asked to "forgive sins" specifically those sins that are undergone through the breaking of the Commandments, the: τῶν σῶν ἐντολῶν. So the author both underscores Christ as the giver of the law, the God of the Old Testament,

---

[1258] See, for example, a similar Structure in the opening prayer of the text. Though this prayer may be, in part, adopted from the Greek-Syrian Liturgy of St. James the neo-Platonic structure of ascent evident in both the prayers adapted by the original author and in the texts original to the Liturgy itself, show a strong reliance on and knowledge of the neo-Platonic school of philosophy, in a Christianized context.

and as the God of the New Testament, who fulfills the law.[1259] The following two imperatives beg Christ to first bind: πᾶσαν ἐνθύμησιν, καὶ πάσαις πράξεσι, καὶ πάσαις κινήσεσι γεγωνυίαις ἐν ἑαυταῖς, and then to prevail: κατὰ τῆς ψυχῆς, juxtaposing the sins of the body and the sins of the soul. This juxtaposition continues in a second request for forgiveness from: συνειδήσεως πονηρῶν, καὶ πάσης ἀκάρπου πράξεως, καὶ παντὸς λογισμοῦ πεπυρωμένου ἅτινα ἐστὶν παρὰ βεβηλὰ τὴν τῆς ψυχῆς καθαρότητα. The author uses this juxtaposition, first of all, to create the illusion of movement in the text, as the individual progresses from the earthly to the heavenly, the text progresses from the bodily sins to the spiritual sins.

The following two imperatives Χάρισαι and Δώρησαι are possible because the individual has now been forgiven by Christ, they show the progression that has been made along the upward journey, the requests made before, that Christ ‚bind up' the sins of the body and "rule over" the soul are no longer necessary following the forgiveness of first the bodily and then the spiritual sins. In these requests, the responsibility of not sinning, of recognizing sin and repenting, is transferred from Christ back to the individual.

The final imperatives: Φεῖσαι πάντων and ἔμπλησον ἡμᾶς discuss the final arrival of the individual at the end of the journey, the reason given, why Christ should ‚spare' those praying, is that they have become: δοῦλα σά, they have reached the goal of the Christian life, to become servants of Christ, here another allusion to a Gospel passage, in which the person who has reached salvation is referred to as the ‚good and faithful servant.'[1260] Referring back to the first part of the prayer, in which those who fear Christ are heard by Him and receive salvation, the request, that "we" be filled with: τοῦ σοῦ φόβου. The filling of the individual with the fear of Christ also leads into the final imperative of the section, which does not stand on its own, but is dependant on this fear: κατεύθυνον εἰς τὸ ἀγαθόν σου θέλημα, it is through the fear of Christ, that the individual is brought into and completes his journey.

6. (Section III.8 lines 19-22 and 22-25): σὺ γὰρ Δέσποτα Κύριε ἐπτώχευσας ἑκουσίως ἐν τῷ σε σαρκωθῆναι διὰ τὴν τοῦ γένους ἡμῶν σωτηρίαν. Καὶ διέρρηξας τὸ καθ' ἡμῶν χειρόγραφον, διὰ τὴν ἐπὶ τοῦ σταυροῦ τῶν θείων σου παλάμων ἐφ' ἅπλωσιν...Καὶ παρὰ σοῦ ἡμέτερα ἀφετήρια, καὶ οὐδὲν τῶν ἐπιτηδευμάτων τῶν χειρῶν ἡμῶν. Δι' ὃ τὴν σὴν βασιλείαν δοξάζομεν καὶ ἀνυμνοῦμέν σε Χριστὲ ὁ Θεὸς ἡμῶν. Ἅτινα ν...λου...ων...θόρων... Πάσαις ἁμαρτίας ἕως, αἱρετικῶν καὶ ἐθνικῶν·

[1259] Cf. the Gospel of Matthew 5:17
[1260] Cf. the Gospel of Matthew 25:21

The Commentary

Twice in this second section of the text are insertions between the imperatives. These occur between the eighth and ninth and ninth and tenth imperatives respectively. These interpolations serve to expand the discussion of the imperatives they follow, as well as to shift the focus of the section back to Christ. The eighth imperative requests a true repentance and the ability to turn towards Christ, these requests result in the ability of the individual to drive his own salvation forward, the author cannot leave this as is, since his purpose is to emphasize Christ, and this request ultimately negates any further need for Christ to interact with the individual, since the individual can now complete the process of salvation on his own. In order to shift the focus back to Christ, the author takes a break from the stream of imperatives and discusses again the process of Salvation, through the Incarnation and the cross. Striking here too is the use of the phrase: καὶ διέρρηξας τὸ καθ' ἡμῶν χειρόγραφον, a legalistic term, unusual in the more mystical and less legalistic Eastern tradition, but a term found in the Liturgy of St. John Chrysostom.

Following the shift of focus back to the salvific efforts of Christ the author returns to the row of imperatives, continuing with a plea that Christ spare ‚us' as His servants. This is followed by the second of the interpolated passages, which lays out the feebleness of humanity: οὐδὲν τῶν ἐπιτηδευμάτων τῶν χειρῶν ἡμῶν and once more shifts the focus of the listener to Christ, and away from the individual who is making the journey upward, and has, in fact, nearly reached the goal. Despite the upward journey of the individual toward salvation, the author makes clear that it is never he who accomplishes this, it is only through Christ that this salvation can occur. In light of this the author switches tracks, it is no longer the human who is denigrated, but Christ who is exalted: δι' ὃ τὴν σὴν βασιλείαν δοξάζομεν καὶ ἀνυμνοῦμέν σε, Χριστὲ ὁ Θεὸς ἡμῶν, it seems to be the verbal equivalent of the prostrations that are so common in the Eastern Church, overwhelmed by his own unworthiness as a human and the greatness of Christ as God, the author has only one option left, to praise and worship Christ as God.

Unfortunately the majority of the rest of this insertion is lost in a *crux*, and it is difficult to say what may have stood there originally. The *crux* lasts only few lines in the Paris manuscript, so not very much text has been lost, what is missing is the transition from what is written on the one side of the *crux* to what comes after. The exaltant tone is gone and the focus has shifted to the: ἁμαρτίας...αἱρετικῶν καὶ ἐθνικῶν, what is possible is that the section shifts from the exaltation of Christ and His kingdom to a request for the stability of that kindom on earth in the face of these "heretics and nations."

7. (Section III.8 line 27): Σὺ γὰρ, εἶ, ὁ Θεὸς ἡμῶν, καὶ πρέπει σοι δόξα τιμὴ καὶ προσκύνησις.

The Liturgy of Saint Gregory the Theologian

Closing the prayer is an *ekphonesis*, which is slightly different from the usual form found in the Liturgy. The beginning of the *ekphonesis* usually includes the name of Christ, but this is unecessary here, since the other members of the Trinity are not included in this prayer (with the exception of a short mention of God the Father: ὁ ἀμνὸς τοῦ Θεοῦ). The lack of the Trinitarian formula may also be explained in this way, though there are examples of prayers without a Trinitarian formula, these are usually found in prayers without a proper *ekphonesis*, the lack of the formula may, then, reflect the lack of the name of Christ which should balance it on the other side of the discussion of the types of worship due to Christ.

III.X. The Preparation for the Eucharist: The Σῶμα καὶ αἷμα.

Following the "Prayer of Freedom," a dialogue between the priest, the deacon and the people begins, which culminates in the reception of the Eucharist by the clergy and the distribution of the Eucharist to the people. Though Hammerschmidt does not include the section in his commentary, the Coptic text and translation are included in his edition, in which we see that, despite the disproportionally large amount of Greek phrases still used in the Coptic text, there are still a large number of differences between the Greek text and the Coptic translation. In order to illustrate this, the Coptic (in Hammerschmidt's translation) and the Greek text are placed opposite each other in the following table and the differenes underlined:

Table III.X.1: The Greek text vs. the Coptic translation.

1. The Greek text[1261]	2. The Coptic text[1262]
Ὁ Διάκονος λέγει· Σῶμα καὶ αἷμα. Μετὰ φόβου θεοῦ προσχῶμεν. Ὁ Ἱερεὺς ὑψοῖ τὸ σπουδικὸν καὶ ἐκφωνήσει. Τὰ ἅγια τοῖς ἁγίοις. Ὁ Λαὸς λέγει· Κύριε ἐλέησον. Εἷς Πατὴρ ἅγιος, εἷς Υἱὸς ἅγιος, ἓν Πνεῦμα ἅγιον.	Der Diakon spricht: <u>Gerettet. Amen. Und deinem Geiste.</u> Mit Gottesfurcht lasst uns aufmerken. <u>Das Volk spricht:</u> <u>Herr, erbarme dich. Herr, erbarme dich. Herr, erbarme dich.</u>

[1261] Cf. Section III.9 lines 1-37.
[1262] Cf. Hammerschmidt (1957). pp. 69-73

The Commentary

Ἀμήν. Ὁ Ἱερεὺς λέγει. Ὁ Κύριος μετὰ πάντων ὑμῶν. Ὁ Λαὸς λέγει· Καὶ μετὰ τοῦ πνεύματός σου. Ὁ Ἱερεὺς λέγει· Εὐλογητὸς Κύριος εἰς τοὺς αἰῶνας, Ἀμήν. Ὁ Λαὸς λέγει· Ἀμήν. Ὁ Ἱερεὺς λέγει· Εἰρήνη πᾶσιν. Ὁ Λαὸς λέγει· Καὶ τῷ πνεύματί σου. Ὁ Ἱερεὺς λέγει· Σῶμα ἅγιον καὶ αἷμα τίμιον, ἀληθινὸν Ἰησοῦ Χριστοῦ υἱοῦ τοῦ Θεοῦ. Ἀμήν. Ὁ Λαὸς λέγει· Ἀμήν. Ὁ Ἱερεὺς λέγει· Ἅγιον τίμιον σῶμα καὶ αἷμα ἀληθινὸν Ἰησοῦ Χριστοῦ τοῦ Θεοῦ. Ἀμήν. Ὁ Λαὸς λέγει· Ἀμήν. Ὁ Ἱερεὺς λέγει· Σῶμα καὶ αἷμα Ἐμμανουὴλ τοῦ Θεοῦ ἡμῶν, τοῦτό ἐστιν ἀληθῶς. Ἀμήν. Ὁ Λαὸς λέγει· Ἀμήν. Πιστεύω, πιστεύω, πιστεύω, καὶ ὁμολογῶ ἕως ἐσχάτης ἀναπνοῆς. Ὅτι αὕτη ἐστὶν ἡ σὰρξ ἡ ζωοποιὸς, ἣν ἔλαβες Χριστὲ ὁ Θεὸς ἡμῶν, ἐκ τῆς ἁγίας δεσποίνης ἡμῶν Θεοτόκου, καὶ ἀειπαρθένου Μαρίας. Καὶ ἐποίησας αὐτὴν μίαν σὺν τῇ θεότητί σου, μὴ ἐν μίξει, μηδὲ ἐν φυρμῷ, μηδὲ ἐν ἀλλοιώσει. Καὶ ἐμαρτύρησας ἐπὶ Ποντίου Πιλάτου τὴν καλὴν ὁμολογίαν, καὶ παρέδωκας αὐτὴν ἡμῶν πάντων ἡμετέρων ἐπὶ τοῦ ξύλου τοῦ σταυροῦ τοῦ ἁγίου, ἐν τῷ θελήματί σου. Ἀληθῶς πιστεύω, ὅτι θεότης σου, οὐδ' οὐ μηδέποτε χωρισθεῖσα ἐξ ἀνθρωπότητός σου, ἐν ἀτόμῳ, οὐδὲ ἐν ῥιπῇ ὀφθαλμοῦ.	[Der Priester spricht: (indem er das isbadiyaqun [=δεσποτικόν] in die Höhe hebt und sein Haupt neigt):] Das Heilige den Heiligen (das ganze Volk wirft sich nieder). Gepriesen ist der Herr Jesus Christus, Sohn Gottes (und) die Heiligung der heilige Geist. Amen. [Das Volk (erhebt sich und) spricht:] Amen. Ein heiliger Vater, ein heiliger Sohn, ein heiliger Geist. Amen. Der Priester spricht: Friede allen. Das Volk spricht: Und deinem Geiste. [Der Priester spricht:] Der heilige Leib und das erwürdige warhafte Blut Jesu Christi, des Sohnes unseres Gottes. Amen. Das Volk spricht: Amen. Der Priester spricht: Der heilige ehrwürdige Leib und das warhafte Blut Jesu Christi, des Sohnes unseres Gottes. Amen. Das Volk spricht: Amen. Der Priester spricht: Der Leib (σῶμα) und das Blut des Emmanuel, unseres Gottes, dies ist wahrhaft. Das Volk spricht. Amen. Ich glaube. Der Priester spricht: Amen. Amen. Amen. Ich glaube. Ich glaube und bekenne (ὁμολογεῖν) bis zum letzten Atemzuge, dass dies das belebende Fleisch (σάρξ) ist, das du, o Christus, mein Gott, aus unser aller Herrin, der heiligen Gottesgebärerin (θεοτόκος) der heiligen (ἁγία) Maria, angenommen hast. Du hast es vereint mit

Μετέδωκας αὐτὴν εἰς λύτρωσιν, καὶ εἰς ἄφεσιν ἁμαρτιῶν, καὶ εἰς ζωὴν τὴν αἰώνιον, τοῖς ἐξ αὐτῆς μεταλαμβάνουσι. Πιστεύω ὅτι αὕτη ἐστὶν ἀληθῶς, ἀμήν. Ὁ Λαὸς λέγει· Ἀμήν. Ὁ Διάκονος λέγει· Ἐν εἰρήνῃ καὶ ἀγάπῃ. Ὁ Ἱερεὺς ἐκφωνήσει· Ἀκατάληπτε Θεέ Λόγε ἀχώρητε· ἀΐδιε, δέχου παρ' ἡμῶν τῶν ἁμαρτωλῶν ἐξ ἀναξίων χειλέων ὕμνον μετὰ τῶν ἄνω δυνάμεων. *Σοὶ γὰρ πρέπει πᾶσα δόξα τιμὴ καὶ προσκύνησις, σὺν τῷ ἀνάρχῳ σου Πατρὶ, καὶ τῷ ζωοποιῷ σου Πνεύματι, εἰς πάντας τοὺς αἰῶνας τῶν αἰώνων. Ἀμήν.* Ὁ Λαὸς λέγει ψαλμὸν ρ´ν. Ὁ Διάκονος λέγει· Συνάχθητε καὶ εἰσέλθετε οἱ διάκονοι μετ' εὐλαβείας.	deiner Gottheit, unvermischt und un-vermischbar und ohne Veränderung; indem du vor Pontios Pilatos das gute Bekenntnis (ὁμολογία) abgelegt hast (ὁμολογεῖν). Du hast es durch das heilige Holz des Kreuzes (σταυρός) für uns abgelegt, nach deinem eigenen Willen für uns alle. Ich glaube, dass sich deine Gottheit von deiner Menschheit weder einen einzigen Augenblick noch (οὐδέ) ein Augenzwinkern (=Augenblick) lang getrennt hat. Sie wird (nun) für uns zur Rettung und zur Vergebung der Sünden und zu ewigem Leben denen gegeben, die von ihr nehmen werden. Ich glaube, dass dies wahrhaft do ist. Amen. Der Diakon spricht: Betet für uns für alle Christen, deretwegen uns gesagt worden ist: Gedenkt user im Hause des Herrn: DerFriede und (die) Liebe Jesu Christi sei mit euch. Singt. [Der Priester spricht:] Du bist es, dem der Lobpreis (δοξολογία), in einer Stimme aller gebührt (πρέπει), der Ruhm und die Ehre, die Herrlichkeit (eigentl.: Grösse) (und) die Anbetung (προσκύνησις), und deinem guten (ἀγαθός) Vater und dem lebenspendenden und dir wesensgleichen (ὁμοούσιος) heiligen Geist (πνεῦμα), jetzt und zu jeder Zeit bis zur Ewigkeit aller Ewigkeiten. Amen. Das Volk spricht: Hunder Jahre [oder] Ehre dir, Herr, Ehre dir. [Dann singt das Volk den Ps. 150, währenddessen empfängt der Priester und die anderen das Abendmahl.] [Der Diakon spricht:] Betet für den würdigen Empfang der unbefleckten und himmlischen heiligen Gaheimnisse. Das Volk spricht:

	Herr, erbarme dich.[1263]

The majority of this dialogue is paralleled more closely in another text, in the introduction to the Eucharist in the Egyptian Liturgy of St. Basil,[1264] the differences are shown in the following table:

Figure III.X.2: comparing the parallel dialogues in the Liturgies of St. Gregory and St. Basil

1. The Liturgy of St. Gregory[1265]	2. The Liturgy of St. Basil
Ὁ Διάκονος λέγει· Σῶμα καὶ αἷμα. Μετὰ φόβου θεοῦ προσχῶμεν. Ὁ Ἱερεὺς ὑψοῖ τὸ σπουδικὸν καὶ ἐκφωνήσει. Τὰ ἅγια τοῖς ἁγίοις. Ὁ Λαὸς λέγει· Κύριε ἐλέησον. Εἷς Πατὴρ ἅγιος, εἷς Υἱὸς ἅγιος, ἓν Πνεῦμα ἅγιον. Ἀμήν. Ὁ Ἱερεὺς λέγει· Ὁ Κύριος μετὰ πάντων ὑμῶν. Ὁ Λαὸς λέγει· Καὶ μετὰ τοῦ πνεύματός σου. Ὁ Ἱερεὺς λέγει· Εὐλογητὸς Κύριος εἰς τοὺς αἰῶνας, Ἀμήν.	Ὁ Ἱερεὺς ὑψοῖ τὸ σουδικὸν καὶ ἐκφωνήσει. Τὰ ἅγια τοῖς ἁγίοις. Ὁ Λαὸς λέγει. Κύριε ἐλέησον. γ΄. Εἷς πατὴρ ἅγιος· εἷς υἱὸς ἅγιος, ἓν πνεῦμα ἅγιον. Ἀμήν. Ὁ Ἱερεὺς λέγει. Ὁ κύριος μετὰ πάντων ὑμῶν. Ὁ Λαὸς λέγει. Καὶ μετὰ τοῦ πνεύματος σου. Ὁ Ἱερεὺς λέγει. Εὐλογητὸς κύριος εἰς τοὺς αἰῶνας. Ἀμήν. Ὁ Λαὸς λέγει. Ἀμήν. Ὁ Ἱερεὺς λέγει. Εἰρήνη πᾶσιν. Ὁ Λαὸς λέγει. Καὶ τῷ πνεύματί σου.

[1263] "The deacon says: Saved. Amen. And with your spirit. With fear of God let us attend. The people say: Lord, have mercy; Lord, have mercy; Lord, have mercy. The priest says: (As he raises the dadiyaqun [δεσποτικόν] up high and bows his head) The holy for the holy (the whole people throw themselves down). Blessed is the Lord Jesus Christ the SOne of God and the sanctification of the Holy Spirit. Amen. The people (rising) say: Amen. A holy Father, a holy Son, a holy Spirit. Amen. The priest says: Peace be with all. The people say: And with your spirit. The priest says: The holy Body and precious Blood of Jesus Christ the Son of God. Amen. The people say: Amen. The priest says: The holy precious Body and the true Blood of Jesus Christ the Son of our God. Amen. The people say: Amen. The priest says: The Body and Blood of Emmanuel our God, this is true. The people say: Amen. I believe. The priest says: Amen. Amen. Amen. I believe, I believe and confess until my last breath, that this is the life-giving flesh, which You, O Christ my God, took from our Lady the holy Theotokos the holy Mary. You unified it with Your divinity, unmixed and unmixable and without change; in that You endured the good confession before Pontius Pilate. You set it off for us through the holy wood of the Cross, according to Your own will for us all. I believe that Your divinity was separated from Your humanity not for an instance, not for the twinkling of an eye. Now it becomes for us salvation and forgiveness of sins and eternal life for those who partake of it. I believe that this is truly so. Amen. The deacon says: Pray for us, for all Christians, on whose behalf it was said to us: Think about ours who are in the House of the Lord. The peace and the love of Jesus Christ be with you. The priest says: You are He who deserves the doxology of all in one voice, the glory, the honor, the might and the worship and Your good Father and the life-giving, consubstantial Holy Spirit, now and ever and to the ages of ages. Amen. The people say: Hundred years (or) Honor to You, Lord, Honor to You. [then the people sing the 150th Psalm, meanwhile the priest and the others receive the Supper.] The deacon says: Pray for the worthy participation in the spotless and heavenly holy mysteries. The people say: Lord, have mercy."

[1264] The text can be found in Renaudot (1847) I. pp. 80-81

[1265] Section III.9 lines 1-37.

The Liturgy of Saint Gregory the Theologian

Ὁ Λαὸς λέγει· Ἀμήν.
Ὁ Ἱερεὺς λέγει· Εἰρήνη πᾶσιν.
Ὁ Λαὸς λέγει· Καὶ τῷ πνεύματί σου.
Ὁ Ἱερεὺς λέγει· Σῶμα ἅγιον καὶ αἷμα τίμιον, ἀληθινὸν Ἰησοῦ Χριστοῦ υἱοῦ τοῦ Θεοῦ. Ἀμήν.
Ὁ Λαὸς λέγει· Ἀμήν.
Ὁ Ἱερεὺς λέγει· Ἅγιον τίμιον σῶμα καὶ αἷμα ἀληθινὸν Ἰησοῦ Χριστοῦ τοῦ Θεοῦ. Ἀμήν.
Ὁ Λαὸς λέγει· Ἀμήν.
Ὁ Ἱερεὺς λέγει· Σῶμα καὶ αἷμα Ἐμμανουὴλ τοῦ Θεοῦ ἡμῶν, τοῦτό ἐστιν ἀληθῶς. Ἀμήν.
Ὁ Λαὸς λέγει· Ἀμήν.
Πιστεύω, πιστεύω, πιστεύω, καὶ ὁμολογῶ ἕως ἐσχάτης ἀναπνοῆς. Ὅτι αὕτη ἐστὶν ἡ σὰρξ ἡ ζωοποιός, ἣν ἔλαβες Χριστὲ ὁ Θεὸς ἡμῶν, ἐκ τῆς ἁγίας δεσποίνης ἡμῶν Θεοτόκου, καὶ ἀειπαρθένου Μαρίας. Καὶ ἐποίησας αὐτὴν μίαν σὺν τῇ θεότητί σου, μὴ ἐν μίξει, μηδὲ ἐν φυρμῷ, μηδὲ ἐν ἀλλοιώσει. Καὶ ἐμαρτύρησας ἐπὶ Ποντίου Πιλάτου τὴν καλὴν ὁμολογίαν, καὶ παρέδωκας αὐτὴν ἡμῶν πάντων ἡμετέρων ἐπὶ τοῦ ξύλου τοῦ σταυροῦ τοῦ ἁγίου, ἐν τῷ θελήματί σου.
Ἀληθῶς πιστεύω, ὅτι θεότης σου, οὐδ᾽ οὐ μηδέποτε χωρισθεῖσα ἐξ ἀνθρωπότητος σου, ἐν ἀτόμῳ, οὐδὲ ἐν ῥιπῇ ὀφθαλμοῦ. Μετέδωκας αὐτὴν εἰς λύτρωσιν, καὶ εἰς ἄφεσιν ἁμαρτιῶν, καὶ εἰς ζωὴν τὴν αἰώνιον, τοῖς ἐξ αὐτῆς μεταλαμβάνουσι.
Πιστεύω ὅτι αὕτη ἐστὶν ἀληθῶς, ἀμήν.
Ὁ Λαὸς λέγει· Ἀμήν.
Ὁ Διάκονος λέγει· Ἐν εἰρήνῃ καὶ ἀγάπῃ.
Ὁ Ἱερεὺς ἐκφωνήσει· Ἀκατάληπτε Θεέ

Ὁ Ἱερεὺς λέγει τὴν Ὁμολογίαν.
Ὁ Ἱερεὺς λέγει. Σῶμα ἅγιον καὶ αἷμα τίμιον, ἀληθινὸν Ἰησοῦ Χριστοῦ υἱοῦ τοῦ Θεοῦ. Ἀμήν.
Ὁ Λαὸς λέγει. Ἀμήν.
Ὁ Ἱερεὺς λέγει. Ἅγιον τίμιον σῶμα καὶ αἷμα ἀληθινὸν Ἰησοῦ Χριστοῦ τοῦ Θεοῦ. Ἀμήν.
Ὁ Λαὸς λέγει. Ἀμήν.
Ὁ Ἱερεὺς λέγει. Σῶμα καὶ αἷμα Ἐμμανουὴλ τοῦ Θεοῦ ἡμῶν, τοῦτό ἐστιν ἀληθῶς. Ἀμήν.
Ὁ Λαὸς λέγει. Ἀμήν.
Πιστεύω, πιστεύω, πιστεύω καὶ ὁμολογῶ ἕως ἐσχάτης ἀναπνοῆς, ὅτι αὐτή ἐστιν ἡ σὰρξ ζωοποιὸς τοῦ μονογενοῦς σου υἱοῦ, τοῦ κυρίου δὲ καὶ θεοῦ καὶ σωτῆρος ἡμῶν Ἰησοῦ Χριστοῦ. Ἔλαβεν αὐτὴν ἐκ τῆς ἁγίας δεσποίνης ἡμῶν θεοτόκου καὶ ἀειπαρθένου Μαρίας, καὶ ἐποίησεν αὐτὴν μίαν σὺν τῇ θεότητι αὐτοῦ, μὴ ἐν μίξει, μηδὲ ἐν φυρμῷ, μηδὲ ἐν ἀλοιώσει. Καὶ ἐμαρτύρησε ἐπὶ Ποντίου Πιλάτου τὴν καλὴν ὁμολογίαν· καὶ παρέδωκεν αὐτὴν ὑπὲρ ὑμῶν πάντων, ἐπὶ τοῦ ξύλου τοῦ σταυροῦ τοῦ ἁγίου, ἐν τῷ θελήματι αὐτοῦ. Ἀληθῶς πιστεύω ὅτι θεότης αὐτοῦ οὐδ᾽ οὐ μηδέποτε χωρισθεῖσα ἐξ ἀνθρωπότητος αὐτοῦ, ἐν ἀτόμῳ, οὐδὲ ἐν ῥιπῇ ὀφθαλμοῦ. Μετέδωκεν αὐτὴν εἰς λύτρωσιν, καὶ εἰς ἄφεσιν ἁμαρτιῶν καὶ εἰς ζωὴν τὴν αἰώνιον τοῖς ἐξ αὐτῆς μεταλαμβάνουσι. Πιστεύω ὅτι αὐτή ἐστιν ἀληθῶς. Ἀμήν.
Ὁ Λαὸς λέγει. Ἀμήν.
Ὁ Διάκονος λέγει. Ἐν εἰρήνῃ καὶ ἀγάπῃ.
Ὁ Ἱερεὺς ἐκφωνήσει. Δι᾽ οὗ καὶ μεθ᾽ οὗ πρέπει πᾶσα δόξα, τιμὴ καὶ προσκύνησις τῷ πατρὶ καὶ τῷ ἁγίῳ πνεύματι νῦν, κλ΄.

Λόγε ἀχώρητε· ἀΐδιε, δέχου παρ' ἡμῶν τῶν ἁμαρτωλῶν ἐξ ἀναξίων χειλέων ὕμνον μετὰ τῶν ἄνω δυνάμεων. *Σοὶ γὰρ πρέπει πᾶσα δόξα τιμὴ καὶ προσκύνησις, σὺν τῷ ἀνάρχῳ σου Πατρί, καὶ τῷ ζωοποιῷ σου Πνεύματι, εἰς πάντας τοὺς αἰῶνας τῶν αἰώνων. Ἀμήν.* Ὁ Λαὸς λέγει ψαλμὸν ρ΄ν. Ὁ Διάκονος λέγει· Συνάχθητε καὶ εἰσέλθετε οἱ διάκονοι μετ' εὐλαβείας.	Ὁ Λαὸς λέγει *Ψαλμὸν ν΄. καὶ τὸ κοινωνικὸν τῇ ἡμέρᾳ*. Ὁ Διάκονος λέγει. Συνάχθητε καὶ εἰσέλθετε οἱ διάκονοι μετ' εὐλαβείας.

The major difference between the section lies in the style. While both Liturgies deal with Christ in this section, in the Liturgy of St. Gregory the section is written in the dialogue style which further emphasizes the connection of the worshipper with Christ in the Liturgy; in the Greek-Egyptian Liturgy of St. Basil the section is written in a narrative style, using third person singular verbs instead of second person singular. A portion of this section, that surrounding the exclamation: Τὰ ἅγια τοῖς ἁγίοις belongs to the standard exclamations of the liturgical genre and similar phrases and responses are found in almost all liturgical types, so for example in the Greek-Egyptian Liturgy of St. Mark: Ὁ Ἱερεὺς λέγει· Τὰ ἅγια τοῖς ἁγίοις. Ὁ Λαός· Εἷς πατὴρ ἅγιος, εἷς υἱὸς ἅγιος, ἓν πνεῦμα ἅγιον, εἰς ἑνότητα πνεύματος ἁγίου. Ἀμήν.[1266] The remainder of the section does not conform, however, to the established Egyptian form of Eucharistic preparation, as laid out in the Liturgy of St. Mark.[1267] Since both versions of the prayer add nearly equal amounts the observation that prayers do not decrease in length does not help in identifying the origin of this prayer. Another criterion must then be found to determine to which Liturgy this section originally belongs. If we examine the prayers surrounding this section, especially other prayers that lead into the Eucharist, we see that the prayers in the Liturgy of St. Basil are all addressed to the Father; so we see in the prayer following this section: εἶ ὁ θεός, ὁ πατὴρ τοῦ κυρίου, δὲ καὶ θεοῦ, καὶ σωτῆρος ἡμῶν Ἰησοῦ Χριστοῦ,[1268] and following this in the "Prayer of the Bowing of the Head:" Δέσποτα κύριε ὁ θεός, ὁ πατὴρ ὁ παντοκράτωρ,[1269] even in the prayer

---

[1266] Renaudot (1847) I. pg. 145
[1267] This begins with the prayer: Ἅγιε, ὕψιστε, φοβερέ, ὁ ἐν ἁγίοις ἀναπαυόμενος, κύριε... and then continues with a dialogue between the priest, deacon and people, this dialogue has, however, a very different form than the one found in the Liturgies of St. Gregory and of St. Basil. Cf. Renaudot (1847) I. pg. 144-146.
[1268] Renaudot (1847) I. pg. 81. "You are God, the Father of our Lord and God and Savior Jesus Christ."
[1269] Ibid. "Master, Lord, God the Father, all-powerful."

preceeding the section, following a blessing of the peace: Δέσποτα κύριε ὁ θεός, ὁ πατὴρ ὁ παντοκράτωρ.[1270] While this prayer does initially address itself to the Father, it immediately shifts focus and discusses Christ. This, then fits more easily into the Christ centered style of the Liturgy of St. Gregory.

Along with the stylistic argument is the theological; other prayers that are adopted into the Liturgy of St. Gregory later tend to show Monophysite, or more precisely Miaphysite theological positions on the Incarnation and on the nature of Christ.[1271] In this section, however, we see: καὶ ἐποίησας αὐτὴν μίαν σὺν τῇ θεότητί σου, μὴ ἐν μίξει, μηδὲ ἐν φυρμῷ, μηδὲ ἐν ἀλλοιώσει, the theological position of this prayer is then firmly aligned with the Chalcedonian position on the dual natures of Christ, a position espoused in the rest of the Liturgy whenever the Incarnation is discussed. We can, then, conclude that this section was adopted into the Liturgy of St. Basil under the influence of the Liturgy of St. Gregory.

Another possibility is offered by the the Coptic Liturgy of St. Mark, in which this section is found again:

The body and blood of Emmanuel our God this is in truth. Amen. I believe, I believe, I believe and I confess unto the last breath that this is the quickening flesh which thine only-begotten Son our Lord and God and our Saviour Jesus Christ took of the lady of us all the holy theotokos S. Mary: he made it one with his godhead without confusion and without mixture and without alteration. Having confessed the good confession before Pontius Pilate he gave it also for us on the hoy tree of the cros by his own will, himself for us all. I verily believe that his godhead was not severed from his manhood for one moment nor for the twinkling of an eye. It is given for us to be salvation and forgiveness of sins and life everlasting to them that shall receive of it. I believe that this is so in truth. Amen."he made it one with his godhead without confusion and without mixture and without alteration.[1272]

In this version, like that of the Liturgy of St. Basil the focus of the prayer shifts from the Father to Christ and what Christ does to the exclusion of the Father. Here, though, the strong Chalcedonian nature of the theology: "...he made it [his humanity] one with his godhead without confusion and without mixture and without alteration..." makes this an

---

[1270] Renaudot (1847) I. pg. 77
[1271] See, for example, the first of the three "Prayers of the Breaking."
[1272] Hammond and Brightman (1896). pg. 185

awkward fit at best into a Miaphysite Liturgy. Here too we must conclude that the original prayer was replaced with a borrowing from the Liturgy of St. Gregory.

Since the influence of the Liturgy of St. Gregory, the origins of which lie in the Cappadocian-Syrian liturgical family, on the Egyptian Liturgy of St. Basil obscures the original rituals surrounding the Eucharist, and the influence of the Syrian rite colors the Eucharistic ritual of the Liturgy of St. Mark, it is difficult to determine what the original Egyptian rite may have looked like. This is an excellent example, then, to see how a liturgical family can evolve under the influence of another.

1. Structure

Unlike the majority of the chapters we have discussed so far, we see not one prayer, but a text passage encompassing two semi-independant prayers and a dialogue style section, in which the priest, deacon and people profess their belief in the true transformation of the bread and wine of the Eucharist into the Body and Blood of Christ.

This chapter begins with the exclamation of the deacon: Σῶμα καὶ αἷμα. Μετὰ φόβου θεοῦ προσχῶμεν. This begins a dialogue section based around two focal points, the exclamation: Τὰ ἅγια τοῖς ἁγίοις and the triple affirmation of Christ's presence in the Eucharist: Σῶμα ἅγιον καὶ αἷμα τίμιον, ἀληθινὸν Ἰησοῦ Χριστοῦ υἱοῦ τοῦ Θεοῦ. Ἀμήν, which is repeated, slightly altered, twice more. Between these two focal points the dialogue consists of standardized liturgical phrases and their responses.[1273]

Central to this chapter is the prayer that begins: Πιστεύω, πιστεύω, πιστεύω. This prayer can be divided into two large sections, the second of which echoes, in an abbreviated fashion, the topics discussed in the first. Both these sections begin with a statement of faith, then discuss the incarnation and finally culminate in a discussion of salvation.

Following another exclamation: Ἐν εἰρήνῃ καὶ ἀγάπῃ, the priest recites the second prayer of this section. This, much shorter prayer, is also in two parts, the first consists of a short discussion of Christ as divine, and a request in the form of an imperative. The second section is an *ekphonesis*.[1274]

This section ends with the recitation of the 150th psalm by the people and the final exclamation: Συνάχθητε καὶ εἰσέλθετε οἱ διάκονοι μετ' εὐλαβείας. The Structure of this section can also be seen in the following table:

[1273] See the table below.
[1274] See the funiction section below for a discussion of this *ekphonesis* and the relationship between the two prayers of this section.

The Liturgy of Saint Gregory the Theologian

Table III.X.3: The structure of the Σῶμα καὶ αἷμα section.[1275]

The structure of the Σῶμα καὶ αἷμα section
1. Opening.   a. the deacon introduces the dialogue section by exclaiming: Σῶμα καὶ αἷμα. Μετὰ φόβου θεοῦ προσχῶμεν.

2. First focal point of the dialogue.
   a. The priest raises the ‚zealous piece:' Ὁ Ἰερεὺς ὑψοῖ τὸ σπουδικὸν
   b. The priest cries out: Τὰ ἅγια τοῖς ἁγίοις.
   c. The people respond: Κύριε ἐλεήσον. Εἷς Πατὴρ ἅγιος, εἷς Υἱὸς ἅγιος, ἓν Πνεῦμα ἅγιον. Ἀμήν.

3. Intermediate dialogue between priest and people
   a. First couplet: Ὁ Ἰερεὺς λέγει· Ὁ Κύριος μετὰ πάντων ὑμῶν.
       Ὁ Λαὸς λέγει· Καὶ μετὰ τοῦ πνεύματος σου.
   b. Second couplet: Ὁ Ἰερεὺς λέγει· Εὐλογητὸς Κύριος εἰς τοὺς αἰῶνας, Ἀμήν.
       Ὁ Λαὸς λέγει· Ἀμήν.
   c. Third and final couplet: Ὁ Ἰερεὺς λέγει· Εἰρήνη πᾶσιν.
       Ὁ Λαὸς λέγει· Καὶ τῷ πνεύματί σου.

4. Second focal point of the dialogue.
   a. The priest exclaims the first time (the people respond each time with: Ἀμήν): Σῶμα ἅγιον καὶ αἷμα τίμιον, ἀληθινὸν Ἰησοῦ Χριστοῦ υἱοῦ τοῦ Θεοῦ. Ἀμήν.
   b. The priest exclaims the second time: Ἅγιον τίμιον σῶμα καὶ αἷμα ἀληθινὸν Ἰησοῦ Χριστοῦ τοῦ Θεοῦ. Ἀμήν.
   c. The priest exclaims the third time: Σῶμα καὶ αἷμα Ἐμμανουὴλ τοῦ Θεοῦ ἡμῶν, τοῦτό ἐστιν ἀληθῶς. Ἀμήν.

[1275] Section III.9 lines 1-37.

5. The first prayer.
    a. Part One.
        i. Confession of faith: Πιστεύω, πιστεύω, πιστεύω καὶ ὁμολογῶ ἕως ἐσχάτης ἀναπνοῆς. Ὅτι αὕτη ἐστιν ἡ σὰρξ ἡ ζωοποιὸς, ἣν ἔλαβες Χριστὲ ὁ Θεὸς ἡμῶν, ἐκ τῆς ἁγίας δεσποίνης ἡμῶν Θεοτόκου, καὶ ἀειπαρθένου Μαρίας.
        ii. Discussion of Christ's dual nature: Καὶ ἐποίησας αὐτὴν μίαν σὺν τῇ θεότητί σου, μὴ ἐν μίξει, μηδὲ ἐν φυρμῷ, μηδὲ ἐν ἀλλοιώσει·
        iii. The discussion of salvation, through the death on the Cross: Καὶ ἐμαρτύρησας ἐπὶ Ποντίου Πιλάτου τὴν καλὴν ὁμολογίαν, καὶ παρέδωκας αὐτὴν ἡμῶν πάντων ἡμετέρων ἐπὶ τοῦ ξύλου τοῦ σταυροῦ τοῦ ἁγίου, ἐν τῷ θελήματί σου.
    b. Part Two.
        i. Second Confession of faith: Ἀληθῶς πιστεύω,
        ii. Second discussion of Christ's nature: ὅτι θεότης σου οὐδ᾽ οὐ μηδέποτε χωρισθεῖσα ἐξ ἀνθρωπότητός σου, ἐν ἀτόμῳ, οὐδὲ ἐν ῥιπῇ ὀφθαλμοῦ.
        iii. Second discussion of salvation, through the partaking of the Eucharist: Μετέδωκας αὐτὴν εἰς λύτρωσιν, καὶ εἰς ἄφεσιν ἁμαρτιῶν, καὶ εἰς ζωὴν τὴν αἰώνιον, τοῖς ἐξ αὐτῆς μεταλαμβάνουσι.

        iv. Final affirmation of faith: Πιστεύω ὅτι αὕτη ἐστὶν ἀληθῶς, ἀμήν.

6. Interlude.
    a. The deacon exclaims: Ἐν εἰρήνῃ καὶ ἀγάπῃ.

7. The second prayer.
    a. Part One.
        i. Discussion of Christ as divine: Ἀκατάληπτε Θεέ Λόγε ἀχώρητε· ἀίδιε
        ii. Request in the form of an imperative: δέχου παρ᾽ ἡμῶν τῶν ἁμαρτωλῶν ἐξ ἀναξίων χειλέων ὕμνον μετὰ τῶν ἄνω δυνάμεων.
    b. Part Two, the *ekphonesis*.

> i. What worship is due to Christ: Σοὶ γὰρ πρέπει πᾶσα δόξα τιμὴ καὶ προσκύνησις,
> ii. The Trinitarian formula: σὺν τῷ ἀνάρχῳ σου Πατρὶ, καὶ τῷ ζωοποιῷ σου Πνεύματι, εἰς πάντας τοὺς αἰῶνας τῶν αἰώνων. Ἀμήν.

> 8. The Conclusion of the section.
>   a. The people recite the 150th psalm.
>   b. The Deacon exclaims: Συνάχθητε καὶ εἰσέλθετε οἱ διάκονοι μετ' εὐλαβείας.

2. Function

The focus of this section is unusual when compared to other parts of the Liturgy. Whereas the majority of the prayers do include theological statements about Christ's divinity, about Christ's dual nature, about the Incarnation and Salvation, they also include large sections of requests and often focus on the purification of the individual for the approaching Eucharist. These two prayers, however, with the exception of one request in the second prayer, functions entirely as a confession of faith, discussing Christ's place as God, salvation through the Cross, the presence of Christ in the Eucharist, and the dual nature of Christ. In this function, as well as the style in which it is written, these prayers are reminiscent of the private prayers of the priest recited before he partakes of the Eucharist in the Byzantine Liturgy of St. John Chrysostom:

> Πιστεύω, Κύριε, καὶ ὁμολογῶ ὅτι σὺ εἶ ἀληθῶς ὁ Χριστός, ὁ Υἱὸς τοῦ Θεοῦ τοῦ ζῶντος, ὁ ἐλθὼν εἰς τὸν κόσμον ἁμαρωλοὺς σῶσαι, ὧν πρῶτός εἰμι ἐγώ. Ἔτι πιστεύω ὅτι τοῦτο αὐτό ἐστι τὸ τίμιον Αἷμα σου.[1276]

The similar Structure of these two texts, beginning the prayer with a first person singular verb, rather than a first person plural: Πιστεύω...ὁμολογῶ rather than in the first person plural suggests that both prayers share the same function, that both serve as the private prayer of the priest.

[1276] Hammond and Brightman (1896). pg. 394 and Trempelis (1982). pg. 140. "I believe Lord, and I confess that You are truly the Christ, the Son of God, who came into the world in order to save sinners, of whom I am the first."

The Commentary

1. (Section III.9 lines 1-5): Ὁ Διάκονος λέγει· Σῶμα καὶ αἷμα. Μετὰ φόβου θεοῦ προσχῶμεν.
Ὁ Ἱερεὺς ὑψοῖ τὸ σπουδικὸν καὶ ἐκφωνήσει. Τὰ ἅγια τοῖς ἁγίοις.
Ὁ Λαὸς λέγει· Κύριε ἐλέησον. Εἷς Πατὴρ ἅγιος, εἷς Υἱὸς ἅγιος, ἓν Πνεῦμα ἅγιον. Ἀμήν.

The opening phrase of this section: Σῶμα καὶ αἷμα. Μετὰ φόβου θεοῦ προσχῶμεν is problematic, as it appears neither in the parallel text of the Egyptian Liturgy of St. Basil, which skips the deacons exclamation entirely and begins with the priest raising the σπουδικὸν; nor does it appear in the Coptic translation of this text: "Gerettet. Amen. Und deinem Geiste. Mit Gottesfurcht lasst uns aufmerken."[1277] The first part: "Gerettet. Amen." seems to be an interpolation or a response to a prayer found in the *crux* which preceeds this text, this leaves only the translation of the Μετὰ φόβου θεοῦ προσχῶμεν, this begs the question: is the exclamation Σῶμα καὶ αἷμα original to the text, and if not, where does it come from? Despite the other differences in the text between the Coptic translation, the Liturgy of St. Basil and the Liturgy of St. Gregory, the fact that both other versions of the text differ from that found in the Liturgy of St. Gregory may point to the fact that it is not originally a part of the Liturgy. Where then does the phrase come from? It is possible that this phrase was inserted as a title for this section of the text, in reference to the triple affirmation of the presence of Christ in the Eucharist, each one of which includes the phrase. In the post Anaphora every prayer has a title, these were certainly added secondarily, which would account for the lack of this phrase in the other texts. This title could then have been misinterpreted as part of the text by a later scribe, and in this way became part of the text of the prayer. Unfortunately it will be impossible to settle this question in this study, if older manuscripts of the Liturgy were available it would be possible to see if and when this phrase was added, since the earliest extant manuscript is from the fourteenth century, however, this question must remain without a definitive answer.

Another question in this section is: what is it that the priest raises before his exclamation? Hammerschmidt identifies it as the *isbadiyaqun,* which he equates to the Greek word: δεσποτικόν, the "Lord's piece."[1278] The δεσποτικόν is part of the *corban*, it is the square piece formed by the intersection of the vertical and horizontal sections of the cross. This piece is also known as the σπουδικόν, the "zealous piece."[1279] Despite the use of the term *isbadiyaqun* in the Hammerschmidt edition, and the use of the term δεσποτικόν in the Renaudot/Migne editions, this is not the term used in the Paris manuscript, which has the

---

[1277] Hammerschmidt (1957). pg. 69 "Saved. Amen. And with your spirit. With the fear of God let us be attentive."
[1278] Hammerschmidt (1957). pg. 69
[1279] Renaudot (1847). I. pg. 80

term: σπουδικόν, since these are all equally valid terms for this element of the Eucharist, and since this is the same term used in the Liturgy of St. Basil, we can conclude that this is the term originally part of the Liturgy.

The response to the priest's exclamation: Τὰ ἅγια τοῖς ἁγίοις is interesting, as it shows, once again, the dependance of the Egyptian rite on the Syrian, as all the Egyptian liturgies show the same response to this phrase: Εἷς Πατὴρ ἅγιος, εἷς Υἱὸς ἅγιος, ἓν Πνεῦμα ἅγιον. Ἀμήν. This response originates in the Syrian Liturgy of St. James, and is adopted into the Egyptian Liturgy. The Byzantine Liturgies use a similar phrase as a response: Εἷς ἅγιος, εἷς κύριος Ἰησοῦς Χριστός εἰς δόξαν Θεοῦ Πατρός.[1280] It seems strange that the Liturgy of St. Gregory, which we have argued is part of the Cappadocian rite would use the strictly Syrian phrase, rather than the Byzantine, but it is possible that the original response in Liturgy of St. Gregory was altered along with the other Egyptian liturgies under the influence of the Syrian Liturgy of St. James. Another possibility is that this phrase is original to the Liturgy of St. Gregory since the Cappadocian rite is a subgroup of the Syrian, which would suggest that the Liturgy of St. Gregory may have acted as a vector for transmitting this phrase from the Syrian into the Egyptian rite.

2. (Section III.9 lines 6-11): Ὁ Ἱερεὺς λέγει· Ὁ Κύριος μετὰ πάντων ὑμῶν. Ὁ Λαὸς λέγει· Καὶ μετὰ τοῦ πνεύματός σου. Ὁ Ἱερεὺς λέγει· Εὐλογητὸς Κύριος εἰς τοὺς αἰῶνας, Ἀμήν. Ὁ Λαὸς λέγει· Ἀμήν. Ὁ Ἱερεὺς λέγει· Εἰρήνη πᾶσιν. Ὁ Λαὸς λέγει· Καὶ τῷ πνεύματί σου.

The dialogue between the two focal points of this section is made up of standard liturgical phrases and their responses: two blessings and an exclamation of praise. The blessings "The Lord be with you" and "Peace be with all" are both blessings very common in the liturgical context. The other phrase: "Peace be with all" we have seen already six times in this Liturgy alone. The exclamation: "Blessed is the Lord unto the Ages."

3. (Section III.9 lines 12-20): Ὁ Ἱερεὺς λέγει· Σῶμα ἅγιον καὶ αἷμα τίμιον, ἀληθινὸν Ἰησοῦ Χριστοῦ υἱοῦ τοῦ Θεοῦ. Ἀμήν. Ὁ Λαὸς λέγει· Ἀμήν. Ὁ Ἱερεὺς λέγει· Ἅγιον τίμιον σῶμα καὶ αἷμα ἀληθινὸν Ἰησοῦ Χριστοῦ υἱοῦ τοῦ Θεοῦ. Ἀμήν. Ὁ Λαὸς λέγει· Ἀμήν. Ὁ Ἱερεὺς λέγει· Σῶμα καὶ αἷμα Ἐμμανουὴλ τοῦ Θεοῦ ἡμῶν, τοῦτό ἐστιν ἀληθῶς. Ἀμήν. Ὁ Λαὸς λέγει· Ἀμήν.

The second focal point of the dialogue section of this chapter is the triple emphasis on the true presence of Christ in the Eucharist. It is possible that the phrase Σῶμα καὶ αἷμα that opens the section is a title for the section based on this triple repetition. The triple rep-

---

[1280] Hammond and Brightman (1896). Pg. 62. "One holy, one lord, Jesus Christ, for the glory of God the Father."

etition shows the emphasis that the author wishes to place on this idea. In the Byzantine Liturgy of St. John Chrysostom the same strategy is used in the *epiklesis* in the invocation of the Holy Spirit on the gifts: Καὶ ποίησον τὸν μὲν ἄρτον τοῦτον, τίμιον Σῶμα τοῦ Χριστοῦ σου. Ἀμήν...Τὸ δὲ ἐν τῷ ποτηρίῳ τούτῳ, τίμιον Αἷμα τοῦ Χριστοῦ σου. Ἀμήν...Μεταβαλὼν τῷ Πνεύματί σου τῷ Ἁγίῳ. Ἀμήν. Ἀμήν. Ἀμήν.[1281] We see in both sections not only the triple repetition meant to emphasize the point, but also many of the same terms. This is not to say that either of these texts owes the other for these sections, but it does show that Liturgy as a genre has certain components, stylistically and in word choice, that are universal. This is one reason why the question of authorship is difficult, Gregory Nazianzus, for example, if he was the author of this Liturgy, would not have been able to use only his usual style, since liturgical writing has its own style within which he would have had to write.

Another commonality between this triple affirmation in the Liturgy of St. Gregory and the *epiklesis* in the Liturgy of St. John Chrysostom is the progression from the first two phrases to the third. In both texts the first two phrases are equal or identical, but the third shifts the parameters of the discussion and completes it. In the Liturgy of St. Gregory, despite the difference in phrasing, the first two phrases are identical, identifying the Eucharist as the Body and Blood of Ἰησοῦ Χριστοῦ υἱοῦ τοῦ Θεοῦ This description in the first two phrases is ammended by the author in the third, in order to refocus the discussion on the point of the text, the establishment of Christ as God. By shifting the term from Ἰησοῦ Χριστοῦ υἱοῦ τοῦ Θεοῦ to Ἐμμανουὴλ τοῦ Θεοῦ ἡμῶν, the author shifts the discussion from a subordinate member of the Trinity to God Himself. A similar progression is seen in the three phrases of the *epiklesis* of the Liturgy of St. John Chrysostom, the first two phrases are not identical, as the phrases in St. Gregory, but they are equal in value, each one asking that the gift in question, either the bread or the wine, be transformed into the Body or Blood of Christ. These two phrases culminate in the third, which asks the Holy Spirit to descend upon both of the gifts, completing the thought of the entire section.

The triple affirmation in the Liturgy of St. Gregory is also reflected in the Liturgy of St. Mark: Καὶ εἰς τὸ ποτήριον λέγει. Αἷμα τίμιον τοῦ κυρίου καὶ θεοῦ καὶ σωτῆρος ἡμῶν,[1282] this phrase in the Liturgy of St. Mark shows that it was used outside of the Liturgy of St. Gregory and the Liturigies into which it was adopted. Intersting, though, is that

---

[1281] Holy Cross (1985). pg. 22 and Trempelis (1982). pp. 114-115. "And make this bread the precious Body of Your Christ. Amen. And that in this cup, the precious Blood of Your Christ. Amen...changing them through Your Holy Spirit."

[1282] Hammond and Brightman (1896). pg 140 and Cuming (1990). pg. 57. "And for the cup he says: Precious Blood of our Lord and God and Savior."

The Liturgy of Saint Gregory the Theologian

the Liturgy of St. Mark does not have the repetition of the phrase, nor the culmination in a third. The triple repetition in the Liturgy of St. Gregory may then be an allusion back to the *epiklesis*, back to the hallowing of the gifts that are to be received in the Eucharist.

4. (Section III.9 lines 21-23): Πιστεύω, πιστεύω, πιστεύω καὶ ὁμολογῶ ἕως ἐσχάτης ἀναπνοῆς. Ὅτι αὕτη ἐστιν ἡ σὰρξ ἡ ζωοποιὸς, ἣν, ἔλαβες Χριστὲ ὁ Θεὸς ἡμῶν, ἐκ τῆς ἁγίας δεσποίνης ἡμῶν Θεοτόκου καὶ ἀειπαρθένου Μαρίας.

Here again the author uses a triple repition to underscore the importance of an idea. The term "I believe" is repeated three times in order to emphasize the focus of this prayer as a confession of faith. The priest confesses his belief that the bread is, in fact, the body of Christ: ὅτι αὕτη ἐστιν ἡ σὰρξ ἡ ζωοποιὸς. Despite the change in function here, not the usual prayer of purification, the style of the prayer, a second person dialogue with Chirst, puts this prayer into the correct context. Following this confession of faith is a discussion of the Incarnation: ἣν ἔλαβες Χριστὲ ὁ Θεὸς ἡμῶν. The description of the Incarnation, that Christ took flesh ἐκ τῆς ἁγίας δεσποίνης ἡμῶν Θεοτόκου, καὶ ἀειπαρθένου Μαρίας differs from the description of the Incarnation found in the Nicene Creed: καὶ σαρκωθέντα ἐκ Πνεύματος Ἁγίου καὶ Μαρίας τῆς Παρθένου καὶ ἐνανθρωπήσαντα.[1283] The discrepancy can be explained by the author's purpose, in emphasizing the divinity of Christ. By taking the Holy Spirit out of the Incarnation, the author focuses the Incarnation on Christ to the exclusion of the other members of the Trinity, underscoring His divinity and His part in Salvation. This is the same strategy is used by the author throughout the text in order to deemphasize the other members of the Trinity in favor of Christ.

The mention of the Virgin Mary here: ἁγίας δεσποίνης ἡμῶν Θεοτόκου, καὶ ἀειπαρθένου Μαρίας, is unusual for this text. There are only three other mentions of the Virgin Mary in the text, and one is in the first "Prayer of the Breaking" which is almost certainly a later addition to the text. The other mentions of the Virgin Mary are usually found in commemorations, such as the commemorations at the end of the Anaphora: Ἐξαιρέτως τῆς παναγίας ὑπερενδόξου, ἀχράντου, ὑπερευλογημένης δεσποίνης ἡμῶν Θεοτόκου καὶ ἀειπαρθένου Μαρίας.[1284] Note that the epithets of the Virgin Mary are the same in both parts of the Liturgy, making it more than likely that the phrases are original to the Liturgy.

[1283] Cf. Holy Cross (1985). Pg. 18. "and taking flesh from the Holy Spirit and the Virgin Mary and becoming man."
[1284] See the Intercessions lines 421-422.

The Commentary

5. (Section III.9 line 23-24): Καὶ ἐποίησας αὐτὴν μίαν σὺν τῇ θεότητί σου, μὴ ἐν μίξει, μηδὲ ἐν φυρμῷ, μηδὲ ἐν ἀλλοιώσει·

This section continues the discussion of the Incarnation, but progresses the discussion from the physical Incarnation to a discussion of how the natures of Christ interact following the Incarnation. The theology presented here, as all discussions of the nature of Christ original to this text have been, is consistent with what becomes the position of the Chalcedonian Church. The human nature of Christ, the σὰρξ mentioned in the last section, is united with the divine nature μίαν σὺν τῇ θεότητί. This unification is then qualified. Although united, the author emphasizes that the two natures are not the same: μὴ ἐν μίξει, μηδὲ ἐν φυρμῷ, μηδὲ ἐν ἀλλοιώσει they are not mingled, nor are they altered.

6. (Section III.9 lines 24-26): Καὶ ἐμαρτύρησας ἐπὶ Ποντίου Πιλάτου τὴν καλὴν ὁμολογίαν, καὶ παρέδωκας αὐτὴν ἡμῶν πάντων ἡμετέρων ἐπὶ τοῦ ξύλου τοῦ σταυροῦ τοῦ ἁγίου, ἐν τῷ θελήματί σου.

The confession of faith continues following the completion of the discussion of the Incarnation and the dual natures of Christ. Here the author progresses to a discussion of the way that salvation was accomplished by Christ through the Incarnation. The author's argument mirrors, to a certain extent, the progression of the Nicene Creed: 1. Incarnation through the Virgin Mary; 2. Pontius Pilate; 3. the Crucifixion.[1285] Again the author uses the second person singular in order to make Christ's presence among the congregation, and by extension in the Eucharist, more tangible to the listener, this also takes the other members of the Trinity out of the history of salvation, underscoring once again, Christ's place as God, this is especially emphasized by the phrase: ἐν τῷ θελήματί σου, this claims that salvation came about not only through Christ's action in the Incarnation and Crucifixion etc..., but through Christ's will, this interpretation goes against what is found in the Anaphora of the Liturgy of St. John Chrysostom, in the prayer before the *Sanctus*: Σὺ ἐκ τοῦ μὴ ὄντος εἰς τὸ εἶναι ἡμᾶς παρήγαγες, καὶ παραπεσόντας ἀνέστησας πάλιν, καὶ οὐκ ἀπέστης πάντα ποιῶν, ἕως ἡμᾶς εἰς τὸν οὐρανὸν ἀνήγαγες καὶ τὴν βασιλείαν σου ἐχαρίσω τὴν μέλλουσαν.[1286] In this prayer it is God the Father who is the source of both Creation and salvation, by taking the Father out of the equation, the author is able to underscore the importance of Christ in the history of salvation.

[1285] Cf. lines 11-16 of the Nicene Creed.
[1286] Holy Cross (1985). Pg. 20. "You led us from not being into being and falling, You raised us again, and You did not hold off doing everything until You led us up into heaven and give over Your kingdom to come."

7. (Section III.9 26-28): Ἀληθῶς πιστεύω, ὅτι θεότης σου οὐδ' οὐ μηδέποτε χωρισθεῖσα ἐξ ἀνθρωπότητος σου, ἐν ἀτόμῳ, οὐδὲ ἐν ῥιπῇ ὀφθαλμοῦ.

With the phrase: Ἀληθῶς πιστεύω the author opens the second section of this prayer, but also reopens the confession of faith. We have seen this strategy used by the author before; this strategy allows the author to change the topic of the discussion, while being able to connect the new topic back to the completed discussion.

The newly opened discussion deals with the divine nature of Christ: θεότης σου, as opposed to the human nature of the past discussion. Whereas the distinctness of the two natures was the topic of the discussion above, here the unity of these natures is emphasized: μηδέποτε χωρισθεῖσα ἐξ ἀνθρωπότητος σου. The terms used to describe the union of the two natures of Christ come from Paul's first letter to the Corinthians 15:51-52. Interestingly the author uses this passage in a context that seems almost opposite of that in Scripture. St. Paul discusses the change undergone by humans in order to rise to heaven at the last day, the author of this text uses this change to discuss how the nature of Christ stays the same and was never separated.

8. (Section III.9 28-29): Μετέδωκας αὐτὴν εἰς λύτρωσιν, καὶ εἰς ἄφεσιν ἁμαρτιῶν, καὶ εἰς ζωὴν τὴν αἰώνιον, τοῖς ἐξ αὐτῆς μεταλαμβάνουσι. Πιστεύω ὅτι αὕτη ἐστὶν ἀληθῶς, ἀμήν.

This section continues the parallelism of the first half of the prayer, both discuss the saving effort of Christ. The first half of the prayer discusses salvation in the historic context of Christ's death on the Cross, while this section discusses salvation through the participation in the Eucharist.

The prayer concludes in a final confession of faith: Πιστεύω ὅτι αὕτη ἐστὶν ἀληθῶς, this phrase is structured opposite to the first confession of faith in this second half of the prayer: Ἀληθῶς πιστεύω. By doing so, the author closes the discussion opened by this first confession, however, there is no *ekphonesis* in this prayer, making it one of the only prayers in the Liturgy without one. One possible explanation is that this is another parallel to the Nicene Creed, which also has no *ekphonesis*, but another possibility is that this is a false conclusion, and the next prayer is not an independent prayer at all, but continues and concludes this first prayer.

9. (Section III.9 lines 31-35): Ὁ Διάκονος λέγει· Ἐν εἰρήνῃ καὶ ἀγάπῃ. Ὁ Ἱερεὺς ἐκφωνήσει· Ἀκατάληπτε Θεέ Λόγε ἀχώρητε ἀΐδιε δέχου παρ' ἡμῶν τῶν ἁμαρτωλῶν ἐξ ἀναξίων χειλέων ὕμνον μετὰ τῶν ἄνω δυνάμεων. *Σοὶ γὰρ πρέπει πᾶσα δόξα, τιμὴ καὶ προσκύνησις σὺν τῷ ἀνάρχῳ σου Πατρὶ, καὶ τῷ ζωοποιῷ σου Πνεύματι εἰς πάντας τοὺς αἰῶνας τῶν αἰώνων. Ἀμήν.*

The exclamation of the deacon: Ἐν εἰρήνῃ καὶ ἀγάπῃ, separates the first prayer from what, at first, seems to be a second prayer. When the elements of both prayers are examined, however, the more likely conclusion is that this second prayer is a continuation of the first. The "second" prayer contains a request of Christ in the form of an imperative to "accept" the hymn from the sinners, to accept the worship of the congregation and through this acceptance to make them: μετὰ τῶν ἄνω δυνάμεων to put them on the same level as the angelic powers, i.e. bring them into the presence of God through the Eucharist. Interpreting this prayer as a continuation of the first also connects it more closely with the private prayer of the priest before the Eucharist in the Liturgy of St. Basil, which too begins with a confession of faith and continues with the request that the priest be made worthy to receive the Eucharist.

One of the differences between the Coptic and Greek texts is interesting here. While the Coptic text describes the Holy Spirit as ‚homoousios' in the *ekphonesis*, this epithet is missing in the Greek. This is one of the instances that shows that the author of the text did not use the term homoousios for the Holy Spirit as ofen as it is seen in the Monophysite Liturgies, and the use of the term for the Holy Spirit in the original prayers by the author is used deliberately against the Macedonian heresy, assisting in the dating of the text.

10. (Section III.9 lines 36-37): Ὁ Λαὸς λέγει ψαλμὸν ρ΄ν. Ὁ Διάκονος λέγει· Συνάχθητε καὶ εἰσέλθετε οἱ διάκονοι μετ' εὐλαβείας.

The final part of this section is the recitation of a psalm by the congregation and an exclamation by the deacon: Συνάχθητε καὶ εἰσέλθετε οἱ διάκονοι μετ' εὐλαβείας. The recitiation of the 150th Psalm fills the time while the priest receives the Eucharist. Following the Communion of the priest, the exclamation of the deacon invites the other deacons to come forward to receive the Eucharist, this also shows that there is, at least hypothetically, more than one deacon present at every Liturgy, the traditional number of deacons at a Liturgy is seven, to coincide with the seven lamp stands mentioned in the description of the heavenly Liturgy in Revelations.[1287]

III.XI. The "Prayer of Thanksgiving"[1288]

The Liturgy has reached its climax, the Eucharist is distributed and the journey is complete. Nothing shows the vital importance of the Eucharist in the liturgy more clearly

---

[1287] Revelation 1: 10-15.
[1288] lit. The Prayer of Thanksgiving after the reception of the Holy Mysteries.

The Liturgy of Saint Gregory the Theologian

than the position it holds within the text, leading up to it are the entirety of the pre-Anaphora, the Anaphora itself, the prayer of the Breaking; the prayer of Freedom and the private prayer of the priest. Following the Eucharist is a prayer of thanksgiving and the dismissal.

There are a number of difficulties in the Coptic translation of this text, these difficulties are laid out by Hammerschmidt,[1289] along with these difficulties within the Coptic itself, there are a number of differences between the Greek and the Coptic. The first difference is that the dialogue included as the introduction to this text in the Greek: Ὁ Διάκονος λέγει· Ἐπὶ προσευχῆς στάθητε. Ὁ Ἱερεὺς λέγει· Εἰρήνη πᾶσιν. Ὁ Λαὸς λέγει· Καὶ τῷ πνεύματί σου. Ὁ Διάκονος λέγει· Προσεύξασθε ὑπὲρ τῆς ἀξίας μεταλήψεως. Ὁ Λαὸς λέγει· Κύριε ἐλέησον, is counted as the end of the previous section in the Coptic. The Coptic text also skips the exclamation of the deacon and the blessing of peace given by the priest and adds "...der unbefeckten und himmlischen heiligen Geheimnisse..."[1290] to the end of the exclamation: Προσεύξασθε ὑπὲρ τῆς ἀξίας μεταλήψεως.[1291] The Coptic adds: "...Herr Christus, unser Gott..."[1292] between: Εὐχαριστοῦμέν σοι and Λόγε Θεοῦ ἀληθινέ in the Greek text.[1293] The Coptic text has: "...reinen heiligen Vaters..."[1294] instead of: τοῦ ἀνάρχου Πατρός. Hammerschmidt postulates that this is occured through a mistake of the translator, who seems to have mistook ἀχράντου for ἀνάρχου.[1295] The Coptic text states that Christ gave himself: "...für unsere Sünden..."[1296] while the Greek text states only: ὑπὲρ ἡμῶν. This is where the Coptic text breaks off, while the Greek text continues:

> Κεχάρισας ἡμῖν, διὰ τοῦ ἀχράντου σου σώματος, καὶ τοῦ τιμίου σου αἵματος, τὴν ἀπολύτρωσιν. Ὡς κατηξίωσας ἡμᾶς νῦν φιλάνθρωπε, ἵνα λάβωμεν ἐξ αὐτῶν εὐχαριστια. Διὸ ἐξομολογοῦμεν σοι νῦν, φιλάνθρωπε ἀγαθέ καὶ σοι τὴν δόξαν καὶ τὴν τιμὴν καὶ τὴν προσκύνησιν διηνεκῶς ἀναπέμπομεν, σὺν τῷ ἀνάρχῳ σου Πατρὶ καὶ τῷ ἁγίῳ σου Πνεύματι, νῦν, καὶ

The "Prayer of Thanksgiving" has its origins, postulates Hammerschmidt, in the mealtime custom of Jewish households for the father to offer prayers of thanksgiving fol-

---

[1289] Hammerschmidt (1957). pg. 165-167
[1290] "of the spotless and heavenly, holy mysteries."
[1291] Hammerschmidt (1957). pg. 73
[1292] "Lord Christ, our God"
[1293] Ibid.
[1294] Ibid. "spotless holy Father"
[1295] Hammerschmidt (1957). pg. 165
[1296] Hammerschmidt (1957). pg. 73. "for our sins"

lowing the blessing of the food.¹²⁹⁷ This is one of a number of phrases in the liturgy borrowed from Jewish ritual, several others of which are also from the rituals surrounding the eating of a meal.¹²⁹⁸ Hammerschmidt also notes that a "Prayer of Thanksgiving" is universally found in every liturgy of the Egyptian rite.¹²⁹⁹ Though he limits his discussion to the Egyptian rite, the same could be said of every major Liturgy in the Eastern Churches. Both major Byzantine liturgies have a "Prayer of Thanksgiving" like the Egyptian liturgies, the two Byzantine liturgies, other than the opening phase and the *ekphonesis*, have different prayers. In the Liturgy of St. Basil we see:

> Εὐχαριστοῦμέν σοι Κύριε ὁ Θεὸς ἡμῶν ἐπὶ τῇ μεταλήψει τῶν ἁγίων ἀχράντων ἀθανάτων καὶ ἐπουρανίων σου μυστηρίων ὧν ἔδωκας ἡμῖν ἐπὶ εὐεργεσίᾳ καὶ ἁγιασμῷ καὶ ἰάσει τῶν ψυχῶν καὶ τῶν σωμάτων· αὐτὸς δέσποτα τῶν ἁπάντων δὸς γενέσθαι ἡμῖν τὴν κοινωνίαν τοῦ ἁγίου σώματος καὶ αἵματος τοῦ Χριστοῦ σου εἰς πίστιν ἀκαταίσχυντον, εἰς ἀφάπην ἀνυπόκριτον, εἰς πλησμομὴν σοφίας, εἰς ἴασιν ψυχῆς καὶ σώματος, εἰς ἀποτροπὴν παντὸς ἐναντίου, εἰς περιποίησιν τῶν ἐντολῶν σου, εἰς ἀπολογίαν εὐπρόσδεκτον τὴν ἐπὶ τοῦ φοβεροῦ βήματος τοῦ χριστοῦ σου. ὅτι σὺ εἶ ὁ ἁγιασμὸς ἡμῶν καὶ σοὶ τὴν δόξαν ἀναπέμπομεν τῷ Πατρὶ καὶ τῷ Υἱῷ καὶ τῷ ἁγίῳ Πνεύματι νῦν καὶ ἀεὶ καὶ εἰς τοὺς αἰῶνας τῶν αἰώνων. Ἀμήν.¹³⁰⁰

While in the Liturgy of St. John Chrysostom we see:

> Εὐχαριστοῦμεν σοι δέσποτα φιλάνθρωπε εὐεργέτα τῶν ψυχῶν ἡμῶν ὁ καὶ τῇ παρούσῃ ἡμέρᾳ καταξιώσας ἡμᾶς τῶν ἐπουρανίων σου καὶ ἀθανάτων μυστηρίων· ὀρθοτόμησον ἡμῶν τὴν ὁδόν, σῶσον ἡμᾶς ἐν τῷ φόβῳ σου τοὺς πάντας, φρούρησον ἡμῶν τὴν ζωήν, ἀσφάλισαι ἡμῶν τὰ διαβήματα, εὐχαῖς καὶ

---

¹²⁹⁷ Hammerschmidt (1957). pg. 166-167
¹²⁹⁸ The Sursum Corda dialogue, for example.
¹²⁹⁹ Hammerschmidt (1957). pg. 166-167
¹³⁰⁰ Hammond and Brightman (1896). pg. 342 and Trempelis (1982). pg. 192; The ‚Prayer of Thanksgiving' found in the Greek-Egyptian Liturgy of St. Mark is nearly identical to this prayer. This is one of the few instances in which it is not the Liturgy of St. Gregory or the Greek-Egyptian Liturgy of St. Basil that show congruence with the Byzantine Liturgy of St. Basil. "We thank You Lord our God for the participation in Your holy, pure, immortal and heavenly mysteries, which You gave to us for a benefit and sanctification and healing of our souls and bodies. Grant Yourself, Lord of all, that the communion of the holy Body and Blood of Your Christ to become for us an unshamed faith, genuine love, fullness of wisdom, healing of soul and body, a defense against every adversary, a keeping of Your commandments, an acceptable defense before the fearful tribunal of Your Christ. For You are our sanctification and to You we send up glory, to the Father and to the Son and to the Holy Spirit, now and ever and to the ages of ages. Amen."

ἱκεσίαις τῆς ἁγίας ἐνδόξου δεσποίνης ἡμῶν θεοτόκου καὶ ἀειπαρθένου Μαρίας καὶ πάντων τῶν ἁγίων σου τῶν ἀπ' αἰώνων σοι εὐαρεστησάντων.[1301]

Comparing these texts to those of the Egyptian rite, we can come to some conclusion about this type of prayer. We see that the majority of these texts begin with the word: Εὐχαριστοῦμεν, from which the prayer takes its name, this seems to have an exception in the Coptic Liturgy of St. Mark, which begins: "...We that have received of spiritual incorruption have been healed in the powers of our soul, and unto thee, beneficient God...we offer songs of thankfulness..."[1302] This is, however, not a prayer original to this liturgy, but comes from a much later, Syrian, Liturgy, that of John of Bostra.[1303] It is in the Syrian rite that we see the greates variety in these "Prayers of Thanksgiving." Not only is the standard: Εὐχαριστοῦμεν not always present, the prayer is also not always addressed to the Father, a norm in the majority of these prayers. In the Greek-Syrian Liturgy of St. James, there are two of these prayers, one sung by the people and one recited by the priest, it is the hymn of the people that breaks out of the excpected paradigm: Εὐχαριστοῦμέν σοι Χριστὲ ὁ θεὸς ἡμῶν ὅτι ἠξίωσας.[1304] This discrepancy is not shared by the prayer of the priest, however: Εὐχαριστοῦμέν σοι τῷ σωτῆρι τῶν ὅλων Θεῷ.[1305] Seeing the numerous variations on the single theme, we can conclude that the majority of these prayers, including that in the Liturgy of St. Gregory, are original to their respective liturgies.

This prayer, along with the puroseful use of the term: ὁμοούσιος with the Holy Spirit, is important, as noted by Hammerschmidt, in the dating of the text. This is, at the same time, another text that suggests the authorship of Gregory the Theologian, or one close to him. Hammerschmidt discusses the phrase: ἐκ τῆς οὐσίας τοῦ πατρός. This phrase fits well into the established, anti-Arian, function of the text, as Hammerschmidt himself notes: "Man hört durch diese Worte deutlich das antiarianische Anliegen hindurch."[1306] It is, however, the historical use of the term: οὐσία that makes this prayer so important:

[1301] Hammond and Brightman (1896). pg. 342 and Trempelis (1982). pg. 153; The *ekphonesis* is the same as that of the Liturgy of St. Basil. "We thank You Master, lover of man, benefactor of our souls, who deemed us worthy, on this day of Your coming, of Your heavenly and immortal mysteries. Set us aright on the path, save us all in Your fear, guard our lives, secure our steps, through the prayers and supplications of our holy, glorious lady the Theotokos and ever virgin Mary and all Your saints, who were well pleasing to You from all ages."

[1302] Hammond and Brightman (1896). pg. 186

[1303] Ibid.

[1304] Hammond and Brightman (1896). pg. 64 and Mercier (1944). pg. 236. "We thank You Christ our God, since You deemed."

[1305] Ibid. "We thank You, God, the salvation of all."

[1306] Hammerschmidt (1957). pg. 168. "One hears the anti-Arian coming through these words."

> Gregor von Nazianz übernahm von Basilios d. Gr. die Unterscheidung von Usia und Hypostasis und von Gregor von Nyssa die Identifizierung von Prosopon und Hypostasis. In seiner berühmten Abschiedsrede, der Oratio 42, schlug er vor, die Terminologie zu vereinheitlichen, indem man Usia für die allgemeine Wesenheit, Hypostasis und Prosopon aber identifizierte und für das konkrete, individuelle Einzelwesen verwandte... die Zeit des theologischen Kampfes gegen den zurückweichenden Arianismus, der ja dann in dem vom Konzil von Konstantinopel 381 verurteilten Makedonianismus einen späten Ausläufer fand.[1307]

Hammerschmidt is very careful to emphasize that he does not himself believe that Gregory the Theologian wrote this text: "Es soll hier mit der Anführung des Gregor von Nazianz nicht etwa auf seine Autorschaft der Greglit angespielt...werden..."[1308] Hammerschmidt was working, though, in a time when the assumption was that the authors to whom these Liturgies were attributed were pseudonyms.

1. Structure

The Greek text of this prayer begins with an introductory dialogue between priest, deacon and people. The prayer proper begins with the expression of thanks: Εὐχαριστοῦμέν σοι, the direct address of Christ is combined with a theological exposition of His nature, He is addressed not as Jesus Christ, but as the Logos. Following this theological discussion the actual thanksgiving takes place. This thanksgiving is divided into two parts, the first is in the first sentence and offers thanks for Christ's participation in salvation. The second sentence continues the thanksgiving, but shifts the focus to the actual participation in the Eucharist.

The prayer culminates in the *ekphonesis*, which begins in an unusual manner, instead of a second direct address of Christ, this *ekphonesis* begins by looking back to the thanksgiving and using what Christ has done as the catalyst for the worship owed to Christ: Διὸ ἐξομολογοῦμεν σοι, this transition is then followed by the direct address of Christ, the

---

[1307] Hammerschmidt (1957). pg. 169. "Gregory of Nazianzus adopted the difference between Usia and Hypostasis from Basil the Great and he adopted the identification of Prosopon and Hypostasis from Gregory of Nyssa. In his famous farewell speech, the Oratio 42, he suggested that the terms be unified, in that Usia be used for general being, Hypostasis and Prosopon be identified and used for the concrete, individual being...(this belongs to) the time of the theological battle against the retreating Arianism, which found a late resurgence in Macedoniansim, which was condemned at the Council of Constantinople in 381."
[1308] Ibid. "The mention of Gregory of Nazianzus here is not meant to play on the authorship of the Liturgy of St. Gregory."

The Liturgy of Saint Gregory the Theologian

description of the worship due to Christ and, finally, the Trinitarian formula. The Structure of this prayer can also be seen in the following table:

Table III.XI.1: The Structure of the "Prayer of Thanksgiving."[1309]

The ‚Prayer of Thanksgiving'

1. The Introductory dialogue:
    a. The deacon introduces the prayer with the exclamation: Ἐπὶ προσευχῆς στάθητε.
    b. The priest gives a blessing of peace: Εἰρήνη πᾶσιν.
    c. The people respond: Καὶ τῷ πνεύματί σου.
    d. A second introduction of the prayer by the deacon: Προσεύξασθε ὑπὲρ τῆς ἀξίας μεταλήψεως.
    e. The people respond: Κύριε ἐλέησον.

2. The initial thanksgiving:
    a. The Thanksgiving proper: Εὐχαριστοῦμέν σοι
    b. A theological discussion of Christ's nature: Λόγε Θεοῦ ἀληθινέ, ὁ ἐκ τῆς οὐσίας τοῦ ἀνάρχου Πατρός.

3. Thanksgiving for salvation through the historical acts of Christ:
    a. For Christ's love: Ὅτι οὕτως ἠγάπησας ἡμᾶς
    b. That Christ gave Himself over: καὶ ἔδωκας σεαυτὸν ὑπὲρ ἡμῶν
    c. That Christ was crucified: ἐσφαγιάσθης.

4. Thanksgiving for salvation through the Eucharist:
    a. Deliverance through the Eucharist: Κεχάρισας ἡμῖν διὰ τοῦ ἀχράντου σου σώματος, καὶ τοῦ τιμίου σου αἵματος, τὴν ἀπολύτρωσιν.
    b. Thanks for the ability to partake in the Eucharist: Ὡς κατηξίωσας ἡμᾶς νῦν

[1309] Cf. Section III.10 lines 1-15.

φιλάνθρωπε, ἵνα λάβωμεν ἐξ αὐτῶν εὐχαριστια.

> 5. The *ekphonesis*:
>   a. Transition: Διὸ ἐξομολογοῦμέν σοι νῦν
>   b. Direct address of Christ: φιλάνθρωπε ἀγαθέ·
>   c. Worship due to Christ: καὶ σοι τὴν δόξαν καὶ τὴν τιμήν καὶ τὴν προσκύνησιν διηνεκῶς ἀναπέμπομεν,
>   d. Trinitarian formula: σὺν τῷ ἀνάρχῳ σου Πατρὶ καὶ τῷ ἁγίῳ σου Πνεύματι, νῦν, καὶ.

2. Function

1. (Section III.10 line 8): Εὐχαριστοῦμέν σοι Λόγε Θεοῦ ἀληθινέ, ὁ ἐκ τῆς οὐσίας τοῦ ἀνάρχου Πατρός.

In this section, the author's wish to establish Christ's relationship with the Father supercedes the usual tendency to deemphasize the other members of the Trinity. So we see here that Christ is the "true Word of the Father" and "of the essence of the eternal Father," defining the relationship in terms of the Father, rather than the usual ‚your Father' we have seen in other prayers. The danger, that Christ is overshadowed by the Father, is avoided by the author assigning all the thanks for the Eucharist and for salvation to Christ. This is perhaps the most important section of this prayer because of the theological statement made about Christ: ὁ ἐκ τῆς οὐσίας τοῦ ἀνάρχου Πατρός, this is one of the few times that the term ὁμοούσιος occurs in a liturgical setting, outside of the Monophyiste liturgies. This term puts this prayer in the context of the anti-Arian Nicene party, despite the connection to the theology of the Nicenes, this cannot be attributed directly to the Nicene Creed, since it does not use the term ὁμοούσιος as such, but only indirectly, the term Logos, which is not found in the Nicene Creed, also shows that it is an indirect theological connection, it is in the theological context of Gregory the Theologian himself, where he uses this, especially in his Oration 42.[1310]

2. (Section III.10 lines 8-9): Ὅτι οὕτως ἠγάπησας ἡμᾶς καὶ ἔδωκας σεαυτὸν ὑπὲρ ἡμῶν ἐσφαγιάσθης.

Here, following the discussion of Christ's relationship with the Father, the author returns to the description for what humanity thanks Christ. This description follows the es-

---
[1310] Cf. Hammerschmidt (1957). pg. 168

The Liturgy of Saint Gregory the Theologian

tablished paradigm of progression either progressing the worshipper heavenward or progressing the narrative historically forward. In this case the author uses the historical progression, but also goes from the general to the specific. The author begins with thanking Christ for loving "us," a general term that covers everything from the Incarnation to the Crucifixion and Ressurection. The next stage in the list: ἔδωκας σεαυτὸν ὑπὲρ ἡμῶν is more specific, but could still refer to one of a number of occasions, the Crucifixion itself, the trial before Pontius Pilate or the entire Passion story. Finally, the discussion culminates in the specific: ἐσφαγιάσθης, the Crucifixion and in the Ressurection that is implicit with it.

3. (Section III.10 lines 10-12): Κεχάρισας ἡμῖν διὰ τοῦ ἀχράντου σου σώματος, καὶ τοῦ τιμίου σου αἵματος, τὴν ἀπολύτρωσιν. Ὡς κατηξίωσας ἡμᾶς νῦν φιλάνθρωπε, ἵνα λάβωμεν ἐξ αὐτῶν εὐχαριστια.

This section is not in the Coptic translation and Renaudot believes that it may be a later addition to the text.[1311] While this seems, at first, to be a distinct possibility, as this section does not seem to fit stylistically with the first section, as there seems to be no progression of the discussion. This progression is seen, however, in the comparison of the focus of the first section, Salvation, to that of the second section, the Eucharist. Historical Salvation through the sacrifice of Christ is discussed in the historical progression of the first section, salvation: τὴν ἀπολύτρωσιν is then described as being: διὰ τοῦ ἀχράντου σου σώματος. So the historical salvation is transformed into the mystical salvation through the Eucharist. The final thanksgiving is then given for the participation in the Eucharist: λάβωμεν ἐξ αὐτῶν εὐχαριστια. The progression of this section goes then from thanks for historical salvation to the description of historical salvation in terms of the Eucharist to thanks for the Eucharist. This is, then, an integral section of the prayer and seems to be an original part of it.

4. (Section III.10 lines 13-15): Διὸ ἐξομολογοῦμεν σοι νῦν, φιλάνθρωπε ἀγαθέ· καὶ σοι τὴν δόξαν καὶ τὴν τιμήν καὶ τὴν προσκύνησιν διηνεκῶς ἀναπέμπομεν, σὺν τῷ ἀνάρχῳ σου Πατρὶ καὶ τῷ ἁγίῳ σου Πνεύματι, νῦν, καὶ.

The *ekphonesis* begins in an unusual manner, it neither refers directly back to the prayer it completes, nor does it reopen the prayer with a direct address of Christ. Instead, this *ekphonesis* continues the thought of the prayer directly, marking the transition with the

---
[1311] Hammerschmidt (1957). pp. 166-167

word: Διό. This transition puts the worship due to Christ: ἐξομολογοῦμεν...καὶ σοι τὴν δόξαν καὶ τὴν τιμήν καὶ τὴν προσκύνησιν διηνεκῶς ἀναπέμπομεν in the context of salvation and of the Eucharist, the congregation thanks Christ for His participation in salvation then worships Him for it. Finally the usual Trinitarian formula, the Father and the Holy Spirit named in reference to Christ, completes the prayer.

III.XII. The Prayer of the "Bowing of the Head"

The final prayer of this liturgy is entitled the prayer of the "Bowing of the Head." This is the second of two prayers with this title in this liturgy. The topics of these prayers seem, at first, not to have much to do with one another. The first prayer of ‚the Bowing of the Head' focuses on purification, while the second is a historical discussion of salvation. The technical connection between the two prayers, however, is seen in the exclamation of the deacon that introduces the prayer: Τὰς κεφαλὰς ὑμῶν τῷ Κυρίῳ κλίνατε, but another connection exists between the two, in their openings: Ὁ κλίνας οὐρανοὺς καὶ κατελθὼν ἐπὶ τῆς γῆς, εἰς σωτηρίαν τοῦ γένους τῶν ανθρώπων and Ὁ ὤν, ὁ ἦν, ὁ ἐλθὼν εἰς τὸν κόσμον τοῦ φωτίσαι αὐτόν. Both prayers open by describing Christ as coming into the world, coming down, verbally mimicking the physical action of bowing the head.

It is quite common to have a "Prayer of the Bowing of the Head" in this position in a Liturgy, so in the Syrian Liturgy St. James:

> Let us bow down our heads to the Lord...O God, who art great and marvellous, who didst bow the heavens and come down fort he salvation of the race of the sons of men: turn thee unto us in thy mercies and pity and bless thy people and preserve thine inheritance that in very truth and at all times we may glorify thee who alone art our true God, and God the Father who begat thee and thine Holy Spirit now and at all times for ever...[1312]

Note that this prayer is also directed to Christ, rather than to the Father, and the beginning: "O God, who art great and marvellous, who didst bow the heavens and come down fort he salvation of the race of the sons of men..." seems to reflect the beginning of the first "Prayer of the Bowing of the Head" in the Liturgy of St. Gregory: Ὁ κλίνας οὐρανοὺς καὶ κατελθὼν ἐπὶ τῆς γῆς, εἰς σωτηρίαν τοῦ γένους τῶν ανθρώπων. We see that the same quotation is used to poetically evoke the image of bending, as Christ bent the heavens, so the congregation bends its neck. The majority

---

[1312] Hammond and Brightman (1896). pg. 105 and Day (1972). pg. 193.

of these types of prayers, however, do not make the connection between the Incarnation and the bowing of the congregation, but explicitly discuss the bowing of the head of the congregation: ὁ Θεὸς ὁ μέγας καὶ θαυμαστὸς ἔπιδε ἐπὶ τοὺς δούλους σου ὅτι σοὶ τοὺς αὐχένας ἐκλίναμεν.[1313] The prevelance of this prayer type in the Syrian must be compared to the lack of a prayer of this sort in the Byzantine rite, both major Byzantine Liturgies go directly from the "Prayer of Thanksgiving" to the dismissal. In the Egyptian family of Liturgies the consistency varies, the Coptic Liturgy of St. Mark, for example does not contain an original prayer of this type,[1314] while the Greek-Egyptian Liturgy of St. Mark does: τὰς κεφαλὰς ὑμῶν ἐπὶ εὐλογίαις τῷ Κυρίῳ κλίνατε...Ἄναξ μέγιστε καὶ τῷ Πατρὶ συνάναρχε ὁ τῷ σῷ κράτει τὸν ᾅδην σκυλεύσας καὶ τὸν θάνατον πατήσας.[1315] Note that this prayer too is directed to Christ.

This prayer poses some problems in the Liturgy of St. Gregory as well. The text of the Paris Codex contains a *crux* that obscures the entire middle of the prayer, unfortunately the Kacmarcik Codex cuts off at the end of the Anaphora and therefore does not contain this prayer. The Coptic text can also not be used to fill in this *crux*, since only the first part of the texts coincide. In fact, the Coptic text, as Hammerschmidt explains, has more in common with one of the Syrian Liturgies than with the Greek text: "Eine weitere Parallele zu diesem Gebet der kopt Greglit bildet das Inklinationsgebet der syrischen Timotheosanaphora, wo es auch am Ende der Liturgie steht. Es ist sehr auffallend, dass dieses syrische Gebet weit mehr mit dem koptischen zusammengeht, als das der gr. Greglit. Einzelne Stellen weichen aber auch im Syrischen ab..."[1316] Hammerschmidt uses this to show the: "grosse Nähe der syrischen Timotheusanaphora zu der kopt Greglit...Die Übereinstimmung des syrischen Textes mit dem koptischen ist viel grösser als die des griechischen mit dem

---

[1313] Hammond and Brightman (1896). pg. 67 and Mercier (1944). pg. 238-240. "O great and marvelous God, look upon Your slaves, since we bow our necks to You."
[1314] Hammond and Brightman (1896). pp. 186-187. The prayer here is taken from the liturgy of St. John of Bostra.
[1315] Hammond and Brightman (1896). pg. 142 and Cuming (1990). pg. 60 footnote 1. "Bow your heads to the Lord for blessing...greatest king."
[1316] Hammerschmidt (1957). pg. 171. He goes on to describe the few differences between the Syrian and Coptic texts pp.171-172. "A further parallel to this prayer of the Coptic Liturgy of St. Gregory is found in the 'Prayer of the Bowing of the Head' in the Syrian Anaphora of Timothy, in which it also stands at the end of the liturgy. It is quite noticeable that the Syrian prayer hangs together fare more with the Coptic, than that of the Greek Liturgy of St. Gregory. Individual sections differ in the Syrian as well..."

koptischen."[1317] It is this closeness between the Coptic and Syrian texts, both in this case and in certain others,[1318] that lead Hammerschmidt to place the Liturgy of St. Gregory in the Syrian family of Liturgies, in doing so, however, he overlooks several pieces of evidence that point rather to the Cappadocian, the subset of the Syrian that becomes so influential in the Byzantine rite.

Hammerschmidt is able to show that this part of the Coptic text is adopted from the Syrian: "Da die angeführten Abweichungen des syrischen Textes[1319] vom koptischen wegen der typisch sekundären Erweiterungen des koptischen Gebetes auf eine Abhängigkeit des Koptischen vom Syrischen hinzuweisen scheinen, muss man wohl eine spätere Einfügung in die Greglit annehmen."[1320] If the second part of the Coptic text is secondarily adopted, then the text of the Greek Liturgy,[1321] despite the *crux*, seems to be original. The Greek text consists of a row of remembrances: Gabriel and Raphael are remembred, as are the angels, the Cherubim, the elders,[1322] John the Baptist, St. Stephen, the Apostles, the prophets, the martyrs, St. Mark and all of the saints. This section echoes the ending of the Anaphora:

Ἐξαιρέτως τῆς παναγίας ὑπερενδόξου ἀχράντου ὑπερευλογημένης δεσποίνης ἡμῶν Θεοτόκου καὶ ἀειπαρθένου Μαρίας. Τοῦ ἁγίου ἐνδόξου προφήτου προδρόμου βαπτιστοῦ καὶ μάρτυρος Ἰωάννου. Τοῦ ἁγίου Στεφάνου τοῦ πρωτοδιακόνου καὶ πρωτομάρτυρος. Καὶ τοῦ ἁγίου καὶ μακαρίου πατρὸς ἡμῶν Μάρκου, τοῦ ἀποστόλου καὶ εὐαγγελιστοῦ. Καὶ τοῦ ἐν ἁγίοις πατρὸς θεολόγου Γρηγορίου. Καὶ ὧν, ἐν τῇ σήμερον ἡμέρᾳ τὴν ὑπόμνησιν ποιούμεθα καὶ παντὸς χοροῦ τῶν ἁγίων σου. Ὧν ταῖς εὐχαῖς καὶ πρεσβείαις καὶ ἡμᾶς ἐλέησον καὶ σῶσον διὰ τὸ ὄνομά σου τὸ ἅγιον τὸ ἐπικληθὲν ἐφ' ἡμᾶς.[1323]

[1317] Hammerschmidt (1957). pg. 172. "great closeness of the Syrian Anaphora of St. Timothy to the Coptic Liturgy of St. Gregory…The commonalities of the Syrian text with the Coptic is much greater than the Greek with the Coptic."
[1318] For a list of Hammerschmidt's reasons see pp. 176-180.
[1319] Hammerschmidt places the Anaphora of St. Timothy in the Syrian rite despite the arguments of Rücker that it is also an Egyptian Litugry. pg. 172
[1320] Hammerschmidt (1957). pg. 173. "Since the mentioned variations of the Syrian text from the Coptic seem to point to a dependency of the Coptic on the Syrian, because of the typical secondary expression of the Coptic prayer, one must assume a later addition into the Greek Liturgy of St. Gregory."
[1321] The text that Hammerschmidt does not deal with: "…den griechischen wollen wir wegen seiner starken Abweichung ausser Betracht lassen..." pg. 173. "We will leave the Greek text out, because of the strong variations."
[1322] References to those present at the heavenly Liturgy in Revelation.
[1323] Section II.7 lines 105-112.

The Liturgy of Saint Gregory the Theologian

This points to the author wishing to establish an intratextual link between the end of the entire Liturgy and the end of the end of the Anaphora. This may be the author's way of emphasizing the importance of the Anaphora as the central part of the Liturgy, and by extension the importance of the Eucharist. The phrasing may be borrowed from the Coptic Liturgy of St. Mark: "...by the intercessions of the holy glorious evervirgin theotokos S. Mary and the prayers and supplications of the holy archangels Michael and Gabriel, and S. John the forerunner and baptist and martyr, and S. Stephen the protdeacon and protomartyr, and our holy fathers the apostles, and S. Mark the apostle and evangelist and martyr, and the holy patriarch Severus ..."[1324] This would then have to be a later addition into the Liturgy, as the Coptic texts are later in date than the proposed date of the Liturgy of St. Gregory. The problem with this interpretation is, first of all, that Coptic is translated into Greek and not the other way. Second of all, this text in the Coptic Anaphora of St. Gregory is also changed, and if the Greek were modified to conform more to the Coptic Liturgy, why does the Coptic adopt a prayer from a Syrian Anaphora, rather than also adopting this type of conclusion? A more logical conclusion is that the Liturgy of St. Gregory influences the Coptic Liturgy of St. Mark.

In exploring the origins of this text there is an interesting phrase: Χριστέ, ὁ ἀληθινὸς θ...μ... in the *crux*, which the Renaudot edition fills out to: Χριστέ, ὁ ἀληθινὸς θεὸς ἡμῶν[1325] this phrase is reflected in the final dismissal of the modern usage of the Byzantine Liturgies: Χριστὸς ὁ ἀληθινὸς Θεὸς ἡμῶν,[1326] which then go through a list of remembrances and end in a request for salvation:

ταῖς πρεσβείαις τῆς παναχράντου καὶ παναμώμου ἁγίας αὐτοῦ μητρός· δυνάμει τοῦ τιμίου καὶ ζωοποιοῦ Σταυροῦ· προστασίαις τῶν τιμίων ἐπουρανίων Δυνάμεων ἀσωμάτων· ἱκεσίαις τοῦ τιμίου, ἐνδόξου, προφήτου, προδρόμου καὶ βαπτιστοῦ Ἰωάννου· τῶν ἁγίων, ἐνδόξων καὶ πανευφήμων Ἀποστόλων· τῶν ἁγίων, ἐνδόξων καὶ καλλινίκων Μαρτύρων· τῶν ὁσίων καὶ θεοφόρων Πατέρων ἡμων...τῶν ἁγίων καὶ δικαίων θεοπατόρων Ἰωακεὶμ καὶ Ἄννης...καὶ πάντων τῶν ἁγίων, ἐλεήσαι καὶ σῶσαι ἡμᾶς ὡς ἀγαθὸς καὶ φιλάνθρωπος καὶ ἐλεήμων Θεός.[1327]

[1324] Hammond and Brightman (1896). pg. 169
[1325] Renaudot (1847). I. pg.116
[1326] Holy Cross (1985). pg. 36 and Trempelis (1982). pg. 159
[1327] Ibid. Pp. 36-37. "May Christ our true God, through the prayers of His all pure and all blameless holy mother; through the power of the precious and life-giving Cross; through the defense of the precious heavenly bodiless powers; through the prayers of the precious, glorious, prophet, forerunner and Baptist John; of the glorious glorious and all lauded apostles; of the holy and glorious and victorious martyrs; of our blessed and

The Commentary

The marked similarity between these two texts in content, style and in position within the Liturgy cannot be ascribed to coincidence, which begs the question: how are these texts related to one another? The possibilty that the Liturgy of St. Gregory adopts the form of the text from the Byzantine Lliturgies can be discarded, since this conclusion is not original to the Byzantine liturgy,[1328] nor is there a hint of a similar adoption into the other major Egyptian liturgies, both of which end in closing doxologies.[1329] One possibility is that the text was not, in fact, adopted into the Byzantine liturgy from the Vespers service, but from the Liturgy of St. Gregory, we have seen numerous other instances in which a prayer, especially in the Liturgy of St. Basil, adopted from the Liturgy of St. Gregory, however, these were early borrowings, and, if this text were adopted, it would necessitate a knowledge of the Liturgy of St. Gregory much later in the Byzantine world than there is any evidence for. Unfortunately the badly degraded state of the Paris Manuscript here makes it impossible to tell how the text progresses within the *crux*, whether this phrase belongs to the remebrances, making a case for a much later interaction with the Byzantine rite than hitherto thought, or if it is the ending of the first part of the prayer, and until the other manuscripts of this Liturgy can be found, it will be impossible to come to a full conclusion.

Like the rememberances seem to look back to the closing of the Anaphora, the first section of the prayer forms an intratextual link with the closing prayer of the pre-Anaphora. The striking similarity between the two prayers can be seen in the following table:

God-bearing fathers…of the holy and just ancestors of God Joachim and Anna…and all the saints, have mercy on us and save us as good and man loving and merciful God."

[1328] Note that in Brightman's edition of the Byzantine text as it was in the ninth century, this prayer is not included. Cf. Hammond and Brightman (1896). pg. 344

[1329] Renaudot (1847). volume 1. pp. 84-85 and 147-148

The Liturgy of Saint Gregory the Theologian

Table III.XII.1: the "Prayer of the Bowing of the Head"[1330] *and the "Prayer of the Kiss of Peace."*[1331]

1. The "Prayer of the Greeting"	2. The "Prayer of the Bowing of the Head"
Ὁ ὤν, καὶ προὼν, καὶ διαμένων εἰς τοὺς αἰῶνας. Ὁ τῷ Πατρὶ συναΐδιος καὶ ὁμοούσιος καὶ σύνθρονος καὶ συνδημιουργός. Ὁ διὰ μόνην ἀγαθότητα ἐκ τοῦ μὴ ὄντος εἰς τὸ εἶναι παραγαγὼν τὸν ἄνθρωπον, καὶ θέμενος αὐτὸν ἐν παραδείσῳ τρυφῆς. Ἀπάτῃ δὲ τοῦ ἐχθροῦ καὶ παρακοῇ τῆς σῆς ἐντολῆς παραπεσόντα, ἀνακαινίσαι βουλόμενος καὶ πρὸς τὸ ἀρχαῖον ἀναγαγεῖν ἀξίωμα. Οὐκ ἄγγελος, οὐκ ἀρχάγγελος, οὐ πατριάρχης, οὐ προφήτης τὴν ἡμῶν ἐνεχείρησας σωτηρίαν, ἀλλ' αὐτὸς ἀτρέπτως σὰρξ γενόμενος καὶ ἐνηνθρώπησας. Κατὰ πάντα ὡμοιώθης ἡμῖν ἐκτὸς μόνης ἁμαρτίας. Μεσίτης ἡμῶν γέγονας καὶ τοῦ Πατρὸς, καὶ τὸ μεσότοιχον τοῦ φραγμοῦ· καὶ τὴν χρονίαν ἔχθραν καθελών. Τὰ ἐπίγεια τοῖς ἐπουρανίοις συνῆψας, καὶ τὰ ἀμφότερα εἰς ἓν συνήγαγες, καὶ τὴν ἔνσαρκον ἐπλήρωσας οἰκονομίαν. Καὶ μέλλων σωματικῶς ἐλαύνειν εἰς οὐρανοὺς, θεϊκῶς τὰ πάντα πληρῶν, τοῖς ἁγίοις σου μαθηταῖς καὶ ἀποστόλοις ἔλεγες· εἰρήνην ἀφίημι ὑμῖν, εἰρήνην τὴν ἐμὴν δίδωμι ὑμῖν...	Ὁ ὤν, ὁ ἦν, ὁ ἐλθὼν εἰς τὸν κόσμον τοῦ φωτίσαι αὐτόν. Ὁ σαρκωθεὶς καὶ ἐνανθρωπήσας, καὶ σταυρωθεὶς δι' ἡμᾶς, καὶ παθὼν ἑκουσίως σαρκί, καὶ μείνας ἀπαθής, ὡς Θεός. Καὶ ταφεὶς καὶ ἀναστὰς τῇ τρίτῃ ἡμέρᾳ καὶ ἀνελθὼν εἰς οὐρανούς, καὶ καθίσας ἐν δεξιᾷ τῆς μεγαλωσύνης δόξης τοῦ Πατρός· τό τε θεῖον καὶ ἅγιον καὶ ὁμοούσιον καὶ ὁμοδύναμον καὶ ὁμόδοξον καὶ συναΐδιον Πνεῦμα καταπέμψας ἐπὶ τοὺς ἁγίους σου μαθητὰς καὶ ἀποστόλους, καὶ διὰ τούτου φωτίσας μὲν αὐτούς

By evoking imagery from prior sections of the Liturgy in this prayer, the rememberances of the end of the Anaphora; the discussion of the history of salvation, and especially the near repetition of the phrase: Ὁ ὤν, καὶ προὼν, καὶ διαμένων εἰς τοὺς αἰῶνας.../...Ὁ ὤν, ὁ ἦν, ὁ ἐλθὼν εἰς τὸν κόσμον τοῦ φωτίσαι αὐτόν from the "Prayer of the Greeting;" and the use of the imagery and the name of the "Prayer of the Bowing of the Head," which is said prior to the distribution of the Eucharist, instead of ending the Liturgy with a new prayer of

---

[1330] Section I.6 lines 2-21.
[1331] Section III.11 lines 2-8.

doxology, the author is able to tie in the various sections of the Liturgy together and close the Liturgy as a whole literary work.

1. Structure.

This prayer is divided into two main parts, the first of which deals with the history of salvation, and the second of which requests for salvation for all Christians through a string of intercessory rememberances.

Opening the prayer is a direct address of Christ: Ὁ ὤν, ὁ ἦν, ὁ ἐλθὼν εἰς τὸν κόσμον τοῦ φωτίσαι αὐτόν. This is followed by a description of the history of salvation. The author begins with the Incarnation and discusses, in a list of six historical events, the events of Christ's life until the Ascension into heaven and Pentecost.

Following this first section there is a *crux* in the text, and precicely how and where the transition to the second section of the prayer takes place is difficult to pinpoint. It seems, however, that the phrase: Χριστέ, ὁ ἀληθινὸς θεὸς ἡμῶν acts as the second opening in the form of a renewed address of Christ. The beginning of this section, like the ending of the last, lost in the *crux*, but from the content of what is legible, we can insert in the beginning of the text a rememberance of the Virgin Mary, as we saw in the ending of the Anaphora: τῆς παναγίας ὑπερενδόξου ἀχράντου ὑπερευλογημένης δεσποίνης ἡμῶν Θεοτόκου καὶ ἀειπαρθένου Μαρίας, the legible rememberances go through twelve steps, beginning with the bodiless powers of heaven, then specific saints, and finally a general rememberance of the whole body of the saints. This section of the prayer ends with the request which Christ is to acquiesce to through the prayers of the various saints mentioned, that he save the whole body of Christians.

The prayer closes with an *ekphonesis*, which, unlike the doxology found in the Coptic text, is written in the normal style that we have seen: description of the worship to Christ and a final Trinitarian formula.

Finally, the Liturgy ends: Ἐν εἰρήνῃ τοῦ Θεοῦ ἐτελειώθη ἡ θεία λειτουργία this phrase is then used to identify the author, according to Church tradition: ἡ ὡρισμένη τῷ ἐν ἁγίοις πατρὶ ἡμῶν θεολόγῳ Γρηγορίῳ. The Structure of this prayer can also be seen in the following table:

The Liturgy of Saint Gregory the Theologian

Table III.XII.2: the Structure of the "Prayer of the Bowing of the Head."[1332]

The "Prayer of the Bowing of the Head"

1. Part I.
    a. Opening, the discussion of Christ's nature as God: Ὁ ὤν, ὁ ἦν, ὁ ἐλθὼν εἰς τὸν κόσμον τοῦ φωτίσαι αὐτόν·
    b. The discussion of the history of Salvation.
        i. The Incarnation: ὁ σαρκωθεὶς καὶ ἐνανθρωπήσας,
        ii. The Crucifixion: καὶ σταυρωθεὶς δι' ἡμᾶς, καὶ παθὼν ἑκουσίως σαρκί, καὶ μείνας ἀπαθής, ὡς Θεός.
        iii. The Burial: Καὶ ταφείς,
        iv. The Resurrection: καὶ ἀναστὰς τῇ τρίτῃ ἡμέρᾳ
        v. The Ascension into Heaven: καὶ ἀνελθὼν εἰς οὐρανούς, καὶ καθίσας ἐν δεξιᾷ τῆς μεγαλοσύνης δόξης τοῦ Πατρός·
        vi. Pentecost and the descent of the Holy Spirit: τό τε θεῖον καὶ ἅγιον καὶ ὁμοούσιον καὶ ὁμοδύναμον καὶ ὁμόδοξον καὶ συναΐδιον Πνεῦμα καταπέμψας ἐπὶ τοὺς ἁγίους σου μαθητὰς καὶ ἀποστόλους, καὶ διὰ τούτου φωτίσας μὲν αὐτούς…

2. Part II.
    a. Reopening: Χριστέ, ὁ ἀληθινὸς θ…μ…
    b. Rememberances
        i. The bodiless powers: *(crux)* καὶ Γαβριὴλ καὶ Ῥαφαήλ. *(crux)*…Καὶ τῶν ἀγγέλων τετραμόρφων ζώων ἀσωμάτων· καὶ τῶν ἀγγέλων, καὶ τῶν εἰκοσιτεσσάρων πρεσβυτέρων.
        ii. The specific saints and groups of saints (St. John the Baptist, St. Stephen, the apostles, the prophets, the martyrs and St. Mark): Τοῦ ἁγίου ἐνδόξου προφήτου προδρόμου βαπτιστοῦ καὶ μάρτυρος Ἰωάννου. Τοῦ ἁγίου Στεφάνου τοῦ πρωτοδιακόνου καὶ πρωτομάρτυρος. Τῶν θείων ἱερῶν ἐνδόξων ἀποστόλων ἀθλοφόρων, προφητῶν καὶ καλλινίκων μαρτύρων. Καὶ τοῦ ἁγίου καὶ μακαρίου πατρὸς ἡμῶν Μάρκου τοῦ ἀποστόλου καὶ εὐαγγελιστοῦ,

---

[1332] Section III.11 lines 1-20.

iii.   The general rememberance of the saints: Καὶ πάντων τῶν χόρων τῶν ἁγίων σου.   c. The Request, salvation for all Christians: Καὶ σῶσον, καὶ ἐλέησον, καὶ εὐλόγησον, πάντα χριστιανόν.

3. Part III. The *Ekphonesis*.
  a. Direct address of Christ: Καὶ σοι
  b. The worship due to Christ: τὴν δόξαν, καὶ τιμήν, καὶ προσκύνησιν,
  c. The Trinitarian formula: σὺν τῷ ἀνάρχῳ σου Πατρὶ, καὶ τῷ ἁγίῳ Πνεύματι νῦν καὶ ἀεί, καὶ εἰς.

4. Part IV. The conclusion of the Liturgy: Ἐν εἰρήνῃ τοῦ Θεοῦ ἐτελειώθη ἡ θεία λειτουργία ἡ ὡρισμένη τῷ ἐν ἁγίοις πατρὶ ἡμῶν θεολόγῳ Γρηγορίῳ.

2. Funcion

1. (Section III.11 line 2): Ὁ ὤν, ὁ ἦν, ὁ ἐλθὼν εἰς τὸν κόσμον τοῦ φωτίσαι αὐτόν.

    The author uses this phrase to connect back to the "Prayer of the Greeting," however, this phrase also establishes Christ's nature as the eternal God, who exists from all time and to all time. This becomes, then, not only an intratextual reference, but a part of the description of the history of salvation that follows. Christ is referred to as: Ὁ ὤν, the Greek translation of the Hebrew Yahweh, and is so identified as the God of the Old Testament and the God of Creation. He is also reffered to as: ὁ ἐλθὼν εἰς τὸν κόσμον τοῦ φωτίσαι αὐτόν, here it is the *Parousia* and the Day of Judgement that is referred to, the ‚enlightenment' that Christ is coming to bring is contrasted to that sent upon the Apostles at Pentecost: καὶ διὰ τούτου φωτίσας μὲν αὐτούς, the enlightenment at Pentecost was an incomplete one, given only to the apostles and through them to what becomes the Church, when Christ returns, however, he will enlighten not only the Church, but the entire creation. In this way the incomplet action of the Holy Spirit is completed by Christ, once again underscoring His position as God. The author is able to encapsulate the entire history of salvation in one phrase, but decides to expand on the third description: ὁ ἦν by discussing the events of Christ's life on earth.

2. (Section III.11 lines 3-8): Ὁ σαρκωθεὶς καὶ ἐνανθρωπήσας, καὶ σταυρωθεὶς δι' ἡμᾶς, καὶ παθὼν ἑκουσίως σαρκί, καὶ μείνας ἀπαθής, ὡς Θεός. Καὶ ταφεὶς καὶ ἀναστὰς τῇ τρίτῃ ἡμέρᾳ καὶ ἀνελθὼν εἰς οὐρανούς, καὶ καθίσας ἐν δεξιᾷ τῆς μεγαλοσύνης δόξης τοῦ Πατρός· τό τε θεῖον καὶ ἅγιον καὶ ὁμοούσιον καὶ ὁμοδύναμον καὶ ὁμόδοξον καὶ συναΐδιον

The Liturgy of Saint Gregory the Theologian

Πνεῦμα καταπέμψας ἐπὶ τοὺς ἁγίους σου μαθητάς καὶ ἀποστόλους, καὶ διὰ τούτου φωτίσας μὲν αὐτούς.

In this section, the author uses the language of the Nicene Creed, specifically the section which deals with Christ's Incarnation, to describe Christ's action in the world, as can be seen in the following table:

Table III.XII.3: The Nicene Creed and the historical actions of Christ.

1. The Nicene Creed	2. The Liturgy of St. Gregory
1. καὶ σαρκωθέντα	1. ὁ σαρκωθείς
2. καὶ ἐνανθρωπήσαντα	2. ἐνανθρωπήσας
3. Σταυρωθέντα τε ὑπὲρ ἡμῶν	3. καὶ σταυρωθεὶς δι' ἡμᾶς
4. καὶ παθόντα	4. καὶ παθὼν
5. καὶ ταφέντα	5. καὶ ταφείς
6. Καὶ ἀναστάντα τῇ τρίτῃ ἡμέρᾳ κατὰ τὰς Γραφάς	6. καὶ ἀναστὰς τῇ τρίτῃ ἡμέρᾳ
7. Καὶ ἀνελθόντα εἰς τοὺς οὐρανοὺς καὶ καθεζόμενον ἐκ δεξιῶν τοῦ Πατρός	7. καὶ ἀνελθὼν εἰς οὐρανούς, καὶ καθίσας ἐν δεξίᾳ τῆς μεγαλοσύνης δόξης τοῦ Πατρός

The other statements in the Creed about Christ were already covered by the author in the opening statement, the theological exposition of Christ's nature correspond to the: Ὁ ὤν, ὁ ἦν, ὁ ἐλθὼν, but the author does not wish to discuss Christ's nature using the Father as a point of reference, instead he focuses only on Christ. The: εἰς τὸν κόσμον τοῦ φωτίσαι αὐτόν, the second coming, corresponds to the last portion of the Nicene Creed that discusses Christ: Καὶ πάλιν ἐρχόμενον μετὰ δόξης κρῖναι ζῶντας καὶ νεκρούς, οὗ τῆς βασιλείας οὐκ ἔσται τέλος.[1333]

The reflection of the entire section of the Creed that discusses Christ can be explained on two levels. It shows the theological dependance of the author on the Nicene Christian position, to which he adheres completely. On a functional level, the author uses the Nicene Creed as a ‚trump card' in his final prayer to make a strong final push in his fight against resurgent Arianism.

[1333] "And coming again with glory to judge the living and dead, whose kingdom does not have an end."

The Commentary

The strongly Nicene, anti-Arian, arguments of this prayer are augmented by the qualifying phrase: καὶ παθὼν ἑκουσίως σαρκί, καὶ μείνας ἀπαθής, ὡς Θεός, the author uses the dichotomy of Christ's nature, that he did suffer as human, but remained without suffering as God to underscore the truth of His divinity, and to further the polemic purpose of the author by being able to add the word "God" one more time. The dual natures of Christ have been a topic in a number of other prayers as well, all of which have been consistently Chalcedonian. The numerous affirmations of the dual nature of Christ and their unity and independance rule out the interpretation of this Liturgy postulated by Jungmann, that the Christ centered style of this liturgy must be understood as Monophysite theology.

Knowing that this liturgy is not Monophysite in origin is also important in the interpretation of the phrase: τό τε θεῖον καὶ ἅγιον καὶ ὁμοούσιον καὶ ὁμοδύναμον καὶ ὁμόδοξον καὶ συναΐδιον Πνεῦμα, especially the term ὁμοούσιον. In the context of the Holy Spirit. Although seen frequently in Syrian and Egyptian liturgies, the Spirit "of one essence" is seen only rarely in, for example, the Byzantine theological world. In this liturgy the author refrains from calling the Spirit "of one essence" in a number of places where even in the Coptic translation the term is used, this means that when the term is used in the Greek, in an original prayer, the author is using it deliberately, rather than as a liturgical stock phrase. This use puts this liturgy in the context of the Pneumatic theology of St. Gregory the Theologian and his fight against the Macedonian semi-Arians that culminated in the First Council of Constantinople in 381. This phrase is also composed of a number of homophonic epithets, a style seen in the "Prayer of the Beginning of the Proskomide:" ἄφραστον τὸν ἀόρατον τὸν ἀχώρητον τὸν ἄναρχον τὸν αἰώνιον τὸν ἄχρονον τὸν ἀμέτρητον τὸν ἄτρεπτον in this case, however, it is Christ who is being described. The use of a similar style, however, creates another intratextual reference, which connects the Holy Spirit with Christ, and equates the divine position of the Holy Spirit with that of Christ, which has been the focus of this work.

3. (Section III.11 lines 19-20): Ἐν εἰρήνῃ τοῦ Θεοῦ ἐτελειώθη ἡ θεία λειτουργία ἡ ὡρισμένη τῷ ἐν ἁγίοις πατρὶ ἡμῶν θεολόγῳ Γρηγορίῳ.

Imporant in this section is the naming of the author of the Liturgy: θεολόγῳ Γρηγορίῳ. This declaration expresses the historical tradition of the Church, which has in recent scholarship lost much of the stigma it endured in the scholarship of earlier in the century, when both Hammerschmidt and Gerhardts were writing. In the meantwhile both the Byzantine liturgies of St. Basil and of St. John Chrysostom have been recognized as having their origin, at least in part, with those famous figures. The historical tradition of the Church can certainly not be taken at face value, but can no longer be merely dismissed.

Part IV: Conclusions

The preceding commentary, while covering a variety of subjects, such as the textual variations between the Greek and Coptic versions of the text, is defined by three overarching themes: 1. intertextual connections between this and other liturgical and theological works and the question of what is original to the text and what is a later addition;2. the question of authorship; and 3. the questions of function, the agenda of the author and the audience for the text.

1. Intertexuality and the Problem of Originality

A discussion of intertextuality and adaptation in a liturgical text is really a discussion of Liturgy as a living text. As a living text, and a functional text, a Liturgy can borrow prayers from other texts, and can add and change prayers depending on the theological and aesthetic preferences of the community and age. This makes the establishment of an edition of a Liturgy different than the establishment of a critical text of other texts of antiquity, since changes from the *Urtext* are not necessarily mistakes or false readings, but deliberate alterations which help to understand the cultural context in which the Liturgy existed, and, as such, these additions and changes cannot be taken out, but explained. This difficult situation is exacerbated in the Liturgy of St. Gregory by the poor state of the manuscript evidence, due perhaps to the fact that the Liturgy fell out of use in the Cappadocian/Constantinopolitan area in which it originated,[1334] as the late date of even the earliest manuscripts make it impossible to see the process of change in the text and this must be discovered from internal evidence, such as anachronistic theology.

I. While the discussion of this topic permeated the commentary, there are several prayers which stand out as excellent examples of the problems associated with this living text. The first prayer of the Liturgy, "The Prayer which the Priest Reads Silently,"[1335] is a prayer of access, through which the priest hopes to receive absolution from his sin and gain approval to begin the Liturgy. This prayer is almost identical to a prayer found in the Liturgy of St. James,[1336] in which it is used as a prayer of offering. As noted in the commentary, the few differences in the texts are focused on the person being addressed in the prayer, Christ in the Liturgy of St. Gregory and God the Father in the Liturgy of St. James. The difficulty lies in determining in which Liturgy this prayer has its origin, which has great implications in determining points of influence on the Liturgy of St. Gregory. In his com-

---

[1334] In the Christian west, local liturgical traditions that are replaced by the Tridentine rite also often have a poor manuscript tradition, as the manuscripts of the Liturgy, which are no longer in use, are repurposed.
[1335] Cf. Section I.1.
[1336] Mercier (1944). Pp. 190-192

mentary of the Bohairic Coptic text, Hammerschmidt postulates that the text was adopted into the Liturgy of St. Gregory and rewritten to reflect the Christ centered nature of the Liturgy of St. Gregory, he comes to this conclusion because the text in the Liturgy of St. Gregory is longer, and early liturgies tend not to subtract when adopting prayers, but to add to them. There is language in the prayer, however, that is also used in the anti-Arian writings of, among others, Athanasius of Alexandria, this would seem to support the origin of this prayer in the Liturgy of St. Gregory. Despite this glimmer of evidence, Hammerschmidt's theory must be adopted, as one phrase is not enough evidence to overturn established liturgical theory. This prayer, then, shows how the original author of the text treats adoptions into his Liturgy, by rewriting them so that they fit more seamlessly into the larger context of the text.

In the post-Anaphora there are three alternate "Prayers of the Breaking,"[1337] which illustrate well how changing theological climate has an effect on a liturgical text. The final of these three prayers seems to be the original, as it is the most functional of the three, and contains all of the necessary components of a "Prayer of the Breaking." This prayer also uses a phrase: λόγε ὅν νοοῦσιν, ἄνθρωπε ὅν θεωροῦσιν, this is not, as Hammerschmidt notes, Alexandrian Greek, rather it is the Atticistic Greek used by authors like St. Gregory the Theologian and once again points the origin of this text outside of Egypt. This is a theological statement unusual in this type of prayer, which focuses on the preparation for the reception of the Eucharist and the recitation of the Lord's Prayer, and it is this unusual statement that causes the insertion of the other two prayers, as the Christology of Egypt changed. This is best exemplified in the first of the three prayer, which was the most recent addition. This prayer is difficult to interpret as a "Prayer of the Breaking," as the focus has entirely shifted from the Eucharist and the Lord's Prayer to a discussion of the Incarnation, drawing on the Nicene Creed and the *Monogenes* Hymn of Justinian to create a statement of faith in which the Incarnation is expressed in terms of Miaphysite theology.[1338] As this prayer is found in no other extant Liturgy, it seems to have been written specifically for this Liturgy, that such an important section of the Liturgy reflect the theology of the audience of the text later in the life of the Liturgy.

II. Along with the prayers that are adapted by the original author to fit the style of the Liturgy and those that are written specifically to be added to this text, there are some

---

[1337] Cf. Section III. 2,3 and 4.
[1338] The Nicene Creed is not only used in this later prayer, however, and is one of the most important sources for the theology of the text. Other important sources include the works of St. Gregory the Theologian. St. Gregory's Christology, as laid out in his *Third* and *Fourth Theological Oration* is seen in the post-*Sanctus* prayers, as discussed by Sanchez Caro. The theological sources used in this Liturgy helps in determining the origin of this Liturgy.

prayers that were adopted wholesale into the Liturgy to make it more familiar to the audience in Egypt. These prayers are more easily identifiable, as they are usually adopted from the Egyptian liturgies, and are adopted whole, without any alterations to adapt them to the style of the Liturgy of St. Gregory. The most prominent example of this type of adoption is in the pre-Anaphora, the "Alternate Prayer of the Veil among the Egyptians."[1339] This prayer can be counted as a later adoption into the Liturgy of St. Gregory by its name, as we have established the origins of this text are not in Egypt, but in the Cappadocian/Constantinopolitan liturgical family, more telling, however, is the language used in the prayer: not only is this the only prayer in the Liturgy that is not addressed to Christ and so does not fit into the established theme of the Liturgy. Hammerschmidt also points out that the use of the term λογικός in the prayer also helps to localize the prayer as Egyptian in origin, and therefore not an original part of the Liturgy. Another prayer, the "Prayer of the Gospel,"[1340] fits into this category as well. Although this prayer is addressed to Christ it seems to have been adopted into the Liturgy as a whole from the Coptic Liturgy of St. Mark, in which the prayer appears as well. Unlike the previous prayer, this is not an alternate prayer, but the only prayer in the Liturgy for the Gospel reading, which leads to the conclusion that an original "Prayer of the Gospel" was cut out of the Liturgy and replaced by this prayer.

    III. In looking for intertextual connections in this Liturgy the reader is struck by numerous commonalities between the Liturgy of St. Gregory and the Byzantine Liturgy of St. Basil, even more so than with the Egyptian Liturgy of St. Basil, with which it is often found in manuscripts, such as the Paris Manuscript and the Kacmarcik Codex.[1341] These commonalities are found throughout the text and cannot be explained only by the Byzantine character of much of the Anaphora of the Liturgy of St. Gregory. In the Anaphora, these commonalities tend to be phrases, or the similar setup of prayers, such as the Consecration, it is outside the Anaphora, however, that the close connection between these prayers is truly seen. In the post-Anaphora, following the rituals and prayers surrounding the Lord's Prayer is a "Prayer of the Bowing of the Head"[1342] and an alternate, the alternate is nearly identical with the corresponding prayer in the Byzantine Liturgy of St. Basil. In the pre-Anaphora another prayer, the "Prayer of the Veil,"[1343] is also nearly identical with its counterpart in the Byzantine Liturgy of St. Basil. These prayers both play an important role

---

[1339] Cf. Section I. 5.
[1340] Cf. Section I. 3.
[1341] Because they are found together in manuscripts so often the two texts are referred to as sister liturgies.
[1342] Section III.7.
[1343] Section I.4.

in the Liturgy and the "Prayer of the Veil" is quite lengthy, it is important, then, to identify which Liturgy these prayers originate in, and into which Liturgy they are adopted, as this gives a glimpse into the interplay between these two liturgies and hints at the origin of the Liturgy of St. Gregory. How, however, is it possible to determine in which Liturgy these prayers originate and which adopts them? In this discussion it is the style of these liturgies that tells, the Liturgy of St. Gregory is, uniquely, addressed to Christ,[1344] while the Byzantine Liturgy of St. Basil is written in a more liturgically standard style and addresses its prayers to God the Father. As the prayers held in common between these two are all addressed to Christ, their origin in the Liturgy of St. Gregory seems logical. Such borrowing into the Byzantine Liturgy of St. Basil also gives a clue as to the identity of the original "Prayer of the Gospel," which was replaced in the Liturgy of St. Gregory by a borrowing from the Egyptian Liturgy of St. Mark. The "Prayer of the Gospel" in the Byzantine Liturgy of St. Basil is the only prayer in this text, other than those apparently adopted from the Liturgy of St. Gregory, it seems probable, then, rather than postulating one prayer in the entire text written in a different style, that this prayer too was adopted from the Liturgy of St. Gregory and is the original "Prayer of the Gospel" in the Liturgy of St. Gregory, which was later replaced.

2. *The Question of Authorship*

Another question of importance in the commentary is the question of authorship, and the origins in general of this text. Unfortunately, there is no discussion of this text in liturgical commentaries of late antiquity, making a determination of the source dependent solely on internal evidence of the Liturgy itself. This lack of evidence has led to theories on the origin of the Liturgy that are difficult to substantiate, such as the Syrian origin theory that has become the *communis opinio*. In the commentary to this text clues to the origin of the text are discovered in I. the nature of the intertextual connection between the Byzantine Liturgy of St. Basil and the Liturgy of St. Gregory; II. in the theological nature and functionalization of the text and; III. in the stylistic and linguistic nature of the text.

I. It is the intertextual connection between the Liturgy of St. Gregory and the Byzantine Liturgy of St. Basil that allow us to pinpoint the place of origin of this text. Both the fact that the Liturgy of St. Gregory and the Egyptian Liturgy of St. Basil do not share nearly as many prayers and phrases as the Liturgy of St. Gregory does with the Byzantine Liturgy of St. Basil and that it seems that the prayers are adopted from the Liturgy of St.

[1344] The uniqueness of this Liturgy is still remarkable even if Gerhards is correct and the Christ centered style of the Liturgy of St. Gregory is not part of the functionalization of the text, as I contend, but is an extension of the Christ centered prayers one sees in other liturgies as well.

Gregory point to the fact that this is not a Liturgy of the Egyptian family.[1345] As the main liturgical text of the capital of the Byzantine Empire, the Byzantine Liturgy of St. Basil exerts great influence on other liturgies of the eastern Christian world. If, then, the Byzantine Liturgy of St. Basil is influenced by another text, this must have taken place early in its history, and in its place of origin, the Cappadocian/Constantinopolitan liturgical world. That this Liturgy has its origin in Cappadocia/Constantinople has an important bearing on the discussion of the author, as this is both the time period and the geographic area in which St. Gregory the Theologian was active.

II. The theological functionalization of this text by the author is an important part of the commentary by itself, it is, however, also important in the discussion of who the author of the text could be. In the commentary, the theology of this Liturgy is shown to be entirely in line with the Christology and Pneumatic theology espoused by St. Gregory the Theologian and that found in the Nicene Creed. This theology, which comes through so strongly in the prayers that it is possible to identify prayers that are added later, such as the first "Prayer of the Breaking," because they present a different theological position than the other prayers in the Liturgy. This theology is exemplified by the use of the term *homoousios* in the text. This term, which is adopted by the Nicene Fathers from late antique philosophy to describe the relationship between the Father and the Son in the Trinity, was initially not widely used in liturgical texts, the Byzantine Liturgy of St. Basil, for example, only has one instance of this term, and in one of the hymns of the people. Eventually, however, the term is adopted in liturgies of the Syrian and Coptic families in a string of epithets of the Holy Spirit during the *ekphonesis* of prayers. In the Liturgy of St. Gregory, however, this use of *homoousios* as a stock phrase is not found.[1346] The author does use the term twice in his Liturgy, once in the first "Prayer of the Greeting:" Ὁ ὢν καὶ προὼν, καὶ διαμένων εἰς τοὺς αἰῶνας. Ὁ τῷ Πατρὶ συναΐδιος καὶ ὁμοούσιος καὶ σύνθρονος καὶ συνδημιουργός.[1347] The other is in the "Prayer of the Bowing of the Head," the final prayer of the Liturgy: τό τε θεῖον, καὶ ἅγιον, καὶ ὁμοούσιον, καὶ ὁμοδύναμον, καὶ ὁμόδοξον, καὶ συναΐδιον Πνεῦμα...[1348] The two sections share an intratextual connection through the alliterated lists of epithets, and in doing so the author uses the Christological background of the Nicene

---

[1345] In addition to this, there are numerous smaller indications that this is a Byzantine liturgical text in origin, rather than an Egyptian. The most important of these is the form of the *Post-Sanctus* prayer, which is lengthy and discusses the entirety of the history of salvation, instead of the shorter prayers found in the Egyptian liturgies that focus on the preparation of the Eucharist.

[1346] The author seems to intentionally avoid using the term in this manner. So, for example in the *ekphonesis* of the initial prayer of the Liturgy, the Syrian version of which contains the term *homoousios*.

[1347] Cf. Section I. 6 lines 2-3.

[1348] Cf. Section III. 11 lines 6-7.

Creed to emphasize both the divinity of Christ and of the Holy Spirit. This falls in line with the theology of St. Gregory the Theologian, who is one of the first to use the term *homoousios* with the Holy Spirit in his *Fifth Theological Oration*.

The most striking aspect of the functionalization of the text is in the address of the entire Liturgy to Christ, this allows the author to underscore and emphasize Christ's divinity in a way that is both inescapable to the audience of the text, both the clergy celebrating the Liturgy and the laity attending it and serves to marginalize those who do not accept Christ's divinity, such as the Arians and the semi-Arians, such as the Pneumatomachians. St. Gregory the Theologian spent much of his career combating the Arians and semi-Arians entrenched in Constantinople, which came to a head at the Second Ecumenical Council at Constantinople in 381. In 379, St. Gregory the Theologian presented his *Theological Orations*, each of these orations is concluded with a prayer, in the first, third and fourth of these orations, these prayers are addressed to Christ, underscoring Christ's divinity as it is in this liturgical text.

As the intertextual connections between this Liturgy and the Byzantine Liturgy of St. Basil helps to pinpoint the geographical origin of the Liturgy, the theological content and functionalization of the text helps to pinpoint the approximate date of the Liturgy. The Christology and the emphasis on Christ's divinity seen in the text only makes sense in the context of a controversy in which the divinity of Christ is called into question, the Arian controversy of the fourth century. That this text belongs in the timeframe of the Arian controversy and is not, as has been postulated by some because of the strong emphasis of Christ's divinity, a text meant to promote the Monophysite position in the conflict leading up to the Council of Chalcedon in the fifth century can be seen in the consistent description of Christ's dual nature.[1349] It is possible the narrow the date of authorship down even further, the Arian controversy raged from the beginning of the fourth century to ~381 when it was condemned for the second time at the Second Ecumenical Council, when one takes the use of *homoousios* with the Holy Spirit into account as well. It was only in the second half of the fourth century that the semi-Arian Pneumatomachians denied the divinity of the Holy Spirit, and it was in 379 that St. Gregory the Theologian used *homoousios* in terms of the Holy Spirit for the first time, the text, then must stem from the time of the Pneumatomachian controversy, in the years following 379.

III. In discussing what the style of this text can reveal about the author the genre of the text poses some problems. In a liturgical text each prayer has a specific form and func-

---

[1349] Except for the first *Prayer of the Breaking*, the Miaphysite leanings of which betray its later addition into the text.

tion, and despite the functionalization of the text, the author does attempt to stick to the stylistic forms used in these types of prayers. The standardized liturgical phraseology and the elements of a Liturgy which must be present[1350] makes it difficult for the individuality of the author to shine through. In a study of the style and theology of the post-*Sanctus* prayer, Sanchez Caro shows that the author of this text emulates the writing style and the theology seen in the works of St. Gregory, at least as much as possible in a liturgical setting. This style is seen in other parts of the text as well and is especially expressed in the use of *epitheta* of Christ. In the introduction the use of these *epitheta* outside of the post-*Sanctus* hymn was investigated and compared to the *epitheta* of Christ in an excerpt from the *Theological Orations* of St. Gregory. In this investigation the sheer number of *epitheta* used in both texts was of interest, as were the number *epitheta* this excerpt and the Liturgy held in common.

A number of prayers of the Liturgy, for example in the first and second prayers of the pre-Anaphora, are marked by a progression of the priest and the people from the earthly to the heavenly. The initial prayer sets up the worshipper and Christ in two very separate positions, Christ is the one who ἐπισκεψάμενος ἡμᾶς. This sets up two levels, the heavenly level from which Christ looks down and an earthly in which "we" are and on which Christ looks down. This juxtaposition is further emphasized by the epithets used to describe "us," such as "sinful" and "unworthy." In the second prayer, which is set up as a continuation of the first, this unworthiness has been transformed into sanctity: καὶ ἀξίωσον ἡμᾶς ἐν καθαρῷ συνειδότι λατρεῦσαί σοι πάσας τὰς ἡμέρας τῆς ζωῆς ἡμῶν, καὶ ἐν ἁγιασμῷ ταύτην σοι τὴν προσενέγκειν λειτουργίαν.[1351] The priest and the people have progressed to a state of holiness through these prayers of access, and are now able to embark on the further journey of the Liturgy, which culminates in the Eucharist. While this style is not unusual in a Liturgy, it is also reminiscent of the treatises of Neoplatonic philosophy, such as *Peri tou Kalou* by Plotinus, in which the cosmos is understood as a progression upward to perfection. The Cappadocian Fathers, as well aristocrats of late antiquity were educated in the Neoplatonic method.

An important question in the stylistic analysis of this text is if the language is Atticistic, as the works of St. Gregory the Theologian are, or not. This question too is obscured by the standardization of liturgical language and phrasing, the third "Prayer of the Breaking,"[1352] however, contains a phrase: ὦ Λόγε ὃν προνοοῦσιν αὐτόν, καὶ ἄνθρωπε ὃν προθεωροῦσιν αὐτόν. As Hammerschmidt and Renaudot point out, this is not the expected

---

[1350] Such as a *Sanctus* Hymn, the Lord's Prayer, the Consecration and *epiklesis* etc…
[1351] Cf. Section I.2 lines 7-8.
[1352] Cf. Section III.4.

phrasing in for Alexandrian Greek, which should have: λόγε ὃν νοοῦσιν, ἄνθρωπε ὃν θεωροῦσιν. This leads Hammerschmidt to postulate that the phrasing of the Coptic translation affected the Greek text, a direction of influence which is very rare. This phrase may not be what is expected in an Alexandrian Liturgy, but is proper Atticistic Greek and, rather than leading us to postulate such a radical departure from the standard interaction between the Greek original and the Coptic translation, this phrase underscores the origin of this Liturgy outside of the Alexandrian liturgical world and in the Cappadocian/Constantinopolitan tradition.[1353] This phrase is also an indication that the author is at least attempting to, despite the standardized language of the Liturgy, write in the same Atticistic style that marks the writings of the church Fathers including St. Gregory the Theologian.

IV. Through the investigation in the commentary, several aspects of the discussion surrounding the authorship of the Liturgy of St. Gregory the Theologian become clear. The Liturgy was written in the late fourth century in Cappadocia or Constantinople, and while we were not able to pinpoint the origin as exactly as Baumstark, who gives the origin as in Nazianzus,[1354] an origin in Cappadocia points to St. Gregory as a possible author. The text is written in Atticistic Greek and shows influence from the Neoplatonic school of late antique philosophy. More importantly, the text shows very strong anti-Arian and anti-Pneumatomachian functionalization. All of this would fit a text written by St. Gregory the Theologian, and suggests him as the author.[1355] Unfortunately, as there is no discussion of this text in other sources, scholars working on this Liturgy face the same difficulty as those working on the Liturgy of. St. John Chrysostom, the authorship can only be reconstructed from internal evidence. This means that, despite the internal evidence, it is impossible to say without any doubt that St. Gregory the Theologian is the author. It is also possible that the text was written by one of his disciples, or another contemporary who shared his theological views and admired his writing style and the text was later attributed to St. Gregory in order to lend the text greater importance.

3. Functionalization and Audience

The way that the author functionalizes this text and the agenda the author has are two inexorably linked questions. We have discussed the agenda of the author in the previous section, how he uses the direct address of Christ in the text in order to combat the Ariana

---

[1353] As postulated by Baumstark (1908) and Beck (1959)
[1354] Beck (1959). pp. 40-41
[1355] Despite initial rejection of St. Gregory the Theologian as the author of the text, there seems to be a progression towards accepting him as the author, each new scholar going a little further.

and the Pneumatomachians. Gerhards suggested that this direct address of Christ is not, in fact, used to combat these heresies, but is a logical progression from the tradition of prayers *ad Christum* one sees in, for example, the Anaphora of Sts. Addai and Mari or in the Byzantine Baptismal liturgies. One issue with this theory are the sheer number of prayers in the Liturgy which are addressed to Christ. In the examples given by Gerhards, there are individual prayers addressed to Christ, but they are part of larger texts in which other prayers addressed to God the Father or the Trinity as a whole are addressed. The Liturgy of St. Gregory the Theologian, however, is addressed entirely to Christ, with two exceptions, one being the Lord's Prayer and the second being a prayer added after the Liturgy was introduced into Egypt. Such focus on Christ does not seem to be a mere expansion of the tradition of prayers *ad Christum*, but a deliberate marginalization of the Arian and Pneumatomachian groups. In the Commentary the functionalization of the text is explored from two angles: 1. How does the author functionalize the text? And 2. What is the audience for this text?

I.   Addressing Christ in the prayers of the Liturgy is, perhaps, the most obvious way in which the author functionalizes the text, it is not, however, the only way he does so. Along with this direct address, the author transfers *epitheta*, attributes and objects associated with other members of the Trinity to Christ. He does this using the qualifier σου in these various references. By doing so, Christ seems to take a dominant role in the Trinity, almost, at times, seeming to replace God the Father, who is not even mentioned in the first prayer until the *ekphonesis*. So, for example, the Holy Spirit and the Altar, both usually associated with God the Father are associated with Christ instead. In this way, as is the case with the address of Christ, the author shifts the focus of the Liturgy from God the Father to Christ thus making it impossible for Arians and Pneumatomachians to participate in the Eucharist in churches which use this Liturgy, since they would consider it blasphemy to pray to Christ, as they do not accept his divinity.[1356] The author's positioning of Christ in the Trinity can even approach the extreme, as it does in the *epiklesis*. The *epiklesis* is the section of the Anaphora following the Consecration in which the congregation prays that the Holy Spirit be sent down to transform the bread and the wine into the Body and Blood of Christ, in nearly every Liturgy containing this prayer, it is God the Father who is asked to send down the Holy Spirit.[1357] In the Liturgy of St. Gregory the Theologian, however, this prayer, too is addressed to Christ and it is Christ who is asked to

---

[1356] We see a similar example of this type of functionalization in the Jewish *Birkat Haminim*. In this prayer, the *Minim*, the Christians, are condemned and effectively forced out of the praying community of the Jews, since it is counterproductive to pray for one's own condemnation.
[1357] See, for example the Liturgy of St. John Chrysostom.

send the Holy Spirit. This is reminiscent of the way in which the Council of Toledo combated the Arianism of the Visigoths, inserting the *filioque* into the Nicene Creed, also in order to underscore Christ's position in the Trinity. It is this quite radical expression of Christ's divinity that could be evidence that this Liturgy was not written by St. Gregory himself, but by one of his disciples. St. Gregory himself rarely exhibits "radical" theology, a disciple, however, or another author who is emulating St. Gregory's style and theology would be more likely to take a step further that St. Gregory himself would be unlikely to take. In the context of this Liturgy, however, the seemingly "radical" departure from the normal is a logical culmination of what is occurring in the other prayers, the author must address this prayer to Christ or risk undoing the image of a Christ centered cosmos created in this text.

The position of Christ within the Trinity is not the only way in which the author emphasizes His divinity. The relationship between Christ and humanity presents another place the author is able to do this, the Arian view of creation was an anthropocentric one, in which Christ's role in creation is for the benefit of humanity and the author is vehement in his combating of this view of the relationship between Christ and humanity. We see the author setting up the relationship between humanity and Christ using a variety of adjectives.[1358] Humanity is often referred to with adjectives emphasizing unworthiness and extreme humility in the face of Christ's divine power. Adjectives such as humble, unworthy etc… underscore the position of the worshipper as the *doulos*, the slave of Christ. While other Eastern liturgies do not hesitate to use similar adjectives when describing the members of the congregation, their use in this Liturgy, in which Christ's status in the Trinity is also emphasized and in which all of the prayers are addressed to Christ, this leaves little doubt as to the cosmic order as envisioned by the author. The danger of setting Christ so far above humanity is that His human nature can be obscured, and this, as well as the address of Christ, has led some scholars to interpret the text in the context of the Monophysite controversy. The author mitigates this by coupling the adjectives emphasizing humility in humanity with adjectives emphasizing Christ's love for and closeness to humanity.

II. The author functionalizes this text in order to influence those who participate in the celebration of the Eucharist. This means that the target audience of the text is not those who are marginalized by it, the Arians and Pneumatomachians, as they would not be present at a celebration of this Liturgy to begin with. The audience, then, are the Nicene Christians who were present at the Liturgy, especially the clergy, who, because they are

---

[1358] This is an interesting example of how the author uses the standard liturgical phrasing to underscore his position. It is not unusual to see this type of language in a liturgical text, in the context of this Liturgy, however, the standard phrasing is functionalizes as anti-Arian polemic.

officiating over the service, would be able to pick up on aspects of the functionalization lost on members of the congregation who were listening.[1359]

4. Further Study

There is always room for further study in any project, in the case of the Liturgy of St. Gregory the Theologian, further study must focus on the manuscripts, both taking the two later manuscripts into account as well as investigating the possibility of further manuscripts of the Liturgy in other monastery libraries. It would also be interesting to look further into the relationship, if any, between the Syrian and Greek versions of the Liturgy.

[1359] Although it was common to read all prayers in the Liturgy aloud until the time of Justinian, when silent prayers became more common, it would still have been difficult for the laity to understand every word.

Appendix I: Select Bibliography

I. Monographies:

1. *A Dictionary of Early Christian Beliefs*. Bercot, David (ed). Hendrickson Publishers. 1998.
2. A Monk of the Eastern Church. *Orthodox Spirituality: An Outline of the Orthodox Ascetical and Mystical Tradition*. St. Vladimir's Seminary Press. 1987.
3. Altaner, Berthold und Stuiber, Alfred (editors). *Patrologie: Leben, Schriften und Lehre der Kirchenväter*. Verlag Herder. 1978.
4. *Anti-Nicene Fathers Volume 7: Lactatantius, Venantius, Asterius, Victorianus, Dionysius, Apostolic Teachings and Constitutions, 2 Clement, Early Liturgies*. Roberts, Alexander and Donaldson, James (ed). Hendrickson Publishers. 1994.
5. *Apocrypha Anecdota*. James, M.R. (ed). The Cambridge University Press. 1893.
6. *Apocryphal New Testament*. James, M.R. (trans). Oxford at the Claredon Press. 1924.
7. Aquilina, Mike. *The Mass of the Early Christians*; Our Sunday Visitor Publishing Division, Huntington, Indiana. 2001.
8. *Arianism: Historical and Theological Reassessments; Papers from the Ninth International Conference on Patristic Studies*. Gregg, Robert C. (ed). The Philadelphia Patristic Foundation Ltd. 1985.
9. Arnold, Robert Lloyd. *Orthodoxy Revisited: Contrasting the Faith and Practice of the Eastern Orthodox Church with Evangelical Doctrine*. Regina Orthodox Press Inc.
10. Athanasius. *On the Incarnation of the Word*. ed. by Archibald Robertson. David Nutt. 1891.
11. Athanasius. *Zwei Schriften Gegen die Arianer: Verteidigungsschrift Gegen die Arianer, Geschichte der Arianer*. Portmann, Werner (übersetzt). Anton Hiersemann. 2006.
12. Barnes, Michael R. and Williams, Daniel H. (ed.). *Arianism after Arius: Essays on the Development of the Fourth Century Trinitarian Conflicts*. T&T Clark Ltd. 1993.
13. Baumstark, A. *Die Chrysostomusliturgie und die Syrische Liturgie des Nestorios*. Chrysostomika. 1908.
14. Beck, H.G. *Kirche und Theologische Literatur im Byzantinischen Reich*. In *Byzantinisches Handbuch* Band I, Teil II. C.H. Beck'sche Verlagsbuchhandlung. 1959.
15. Bedingfield, M. Bradford. *The Dramatic Liturgy of Anglo-Saxon England*. The Boydell Press. 2002.

16. Behr, John. *Formation of Christian Theology Volume I: The Way to Nicaea*. St. Vladimir's Seminary Press. 2001.
17. Bendedictus. *The Rule of St. Benedict*. Rev. Boniface Verheyen (trans.). St. Benedict's Abbey. 1949.
18. Berry, Paul. The *Bobbio Missal: A.D. 700*. The Edwin Mellen Press. 2010.
19. Binns, John. *An Introduction the Christian Orthodox Churches*. Cambrdige University Press. 2002.
20. Bouyer, Louis. *Eucharist: Theology and Spirituality of the Eucharistic Prayer*. Univeristy of Notre Dame Press. 1989.
21. Bradshaw, Paul. *The Search for the Origins of Christian Worship*. Oxford University Press. 2002.
22. Brock, Sebastian. *The Harp of the Spirit: Eighteen Poems of Saint Ephraim*. The Borgo Press. 1984.
23. Brock, Sebastian. *The Syriac Version of the Pseudo Nonnos Mythological Scholia*; Cambridge at the University Press, Cambridge, England. 1971.
24. Budde, Achim. *Die ägyptische Basilios-Anaphora. Text – Kommentar- Geschichte*. Aschendorff Verlag. 2004.
25. *Cambridge Illustrated History: Islamic World*. Robinson, Francis (ed). Press Syndicate of the University of Cambridge. 1996.
26. Caro, J.M.S. *Eucharistia e Historia de la Salvacion*. Biblioteca de Autores Cristianos. 1984.
27. *Christian Origins*. Horsley, Richard (ed.). Fortress Press. 2010.
28. Coniaris, Anthony. *These are the Sacraments: the Life Giving Mysteries of the Orthodox Church*. Light and Life Publishing Company. 1981.
29. Constantine and Licinius. *The Edict of Milan*. H. Bettenson (trans). in Documents of the Christian Church. Oxford University Press. 1963.
30. Cuming, Geoffrey, J. *The Liturgy of St. Mark: edited from the manuscripts with a commentary*. in Orientalia Christiana Analecta 234. Pontificium Institutum Studiorum Orientalium. 1990.
31. Day, Juliette. *The Baptismal Liturgy of Jerusalem*. Ashgate. 2007.
32. Day, Juliette. *Reading the Liturgy: An Exploration of Texts in Christian Worship*. T&T Clark. 2014.
33. Day, Peter. *Eastern Christian Liturgies: The Armenian, Coptic, Ethiopian and Syrian Rites. Eucharistic Rites with Introductory Notes and Rubrical Instructions*. Irish University Press. 1972.
34. Deiss, Lucien C.S.Sp; trans by Matthew O'Connell. *Springtime of the Liturgy*; The Liturgical Press, Collegville Minnesota. 1979.

Appendix I: Selected Bibliography

35. *Dictionary of the Middle Ages*. Joseph Strayer (ed). Charles Scribner's Sons. 1989.
36. *Die Melodien der Jakobitischen Kirche*. Hutsmann, Heinrich (ed). Kommissionsverlag der Österreichischen Akademie der Wissenschaften. 1969.
37. Dijkstra, Klaas. Life *and Loyalty: A Study in the Socio-Religious Culture of Syria and Mesopotamia in the Graeco-Roman Period Based on Epigraphical Evidence*. E.J. Brill. 1995.
38. Easton, Burton Scott. *The Apostolic Tradition of Hippolytus: Translated into English with Introduction and Notes.* Cambridge University Press. 1962.
39. Eusebius. *Vita Constantini*. P. Schaff and H. Wace (ed.) in. Volume I of the Nicene and Post-Nicene Fathers. Wm. B. Eerdmans. 1955.
40. Fuller, J.M. *Macedonius Bishop of Constantinople*. Wace, H. and Piercy, W. (ed.) in the *Dictionary of Christian Biography and Literature to the End of the Sixth Century*. John Murray (ed). 1911.
41. Gain, Benoit. *L'Eglise de Cappadoce au IVe Siecle D'apres la Correspondance de Basile de Cesaree (330-379)*. Pontificium Institutum Studiorum Orientalium. 1985.
42. Gamber, Klaus. *Ordo Antiquus Gallicanus: Der gallikanische Messritus des 6. Jahrhunderts*. Verlag Friedrich Pustet Regensburg. 1965.
43. Geanakopolos, Deno John. *Byzantium: Church, Society and Civilization Seen through Contemporary Eyes.* University of Chicago Press. 1984.
44. Gerberding, R. and Moran Cruz, J.H. *Medieval Worlds*. Houghton Mifflin Company. 2004.
45. Gerhards, Albert. *Die Griechsische Gregoriosanaphora: Ein Beitrag zur Geschichte des Eucharistischen Hochgebets*. Aschendorff. 1984.
46. Gilbert, Peter. *On God and Man: The Theological Poetry of St. Gregory of Nazianzus*; St. Vladimir's Seminary Press, Crestwood, NY. 2001.
47. Goehring, James E. and Timbie, Janet A. *The World of Early Egyptian Christianity: Language, Literature, and Social Context*. The Catholic University of America Press. 2007.
48. Graf, Georg. *Ein Reformversuch innerhalb der koptischen Kirche im zwölften Jahrhundert*. Paderborn. 1923.
49. Gregory or Nazianzus. *The Five Theological Orations*. Arthur James Mason (ed). Cambridge at the University Press. 1899.
50. Grillmeier, Aloys. *Christ in Christian Tradition*. A.R. Mowbray & Co. 1975.
51. Hamilton, Alistair. *The Copts and the West, 1439-1822: The European Discovery of the Egyptian Church*. Oxford University Press. 2006.
52. Hammerschmidt, Ernst. *Die Koptische Gregoriosanaphora: Syrische und Griechische Einflüsse auf eine Ägyptische Liturgie*. Akademie Verlag Berlin. 1957.
53. Hammerschmidt, Ernst. *Studies in the Ethiopic Anaphoras*. Akademie Verlag Berlin. 1961.

54. Hammond, C.E. and Brightman, F.E.: *Liturgies Eastern and Western; Being the Texts Original or Translated of the Principal Liturgies of the Church, Eastern T*
55. Hanson, R.P.C. *The Search for the Christian Doctrine of God*: The Arian Controversy, 318-381; Baker Academic, Grand Rapids, Michigan. 2005.
56. Hanssesn, J.M. *Institutiones Liturgicae de Ritibus Orientalibus Volume I, II and III.* Collegium Romanum Societatis Jesu. 1930-31.
57. Heinz, Andrea. *Die Heilige Messe nach dem Ritus der Syrisch-maronitischen Kirche.* Paulinus Verlag. 1996.
58. Hieromonk Gregorios. *The Divine Liturgy: A Commentary in the Light of the Fathers.* The Cell of St. John the Theologian Koutloumousiou Monastery. 2012.
59. Hughes, Phillip. *A History of the Church Volume I.* Sheed and Ward. 1949.
60. Humphries, Mark. *Early Christianity*; Routledge Publishings, London and New York. 2006.
61. Isaac, Jaques. *Taksa D-Hussaya: Le Rite du Pardon dans l'Eglise Syriaque Orientale.* Pontificium Institutum Studiorum Orientalium. 1989.
62. Jammo, Sarhad Y. Hermiz. *La Structure de la Messe Chaldeenne: du Debut jusqu'a l'Anaphore.* Pontificium Institutum Studiorum Orientalium. 1979.
63. John Chrysostom. *Baptismal Homily II.* in Harkins, Paul W. *Ancient Christian Writers: St. John Chrysostom Baptismal Instructions.* Pauline Press. 1962.
64. Jones, Garth and O'Donell, Victoria. *Propaganda and Persuasion.* Sage Publications Inc. 1999.
65. Jungmann, Josef A. S.J. *Die Stellung Christi im liturgischen Gebet.* Verlag der Aschendorffschen Verlagsbuchhandlung. 1925.
66. Jungmann, Josef A. S.J.: *The Early Liturgy; To the Time of Gregory the Great;* University of Notre Dame Press Notre Dame, Indiana. 1959.
67. Khalil, Samir. *La Version Arabe de la Liturgie Alexandrine de Saint Gregoire. (Codex Kacmarcik).* In Orientalia Christiana Periodica. 1979. pp 308-358.
68. Khs-Bumester, O.H.E. *The Egyptian or Coptic Church: A Detailed Description of Her Liturgical Services and the Rites and Ceremonies Observed in the Administration of Her Sacraments.* Le Claire. 1967.
69. Kilgallen, John J. *A Brief Commentary on the Gospel of Luke.* Paulist Press. 1988.
70. Kucharek, Casimir. *The Byzantine-Slav Liturgy of St. John Chrysostom.* Alleluia Press. 1971.
71. *Liturgiarum Orientalium Collectio: Volumes I and II.* Renaudot, Eusebe (ed). Gregg International Publishers Limited. 1970 (Original Publication 1847).
72. Lossky, Vladimir. *The Mystical Theology of the Eastern Church.* St. Vladimir's Seminary Press. 1997.

Appendix I: Selected Bibliography

73. Martyn, John R.C. *Arians and Vandals of the 4th-6th Centuries*. Cambridge Scholars Publishing. 2008.
74. Mercier, Dom B.-CH. *La Liturgie de Saint Jacques: Edition Critique du Texte Grec avec Traduction Latine.* in *Patrologia Orientalis*. Paris. 1944.
75. McGuckin, John. *Saint Cyril of Alexandria and the Christological Controversy*. St. Vladimir's Seminary Press. 2004.
76. Meinardus, Otto F.A. *Two Thousand Years of Coptic Christianity*. The American University in Cairo Press. 1999.
77. Mercier, Dom B.-CH. *La Liturgie De Saint Jacques: Edition Critique du Texte Grec avec Traduction Latine.* in Patrologia Orientalis 26. Paris. 1944.
78. Migne, J.P. *Gregorii Theologi: Opera Quae Extant Omnia.* in Patrologia Graeca Cursus Completus. Vol. 38. Francis Gallicis. 1862.
79. *Missale Parvum: ad Usum Sacerdotis Itinerantis.* Libreria Editrice Vaticana. 1972.
80. *Missale Parvum: ad Usum Sacerdotis Itinerantis*.edito iuxta typicam. Libreria Editrice Vaticana. 1977.
81. *Missale Romanum: Ex Decreto Concilii Tridentini Restitutum.* Bonnae ad Rhenum. 2004.
82. *Missale Romanum: Ex Decreto Sacrosancti Concilii Tridentini*; Typis Alfredi Mame et Filiorum, Turonibus. M CM XXII.
83. Müller-Wiener, Wolfgang. *Bildlexikon Zur Topographie Istanbuls: Byzantion, Konstantinupolis, Istanbul bis zum Beginn d. 17 Jh*. Tübingen. 1977.
84. Nicozisin. Fr. George. *The Orthodox Church: A Well Kept Secret, A Journey Through Church History.* Light and Life Publishing. 1997.
85. Norwich, John Julius. Byzanz Band I, II, III. (trans) Esther Mattile, Ulrike und Manfred Halbe. Econ Verlag GmbH. 1988 (Deutsche Fassung 1993).
86. *Novum Testamentum Graece*. D. Eberhard Nestle (ed). Privilegierte Wüttembergische Bibelanstalt. 1941.
87. *Novum Testamentum Latine*. Nestle-Aland (ed). Deutsche Bibelgesellschaft Stuttgart. 1906.
88. Ostrogorsky, George. *History of the Byzantine State.* Rutgers University Press. 1969.
89. *Oxford Classical Dictionary.* Oxford University Press. 1970.
90. Palmer, G.E.H., Sherrard, Phillip and Ware, Kallistos. *The Philokalia: The Complete Text Volumes I-IV*. Faber and Faber. 1981-1995.
91. Pappas, Barbara. *First and Second Corinthians: A Study of Paul's Letters.* Regina Orthodox Press. 2005.
92. Parvis, Sara. *Marcellus of Ancyra and the Lost Years of the Arian Controversy 325-345*. Oxford University Press. 2006.

93. Pelikan, Jaroslav. *Jesus Through the Centuries.* Yale University. 1985.
94. Pelikan, Jaroslav. *Mary Through the Centuries.* Yale University. 1996.
95. Pereira, Rodrigues A.S. *Studies in Aramaic Poetry (c. 100 B.C.E. – c. 600 C.E.) Selected Jewish, Christian and Samaritan Poems.* Studia Semitica Neederlandica. Van Gorcum. 1997.
96. *Perspectives on Christian Worship.* Pinson, Matthew J (ed.). B and H publishing. 2009.
97. Popovich, St. Justin. *The Life and Ascetical Feats of our Venerable and God-Bearing Father Theodore the Studite, Confessor.*
98. Pott, Thomas. *Byzantine Liturgical Reform.* St. Vladimir's Seminary Press. 2010.
99. *Qurbono; The Book Of Offering: The Service of the Holy Mysteries According to the Antiochene Syriac Maronite Church*; Saint Maron Publications, Brooklyn, New York. 1994.
100. Rhee, Helen. *Early Christian Literature: Christ and Culture in the Second and Third Centuries; The Apologies, Apocryphal Acts and Martyr Acts*; Routledge Publishing, London and New York. 2005.
101. Rordorf Willy and Others; trans by Matthew O'Connell. *The Eucharist of Early Christians*; Pueblo Publishing Company, New York. 1978.
102. Sabra, Adam. *Poverty and Charity in Medieval Islam: Mamluk Egypt, 1250-1517.* Cambridge University Press. 2000.
103. *Sacraments and Services Book One.* Contos, Leonidas (trans). Narthex Press. 1995.
104. Saliers, Don. *Worship as Theology: Foretaste of Glory Divine*; Abingdon Press, Nashville. 1994.
105. *Sancti Gregorii Nazianzeni Ope*ra: Versio Syriaca IV; Orationes XXVIII, XXIX, XXX et XXXI. Haelewyck, Jean-Claude (ed). Turnhout Brepolis Publishers. 2007.
106. Schaff, Phillip. *The Creeds of the Greek and Latin Churches.* Harper and Brothers. 1877.
107. Scherman, Theodor. Einleitung zu Storf, Remigius. *Griechische Liturgien.* Kempten und Muenchen. 1920.
108. Schreiner, Peter. *Byzanz: 565-1453.* R. Oldenbourg Verlag. 2008.
109. Sheerin, Daniel. *The Eucahrist: Message of the Fathers of the Church 7*: Michael Glazier Inc, Washington D.C. 1986.
110. Shepardson, Christine. *Anti-Judaism and Christian Orthodoxy: Ephrem's Hymns in Fourth-Century Syria.* The Catholic University of America Press. 2008.
111. Shulz, Hans-Joachim, trans by Matthew O'Connell. *The Byzantine Liturgy*; Pueblo Publishing Company, New York. 1986.
112. *St. Gregory Nazianzen: Select Orations.* Brown, Charles Gordon (trans). In Nicene and Post Nicene Fathers of the Christian Church. W.M.B. Eerdman's Publishing Company. 1893.

Appendix I: Selected Bibliography

113. Sterk, Andrea. *Renouncing the World Yet Leading the Church*; Harvard University Press, Cambridge, MA. 2004.
114. Stevenson, Kenneth. *The First Rites: Worship in the Early Church*; The Liturgical Press, Collegville, MN. 1989.
115. Stokstad Marilyn. *Medieval Art.* Westview Press. 2004.
116. *Summa Poetica: Griechische und lateinische Lyrik von der christliche Antike bis zum Humanismus.* Fischer, Carl (ed).Winkler Verlag.
117. Swainson, Charles Anthony. *The Greek Liturgies: Chiefly from Original Authorities.* Cambridge at the University Press. 1884.
118. Taft, Robert J. S.J. *A History of the Liturgy of St. John Chrysostom Volume IV; The Diptychs.* Pontificium Institutum Studiorum Orientalium. 1991.
119. Taft, Robert J. S.J. *Beyond East and West: Problems in Liturgical Understanding.* The Pastoral Press. 1984.
120. Taft, Robert J. S.J. *The Great Entrance: A History of the Transfer of Gifts and other Preanaphoral Rites of the Liturgy of St. John Chrysostom.* Pontificium Institutum Studiorum Orientalium. 1975.
121. Taft, Robert S.J. *The Pontifical Liturgy of the Great Church According to a Twelfth-Century Diataxis in Codex British Museum Add. 34060.* In Orientlia e
122. Tagher, Jaques. *Christians in Muslim Egypt: An Historical Study of the Relations between Copts and Muslims from 640 to 1922.* Oros Verlag. 1998.
123. Tamcke, Martin. *Das Orthodoxe Christentum.* Verlag C.H. Beck. 2004.
124. Teppler, Yaakov. *Birkat haMinim: Jews and Christians in conflict in the Ancient World.* Weingarten, Susan (trans). Mohr Siebeck. 2007.
125. Tereriatnikov, Natalia. *The Liturgical Planning of Byzantine Churches in Cappadocia.* Pontificium Institutum Studiorum Orientalium. 1996.
126. *The Divine Euchologion and the Divine Liturgy of S. Gregory the Theologian.* trans by Malan, S.C. D. Nutt. 1875.
127. *The Divine Liturgy of Our Father Among the Saints Basil the Great*; Holy Cross Orthodox Press, Brookline, MA. 1988.
128. *The Divine Liturgy of Saint James the Brother of the Lord*; Holy Cross Orthodox Press, Brookline, MA.
129. *The Divine Liturgy of Saint John Chrysostom*; Holy Cross Orthodox Press, Brookline, MA. 1985.
130. *The Fathers of the Church: St. Gregory of Nazianzus, Three Poems.* Denis Molaise Meehan, O.S.B (trans). The Catholic University of America Press, Washington D.C. 1987.

131. *The Festal Meanaion.* trans by Mother Mary and Kallistos Ware. St. Tikhon's Seminary Press, South Canaan, PA. 1998.
132. *The Lenten Triodion.* Mother Mary and Kallistos Ware (trans). St. Tikhon's Seminary Press, South Canaan, PA. 2002.
133. *The Life of St. Nikon.* Sullivan, Denis (trans). Hellenic College Press. 1987.
134. *The Liturgikon.* Leonidas Contos (trans). Narthex Press; Northridge, CA. 1993.
135. *The Order of Common Prayer of the Armenian Apostolic Orthodox Church.* Samoorian, V.Rev. Ghevont (ed). Published in Chelmsford MA by the author. 1986.
136. *The Orthodox Study Bible.* St. Athanasios Academy (ed). Thomas Nelson. 2008.
137. *The Oxford Dictionary of Byzantium.* Kazdhan, Alexander (ed). Oxford University Press. 1991.
138. *The Oxford History of the Biblical World.* Coogan, Michael (ed.). Oxford University Press. 1998.
139. *The Sarum Missal Edited from Three Early Manuscripts.* Legg, Wickham J. (ed). Oxford at the Claredon Press. 1916.
140. *The Seven Ecumenical Councils of the Undivided Church: Their Canons and Dogmatic Decrees.* Percival, Henry (trans). In the Nicene and Post Nicene Fathers of the Christian Church series. W.M.B. Eerdman's Publishing Company. 1971.
141. *The Study of Liturgy.* Jones, Cheslyn; Wainwright, Geoffrey; Yarnold, Edward SJ (ed). Oxford University Press, New York. 1978.
142. *The Synaxarion: The Lives of the Saints of the Orthodox Church, Volume Three: January and February.* Christopher Hookway (trans). Holy Convent of The Annunciation of Our Lady, Ormylia (Chalkidike). 2001.
143. Thompson, Bard. *Liturgies of the Western Church.* Fortress Press, Philadelphia. 1989.
144. Trempelis, Panagiotis. *ΑΙ ΤΡΙΕΣ ΛΕΙΤΟΥΡΓΙΑΙ: ΚΑΤΑ ΤΟΥΣ ΕΝ ΑΘΗΝΑΙΣ ΚΩΔΙΚΑΣ.* Αδελφότης Θεολόγων "ο Σωτηρ." 1982.
145. Vaggione, Richard Paul OHC. *Eunomius of Cyzicus and the Nicene Revolution.* Oxford University Press. 2000.
146. Vasiliev, A.A. *History of the Byzantine Empire Volumes I and II.* The University of Wisconsin Press. 1958.
147. *Von Arius zum Athanasianum: Studien zur Edition der "Athanasius Werke."* von Stockhausen, Anette and Brennecke, Hanns Christof (ed). Berlin-Brandenburgische Akademie der Wissenschaft. Walter de Gruyter GmbH & Co. 2010.
148. Watterson, Barbara. *Coptic Egypt.* Scottish Academic Press. 1988.
149. Wegman, Herman A.J. *Christian Worship in East and West: A Study Guide to Liturgical History.* Gordon W (trans). Lathrop. Pueblo Publishing Company. 1976.

150. Wellesz, Egon. *A History of Byzantine Music and Hymnography*. Claredon Press. 1961.
151. White, Hugh G. Evelyn. *The Monasteries of the Wadi ,N Naturn: Part I New Coptic Texts from the Monastery of Saint Macarius*. Arno Press. 1926 (reprinted 1973).
152. Williams, Benjamin; Anstall, Harold. *Orthodox Worship: A Living Continuity with the Synagogue, the Temple and the Early Church*; Light and Life Publishing Company, Minneapolis, Minnesota. 1990.
153. Williams, Rowan. *Of Arius: Heresy and Trandition*; William B. Eerdmans Publishing Company. 1987.
154. Williams, Stephen and Friell, Gerard. *Theodosius: The* Empire at *Bay*. Yale University Press. 1994.
155. Winkler, Gabriele. *Trinity and Liturgy: The Syrian Tradition (abstract)*. Liturgy: a Conference 2005. Yale Institute of Sacred Music. 2005.
156. Wybrew Hugh. *The Orthodox Liturgy: The Development of the Eucharistic Liturgy in the Byzantine Rite*; St. Vladimir's Seminary Press, Crestwood, NY. 1990.
157. Zaki, Nagdi Sami. *Histoire des coptes d'Egypte*. Editions de Paris. 2005.
158. Zizoulas, John D. *Eucharist Bishop Church: The Unity of the Church in the Divine Eucharist and the Bishop During the First Three Centuries*. Holy Cross Orthodox Press. 2001.
159. *ΙΕΡΑΤΙΚΟΝ:* Ἀποστολικὴ Διακονία τῆς Ἐκκλησίας τῆς Ἑλλάδος, Ἀθῆναι. 1987.
160. *ΜΙΚΡΟΝ ΕΥΧΟΛΟΓΙΟΝ*; Ἀποστολικὴ Διακονία τῆς Ἐκκλησίας τῆς Ἑλλάδος, Ἀθήνα. 2004.

II. Articles:

1. Barkhuizen, Jan. *Justinian's Hymn"O monogenes uios tou Theou."* Byzantinische Zeitschrift. Vol 77. pp. 3-5.
2. Beagon, Phillip M. *The Cappadocian Fathers, Women and Ecclesiastical Politics*. Vigiliae Christianae. Vol. 49. No. 2. pp. 165-179. 1995.
3. Beatrice, Pier Franco. *The Word 'Homoousios' from Hellenism to Christianity*. The American Society of Church History. 71:2. 2002. pp. 243-272.
4. Bernicolas-Hatzopoulos, Dionysios. *The First Siege of Constantinople by the Ottomans (1394-1402) and its Reprecusions on the Civilian Population of the City*. Byzantine Studies 10, 1. 1983. pp. 39-51.
5. Bonner, G. *A New Patristic Manuscript*. The British Museum Quarterly. Vol. 21. No. 4. pp. 91-92. 1959.

6. Bouman, C.A. *Variants in the Introduction to the Eucharistic Prayer*. Vigiliae Christianae, Vol. 4, No. 2, pp 94-115. Published by Brill. April 1950.
7. Brakmann, H. *Zur stellung des Parisinus Graecus 325 in der alexandrinisch-ägyptischen Liturgie*. Studi sull' Oriente Cristiano 3 1999. pp. 97-110.
8. Crivalleto, E. and Ribatti, D. *Soul, mind, brain: Greek philosophy and the birth of neuroscience*. Brain Research Bulletin 71. 2007. pp. 327-336.
9. Davis, Natalie Zemon. *Gregory Nazianzen in the Service of Humanist Social* Vol. 5. Number 1. 1961. pp. 17-32.
10. Edwards, M.J. *Did Origen apply the Word 'Homoousios' to the Son?* The Journal of Theological Studies. Oxford University Press. 1998.
11. Engberding, H. *Das chalkedonische Christusbild und die Liturgien der monophysitischen Kirchengemeinschaften*. A. Grillmeier (ed). Das Konzil von Chalkedon II. 1953. pp. 697-733.
12. Engberding, H. *Die syrische Anaphora der zwölf Apostel und ihre Paralleltexte*. in OrChr 34. 1937. pp. 213-247.
13. Engberding, H. *Ein Problem in der Homologia vor der heiligen Kommunion in der ägyptischen Liturgie*. Orientalia Christiana Periodica 2. 1936. pp. 145-154.
14. Ferhat, P. *Denkmäler altarmenischer Messliturgie 1. Eine dem hl. Gregor von Nazianz zugeschrieben Liturgie*. Oriens Christianus NS 1. 1911. 201-214.
15. Gilliard, Frank. *Senatorial Bishops of the Fourth Century*. The Harvard Theological Review, Vol. 77, No. 2, pp. 153-175. April 1984.
16. Haas, Christopher. *The Arians of Alexandria*. Vigiliae Christianae Vol. 47, No 3, pp234-245. Published by Brill. Sep 1993.
17. Hausherr, I. *Anaphora Gregorii Nazianzeni*. Anaphorae Syriacae Vol. 1, Fasc. 2. pp. 106-145. Pontificii Instituti Studiorum Orientalium. 1940.
18. Karavites, Peter. *Gregory Nazianzinos and Byzantine Hymnography*. The Journal of Hellenic Studies. Vol. 113. pp. 81-98. 1993.
19. Kienzle, Beverly Mayne. *Preaching the Cross: Liturgy and Crusade Propaganda*. Medieval Sermon Studies. Vol 53. 2009. pp. 11-32.
20. Kopecek, Thomas. *The Cappadocian Fathers and Civic Patriotism*. Church History. Vol. 43. No.3. pp. 293-303. 1974.
21. Kopecek, Thomas. *The Social Class of the Cappadocian Fathers*. Church History. Vol. 42, No. 4. pp. 453-466. Dec, 1973.
22. Le Boulluec, Alain. *Pagan and Biblical Exempla in Gregory Nazianzen. A Study in Rhetoric and Hermeneutics*. Rhetorica: A Journal of the History of Rhetoric. Vol. 16. No. 3. pp. 329-333. 1998.

Appendix I: Selected Bibliography

23. Lietzmann, Hans. *Sahidische Bruchstücke der Gregorios- und Kyrillosliturgie.* Oriens Christianus. N. S. 9. 1920. 1-19.
24. Login, Cezar. *The Pre-Anaphoral Rites of the Greek Egyptian Liturgies of St. Basil the Great and St .Gregory the Theologian.* Altarul Reintegirii. Nr. 2. 2010. pp. 243-262.
25. Maas, Paul. *Kleine Schriften.* C.H. Beck.1973.
26. MacMullen, Ramsay. *Cultural and Political Changes in the 4th and 5th Centuries.* Historia: Zeitschrift für Alte Geschichte. 52, 4. 2003. pp. 465-495.
27. Macomber, W. F. S. J. *The Greek Text of the Coptic Mass and of the Anaphoras of Basil and Gregory According to the Kacmarcik Codex.* Orientalia Christiana Periodica. 1977. pp 308-334.
28. Macomber, W.F. S. J. *The Oldest Known Text of the Anaphora of the Apostles Addai and Mari.* Orientalia Christiana Periodica. 1966 pp 335-371.
29. Majercik, Ruth. *A Reminiscence of the "Chaldean Oracles" at Gregory of Nazianzus, Or. 29,2: oion krathp tiΣ yΠepeppyh.* Vigiliae Christianae. Vol. 52. No. 3. pp. 286-292. 1998.
30. Margoulith, G. *The Liturgy of the Nile.* Journal of the Royal Asiatic Society of Great Britain and Ireland. 1896. pp. 677-731.
31. Maslov, B. *The Limits of Platonism: Gregory of Nazianzus and the Invention of theōsis.* Greek Roman and Byzantine Studies 52 2012. pp. 440-468.
32. McGuckin, J.A. *Deification in Greek Patristic Thought: The Cappadocian Fathers' Strategic Adoption of a Tradition.* From. M Christensen & J Wittung (ed). *Partakers of the Divine Nature. The History and Development of Deification in the Christian Tradition* Farleigh Dickinson University Press. 2006.
33. Milovanovic-Barham, Celica. *Three Levels of Style in Augustine of Hippo and Gregory of Nazianzus.* Rhetorica: A Journal of the History of Rhetoric. Vol. 11. No. 1. pp. 1-25. 1993.
34. Newman, Fr. Constantine. *The Poetry of Theology: An Analysis of Justinian's Hymn 'Ο Μονογενὴς Υἱός.* The Greek Orthodox Theological Review.Vol. 43. Nos 1-4. pp. 85-91. 1998.
35. Newman, Nicholas. *The Origin of the "Egyptian" Liturgy of St. Gregory the Theologian.* The Greek Orthodox Theological Review Vol. 58. Nos 1-4. pp. 119-139. 2013.
36. Newman, Nicholas. *The Use of the Term Homoousios in the Liturgy of St. Gregory the Theologian.* St. Vladimir's Theological Quarterly. Vol. 58. No 3. 2014.
37. Norris, F.W. *The Tetragrammation in Gregory Nazianzen (Or. 30.17).* Vigiliae Christianae. Vol. 43. No. 4. pp. 339-344. 1989.
38. Norris, Frederick. *Of Thorns and Roses: The Logic of Belief in Gregory Nazianzen.* Church History. Vol. 53. No. 4. pp. 455-464. 1984.

39. Norris, Frederick. *The Authenticity of Gregory Nazianzen's Five Theological Orations.* Vigiliae Christianae. Vol. 39. No. 4. pp. 331-339. 1985.

40. Otis, Brooks. *Cappadocian Thought as a Coherent System.* Dumbarton Oaks Papers. Vol. 12. pp. 95+97-124. 1958.

41. Otis, Brooks. *The Throne and the Mountain: an Essay on St. Gregory Nazianzus.* The Classical Journal. Vol. 56, No. 4. pp. 146-165. Jan., 1961.

42. Papadeas, George. *Greek Orthodox Holy Week and Easter Services.* Papadeas. 1977.

43. Piper, Otto A. *The Apocalypse of John and the Liturgy of the Ancient Church.* Church History. Vol. 20, No. 1. pp. 10-22. Mar., 1951.

44. Richardson, Canon D.R. *The Docturne of the Trinity: Its Development, Difficulties and Value.* The Harvard Theological Review. Vol. 36. No. 2. pp. 109-134. 1943.

45. Rose, H.J. *St. Gregory Nazianzen and Pauline Rhythm.* The Harvard Theological Review. Vol. 24. No. ¾. pp. 323-324. 1933.

46. Sanchez, Caro. *Historia de la Salvacion en la anafora alejandrina de San Gregorio Nacianceno.* Salmaticenses. 24. 1977. pp. 49-82.

47. Schechter, S. *Genizah Specimens.* JQR. 10. 1898. 657.

48. Schmemann, Protobresbyter Alexander. *Byzantium, Iconoclasm and the Monks.* St. Vladimir's Seminary Quarterly. Vol. 3. No. 3. pp 18-34. 1959.

49. Schmemann, Protobresbyter Alexander. *Easter in the Liturgical Year.* Excerpts from the lecture *The Sanctification of Life.* July 1963.

50. Schmemann, Protobresbyter Alexander. *Fast and Liturgy.* St. Vladimir's Seminary Quarterly. Vol. 3. No. 1. pp 2-9. 1959.

51. Schmemann, Protobresbyter Alexander. *The Historical Background of the Council [Chalcedon].* The Ecumenical Review. Vol. 4. No. 4. pp 400-402. 1952.

52. Schmemann, Protobresbyter Alexander. *The Liturgical Structure of Lent.* The Russian Orthodox Journal. pp. 6-8. 1959.

53. Schmemann, Protobresbyter Alexander. *Theology and Eucharist.* St. Vladimir's Seminary Quarterly. Vol. 5. No. 4. pp 10-23. 1961.

54. Shepherd, Massey H. *Liturgical Expressions of the Constantinian Triumph.* Dumbarton Oaks Papers. Vol. 21. pp. 57-78. 1967.

55. Shepherd, Massey H. *The Formation and Influence of the Antiochene Liturgy.* Dumbarton Oaks Papers. Vol. 15. pp. 23+25-44. 1961.

56. Sivan, Hagith. *Ulfila's Own Conversion.* The Harvard Theological Review. Vol. 89, No. 4, pp 373-386. Oct, 1996.

57. Snee, Roger. *Gregory Nazianzen's Anastasia Church; Arianism, the Goths and Hagiography.* Dunbarton Oaks Papers. Vol. 52, pp157-186. 1998.

Appendix I: Selected Bibliography

58. Taft, Robert. *The Liturgy of the Great Church: An Initial Synthesis of Structure and Interpretation on the Eve of Iconoclasm*. Dunbarton Oaks Papers. Vol. 34. pp 45-75. 1980-1981.
59. van Steenbergen, Jo. *The Alexandrian Crusade and the Mamluk Sources: Reassesment of the Kitab al-Ilmam of An-Nuwayri Al Iskandarani*. East and West in the Crusader States. Vol. 3. 2003.
60. Velimirovic, Milos. *Liturgical Drama in Byzantium and Russia*. Dumbarton Oaks Papers. Vol 16. 1962. 349-385.
61. Weitzmann, Kurt. *A Codex with the Homilies of Gregory of Nazianzus*. Record of the Museum of Historic Art. Princeton University. Vol. 1. No. 1. pp. 14-17. 1942.
62. Wellesz, Egon. *Words and Music in Byzantine Liturgy*. The Musical Quarterly. Vol. 33. No. 3. pp. 297-310. 1947.
63. Winslow, Donald F. *Christology and Exegesis in the Cappadocians*. Church History. Vol. 40. No. 4. pp. 389-396. 1971.
64. Wolfson, Harry A. *Philosophical Implications of Arianism and Apollinarianism*. Dumbarton Oaks Papers. Vol. 12, pp. 3+5-28. 1958.
65. Zheltov, Michael. *The Anaphora and the Thanksgiving Prayer from the Barcelona Papyrus: An Underestimated Testimony to the Anaphoral History in the Fourth Century*. Vigiliae Christianae. Vol. 62. pp. 467-504. 20

www.ingramcontent.com/pod-product-compliance
Lightning Source LLC
Chambersburg PA
CBHW051359070526
44584CB00023B/3220